A-Level
Politics

Exam Boards: Edexcel & AQA

A-Level Politics is specialist stuff, but use this all-in-one guide from CGP and you'll show your exams who's in charge!

It's packed with clear notes and case studies completely covering the Edexcel and AQA courses, including all the optional modules. You'll also find lots of revision tasks throughout, from quick recap activities to exam-style questions.

We've even included annotated answers to exam questions for both exam boards. After all that, you'll be feeling as confident as a well-briefed Prime Minister before PMQs!

Unlock your Online Edition

Just scan the QR code below or go to cgpbooks.co.uk/extras and enter this code!

2124 8770 6227 5182

By the way, this code only works for one person. If somebody else has used this book before you, they might have already claimed the code.

A-Level revision? It has to be CGP!

Contents

Exam Breakdown — Edexcel 1
Exam Breakdown — AQA 2

UK Politics and Core Political Ideas

UK Politics

Democracy and Participation
Democracy in the UK 3
Referendums 5
Reforms to Voting 6
Pressure Groups in the UK 9
Corporations, Lobbyists and Think Tanks 12
Rights in the UK 13

Political Parties
Political Parties in the UK 15
Party Funding 17
Conservative Policies 19
Labour Policies 20
Other Parties' Policies 21
Comparing Party Policy 22
Factors Affecting Parties' Chances of Success 23

Electoral Systems
Electoral Systems in the UK 25
First-Past-the-Post 26
Additional Member System 27
Single Transferable Vote 28
Supplementary Vote 29
Alternatives to First-Past-the-Post 30

Voting Behaviour and the Media
Voting Behaviour 32
Demographic Factors 34
Campaigning, Manifestos and Policies 36
Opinion Polls 39
The Role of the Media in Elections and Referendums 41
Impact of the Media on the UK Political System 43

Core Political Ideas

Conservatism
Conservatism 44
Traditional Conservatism 45
One Nation Conservatism 46
The New Right 47
Comparing Conservative Ideas 48

Liberalism
Liberalism 49
Classical Liberalism 50
Transition from Classical to Modern Liberalism 51
Modern Liberalism 52
Comparing Liberal Ideas 53

Socialism
Socialism 54
Revolutionary Socialism 55
Social Democracy 57
The Third Way 58
Comparing Socialist Ideas 59

UK Government and Non-core Political Ideas

UK Government

The Constitution
The UK Constitution 60
Constitutional Reforms Under New Labour 62
Constitutional Reforms Since 2010 64
Taking Previous Constitutional Reforms Further 65
Has Devolution Been a Success? 66
Devolution in England 68
Codifying the UK Constitution 69

Parliament
Parliament 70
The House of Commons 71
The House of Lords 72
Comparing the Commons and the Lords 74
The Role of Backbenchers 75
Parliament's Legislative Function 76
Parliamentary Scrutiny 78
Parliament's Representative Function 81

Prime Minister and the Executive
Prime Minister and the Executive 83
Prime Ministerial Power 85
Prime Minister and the Cabinet 88
Collective and Individual Ministerial Responsibilty 91
Does the PM Have Too Much Power? 94

Relations Between the Branches
The Executive and Parliament 96
The Supreme Court 97
The Impact of the Supreme Court 98
The Executive and the Judiciary 100
Judicial Independence and Neutrality 101
Parliament and the Judiciary 102
The European Union 103
The Impact of the European Union 105
Is Parliament Sovereign? 106

Non-core Political Ideas

Anarchism
Anarchism 108
Collectivist Anarchism 110
Individualist Anarchism 113
Comparing Anarchist Ideas 114

Ecologism
Ecologism 115
Deep Green Ecology 117
Social Ecology 119
Shallow Green Ecology 121
Comparing Ecologist Ideas 122

Feminism
Feminism 123
Liberal Feminism 125
Socialist Feminism and Radical Feminism 126
Post-modern Feminism 128
Comparing Feminist Ideas 129

Multiculturalism
Multiculturalism 130
Liberal Multiculturalism 132
Pluralist and Cosmopolitan Multiculturalism 133
Criticisms of Multiculturalism 135
Comparing Multiculturalist Ideas 136

Nationalism
Nationalism 137
Nationalism and Internationalism 138
Liberal Nationalism 139
Conservative and Expansionist Nationalism 141
Post-colonial Nationalism 143
Comparing Nationalist Ideas 144

Comparative Politics

Government and Politics of the USA

Comparative Theories
Comparative Theories 145

The Constitution and Federalism
The US Constitution 146
Interpreting the US Constitution 148
Checks and Balances 150
Bipartisanship 153
Federalism 155
Democracy in the United States 157
Amendments to the US Constitution 159
Comparing the US and UK Constitutions 161
Analysing the US and UK Constitutions 163

Congress
Congress 166
The House of Representatives and the Senate 167
Congress's Legislative Function 169
Congressional Oversight 171
Representation and Political Parties 174
Comparing Congress and Parliament 177

The Presidency
The Executive Branch 179
Presidential Powers 181
Congressional Checks on Presidential Power 183
Judicial Checks on Presidential Power 185
Imperial and Imperilled Presidencies 186
Judging the Effectiveness of Presidencies 188
Comparing the US President and UK PM 190

US Supreme Court and Civil Rights
The US Supreme Court 192
Notable Supreme Court Rulings 194
Influence of the Supreme Court 196
Is the Supreme Court Political or Judicial? 198
Civil Rights and Racial Equality in the US 199
Comparing the US and UK Supreme Courts 201
Comparing Rights Protections in the US & UK .. 203

Democracy and Participation
Presidential Elections 205
The Electoral College 208
Campaign Finance and Election Performance 210
Comparing US and UK Elections 213
Interest Groups in the US 215
Comparing Interest Groups in the US and UK ... 218
The Democratic and Republican Parties 220
Comparing US and UK Party Policies 223
Comparing US and UK Party Unity 225
Comparing US and UK Party Systems 227

Global Politics

The State and Globalisation
State and Nation State 228
Sovereignty 229
Globalisation 231
Impact of Globalisation on the State System 233
Debate on the Impact of Globalisation 234

Global Governance — Political and Economic
Global Governance and the UN 237
Role and Significance of the UN 239
Strengths and Weaknesses of the UN 240
How the UN Resolves Issues 242
NATO 244
Economic Global Governance 246
Criticisms of the IMF and World Bank 248
The World Trade Organisation 250
The G7 and G20 252
Economic Development Theories and Poverty .. 254
Theories on the Causes of Poverty 256
Independent International Bodies 258
Realism and Liberalism in Global Politics 259

Global Governance — Human Rights and Environmental

ID: The ICJ, ECHR and ECtHR 260
Enforcing and Protecting Human Rights 261
Humanitarian Intervention 263
Responsibility to Protect Human Rights 264
Different Perspectives on Human Rights 265
Environmental Issues and Climate Change 266
The IPCC, UNFCCC and UN Conferences 267
Competing Views on the Environment 269
Obstacles to International Cooperation 270
Non-state Actors and Environmentalism 272

Power and Development

Hard Power and Soft Power 273
Classifications of Power 275
Polarity 277
Developments in Global Politics 279
States, Governments and Global Politics 280
The Impact of Changes in Global Power 282

Regionalism and the EU

Regionalism 283
Regionalism, Globalisation and Sovereignty 284
Significant Regional Bodies 285
The Development of the EU 287
The Euro and Institutions of the EU 289
The EU as a Global Actor 291
Regionalism and Contemporary Issues 293

Comparative Theories

Comparative Theories 294

Exam Skills

Planning Your Essays 298
Sentence Frames — Edexcel 299
Sentence Frames — AQA 300
Helpful Phrases 301
Annotated Essay — Electoral Systems 302
Annotated Essay — Socialism 303
Annotated Essay — US Presidency 304
Annotated Short Answers — Edexcel & AQA 305
Annotated Source Essay — Edexcel-style 306
Annotated Extract Essay — AQA-style 308
Edexcel-style Source Questions (30 marks) 310
Edexcel-style Essay Questions (30 marks) 312
Edexcel-style Political Ideas Qs (24 marks) 314
Edexcel-style Exam Questions (12 marks) 315
AQA-style Extract Questions (25 marks) 316
AQA-style Essay Questions (25 marks) 318
AQA-style Exam Questions (9 marks) 320

Sample Answers 322
Acknowledgements 329
Index 331

Published by CGP

Written by Tony Cains and Robin Hardman

Editors: Aimee Ashurst, Emma Cleasby, Ruth Greenhalgh, Chris Lindle, Duncan Lindsay, Sam Norman and Adam Worster

Reviewers: Rebecca Brattle

With thanks to Evangeline Bell, Catherine Heygate, Sean McParland, Elisabeth Page, Glenn Rogers and Elizabeth Teplizki for the proofreading.
With thanks to Alice Dent for the copyright research.

This book does not include any official AQA or Edexcel questions and is not endorsed by either body.

ISBN: 978 1 83774 148 9

Printed by Sterling, Kettering.
Clipart from Corel®

Based on the classic CGP style created by Richard Parsons.

Text, design, layout and original illustrations © Coordination Group Publications Ltd (CGP) 2025 All rights reserved.

Photocopying more than one section of this book is not permitted, even if you have a CLA licence.
Extra copies are available from CGP with next day delivery • 0800 1712 712 • www.cgpbooks.co.uk

Exam Breakdown — Edexcel

Before you dive into all that juicy A-Level Politics information, it's worth familiarising yourself with what you'll be faced with when exam season rolls around. Let's look at the exams you'll be sitting for the Edexcel course. Hop to the next page for AQA.

You'll have to do **three exams**

If you're doing AS Politics, the structure of your exams will be different — ask your teacher for more information.

Paper 1 — UK Politics and Core Political Ideas

1) It's **2 hours** long and there are **84 marks** available (worth a **third** of your A-Level grade).
2) It tests your knowledge of **UK politics** and the three **core** political ideas — **conservatism**, **liberalism** and **socialism**.
3) There are **two sections** in the paper — **A** and **B**:

NOT a suitable exam structure

Section A

This section will be about **UK politics**.

You **must** answer:
- **ONE** question from a choice of two questions that use **sources**.
- **ONE** question from a choice of two questions that **don't** use sources.

Each question is worth **30 marks**.

Section B

This section will be about the **core political ideas**.

You **must** answer **ONE** question from a choice of two questions.

The question is worth **24 marks**.

Paper 2 — UK Government and Non-core Political Ideas

1) It's **2 hours** long and there are **84 marks** available (worth a **third** of your A-Level grade).
2) It tests your knowledge of **UK government** and the **non-core political idea** you are studying — **anarchism**, **ecologism**, **feminism**, **multiculturalism** or **nationalism**.
3) There are **two sections** in the paper — **A** and **B**:

Section A

This section will be about **UK government**.

You **must** answer:
- **ONE** question from a choice of two questions that use **sources**.
- **ONE** question from a choice of two questions that **don't** use sources.

Each question is worth **30 marks**.

Section B

This section will be about the **non-core political idea** you are studying.

You **must** answer **ONE** question from a choice of two questions.

The question is worth **24 marks**.

There will be a pair of questions for each non-core political idea. You only need to look at the ones on the idea you are studying.

Paper 3 — Comparative Politics

1) It's **2 hours** long and there are **84 marks** available (worth a **third** of your A-Level grade).
2) Depending on what you are studying, you'll either sit **Paper 3A** or **Paper 3B**:
   - **Paper 3A** (Paper 3: Comparative Politics — USA) tests your knowledge of **US politics** and how it **compares** to politics in the **UK**.
   - **Paper 3B** (Paper 3: Comparative Politics — Global Politics) tests your knowledge of **global politics** and how the perspectives of liberalism and realism **compare** and are **applied** to global politics.
3) Both Paper 3A and Paper 3B have **three sections** — **A**, **B** and **C**:

Section A

You **must** answer **ONE** question from a choice of two questions.

The question is worth **12 marks**.

Section B

You **must** answer **ONE** compulsory question on **comparative theories**.

The question is worth **12 marks**.

Section C

You **must** answer **TWO** questions from a choice of three questions.

Each question is worth **30 marks**.

Exam Breakdown — AQA

Knowing how your exams are going to be structured can really help avoid you being taken by surprise when you sit down in that exam hall. So grab a cuppa, get cosy and have a nosey below to find out about the papers you'll be sitting for AQA Politics.

There are **three exams** you'll have to sit

Paper 1 — Government and politics of the UK

1) It's **2 hours** long and there are **77 marks** available (worth a **third** of your A-Level grade).
2) It tests your knowledge of **UK politics** and **UK government**.
3) There are **three sections** in the paper — **A**, **B** and **C**:

Section A
You **must** answer **THREE** compulsory, medium-length questions.
Each question is worth **9 marks**.

Section B
You **must** answer **ONE** compulsory question that uses **sources**.
The question is worth **25 marks**.

Section C
You **must** answer **ONE** question from a choice of two questions.
The question is worth **25 marks**.

Paper 2 — Government and politics of the USA and comparative politics

1) It's **2 hours** long and there are **77 marks** available (worth a **third** of your A-Level grade).
2) It tests your knowledge of **US politics** and **comparative theories**.
3) There are **three sections** in the paper — **A**, **B** and **C**:

Polly and Mona were very into comparrotive politics

Section A
You **must** answer **THREE** compulsory, medium-length questions.
Each question is worth **9 marks**.

Section B
You **must** answer **ONE** compulsory question that uses **sources**.
The question is worth **25 marks**.

Section C
You **must** answer **ONE** question from a choice of two questions.
The question is worth **25 marks**.

Paper 3 — Political ideas

1) It's **2 hours** long and there are **77 marks** available (worth a **third** of your A-Level grade).
2) It tests your knowledge of:
   - the three **core** political ideas — **conservatism**, **liberalism** and **socialism**
   - the **non-core political idea** you are studying — **anarchism**, **ecologism**, **feminism**, **multiculturalism** or **nationalism**.
3) There are **three sections** in the paper — **A**, **B** and **C**:

Section A
You **must** answer **THREE** compulsory, medium-length questions.
Each question will be about a **different core political idea**.
Each question is worth **9 marks**.

Section B
You **must** answer **ONE** compulsory question that uses **sources**.
The question will be about **core political ideas**.
The question is worth **25 marks**.

Section C
You **must** answer **ONE** compulsory question on the **non-core political idea** you are studying.
The question is worth **25 marks**.

There will be five questions on the paper, one for each non-core political idea.

Democracy in the UK

Democracy in the UK comes in many forms — MPs, Lords, devolved parliaments, referendums and petitions all play a part.

The UK has traditionally been a **representative democracy**

In a **representative democracy**, **representatives** make political decisions **on behalf of citizens**.

- In the UK, citizens **elect** Members of Parliament (MPs) to the **House of Commons** (see p.71).
- The **House of Lords** is **unelected**, but its members also **amend** and **approve** laws (see p.72-73).
- The **Scottish Parliament**, **Welsh Parliament** and **Northern Ireland Assembly** also form part of the UK's representative democracy (see p.66-67).

Direct democracy has been used more in recent decades

Switzerland has the highest level of direct democracy in the world. Swiss voters can take part in several public votes each year.

In a **direct democracy**, **citizens** make political decisions **themselves**.

- **Referendums** are the best-known form of direct democracy in the **UK**. Between 1997 and 2016, **9** referendums have been held on **constitutional issues** (see p.5).
- The UK also uses **e-petitions**, which allow citizens to express their views on any **political** or **social** issue. Any petition that attracts over **100 000 signatures** is **considered for debate** in Parliament.

Recall of MPs Act (2015)

1) Under this act, constituents can **recall** their **local MP** (vote to remove them from office) if the MP has been:
   - convicted of a **crime** and **handed a prison sentence**.
   - **suspended** from the House of Commons for **10 days or more**.
   - convicted of making **false expenses claims**.
2) A **by-election** is triggered if 10% of eligible voters sign a **petition**.

Margaret Ferrier was **recalled** in **2023** after admitting to **breaking lockdown** and **social distancing guidance** by travelling from London to Glasgow after a positive COVID-19 test.

There are **defenders** and **critics** of the UK's political system

Democracies can be **judged** against the following **criteria**:

1) Levels of **participation**
2) How far **all groups** and **individuals** have **opportunities** for **political influence**
3) Levels of **trust** in the political system
4) How **effectively rights** are **protected**

Elitist political systems allow those with wealth and connections to exercise disproportionate amounts of power.

Defenders of the UK's political system argue that it upholds the principles of **pluralist democracy** (where **many groups** and **individuals** are able to have political influence).

- The **Human Rights Act (1998)** set out **fundamental rights** that belong to **all in the UK**, including **freedom of speech** and **freedom of assembly** (the right to gather, e.g. for meetings, political rallies, protests).
- **Parliament** has passed many other laws that **protect** the **rights** of **minorities** and **vulnerable individuals** (see p.13).
- The **Supreme Court** frequently **defends minority rights** in its rulings (see p.98-99).

Critics believe that the UK is becoming increasingly **elitist**.

- There have been high-profile examples of **wealthy party donors** achieving significant **political influence** in recent years (see p.17-18).
- The influence of **corporations** and **lobbyists** is seen as an example of **elitism** (see p.12).
- The **privileged backgrounds** of many **MPs** can also be seen as evidence of **elitism** — see p.81.
- The **appointments process** for the **House of Lords** has been **criticised** for a **lack** of democracy. The **prime minister** oversees most **nominations**, with **no opportunity** for **voters** to express their views. For example, **29 peers** were appointed to the House of Lords during **Liz Truss's premiership**, despite her short term in office.

Democracy in the UK

Representative democracy has three main advantages...

1) Political decisions are made by **specialists** who should understand the **complexity** of the **issues** they're voting on. They can then be **held accountable** for their decisions.
2) Representatives have **time** to consider the **impact** of legislation, whereas many **members of the public** may not.
3) Representatives can take **minority interests** into account when making decisions, whereas **referendums** reflect **majority views**.

"Ann said you were a specialist, but I didn't know you were this good"

...but it also has significant disadvantages

1) Representative democracy relies on the **good performance** and **conduct** of those in power.
   - There have been several **high-profile scandals** in Parliament. Between **2019** and **2024**, at least 20 MPs were either **suspended** from the **House of Commons**, **suspended** by their **party** or chose to **resign their seats** following accusations of **misconduct**.
2) If **turnout** in elections is **low**, there can be **questions** about the **mandate** of the **representatives**.
   - Turnout in **general elections** between **2001** and **2019** was between 59% and 69%. In the **2024 general election**, turnout dipped **below 60%** for the first time since **2001**.
   - As of 2021, elections to the **Welsh Parliament** have never attracted turnout above 47%.
3) Because representatives are mindful of the need to **remain popular** with the electorate, they can sometimes **avoid** making **necessary reforms** that are **unpopular** with **influential groups** of voters. For example, the Public Accounts Committee has consistently called for a **long-term funding** agreement for **adult social care**, but **neither major party** has been willing to introduce either **tax increases** or **cuts** in **other policy areas** in order to **fund** the spending increase.

Key Terms
mandate
The extent to which a politician, party or policy can be said to possess legitimate authority by virtue of an election or referendum result.

Supporters of direct democracy say it's preferable to representative democracy

- Direct democracy is the **form of democracy** that gives **the people** the **most power**.
- Referendums give **decision-making power** to **the people**, which can lead to **reforms** that would be **very unlikely** under **representative democracy**.
- Direct democracy can help to **engage** the **electorate** when **participation** is **low** in **general elections** and other forms of representative democracy.

> An estimated 75% of MPs supported Remain during the Brexit referendum in 2016, whereas only 48% of voters voted to remain in the EU.

> The **2014 Scottish independence referendum** had a turnout of 85% and the **2016 Brexit referendum** had a turnout of 72%. Both of these turnouts were higher than those for general elections between 2001 and 2019 (see above).

Critics of direct democracy emphasise the problems it can involve

- **Referendums** can **over-simplify** complex issues. There was **no consensus** over the **terms** on which the UK could **leave the EU**, so **Brexit** was **much more complex** than the choice to **remain** or **leave**.
- **Referendums** can only be held in the UK via an **Act of Parliament**, which means that a referendum is **highly unlikely** to happen unless it is **supported** by the **prime minister**.
- The **outcomes** of **referendums** only take into account the views of the **majority**, which is especially **problematic** when the **results** are **close**.
- **E-petitions** can create the **illusion** of democracy without offering **meaningful influence**.

> In some US states, citizens can propose questions that are put to a public vote. In California, a vote called a 'proposition' is scheduled if it has enough support. To trigger a vote, there need to be signatures amounting to 5% of the turnout from the last election for state governor.

Exam Practice

For Edexcel students: Evaluate the view that representative democracy has more advantages than direct democracy. [30]
For AQA students: Explain and analyse three criticisms of direct democracy. [9]

Who would win in a fight between representative and direct democracy?

Okay, I'll admit that this isn't quite as thrilling a battle as a T-rex vs the Loch Ness Monster (my money's on the monster), but you may be asked to analyse these types of democracy, so it's handy to understand the advantages and disadvantages of both.

UK Politics — Democracy and Participation

Referendums

Ref-er-en-dums — it has a nice ring to it. Try saying it five times really fast though* — you'll wish it was called something else.

The UK has held **three nationwide referendums**

Remaining in the European Economic Community (1975)
- 67% Yes | 33% No
- 64% Turnout

Replacing First-Past-the-Post with the Alternative Vote electoral system (2011)
- 32% Yes | 68% No
- 42% Turnout

Leaving the European Union (2016)
- 52% Yes | 48% No
- 72% Turnout

There have been **several referendums** in specific parts of the UK

Creation of a Scottish Assembly (1979)
- 52% Yes | 48% No
- 64% Turnout

Although a majority voted to create a Scottish Assembly, this wasn't enough. Parliament had decided that 40% of the registered electorate had to vote in favour for the reform to happen.

Creation of a Scottish Parliament (1997)
- 74% Yes | 26% No
- 60% Turnout

Northern Ireland Remaining in the United Kingdom (1973)
- 99% Yes | 1% No
- 59% Turnout

This referendum was boycotted by nationalists, who feared that it would inflame tensions.

Scottish Independence (2014)
- 45% Yes | 55% No
- 85% Turnout

Creation of a North East Assembly (2004)
- 22% Yes | 78% No
- 48% Turnout

Good Friday Agreement (1998)
- 71% Yes | 29% No
- 81% Turnout

Creation of a Welsh Assembly (1979)
- 20% Yes | 80% No
- 59% Turnout

Creation of a Welsh Assembly (1997)
- 50.3% Yes | 49.7% No
- 50% Turnout

There are arguments **for** and **against** holding **more referendums** in the UK

Some believe that the UK should hold more frequent referendums...	Others argue that more referendums would harm the UK's political system...
✓ Referendums can help to **legitimise** major **constitutional changes**. Many would expect a referendum to be held on proposals to further change the UK Constitution.	✗ Referendum **campaigns** are **divisive** and their **outcomes** can cause even more division.
✓ Holding **more referendums** in the UK would allow the **public** to **express their views** on areas of **policy** that politicians might not want to tackle.	✗ Referendums can **take attention away** from **other important issues**. There was a fall in parliamentary productivity in the years after the 2016 EU referendum — this was partly caused by the Conservatives losing their majority in the 2017 general election, but also by the attention that needed to be given to Brexit.
✓ In **other political systems**, referendums are held on **social issues** like the legalisation of drugs.	✗ Holding **more public votes** can create **voter fatigue**.

More Maths Lessons in the UK (2024) — Yes: 23%, No: 99%, Turnout: 105%...
You might need to evaluate the use of referendums in the UK, so make sure you know the arguments for and against their use.

* *You tried it, didn't you?*

UK Politics — Democracy and Participation

Reforms to Voting

Voting rights in the UK have changed a lot in the last few centuries, and there are ongoing debates about voting reforms.

There have been some **major milestones** in **voting rights**

franchise/suffrage
The right to vote

Campaigns in the **19th** and **20th century** succeeded in **expanding** the **franchise**.

1) In the **early 19th century**, only a small number of **men** could **vote** in elections for the **House of Commons**.
2) The **criteria** for being allowed to vote **differed** depending on the **local area**, but most boroughs required men to **own property** in order to have the right to vote. This often meant that only **wealthy men** could vote.

The Great Reform Act (1832) began the extension of voting rights

- This act **abolished** 'rotten boroughs' (areas with **representatives** chosen by a **small electorate**). As the electorate was so small, voters could be more easily **manipulated** into voting a certain way by **wealthy patrons** in the area.
- **Cities** like **Manchester** and **Birmingham**, which had grown rapidly during the **Industrial Revolution**, were rewarded with **new constituencies** to reflect their **increase** in **population**.

The Chartists campaigned for voting rights for the working class

1) The **Chartists** believed that the **Great Reform Act (1832)** had not gone far enough — men still had to **own property** to vote, which effectively prevented **working-class people** from voting. The Chartists **campaigned** for **universal male suffrage** (giving all men the vote). By 1842, over **three million** people had signed one of their **petitions** to Parliament.
2) Parliament didn't expand **working-class suffrage** until the second half of the 19th century:
   - The **Representation of the People Act (1867)** extended the franchise to **all men** who were **property owners** or **responsible** for **paying** their household's **rent**.
   - The **Representation of the People Act (1884)** further extended suffrage by addressing **differences** between voters in **cities** and **towns** — after this act, **60% of men** could vote.
   - The **Representation of the People Act (1918)** enabled **all men over the age of 21** to vote.

Suffragettes and suffragists successfully campaigned for women's suffrage

- **Mary Wollstonecraft** (p.50) had first written about the need for **women's suffrage** in the **late 18th century**, and in the mid-19th century, MP **John Stuart Mill** (p.50) prominently **spoke in favour** of extending the franchise to women.
- By the early 20th century, there were **two main organisations** in the **women's suffrage movement** — the **suffragettes** used radical methods to draw attention to their cause, and the **suffragists** tried to build closer links with politicians.

Emmeline Pankhurst, leader of the Women's Social and Political Union, is arrested while campaigning for women's suffrage in 1914

1 Representation of the People Act (1918)

- After decades of campaigning, the **women's suffrage movement** finally persuaded MPs and peers to extend the franchise to **women**. This was done through the **Representation of the People Act (1918)** (also known as the **Fourth Reform Act**).
- However, under this Act, only women **over the age of 30** who **owned property**, or who were **married** to someone who did, were able to vote.

2 Representation of the People (Equal Franchise) Act (1928)

Ten years later, the **Representation of the People (Equal Franchise) Act (1928)** extended the franchise to **all women over the age of 21**.

The voting age has been lowered again since the early 20th century

1 In the **Representation of the People Act (1969)**, the voting age was lowered to **18** for **men** and **women**. This made the UK one of the **first democratic countries** in the world to lower its voting age to include those aged 18-20.

2 While the **voting age** is still **18** for **general elections**, some **16- and 17-year-olds** can vote in other elections in Scotland and Wales.

- In Scotland, the voting age was lowered to **16** for the **2014 Scottish independence referendum**, and **all Scottish elections** from **2015**.
- The voting age for **Welsh elections** was lowered to **16** in **2021**.

UK Politics — Democracy and Participation

Reforms to Voting

There are other **possible reforms** to the UK's democracy

As well as holding **more referendums** (see page 5), there are debates about other possible **voting reforms** in the UK:

Lowering the **voting age** to **16** | Allowing **electronic voting** | Introducing **compulsory voting** | Giving **all prisoners** the right to **vote**

There are **supporters** and **opponents** of **lowering** the **voting age**

Although some 16- and 17-year-olds can vote in certain elections in Scotland and Wales (see p.6), the voting age is still 18 for general elections. Some argue this should be **lowered**.

✓ For Lowering Voting Age

1) Lowering the voting age to 16 across the UK could be a **solution** to the UK's **participation crisis**:
   - **75%** of registered 16- and 17-year-olds **voted** in the **2014 Scottish independence referendum**.
   - Studies showed that **high turnout** of 16- and 17-year-olds continued in the **2016** and **2021 Scottish Parliament elections**.
   - This is much **higher** than turnout among those aged **18-24** in **general elections** — only **47%** of registered voters in this age category voted in the **2019 general election**.
   - Supporters argue that people are **more likely** to develop a **lifelong habit** of **voting** if they are **encouraged to vote** while they are at **school** or **college**.
2) Some campaigners feel that it's **undemocratic** for 16- and 17-year-olds to be able to vote in **Scotland** and **Wales**, but **not** in **England** or **Northern Ireland**.
3) Research carried out after the 2014 independence referendum revealed that 16- and 17-year-old voters in **Scotland** used a **broader range** of **sources** than **other age groups** while considering how to vote.

Labour, the Liberal Democrats, the SNP and Plaid Cymru have all supported lowering the voting age to 16 across the UK, but the Conservatives have opposed this.

✗ Against Lowering Voting Age

Kwame wasn't very pleased when MPs rejected proposals to lower the voting age again

1) Opponents of lowering the voting age argue that 16- and 17-year-olds may be **swayed** by the **political views** of their **parents** or **guardians**.
2) Currently, there is very **limited compulsory political education** in the UK.
3) Lowering the voting age could expose young voters to **important decisions before** they are **ready**.
4) Most 16- and 17-year-olds **don't pay taxes** — **opponents** of lowering the voting age argue that this means they have **less to gain** or **lose** from their vote than **adults** who **do pay taxes**.

In a survey in 2018, **only 34%** of those of voting age **supported lowering** the **voting age** to give 16- and 17-year-olds the **right to vote**.

The original basis of the right to vote in the UK was that voters were adults who paid taxes.

Electronic voting involves voting **online** or using **electronic devices**

For Electronic Voting

1) Electronic voting could help **engage reluctant voters** by making voting **more accessible**.
2) **Turnout** among **18-24-year-olds** for **general elections** is **low** compared to older age groups. Some believe that only a **radical** solution will **improve levels of participation** in this age group.
3) Now that many aspects of **society** and the **economy** are conducted **digitally**, it could be seen as **outdated** that people can only vote **in person**, **by proxy** (where someone votes in person on behalf of someone else) or **by post**.

However, when internet voting was introduced in Geneva, Switzerland, research shows that turnout among voters over the age of 80 increased, but there was no statistically significant impact on other groups.

✗ Against Electronic Voting

1) There are **concerns** over the **security** of **online systems**. For example, electronic voting in Estonia has been found to be vulnerable to **hacking** and **fraud**.
2) This **compromises** the important **democratic principle** of **voters' secrecy**.

UK Politics — Democracy and Participation

Reforms to Voting

Compulsory voting means that **all** eligible voters **must vote**

✓ For Compulsory Voting

Supporters of **compulsory voting** argue it would **strengthen politicians' mandates** and **increase political engagement**:

1) **Turnout increases** when voting is made compulsory.
   - Since voting was made compulsory in **Australia** in **1924**, turnout has nearly always been **over 90%** or just below this figure.
   - If the **same** happened in the UK, an estimated **fifth of the population** who currently **choose not to vote** would likely take part in elections.
2) Supporters of compulsory voting hope that this would make **Parliament more representative** of **UK society**.

✗ Against Compulsory Voting

Opponents of **compulsory voting** argue that it **masks deeper issues** with political systems:

1) Compulsory voting can create the **illusion** that the **electorate** is **engaging with politics** when many would **choose not to** if they could.
2) There are **fears** that those who vote **only** because they have to wouldn't take their vote **seriously**, which might **distort the result**.

The Electoral Reform Society, a pressure group (see p.9-10) that supports introducing a proportional electoral system and lowering the voting age to 16, does not support compulsory voting for this reason.

There is debate over whether **prisoners** should have the **right to vote**

✓ For Votes for Prisoners

- The **Howard League**, a **pressure group** that campaigns for **prison reform**, believes that extending the right to vote to **all prisoners** would **improve** the **UK's democracy** and **society**. It argues that voting offers a **stake** in society that can help to **rehabilitate** them.
- **Civil prisoners** (who have been sent to prison for **offences** like not paying fines or debts) are already **able to vote**. This is due to a **2005 European Court of Human Rights ruling** which stated that the UK was **in breach** of the **ECHR** (p.260). However, this has created a **hierarchy of offenses** that critics believe is **unfair**.

✗ Against Votes for Prisoners

- Others believe that voting is a **privilege** that prisoners **forfeit** when committing a crime.
- There was **cross-party consensus against** extending the right to vote to all prisoners when the issue was debated in Parliament in **2011**.

Former prime minister **David Cameron** said in 2010 when asked in the House of Commons if **convicted prisoners** should still be able to vote:
"Frankly, when people commit a crime and go to prison, they should lose their rights, including the right to vote."

Quick Questions

1) For which referendum was the voting age lowered to 16 in Scotland?
2) When was the voting age lowered to 16 for Welsh elections?
3) What problems with electronic voting have been discovered in Estonia?
4) What happened in Australia after compulsory voting was introduced?
5) Which pressure group supports extending the right to vote to all prisoners?

Exam Practice

For Edexcel students: Evaluate the view that further reforms to suffrage would improve democracy in the UK. [30]
For AQA students: Explain and analyse three ways in which suffrage could be reformed further in the UK. [9]

Swayed by parents? My little sister always does the opposite of what they say...

These debates are about expanding the franchise and reforming the process of voting. There are lots of issues to consider in each debate, but many of the reforms have a similar motive — to improve democracy in the UK by increasing participation.

Pressure Groups in the UK

Pressure groups are organisations that try to influence the government. There are lots of factors that affect how well a pressure group is able to achieve its aims — it's not just about coming up with a snappy name and rocking up at a protest.

There are **two main types** of pressure group

1) **Causal pressure groups** — pressure groups that **unite** around a particular cause.
   E.g. **Justice for Subpostmasters Alliance (JFSA)**, **Just Stop Oil** and **Action on Smoking and Health (ASH)**.

2) **Sectional pressure groups** — pressure groups that **represent** a particular **section** of **society**.
   E.g. The **Muslim Council of Britain**, the **National Farmers' Union** and the **British Medical Association**.

Pressure groups can either be **insider** or **outsider** groups

Insider Groups
- Insider groups have **close relationships** with those in **government** and in **other influential positions**.
- Examples of insider groups include **ASH**, the **National Farmers' Union** and the **Institute of Directors**.

Outsider Groups
- Outsider groups **don't have close relationships** with **political decision-makers**, often because their **agendas** go **against** the **government's policies**.
- Examples of outsider groups include **Just Stop Oil**, **Extinction Rebellion** and **Countryside Alliance**.

The outsider or insider status of a group can change over time...

Stonewall (an LGBTQI+ campaign group) became an **insider group** in the **mid-2000s**, but then returned to being an **outsider group** in the early 2020s. This happened when its stance on **transgender rights** began to **clash** with the **Conservative government's policy**.

Pressure groups use **different methods** to achieve their **aims**

Direct Action
1) Direct action is where pressure groups attempt to **raise awareness** of their campaigns **directly**.
2) **Protests**, **marches**, **demonstrations** and **sit-ins** are all forms of direct action.
3) **Outsider groups** often rely on **direct action**.

A sit in is a form of protest where protestors occupy a location and refuse to move.

Just Stop Oil protestors marching across Westminster Bridge in 2022 on the way to stage a sit-in protest

Lobbying
1) **Lobbying** is when a **group** or **individual** tries to persuade **politicians** to **support** their campaign.
2) Although anyone can attempt to lobby politicians, **wealthy insider groups** are **more likely** to be able to **offer incentives**.
3) **Insider groups** usually use **lobbying** as their **main method**.

Some wealthy insider groups offer MPs generous corporate hospitality and payment for work done. This can lead to accusations of these groups having undue influence on politicians.

Other methods used by pressure groups:
- Petitions
- Celebrity endorsements
- Media campaigns
- Judicial review (see p.98)
- Collaborations with think tanks (see p.12)
- Strike action

UK Politics — Democracy and Participation

Pressure Groups in the UK

Pressure groups can be very influential...

1) **ASH** has frequently been **consulted** by the **government** and **Parliament** about **anti-smoking measures**. The group has helped to **draft policies** on **plain packaging**, **health warnings** and **banning disposable vapes**.
2) Senior doctors represented by the **British Medical Association** managed to negotiate a **pay increase** with the **government** after taking **strike action** in 2023.
3) **Surfers Against Sewage** and **CPRE** (formerly **The Campaign to Protect Rural England**) have raised awareness of **sewage dumping** by **water companies**. **Legislation** to **prevent** this practice was introduced by the Labour government after the 2024 general election, and **water companies** have planned to spend **£272 billion** over 25 years on cleaning the UK's rivers, lakes and coastline.

> Labour MP Jim McMahon proposed the Water Quality (Sewage Discharge) Bill in 2022. However, like most bills not proposed by the governing party, it failed to make it past the second reading (see p.76).

...but groups don't always achieve their goals

1) Environmental groups **Friends of the Earth** and **Plan B** teamed up to challenge the planned construction of a **third runway** at **Heathrow Airport**, but their legal challenge was **defeated** in the **Supreme Court** in **2020** (see p.98).
2) The pro-smoking group **FOREST** campaigns against regulation of smoking and tobacco use. FOREST has **some supporters** in the **House of Lords**, but its **agenda** has been **rejected** by both the **Conservative** and **Labour** parties.
3) The civil rights pressure group **Liberty** campaigned against **lockdown** and **social distancing** during the COVID-19 pandemic. However, its aims **conflicted** with the stances adopted by the **governments** of **all four UK nations** for most of 2020 and some of 2021

Social media has allowed individuals to run successful campaigns in recent years

Marcus Rashford — Footballer Marcus Rashford's campaign against **food poverty** during the COVID-19 pandemic led to the government **changing** its policy on **providing free meals** to **disadvantaged schoolchildren** through **school holidays**.

3 Dads Walking — Three fathers, known together as 3 Dads Walking, started a campaign on **suicide prevention**. They have raised over **£1 million** and met with **Rishi Sunak** at Number 10 in 2023.

Some believe that pressure groups improve the UK's democracy

1) Pressure groups offer many opportunities for **informal political participation**:
   - This is particularly important when there is **low formal participation**.
   - An estimated **400 000** people marched in **London** to support the **People's Vote** campaign in 2019.

2) Their activities help to **represent the interests of minorities** who many feel are **underrepresented** in the UK's political system:
   - Tens of thousands joined **Black Lives Matter** protests against **police brutality** and **structural racism** across the UK in 2020.
   - Parliament remains **unrepresentative** of **British society** — **sectional pressure groups** like the **Muslim Council of Britain** and **Stonewall** provide representation outside of Parliament to groups who are not well represented in Parliament.

Anita regretted letting Logan join her pressure group

3) Pressure groups can also provide **expertise** in the **policy-making process**:
   - **ASH** has used its **knowledge** to **help shape anti-smoking policies** (see above).
   - **Refuge**, a charity that supports people experiencing domestic abuse, provided **expert guidance** to the government during the passage of the Domestic Abuse Act (2021).

UK Politics — Democracy and Participation

Pressure Groups in the UK

Others say that **some pressure groups** can cause **more harm than good**

1) Some pressure groups are thought to have **disproportionate influence**:

   The Betting and Gambling Council has successfully managed to lobby against tighter gambling regulations, despite increases in the number of bankruptcies caused by gambling.

2) Some have been accused of **spreading misinformation**:

   An anti-vaccination pressure group, the Health Advisory and Recovery Team, was accused of spreading conspiracy theories about the COVID-19 vaccine in 2021.

3) **Direct action** by pressure groups can cause **disruption** and **lead to police action**:

   Eight members of Extinction Rebellion were arrested in 2022 after they glued and locked themselves to parts of the Parliamentary Estate.

Many protest groups feel that direct action is over-policed, especially since the passage of the Police, Crime, Sentencing and Courts Act (2022) and the Public Order Act (2023).

Extinction Rebellion protestors locked at the neck to fences outside Parliament in September 2022

Quick Questions

1) Give an example of a causal pressure group.
2) What is meant by the term 'direct action'?
3) Give an example of lobbying.
4) Which two pressure groups have campaigned against sewage dumping?
5) How many members of Extinction Rebellion were arrested during a protest in Westminster in 2022?
6) Which charity was consulted during the passage of the Domestic Abuse Act (2021)?

Revision Task

For Edexcel students: Analyse the view that pressure groups are rarely able to achieve their aims in the UK. [30]
For AQA students: 'Pressure groups are rarely able to achieve their aims in the UK.' Analyse this statement. [25]

Imagine you're answering one of the essay questions above. Practise your **analysis skills** by explaining the significance of the examples below. You can use the sentence frames on pages 299-300.
1) ASH's role in drafting anti-smoking legislation
2) The British Medical Association's success in negotiating a pay increase for senior doctors
3) Friends of the Earth and Plan B's Supreme Court defeat

Exam Practice

For Edexcel students: Evaluate the view that pressure groups have an overwhelmingly positive impact on the UK's democracy. [30]
For AQA students: Explain and analyse three methods used by pressure groups in the UK. [9]

Chocolate, avocado and tuna works really well on a sandwich. Fight me...
When you're evaluating pressure groups, don't just focus your attention on one side of the argument. Consider examples of both the positive and negative impact of pressure groups and how they're likely to have an effect on the UK's democracy.

UK Politics — Democracy and Participation

Corporations, Lobbyists and Think Tanks

Sorry, that title was a bit of a mouthful, but it was that or 'other organisations that try to influence government policy'...

Corporations, lobbyists and think tanks try to influence the government

Corporations — Criticisms

Critics argue that corporations have **disproportionate influence**, which can lead to **improper behaviour**:

- **Randox Health** and **Lynn's Country Foods** were caught up in a **scandal** in 2021 when it emerged that they had paid Conservative MP **Owen Paterson**, who was **lobbying** on their behalf, an estimated £500 000. This was controversial because **Randox** had won **government contracts** worth £777 million during the COVID-19 pandemic.
- The **House of Commons Science and Technology Committee** was criticised in 2018 for producing a report that promoted the **health benefits** of **e-cigarettes** without disclosing its members' links to the **vaping industry**.
- Financial firm **Greensill Capital** employed former PM **David Cameron** as an advisor. Cameron used his private contacts to set up **meetings** with **senior government ministers** where he tried to persuade them to give Greensill access to a Covid loan scheme.

Corporations are profit-seeking businesses, so it's not surprising that they use their influence over the political process to try to maximise their own profits and reputations.

Corporations — Benefits

Others feel that corporations are **important stakeholders** in the **UK's economy**:

- **Government** needs to **work with corporations** to carry out many aspects of public policy. For example, transitioning to **renewable energy** would be difficult without **close relationships** between government and firms like **BP** and **Shell**.
- Some corporations help to **sponsor policy initiatives** that have a much **wider benefit** than their own profits. **Santander®** and **Barclays** have provided **funding** for **bike rental schemes** in London, which have helped to **reduce air pollution** and **traffic congestion**.
- Corporations can help to **boost employment** and **stimulate economic growth**. In 2023, **Nissan™** signed a £2 billion deal to **build electric cars** in **Sunderland**.

Lobbyists

Corporations often use **lobbyists** to manage their **relationships** with **politicians**:

- **Hanbury Strategy** has been one of the most influential lobbyists in recent years, with close links to the **Vote Leave campaign** and **the Conservative Party**. It has also represented corporations such as **Deliveroo**.
- In **2020**, Hanbury Strategy was asked to hire **special advisors** to work in No. 10. This caused **controversy** because it was thought this could give its clients a direct line to the then prime minister **Boris Johnson**.
- Lobbyists can also represent **non-profit groups** — **Solidarity Consulting** has lobbied on behalf of **trade unions** and **charities**, and has close links with **Labour MPs**.

Key Terms

lobbyist
A person or organisation that seeks to form close relationships with political decision-makers on behalf of clients.

think tank
A privately-funded research organisation that produces reports and policy proposals to try to influence the political agenda.

Think Tanks

Think tanks try to **persuade politicians** to adopt their **agenda**:

- Some think tanks have **close links** to both **major UK parties**. **Chatham House** specialises in foreign affairs and frequently provides **advice** to both parties on issues of **national security** and **foreign policy**.
- Other think tanks have a **clearer political agenda**. The centrist **Tony Blair Institute for Global Change**, founded by the former prime minister, has close links with the **Labour Party**. Reports by the right-wing **Institute of Economic Affairs (IEA)** influenced Liz Truss and Kwasi Kwarteng's mini-budget in 2022, where the highest rate of income tax was cut (see p.86).

There is a lack of transparency around some think tanks. Both the IEA and the Adam Smith Institute receive funding from the tobacco industry and have produced research that warns against regulating smoking.

Exam Practice

For Edexcel students: Evaluate the view that corporations and lobbyists have a negative impact on the UK's democracy, but pressure groups and think tanks do not. [30]

For AQA students: 'Corporations and lobbyists have a negative impact on the UK's democracy, but pressure groups and think tanks do not.' Analyse and evaluate this statement. [25]

Practise your **evaluation skills** by writing a **conclusion** to one of the essay questions above. There are sentence frames for you to use on pages 299-300.

I lobby, you lobby, we lobby — nope, it still doesn't sound like a real verb...

The impact of some groups can be hard to judge. Even though all paid lobbying needs to be declared, lobbyists usually act away from the public eye, so it's unclear how influential they are. The influence of think tanks can depend on who's in power.

Rights in the UK

Protecting rights is a key part of a healthy democracy. Try telling my housemates that though — they're still denying me my right to keep a llama in the garden. What do you mean that's not a right? Well it should be. Time to start a petition...

There are **two categories** of **rights**

1) **INDIVIDUAL RIGHTS** — Rights enjoyed by **individuals**.
   E.g. **Free speech** and the **right to a fair trial**.
2) **COLLECTIVE RIGHTS** — Rights enjoyed by **society as a whole**.
   E.g. The **right to safety** from **criminal** and **public health threats**.

Cheese and Pickle's owners had no respect for their right to freedom from ridiculous outfits

There have been some **major milestones** in **rights protection**

1) Magna Carta (1215)

Nobles forced **King John I** to sign a **charter** in which he agreed **not to impose taxes** without their **consent**. The charter also laid out the right to a **fair and impartial trial**.

2) Bill of Rights (1689)

This established the principles of **free elections** and **free speech** within **Parliament** (known as parliamentary privilege — see p.60).

Parliament has passed several **landmark laws** on **rights** in recent decades

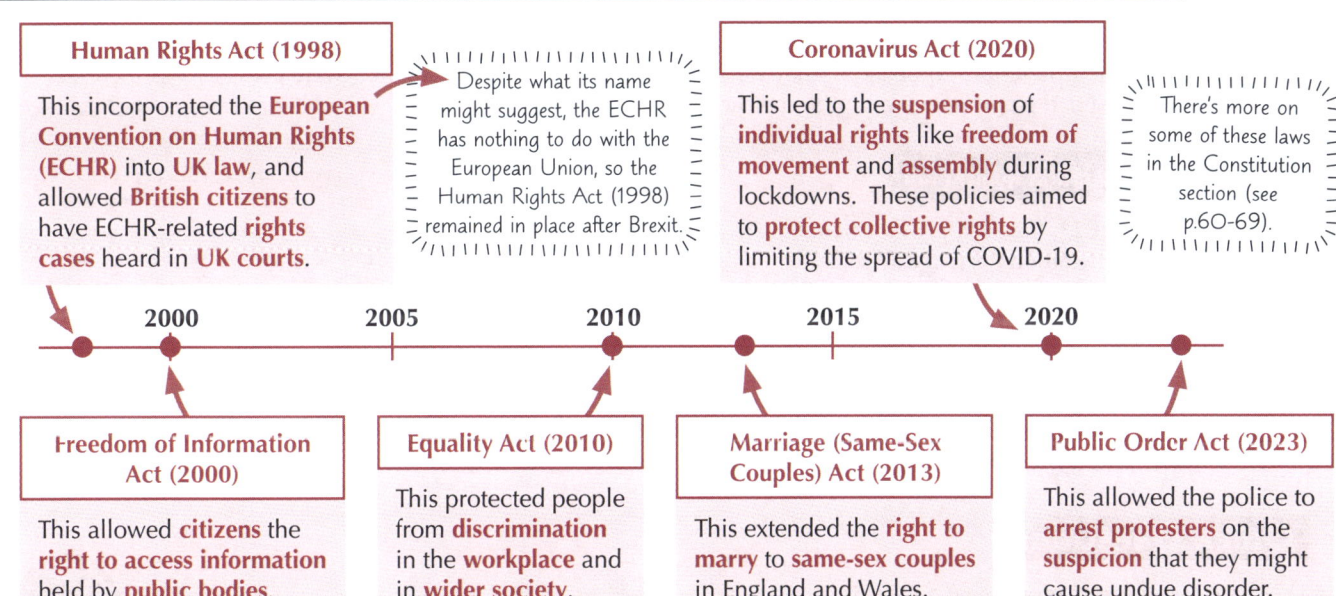

Human Rights Act (1998)

This incorporated the **European Convention on Human Rights (ECHR)** into **UK law**, and allowed **British citizens** to have ECHR-related **rights cases** heard in **UK courts**.

Despite what its name might suggest, the ECHR has nothing to do with the European Union, so the Human Rights Act (1998) remained in place after Brexit.

Coronavirus Act (2020)

This led to the **suspension** of **individual rights** like **freedom of movement** and **assembly** during lockdowns. These policies aimed to **protect collective rights** by limiting the spread of COVID-19.

There's more on some of these laws in the Constitution section (see p.60-69).

Freedom of Information Act (2000)

This allowed **citizens** the **right to access information** held by **public bodies**.

Equality Act (2010)

This protected people from **discrimination** in the **workplace** and in **wider society**.

Marriage (Same-Sex Couples) Act (2013)

This extended the **right to marry** to **same-sex couples** in England and Wales.

Public Order Act (2023)

This allowed the police to **arrest protesters** on the **suspicion** that they might cause undue disorder.

Some believe that **rights** are **well protected** by the UK's democracy

Both **individual** and **collective** rights are protected in a number of ways:

- **The UK's Constitution** is **more flexible** than the constitutions of many other countries, allowing rights to be **updated** more easily.

  > This **flexibility** meant that **same-sex marriage** could be introduced through an Act of Parliament (a law) in the **UK** (see p.61), whereas a **referendum** was needed to introduce this in the **Republic of Ireland**.

- **Pressure groups** like **Stonewall**, **Liberty** and **ASH** help to **raise awareness** of rights-related issues (see p.9-11).
- **Media campaigns** frequently **expose rights abuses** by **public bodies** and **criminal** networks (see p.43).
- **Court rulings** often protect the rights of the **most vulnerable** in society (see p.98-99).

Guardian journalist Amelia Gentleman helped to uncover the Windrush scandal in 2018, which led to a campaign for justice for the victims

UK Politics — Democracy and Participation

Rights in the UK

Some argue that **individual rights** have taken **priority** over **collective rights**

Court rulings have often **protected individual rights** over **collective rights**.

1) In **2017**, the **Supreme Court** ruled that the **May** government's 'deport first, appeal later' policy for dealing with **foreign nationals** convicted of **crimes** in the UK was **unlawful**.

2) In this case, **critics** of the Supreme Court ruling believed that the **individual rights** of the foreign nationals were being **prioritised** over the **collective rights** of members of society affected by their **crimes**.

3) In **2023**, the **Supreme Court** also ruled that the **Sunak** government's **Rwanda policy** was **unlawful**. The court's decision rested on whether Rwanda could be considered a **safe destination** for **deportations**.

4) **Supporters** of the government's policy argued that the ruling failed to take into account both the **collective rights** of **society** and the **individual rights** of **asylum seekers** travelling to the UK on unsafe small boats. **Opponents** of the policy welcomed the ruling as a **protection** of the **right** to seek a **safe haven**.

This policy prevented foreign nationals who had been convicted of serious crimes from appealing their deportation while they were still in the UK. Instead, they could only appeal after they had been deported.

See pages 98-99 for more on the impact of the Supreme Court in the UK.

There are other **tensions** relating to **rights** in the UK

1) Public Order Act (2023)

- The **Public Order Act (2023)** aimed to **protect collective rights** by **reducing** pressure groups' ability to cause **disruption**, but critics argued that it **eroded** the right of **freedom of assembly**.
- Within a **week** of the Act's passage, it had been used to **arrest** six members of **Republic** (an anti-monarchy pressure group) before Charles III's coronation. They were arrested on the suspicion that they were going to lock themselves to something to **disrupt** the event (a protest tactic known as **locking-on**), but they were later released without charge.

2) Gender Recognition Reform Bill

- In January 2023, the Sunak government blocked the Scottish Parliament's **Gender Recognition Reform Bill** (see p.62 and p.64 for more on Scottish devolution). This decision **divided opinion**.
- The bill's **supporters** felt that allowing **self-identification** was an important way to **progress transgender rights**, because this would remove what they considered to be **unfair requirements** for gaining legal gender recognition.
- However, **opponents** felt the bill could lead to **fraudulent applications** to **change legal sex** and that **under-18s** are **too young** to make the decision to legally change their sex.

The bill would have allowed people in Scotland aged 16 or over to change their legal sex (the sex recorded on a person's birth certificate and other official documents) without a medical diagnosis of gender dysphoria. This is known as gender self-identification.

Quick Questions

1) Name two pressure groups that aim to protect rights.
2) Which act gave same-sex couples in England and Wales the right to marry?
3) What is the difference between individual and collective rights?
4) Under which law were six members of the pressure group Republic arrested at Charles III's coronation in 2023?
5) Which Scottish Parliament bill did the Sunak government block in 2023?
6) Which government policy did the Supreme Court rule unlawful in 2023?

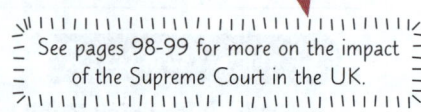

Revision Task

Practise **selecting the best evidence** by choosing examples that support the following arguments:
1) *The court system helps to protect rights in the UK.*
2) *Individual and collective rights can often be in conflict.*
3) *The government has sometimes prioritised collective rights.*

Are you alright? No, I'm half left...

I know... But did you really expect me to make a joke about such an important topic? It wouldn't be right. Okay, I'm done now. Make sure you're familiar with key debates around rights in the UK, such as how they might be limited or be in conflict.

Political Parties in the UK

Political parties may not be as fun as regular parties, but they're a bit more important when it comes to running the country. You'll need to understand the main functions of political parties in the UK and some key terms associated with them.

Political parties have **five main functions** in the **UK's democracy**

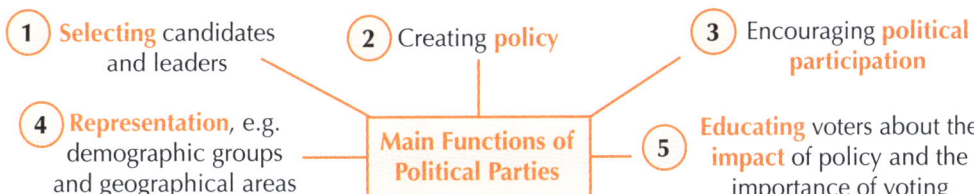

1) **Selecting** candidates and leaders
2) Creating **policy**
3) Encouraging **political participation**
4) **Representation**, e.g. demographic groups and geographical areas
5) **Educating** voters about the **impact** of policy and the importance of voting

Main Functions of Political Parties

The **UK's party system** has three **main features**

Make sure you know these **three features** of the UK's party system:

1) Long-term dominance by the **Conservatives** and **Labour**.
2) Parties are mostly **self-funding** (they don't receive large **sums of money** from the state).
3) The two main parties have traditionally been **ideologically big tents**. This means they have several **factions** which span from the **left wing** (in Labour's case) or the **right wing** (in the Conservatives' case) to the **centre-ground**.

At their recent party conference, members started to feel that their tent wasn't ideologically big enough

The Political Spectrum

Left wing — policies linked with **socialist** ideology (see p.54) that tend to support **significant state intervention** in the economy and society to increase levels of equality.

Centre-ground/centrist — policies that **blend** left wing and right wing positions to create **targeted state interventions** in the economy and society.

Right wing — policies linked with **conservative** ideology (see p.44) that tend to support **minimal state intervention** in the economy and a return to traditional social values.

Make sure you know the definitions of these **key terms**:

consensus
Areas of agreement between two or more parties.

faction
A group within a political party that has a shared ideological position.

two-party system
A political system in which only two parties can consistently influence policy-making or have a realistic chance of forming part of the government.

multi-party system
A political system in which more than two parties are consistently able to influence policy and form part of the government.

The UK is generally seen as a **two-party system**...

Here are some **facts** and **figures** which show how the UK system is **dominated** by **Labour** and the **Conservatives**.

1) Only **three elections since 1929** have failed to produce a Conservative or Labour **majority government**.
2) Labour has been the **biggest party in Wales** since the first devolved election in 1999.
3) The two main parties' share of the popular vote increased to **82% in 2017**, and was **76% in 2019**.
4) After the **2019 general election**, Labour and the Conservatives shared **87%** of the seats in the **House of Commons**.
5) In 2019, **Boris Johnson refused** to take part in a TV debate with any other party leaders except **Jeremy Corbyn**.
6) The Conservatives and Labour accounted for over **80% of the combined fundraising total** across all parties for the 2019 general election.
7) In **2024**, **Labour** once more won the **majority** of the **Scottish seats** in the **UK general election**, after a period of **ten years** where they had fallen **behind** the **SNP**.

Political Parties in the UK

...but you can make a case for the UK being a **multi-party system** in recent years

While Labour and the Conservatives still largely dominate the UK system, the **influence** of the other parties is **growing**:

- The **SNP** has been the **biggest party** in the Scottish Parliament since **2007**.
- The SNP's rise led to the **2014 Scottish independence referendum**. Between **2015** and **2024**, the **SNP** replaced **Labour** as the **biggest party** in Scotland in **general elections** to the **UK Parliament** (winning 56 out of 59 available seats in 2015).
- In 2023, the **Scottish Green Party** had **two ministers** in the devolved Scottish government.

- The Conservatives formed a **coalition government** with the **Liberal Democrats** from 2010-2015. This gave the Lib Dems **five ministerial posts** (including two members of **the Quad** — see p.89).
- In the **2024 general election**, the two main parties (the Conservatives and Labour) shared only **57%** of the vote — a record low.
- In 2024, the Lib Dems took **59 seats** from the Conservatives, including previously safe seats like **Chichester** and **Cheltenham**.

- The last two **European Parliament** elections held in the UK were won by **UKIP** (in 2014) and the **Brexit Party** (in 2019).
- The **threat** posed by UKIP **influenced** David Cameron's decision to hold the **Brexit referendum** in 2016.
- However, UKIP has only had **two MPs** and the Brexit Party **never held a seat** in the House of Commons. In **2024**, **Reform UK** won a record **5 seats**, having gained **14%** of the popular vote.

- Neither Labour nor the Conservatives stand in Northern Ireland in devolved or general elections. **Sinn Féin** and the **DUP** are consistently the two **most successful parties** in Northern Ireland.
- Theresa May signed a **confidence and supply deal** with Northern Ireland's DUP in 2017. As part of this, the DUP **negotiated** an extra **£1 bn** in infrastructure spending for Northern Ireland.

Key Terms

confidence and supply deal
An agreement between the governing party and a smaller party to support the government in confidence votes and all budget votes. The smaller party also supplies votes in other policy areas on a case-by-case basis.

Quick Questions

1) For how long has the SNP been the biggest party in the Scottish Parliament?
2) How many ministerial posts did the Liberal Democrats have as part of the coalition government?
3) What percentage of the popular vote was shared by the two main parties in elections in 2015, 2017 and 2019?
4) How much did the DUP secure in extra infrastructure spending in Northern Ireland in 2017?
5) How many elections since 1929 have failed to produce a single-party majority?

Exam Practice

For students studying...

Edexcel: Evaluate the view that the UK should no longer be seen as a two-party system. [30]

AQA: 'The UK should no longer be described as a two-party system.' Analyse and evaluate this statement. [25]

Using the sentence frames on pages 299-300, write a **conclusion** to the question above.

A great conclusion to this question would think about the different levels of influence for the two main parties in Westminster compared with at a devolved level.

Top Tip for Politicians #8: Always have a hard hat readily available...

Do some research of your own and compare the coalition government of 2010-2015 to the confidence-and-supply deal in 2017. Why did these collaborations between political parties happen and what compromises did each party have to make?

Party Funding

Political parties need to do fundraising in order to gather the money required for running election campaigns.

There are **four main sources** of **party funding** in the UK

1) **Individuals** — Either large sums from **wealthy donors**, or small donations from **the general public**.
2) **Businesses** — Usually made to the **Conservative Party**.
3) **Trade Unions** — Usually made to the **Labour Party**.
4) **The state** — Opposition parties receive **Short money** and **Cranborne money** from the state. These funds help **shadow ministers** to employ **specialist researchers** and **advisers**.

Funding from the state is a small part of the overall funding for parties.

The **Conservatives** have **raised** and **spent** the **most money** in recent elections

2017 general election

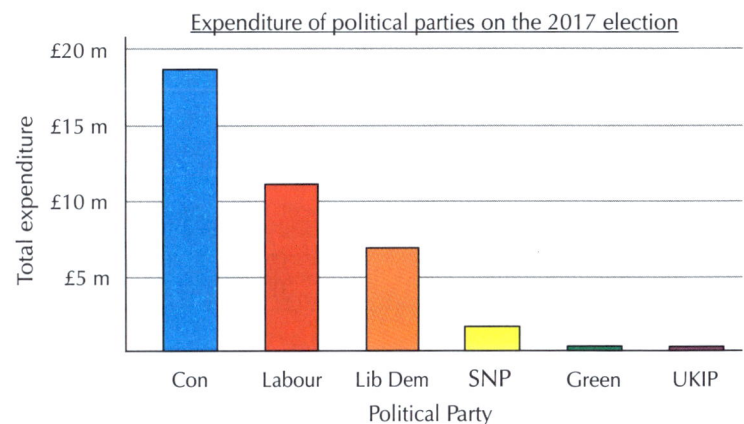

- As the graph to the right shows, the **Conservatives** spent the **most money** on the 2017 election.
- The **Conservatives** spent £18.6 m, **Labour** spent £11 m, the **Lib Dems** spent £6.8 m, the **SNP** spent £1.6 m, the **Green Party** spent £299 000 and **UKIP** spent £273 000.
- The Conservatives spent **more** than Labour and the Liberal Democrats **combined**.

2019 general election

- The table below shows the **funding sources** for five political parties in the **run up** to the 2019 election.

Party	Individuals	Trade Unions	Businesses	Other	Total
Conservatives	£13.3 m		£6 m	£100 000	£19.4 m
Labour	£160 000	£5 m	£200 000	£10 500	£5.4 m
The Brexit Party	£4 m				£4 m
Liberal Democrats	£1 m		£200 000		£1.2 m
The Green Party	£232 000		£10 000		£242 000

- The **£19.4 m** raised by the Conservatives was over **60%** of the total amount raised by all the parties.
- The **£5 m** Labour raised from trade unions made up **93%** of all the donations they received.
- The Brexit Party **failed** to win any seats despite receiving the third highest amount of donations.

Fundraising allows parties to spend more money on **campaigning**

1) In 2017, Labour spent over **£1.3 m** on digital strategy. This included over **£250 000** on advertising through Google (including YouTube and over **£100 000** through Snapchat — this involved creating a Jeremy Corbyn filter.
2) In 2019, the Conservatives' fundraising success allowed them to spend nearly **£6 m** on a mail campaign — more than Labour raised for their whole campaign.
3) The Conservatives also spent **£2 m** on **Facebook adverts** in 2017 and **£1 m** in 2019.

Tom and Debbie really put the fun into fundraising

Party Funding

Many believe that the current **party funding system** is **unfair**

1) Some feel that allowing **large donations** from individuals adds to the problem of **elitism** (see p.3) in UK politics, giving more influence to the most wealthy.
   - The Conservatives' **dominance** (especially among wealthy individual donors) makes it difficult for other parties to campaign on **equal terms**.
   - Critics argue that **wealthy individuals** and **large companies** are able to gain **disproportionate influence and access** by donating money to parties.
   - Companies linked to **Conservative donors** were awarded government contracts worth an estimated **£880 m** during the **COVID-19 pandemic**.
   - Boris Johnson was criticised for driving a **JCB digger** during the 2019 election campaign — the owner of JCB was an important **Conservative donor**.

Boris Johnson speaking at JCB headquarters in 2019

2) There have been allegations that **senior Labour figures** may also be **influenced** by **donations**.
   - For example, **Lord Alli**, a TV executive, made **gifts** to **Keir Starmer** of clothing and accommodation in 2023-2024. It later emerged that he had been offered a **temporary security pass** to Downing Street.
3) The influence of **trade unions** over Labour has also created **controversy**.
   - For example, the involvement of the Trade union **Unite** in the **anti-Semitism** scandal.
4) A **funding scandal** led to the **arrest** of the **former FM**, Nicola Sturgeon, and the **resignation** and **arrest** of both the **SNP's chief executive** and **treasurer** in 2023. It was **alleged** that the party had **misspent funds** that had been donated to campaigning for independence.

But others argue the current system is **better** than any of the **possible reforms**

1) **Reforming** the current funding system could make it **unfair** in other ways:
   - **State funding** — This would solve the problem of donors' influence, but it would mean that taxpayers' money would be used to fund parties that they **don't support**.
   - **Capping donations** — Placing a cap on **individual donations** would disproportionately affect the **Conservatives**, while capping donations from **trade unions** would disproportionately affect **Labour**.
2) Parties are able to **perform well** without reforms to the current funding system:
   - The Brexit Party's successful fundraising for the 2019 election (see previous page) shows that **smaller parties** can attract significant sums of money.
   - The fact that the SNP won **48 more seats** than the Brexit Party (despite raising only around 5% of their total during the course of the campaign) suggests that **funding** doesn't always translate into **performance**.

Some people in the UK agree with the US Supreme Court's ruling in 2010 that restricting donations is a breach of free speech (see p.194).

Quick Questions

1) What are Short money and Cranborne money?
2) What was the total expenditure of the Liberal Democrats for the 2017 general election?
3) How much did the Conservatives raise for the 2019 general election campaign?
4) How much did the Brexit Party raise in 2019?
5) How much did the Conservatives spend on their mail campaign in 2019?
6) What was the total value of government contracts awarded to companies with links to the Conservatives' donors during the COVID-19 pandemic?
7) Which party would be disproportionately affected if donations from trade unions were capped?

Exam Practice

For Edexcel students: Analyse the view that the current system of party funding in the UK requires reform. [30]
For AQA students: Explain and analyse three criticisms of the current party funding system in the UK. [25]

I spent over £100 on a pair of shoes — it was a real funding sandal...

Statistics are always going to help you out when it comes to backing up your points in the exam, and luckily for you these last two pages have been filled with them. Go through these pages and write out the most important figures on a piece of paper.

UK Politics — Political Parties

Conservative Policies

The Conservative Party, officially called the Conservative and Unionist Party, was founded in 1834 by Robert Peel.

There are **two** main ideological traditions in the Conservative Party

One Nation (centrist)	Thatcherite (centre-right/right wing)
• Supports necessary **economic** and **social interventions** by the state and sees the government as a tool for achieving a fair and prosperous society. • Favours co-operation with international bodies such as the **EU**. • Inspired by **Benjamin Disraeli's 19th-century government** and the post-war policies of **Winston Churchill** and **Harold Macmillan** (see p.46).	• Supports a blend of **neo-liberal** economic policy and **neo-conservative** social policy. • Favours **minimal state intervention** in the economy, including low taxes and public spending • Believes foreign policy should be based on the UK's national interest and is **Eurosceptic**. • Inspired by **Margaret Thatcher's** policies of **privatisation** and **deregulation**.

Key Terms

neo-liberalism
A form of non-interventionist capitalism.

neo-conservatism
A movement aiming to revive traditional values such as encouraging marriage and taking a tough approach to law and order.

Euroscepticism
Opposing the integration between UK and European institutions, such as the EU.

deregulation
Reducing the influence of state regulation to increase the freedom of private companies.

Boris Johnson took a One Nation **and** Thatcherite approach as Conservative leader

One Nation

- **Approach to COVID-19** — Johnson and Rishi Sunak (his Chancellor at the time) committed over **£70 billion** to the **furlough scheme**, which saw the state pay up to 80% of the wages of workers affected by the pandemic. The government also **temporarily increased** welfare payments by £20 per week and collaborated with **Marcus Rashford** on his **free school meals campaign** (see p.10).
- **Net zero agenda** — The Conservatives' 2019 manifesto pledged to reach **net zero carbon emissions** by 2050. Johnson's government also announced significant funding **increases** for **renewable energy** and **electric vehicles**.
- **Levelling up** — Disadvantaged parts of England were encouraged to bid for **increased funding** to stimulate economic growth.
- **Windfall tax** — To fund support for households struggling with **rising bills**, Johnson's government imposed a **25% windfall tax** on energy companies' profits in 2022.

Thatcherite

- **Welfare** — Under Johnson **welfare** wasn't linked to **inflation**, so the overall value of payments **decreased**.
- **Immigration** — Johnson approved **Priti Patel's plan** to deport asylum seekers who had illegally entered the UK to **Rwanda**.
- **Foreign aid cuts** — During the COVID-19 pandemic, the Johnson government reduced spending on foreign aid from **0.7%** of GDP to **0.5%**.
- **Brexit** — Johnson's Brexit deal saw the UK leave the **EU**, the European **single market** and the **customs union**.

Liz Truss pursued a **radical Thatcherite** approach

1) Truss and her Chancellor, **Kwasi Kwarteng**, announced plans to **cut** the top rate of **income tax** from **45%** to **40%**.
2) Truss and Kwarteng planned to keep **corporation tax** at **19%**, reversing the planned increase to **25%**.
3) She also pledged to **reduce regulations** on **fracking** (a way of extracting gas from underground).

Rishi Sunak mostly pursued a **Thatcherite** approach

1) Sunak's government **blocked** the Scottish Parliament's **Gender Recognition Reform (Scotland) Bill**.
2) His government pursued a **tougher** approach to law and order, including the **Public Order Act (2023)**, and **James Cleverly**, Sunak's **Home Secretary**, continued Priti Patel's **Rwanda plan** (see above).
3) However, Sunak was not as **radically Thatcherite** as Truss:
   - He maintained the **45%** income tax rate and his Chancellor, **Jeremy Hunt**, increased **corporation tax** for larger companies from **19%** to **25%**.
   - Sunak also announced plans for the **state** to **help** with the costs of **childcare** — a **One Nation** policy.

UK Politics — Political Parties

Labour Policies

The Labour Party sits on the centre-left of the political spectrum. Like the Conservatives, they're a big deal in UK politics.

There are **three** main ideological traditions in the Labour Party

Hard Left (democratic socialists)

The Hard Left supports:
- **Significant state intervention** to address economic and social inequalities.
- **High taxation** to re-distribute wealth.
- **Full nationalisation** of industry.
- **Non-interventionist** foreign policy that prefers **diplomatic solutions** to military ones.

Soft Left (social democrats)

The Soft Left supports:
- **Significant state regulation** of business.
- **Progressive taxation** to fund public spending.
- **Some nationalisation** of industry.
- Some **foreign military interventions**.

Key Terms

progressive taxation — Introducing higher tax rates for those with higher income or wealth, so that those who earn more money are taxed at a higher rate.

New Labour (Third Way socialists)

New Labour supports:
- **Limiting regulation**, maintaining **low corporation taxes** and working with the private sector to deliver **public services** (including healthcare).
- Thatcher's policies of **privatisation** and **deregulation** (see previous page).
- The idea that the UK has a moral and strategic duty to **intervene overseas** to **protect** its interests and those of other democracies.

Tony Blair launching the New Labour manifesto in 1997

Under **Jeremy Corbyn**, Labour's policies moved towards the **Hard Left**

1) The **2017 and 2019 manifestos** promised to **nationalise** rail, energy and water companies.
2) The 2019 manifesto also pledged to **nationalise** broadband, **abolish** university tuition fees and **increase** income tax for people earning over **£80 000** a year.
3) In total, the 2019 manifesto would have led to an **annual increase** in government spending of **£83 billion**.
4) Corbyn opposed **air strikes** against the Bashar al-Assad regime in **Syria**.

Under **Keir Starmer**, there has been a **blend** of New Labour and Soft Left policies

New Labour

- Labour **scrapped** its 2019 pledge to **abolish university tuition fees**.
- Starmer supported the **UK's military aid to Ukraine** since the Russian invasion in 2022.
- In 2024, the only **nationalisation** that Starmer publicly proposed was the creation of a state-owned company called **Great British Energy** to oversee the shift towards **renewable energy**.

Soft Left

- Starmer supported **Marcus Rashford's campaign** to extend **state-funded meals** during the school holidays in 2020 (see p.10).
- Labour called for an **increase in welfare payments** in 2021, proposed a **windfall tax** on energy companies' profits in 2022 and announced £40 bn worth of **tax increases** in 2024.
- In 2024, Labour introduced **VAT** on **independent school fees** and **increased employers'** national insurance contributions.

Exam Practice

Which **examples** from the last two pages would **best support** the following arguments in an essay?
1) *Labour and the Conservatives now share a **similar** economic policy.*
2) *The Conservatives have moved to the **right** on **social policy** in recent years.*
3) *Labour has moved to the **centre** on **foreign policy** in recent years.*

When you get to a fork in the road, take a hard left to nationalisation...

You need to think about the subtle differences between the different attitudes and beliefs in each political party. Have a go at creating a timeline to show the changes in policy for both Labour and the Conservatives in the last twenty years.

UK Politics — Political Parties

Other Parties' Policies

Those last couple of pages might have you feeling all partied out. However, it's not all about the Conservatives and Labour. There are also lots of smaller political parties that have an impact in the UK. And here's a lovely selection just for you.

Smaller parties tend to occupy narrower ideological positions than Lab or Con

Here are some of the key **policies** and **positions** for each of these smaller parties:

Party	Position on spectrum	Policies
Scottish National Party	Left wing / Centre-left	• Scottish independence • Re-join the EU • Free university tuition for Scottish students at Scottish universities • Implemented current top income tax rate of 47% (compared with 45% in England, Wales and Northern Ireland) • Net zero by 2045
Liberal Democrats	Centrist	• Net zero emissions by 2045 • Windfall tax on energy companies' profits • Re-join the EU single market (see p.103-104)
Sinn Féin	Left wing	• Unite Northern Ireland and the Republic of Ireland • Re-join the EU • Higher income tax for top earners • Recognise Irish as an official language of Northern Ireland
Democratic Unionist Party	Right wing	• Maintain Northern Ireland's place in the UK • Support for Brexit • Opposition to recognising Irish as an official language of Northern Ireland • Tax cuts
Green Party	Left wing	• Net zero as soon as possible • Free university tuition across the UK • Reduce consumption of meat and dairy in the UK • Taxes on carbon and frequent flyers
Plaid Cymru	Left wing	• Gradual move towards Welsh independence • Investment to protect the Welsh language and culture • Free university tuition for Welsh students at Welsh universities

The DUP is a political party in Northern Ireland, while Sinn Féin is in both Northern Ireland and the Republic of Ireland.

Quick Questions

1) By how much did the 2019 Labour manifesto plan to increase annual public spending?
2) What is the top rate of income tax in:
   a) England, Wales and Northern Ireland? b) Scotland?
3) Name one party that wants Irish to be made an official language in Northern Ireland.
4) What is Great British Energy?
5) By which years do the following parties want to reach net zero?
   a) Conservatives   b) Liberal Democrats   c) SNP
6) Name three parties that have supported a windfall tax in recent years.

Daniel was not familiar with the ideological position

I'm rubbish at basketball — my games always end in net zero...

These smaller parties offer an alternative to Labour and the Conservatives. They're really important as they help to strengthen the democracy of the UK and give a voice to people who don't agree with the policies of the two main parties.

Comparing Party Policy

Some people argue that the different political parties have plenty in common, while others think that there are too many policy disagreements between the parties to say that there's now a centre-ground consensus in the UK.

There are areas of **agreement** and **disagreement** between parties...

Policy Area	Agreements	Disagreements
Economy	• The Conservatives, Labour and the Liberal Democrats all support the **45% tax rate** for **top earners**. • All parties supported the **windfall tax** on energy companies' profits. • Labour and the Liberal Democrats supported the Conservatives' decision to increase **corporation tax** from **19%** to **25%** in 2023.	• Labour has proposed an **extended windfall tax** to provide more money for reducing the **cost of living**, which the Conservatives oppose. • In her **2024 Budget**, Labour **Chancellor Rachel Reeves** announced **£40 bn** worth of **tax increases**.
Welfare	All parties supported an **increase** in **universal credit payments** during the COVID-19 pandemic.	Labour has promised to replace **universal credit**. The Conservatives are **against** this.
Healthcare	All parties support the continued existence of the **NHS** as a free, state-run health system.	Labour and the Conservatives are in favour of some **private sector delivery** of **NHS services**, whereas the SNP and the Greens argue that all NHS provision should be delivered by the **public sector**.
Education	Labour, the Conservatives and the Liberal Democrats all support the principle of **university tuition fees**.	Labour have introduced **Value Added Tax** (**VAT**) on **independent school fees**. The Conservatives and the Liberal Democrats both oppose this policy.
Environment	All parties share a commitment to achieving **net zero**.	Labour want to create **Great British Energy**. The Conservatives argue that renewable energy is best delivered by the **private sector**.
Law and Order	Labour and the Liberal Democrats voted in favour during the second reading of the Conservatives' **Public Order Act** in 2023 (see p.14).	• Labour, the Liberal Democrats and the SNP all oppose the Conservatives' plan to deport asylum seekers who had illegally entered the UK to **Rwanda**. • The Liberal Democrats supported the **legalisation of marijuana** in their 2024 manifesto, whereas Labour and the Conservatives opposed this.
Foreign Policy	• There has been **cross-party agreement** over significant UK financial and military aid to support **Ukraine** in its war against Russia. • Since 2019, Labour and the Liberal Democrats have **stopped** calling for a **second referendum** on **Brexit**.	• The SNP and Sinn Féin support **re-joining the EU** whereas the Conservatives and Labour have both accepted **Brexit**. • Labour and the Liberal Democrats oppose the Conservatives' decision to cut **foreign aid** to **0.5%** of GDP.

Exam Practice

For Edexcel students: Evaluate the view that political parties in the UK now offer broadly similar policy solutions. [30]

For AQA students: Explain and analyse three differences between the policies of the Labour Party and the Conservative Party. [9]

All guests must bring a balloon — inflation is one of my party policies...

Trying to get your head around all these agreements and disagreements can be tricky. On some paper, draw a Venn diagram with the policy disagreements between Labour and the Conservatives in the two circles and the agreements in the overlap.

UK Politics — Political Parties

Factors Affecting Parties' Chances of Success

As I found out when nobody came to my birthday, some parties are more successful than others. Success can mean different things — for major parties it means winning a majority, but minor parties usually aim for things like policy influence.

Parties tend to **succeed** or **fail** based on a combination of different factors

1) The success of parties can be affected by how party **leaders** are seen by the public, what the general public thinks of party **policies** and **campaigns**, **public perceptions** of party performance and how the **media** covers a party.
2) There are arguments **for** and **against** the **impact** of each of the **four factors** below:

Party **leaders**

1) Leaders often shape their parties' **public profile**, for better or for worse.
   - In 1992, **John Major** polled far better than **Neil Kinnock**, the leader of the Labour Party. Although Labour led the national **polls** in 1992, the Conservatives managed to keep their **majority**.
   - Every time **Jo Swinson**, leader of the Liberal Democrats, appeared on radio or television in 2019, the Lib Dems' poll ratings **fell**.
2) Campaigns are becoming increasingly '**presidential**', simplifying general elections as contests between the leaders of the major political parties.
   - Every campaign since **2010** has featured at least one **leaders' TV debate** (although Theresa May **did not participate** in the 2017 debate).
3) Prime ministers lead the **largest party** in the House of Commons, which makes them the **highest-profile spokesperson** for their party's policies.
   - Other than on **Northern Ireland**, Boris Johnson's **Brexit** deal didn't differ substantially from Theresa May's. However, his leadership of that policy area was **more successful** because **Eurosceptic** Conservative MPs and voters had more **faith** that he would carry out their wishes. This was a significant factor in the Conservatives' 2019 election victory.

However, you can also make a case for the party leader **not** being so crucial.
- **Minor parties** often have **popular leaders**, but **first-past-the-post** (see p.26) makes it **difficult** for these parties to achieve **electoral success**.
- During his time as leader of the Liberal Democrats, **Charles Kennedy** polled **above** Tony Blair and Michael Howard (the Conservatives' leader at the time). However, the Lib Dems won under **10%** of the seats in the **2005 election** despite winning **22%** of the popular vote. This shows that there's a **limit** to the leader's influence on party success.

Charles Kennedy speaking at a Liberal Democrat conference in 2003

Policy and **campaigning**

Popular policies and **effective campaigning** allow parties to target specific seats and groups of voters that can **swing** the election result.
- Theresa May's 2017 policy proposal for adult social care was **unpopular** with the **general public** and contributed to the Conservatives **losing their majority**. The policy was nicknamed the '**dementia tax**' by Labour.
- The Conservatives had huge success with their '**Get Brexit Done**' slogan in the 2019 general election. This helped them to win many **Brexit-supporting constituencies** in Labour's '**Red Wall**' (see p.36).
- In 2024, Rishi Sunak's decision to leave **D-Day commemorations** to return to general **election campaigning** harmed the public's opinion of him, which disadvantaged the rest of his campaign.

In some cases, **popular policy** and **effective campaigning** doesn't directly lead to **success** for a political party.
- **Nick Clegg** was seen to have run a **highly effective campaign** for the Liberal Democrats in 2010. He was considered the **best performer** in the televised leaders' debates, and the party's pledge to **scrap university tuition fees** was **popular** among younger voters. But the Lib Dems still won **5 seats fewer** than in **2005**.
- In the 2019 general election, Labour's **economic policies** were **more popular** than the Conservatives'. However, Jeremy Corbyn was significantly **less popular** as a **leader** than Boris Johnson, which contributed to Labour losing the election.

Factors Affecting Parties' Chances of Success

Public perceptions of their performance

1) Voters' perceptions of a party's **economic competence** often shape their chances of **success**. For example, the past **three** elections when the party in government changed (**1979, 1997, 2010**) all followed, or were held during, **economic crises**.
2) **Scandals** can also harm parties' chances. The Conservatives were **punished** for '**sleaze**' in the 1997 election.
3) A **strong performance** as the main opposition party **boosted** the chances of the Conservatives in **1979**, Labour in **1997**, the Conservatives in **2010** and Labour in **2024**.

Although the UK's economy had recovered by the 1997 election, it had been in recession earlier in the decade. The Tories' previous reputation for economic competence had been harmed by the UK's forced withdrawal from the Exchange Rate Mechanism in 1992 (see p.38.).

However, there are examples of parties performing well or badly **in spite of** public perception.
- Polls suggested that the public had a **negative** view of the Conservatives' performance in government during the 2019 election campaign, but they were far more **trusted** to carry out **Brexit** than Labour.
- This suggests that sometimes **individual issues** can have a **greater impact** on party success than public perception of a party's overall performance.

Media coverage

1) *The Sun*, which has traditionally had the **highest readership** of any UK newspaper, has endorsed the **winning party** in every general election since **1979**. This suggests that its support can help to sway its readers' voting decisions.
2) An estimated **6.7 million people** watched the 2019 TV debate between Johnson and Corbyn, making it the **most-watched** political TV programme of the year. However, the number of viewers **fell** to **under 5 million** for the leaders' televised debate between Sunak and Starmer in **2024**.
3) The Conservatives used their higher **fundraising** in 2019 to spend over **£1 m** on targeted campaigns on **Facebook** and **YouTube**, which were credited with helping the party target the Brexit-supporting swing voters who were crucial to winning '**Red Wall**' seats.

Harpreet thought the newspaper would provide excellent coverage from the rain

However, there's debate over whether **newspapers** do **influence public opinion**, or whether they confirm existing biases (see p.41-42).
- Many (including Tony Blair himself) felt that Labour's chances of winning the 1997 election were **boosted** by *The Sun*'s **endorsement**, which was the first time the paper had supported Labour since **1970**. However, support for Labour actually **fell** after *The Sun*'s endorsement. This was due to a combination of factors, but it suggests that the newspaper's support was **not a significant factor** in Labour's victory.
- The Liberal Democrats **gained 28 seats** in 1997 and **Reform UK** won **14%** of the **vote** in **2024** despite having **no** national newspaper endorsements.
- **Theresa May's Conservatives** had the endorsement of **twice** as many daily national newspapers as **Jeremy Corbyn's Labour** in 2017, but a **poor campaign** and **public concerns** over May's leadership meant her party **lost its majority**, while Labour gained **30** seats.

Exam Practice

For Edexcel students: Evaluate the view that leadership is the most important factor determining a political party's chances of success. [30]

For AQA students: Explain and analyse three factors that influence a political party's chances of success. [9]

I already loved CGP, but this page has just confirmed my existing bias...

Apologies to any aspiring politicians, but the path to political success isn't straightforward. However, looking out for these factors and how they affect a party's chances of success is a good idea — even if you're not aiming for political stardom. Choose an election from the last ten years and weigh up which factor had the biggest impact on the winning party's success.

UK Politics — Electoral Systems

Electoral Systems in the UK

You'd think that one electoral system would do, but the UK has used a few types. Luckily for you, this page introduces them all.

There are **four main types** of **election** that take place in the UK

1 General election
- Elects MPs to represent **constituencies** in the House of Commons.
- The party with the **most seats** then forms the executive branch of government (see p.83)…
- …unless they don't win a **majority** — then they form either a **minority government** or a **coalition government** with another party.

2 Devolved legislative election
- Elects members of a **devolved legislature**.
- E.g. the Scottish Parliament, the Senedd (Welsh Parliament) and the Northern Ireland Assembly.

3 Mayoral election
- Elects **mayors** who are responsible for running a **city** or **regional government**.
- E.g. the Mayor of London and the Mayor of Greater Manchester.

4 Local election
Elects **councillors** who represent local wards on a **borough** or **county council**.

Sadiq Khan (left), who became Mayor of London in 2016, and Andy Burnham (right), who became Mayor of Greater Manchester in 2017

Key Terms

legislature
A parliament or assembly that is responsible for passing laws.

majority government
When one party wins more than half of the seats in the legislature, meaning they can govern without the help of another party.

minority government
When the largest party in a legislature does not have a majority of seats, but still forms a government on its own.

coalition government
When two or more parties come together to form a government.

You don't need to know about local elections in detail, but it's worth remembering for the Prime Minister and the Executive topic (see p.83-95) that poor results can often put pressure on the PM. The Conservative party lost over 1300 council seats in 2019, shortly before Theresa May's failure to pass her Brexit bill led to her stepping down as PM.

There are also **four types** of **electoral system** in the UK

Type of System	Constituencies	Examples and Usage in the UK
Plurality Where the candidate with the most votes is elected.	Single-member	**First-past-the-post (FPTP)** Local elections in England and Wales, general elections and mayoral elections
Proportional Where candidates are elected proportionally depending on the percentage of the popular vote won.	Multi-member	**Single transferable vote (STV)** Northern Ireland Assembly elections **Regional party list** (Regional party list was formerly used in European Parliament elections.)
Mixed Hybrid systems where some candidates are elected under a plurality system. Other candidates are elected proportionally.	Mix of single-member and multi-member	**Additional member system (AMS)** Scottish Parliament and Senedd elections
Majoritarian Where candidates need to receive over 50% of the vote to be elected. This can result in multiple rounds of voting.	Single-member	**Supplementary vote (SV)** Used in English mayoral elections until 2023. **Alternative vote (AV)** AV has never been used in the UK, but it was the subject of a referendum in 2011 (see p.30).

constituency
A geographical area that receives representation in a legislature. Depending on the electoral system, constituencies can either have one representative (single-member) or several representatives (multi-member).

A majoritarian system (SV) has been used in the UK in the past, but now only the other three types of system are used.

Patisserie System — where voters chuck a pastry at their chosen candidate...

The candidate with the biggest pile of pastries wins. Candidates can eat their votes if they like, but consumed votes won't be counted. Sounds like a perfect system to me. You should still learn about all the others though, just in case it doesn't take off.

First-Past-the-Post

First-past-the-post (FPTP) features in most UK elections, which is bad news for hyphen-haters but great news for parties that can drum up strong support in many constituencies. Here's a handy overview of the advantages and disadvantages of FPTP.

First-past-the-post produces **disproportionate outcomes**...

1) The **winner-takes-all** nature of FPTP means that the proportion of seats won by a party doesn't accurately reflect the proportion of votes that they received nationally.
2) Minor parties with **dispersed support** tend to perform **poorly** because they come **second** and **third** in lots of constituencies:

- In 1983, the **SDP-Liberal Alliance** (now called the Liberal Democrats) won 25% of the vote but only 23 seats (4% of the total).
- In 2015, **UKIP** won 13% of the vote but only 1 seat (0.2% of the total).
- In 2019, the **Liberal Democrats** won 12% of the vote but only 11 seats (2% of the total).
- In 2024, Reform UK won 14% of the vote but only 5 seats (around 1% of the total)

3) But parties with **concentrated support** tend to perform **well**:

- In 2015, the **SNP** won 5% of the vote and 9% of the seats.
- In 2019, the **Conservatives** won 44% of the vote and 56% of the seats.
- In 2024, **Labour** won 34% of the vote and 63% of the seats.

Alan misunderstood when they said he had to be first past the post to win

Key Terms

dispersed support
Support that is thinly spread across a wide geographical area.

concentrated support
Strong support in a small geographical area.

...which means that it usually produces a **majority government**

1) FPTP has only failed to produce a majority government **three times** since 1929 — in February 1974, and in 2010 and 2017.
2) This creates a **two-party system** dominated by the **Conservatives** and **Labour**.

- Every government between 1922 and 2023 has been led by the **Conservatives** or **Labour**.
- The **2010-2015 Conservative-Liberal Democrat** government was the **first peacetime coalition** in nearly a hundred years.

First-past-the-post helps to create **safe seats**

FPTP rewards **concentrated support**, which leads to the creation of many **safe seats** where one party **dominates**.

- In **Liverpool Walton** in 2019, **Labour** won 85% of the vote.
- This made Liverpool Walton the **safest seat** in the UK.
- No other party has been elected there since **1964**.

Safe seats **benefit** the **two main parties** — the 30 safest seats in 2019 were all won by the **Conservatives** or **Labour**.

General elections are often decided by marginal seats

1) Under 100 **marginal seats** usually decide the **outcome** of a UK general election.
2) This means that **some votes** matter **more** than others.
3) It also leads to some MPs being elected with a **weak mandate**.
   - In 2019, Sinn Féin beat the Ulster Unionist Party by just 57 votes in **Fermanagh and South Tyrone** in Northern Ireland. See p.28 for how results in this constituency differ under a proportional electoral system.
   - In 2024, David Pinto-Duschinsky was elected as MP for **Hendon** with **21%** of the vote and by a **margin** of only **15 votes**.

Key Terms

safe seat
A seat in Parliament that is likely to be won by the same party at the next election because the incumbent (current holder) has a large majority.

marginal seat
A seat that could be lost to another party at the next election because the incumbent was elected with only a small majority.

What's every postie's favourite electoral system? First-pass-the-post...

The trouble with FPTP is that it's hard to win seats with dispersed support. It's like trying to cover a slice of toast with the dregs of the jam jar when someone else is dropping dollops of marmalade on top — no one will notice the jam in the end.

Additional Member System

Additional member system (AMS) might sound like a machine for growing limbs, but it's just a mixed electoral system (see p.25).

AMS gives voters **two chances** to vote

AMS is used in **Scotland** and **Wales** in Scottish Parliament and Senedd elections:

From 2026, the Senedd will use a new proportional system in which voters cast one vote for a party or an independent candidate in their local constituency. Each of the 16 constituencies will elect 6 MSs to the Senedd (96 in total).

1) Voters get **one vote** under **first-past-the-post** for their **local constituency representative**, called a Member of the Scottish Parliament (MSP) in Scotland and a Member of the Senedd (MS) in Wales.

Scottish Parliament — 73 MSPs elected
Senedd — 40 MSs elected

2) Voters then vote **once** for a **party** to represent their **region** under a **directly proportional** system called **Regional Party List** (see below).

Scottish Parliament — 56 MSPs elected to represent 8 regions
Senedd — 20 MSs elected to represent 5 regions

Supporters of AMS say it uses the **best parts** of other **voting systems**...

Supporters argue that AMS **combines** the best elements of **first-past-the-post** with the best elements of **proportional systems**.

Elements of First-past-the-post

1) AMS maintains the **direct link** between a **single representative** and their **local constituents**.
2) AMS produces **governments** that are able to **survive** and pass **meaningful policy** (see p.66-67).

Elements of Proportional Systems

1) The **number of seats won** by a party is usually **more in proportion** with the **number of votes cast** for that party.
   - In 2021, the **SNP** won just under half of the seats in the Scottish Parliament and 44% of the vote across the constituency and regional elections.
   - In the same year, **Plaid Cymru** won 22% of the seats in the Senedd and 21% of the vote.

2) **Smaller parties** are **not punished** for having **dispersed support**.
   The **Greens** won only 1% of the constituency vote in 2021 but 8% of regional votes, allowing them to win 8 seats in the **Scottish Parliament**.

...but there are **criticisms** of AMS too

1) **Critics** of AMS believe that it creates **unequal mandates**.
   - Representatives elected under **first-past-the-post** have a **direct mandate** from their **local constituency**, whereas those elected **regionally** owe their mandate to their **parties**, who choose each candidate's position on the **regional list**.
   - This is especially **problematic** when regional representatives choose to **switch parties**:

Michelle Ballantyne left the **Scottish Conservatives** in 2020 and joined **Reform UK** in 2021.

Mark Reckless switched his party affiliation in the Senedd **four times** between 2016 and 2021.

Under the regional party list system, parties provide a list of candidates for each region, and the candidates are elected in the order they appear on the regional list. The number of candidates elected depends on how much of the vote the party receives, so candidates at the top of the list are more likely to be elected.

2) Critics also believe AMS often fails to deliver **outcomes** that are **significantly different** from **first-past-the-post**.
   - Both Wales and Scotland have been dominated by a **single party** for most of devolution's history.
   - **Labour** has been in government in Wales since devolution began and the **SNP** has been in power in Scotland since 2007.

Welsh Labour particularly benefits from AMS. In 2021, the party won an average of **38% of the vote** across the **constituency** and **regional elections**, but managed to gain **50% of the seats** in the **Senedd**.

This is a similar level of **disproportionality** to first-past-the-post (see previous page).

How many words with AMS in can you get into one sentence?*

Don't assume minority or coalition governments must be weak or unstable. AMS rarely produces majorities, but government has been very stable in Scotland and Wales, with no suspensions in the Scottish Parliament or the Senedd since their devolution.

*Pam's mam went to Amsterdam to buy some hamsters in prams. Ha! Beat that.

Single Transferable Vote

Single transferable vote (STV) is used to elect multi-member constituencies that often have representatives from a range of parties.

STV is a **proportional** system where voters **rank** candidates

1) Under STV, voters **rank candidates** by numbering them in order of **preference**.
2) Once a party has received enough votes to meet a **quota** (usually the **minimum number of votes** or a **percentage of the total vote** needed to **win a seat**), their **top-ranking candidate** is elected.
3) The second, third, fourth and further **preferences** of voters are counted until **all seats** in the constituency have been won.

STV is the **most proportional** system used in the **UK**

STV is used to elect **Members of the Legislative Assembly** (MLAs) in the Northern Ireland Assembly.
In the 2022 **Northern Ireland Assembly** election, parties received the following share of the vote and seats:

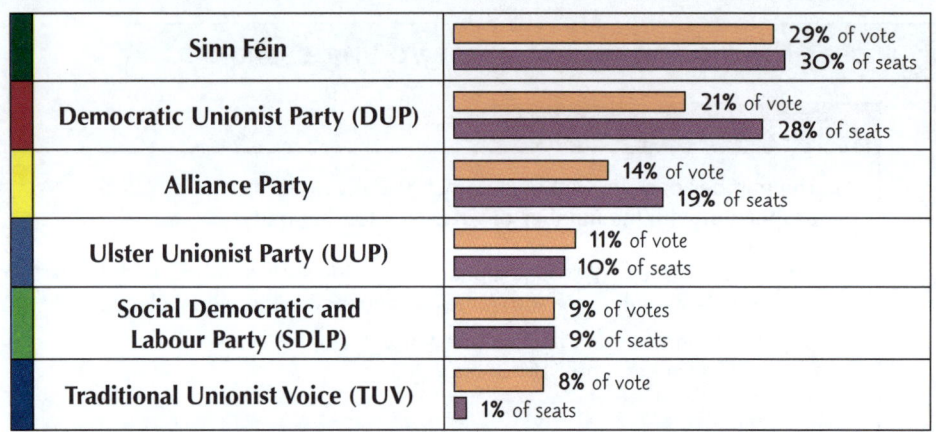

Party	% of vote	% of seats
Sinn Féin	29%	30%
Democratic Unionist Party (DUP)	21%	28%
Alliance Party	14%	19%
Ulster Unionist Party (UUP)	11%	10%
Social Democratic and Labour Party (SDLP)	9%	9%
Traditional Unionist Voice (TUV)	8%	1%

Although STV is the **most proportional** system that's used in the UK, it's not a **directly** proportional system — most **parties** are rewarded with proportional results, but **not all**.

This is because STV still **splits representation** into **constituencies**. Having **concentrated support** is still helpful, but it has much **less impact** than it does under first-past-the-post.

STV guarantees coalition governments...

1) STV was chosen for **Northern Ireland Assembly** elections because it **guarantees** coalition governments. This guarantee satisfies the need for '**power-sharing**' under the **Good Friday peace agreement** of 1998 (p.62).
2) Every Northern Irish government **since devolution** has been a coalition. The Northern Ireland Assembly was initially led by the **UUP** and the **SDLP**, and more recently it has been led by **Sinn Féin** and the **DUP**.

...and it creates nuanced constituency representation

- Under **FPTP**, **Fermanagh and South Tyrone** was the most marginal constituency in the UK in the **2019 general election** (p.26).
- This was problematic because **Sinn Féin**, a Republican party, very **narrowly beat** the **UUP**, a Unionist party.
- This left **Unionist voters** feeling **unrepresented** in Westminster.

However, under **STV** in the **2022 Northern Ireland Assembly elections**, this constituency elected 3 MLAs from **Sinn Féin**, 1 from the **UUP** and 1 from the **DUP**. This gave representation to **both Republicans** and **Unionists**.

17 out of 18 constituencies elected MLAs from at least three different parties.

Critics of STV say it has two key weaknesses

1 STV can fail to create strong governments

- **Coalition governments** can be **unstable**, especially in a **divided political system** like Northern Ireland's.
- **Disagreements** between **coalition partners** have meant that the **Northern Ireland Assembly** has now been **suspended** for over 40% of its history.

2 Candidates can be elected with a weak mandate

- STV elects **multi-member constituencies** with several representatives, so candidates can often be elected with a **low percentage** of **first preference votes**.
- The SDLP's **Sinéad McLaughlin** won **under 7%** of **first preference votes** in **Foyle** in 2022, but she was still elected as an MLA.

SSSSSSSSSSSTV — the most proportional voting system used by snakes...

STV didn't cause the disagreements in the Northern Ireland Assembly, but seeing the effects of unstable coalition governments could make voters less open to the idea of using STV as an alternative to FPTP in general elections in the UK.

Supplementary Vote

Another page, another round of acronyms. This page will help you tell your SV from your STV. I know, not confusing at all...

Supplementary Vote (SV) allows voters to express up to two preferences

1) A candidate is elected if they win **over 50%** of **first preference votes**.

2) If **no** candidate passes this threshold, **all** but the **top two candidates** are **eliminated**.

3) Then **second preference votes** are counted and the candidate who has the **most votes** is elected.

A postal ballot paper for the 2016 London mayoral election, which used a supplementary vote system. UK mayoral elections stopped using SV voting in 2022.

There are advantages and disadvantages to using SV

This wasn't quite what Fred had in mind when he said he wanted a strong mandate

✓ SV gives elected representatives a **strong mandate**:
- **Sadiq Khan** won 40% of first preference votes in the **2021 London mayoral election**, but 55% of the total vote once second preference votes had been counted.
- **Andy Street** won 49% of first preference votes in the **West Midlands mayoral election** in the same year, but 54% of the total vote once second preference votes had been counted.

✓ Since candidates often need **support** from voters who are initially drawn to **other parties**, they are more likely to reach across **party political divides** in their campaigning.

✓ If adopted in general elections, SV would be **likely** to produce a **majority government**.

✗ **Critics** of SV argue that it can be just as **disproportionate** as **first-past-the-post**.

✗ Votes for **smaller parties** with **more dispersed support** will often be '**wasted**' because their candidates are unlikely to finish in the top two.

✗ As a **majoritarian system**, SV still gives **most benefit** to the **more established parties** that enjoy **concentrated support**.

Under SV, most directly elected mayors in England represented Labour, with some representing the Conservatives. Because the system rewards concentrated support, it remained difficult for other parties and independent candidates to have a realistic chance of election.

Quick Questions

1) How many MLAs were elected to represent Fermanagh and South Tyrone in the Northern Ireland Assembly in 2022?
2) Which parties did they come from, and why is this significant?
3) How many seats did the Scottish Greens win under AMS in 2021?
4) Which party has always been in government in Wales since the beginning of devolution?
5) What percentage of the vote, and how many seats, did UKIP win in 2015?
6) Which parties did nearly all of England's directly elected mayors represent under SV?
7) What was the safest seat in the 2019 general election?

Exam Practice

There's a lot of **data** to deal with in the Electoral Systems topic, and the number of **statistics** on these pages might seem a bit overwhelming. Practise **using data** in an exam context by selecting relevant **examples** from the last four pages and explaining how you could use them to illustrate the following **arguments** in an essay:

1) *FPTP harms parties with dispersed support.*
2) *AMS produces more proportional outcomes than FPTP.*
3) *STV is the most proportional system used in the UK.*
4) *SV produces stronger mandates than FPTP.*

Who doesn't love a good acronym? Just us at CGP? Awkward...

Make sure you learn some statistics that show the impact of all four systems covered in this section — first-past-the-post, additional member system, single transferable vote and supplementary vote. It'll help you pick up AO1 and AO2 marks.

UK Politics — Electoral Systems

Alternatives to First-Past-the-Post

There's been a lot of debate about whether an alternative to first-past-the-post should be adopted for UK general elections. There are lots of arguments to consider, so take a look at these pages and decide which one gets your vote. *Sorry, couldn't resist.*

Governments have considered **replacing** first-past-the-post

1) When **devolution** was introduced by **Tony Blair's government**, the new electoral systems were intended to **improve** the **quality** of the UK's **democracy**.
2) The **1997 Labour manifesto** also promised a referendum on **replacing first-past-the-post** for general elections, but this **never happened**.
3) A **commission** that Blair established to **investigate electoral reform** judged electoral systems based on **four criteria**:

There's still intense debate over whether this aim has been achieved with these systems.

- broad proportionality
- the need for **stable government**
- an extension of **voter choice**
- maintaining a **link** between **MPs** and **geographical constituencies**

Election results are **broadly proportional** if there is a **close link** between the **percentage of votes** for a party and the **percentage of seats** they win. For example, if Labour won 40% of the votes and 45% of the seats, this would be a broadly proportional outcome. If the percentage of votes and seats were **almost exactly the same**, the results would be described as directly proportional.

You could use these criteria in an essay if you have to analyse and evaluate electoral reform.

There was a **referendum** on adopting the **alternative vote** system in **2011**

1) In **2011**, under the **Conservative-Liberal Democrat coalition**, a referendum was held on adopting the **alternative vote (AV) system** for general elections.
2) **68%** voted **against** replacing first-past-the-post with AV.
3) Some believe this **rejection** of AV shows that there's **not enough desire** for **electoral reform**.
4) The fact that **turnout** was only **42%** further suggests a lack of public engagement.

The rejection of AV doesn't mean that **proportional representation** has been **rejected** by British voters:

- The **alternative vote** system is **majoritarian**, which means that it can sometimes produce **even less proportional** outcomes than first-past-the-post.
- Therefore, voters in the UK have never been offered a **proportional alternative** to FPTP in a referendum.

There are arguments **for** and **against** keeping **first-past-the-post**

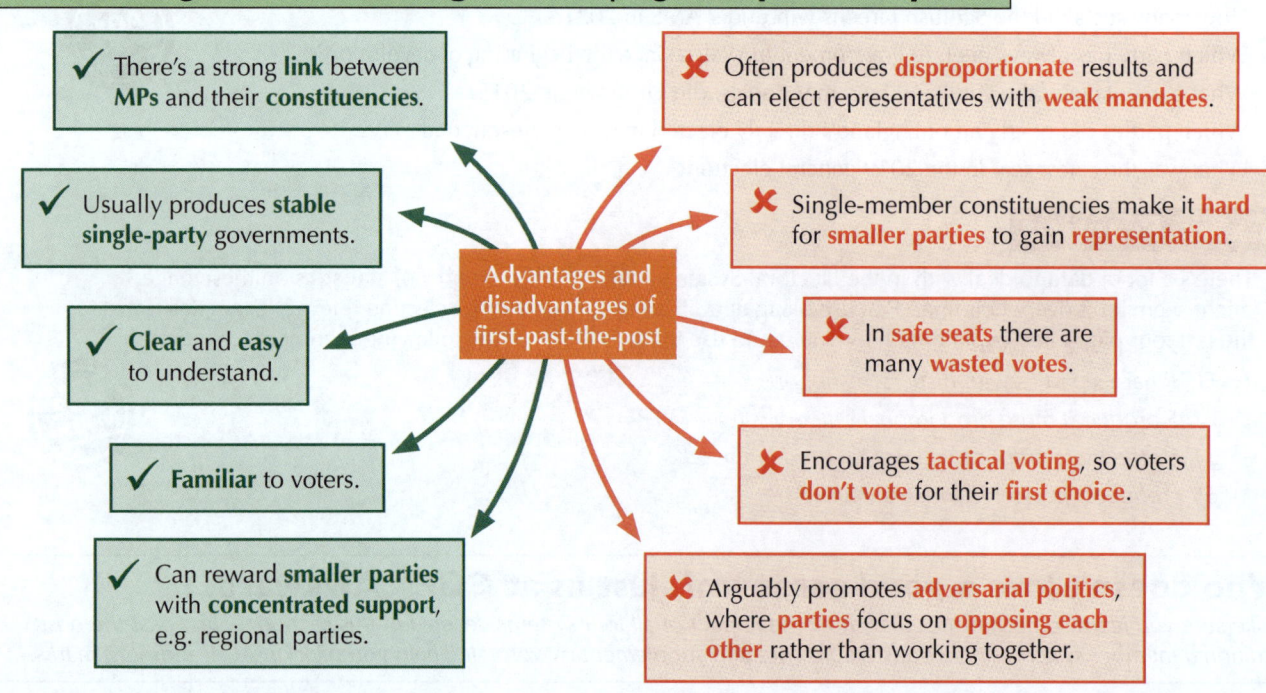

✓ There's a strong **link** between **MPs** and their **constituencies**.

✓ Usually produces **stable single-party** governments.

✓ **Clear** and **easy** to understand.

✓ **Familiar** to voters.

✓ Can reward **smaller parties** with **concentrated support**, e.g. regional parties.

✗ Often produces **disproportionate** results and can elect representatives with **weak mandates**.

✗ Single-member constituencies make it **hard** for **smaller parties** to gain **representation**.

✗ In **safe seats** there are many **wasted votes**.

✗ Encourages **tactical voting**, so voters **don't vote** for their **first choice**.

✗ Arguably promotes **adversarial politics**, where **parties** focus on **opposing each other** rather than working together.

Advantages and disadvantages of first-past-the-post

UK Politics — Electoral Systems

Alternatives to First-Past-the-Post

Some want a referendum on a system that has already been used in the UK

Here are some **arguments** you could consider when evaluating the **advantages** and **disadvantages** of replacing FPTP:

Additional Member System

👍
- Combines the constituency representation of FPTP with **better party representation**.
- Has consistently produced **stable governments** in Scotland and Wales.
- Promotes **more power-sharing** and **compromise** than FPTP.
- Allows voters **greater choice** than FPTP.
- Allows parties with **either** concentrated or dispersed support to gain **representation**.

👎
- **Less likely** than FPTP to produce a **single-party majority** government, which can lead to **slower** decision making.
- Creates **two tiers** of **representatives** with **unequal mandates**.
- The **party list system** gives lots of **power** to **party bosses**, rather than to voters.
- Can still produce **disproportionate outcomes**.
- May allow fringe parties with **extremist views** to gain representation (though it hasn't in Scotland or Wales).

Single Transferable Vote

👍
- Multi-member constituencies offer **more nuanced representation** than single-member constituencies.
- **Most proportional** system used in the UK.
- Designed to promote a **consensus-based** style of politics.
- Far **fewer wasted votes** than under FPTP.
- The process of **ranking candidates** is **fairly easy** to explain.

👎
- Tends to produce **multi-party coalition governments**, enhancing representation but potentially **slowing** legislative efficiency and decision making.
- **Coalitions** can take a **long time** to form, and can give **disproportionate** amounts of **power** to **small parties**.
- The **quota** used to **allocate seats** is **complex**.
- Multi-member **constituencies** would be **larger** than current seats if adopted in general elections. This would **weaken** the **local connection** between **representatives** and **voters**.
- May allow fringe parties with **extremist views** to gain representation.

Supplementary Vote

👍
- Offers **greater choice** than FPTP.
- **Fewer wasted votes** than under FPTP.
- Representatives will have **stronger mandates** than most MPs who are elected under FPTP.
- Maintains a **strong link** between **MPs** and their **constituencies**.
- **Voting process** is fairly easy to explain.

👎
- Can produce **results** that are even **less proportional** than under FPTP.
- Likely to maintain the **two-party system**.
- More likely to produce **single-party majority** governments, ensuring **strong mandates** but **reducing opportunities** for smaller parties.
- Ballots have caused **confusion** in some elections — thousands of ballots in the **2021 London mayoral elections** were **void** because **voters** filled them out **incorrectly**.

Exam Practice

For students studying...

Edexcel: Evaluate the view that the advantages of first-past-the-post outweigh the case for replacing it with an alternative electoral system in Westminster general elections. [30]

AQA: Explain and analyse three arguments in favour of replacing first-past-the-post in UK general elections. [9]

As well as discussing the alternative systems, you can also refer to the disadvantages of first-past-the-post when answering this question. Just make sure you refer back to the question throughout your essay.

I've already suggested an excellent alternative on p.25...

If you're asked to evaluate electoral reform, it's a good idea to back up your arguments with statistics. Think about how the election data on pages 26-29 could be used to support arguments for and against replacing FPTP with a different system.

Voting Behaviour

Step 1: check where your polling station is. Step 2: grab your photo ID. Step 3: go to polling station. Step 4: give your name and address to — Oh sorry, this isn't about election day etiquette? Ah well, still all useful info, but let's get back on track.

Voting behaviour **varies** significantly between **general elections**...

1) In recent decades, the UK has witnessed a process known as **partisan dealignment**.
2) This means that many voters no longer **identify** with just **one political party**. Instead, they make a **decision** over which party they vote for depending on a **range of factors** which may **change** from one election to the next.

- Only **52%** of **Conservative voters** from 2019 **supported** the party again in 2024. Voters' **shifting loyalties** were especially noticeable in the **red wall** seats in the **north of England** and the **Midlands**.
- These constituencies had been **dominated** by **Labour** until **2019**, when the **Conservatives won 28 seats** in these areas.
- However, in **2024**, the Conservatives didn't win **any** of the 38 red wall seats. **Labour** won **37 seats**, and **Reform UK** won the remaining seat (Ashfield).

In 2024, the Conservatives also performed poorly in the blue wall seats — rural and suburban seats that had previously been safe seats for the party. The Liberal Democrats made significant gains in these areas, winning 23 of the 43 blue wall seats that the Conservatives had won in 2019.

Voters in **Scotland** have also been prepared to **shift** their **allegiances** in recent **general elections**:

- In **2010**, **Labour** won **42%** of **Scottish votes**, compared with **under 20%** for the **SNP**.
- By **2015**, this had **shifted** to just **24%** of votes for **Labour**, with the **SNP** vote share increasing to **50%** of **Scottish votes**.
- The **SNP's dominance** continued in the **2017** and **2019** general elections. However, in **2024**, **Labour** gained **35%** of the vote, with the **SNP** receiving **30%**.

...but there are some **influences** on voting behaviour that remain **consistent**

Age

1) Increasingly, **age** is seen as the **most reliable indicator** of voting behaviour, with **older voters** more likely to support the **Conservatives** and **younger voters** more likely to support **Labour**.
2) In the **2024** general election, **younger voters** were also much **more likely** to support the **Green Party** or the **Liberal Democrats**, while **older voters** were more likely to support **Reform UK**.

Younger voters are generally seen as more progressive on social and economic issues, whereas older voters are seen as having more conservative views on these issues.

There's more on demographics on p.34-35.

Safe Seats

1) Many formerly **safe seats** in the **red wall** and **blue wall** have become **more marginal** in recent years. However, there are still some constituencies that remain **extremely safe seats** for either Labour or the Conservatives.
2) **Liverpool Walton** has had only **Labour MPs** since **1964**. It had the **largest margin** of victory of any constituency across the UK in **2010**, **2015** and **2019**, and the **second-largest margin** of victory in **2024**.
3) The constituency of **Richmond and Northallerton** (which was known as Richmond before boundary changes were implemented in 2024) has been held by the **Conservatives** since **1910**. It was the **safest Conservative seat** in **2010** and **2024**.

Not to be confused with a saved seat

Public Approval

1) In most elections, **public perceptions** of the party leaders' **competence** and **suitability** to serve as prime minister have a significant impact on voting behaviour.
2) Many commentators argued that **low public approval ratings** for **Ed Miliband** in 2015 and **Jeremy Corbyn** in **2019** influenced **Labour's poor performance** in those **elections**.

Corbyn's approval ratings were significantly higher in 2017, when Labour gained 30 seats. According to YouGov polls, he slipped from a 46% approval rating just after the 2017 general election to a 22% approval rating just before the 2019 general election.

Voting Behaviour

The performance of the economy has a key role in most election campaigns

1) The last four elections that were **lost** by the **governing party** have all taken place during or shortly after **economic crises**:
   - In **1979**, **2010** and **2024**, the **opposition** successfully persuaded enough voters that a **change of government** would be more likely to **solve** the UK's **economic problems**.
   - In **1997**, **Labour's** campaign drew on the public's **mistrust** of the **Conservatives** after the **Black Wednesday crisis** in **1992** and the **recession** that followed (see p.38).

   > Some political commentators use rational choice theory to explain voting behaviour. This is the idea that many voters tend to base their vote on self-interest, calculating which party is most likely to benefit them.

2) When the economy is **performing well** or showing signs of **recovery**, the **governing party** is generally **very likely** to **win** general elections:
   - In **1987**, Margaret Thatcher's **Conservatives** benefited from **economic growth**, maintaining a **large majority**.
   - In **2001**, Tony Blair's **Labour** did the same. In **2005**, the economy's **continued strength** helped Labour to hold onto a **majority** in the general election, despite the unpopularity of the **Iraq War**.
   - In **2015**, David Cameron's **Conservatives'** campaign was based on **persuading voters** that they were dealing with the **deficit** that they'd **inherited** from the **last Labour government** in 2010. Their campaign was **successful**, although they won a **majority** of only 12 seats.

   > There's more about the influence of the economy on voting on page 38.

Some issues rise and fall in importance depending on the political context

TRADE UNIONS:
- Following the **Winter of Discontent** in **1978-79**, the power of **trade unions** was a **major factor** in the **1979 general election**. Margaret Thatcher's **Conservative opposition** accused Jim Callaghan's **Labour government** of being **too close** to the unions to **prevent strikes**.
- The Conservatives' **campaign slogan** ('Labour isn't working') was designed to **emphasise** this point and make the case for a **change of government**. The Conservatives **gained 62 seats** to win a **Commons majority** of **44**. They spent the next **18 years** in government before Tony Blair's **landslide victory** in 1997.

FOREIGN POLICY:
Most election campaigns focus on domestic policy, but **foreign policy** has played a **pivotal role** in several elections:
- **FALKLANDS WAR** — In **1983**, the **Conservatives** benefited from a surge in Margaret Thatcher's **public approval ratings** after the successful conclusion of the **Falklands War**.
- **IRAQ WAR** — In **2005**, **Labour** lost **48 seats** and **over 5%** of the **popular vote**. This was largely due to Tony Blair's decision to join the US-led **invasion of Iraq** in **2003** without clear evidence of the 'weapons of mass destruction' that he and US President George W. Bush believed Iraq was developing.
- **BREXIT** — **Brexit** was a **key factor** in both the **2017** and **2019** general elections, with the **Conservatives** benefiting from the support of the **majority** of **Leave voters**. David Cameron's decision to promise a **referendum** on the UK's membership of the **European Union** was seen as an important factor in the Conservatives' **surprise majority** in **2015** — it helped them to limit **UKIP** to only **one seat**.

> See pages 37-38 for more on the influence of these factors on voting.

> Following the defections of Conservative MPs Mark Reckless and Douglas Carswell in 2014, UKIP went into the general election with two seats in the House of Commons. Despite winning its highest-ever share of the popular vote (12.6%), the disproportionality of the first-past-the-post system meant that they only won Carswell's seat of Clacton.

Quick Questions

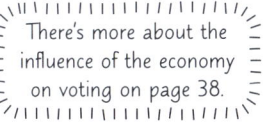

1) What is meant by partisan dealignment?
2) How many red wall seats did Reform UK win in 2024?
3) Which factor is seen as the most reliable indicator of voting behaviour?
4) What do the general elections of 1979, 1997, 2010 and 2024 have in common?
5) When was the Winter of Discontent?
6) In which elections has foreign policy played a prominent role?

Voting Bee-haviour — when a hive usurps the queen and starts a democracy...
A fall in the number of safe seats can have a positive effect on the political process. In places where seats aren't safe, politicians will have to campaign and engage more with their constituents. This may lead to more constituents' concerns being addressed.

Demographic Factors

Now, I'm afraid I'll have to disappoint you, but these pages on 'demoGRAPHics' aren't full of graphs. I know, it's truly gutting. Instead, it's all about different types of people. These pages look at how different aspects of identity influence voting behaviour.

Class used to be seen as the most reliable predictor of voting behaviour

1) Following the **decline** of the **Liberal Party** after the First World War, many voting behaviour analysts believed that **social class** was the **best predictor** of someone's **likely voting behaviour**.
2) **Labour** emerged as the **dominant party** among the **working classes**, while the **Conservatives** retained their strong performance among **middle-class** and **upper-class voters**. This is an example of **class alignment**.

> For example, in the **1964 general election**, **Labour** won 22% of middle-class votes and 64% of working-class votes, compared with the **Conservatives'** 62% of middle-class votes and 28% of working-class votes.

3) Modern voting behaviour studies use **different categories** for **different social classes**, based on people's **occupations**:
   - **AB** — People in **higher** or **intermediate managerial**, **administration** and **professional** roles
   - **C1** — People in **supervisory**, **clerical**, or **lower level managerial**, **administration** and **professional** roles
   - **C2** — People in **skilled manual occupations**
   - **DE** — People in **semi-skilled** and **unskilled manual occupations** and **unemployed** people

In recent decades there has been a process of class dealignment:

- In the **2019 general election**, the Conservatives performed **better** with C2DE voters (48%) than with ABC1 voters (43%), suggesting that the **traditional model** of **class alignment** was **no longer relevant**. Labour performed the same (33%) among both groups.
- In the **2024 general election**, there was **little difference** between the Conservative and Labour **vote share** among the **different social classes**. **Labour** comfortably **outperformed** the **Conservatives** among **both** ABC1 voters (36% compared to 25%) and C2DE voters (33% compared to 23%).

Key Term — class dealignment: When people don't follow the traditional voting behaviour of their social class.

In 2024, although social class seemed not to influence the decisions of voters who opted for one of the two main parties, Reform UK performed much better among C2DE voters (20%) than with ABC1 voters (11%).

Age is now considered a better predictor of voting behaviour than class

Data from the **2019** and **2024 general elections** support the role of **age** in **influencing voting behaviour**:

- In **2019**, the **Conservatives** won **67%** of the **over-70 vote** and **22%** of the **under-30 vote**. In **2024**, the Conservatives performed **very poorly** among **under 30s**, winning just **8%** of their vote. They still performed **fairly well** with **over 70s**, winning **46%** of their vote.
- **Labour** has consistently **performed better** with **younger voters** compared to **older** ones. In **2024**, Labour won **43%** of the **under-30 vote**, compared with **55%** in **2019**. Only **20%** of **over 70s** voted Labour in 2024 and just **14%** had done so in **2019**.

Reform UK performed better among under 30s than the Conservatives did, winning 10% of their votes.

Although Labour generally had a much more successful election in 2024 than in 2019, they lost significant amounts of support among younger voters. In contrast, the Green Party gained 11% more of the under-30 vote in 2024 compared to 2019.

Gender seems to have a limited effect on voting behaviour

1) In the **2019 general election**, the **Conservatives** won the support of **46%** of **men** and **44%** of **women**, and **Labour** received **31%** of **men's** votes to **35%** of **women's** votes.
2) The **gender gap** was also small in **2024**. **34%** of **men** and **35%** of **women** voted for **Labour**, while the **Lib Dems** received a very similar **vote share** from men (**12%**) and women (**13%**). In 2024, **26%** of **women** and **23%** of **men** voted for the **Conservatives**.
3) The largest **gender difference** in 2024 was among **Reform UK** voters — **17%** of **men** voted for the party, compared with **12%** of **women**.

Demographic Factors

Ethnicity has become a less stable predictor for voting behaviour

1) In the **2024 general election**, the **Conservatives'** share of the **white vote** fell by **22%** from **2019**.
2) **Labour's** share of the **BME vote** fell from **77%** in **2017** to **64%** in **2019** and then down again to **46%** in **2024**.
3) **Labour lost 13%** of the vote among **Asian voters** in **2024** compared with its performance in **2019**.

> 1) However, statistics suggest that **religion**, rather than **ethnicity**, was the driving force behind this change. Five of the seven seats Labour lost in **2024** were places where **Muslims** made up over a **quarter** of the population.
> 2) This **realignment** benefited:
>   - the **Green Party**, which won **11%** of the **Asian vote** (up 8% from 2019)
>   - **minor parties** (such as the **Workers' Party of Great Britain**), who received a **combined 10%** of the **Asian vote** (up 9% from 2019)

It's possible that this loss in Asian voters was partly due to several Labour-held seats being challenged by pro-Gaza independent candidates.

Education has become a more reliable predictor of voting behaviour

1) In both the **2019** and **2024 general elections**, **Labour** performed much **better** than the **Conservatives** among **graduates**:
   - In 2019, **Labour** won **43%** of graduate votes, compared with **29%** for the **Conservatives**.
   - In 2024, **Labour** won **42%** of their votes, and the **Conservatives** won **18%**.
2) The **Conservatives** now **generally** perform **better** among voters whose **highest level** of **education** is **GCSE** or **lower**. The **Conservatives** won **58%** of this group's vote in **2019**, while **Labour** won **25%**.

In 2024, Reform UK won 23% of this group's vote, compared to only 8% of graduates' votes.

Some demographics may become disillusioned with political parties

1) If voters feel like their **interests aren't** being **represented** by **politicians**, they may become **disillusioned** and this **leads to apathy**. It can be characterised by things such as **low election turnout** or a **lack** of **awareness** of **political events**.
2) In the **2024 general election**, constituencies with **high proportions** of **young voters** or **Muslim voters** had **lower turnouts** than others. This may suggest there's some **disillusionment** within these demographics.

Quick Questions

1) What is meant by class dealignment?
2) What percentages of C2DE voters voted for the Conservatives and Labour respectively in the 2019 election?
3) Which political party had the largest difference in percentage of male and female voters in 2024?
4) What percentage of graduate voters voted for Labour in the 2024 general election?
5) What can lead to voters becoming disillusioned and apathetic?

Exam Practice

For Edexcel students: Evaluate the view that age is the most significant demographic factor influencing voting behaviour in the UK. [30]

For AQA students: 'Age is the most significant demographic factor influencing voting behaviour in the UK.' Analyse and evaluate this statement. [25]

Practise your **evaluation** skills by writing a **conclusion** to one of the questions above. You can use the sentence frames on pages 299-300.

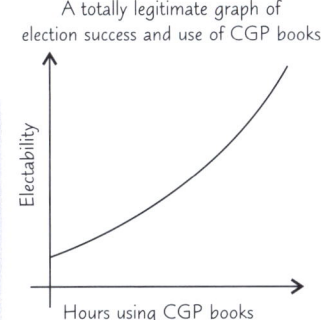
A totally legitimate graph of election success and use of CGP books

OK, you got me, I couldn't resist throwing one graph in there...

The letter codes for class categories can be a bit confusing, but roughly, ABC1 voters are upper and middle-class voters and C2DE voters are working-class voters. Thankfully the other demographics don't have codes like that to worry about.

UK Politics — Voting Behaviour and the Media

Campaigning, Manifestos and Policies

It turns out that the things that politicians say and do, and the legislation that they promise, tend to have a substantial effect on how many votes they get. Shocking, I know. But it's not always clear what policies and proposals will be appealing to voters.

Parties' **campaign strategies** have a big impact on **voting behaviour**

1) **Popular policies** and **effective campaigning** allow parties to **target** specific **seats** and **groups of voters** that swing the election result:

- In **2019**, the **Conservatives** had huge success with their campaign that used the slogan **'Get Brexit Done'**, which helped them to win **support** in **red wall constituencies** that had predominantly voted **Leave** in **2016**. This strategy also helped to reduce the impact of the **Brexit Party**, which had won the **most votes** and **seats** in the **European Parliament elections** earlier that year.
- The Conservatives' **clear message** helped to win the support of **74%** of people who voted **Leave** in 2016. By contrast, Labour's pledge to **renegotiate** the UK's deal with the **European Union** before holding a **second referendum** led to a **lower vote share** among **both Remain** voters (down from 55% in 2017 to 49% in 2019) and **Leave** voters (down from 24% in 2017 to 14% in 2019).

The Conservatives were also helped by the Brexit Party's decision in 2019 to not contest seats that had been won by the Conservatives in 2017. This meant that they could focus their strategy on gaining Labour seats, rather than defending their own.

The **Liberal Democrats** benefited from their strategy of **organising stunts** during the 2024 general election — these allowed **party leader** Ed Davey to gain **media attention** at a very **low cost**. Davey went paddleboarding on **Windermere** in the Lake District to **highlight problems** with the UK's **sewage network**, and **bungee-jumped** from a crane to **encourage voters** to **leave** their **comfort zones** by voting for his party. The effective campaigning of Liberal Democrats helped them to win **72 seats** — the **highest tally** in the party's history and the **highest number** of **seats** won by a **third party** in over a century.

2) Parties' **campaign strategies** can either **benefit** from or be **damaged** by the **public's perception** of their **leader**.

- In **2010**, **Labour** leader **Gordon Brown** was overheard on a microphone calling a **Labour voter** a **"bigoted woman"** after she had raised **concerns** about **immigration** and the **benefits system**. Although **50% of voters** said that the incident made **no difference** to their **opinion** of him, **46%** believed that it presented him as a **hypocrite**.
- In 2019, Labour's **policies** polled well with voters, but **Jeremy Corbyn's leadership** and **Brexit stance** led many Labour **voters** to **abandon** the party. Labour's **share of the vote** (32%) was nearly **8% down** on **2017**, and its **total number of seats** (202) was its **fewest** since **1935**.

- In **2019**, the **Liberal Democrats** placed their leader, **Jo Swinson**, at the **centre** of their **campaign strategy**, but **polling** later **suggested** that the party's **popularity decreased** every time she made a **media appearance**. Swinson began the election expressing **hope** that her party could win **over 100 seats**, but the final total was only **11**, and she **lost** her own **seat** in East Dunbartonshire.
- However, in **2024**, leader **Ed Davey** was **praised** for his appearance in the party's **television campaign broadcast**, when he discussed the **difficulties** of **caring** for his disabled wife and son. The **appeal** of Davey as **leader** helped **contribute** to their **record election success**.

Swinson was criticised for her stance on nuclear weapons and her role in the coalition government of 2010-2015 which had introduced austerity measures.

Reform UK's poll figures **improved** from **11%** to **17%** over the course of the **2024 general election campaign**, mainly due to **Nigel Farage's** decision to **stand** in the Essex constituency of Clacton. As soon as Farage revealed that he would run for **election**, the leader of Reform UK **Richard Tice** announced that he would **step aside** to allow **Farage** to take over as **leader** of the **party**. Reform UK's vote share of 14% was the best popular vote performance by a third party since the Liberal Democrats won 23% of the popular vote in 2010.

UK Politics — Voting Behaviour and the Media

Campaigning, Manifestos and Policies

The **Conservatives'** chances in the **2024** general election may have **suffered** as a result of the **controversy** over **Rishi Sunak's** decision to **leave a D-Day anniversary parade** early to attend a **campaign event**. **Two-thirds** of voters described his decision as **unacceptable**. Having performed marginally **better** than **Keir Starmer** in the **first televised debate** (according to polls of voters who watched), Sunak then had to face **questions** about his **decision** in the **second televised debate**. This prevented him from being able to **control** the **narrative** by talking about the **Conservatives' policies**.

Party manifestos also have a substantial effect on voting behaviour

- Many **commentators** believe that **Labour's 1983 manifesto** harmed the party's chances of beating **Margaret Thatcher's Conservatives**. Under **Michael Foot**, its left-wing leader, Labour pledged to **reverse** Thatcher's **privatisation**, **leave** the **Common Market** and **scrap** the **Trident nuclear deterrent**.
- The Conservatives produced **posters** comparing **Labour's policies** to the **Communist Party's**. **Gerald Kaufman**, a **centrist** Labour MP, described the manifesto as *"the longest suicide note in history"*.

In the **2010** general election, the **Liberal Democrats'** pledge to **prevent** university **tuition fee increases** helped to win the support of **30%** of **18-24 year olds'** votes (on a par with Labour and the Conservatives).

- In the **1997** general election, **Labour** were able to distil their **New Labour manifesto** into **five key pledges**: reducing **school class sizes**, tackling **young offenders**, reducing **NHS waiting times**, getting more **under 25s** into **work** and ruling out **income tax rises**.
- These **concise promises** helped to define the party's **appeal**, and were **communicated quickly** and **easily** on small paper cards.

- In **2017**, the Conservatives' **reforms** to **social care** outlined in their **manifesto** were labelled a '**dementia tax**' by **opposition parties** and the **media**. The policy's **unpopularity** contributed to a **sharp fall** in their **polling figures** and led to **Theresa May** announcing that it would be **removed** from the **manifesto**.
- The Conservatives had **begun** the **election campaign** hoping to win a **majority** of **over 100 seats** to help May carry out Brexit. However, they ended up **losing** their **majority** and needed to sign a **confidence and supply deal** with the **Democratic Unionist Party** (see p.16).

Salient issues can also help to determine voting behaviour

Salient issues is an **umbrella term** used to describe **policy areas** and **events** that have a particularly **important impact** on **election** and **referendum campaigns**.

Aaron's attempts to manifest O were off to a shaky start

Falklands War

- In early **1982**, **Labour led** the **Conservatives** by **3%** in **opinion polls**, and many commentators **predicted** that **Margaret Thatcher** would serve **only one term** as prime minister.
- In **June 1982**, the **Argentine invasion** of the **Falkland Islands** prompted the **Falklands War**. Thatcher's **successful oversight** of the war led to a **drastic increase** in **public support**, which became known as '**the Falklands Factor**'.
- Instead of losing the **1983 election**, the **Conservatives** significantly **improved** on their **performance** from **1979**, winning a landslide **144-seat majority**.

Iraq War

- In **2001**, Tony Blair's **Labour Party retained** nearly all the **seats** that it had won in its **landslide victory** in **1997**, giving him a **majority** of **167 seats** (only **slightly smaller** than the **179 seats** during his **first term**).
- By the **2005** general election though, the **Iraq War** had become a **divisive issue** and many voters **blamed Blair** for having presented **misleading evidence** when making the case for the **invasion** in **2003**. Opposition to the war contributed to **Labour's majority** being cut to **66 seats** after the election.
- Under **Charles Kennedy**, the **Liberal Democrats** had established themselves as the **leading anti-war party**, which helped them to win **62 seats** in the **2005** general election. Until **2024**, this remained the **best performance** in the party's history.

Campaigning, Manifestos and Policies

Economic outlook

1) The **economic outlook** often sets the **tone** for the **campaign**. In particular, **poor economic conditions** may bring the **governing competency** of the party in power into **question**.

governing competency
The perception of the ability of a political party or government to manage a state effectively.

2) The past **four** general elections **lost** by the **governing party** were all **influenced** by **major economic crises**:

- In **1979**, **Margaret Thatcher's Conservatives** capitalised on **public dissatisfaction** with **Labour's** handling of an **economic recession** and **strike action** with their 'Labour isn't working' **campaign slogan** (see p.33). The Conservative Party won a **majority** of **43** seats, its **best performance** since **1959**.
- The **economy** was starting to **recover** from **recession** by the **1997 general election**, but **Labour** still **profited** from the **Conservatives'** handling of the **Black Wednesday crisis** in **1992**, which had led to the **UK crashing out** of the **Exchange Rate Mechanism**, an **international currency union**. Under **Tony Blair's** leadership, Labour based its campaign on the phrase '**Things can only get better**'. The **179-seat majority** that **Labour** won in **2001** remains its **best ever performance**, and the **second-largest** Commons majority of all time.
- In **2010**, **David Cameron's Conservatives blamed Labour** for **causing**, and then **failing** to **solve**, the **economic recession** that had begun in **2007**. Although the Conservatives **didn't** win an **outright majority**, their 'We can't go on like this' strapline helped them to **increase** their **seats** by **96**, which was enough to make them the **largest party** in the **Commons**.
- In **2024**, **Labour** made the case that the **Conservatives** had made the **cost-of-living crisis** worse through **Liz Truss's mini-budget** and **wasteful spending** under **Boris Johnson** during the **COVID-19 pandemic**. Using the simple **campaign slogan** 'Change', **Keir Starmer** led **Labour** to a **172-seat majority**. The **Conservatives** suffered the **worst defeat** for any **governing party** in history, losing **251 seats**.

Brexit

1) Having **failed** to **pass** his **Brexit deal** due to the **Conservatives'** minority **government**, **divisions** within the party and **disagreements** with the **Democratic Unionist Party**, Boris Johnson called a **general election** after his attempt to **prorogue** (suspend) **Parliament** had been ruled **unlawful** by the **Supreme Court** (see p.99).

2) Although **support** for **Brexit** had **fallen** since the **2016 referendum**, the **Conservatives' message** that they would '**Get Brexit Done**' proved **clearer** and **more popular** than **Labour's** manifesto **pledge** to **renegotiate** the UK's deal with the **EU** and then hold a **second referendum** (see page 36).

3) The 2019 election **campaign** was **dominated** by discussions over **Brexit**, helping the **Conservatives** to **win** a **surprise majority** of **80 seats** — their **best** election **performance** since **1987**.

> Voters' views on Brexit continued to be a strong predictor of their voting decisions in the 2024 general election. Among those who had voted Remain, 47% supported Labour, compared with just 16% who voted for the Conservatives.

Revision Task

For Edexcel students: Evaluate the view that demographic factors no longer provide the best explanations of voting behaviour in the UK. [30]

For AQA students: 'Demographic factors no longer provide the best explanations of voting behaviour in the UK.' Analyse and evaluate this statement. [25]

Practise your **analysis** skills by explaining the significance of the following points to one of the essay questions above.

1) Labour's share of the Asian vote fell between 2019 and 2024.
2) Each of the past four general elections lost by the governing party has either taken place during or in the aftermath of an economic crisis.
3) In the 2019 general election, the Conservatives attracted the support of 74% of those who had voted Leave in the 2016 Brexit referendum.

When I pitch my tent on uncomfortable ground — that's a camp-pain...

Political campaigns are a tricky thing to manage. Addressing constituent concerns, presenting appealing policies and tackling ongoing issues, all while putting the best version of yourself forward is a lot to handle. It's no wonder politicians look tired.

UK Politics — Voting Behaviour and the Media

Opinion Polls

Hi there, just before you start this topic, could I ask you how you felt about the last one? Uhuh, and how did you answer the Revision Task? Thank you so much, have a good day. Aaaand scene. You've just done a little opinion poll role play.

Opinion polls can have a significant impact on political campaigns

1) During the **2016 referendum** on the UK's **membership** of the **EU**, the **Remain campaign** were consistently **ahead** of the Leave campaign in the polls. Only a **third** of **polls** carried out between the **announcement** of the **referendum's wording** and **polling day** predicted a **Leave win**.

   > Some have blamed the polls for allegedly low turnout among those who would have voted Remain. Although this is difficult to prove, in London, an overwhelmingly pro-Remain region, the turnout was only 70%, compared with 77% in the South East and the South West.

2) In **2017**, polling helped to **reinforce** the impression that the **Conservatives'** attempt to win a **large parliamentary majority** wasn't going to plan.

   > - Having led by over 20% at the beginning of the campaign, criticism of a social care policy in the Conservative manifesto (see page 37) helped to reduce the gap to nearly 10%.
   > - The closeness of the polls in 2017 has been cited as a reason behind the unusually high turnout among young voters, most of whom tended to vote for Labour.

3) The **Liberal Democrats** amended their most **high-profile manifesto pledge** during the **2019** election campaign. They **initially** promised to **cancel Brexit** if elected to government, however the party returned to an **earlier position** of pledging to hold a **second referendum** after **polls** indicated that its **support** had **fallen** from **over 20%** to around **10%**.

4) Having been **behind** in the **polls** throughout the **campaign** in **2024**, the **Conservatives** shifted their focus to **defending seats** that they had **won** in **2019**, rather than attempting to **make gains** in constituencies that were held by other parties.

   > - During the campaign, Rishi Sunak made many visits to Conservative-held seats such as Witney and Horsham. Witney (David Cameron's former constituency) had only ever elected Conservative MPs since its creation in 1983, and Horsham had been a Conservative seat since 1883.
   > - By contrast, in 2019 the party's poll lead (and the Brexit Party's decision not to contest Conservative-held seats) encouraged Boris Johnson and his strategists to target Labour-held seats in the red wall.

5) **Nigel Farage** was said to have made the **late decision** to enter the **2024 election campaign** after **polling** by **Arron Banks**, a **Reform UK supporter**, indicating he would **comfortably win** the constituency of **Clacton** in Essex.

   > Farage had stood unsuccessfully to become an MP seven times before, but his decision to stand and become Reform UK's leader helped the party to win the highest percentage of the popular vote (14%) of any third party since 2010.

Isaac and Eva answered the opinion pole through interpretive dance

They can also shape political events outside elections and referendums

1) **Conservative backbenchers'** decision to **remove Liz Truss** as **party leader** and **prime minister** in October **2022** was influenced by **polling figures** indicating that the party would **lose over 200 seats** under her leadership.

2) Personal **opinion polls** for **Truss** showed a net approval rating of **-70%** following the **poorly-received mini-budget** announced by her then-Chancellor, **Kwasi Kwarteng** (see page 86).

3) In **December 2024**, **Keir Starmer** made the decision to reset his premiership with the **announcement** of a new set of '**milestone**' promises. This was prompted by **polling figures** suggesting that the **Conservatives** and **Reform UK** were performing **better** than **Labour** in public opinion.

UK Politics — Voting Behaviour and the Media

Opinion Polls

Some believe that the **influence** of **opinion polls** is **limited**

1) In many **recent** general **elections**, **polls** have **inaccurately predicted** the **final result**:

   - In **1992**, Neil Kinnock's **Labour** Party **led** most **polls**, with John Major's **Conservative** Party projected to **lose** their place as the governing party. In reality, the **Conservatives** won a **slim majority** of **21 seats**.
   - In **2015**, most polls **predicted** another **hung Parliament**, which would result either in the formation of a **new coalition government** or a **minority government**. Instead, David Cameron's **Conservatives** won a **12-seat majority**.
   - In **2017**, the majority of polls indicated that the **Conservatives** would either **maintain** or **increase** the **majority** that they had won in **2015**. In reality, **Theresa May** was forced to lead a **minority government** with **support** from the **Democratic Unionist Party**, with whom the Conservatives signed a **confidence and supply agreement**.
   - In **2019**, most polls suggested that there would be a **hung Parliament** or a **narrow Conservative majority**. Instead, Boris Johnson led the **Conservatives** to their **best electoral performance** since **1987**, winning an **80-seat majority**.
   - In **2024**, polls indicated that **45%** of voters **supported Labour** at the **beginning** of the **campaign** — this **fell** to **39%** before election day and the party then received **34%** of the **popular vote**. Despite this, Labour **increased** its **seats** by **211**, winning a **172-seat majority** that was **similar** in size to many pollsters' **predictions** at the **beginning** of the campaign.

2) Some argue that polls simply **reflect existing public opinion**, rather than **shaping** voting behaviour.

3) Some polls are **funded** by **individuals** or **media organisations** that are believed to have a **political bias**, which can be **reflected** in their **results**. In recent years, **Arron Banks** and **Lord Ashcroft** (two **high-profile Brexit supporters**) and **trade unions** such as the **TUC**, have each **funded polls** whose results **reflect** their **political views**.

Quick Questions

1) Which party saw election success due to their 'Get Brexit Done' campaign slogan?
2) Who was the leader of the Liberal Democrats during the 2019 general election?
3) How did the Falklands War affect Margaret Thatcher's electability?
4) Describe how opinion polls may have affected voter turnout in London during the 2016 Brexit referendum?
5) How did the Conservatives change their campaign strategy in response to poor opinion polls in the 2024 general election?
6) What did opinion polls predict as the outcome of the 2019 general election? What was the actual outcome?

Essay Plan

For Edexcel students: Evaluate the view that the most significant influences on voting behaviour change from one general election to the next. [30]

For AQA students: 'The most significant influences on voting behaviour change from one general election to the next.' Analyse and evaluate this statement. [25]

Using the grid on p.298, **plan** an answer to one of the essay questions above.

Exam Practice

For Edexcel students: Evaluate the view that opinion polls have a greater influence on the outcome of elections than any other factor. [30]

For AQA students: 'Opinion polls have a greater influence on the outcome of elections than any other factor.' Analyse and evaluate this statement. [25]

Write an **introduction** to one of the questions above. You can use the sentence frames on pages 299-300.

Hot new pizzeria exit polls on pineapple — 78% in favour, 22% incorrect...

Oops, I let my own bias slip into my polling there. It's important to consider where any political predictions or conclusions are coming from. Bias can crop up not just from the people and organisations running a poll, but also whoever funds it.

UK Politics — Voting Behaviour and the Media

The Role of the Media in Elections and Referendums

The content produced by most media outlets has a political slant, which can be fairly subtle or completely obvious. This means the media tends to have a degree of influence in elections and referendums. Here are three pages to tell you more.

Newspapers play a prominent role during election and referendum campaigns

1) **Party** and **referendum campaigners** place great value on **endorsements** from several of the **most-read newspapers**.

   - The *Daily Mail* and the *Daily Telegraph* have consistently **endorsed** the **Conservatives**.
   - The *Daily Mirror* and *The Guardian* have consistently **endorsed Labour**.
   - *The Sun* and *The Times* have **changed** their **affiliation** at **pivotal moments** during recent campaigns.

2) **Newspapers** have had an impact in **recent campaigns**.

   1992 general election
   - In **1992**, Neil Kinnock's **Labour Party** consistently **led** John Major's **Conservative Party** in **polling** throughout the campaign, but **failed** to win **support** from *The Sun*. *The Sun*'s front-page **headline** on **polling day** predicted a **mass exodus** from Britain **if Kinnock won**.
   - After the **Conservatives'** surprise **victory**, the newspaper's next front-page **headline** was *"It's the Sun Wot Won It"*.

   1997 general election
   - After **Tony Blair** had flown to Australia to **meet** with **Rupert Murdoch**, the **owner** of *The Sun* and the *News of the World*, **both newspapers** supported **Labour** in the **1997** general election. At the time, the combined **readership** of the two papers was **over 8 million**.
   - Commentators believed that these **endorsements** helped Labour to **gain votes** across all **social classes**. The party's **support** among **ABC1 voters** (see p.34) was **12% higher** than it had been in 1992 and **10% higher** among **C2DE voters**.

   2016 Brexit referendum
   - In the **2016 Brexit referendum**, 3 of the **4 most-read** daily **newspapers endorsed** the **Leave campaign**.
   - With a **combined readership** of nearly **4 million**, support from *The Sun*, the *Daily Mail* and the *Daily Telegraph* was seen as a significant victory for the **Leave** campaign, especially given that **75% of MPs** were **campaigning** for **Remain**.

   2017 general election
   - In **2017**, even **Conservative-supporting** newspapers such as the *Daily Mail* and *The Sun* adopted **Labour's** 'dementia tax' **label** for the **Conservatives'** plan to **reform social care**.
   - Although Theresa May **dropped** the **policy** quickly, it's considered one of the **main reasons** why the **Conservatives lost** their **majority**.

Parties are placing a significant emphasis on their social media strategy

Social media enables parties to **target specific groups** of people with **bespoke messaging**:

- The **CONSERVATIVES** spent **over £2 million** on **Facebook** adverts in **2017** and **over £1 million** in **2019**. In **2019**, they made use of **Facebook adverts** targeted exclusively at **specific demographics**. An **advert** sent **exclusively** to accounts belonging to **women** promoted the party's **pledge** to **recruit 20 000** more **police officers**. Another, sent **exclusively** to **men**, asserted the **benefits** of **Brexit** for building **businesses**.
- In **2019**, they also made extensive use of **YouTube**, paying for **adverts** in a bid to attract **younger voters**. Their **most-viewed YouTube advert** was seen by **3.5 million people**.

LABOUR produced a **digital tool** in **2024** called 'Labour Connects'. This was designed to help **local parties** and **individual candidates** produce **targeted advertising** on **Facebook** that showed **up-to-date polling graphics** for their **constituency**. The party's own research estimated that **80% of voters** were **active social media users**.

REFORM UK's leader **Nigel Farage's** posts on **TikTok** gained **more views** and **engagement** than **any other candidate** in the **2024** general election. This may help to explain Reform UK's unexpectedly **strong performance** with voters **under 30**, among whom they won **more votes** than the **Conservatives**.

UK Politics — Voting Behaviour and the Media

The Role of the Media in Elections and Referendums

Televised debates are now considered a significant factor in campaigns

1) Since the introduction of **televised leaders' debates** in **2010**, the leader of the **winning party** in the general election has always **performed better** in **post-debate polling** than the leader of the party that came **second**.

   - In **2010** and **2015**, viewers rated **David Cameron's performances** across the leaders' debates **more highly** than **Gordon Brown's** and **Ed Miliband's** respectively.
   - In **2019**, **Boris Johnson** narrowly **outperformed Jeremy Corbyn** in **polls** following both head-to-head **debates**.
   - In **2024**, **Keir Starmer** led **YouGov's polls** after **two** of his **three televised debates** with **Rishi Sunak**. While **Sunak** narrowly led **Starmer** after the **first debate**, viewers felt that **Starmer** had **performed better** in the **second** and **third debates**.

   > In 2017, Amber Rudd (Theresa May's Home Secretary) represented the Conservatives in the leadership debate, as May and Jeremy Corbyn couldn't agree on the debate's format.

2) The **lack** of **minor party representation** in the **2019 televised debates** between **Johnson** and **Corbyn** was cited as a **barrier** to their electoral **success**. The **Lib Dems**, the **Green Party** and the **Brexit Party** won just **12 seats** between them.

Some argue the media just reflects public opinion without influencing voting

1) *The Sun* has endorsed the **winning party** in **every general election** since **1974**, but its **switches** of **allegiance** have only happened when there's been a **clear** and **sustained poll lead** for the **opposition**. For example, in **1997**, Labour's **poll figures** actually **declined** after *The Sun's* **endorsement** and only **52%** of the newspaper's **readers voted Labour**.

2) Given that the **political leanings** of many **newspapers** are **consistent** and **well known**, many believe that their only effect is **confirmation bias** — they **reinforce** their readers' **existing political views**.

   - In the **2016** Brexit referendum, **70%** of *Sun* **readers** voted **Leave**.
   - In the **2017** general election, **79%** of *Telegraph* **readers** voted **Conservative**, while **73%** of *Guardian* **readers** voted **Labour**.
   - However, polls in the run-up to the **2024** general election suggested that **more readers** of **Conservative-supporting newspapers** were intending to vote **Labour** than **Conservative**.

3) **Newspaper sales** and **subscriptions** have been **falling consistently** in recent years. While nearly **4 million** people read *The Sun* each day in **1997**, it had dropped to just over **1 million** by **2020**. This would suggest that, if **newspapers** do help **shape** their readers' **voting behaviour**, the **scope** of their **influence** has **narrowed**.

Dwindling newspaper sales were no surprise to Ivan

4) The **influence** of **social media** on voting behaviour is **difficult** to **evaluate**. Although the **Conservatives'** spending on **Facebook adverts** was cited as one of the **reasons** why they **won** their surprise **12-seat majority** in **2015**, their **2017 spending** added up to **more than all the other parties combined**, but **failed** to **prevent** them **losing** their **majority**.

5) The **influence** of **televised debates** has also been **questioned**.

   - Despite **Nick Clegg leading polls** after his **performance** in the **first televised debate** in **2010**, the **Liberal Democrats failed** to **break** the **two-party dominance** in the general election. The party won **fewer seats** and a **smaller share** of the **popular vote** than in they did in **2005**.
   - The **Conservatives** were **criticised** for **failing** to send their **leader** to the **Channel 4 climate debate** in **2019**, but the **Conservatives** still went on to **win** a surprise **80-seat majority**.

Revision Task

For Edexcel students: Evaluate the view that the media does not have a significant influence on the outcome of elections or referendums in the UK. [30]

For AQA students: 'The media does not have a significant influence on the outcome of elections or referendums in the UK.' Analyse and evaluate this statement. [25]

> Imagine you're answering one of the essay questions above. Choose the **best examples** from the previous pages or from your own knowledge to **support** these arguments:
> 1) *Some newspapers tend to endorse the winning party in general elections.*
> 2) *Strong performances in televised debates don't always translate into strong election results.*
> 3) *Opinion polls can alter the narrative of a general election or referendum campaign.*

!!!Congratulations!!! You've won! Click HERE to claim your A* in Politics!

Political adverts on social media aren't quite as clickbait-y as that, but they are becoming an important part of campaigns.

Impact of the Media on the UK Political System

You've almost finished this section — it might be a relief to hear that the word 'media' won't be used as much in the next section...

Media coverage helps to set the political agenda

1) **High-profile interviews** with **politicians** on **television** and **radio shows** help to set the **news agenda** for a time.

   > On *Sunday with Laura Kuenssberg* in **October 2022**, **Liz Truss** told Laura Kuenssberg that **Kwasi Kwarteng**, her **then-Chancellor**, had been **responsible** for the unpopular decision to **remove** the **45% income tax rate** for the **highest earners**. Within a week, **Kwarteng** had been **sacked** and the **policy** was **dropped**.

2) Newspapers can impact the **trajectory** of a politician's **career**. A **significant factor** in the **resignations** of **Boris Johnson** and **Liz Truss** as prime minister was that even **Conservative-supporting newspapers** such as the *Daily Telegraph* and the *Daily Mail* had called for them to **step down**.

3) **Social media platforms** have also become a source of **significant influence**. Following **riots** in parts of England and Northern Ireland during the **summer** of **2024**, some **politicians** and **commentators blamed** the **social media** platforms **X** and **Telegram** for **allowing** the spread of **fake news**. False claims that the **perpetrator** of the **Southport stabbings** was a **Muslim** who had **entered** the **UK illegally** were allowed to **remain** on **both platforms**, despite the fact that he had been born in **Cardiff** to a **Christian family**.

Media coverage and investigations provide scrutiny and accountability

1) **Investigations** by **BBC journalist Andrew Gilligan** uncovered **problems** with the **evidence** that **Tony Blair** had presented in **favour** of joining the **US-led invasion** of **Iraq** in **2003**. The **scandal** over this **'sexed up dossier'** led to a **decline** in **support** for the **war** (see p.37). This was reflected in **Labour's** much **smaller majority** and **lower share** of the **popular vote** in the **2005 election**.

2) The *Daily Telegraph* released **details** of **MPs' expenses claims** in **2009**, which led to the **resignation** of the **Speaker of the House of Commons** and several **Cabinet ministers**, as well as **fraud convictions** for **four backbench MPs**.

3) **Amelia Gentleman**, a *Guardian* journalist, led the **investigation** into the **Home Office's** attempt to **deport** members of the **Windrush generation**, which culminated in **Amber Rudd's resignation** as **Home Secretary** in **2018** (see p.92).

4) Allegations about **lockdown-breaking parties** in **No. 10 Downing Street** (a scandal known as **Partygate**) were revealed by *Daily Mirror* journalist **Pippa Crerar**. These allegations contributed to **Boris Johnson's** decision to **resign** as **prime minister**, as did *The Sun's* revelation that **Johnson** had **appointed Chris Pincher** as a **party whip** despite knowing that he had been **accused** of **sexual assault**.

5) In **2024**, sustained **media coverage** influenced the **government response** to the **Post Office scandal**. After the airing of **ITV's** drama *Mr Bates vs The Post Office*, the **Conservative government** promised to pass a **law** that would **overrule convictions** of sub-postmasters who had **wrongly** been **accused** of **fraud** due to a faulty IT system.

6) **Several newspapers** ran **campaigns** on behalf of the **victims** of the **infected blood scandal**. In 2024, the **Labour government** announced that these **victims** could receive a **combined £47 billion** in **compensation**.

Some argue the media doesn't apply equal scrutiny to all aspects of politics

1) Analysis of newspapers during the Partygate scandal and **'Beergate'** (allegations that **Keir Starmer** broke **social distancing** guidelines to drink beer with **Labour campaigners**) suggests that **coverage** often **reflected** the publications' **political biases**. **91%** of the *Daily Mail's* front-page headlines about the stories were **positive** for the **Conservatives**, while **96%** of the *Daily Mirror's* front pages about them were **negative** towards the **Conservatives**.

2) **Critics** of the UK media argue that many **political journalists** prioritise **headline-friendly scandals** over **detailed scrutiny**.

3) Many **newspapers** no longer employ **foreign correspondents** in countries where **UK government** policy has significant **impact**, such as **Afghanistan** or **Iraq**, meaning that **scrutiny** of UK foreign policy is **limited**.

Essay Plan

For Edexcel students: Evaluate the view that the media's biggest impact on the UK's political system is during general election campaigns. [30]

For AQA students: 'The media's biggest impact on the UK's political system is during general election campaigns.' Analyse and evaluate this statement. [25]

Using the grid on p.298, **plan** an answer to one of the essay questions above.

Top Tip for Politicians #432: not *all* publicity is good publicity...
The media can play an important role in holding politicians to account, but when and where it does so can be controversial.

Conservatism

I hope you've conserved some energy from the previous sections and are ready to get to grips with some political ideas. Disraeli, Macmillan and Scruton are not on the spec but are important conservative thinkers. The more the merrier, right?

Conservatism is made up of three main strands

Traditional Conservatism
- **Traditional conservatism** is primarily based on the desire to maintain **traditional social values** as a way to **uphold order**.
- It is sometimes known as **sceptical conservatism** because it involves a belief in **human imperfection** (there's more on this below).

Key Thinkers:
 Thomas Hobbes (1588-1679)
 Edmund Burke (1729-1797)
 Michael Oakeshott (1901-1990)

One Nation Conservatism
- **One Nation conservatism** emerged as a **pragmatic response** to **industrialisation** in the **19th and 20th centuries**.
- It sees a **larger role** for the **state** in **preserving social cohesion**, including **addressing inequalities** of **rights** and **income**.

 Benjamin Disraeli (1804-1881)
 Harold Macmillan (1894-1986)

Disraeli and Macmillan aren't named key thinkers on the spec, but their ideas illustrate this strand well

> **pragmatism** — A core value of many conservative thinkers. This is an approach that involves looking for flexible, evolving solutions to problems as they change over time. **[Key Terms]**

The New Right is associated with the policies of **Margaret Thatcher** and **Ronald Reagan** (see p.85 and p.186). This movement is made up of **two sub-strands**:

The New Right — Neo-conservatism
- **Neo-conservatism** seeks to **renew** the principles of **traditional conservatism** in a **modern context**.
- This strand seeks an **authoritative state** that will **intervene** to **prevent** the development of a **permissive society**. This is where individuals have **too much freedom** at the **expense** of the **collective**.

 *The ideas of Roger Scruton (1944-2020) illustrate this sub-strand well*

The New Right — Neo-liberalism
- **Neo-liberalism** seeks to **maximise individual freedom** and is based on an **optimistic view** of **human nature**.
- Neo-liberal thinkers have a **radical vision** of a **small, largely non-interventionist state**.

Key Thinkers:
 Ayn Rand (1905-1982) — Robert Nozick (1938-2002)

Some core ideas are shared by different strands of conservatism

1) **Human imperfection** — Most conservative thinkers (except neo-liberals) believe that **human nature** is **flawed**.

   - **Thomas Hobbes** (a **traditional conservative**) believed the **natural state** of humans is *"war of all against all"*.
   - **One Nation conservatives** and **neo-conservatives** aren't quite so **pessimistic**. They believe in **paternalism** and therefore accept that a relatively **strong, authoritative state** is needed.

   > **paternalism** — Where the state acts as a father figure to its citizens and guides individuals towards making decisions that benefit themselves and others. **[Key Terms]**

   Hobbes drew on biblical teachings about Original Sin (the belief that all humans are sinful) when constructing his narrative of humans as imperfect, selfish beings.

2) **Hierarchy** — Traditional conservatives and neo-liberals accept **social** and **economic inequalities** as **natural** and **desirable**:

   - **Traditional conservatives** believe that inequality provides a **hierarchy** that promotes an **orderly society**.
   - **Neo-liberals** welcome inequality because they believe that it stimulates **competition** and **economic growth**.

3) **Capitalism** — All conservative thinkers believe that **capitalism** is the **best economic system**, but they **disagree** over **how far** capitalism should be **regulated** or **moderated** by the **state**.

Traditional Conservatism

Ever found yourself being a bit selfish? Well, I've got great news. It's not your fault, according to traditional conservatism...

Traditional conservatives have a **pessimistic view** of **human nature**

Hobbes — Believed that humans are **naturally selfish** and therefore **incapable** of making **rational decisions** that **benefit others**.

Burke — Writing in the **18th century**, Burke believed that only the **ruling aristocracy** had the necessary powers of **reason** to make the **right political decisions**.

> Burke's faith in the aristocracy led him to advocate for the trustee model of representation (see page 81).

Oakeshott — Had **more faith** in the ability of **individuals** to **make decisions** in their **own interests**. Oakeshott **doubted** whether **politicians** could set aside their **own self-interest** for the **public good**.

They believe **traditional structures** should **govern society**...

Traditional conservatives follow **empiricism**, which leads them to argue that **tradition** is the **soundest basis** for government.

> This view contrasts with that of classical liberals, whose belief in rationalism leads them to embrace social change and limited government (see p.49).

- For **Hobbes**, who was writing during the **English Civil War**, following this belief meant **defending** the **authoritarian power** of an **absolute monarchy**.
- For **Burke**, this meant supporting the **right of the aristocracy to rule**. He fiercely **opposed** the ideas behind the **French Revolution**, warning that **radical changes** can have **unintended consequences**. However, Burke followed the idea of *noblesse oblige*, so he believed that those in **power** should use their position to **help** the **less fortunate** in society.
- **Oakeshott** wrote that "*to be conservative... is to prefer the familiar to the unknown, to prefer the tried to the untried*". He believed in "**non-purposive government**", where the **state** acts as an **umpire** — it **upholds rules** but **doesn't intervene**.

empiricism — The belief that decisions should be based on evidence. In political ideas, empiricism contrasts with rationalism.

rationalism — The belief that humans can use their powers of reason to make decisions.

noblesse oblige — The belief that those in power have a duty to look after those underneath them in the social hierarchy.

Key Terms

...and **social** and **economic inequalities** are **natural** and **desirable**

Hobbes — Hobbes wrote that life would be "*nasty, brutish, and short*" without a state. His vision of the state was for it to act like an **awe-inspiring monster**, compelling **citizens** into **obedience**, but **never seeking** to **address inequalities**.

Burke — Burke believed society is "*organic*", which means that it's like a **self-regulating creature** that the **state doesn't** need to **interfere** with. He outlined a view of society made up of "*little platoons*" — **hierarchical**, **military-style units** led by **local aristocrats**.

Oakeshott — Oakeshott's **pessimistic** view of **rationalism** led him to question the "*arrogance*" of politicians who aim for "*utopian bliss*" through interventionist schemes that seek **greater equality**.

Traditional conservatives have **different views** on state intervention

BREAKING: Law and order restored in Ulverston after local menace is finally apprehended.

Hobbes — Hobbes believed that the state should just seek to **uphold law and order**, including by passing laws forcing all healthy citizens to work.

Burke — Although generally **sceptical** of **change**, Burke pragmatically accepted that the state would occasionally need to "*change in order to conserve*", including by **expanding** its **social** and **economic interventions**.

Oakeshott — Oakeshott believed **capitalism** was by far the **best economic system**, but acknowledged that the **state** might occasionally need to **intervene** to **guard** against the **volatility of markets**.

Traditional conservatives look away now — time for a break in tradition...

An activity in a tip? The horror! Well, don't panic — this change will conserve your knowledge. Write a definition for each term:
1) Pragmatism 2) Philosophy of human imperfection 3) Paternalism 4) Empiricism 5) Noblesse oblige 6) Organic society

Core Political Ideas — Conservatism

One Nation Conservatism

One Nation conservatives have different ideas about key issues like state intervention. Variety is the spice of life and all that...

One Nation conservatives **share** the traditional conservative desire for **order**...

1) The term **One Nation** comes from a book written by **Benjamin Disraeli** called *The Two Nations*. In this novel, Disraeli warned that the **increasing gap** between the **rich** and the **poor** was in danger of **splitting Britain** into **two nations**.

2) Disraeli felt that this created the risk of **instability** and possibly even **revolution**, so he argued that the **state** needed to introduce **reforms** to **improve** the **living conditions** of the **poor**.

3) For Disraeli, accepting the need for **reform** was necessary to **maintain** an **orderly** and **peaceful society**. He wrote that **"the palace is not safe if the cottage is not happy"**.

"What do you mean I'm being demolished on Monday?!"

...but they believe the **state** should **intervene more**

One Nation conservatives believe that the state should play a more **active role** in **maintaining social cohesion**, **extending rights** and **reducing inequalities**.

Key Terms

mixed economy
A combination of private and state ownership of industry.

Disraeli
- **Disraeli** believed that the state has a duty to **"elevate the condition of the people"**.
- He embraced **social** and **economic reforms** such as the **Factory Act (1874)**. This act **reduced** the number of **hours** that **women** and **children** could legally **work** each week.

Macmillan
- **Harold Macmillan** supported a **more interventionist state**.
- He believed that a **mixed economy** would allow the state to provide **equality of opportunity** for its citizens.
- His vision for a **welfare state** included the pursuit of **full employment**, as well as high levels of **redistributive taxation** (where the rich are taxed more than the poor) to fund services such as **healthcare**, **education** and **housing**.

Although Macmillan believed that capitalism was the most effective and efficient economic system, his economic ideas are the most interventionist of any of the conservative thinkers on these pages. Macmillan's economic philosophy shares more similarities with social democrats (see p.57) or modern liberals (see p.52) than with neo-liberal thinkers like Ayn Rand or Robert Nozick.

One Nation thinkers use conservative principles to justify changes

The conservative principles of **pragmatism** and **paternalism** (p.44) can be seen in some One Nation ideas.

R. A. Butler, a **One Nation thinker** and a minister in Macmillan's government, believed that **supporting state welfare** and the **Keynesian theory** of an economy with full employment were **"little more than updated expressions of our belief in... paternalism"**.

One Nation thinkers usually welcome change more than traditional conservatives.

Revision Task

Comparing the ideas of different strands is a key skill when writing essays on political ideas.

Explain the similarities and differences between **traditional conservatism** and **One Nation conservatism** by writing two sentences for each of the prompts below.

You can use the sentence frames on pages 299-300 to help you.

1) Traditional conservatives have a more sceptical view of change than One Nation conservatives.
2) Both traditional and One Nation conservatives believe that the state can have a positive impact on society.
3) Traditional conservatives are more accepting of social and economic inequalities than One Nation conservatives.

AO2 Analysis

I've elevated the condition of this box — doesn't it look snazzy...

A good way of linking together conservative ideas is through the shared principles of pragmatism and paternalism. If you're analysing or evaluating conservatism, think about how these principles influence each strand of conservatism.

Core Political Ideas — Conservatism

The New Right

So things seem pretty straightforward so far. Traditional and One Nation conservatives aren't very into change, unless it's to stop *big bad changes* like revolution. But change is inevitable, and ideas move with the times... Enter THE NEW RIGHT.

The New Right is made up of **two separate sub-strands**

1) Neo-conservatism

- Neo-conservatives believe that the **state** needs to **impose traditional values** to prevent the **breakdown** of **social bonds**.
- Neo-conservatism was a **reaction against** the **'permissive'** culture of the **1960s**, when the **US** and the **UK** began to adopt more **liberal attitudes** on **sex**, **relationships** and the **workplace**.
- **Roger Scruton** wrote that *"at the core of every society is a union of man, wife and community"*. This belief led him to **oppose same-sex marriage** and **same-sex adoptions** when they were introduced in the UK.
- His backing of **tough measures** against **drug use** and of **legislation** to **preserve traditional architecture** also highlight his desire to **uphold tradition**.

Margaret Thatcher (1925-2013)
Ronald Reagan (1911-2004)

Ronald Reagan and Margaret Thatcher combined neo-conservative social and foreign policies with a neo-liberal economic agenda.

2) Neo-liberalism

- Neo-liberals believe that the **state** should **limit** its **role** and unleash the **potential of individuals**. They have a **more optimistic** view of **human nature** than the other conservative strands.
- Both **Ayn Rand** and **Robert Nozick** believed humans are **rational** and **capable** of **governing** their **own lives without interference** from the **state** or **social hierarchies**.
- **Rand** described man as *"a heroic being... with reason as his only absolute"*.
- For **Nozick**, humans could only truly be **free** in a *"minarchist state"*, where the state's **only responsibility** would be to **prevent private businesses** from **exploiting individuals**. According to this **vision**, every other **service** traditionally carried out by the **state** (including **policing**) would be carried out by **private organisations**.
- **Rand's** view was similar to Nozick's — she desired a **laissez-faire government**, arguing that *"the small state is the strong state"*.

Key Terms

laissez-faire government
A minimalist style of government where businesses and individuals are largely left to their own devices — 'laissez-faire' is French for 'allow to do'.

Neo-liberals think **individuals** are **capable** of making their **own decisions**

Neo-liberals have different views to other conservatives on **society** and the **economy**:

1) **COMPETITION** — Rand celebrated the **competition** produced by **free-market capitalism** and believed that **social progress** would be **accelerated** by the *"virtue of selfishness"*.
2) **LIBERTARIANISM** — Neo-liberals **reject paternalism** and instead believe that **individuals** should be **trusted** to make their **own choices**. This is part of a **philosophy** called **libertarianism**, which seeks to **maximise** the **freedom** of **individuals**.
3) **ATOMISM** — Atomism is the idea that **society** is made up of **individuals** who are **self-supporting** and will act in their **own interests**. Neo-liberals are said to have an **atomised** view of society because of their emphasis on the **power** of **individuals** over **collectives**.

Nozick's belief that *"individuals own their bodies, talents, and labour"* led him to liken taxation to *"forced labour"*.

Exam Practice

For Edexcel students: To what extent do New Right conservatives accept the ideas of traditional and One Nation conservatives? [24]

For AQA students: 'New Right conservatives accept the ideas of traditional and One Nation conservatives.' Analyse and evaluate this statement. [25]

Practise your **evaluation** skills by writing a **conclusion** to one of the questions above. You can use the sentence frames on pages 299-300.

"What was wrong with the old Right?" — The ghost of Hobbes (probably)...

Neo-liberals and neo-conservatives have very different ideas about human nature, the role of the state and society. These two sub-strands are actually quite distinct from each other, so make sure you explore both when writing about the New Right.

Core Political Ideas — Conservatism

Comparing Conservative Ideas

Here are some handy summaries to show how the three strands of conservatism overlap when it comes to four key themes...

Human Nature

Traditional: Humans are **incapable** of making **rational decisions** and **living peacefully** without a **state** that **compels** them into **order**.

One Nation: Humans are **capable** of fulfilling their potential if they are given **opportunities**, but they need **some help** from the **state**.

Hobbes and Burke believed Most humans lack the necessary **rationality** to **govern** their **own lives**.

Most humans are **selfish** by nature.

Oakeshott, Rand and Nozick all had faith in the ability of individuals to govern their own lives.

The New Right: **Neo-conservatives** believe that humans often exercise their freedom without good judgement. **Neo-liberals** have strong **faith** in human **rationalism**, believing that every **individual** can fulfil their potential if they have enough **freedom**.

State

Traditional: The **state** has **no function** beyond imposing **order**. **Change** should be approached with **great caution**.

One Nation: The state has a **responsibility** to **extend rights** and **improve living conditions**.

An **authoritative** state is necessary for **law and order**. Some **pragmatic change** may be necessary to **uphold order**.

A state is necessary.

Neo-conservatives and **traditional conservatives** believe that **empiricism** and **tradition** should guide **political decisions**. There are similarities between Oakeshott's call for **non-purposive government** and Nozick's **minarchist** state.

The New Right: **Neo-liberals** believe that the state's **role** should be kept as **minimal** as possible.

Society

Traditional: **Hobbes** and **Burke** believed that **social freedoms** should be extremely **limited**.

One Nation: Macmillan believed that society should be underpinned by the **principle** of **equality** of **opportunity**.

Society is **organic**. **Hierarchy** and **paternalism** help to promote **social order**. There are similarities between Burke's *noblesse oblige* and One Nation calls for the state to improve **living standards**.

Social **inequality** is both **natural** and **desirable**.

The New Right: **Neo-conservatives** believe that **permissive societies** threaten to **break down** the **social order**. **Neo-liberals** embrace **individual choice** and **freedom** in society.

Economy

Traditional: Hobbes believed that the state should **pass laws** requiring that **all** citizens who are **able** to **work** do so.

One Nation: Macmillan accepted the principles of a Keynesian **mixed economy** and **redistributive taxation**.

Oakeshott and Disraeli both recognised that the state might **occasionally** need to **intervene pragmatically** in the economy to maintain order.

Capitalism is the most **effective** and **efficient** economic system.

Oakeshott and Scruton both believed that the state might need to introduce **regulations** to **prevent capitalism** from leading to the **destruction** of valuable **traditions**.

The New Right: Nozick believed that all **taxation** was **theft**.

Exam Practice

For Edexcel students: To what extent do conservatives share a common view of the state? [24]

For AQA students: Explain and analyse three ways in which conservative thinkers view human nature. [9]

Unequal letters are both unnatural and highly annoying...
Phew, that's a lot to take in. I'd like to tell you there's an easy way to remember all of this, but that would just be a lie. Soz.

Core Political Ideas — Conservatism

Liberalism

Time for a chapter on liberalism. Best paired with a libation of luscious lemonade while lounging lazily in a library.

Liberalism consists of two main strands

Classical Liberalism
- **Classical liberalism** is based on **rationalist** principles.
- Classical liberals see **state intervention** as an **unnecessary barrier** to **individuals' freedom** and ability to **express** their own **identities**.

 John Locke (1632-1704)
 Mary Wollstonecraft (1759-1797)
 John Stuart Mill (1806-1873)

Modern Liberalism
- **Modern liberals** argue that **targeted interventions** by the **state** are **necessary** if all individuals are to enjoy **comparable rights** and **freedoms**.
- This strand was a **response** to the development of **social** and **economic inequalities** in **industrialised economies**.

 John Rawls (1921-2002)
 Betty Friedan (1921-2006)

Some consider T. H. Green to be a key modern liberal thinker. We'll look at his ideas on page 51.

Wollstonecraft and Friedan were also central figures in the development of liberal feminism (see page 125). Although there are some major differences between their views on the state, it can sometimes be helpful to consider them together in essays on liberalism.

Both strands seek to maximise individual freedom...

All liberals believe that humans are **rational**, **moral** and **capable** creatures. They accept **John Locke's** belief that every human has equal **natural rights** to **life**, **liberty** and **property**. This is known as **foundational equality**.

...but they do this in different ways

	The State and Economics	Equality
Classical Liberals	• Locke, Wollstonecraft and Mill all believed that the **state's intervention** in society and the economy should be **limited** to upholding the **rule of law** and **protecting natural rights**. • Classical Liberals believe that **laissez-faire capitalism** allows individuals to fulfil their **potential**, without the state interfering with the **natural right** of **property ownership**.	**Classical liberals** believe that **formal equality** is enough for individuals to **self-actualise**. Formal equality is where every member of society receives the **same legal protections and rights**.
Modern Liberals	• Green, Rawls, and Friedan all shared classical liberals' view that humans are **inherently rational creatures**, but they believed that the **state** can be a **positive force** in **society** and the **economy**. • Modern liberals call for an **enabling state** that can help people experience **individual freedom** and opportunities for **social progress**. • As well as aiming to **maximise individual liberty**, modern liberals also desire **social justice**.	**Modern liberals** argue that the **state** needs to promote **equality of opportunity**. This means allowing every individual a **fair chance** to realise their potential.

Key Terms

self-actualisation — The process of realising one's potential and striving towards a state of fulfilment.

social justice — The aim for society to be structured so it is fair for every member, regardless of their class or status. Some advocates of social justice emphasise equality of outcomes, but others consider fair opportunities to be more important.

How to self-actualise good exam results: revise, take breaks, don't panic...
All liberals share similar views on human nature. But modern liberal ideas about the state, society and the economy differ significantly from classical liberal ideas. We'll be digging into just how different they are over the next few pages...

Classical Liberalism

Classical liberals dream of a minimal state. Luckily for them, I've got my trusty shrink ray aimed right at 10 Downing Street...

Classical liberals believe that humans are **rational** and **tolerant beings**

1) Locke, Wollstonecraft and Mill all believed that these **traits** allow humans to live **peacefully** and **productively** among one another, without the need for an **overbearing state**.
2) Classical liberals **emphasise tolerance** because they see **humans** as **foundationally equal** and **morally trustworthy**.

LOCKE advocated **religious tolerance** to allow individuals to express their *"personal identity"*, despite writing at a time of **significant tension** between Protestants and Catholics in England in the late 17th century. Locke believed people were **fundamentally moral**, and so capable of **disagreeing peacefully**.

WOLLSTONECRAFT argued that society needed to become more **tolerant** of **women's interests**.

MILL agreed with Wollstonecraft, and was the first MP to speak **in favour of women's suffrage** in the House of Commons. His **harm principle** states that individuals should have **complete liberty** over **self-regarding actions** (those that do not affect others). However, individuals should not use their freedom to **inflict harm** in **other-regarding actions** (those that affect fellow members of society).

Mill wrote *"The liberty of the individual must be thus far limited; he must not make himself a nuisance to other people."*

Locke developed a vision of the **social contract**

1) The **social contract** is an imaginary **agreement** between **citizens** and the **state**, in which individuals **consent** to give up some of their **liberty** in return for **protection**.
2) This is **closely related** to the following two **ideas**:

- **Mechanistic theory** — the concept that the state is a means of preserving individual liberty.
- **Fiduciary power of government** — the concept that political power should only be used for the benefit of society, not for the self-interest of representatives.

Although liberal thinkers disagree over the rights and responsibilities involved, they all accept Locke's idea that political power should be legitimised by the state.

'Fiduciary' means involving trust or being held in trust. Classical liberals describe the government's power as fiduciary because the government only rules by the agreement of the people, who trust them to do what's in the best interests of society.

Mill proposed a **broader vision** of individuals' **responsibilities to society**

1) Mill criticised the idea of **hedonism** — the **pursuit of pleasure** for its own sake.
2) Instead, he advocated **developmental individualism**, where individuals use their **liberty** to **develop themselves**. Mill thought people should use their freedom to discover what he called **higher pleasures**, such as **music**, **science**, **art** and **poetry**.
3) This would have the **dual benefit** of enabling individuals to **self-actualise** while also contributing to **social progress**.
4) Famously, he wrote that it's *"better to be Socrates dissatisfied than a fool satisfied."* This means that individuals should **push themselves** beyond their **intellectual comfort zones**.

Mill's belief in developmental individualism contrasted with the egoistical individualism proposed by Jeremy Bentham, a liberal philosopher who had helped to educate him. Bentham's hedonistic philosophy said individuals should be free to pursue their own pleasures in whatever way they chose, in the belief that this would create a greater degree of happiness within society as a whole.

Wollstonecraft addressed the **role of women**

1) Wollstonecraft believed that **women** had a **responsibility** to **educate themselves** so that they would enjoy **equal social status** to men.
2) Wollstonecraft wrote that *"intellect will always govern"* and that women's *"neglected education"* had allowed the development of *"the tyranny of men"*.
3) Although **supportive** of **free market capitalism**, Wollstonecraft warned that it had made women focus on *"acquisitiveness"* (a desire to own and collect material things), rather than on their own **self-development**.
4) Wollstonecraft placed **significant responsibility** on **women** themselves to **improve** their **position** in **society**. However, she also believed that the **state** should extend **formal equality** to women — particularly in relation to **suffrage**, **property rights** and **representation**.

Wollstonecraft wrote a response to Edmund Burke's *Reflections on the Revolution in France*, as part of an exchange between thinkers known as the 'revolution controversy'. In this exchange, Wollstonecraft criticised Burke's defence of aristocracy, basing her argument on rationalist principles and natural rights. She later similarly attacked republicans for basing their pursuit of liberty on the interests of white men, rather than on the interests of every member of society.

Core Political Ideas — Liberalism

Transition from Classical to Modern Liberalism

As liberal thought developed, people began to question the role of the state in people's lives and the economy...

Some **classical liberals** embraced **self-interest** and **self-preservation**

1) **Classical liberals** believe in a **laissez-faire** form of **capitalism** in which the **state** does **not** need to act to **re-distribute** wealth.

2) **Adam Smith** (1723-1790) was an influential classical liberal thinker. He described the **free market** (unregulated capitalism) as the "*invisible hand*" that guides society.

3) He thought that the actions people took to **pursue** their own **self-interest** in a capitalist system would **naturally benefit society** as a whole.

> Smith's ideas on the benefits of selfishness and competition later influenced neo-liberal thinkers (see page 47). He wrote that "*it is not from the benevolence of the butcher, the brewer, or the baker that we expect our dinner, but from their regard to their own self-interest*".

4) **Herbert Spencer** (1820-1903), another classical liberal, developed a **radical individualist philosophy** called **Social Darwinism**. This applied Charles Darwin's principle of **natural selection** (i.e. 'the survival of the fittest') to **society**.

5) This was very **different** to **Mill's** idea of **developmental individualism**, which stressed **individuals' responsibilities** to wider society.

6) Spencer believed **individuals** are responsible **only** for their own **self-preservation**, and that this **competition** would drive **social** and **economic progress** for the **whole** of society, albeit at the **expense** of some **individuals**.

T. H. Green's ideas marked a **crucial turning point** in the history of **liberalism**

1) **T. H. Green** was an **influential philosopher** who rejected some of the ideas put forward by thinkers like Spencer.

2) He wrote about **two types of liberty**:

1 Negative liberty

Sometimes referred to as '**freedom from**', this concept means that individuals do not have **external constraints** on their liberty. For example, under negative liberty, individuals would be free from **oppression**, **theft** of their property and **violence**.

2 Positive liberty

Sometimes referred to as '**freedom to**', this concept means that individuals are **actively enabled** to realise their **potential**. Under positive liberty, individuals would have **access** to services such as **education**, **healthcare** and **welfare**.

T. H. Green (1836-1882)

3) While **classical liberals** tended to see the **state** as a potential **constraint** on individual liberty, **modern liberals** see **state interventions** as **essential** for guaranteeing freedom.

4) **Classical liberals** believe that the **state** should only be **responsible** for ensuring **negative liberty**. They argue that a **minimal state** helps to promote **individual responsibility**.

5) However, **modern liberals** argue that the **state** should **enable** individuals to enjoy both **negative** and **positive liberty**. They believe that the **inequalities** created by **industrialisation** mean that a minimal state is **insufficient** for maximising the liberty of **all** members of society.

L.T. Hobhouse influenced **modern liberal** thought on the **economy**

L. T. Hobhouse (1864-1929)

1) **L. T. Hobhouse** was a key figure in the **transition** from **classical** to **modern** liberalism.

2) He wrote that "*wealth is a social phenomenon*". This means that all **wealth** is created by **collectives**, rather than by **individuals** in **isolation**.

3) This idea had a significant influence on **modern liberal thought** about the **state's involvement** in the **economy**. It helped to justify the **collection of taxes** to help **fund** an **enabling state**.

The two types of liber-tea — milk-in-first and milk-in-after...

Aaah nothing like a good brew. And what kind of biscuit you dunk in it is entirely up to you. A personal freedom liberals would be proud of. Though I wouldn't say no to some state-enabled biscuits... Custard creams on prescription anyone?

Modern Liberalism

Modern liberals are pretty positive about positive liberty, but this means the state needs to get a little more involved in things.

Modern liberals support a much more **interventionist state** than classical liberals

1) **Betty Friedan** argued that the state needed to pass **legislation** improving **positive liberty**.
2) She campaigned for **laws** on **equal pay** and **maternity rights**.
3) **Friedan** and **John Rawls** both believed that the **state** should provide **education for all** its citizens.
4) Their vision of an **enabling state** leads to a **rejection** of **laissez-faire capitalism**.

> Rawls and Friedan both accepted **Keynesian economic principles**, which called for some **state intervention** — particularly in **stimulating** economies during **recessions** and **depressions**. Keynesianism was considered **essential** for achieving **equality of opportunity**.

While modern liberals believe that education should be provided by the state, classical liberals argue that this responsibility lies with society and with the individuals themselves.

Modern liberals think **society** should be based on **meritocracy** and **social justice**

1) According to **Rawls'** difference principle, in a **just society** any **inequalities** "*are to be to the greatest benefit of the least-advantaged members*".
2) This has been used to **justify** policies based on **positive discrimination**, in which **disadvantaged groups** receive **preferential treatment**.
3) **Friedan** argued that **women** would only be free when "**cultural channels**" like the **media**, **sport**, **education** and **art** stopped reflecting only **male interests**.

Key Terms
meritocracy
A society where people's prospects are based on merit alone. Achievements come from talent and hard work rather than status.

They accept **classical liberal** ideas on **rationalism** and **tolerance**

1) **Rawls** used a **thought experiment** to formulate his **theory of justice**.
2) This experiment imagined individuals behind a **veil of ignorance**, which would mean that they **did not know** details such as their own **sex**, **nationality**, **religion** and **level of education**. Rawls argued that, from this outlook, it was **rational** for everyone to accept **equality of opportunity** and the **difference principle**.
3) **Friedan** believed that **women** bore some **responsibility** for their **inferior status** in society, writing that women needed to stop "*conforming to the conventional picture of femininity*". She wrote:

> *"Men are not the enemy, but the fellow victim. The real enemy is women's denigration of themselves."*

Quick Questions

1) What are Locke's three natural rights?
2) Explain the difference between foundational equality, formal equality and equality of opportunity.
3) What is meant by the enabling state?
4) What did Friedan mean by "cultural channels"?
5) Explain the difference between negative liberty and positive liberty.
6) Which thinker is associated with the veil of ignorance?
7) What did Mill mean by 'higher pleasures'?

Camilla was always looking for higher pleasures

Revision Task

Test your knowledge of liberalism by **defining** the following key terms and concepts:

- Natural rights
- Laissez-faire capitalism
- Harm principle
- Developmental individualism
- Rationalism

Top Tip for Politicians #161: Learn to eat food normally...

Okay, I know this seems like really basic advice, but you'd be amazed at how easily eating can go wrong (just look up some photos from election campaigns). Of course, you're at liberty to eat as messily as you want, but it's a cruel world out there.

Core Political Ideas — Liberalism

Comparing Liberal Ideas

Well, we've gone through the big ideas of the strands of liberalism. If only there was a page that collected all that together...

Human Nature

Classical Liberal

Humans are **sufficiently moral** and **capable** that they need only **negative liberty** if they are to **self-actualise**.

All humans are **foundationally equal**.
All humans have the capacity for **self-actualisation**.
Humans are **inherently rational** creatures.
All humans possess **natural rights** to **life, liberty** and **property**.

Modern Liberal

Humans are **moral** and **capable**, but **unequal social structures** mean that they need both **negative** and **positive liberty** if they are to **self-actualise**.

State

Classical Liberal

A **minimal state** is the best means of **maximising individual liberty**.

Governments require the **consent** of their **people**.
Democracy is the best form of **government**.
The state should **promote tolerance**.
The state should serve the **interests of its citizens**.

Modern Liberal

An **enabling state** is necessary to maximise **individual liberty**.
The state is **responsible** for providing **public services** such as **education** and **healthcare**.

Society

Classical Liberal

Formal equality is **sufficient** for allowing all individuals to **thrive** in society.

Individuals should be **trusted** to enjoy **complete liberty**, as long as they do **not** use their freedom to **inflict harm** on others.
Entrenched social hierarchies are a **barrier** to individual **liberty**.
Individual rights are accompanied by **responsibilities**.
Women should receive the **same education** as **men**.

Modern Liberal

Society should be based on the principle of **equality of opportunity**.
The state should **legislate** to better **protect the rights of women**.
Any **inequalities** should be arranged so that they **benefit the least-advantaged**.

Economy

Classical Liberal

Laissez-faire capitalism is the most effective economic system for preserving **individual liberty**.
Wealth and **property** are created by **individuals**.
Taxation should be kept to a **minimum** to avoid infringing on the **natural right to property**.

Capitalism is the most **effective and efficient economic system**.

Modern Liberal

Wealth and property are created by **collectives**.
Keynesian economics and **re-distributive taxation** are required in order to achieve **equality of opportunity**.

Revision Task

Explain one agreement AND one disagreement between classical and modern liberals in the following areas:
1) Human nature 2) The state 3) Society 4) The economy

Essay Plan

For Edexcel students: To what extent do liberals share a common view on the principle of liberty? [24]
For AQA students: Analyse and evaluate the extent to which liberals share a common view on the principle of liberty. [25]
Using the grid on p.298, **plan** an answer to one of the essay questions above.

Liberals lack alignment on legislation and laissez-faire capitalism...
Ending the section as we started — with a lot of L-iteration. What, you didn't notice? Bah, all my ludicrous labour left unloved.

Core Political Ideas — Liberalism

Socialism

Time to dive into a section about socialism. Unsurprisingly, it has something to say about people as social beings...

There are **three main strands** of socialism

Revolutionary Socialism

- As their name suggests, **revolutionary socialists** place **revolution** at the heart of their philosophy, believing that this is the only way of **achieving socialism**.
- Sometimes known as **fundamentalist socialists**, they desire **complete equality** of outcome and the total **overthrow** of **capitalism**.

Key Thinkers:
Karl Marx (1818-1883), Friedrich Engels (1820-1895), Rosa Luxemburg (1871-1919)

Marx and Engels wrote The Communist Manifesto, published in 1848.

Social Democracy

- **Social democrats**, also known as **evolutionary socialists**, believe that socialism can be achieved peacefully via **democratic** means.
- Rather than overthrowing capitalism, their emphasis is on **gradual reform**.

Key Thinkers:
Beatrice Webb (1858-1943), Anthony Crosland (1918-1977)

The Third Way

- **The Third Way** is given this name because it seeks to find a **middle ground** between socialism and capitalism.
- Third Way thinkers place more emphasis on **eliminating poverty** than on aiming for economic equality.

Key Thinker:
Anthony Giddens (b. 1938)

All three strands have been **influenced** by ideas from *The Communist Manifesto*...

1) **Common humanity** — **All socialists** accept Marx and Engels' belief that humans are **fundamentally equal** because we all belong to the **same species**. This is a **key part** of socialists' **objection** to **social class**.
2) **Exploitative nature of unregulated capitalism** — Although they differ in their views of capitalism, all socialists agree with Marx and Engels that **completely unregulated capitalism** leads to **unfair** and **unstable levels of inequality**.
3) **Role of class** — Because of their belief in **common humanity**, all socialists either want to **eradicate** or **substantially reduce** the role of **class differences** in society and the economy.
4) **Collectivist view of society** — Unlike liberals, who tend to see society in individualist terms, **socialists** believe that **collectives** are **more powerful** and likely to achieve their aims than individuals. As a result, socialists emphasise the importance of **co-operation** over competition.

...but they **disagree** over how **socialism** should be **achieved**

	Views on achieving socialism	Views on the role of the state
Revolutionary Socialism	**Revolutionary socialists** believe that only a **revolution** will be able to **dismantle capitalism**.	They believe a **temporary state** operated by the **proletariat** will be needed to create an **egalitarian society** and **economy** after capitalism has been **overthrown**.
Social Democracy	**Social democrats** are **evolutionary** socialists, meaning that they believe socialism can be achieved **gradually** (and through **democratic processes**).	A **strong, interventionist state** is a **vital** and **permanent** tool for achieving the goals of **social justice** and **equality of opportunity**.
The Third Way	**The Third Way rejects** the traditional socialist aim of **equality of outcome**. They believe **capitalism** can be used by the state as a **tool** for **improving public services** and **living standards**.	**The Third Way** prefers a more **limited state** that is **heavily involved** in **social policy** but much **less interventionist** in the **economy**.

I thought the role of class was to help me pass my A-Levels...
To sum up: we're all equal, capitalism is rubbish, the class system can get in the bin and teamwork makes the dream work. Easy.

Revolutionary Socialism

They say if it ain't broke, don't fix it, but as far as Marx and Engels were concerned, capitalism was seriously broken. And the only way to fix it was to, well, tear it all down, brick by brick. It's not called revolutionary socialism for nothing...

Marx and Engels argued that capitalism could only be overthrown by revolution

1) **Marx** and **Engels** saw capitalism as an **inherently exploitative** economic system that disproportionately **rewards the rich** while **failing** to reward **the poor**.
2) Because the **rich** were also those in possession of **political power**, Marx and Engels **rejected** the idea that **social** or **economic change** could be brought about without **overthrowing** the existing **system**.
3) In one of the most famous lines of *The Communist Manifesto*, they wrote:

   "Workers of the world unite; you have nothing to lose but your chains."

4) They were so confident in their belief that **capitalism** is a **flawed system** that they argued that it would **inevitably** lead to a **violent revolution**.
5) Marx and Engels believed that, because **capitalism** rewards **workers** so **poorly** for their **labours** and **rewards the rich** so well for **working less**, the **working classes** would eventually have **no choice** but to **revolt**.

> This belief is an example of **dialectical materialism** — the idea that history is defined by **conflicts** between different **material** (**economic**) **desires**.

The site of many a violent revolution...

Revolutionary socialists believe that capitalism harms humanity

Revolutionary socialists believe that humans are **fraternal, social beings**, but they say that people have been **alienated** from their **true nature** by **capitalism**.

1) Based on their concept of **common humanity** (see previous page), Marx and Engels shared an **optimistic**, **egalitarian** view of humanity that sees humans as fundamentally **equal**, with the **same capacity** for thriving in society.

2) However, revolutionary socialists also accept that **human nature** is **malleable**, which means that it can **change** according to **social** and **economic circumstances**.

3) Revolutionary socialists argue that the **unequal outcomes** created by capitalism create a culture of **class struggle**, in which the **working classes** are pitted **against** the **upper classes**.
   - **Marx** and **Engels** thought that capitalism had **tricked** members of the **proletariat** into believing that they were in **competition** with **each other**.
   - They also argued that capitalism had made the **bourgeoisie** exploitative and **self-interested**.

4) Revolutionary socialists believe that, to create the conditions in which a **revolution** could happen, the proletariat need to gain **class consciousness**, where they begin to understand that they are being **unfairly exploited** by the bourgeoisie.

Marx once said *"The rich will do anything for the poor but get off their backs"*

Key Terms

fraternity
Enjoying social relationships that are close enough to be like those between brothers.

proletariat
A term used by Marx and Engels to refer to the working classes.

bourgeoisie
A term used by Marx and Engels to refer to the wealthy upper classes, who they blamed for exploiting the proletariat.

Core Political Ideas — Socialism

Revolutionary Socialism

Marx and Engels believed in a form of communism with equality of outcome

1) Marx and Engels' goal was **common ownership** of the **means of production** and the **abolition** of **private property**. **Society** as a whole would **own all property**, including **industries** that would previously have been owned by the upper classes.

2) **Common ownership** would allow society to be based on the guiding principle of **equality of outcome**:

> "from each according to their abilities, to each according to their needs"

In practice, this would mean that everyone would receive a level of pay based on their needs, regardless of the economic value of their occupations.

Key Terms — communism: A radical form of socialism in which all property is owned by the community, rather than by individuals.

Marx and Engels foresaw the need for a supremacy of the proletariat

1) After the **revolution** that they believed was necessary to **overthrow capitalism**, Marx and Engels expected that there would be a period of **proletarian government** to oversee the transition to socialism.

2) This would involve the **working classes** (the proletariat) overseeing the state's efforts to **abolish private property** and **dismantle capitalism**, in order to achieve the goal of **workers' control**.

3) However, Marx and Engels believed that the **state** would eventually **fade away**. Marx believed that the **state** would be **unnecessary** once humans had been **returned** to their true **fraternal, co-operative selves**.

During the Russian Revolution, Lenin re-interpreted this idea to mean a 'dictatorship of the proletariat' in which the Communist Party seized power in the name of the proletariat and instituted an authoritarian form of government.

> This is a **key difference** between **Marxism** and the view of the state offered by **social democracy** and the **Third Way**. Social democrats and the Third Way argue that the **state** will **always** be a **necessary tool** for achieving **social justice**.

Rosa Luxemburg also believed that a form of revolution was necessary

- **Luxemburg** criticised the *"violence of the ruling class"* — the **economic exploitation** of the proletariat by the bourgeoisie.
- She played a leading role in the **Spartacist Uprising**, a revolutionary attempt to seize control of Germany through **strikes** and **demonstrations** in 1919.

> Luxemburg argued that **capitalism** could be **defeated without** resorting to **violence**.
>
> 1) Unlike Marx and Engels, **Luxemburg** felt that **democracy** could help to achieve socialism. She wrote:
>
> > *"Democracy is indispensable to the working class, because only through the exercise of its democratic rights... can the proletariat become aware of its class interests and its historic task."*
>
> 2) As a result, she called for the creation of **socialist political parties** that could help to bring about **class consciousness**.

There's a similar debate in anarchism over whether violent means would be justified in order to overthrow state power — see p.111.

Revision Task

Test your knowledge of revolutionary socialism by defining the following key terms and concepts:

- Common humanity
- Equality of outcome
- Proletarian government
- Dialectical materialism
- Class consciousness
- Common ownership

The capital in this sentence has been successfully overthrown...

Marx and Engels teamed up to write *The Communist Manifesto,* so they're normally considered together when the core philosophy of revolutionary socialism gets examined, even though they might not have seen eye to eye on every single point.

Core Political Ideas — Socialism

Social Democracy

Social democrats (aka 'evolutionary socialists', aka 'revisionist socialists', aka 'why use one name when three will do... socialists) believe that it's better to make a series of small steps — rather than the giant leap that revolutionary socialists aim for.

Social democrats believe socialism should be achieved **gradually**

1) **Beatrice Webb** and **Anthony Crosland** each saw capitalism as **problematic** and **divisive**, but they did **not** believe that it fundamentally **altered human nature** to the same extent that Marx and Engels did.
2) As a result, they believed that it was possible to use **democratic methods**, such as **elections** and **trade union activity**, to move **gradually** towards a more **equal society**.

> **Webb** — Webb was so **confident** that **democratic** means would lead to **socialism** that she wrote of *"the inevitability of gradualness"*.
>
> **Crosland** — Crosland wrote: *"As a democratic socialist profoundly committed to the rule of law, I could not condone, let alone encourage, defiance of the law."*

Unlike Marx, Webb believed that the bourgeoisie could be converted to accept socialist thinking. She co-founded the London School of Economics and Political Science (LSE) in an attempt to achieve this goal.

They believe that **capitalism** needs to be **reformed** rather than **overthrown**

Webb

Webb advocated the establishment of **co-operative movements** to represent **workers' rights** and **distribute profits** more fairly. She wrote about:

- **co-operative individualism** — where **individuals** and **communities** form co-operative movements **themselves**.
- **co-operative federalism** — where **federal co-operatives** made up of smaller **consumer co-operatives** are formed. These federal co-operatives would **purchase** and run things like **farms** and **factories**.

Key Terms
co-operative movements
Organisations that produce goods or offer services in the same way a traditional business might, but whose profits are shared between their workers and the wider community.

Tamal and Sandra realised that co-operative movements were the key to victory

You can draw a connection between Webb's support for co-operative movements and Marx's belief that humans are naturally fraternal, collaborative beings.

Crosland

Crosland embraced **Keynesian economic theory** (p.52), supporting a **mixed economy** (sometimes called **managed capitalism**) that **combined state** and **private ownership**. **Capitalist profits** could then be **redistributed** through **taxation** and **public spending**.

This marked him out from some other social democrats, including Webb, who had argued that **nationalisation of all industries** should be a **central goal** of their movement.

Social democrats aim for **social justice** as their **end goal** instead of **equality of outcome**

1) **Crosland** argued that **capitalism** had **evolved** and **improved** by the 1950s, allowing **social mobility** for some members of the working classes. As a result, he believed that **class differences** were **less pronounced** than Marx and Engels had envisaged, meaning that **equality of outcome** was no longer a **necessary** or **desirable** aim.
2) Social democrats believe achieving **social justice** would **reduce class differences** by offering greater **equality of opportunity** (see page 49).

They see the **state** as a **vehicle** for achieving a **fairer society**

1) **Webb** and **Crosland** were both advocates of **state-funded public services**, such as **education**, **healthcare** and **housing**.
2) **Crosland** argued that the state should play an **active role** in extending individuals' **liberty** — he supported **progressive legislation** such as the **de-criminalisation of homosexuality** and **equal pay**.

Like Harold Macmillan (see p.46), Crosland believed that the state should aim to provide full employment.

My pals all vote on where to hang out — social democracy in action...

Social democrats believe that socialism can be achieved over time, by democratic elections. Socialism would come about through lots of small steps, rather than in one massive revolutionary event. Sounds a bit like my approach to tidying up...

Core Political Ideas — Socialism

The Third Way

Some people thought that the core ideas of socialism about equality and the power of collective action were spot on. They weren't quite as sold on the idea that capitalism was fundamentally broken, though. Say hello to the Third Way...

The Third Way seeks to find a **middle ground** between socialism and capitalism

Anthony Giddens argued that capitalism could be **harnessed** to **improve society**...

1) **Giddens** went **further** than **Crosland** in accepting the **benefits** that capitalism could offer.
2) This led him to **reject nationalisation** completely — instead, he argued that the state should unleash *"the dynamism of markets"* and focus on **re-investing tax yields** (the money received by the state from taxes) into **public services**.

The Third Way is also called 'neo-revisionist socialism'.

- **Giddens** was a major influence on the **New Labour** policies (p.20) developed by **Tony Blair** and **Gordon Brown**. His ideas **combine left-wing social ideas** with **right-wing economic** ones.
- On the economy, his support for the **free market** means that he has more in common with **neo-liberals** (p.47) than with **revolutionary socialists**.
- Blair's **1997 election mantra** of *"education, education, education"* drew on Giddens' belief that the state should **promote equality of opportunity** through heavy **investment** in **public services**.

Sonya knew a thing or two about combining left-wing and right-wing ideas

...and that the **state** should focus on **eradicating poverty** rather than **economic inequalities**

1) Giddens wrote that the **goal of the state** should be to create a *"post-scarcity society"* — one in which every individual and family has access to **sufficient resources** to live a **fulfilled life**.
2) He suggested that the state should aim to **empower individuals** and **communities** to take **more responsibilities** for themselves, rather than becoming **dependent** on **welfare**.

Quick Questions

1) What is meant by managed capitalism?
2) Which thinker is associated with co-operative movements?
3) What is the difference between equality of outcome and equality of opportunity?
4) What did Giddens mean by a post-scarcity society?
5) Discuss the differences between the economic ideas of social democrats and the Third Way.
6) What are the views of each strand on the importance of class differences?

Exam Practice

Practise your **analysis** skills by identifying and explaining one agreement AND one disagreement between socialists' ideas in the following areas:

1) *Human nature*   2) *The state*   3) *Society*   4) *The economy*

Essay Plan

For Edexcel students: To what extent do the Third Way and social democracy accept the ideas of revolutionary socialism? [24]

For AQA students: 'The Third Way and social democracy accept the ideas of revolutionary socialism.' Analyse and evaluate this statement. [25]

Using the grid on p.298, **plan** an answer to one of the essay questions above.

"Chocolate cake, chocolate cake, chocolate cake"...

Sorry, got a bit sidetracked by my own mantra there. Where were we? The Third Way is also called 'neo-revisionist socialism' because (you guessed it) it's a revised approach to socialism. Speaking of revising socialism, the next page is bit of a cracker.

Comparing Socialist Ideas

Have a gander at this page for an overview of where the three strands of socialism agree and disagree on four key issues.

Human Nature

Revolutionary Socialism

Capitalism **corrupts** human nature.

The **bourgeoisie** benefit so **greatly** from capitalism that they can **never** be converted to **support socialist goals**.

The **proletariat** need to achieve **class consciousness** before they can understand their **true nature**.

Social Democracy and The Third Way

Humans are **fundamentally equal**.

Humans are inherently **fraternal, co-operative** and **capable** beings.

Both the **bourgeoisie** and the **proletariat** can be **educated** so that they **support socialist goals**.

Access to **high-quality public services** will allow individuals from every **class** to **thrive**.

State

Revolutionary Socialism

The **capitalist state** must be **overthrown** in order to **achieve socialism**.

A **dictatorship of the proletariat** is necessary before the **state** eventually **withers away**.

Social Democracy

The **democratic state** can be used as a means of **achieving socialism**.

Social democrats and **Luxemburg** (but not Marx or Engels) agree that **democracy** can help to **achieve socialist goals**.

The **state** should seek to **expand** citizens' **rights** and **freedoms**.

A **democratic state** is preferable to a **dictatorship**.

The **state** should aim for **social justice**.

The Third Way

The **state** should be a vehicle for **investment in public services**, rather than a tool for achieving **economic equality**.

The **state** shouldn't own **industries** or aim to **control employment**.

Society

Revolutionary Socialism

A **socialist society** would be based on the principle of **equality of outcome**.

Class shapes human nature.

All societies are shaped by **class conflict**.

Equality of outcome would **eradicate** all **class differences**.

Social Democracy

Class differences can be **narrowed** through education, healthcare, and other **public services**.

Society should be based on **strong, collaborative communities**.

Equality of opportunity is **more important** than **equality of outcome**.

People of **different classes** can live **peacefully** among each other.

Social change is **more important** than **economic change**.

The Third Way

Dealing with **class differences** is **less important** than eliminating **scarcity**.

Economy

Revolutionary Socialism

Capitalism must be **overthrown** by a **revolution**.

The **flawed nature** of **capitalism** makes its downfall **inevitable**.

Social Democracy

Capitalism should be **managed** by the **state** so that it **gradually** begins to **achieve socialist ends**.

Nationalisation helps the state to **improve living standards** by offering **full employment**.

Common ownership provides a much **fairer** economic structure than **private ownership**.

Unregulated free-market capitalism will **not** produce a **fair society**.

Redistributive taxation should be used to **fund** high-quality **public services**.

The Third Way

Free-market capitalism is the most **effective** and **efficient** economic system.

Socialists don't overlap overmuch on overthrow...
Revolutionary socialism has a lot of big ideas, but not all of them are accepted by other socialists. If you're struggling to remember where the three strands overlap, don't overreact (sorry, it's hard to stop) — have another read over this section.

The UK Constitution

The UK's Constitution is based on several different sources and is relatively flexible. This enables the UK political system to evolve, but it also means that problems can arise when it's inconsistently interpreted or applied.

The UK has an **uncodified** constitution that's found in **multiple sources**

- A **common misconception** is that the UK has an **unwritten** constitution. In fact, **four** of the **five** sources **are written**. The Constitution is **uncodified** because it's **not contained** in a **single document**.
- You need to know about the **five sources** of the UK Constitution to understand its key **strengths** and **weaknesses**:

1) **Statute law** — laws made by **Parliament**, e.g. the European Union (Withdrawal Agreement) Act (2020), which saw the UK leave the EU. Most statute laws have been **approved** by a **majority** in the **House of Commons** and the **House of Lords** (there are exceptions to this — see below).

2) **Common law** — rulings issued by the **courts**, including the **Supreme Court**, e.g. R. (Miller) v. The Prime Minister (2019), when Boris Johnson's attempt to **prorogue** (see p.99) Parliament was ruled null and void.

3) **Authoritative works** — **books** and **manuals** that have come to be considered part of the Constitution over time. There's **no definitive list** of authoritative writings, but examples include **Erskine May's Parliamentary Practice** and the **Ministerial Code**.

4) **Treaties** — **international agreements** signed by the UK government, e.g. the **Paris Climate Agreement** (see p.268).

5) **Conventions** — the only **unwritten source** of the Constitution. **Traditions** that are expected to be followed, e.g. the **Salisbury Convention** (see p.70) and the **Sewel Convention** (see p.61). Because they're unwritten, they have **no basis in law**, which means that they're **inconsistently** applied (see p.91-93).

Until Brexit, EU law used to be a sixth source of the UK Constitution, but those regulations have now either been adopted into statute law or abandoned.

The UK Constitution is also **unentrenched**

1) Because the Constitution's **uncodified**, it can be **changed** relatively **easily** — this means it can be described as **unentrenched**. The simplest way of **amending** the Constitution is by passing an **Act of Parliament** (statute law).

2) Here are some examples of laws that have **significantly amended** the UK's Constitution:

Bill of Rights (1689)

- The Bill set out **basic liberties** for all citizens and established **parliamentary sovereignty** by requiring **monarchs** to seek the **consent** of Parliament.
- **Parliamentary sovereignty** is the concept that Parliament, and not the monarch, has the **ultimate legal** and **political authority** over the **state**. It was established in **1689** when Parliament invited **William** and **Mary** (who were Protestants) to **replace James II** (a Catholic) on the throne.
- The Bill of Rights also introduced the **constitutional monarchy** — the idea that the monarch no longer has **absolute power**, and is instead **bound** by the **Constitution**.
- The Bill firmly established the principles of **frequent parliaments**, **free elections** and **freedom of speech** within Parliament (an example of **parliamentary privilege**).

Delilah had a bill to present to the House of Commons

Act of Settlement (1701)

- This reaffirmed **parliamentary sovereignty** and **constitutional monarchy**.
- Parliament decided that **only Protestants** could succeed to the throne.

Acts of Union (1707)

- These Acts formally united the political systems of England and Scotland, creating the **Kingdom of Great Britain**.
- The Acts of Union introduced the **unitary state** — the idea that the UK's political system has a **single location of power** (Westminster).

Parliament Acts (1911 and 1949)

- The Parliament Acts gave the **House of Commons** more power than the **House of Lords**, entrenching **asymmetrical bicameralism** in the UK.
- In 1911, the **House of Lords** lost its **financial privilege** (its ability to amend, block or delay money bills) and could only **delay** other **legislation** for up to **two years**.
- In 1949, the House of Lords' ability to delay legislation was **reduced** to **one year**. If the Commons chose, **laws** could be passed **without** the House of Lords' **consent** after a year had passed.

Key Terms

asymmetrical bicameralism
A term used to describe legislative branches with two chambers that have unequal levels of power.

The Parliament Acts significantly increased the executive's power.

The UK Constitution

The UK's **uncodified constitution** means its political system can **evolve**...

Here are some examples of how the **political system** has **evolved**:

1) **GUN CONTROL** — after the **Dunblane school shooting** in 1996, statute law was quickly amended, with the **Firearms (Amendment) Act (1997)** passing under a year later.
2) **SAME-SEX MARRIAGE** — with support from the Liberal Democrats, Labour and the SNP, **David Cameron** updated the UK Constitution by passing the **Marriage (Same-Sex Couples) Act (2013)**.
3) **COVID-19 PANDEMIC** — when COVID-19 spread to the UK, Parliament passed the **Coronavirus Act (2020)** in under a week, transferring **emergency powers** to the **executive**. This meant **public health** and **economic policies** could be implemented **without** holding **votes** in the Commons or the Lords.

It's often more difficult to make constitutional amendments in countries that have codified constitutions, e.g. the US.

...but it also means there are areas of **vagueness** and **contradiction**

The UK Constitution isn't always applied **consistently**. Here are some examples:

Foreign Interventions

Deploying troops overseas is one of the prime minister's **prerogative powers** (see p.84), but **Tony Blair** held a vote in the House of Commons before invading Iraq in 2003. When **David Cameron** held votes before taking military action in Libya and Syria, many believed that it had become a **convention** to do so. However, **Theresa May** ordered air strikes in Syria **without a parliamentary vote** in 2018 and this created confusion over the limits of prime ministerial power.

Devolution

The **Sewel Convention** states that Parliament should not legislate on devolved responsibilities like healthcare and education. But the **United Kingdom Internal Market Act (2020)** included several UK-wide provisions that directly affected **devolved policy areas**, e.g. agriculture.

Protests

The freedom of assembly is guaranteed under the **Human Rights Act (1998)**. Some people felt that this was challenged by the **Public Order Act (2023)**, which allowed the police to **arrest** protesters on **suspicion** (i.e. without evidence) that they might cause too much **disruption**.

Statute law takes precedence over the other sources of the Constitution

Parliament can **override** court rulings, conventions and treaties by passing statute law. Some examples of this include:

Terrorist Asset-Freezing Act (2010) — This followed a case called **HM Treasury v. Ahmed (2010)** (see p.99), when the **Supreme Court** ruled that the government didn't have the power to **freeze** the **financial assets** of terror suspects. Within a **month**, the House of Commons and the House of Lords passed a law that gave the government the power to do so.

Fixed-Term Parliaments Act (2011) — This act **amended** the **convention** that prime ministers could choose to call an **election** at a time that **suited them politically**. Elections had to be held every **five years** (although there were a couple of loopholes — see p.64). The act was **repealed** (made no longer valid) in **2022**.

Exam Practice

For Edexcel students: Evaluate the view that the UK Constitution is too easily amended. [30]
For AQA students: Explain and analyse three features of the UK Constitution. [9]

I think I need to lie down — I have a weak constitution...

There's plenty of content to get to grips with across these two pages. To help you get your head around it all, take a piece of paper and have a go at creating a table that lists the main strengths and weaknesses of the UK's Constitution.

Constitutional Reforms Under New Labour

New Labour wanted to shake things up, and a big part of this involved making some major reforms to the UK Constitution.

Tony Blair pledged four major reforms to the UK Constitution

1) **Democratisation** — improving the quality of the UK's democracy.
2) **Modernisation** — updating the Constitution so that it would be more relevant to the twenty-first century.
3) **De-centralisation** — reducing Westminster's dominance of the UK's political system.
4) **Maintaining the unity of the United Kingdom** — satisfying the demands of independence movements by transferring political power to Scotland, Northern Ireland and Wales.

Blair later **abandoned** plans for **electoral reform** and **regional devolution in England**, but he did implement the following far-reaching **constitutional changes**.

Devolution — Scotland Act (1998), Northern Ireland Act (1998), Government of Wales Act (1998)

1) **Devolution** is the transfer of **power** from a **central government** to a **regional** or **local** government.
2) As part of devolution, **primary legislative authority** (control over making laws) over areas of policy like **education**, **health**, **transport** and **agriculture** was **transferred** to the newly-created **Scottish Parliament** and the re-instated **Northern Ireland Assembly**.
3) The **National Assembly for Wales** (now called the **Senedd**) gained powers on a more gradual basis.
4) In **Northern Ireland**, devolution carried out the **power-sharing principles** agreed in the **Good Friday Agreement**, which aimed to end decades of political violence. The Northern Ireland **executive** would include **republican** (supportive of a united Ireland) and **unionist** (supportive of remaining in the UK) parties.
5) There have been several **successes** and **failures** to devolution in Scotland, Northern Ireland and Wales:

Successes
- Average **turnout** in Northern Irish (62%) and Scottish (55%) devolved **elections** has been fairly high.
- Policies like the **public smoking ban** (Scotland) and charges for **plastic carrier bags** (Wales) have been implemented across the UK following successful **trials** at a devolved level.
- There has been a significant **decrease** in **political violence** in Northern Ireland since devolution.

Failures
- Devolved elections in **Wales** have always had **below 50% turnout**.
- **Wales** and **Northern Ireland** still have low **economic activity** and **productivity rankings**.
- Because of disagreements between unionists and republicans, the **Northern Ireland Assembly** has been **suspended** for over **40%** of the time between 1998 and 2024.

Human Rights Act (1998)

1) The **Human Rights Act** (HRA) incorporated the **European Convention on Human Rights** (ECHR) into UK statute law.
2) It also enabled courts to issue **declarations of incompatibility** if they think a law is incompatible with the HRA. These are **non-binding recommendations** that Parliament can either choose to **follow** (by amending the law) or **ignore**.
3) The Human Rights Act has had a significant **impact** on **UK law**:

- **17 laws** have been **amended** by Parliament following **declarations of incompatibility** (e.g. the Mental Health Act (1983) was amended in 2007 and the Civil Partnerships Act (2004) was amended in 2019 — see p.99). However, a **total of 34** declarations of incompatibility have been made, meaning **only half** have been **upheld**.
- The HRA has been used to **improve protection** for victims of **domestic abuse** and **modern slavery**.
- The HRA is **often referenced** by politicians when **new laws** are being considered, e.g. the government explained how the **Domestic Abuse Bill** was compatible with its provisions when it was debated in Parliament in 2020.

4) However, the influence of the Human Rights Act is **limited**:

- Rulings by the European Court of Human Rights and UK courts are **often ignored**, e.g. the ruling in **Smith v. Scott (2007)** that denying **prisoners** the right to **vote** was **incompatible** with the HRA.
- As the UK's Constitution is **unentrenched**, the HRA **can be repealed** as easily as any other piece of statute law.

Constitutional Reforms Under New Labour

House of Lords Act (1999)

1) The Act reduced the number of **hereditary peers** (those who inherit their titles) from over **700** to **92**.

2) It promotes a more **even** split between **Conservative** and **Labour** members in the House of Lords and has made the House of Lords a **more effective check** on the **executive**:

> *A proposal to remove all remaining hereditary peers was included in Keir Starmer's King's Speech in 2024.*

- When there was a **Conservative majority** in the House of Lords, **Margaret Thatcher** suffered **156 defeats** in 11 years. In contrast, **Boris Johnson** suffered **243 defeats** in three years.
- **Crossbench peers** (see p.72) now hold the **balance of power** in the House of Lords, meaning that the executive has to reach **across party lines** when passing legislation.

3) However, some people argue that there are still **issues** with the House of Lords that the Act **didn't solve**:

- New Labour's reforms aimed to **modernise** the Constitution, but the UK remains the **only democracy in the world** that **allocates seats** in its Parliament based on **birthright**.
- Many people believe that hereditary peers add **little value** to the House of Lords. On average, **hereditary peers** spoke just **48 times** in the Lords from 2019-2024, compared with **70 times** among **life peers**.
- The continued presence of hereditary peers harms Parliament's **descriptive representation** (see p.81) — as of 2021, over **half** had attended **one school** (Eton), and all were **white** and **male**.
- Those who opposed the Act argued that it would give rise to **cronyism**. This has proven to have some legitimacy given the controversies over **appointments** by Tony Blair, David Cameron, Boris Johnson and Liz Truss.

Constitutional Reform Act (2005)

Ned was a Lord of Appeal in Extraordinary

1) This Act **abolished** the **Lords of Appeal in Ordinary** (also known as the law lords), previously the highest court in the UK. It replaced them with a new, independent **Supreme Court**.

2) It also **reduced** the **executive's influence** over the **judicial appointments** process. **Supreme Court judges** are now appointed by **ad hoc selection panels** (groups formed temporarily to appoint a single judge). All other judges are appointed by the independent **Judicial Appointments Commission**.

> The **Supreme Court** has been involved in many **high-profile cases** since it opened (see p.98-99) and frequently acts as a check on the **executive branch** (see the Gina Miller cases on p.99), without threatening **parliamentary sovereignty**. However, some people argue that the Act still hasn't made the UK court system entirely fair:
> - In 2017, **Liz Truss** (then Lord Chancellor) caused controversy when she **changed** the **age limit** for the post of **Lord Chief Justice**. This **ruled out** the **favourite** for the job — a government critic called **Sir Brian Leveson**.
> - The **Lord Chancellor** (a member of the Cabinet) can still **veto** Supreme Court **nominations** — although this power has **never** been used.

These points show that the executive does still have some influence over the judicial appointments process, which undermines the judiciary's independence.

Quick Questions

1) What does primary legislative authority mean?
2) For what percentage of its history since 1998 has the Northern Ireland Assembly been suspended?
3) How many hereditary peers remain in the House of Lords?
4) Which court case ruled that denying prisoners the right to vote was incompatible with the Human Rights Act (1998)?

Exam Practice

Selecting the most **relevant evidence** is key to succeeding at A-Level Politics. Practise this skill by considering which **examples** from pages 60-63 you would use to illustrate the following **arguments** in an **essay**:

1) *The UK Constitution can be changed **too easily**.*
2) *Constitutional reforms since 1997 have **improved** the UK's protection of rights.*
3) *The UK's political system **remains outdated**, despite recent constitutional reforms.*

With all these Acts, you'd think this was A-Level Drama...
You need to be able to write about how successful these reforms were. If you want to impress the examiner, you can refer to devolved systems as 'policy laboratories' when discussing how their policies have later been adopted across the UK.

Constitutional Reforms Since 2010

Like any film or TV show, all things must eventually come to an end. 2010 marked the end of New Labour and their major reforms to the UK's Constitution. However, there have been some instances of constitutional change since 2010.

The **pace** of **constitutional change** has been **slower** since **2010**

There have been **three** significant developments, which all have their own **successes** and **failures**:

1) Fixed-Term Parliaments Act (2011)

1) It **amended** the PM's **prerogative power** to call a general election at a **politically convenient time**.
2) The Act specified that general elections would take place at exact **five-year intervals**.
3) If a prime minister wanted to call a **snap election** before the end of the five-year parliamentary term, they would need the support of a **two-thirds majority** in the House of Commons.

✓ Provided **stability** during the **coalition** government by ensuring that the government lasted its full **five-year term**.

✗ Although the **2015** general election took place after the government had been in power for their **full five-year term**, there were **two** general elections (in **2017** and **2019**) between 2015 and 2022.

✗ The Act was **repealed** in **2022** as it could be **bypassed** by Parliament passing a **separate Act** which would allow a general election to be called.

2) Devolution — Scotland Act (2016) and Wales Act (2017)

1) **SCOTLAND ACT (2016)** — Transferred full **control** over **income tax** to the **Scottish Parliament** and gave the Scottish Parliament additional powers over **welfare**. It also made the **powers** of the Scottish Parliament a **permanent** part of the UK Constitution, which could **not** be **reduced** without approval from a **referendum**.

✓ Fulfilled **David Cameron's promises** (of **increased powers** for Scotland) during the **2014 Scottish independence referendum**.

✗ The controversy over the UK government's **block** of the **Scottish Gender Recognition Reform Bill** in 2023 (see p.14) suggested that there's still a **lack of clarity** over the relationship between **Westminster** and the **devolved bodies**.

2) **WALES ACT (2017)** — Gave the **Welsh Assembly** (now known as the **Senedd**) the power to **increase** or **decrease income tax** by up to **10%** and began the process of **upgrading** the Welsh Assembly to a **Parliament**.

✓ **Polls** suggest that the **Senedd** has become more **popular** among Welsh voters since it gained power.

✗ The Act granted significant powers to the Senedd **without** the **consent** of the **Welsh people**.

3) Brexit — European Union (Withdrawal Agreement) Act (2020) and European Union (Future Relationship) Act (2020)

1) As a result of the **Withdrawal Agreement Act**, the UK **left** the European Union and the European Common Market (see p.103).
2) Under the **Future Relationship Act**, the UK and the EU must maintain a **'level playing field'** in terms of **trade** — this means that they can't seek to gain a competitive advantage through **tariffs** or **trade barriers**.
3) The **Northern Ireland Protocol** (since revised and re-named as the **Windsor Framework**) means that Northern Ireland maintains **free trade** with the **Republic of Ireland** (and therefore the EU). There are **checks** on **goods** moving between Northern Ireland and the rest of the UK.

✓ The UK Parliament now has more **control** over the **laws** that it can pass governing the **economy**, boosting perceptions of **parliamentary sovereignty**.

✓ The UK can now sign **trade deals** on its **own**, rather than as part of the EU.

✗ Some argue that Brexit hasn't achieved its aims as UK law still **contains thousands** of **EU regulations** and **directives**.

✗ Parliamentary sovereignty is **limited** in practice by the 'level playing field'.

Boris Johnson signing the Withdrawal Agreement in 2020

Exam Practice

For Edexcel students: Analyse the view that constitutional reforms since 1997 have been weak and incomplete. [30]
For AQA students: 'Constitutional reforms since 1997 have been weak and incomplete.' Analyse and evaluate this statement. [25]

There isn't a withdrawal agreement that will get you out of the exam...

It's important to think about the specific words used in an exam question so you understand what's being asked. For example, 'weak' suggests the reforms haven't achieved their goals, while 'incomplete' suggests they need to be taken further.

UK Government — The Constitution

Taking Previous Constitutional Reforms Further

Reforms since 1997 have made significant changes to the UK Constitution, but some people think they should be taken further.

There are **three main areas** where there have been calls for **further change**

There have been calls to change the **House of Lords**, **devolution** and **rights protection**. Here are **key debates** in each area:

House of Lords	Abolition	👍	Some people argue that small changes aren't enough to improve what they see as an **undemocratic** chamber.
		👎	A **unicameral system** (only **one chamber**) would give the **executive** huge amounts of **power**, especially as it tends to have a **majority** in the Commons.
	Reduction in size	👍	The House of Lords would become **less expensive** and **more efficient** if it was smaller. The number of '**absentee peers**' would be reduced, e.g. between 2015 and 2022, **14%** of peers rarely or never attended the chamber.
		👎	Deciding which peers should stay in the chamber and which should be **expelled** would present a large **political challenge**.
	Introduction of a completely or partly elected chamber	👍	The Lords would become more **democratically legitimate**, and therefore more likely to **challenge** the **executive** if it was elected.
		👎	There's a danger that this could create a US-style **gridlock**, or **threaten** the legitimacy of the **House of Commons**.
	Removing the remaining 92 hereditary peers	👍	This would **complete** the **reform** proposed by **Blair** and further modernise the House.
		👎	Some hereditary peers argue that they **work harder** than many **life peers** (see p.72).
Devolution	Increased power for the Northern Ireland Assembly	👍	In 2015, the UK Parliament set out plans to devolve control of **corporation tax** to Northern Ireland, but this still hasn't happened due to the amount of time the NI Assembly has been **suspended** (see p.67).
		👎	Some argue that giving the Assembly more powers is pointless if the **major parties** can't agree to sit in a **power-sharing government** with each other.
	Enlarged Senedd	👍	Increasing the number of **seats** in the Senedd would increase the likelihood of a **multi-party system** developing, and offer more **localised representation**.
		👎	Devolved elections in Wales have always seen **under 50% turnout**, suggesting that there's little public interest in increasing the Senedd's size.
	Repeal Section 35 of the Scotland Act (1998)	👍	Removing the UK government's ability to **block** devolved laws would increase the **integrity** of the **Scottish Parliament**.
		👎	Some people argue this would **challenge** the core principles of **parliamentary sovereignty** and the **unitary state** (see p.60).
	Devolving the ability to call referendums	👍	Giving the Scottish Parliament and the other devolved legislatures the ability to call referendums could **reduce** the UK's **democratic deficit**.
		👎	Some people believe that this would **threaten** the **unitary state**.
Rights protection	Replace the Human Rights Act with a Bill of Rights	👍	Some critics of the Human Rights Act (see p.62) argue that it prioritises **individual rights** over **collective rights**. These critics believe that an **entrenched** Bill of Rights is needed as it would be **harder** to **change** than ordinary statute law.
		👎	A Bill of Rights could give too much **power** to the **executive** and remove the role of the **ECHR** (see p.260). Entrenchment could also lead to the **Constitution** becoming **outdated** as it would be **harder** to **change**.

Exam Practice

For Edexcel students: Evaluate the view that reforms to the Constitution require further extension before they can be considered fit for purpose. [30]

For AQA students: Explain and analyse three ways in which the UK Constitution has been reformed since 1997. [9]

Though not as fun as a 90s band re-forming, these reforms are important...

There's plenty of info on this page, so make your own summary of the debates around further changes to the constitution.

UK Government — The Constitution

Has Devolution Been a Success?

Well, the answer to this question really depends on who you ask. Some argue that devolution has been an overall success, while others are less enthusiastic about devolution for a variety of reasons. Read on to find out more.

There are **supporters** and **opponents** of **Scottish** devolution

1) Supporters of Scottish devolution believe that it has **improved democracy** and led to more **targeted policy-making**.
2) Here are some of the **successes** of Scottish devolution:

   - The **2021 Scottish Parliament election** saw a record **turnout** of **64%**.
   - The adoption of the **Additional Member System** (see p.27) has allowed for broadly **proportional** outcomes and created opportunities for **multi-party influence**.
   - Since 1997, Scotland has benefited from **higher pay growth** (87%) than any other country in the UK.
   - By 2020, Scotland had become the **third-most productive region** in the UK (after London and the South East).
   - Policies created by the Scottish Parliament, like the **public smoking ban** and **mandatory mask-wearing** in supermarkets (during the COVID-19 pandemic), were implemented in the **UK** following **trials** in Scotland.

3) But **opponents** argue that Scottish devolution has **failed** to achieve its **aims**:

   - Despite spending over **£800 more per pupil**, the Scottish **education system** performs **worse** than the English system in **international rankings**.
   - **A&E wait times** are **longer** in Scotland than in England, despite **higher funding** per person.
   - Devolution has failed to stop a **sharp rise** in the number of **drug-related deaths** in Scotland, which was almost **three times higher** than in the **rest of the UK** in 2020.
   - Targeted policy-making was **undermined** when the **UK government** chose to **block** the Scottish Parliament's **Gender Recognition Reform Bill** in **2023**.

People flying flags in support of Scottish independence

4) Others argue that devolution **isn't enough** in a country with strong **nationalist** support:

   - Support for **Scottish independence** rose by **10%** (from 43% to 53%) between **2018** and **2020**.
   - However, it levelled out at **47%** in **2023**.

Devolution has become more **popular** in **Wales**

1) There's been **increased support** for devolution in Wales — **49% voted against** devolution in **1997**, but by **2021**, only **20%** of Welsh voters wanted to abolish the Senedd.
2) There have been some **successes** of Welsh devolution:

   - Devolution in Wales has led to some successful **policies**, e.g. Wales led the way by banning the sale of **single-use plastics** in 2023. The UK government followed suit by banning **single-use cutlery** and **polystyrene cups** in England.
   - Devolution has allowed a much greater focus on preserving and building **Welsh culture** than was possible when Wales was solely governed from Westminster.

Ministers speaking in the Senedd building

3) However, the success of Welsh devolution has been **limited**:

   - There has been an overall **decline** in Welsh speakers in Wales since **2011**, and by **2020** the number of people who considered themselves **fluent** had dropped to as low as **10%**.
   - Like its Scottish counterpart, the Welsh **NHS** has been criticised for providing a **poorer service** than in England: **25%** of Welsh patients waited over a year for treatment in 2022, compared with **5%** in England.
   - Devolved **elections** in Wales have always had a **turnout below 50%**.
   - The **voting age** was **lowered** to **16** for the **2021 Welsh Parliament election**, but only an estimated **40-45%** of 16- and 17-year-olds actually voted.
   - Wales was near the **bottom** of the UK's **economic productivity rankings** according to a 2021 **ONS survey**.

> One of the flaws with devolution is that the Barnett formula, the method by which the devolved nations receive funding from the UK government, doesn't take socio-economic differences into account. Wales has the poorest and oldest population of the four UK nations, but it receives less funding per person than Scotland and Northern Ireland.

Has Devolution Been a Success?

Devolution in **Northern Ireland** has both **defenders** and **critics**

1) There have been some key **benefits** of devolution in Northern Ireland:

   - In the 25 years before the Good Friday Agreement, there were over 3500 deaths due to the Troubles, but there have been under 100 deaths in the 25 years since. Some people argue that this shows that devolution has brought political stability in Northern Ireland.
   - Employment in Northern Irish financial and insurance sectors grew by 36% between 1998-2022, higher than any other UK region.

   When evaluating the successes and failures of devolution in Northern Ireland, remember that peace was the primary aim of the Good Friday Agreement.

2) However, some people argue that devolution hasn't brought **political stability** in Northern Ireland or led to **economic growth**:

   - The Northern Ireland Assembly is often suspended due to disagreements between unionists and republicans, which suggests that the Assembly has done little to promote unity and stability.
   - Northern Ireland remains at the bottom of the regional league table in terms of UK GDP.

There has been some **regional devolution** in **England**

1) Regional devolution in England gives **mayors** more **power** over **policy-making** in their regions. Here are some examples of **successful policies** that mayors have introduced in England:

London has introduced schemes such as 'Boris' bikes (officially called Santander Cycle) and the congestion charge, which have helped to reduce London's carbon footprint by 32% since 2001.

Andy Burnham, mayor of Greater Manchester, introduced a £2 single-journey fare cap on public transport in 2022 to help with cost-of-living pressures.

2) However, there have been some **failures** related to regional devolution in England:
   - **Voter turnout** in mayoral elections has been low — **35%** in the **2021 Greater Manchester** mayoral election and **42%** in the **2021 London mayoral election**.
   - **Bristol** voted to **scrap** the post of **mayor** in a **2022 referendum**, which shows that people in the city were **unhappy** with this form of devolution.
   - The **transfer of power** is **uneven**. While the **London mayor** has significant powers over **transportation** and **housing**, other areas (such as the South West and the East Midlands) have received **no new powers** in recent decades.

Revision Task

Which of the examples from p.66-67 would be best for **supporting** the following arguments in an essay?
1) *Devolution has been **more successful** in Scotland than in England.*
2) *Devolution has **failed to improve** economic inequality.*
3) *Devolution has **successfully modernised** the UK's democracy by removing outdated, traditional elements.*

Exam Practice

For Edexcel students: Evaluate the view that devolution has failed to achieve its aims. [30]
For AQA students: Explain and analyse three successes of devolution in the UK. [9]

We should devolve power to horses — that would bring political stable-ity...

It might seem a bit obvious, but a good way to learn more about the complex topics that crop up in Politics is to do some of your own research into them. It's smart to be appreciative of the broader issues, and to be clued up on current affairs.

Devolution in England

The devolved powers in England have made roses spin around — wait, sorry about that, I'm thinking of the revolved flowers. Devolution has given English regions more power and self-determination. Some people think that it needs to be taken further.

Devolution in **England** is **asymmetrical**

1) This means that each **region** has **different levels** of **political power**.
2) Here's a summary of the **powers** granted to some of England's regions and cities:

Region	Do they have an elected mayor?	Powers granted to region
London	Yes	Oversight of Transport for London, planning permission, policing and economic development
Greater Manchester	Yes	Influence over bus and tram services, education, apprenticeships and waste management
Tees Valley	Yes	Responsible for economic development, regeneration and planning permission
Devon and Cornwall	No	County councils have influence over planning permission and skills investment

Sadiq Khan, Mayor of London from 2016

Some believe that **devolution in England** should be **extended**

Extending devolution would give more **equal** power to the different **regions** in England.

Supporters of further devolution in England give the following arguments:
- Devolution would provide an opportunity to address **economic inequality**.
- Increased **budgetary control** for local leaders would **reduce London's dominance** of **public spending**. E.g. in 2023-24, **investment** per person was **17%** higher in **London** than in the **East Midlands**.
- It would allow more **targeted policy-making**, as seen in Scotland, Wales and Northern Ireland (see p.66-67).

However, there are also several arguments **against** devolution in England:
- Devolution has **failed** to ensure strong **economic growth** in **Wales** and **Northern Ireland**.
- Devolution is **expensive** — **Bristol** allocated an annual budget of **£400 million** to its **metro mayor** before voting to **abolish** the position in 2022.
- **Turnout** in English devolved elections is very **low** — just **34%** voted in the **2021 Tees Valley mayoral election**.
- When voters in the **North East** were offered their own **assembly** in 2004, **78%** voted **against** it.

Others argue that England needs its own **national assembly** or **parliament**

1) **MPs** representing **Scottish**, **Welsh** and **Northern Irish** constituencies can **vote** on **policies** like **education** and **healthcare** affecting England, but **English MPs** can't do the same for the devolved nations. This creates a constitutional problem referred to as the **West Lothian Question** (WLQ).
2) Parliament **experimented** with English Votes for English Laws between 2015 and 2021, but experts believe that it made **no difference** to whether bills were approved or not.
3) The idea of having an English national assembly or parliament has **limited public support**. Polling in 2023 suggested that only around **31%** of the public **supported** the creation of an English Parliament, compared with roughly **46%** who answered 'don't know'.

The West Lothian Question was first raised by the MP for West Lothian, Tam Dalyell, in 1977.

Exam Practice

For Edexcel students: Evaluate the view that there is a compelling case for further devolution in England. [30]
For AQA students: 'There is a compelling case for further devolution in England.' Analyse and evaluate this statement. [25]

Diva-lution — a movement to increase your sense of self-importance...

Make sure you know the main arguments in the debate on extending devolution in England and can support your points (both for and against) with examples. Choosing some key statistics from this page to learn will really help you in the exam.

Codifying the UK Constitution

Some people argue that the UK Constitution should be written in one document rather than having five sources. This would be a pretty drastic change, one that would come with plenty of advantages and disadvantages.

The **most radical** way of reforming the UK Constitution would be **codification**

Here are some **pros** and **cons** to bringing the Constitution together into **one document**:

Pros

Simplicity and accessibility
- Codifying the Constitution would make it **easier** for **citizens** to **understand**.
- It would be **easier** to **access** the Constitution if it was contained in one document.
- For example, the **US Bill of Rights** is just **one page**, whereas the UK's **Human Rights Act** is **28** pages long.

Rights
- Codifying the Constitution would be likely to **increase the protection of rights** in the UK.
- This would make it **more difficult** for rights to be **taken away** from citizens (see the Public Order Act (2023) on p.14).

Checks and balances
- A codified constitution would become **sovereign**, meaning that the **executive** could no longer easily **pass laws** through Parliament that **increase** their **power** (see the Terrorist Asset-Freezing Act (2010) on p.61).

Cons

Practical challenges
- There's **no agreement** over **who** would be **responsible** for drawing up a codified constitution.
- **Parliament** would **no longer** be **sovereign**, meaning that the whole **nature** of the **political system** would also **change**.
- A single document could create a **US-style situation**, where unelected judges frequently rule on social issues like **abortion** and **marriage**.

Loss of flexibility
- Codified constitutions can quickly become **outdated** because it's **harder** to **amend** them.
- The UK's political system has managed to **evolve** significantly in recent years, with **devolution**, **judicial reform**, **same-sex marriage** and **Brexit** all being passed into law by Parliament.

Executive mandate and role of the judiciary
- Because codification would make it more difficult to change the Constitution, the **executive** might find it **harder** to carry out their **mandate**.
- The **unelected judiciary** would need to assume **more power** to **oversee** the newly codified constitution.

Although the most famous **codified constitution** in the world is the **United States Constitution**, it's important to remember that **not all** codified constitutions are as **difficult** to **change**.

> For example, in the **Republic of Ireland**, an amendment requires a simple **majority** in **both legislative chambers** and then a **confirmatory vote** in a **referendum**.

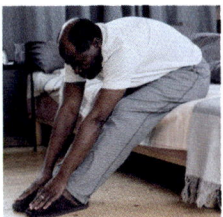

Ade's constitution had lost some flexibility

Exam Practice

For Edexcel students: Analyse the view that codification is the most desirable solution to the UK's constitution problems. [30]

For AQA students: Explain and analyse three arguments in favour of codifying the UK Constitution. [9]

CGP has codified A-Level Politics into one sovereign, authoritative work...

Checking out the constitutions of other countries can give you some interesting comparisons with the UK's Constitution. Understanding how constitutions work in other countries can help you to answer questions like the ones above.

Parliament

There's no denying it, the UK Parliament is a pretty important topic to get to grips with when you're studying politics. So crack those knuckles, get your best game face on and settle down to learn all about the ins and outs of Parliament.

The UK Parliament has **three main functions**

1. **LEGISLATION** — passing, amending and repealing **laws**. In almost all cases, laws have to be agreed by **majorities** in both the **House of Commons** and the **House of Lords**. Parliament is the UK's **sovereign legislative branch**, meaning that it has the **final say** on all legislation.

2. **SCRUTINY AND ACCOUNTABILITY** — Parliament is responsible for checking that the **executive branch** of **government** (led by the prime minister) is operating in the **best interests** of the nation. Weekly sessions called **Prime Minister's Questions** are the most high-profile way of doing this, but **committees**, **ministers' questions** and **urgent questions** also play an important role (see p.78-80).

3. **REPRESENTATION** — the UK is a **representative democracy** where elected representatives make most political decisions **on behalf** of citizens (see p.81). As the **elected chamber**, the **House of Commons** bears this responsibility more than the Lords, which is unelected.

Theresa May at Prime Minister's Questions

Parliament has **two chambers**

The two chambers of the UK Parliament are the **House of Commons** and the **House of Lords**. Their powers have **evolved** over time:

1) The **Lords** was the **dominant** chamber until the **late nineteenth century**, but the **Commons** has been **more powerful** since.
2) In **1911**, a **Parliament Act** was passed that **stopped** the House of Lords from **blocking**, **amending** or **delaying** any bills that involved **money**.
3) The Lords was also limited to blocking **all other legislation** for a maximum of **two years**.
4) This was later reduced to **one year** when another **Parliament Act** was passed in **1949**.
5) The Lords is also expected to follow the **Salisbury Convention**, which states that it should not block, amend or delay any bills that were in the governing party's **manifesto**.
6) There have been calls to further **reform** the House of Lords (see p.63). For the time being, its **unelected** nature means that the Lords recognises it has **no right** to **challenge** the power of the Commons in **disagreements** lasting more than a year (see p.60).
7) Having a parliament that's made up of two chambers, with one more powerful than the other, is known as '**asymmetrical bicameralism**' (see p.60).

A law that is passing through Parliament is called a bill.

Not asymmetrical bicameralism

The **executive branch** has a strong influence on the **House of Commons**

1) The **fusion of powers** in the UK means that **Parliament** also contains members of the **executive branch**:
   - Most **government ministers** (including the prime minister) are members of the **House of Commons**.
   - This gives the government a **significant advantage** — collective responsibility (see p.91) means that **over 100 ministers and aides** are expected to **support** all government bills.

2) **First-past-the-post** (FPTP) tends to produce **majorities** in the Commons (see p.26). This **increases** the executive branch's ability to **dominate** the chamber.

3) But there has **not** always been a single-party majority in recent years:
   - From **2010-2015**, the Conservatives formed a **coalition** government with the Liberal Democrats.
   - Theresa May signed a **confidence and supply deal** with the DUP in **2017** (see p.16).

4) **Peers** (members of the House of Lords) can be **government ministers**, but usually few are. One example is David Cameron, who Rishi Sunak appointed to the Lords and made **Foreign Secretary** in 2023. **No party** has an overall **majority** in the Lords, so the **executive branch** tends to have much **less** influence over the passage of legislation there.

Scrutiny of your answers is one of the main functions of the exam board...
The way in which the executive branch tends to be able to dominate the House of Commons is a recurring theme when you're studying how the UK Parliament works, so make sure you've got the reasons for it all sorted before you move on.

The House of Commons

The Commons is the more powerful of Parliament's two chambers and is made up of elected members.

The House of Commons is made up of **650 MPs**

1) Under the **FPTP** electoral system, each **constituency** elects a single **Member of Parliament (MP)**, which means that every MP has a close link with the **citizens** they represent. For example, in the 2024 general election, **Keir Starmer** was elected as MP for Holborn and St Pancras in London, while **Rishi Sunak** was elected as MP for Richmond and Northallerton in Yorkshire.

See p.26 for further examples of FPTP's impact on the House of Commons.

2) As a **plurality** system, FPTP tends to create **single-party majorities**. This means that one party usually has **more than half** of the total number of MPs.

3) In **all but three** elections since the Second World War, FPTP has given a **majority** to either the **Conservatives** or **Labour**. The exceptions were the elections of **February 1974** (Labour minority), **2010** (Conservative-Liberal Democrat coalition) and **2017** (Conservative minority).

4) **Over 100 MPs** are also members of the **executive branch**:

The House of Commons

- As well as the **prime minister**, most **cabinet ministers**, **junior ministers** and **ministerial aides** serve as MPs as part of the **fusion of powers**.
- They are all expected to follow the convention of **collective ministerial responsibility**. This means that they should **vote for** and support every aspect of **government policy**.

The **executive branch** usually gets its **legislation** through the Commons...

1) **FPTP** and the **fusion of powers** mean the **executive branch** is likely to be **successful** in putting **legislation** through the House of Commons.

2) Prime ministers with **large Commons majorities** suffer **very few defeats** in the Commons (see p.84).

- **Margaret Thatcher's** Conservative government **lost only four votes** in 11 years in the Commons.
- **Tony Blair's** Labour government was **undefeated for eight years** from 1997-2005.
- After the Conservatives won an 80-seat majority under **Boris Johnson's** leadership in the 2019 general election, his government was **undefeated on legislative votes** until his resignation in 2022.

3) Even when prime ministers have **smaller majorities**, they are **rarely defeated** in the Commons.

Theresa May was undefeated for her **first year** in office (2016-2017), with a **majority** that fluctuated **between 10 and 12 MPs**.

...but the **executive branch** is still subject to lots of **scrutiny** in the Commons

1) Every prime minister takes part in **weekly Prime Minister's Questions** sessions in front of the House of Commons.

See p.78-80 for examples of Commons scrutiny of the executive branch.

2) Prime ministers also attend meetings of the **Liaison Committee**, which is made up of the **chairs** of every **select committee** (see p.79).

3) **Ministers** from each **government department** face **question times** in the Commons, during which **backbench** and **opposition MPs** ask questions in order to **scrutinise** the work of the minister and their department.

4) **Select committees** can summon ministers and special advisers to face **questions** about issues they are **responsible** for.

Legislation is scrutinised by the Lords after it's passed by the Commons

The majority of **legislation** that goes through the House of Commons also has to be **agreed** by the **House of Lords**. However, the **Commons** has several **exclusive powers** that the Lords does not possess:

- The Commons can vote on **confidence motions**, which can **bring down a government** (see p.79).
- Since the **Parliament Act (1911)**, the Commons has been the **only chamber** that can block, amend or delay **financial legislation**. In fact, the executive branch has **lost only one vote** on a **finance bill** since **1978** — Theresa May lost a vote on a spending package for **No Deal Brexit** preparations in **2019**.
- Legislation which is **rejected** by the **Commons** can **never** become **law**, whereas the Commons can **overrule** the Lords using the **Parliament Acts**.

UK Government — Parliament

The House of Lords

Yep, that's right — now it's time to get to grips with the ins and outs of Parliament's second chamber, the House of Lords.

The House of Lords is made up of **three types of peer**

The Lords has **nearly 800 members**, who are known as **peers**.

1) Life Peers

1) There are **nearly 700** life peers in total.
2) They are appointed based on **nominations** by the **prime minister** and **opposition party leaders**.
3) Nominations are considered by the non-partisan **House of Lords Appointments Commission**.
4) Prominent examples of life peers in modern times include **Lord Cameron**, prime minister from 2010-2016, **Lord Winston**, a pioneer of fertility treatment, and **Baroness Hale**, former President of the Supreme Court.
5) **Over 200** life peers have **no party affiliation** — most of these are known as **crossbench peers**, e.g. Baroness Hale.

The House of Lords

2) Hereditary Peers

1) These peers have **inherited** their positions through their family line.
2) Limited to a **maximum of 92**, following the **House of Lords Act (1999)** (see p.63 for more details).
3) Examples include the current **Duke of Wellington**, whose ancestor defeated Napoleon at the Battle of Waterloo, and **Lord Younger**, who has filled more than ten ministerial posts.
4) Over half sit as **Conservative** peers, though there is a **growing number** of crossbench hereditary peers. A small number of hereditary peers sit on the **Labour** and **Liberal Democrat** benches.

Former Archbishop Justin Welby

3) Lords Spiritual

1) **26** Church of England **archbishops** and **bishops** sit in the Lords.
2) Most **rarely attend** debates, but there have been a few **notable interventions** in recent decades:
   - In 2002 and 2003, the **Bishop of Chelmsford** led religious **opposition** to the **Iraq War** in the Lords.
   - Justin Welby, then the **Archbishop of Canterbury**, spoke out **against** the government's plan to send **asylum seekers** to **Rwanda** during a Lords debate in May 2023.

Some argue that the Lords' **composition** is its **greatest strength**...

✓ Being a mostly **appointed** chamber can be seen as an advantage because it means the Lords contains many **experts** who might not want to run for election.

✓ As well as the examples above, there have been many peers who have had **wide-ranging experience** of life beyond politics. These include **Baroness Grey-Thompson**, an 11-time Paralympic gold medallist and disability rights campaigner, **Lord Bird**, the founder of the Big Issue, and **Baroness Lawrence**, an anti-racism campaigner.

✓ In **2023**, the Lords contained **five former Chancellors**, **six former Home Secretaries** and **three former Foreign Secretaries**, bringing a wide experience of **government**.

✓ Peers are paid **expenses** for the days that they attend the Lords instead of a **fixed salary**. This means that many are still able to work in their **main jobs**, giving the chamber greater **non-political expertise** than the Commons.

Baroness Lawrence

✓ The presence of **crossbench peers** helps to ensure that there is **no single-party majority** in the Lords. This increases the chamber's effectiveness in holding the **executive branch** to **account**.

✓ Crossbenchers also contribute to the **less partisan** atmosphere in the Lords. As a result, **legislation** tends to be considered on its **merits**, rather than based on party politics.

UK Government — Parliament

The House of Lords

...others believe the **composition** of the Lords is its **greatest weakness**

- ✘ The UK is the **only** democratic country to have **hereditary** legislators — some argue that being born into a particular family should **not** give someone the **right** to sit in Parliament.
- ✘ Many people feel the members of the House of Lords are **unrepresentative** of wider **British society**:
  - The vast majority of hereditary peers who have sat in the House of Lords have been **white men**.
  - In 2021, **nearly half** of the hereditary peers had attended the same school, **Eton College**.
- ✘ Because the Lords is **unelected**, it **lacks** the **authority** to challenge the Commons in so-called **parliamentary ping pong** (see p.77).
- ✘ The **appointments process** has been criticised for promoting **cronyism** (see p.63):
  - **27 major Conservative donors** were given peerages between **2010** and **2022**, while **Labour** was embroiled in its own '**cash for peerages**' scandal during the **Blair government**.
  - Despite only serving as prime minister for **49 days**, **Liz Truss** was able to successfully nominate **three people** to the House of Lords as part of her **resignation honours**.
  - **Boris Johnson** was criticised for appointing **Evgeny Lebedev**, a Russian billionaire whose newspaper, the **Evening Standard**, had supported his **London mayoral campaigns**.

The Lords has **limited powers** compared with the Commons...

1) Since the **Parliament Act (1911)**, the Lords **cannot** block, amend or delay **financial legislation**.
2) The **Parliament Act (1949)** means that the Lords can only **delay** other legislation for a **maximum of one year**. This means that the **House of Commons** can pass laws **without** the **Lords' consent**, which last happened with the **Hunting Act (2004)**.
3) The Lords has **no power** over **military interventions**, whereas the Commons tends to **debate** military interventions and has sometimes been asked to **authorise planned action** through a **vote** (see p.85-86).

...but the Lords has a major role in **amending legislation** and providing **scrutiny**

1) The House of Lords has become a **revising chamber**, responsible for **amending legislation** proposed by the **House of Commons**.
2) The **committee stage** in the Lords happens in the **chamber**, which tends to produce much more **meaningful scrutiny** than public bill committees in the House of Commons (see p.80). For example, the Lords suggested 54 amendments to the **Nationality and Borders Bill** during 2021-2022.
3) Each **government department** has its own **question time** in the House of Lords, similar to the question times that take place in the Commons. This offers a chance for peers to hold the **executive branch** to account.

You should also have a look at the examples on p.77.

Exam Practice

For Edexcel students: Evaluate the view that the House of Lords is not fit for purpose. [30]

For AQA students: 'The House of Lords is not fit for purpose.' Analyse and evaluate this statement. [25]

Imagine that you are answering one of the exam questions above.
Practise your **analysis** skills by explaining the significance of these examples to your question:

- *On average, hereditary peers claimed more than life peers in expenses from 2016-2021, but spoke less often in the chamber.*
- *Over 200 peers (over a quarter of the whole chamber) have no party affiliation.*
- *Tony Blair was undefeated in the Commons from 1997-2005, but his government lost over 300 votes in the Lords during the same period.*

You're probably sitting in your own revising chamber right now...

Sadly the exam board won't award you a peerage for all your hard work, — but it <u>can</u> give you a good grade if you're able to get your head around the different types of peer, the composition of the Lords and the power the Lords has. Much better deal.

Comparing the Commons and the Lords

Now you're an expert on how each House works, it's time to look at some ideas about the significance of the two chambers.

There are **differing views** about which House has **more influence**

1) Although the **House of Commons** has **more exclusive powers** than the **House of Lords**, some argue that the **Lords** possesses **more day-to-day influence** over **legislation**.
2) Others argue that the **Commons** is more politically **influential**.

Arguments that the Lords has more influence	Arguments that the Commons has more influence
• From **2021** to **2022**, the executive branch **lost 128 votes** in the **Lords**, compared with **just one** in the **Commons**. • **FPTP's** tendency to produce **majorities** in the **Commons** means that the Lords is often the only **check** on **executive dominance** (see p.77). • The number of **amendments** suggested by the **Lords** is far **greater** than in the **Commons**. For example, the **Illegal Migration Bill** was **unamended** by the **Commons** in 2023, but the **Lords** suggested **28 amendments**. *Most of these amendments were rejected by the Commons, but peers succeeded in increasing protections for women and children.*	• The **Commons** has been home to **every prime minister** since the beginning of the **twentieth century**. • Most **government ministers** are **MPs**, rather than peers. Only a few peers have run government departments in recent years — **Lord Cameron** was the first peer to do so since **Lord Mandelson** during Gordon Brown's premiership. • The Commons has **direct access** to the PM through **Prime Minister's Questions**. • Most **legislation** is **proposed** in the **House of Commons**. • The **Commons** tends to **win** bouts of so-called **parliamentary ping pong** (see p.77). *The last prime minister to sit in the Lords was the Marquess of Salisbury, who left office in 1902.*

There are also **contrasting views** about which House is **more effective**

1) Some argue that the **Lords** provides a **less partisan**, **more expert** and **more productive** service than the Commons.
2) Those who believe that the **Commons** is more effective highlight its greater **democratic legitimacy**, **geographical representation** and ability to hold the **executive branch** to account.

Arguments that the Lords is more effective:
- The Lords is **less partisan** than the Commons because **over 200 peers** have **no party affiliation**. Only a handful of independent MPs sit in the Commons.
- In recent years, there has been a reported rise in the number of **MPs** who are '**career politicians**', which means that they have never worked outside Westminster. Many **peers** have had extensive and successful careers **outside** of Parliament (see p.72).
- The Lords does **not** have the kind of '**Punch and Judy**'-style sessions that sometimes occur in the Commons (see p.78).

The House of Commons (apparently)

Arguments that the Commons is more effective:
- All 650 **MPs** represent **geographical constituencies** that together span the **entire United Kingdom**. By contrast, the **Lords** has been criticised for being disproportionately made up of peers from **London** and the **South East**.
- The prime minister **cannot** be summoned to give evidence to any **Lords committees**, as they do **two or three times a year** with the **Commons Liaison Committee**.
- Because most **cabinet ministers** are **MPs**, **departmental question times** are more meaningful in the Commons than in the Lords, where **junior ministers** usually answer questions.

Personally I'm not in favour of a less parmesan service — oh, wait, what?

Phew, that's a lot of arguments... Just remembering the fact that the Lords is an <u>unelected</u> chamber and the Commons is <u>elected</u> is a great starting point. From there you can think about questions about democracy and which chamber is more efficient.

UK Government — Parliament

The Role of Backbenchers

The majority of MPs and members of the House of Lords are backbenchers. They've been given this name because (wait for it) they sit on benches behind government ministers or opposition party spokespeople in the Houses of Parliament.

Backbenchers play an **important role** in carrying out **Parliament's functions**

1) Any MP or peer who is **not** part of the **executive branch** or serving in a **shadow ministerial role** is called a **backbencher**.

   Most government ministers have 'shadows' in the largest opposition party. Shadow ministers help to formulate their party's policies and lead departmental questions in the Commons (see p.78).

2) **No bill** can pass without sufficient **backbench support** in both the Lords and the Commons.

3) All members of **Commons select committees**, including their chairs, are backbench MPs. See p.79 for examples of **backbench influence** in select committees.

4) During the **Brexit** process, **backbenchers** managed to gain an extraordinary amount of **influence** due to the weakness of the **minority governments** from 2017-2019:

   - **Remain-supporting backbench MPs** managed to force Theresa May to request **two extensions** to the Brexit **deadline**.
   - They then took control of the **parliamentary timetable** from Boris Johnson in September 2019 (see p.80).

5) Since 2010, the **Backbench Business Committee** has been allocated **35 days per session** to hold debates and votes in the Commons and Westminster Hall. **Individual** backbenchers can suggest subjects for **debate**, which are **evaluated** by the committee. However, their debates tend to be held on **Thursday** afternoons, by which time many MPs have **returned to their constituencies** for their **Friday surgeries**.

6) Backbenchers can sponsor **private members' bills**:

   Conservative backbencher **Pauline Latham** succeeded in passing her **Marriage and Civil Partnerships (Minimum Age) Bill** into law in 2022, raising the minimum age for marrying and entering into civil partnerships to eighteen.

7) Backbenchers tend to have **more time** than ministers and shadow ministers to devote to representing their **constituents**.

Backbench MPs are often **limited** by the **executive dominance** of the Commons

1) For **most days** of the parliamentary year, the **executive branch** controls **timetabling** in both the Commons and the Lords. This means that backbenchers are **powerless** to decide **which issues** they vote on and **how long** they have to **debate**.

   See p.77 for how Boris Johnson tried to restrict Parliament's ability to debate and vote on his Brexit deal in 2019.

2) **Party whips** attempt to **control** backbenchers' **voting decisions** by appealing to their sense of **party loyalty**, and also with **promises** of future promotions or **threats** to derail their careers.

3) The most extreme example of this in recent years came in **2019**, when Boris Johnson **expelled** 21 Conservative backbenchers who voted **against** his **Brexit policy**.

4) Backbenchers sit on **public bill committees**, but they are notoriously **weak** in amending **legislation** — in recent years, **under 1%** of opposition amendments at committee stage have been accepted by the **executive branch**.

   Public bill committees are so unlikely to lead to legislative changes that there are even reports of MPs writing Christmas cards during committee meetings.

5) In the **House of Lords**, the influence of backbench peers is undermined by the Lords' **limited powers** and **unelected status** — see page 73.

Exam Practice

For Edexcel students: Evaluate the view that backbenchers lack the power to play a significant role in Parliament. [30]

For AQA students: 'Backbenchers lack the power to play a significant role in Parliament.' Analyse and evaluate this statement. [25]

Using the sentence frames on pages 299-300, write an **introduction** to one of the questions above.

You know what they say about people who like to sit on the back row...

Make sure you get to grips with both sides of the story when it comes to backbenchers — although they can't control the timetabling of parliamentary business, the executive branch relies heavily on their support to get its policies through.

UK Government — Parliament

Parliament's Legislative Function

Much like my famous opera cake, legislation has to go through quite a few stages before it can get the much-needed Royal Assent. These pages might seem a bit confusing at first, so don't worry if you need to go over them a few times before it all sinks in.

Bills pass through many different stages before they become law

Most bills **begin** in the **Commons** before **progressing** to the **Lords**. Some **start** in the **Lords** instead.

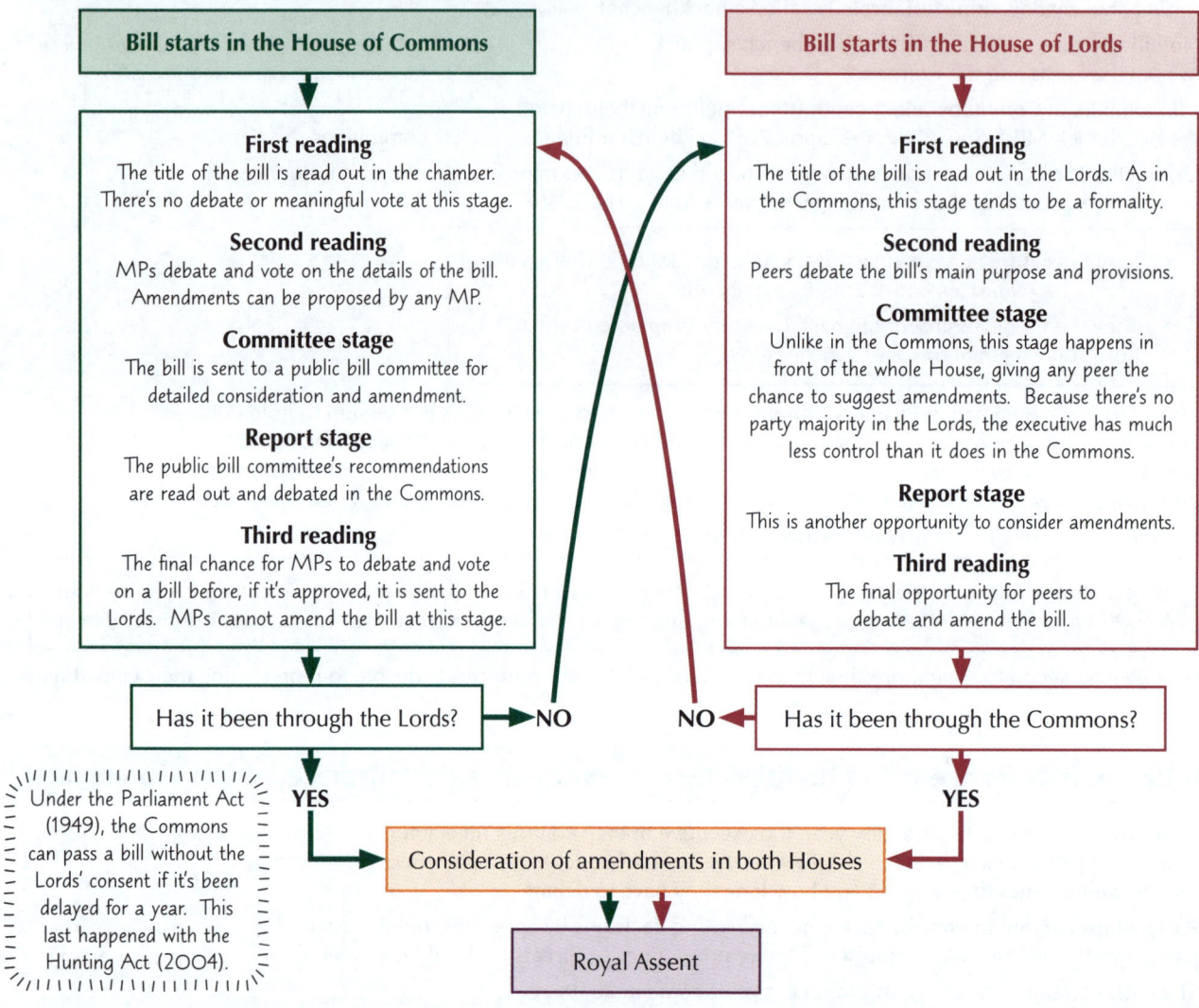

Under the Parliament Act (1949), the Commons can pass a bill without the Lords' consent if it's been delayed for a year. This last happened with the Hunting Act (2004).

The UK Parliament is seen as an efficient legislative branch

1) Because the **executive branch** tends to possess a **majority** in the House of Commons, Parliament is usually one of the **most efficient** legislative branches in the **democratic world**.
2) Some believe this means that Parliament **successfully** fulfils its **legislative function**. Others argue that Parliament's efficiency when passing legislation comes at the **cost of quality**.

In May 2023, it was reported that Parliament had passed into law 43% of bills introduced in 2022-23, whereas the US Congress passed just 2% in 2021-23.

Arguments in favour of Parliament's effectiveness ✓

Parliament has passed many landmark laws in recent decades.
- These include reforms such as the **Constitutional Reform Act (2005)**, which established the **Supreme Court**.
- Other laws have extended people's rights, such as the **Marriage (Same-Sex Couples) Act (2013)**, which allowed same-sex couples to **marry** for the first time in England and Wales.

It has been successful in responding quickly to crises using legislation.
- The **Coronavirus Act (2020)** gave the executive branch **emergency powers** to respond to the **COVID-19 pandemic**. This allowed it to implement and end lockdowns **without** needing to hold **votes** in Parliament.

Parliament's Legislative Function

Even when the Commons quickly approves legislation, the vast majority of bills are still subject to expert and detailed scrutiny from the Lords.

- The **Domestic Abuse Act (2021)** was considered for **eight months** in the House of Lords, hearing expert testimony from **pressure groups** such as Refuge and Women's Aid.
- After passing unamended through the House of Commons in under a month, the **Internal Market Act (2020)** was amended by the House of Lords, **preventing** Boris Johnson from **breaking international law** over the **Northern Ireland Protocol**.
- Although **Tony Blair** was **undefeated** in the **Commons** for eight years from 1997-2005, he suffered **over 300 Lords defeats** during this time.
- Until he resigned as prime minister in September 2022, **Boris Johnson** was **undefeated** on **legislative votes** in the **Commons** after winning a majority in the 2019 election. However, the **Lords** inflicted over **240 defeats** on him in the same period.

Arguments against Parliament's effectiveness

The executive branch can be allowed too much power.

- Critics of the **Coronavirus Act (2020)** felt that it **undermined parliamentary scrutiny** during the pandemic. The **executive branch** was able to make hugely consequential decisions about public health, the economy and education **without** any prior **debate** in either the Commons or the Lords.

There can be insufficient time for Parliament to debate and consider a bill.

- Although **Brexit** had been debated for over two years before the 2019 election, **Boris Johnson** gave the House of Commons just **five hours** to **debate** his **deal**, which was **over 1000 pages long**, after he won his 80-seat majority.
- Parliament faced criticism for allegedly **rushing** the passage of the **Public Order Act (2023)**, which gave the police powers to **arrest protesters** if they suspect they are planning to create undue disorder. See p.14 for more details on how this Act affected citizens' **rights**.

Amendments from the Lords are often ignored by the Commons

1) **All amendments** need to be **agreed** by both the **Commons** and the **Lords** in order to be **retained** in the version of the **bill** that passes into law.
2) When the two chambers **disagree** with each other's amendments, they send the bill **back and forth** in a process known as **parliamentary ping pong**.
3) Because the Lords is an **unelected** chamber, it will usually back down and **accept** the Commons' wishes after a **couple of months**.
4) This happened when the **Trade Bill** was passing through Parliament in **2021**. The **Lords tried** to amend the legislation to give the courts and Parliament **more power** over trading **sanctions**, but eventually **backed down** and accepted the Commons' version of the bill.

His Lordship admits defeat...

Revision Task

For Edexcel students: Evaluate the view that Parliament fails to fulfil its legislative function. [30]
For AQA students: 'Parliament fails to fulfil its legislative function.' Analyse and evaluate this statement. [25]

Imagine that you are answering one of the exam questions above. Choose the **best examples** from the previous pages or from your own knowledge to **support** the arguments below.

1) *The executive dominance of the House of Commons means that Parliament fails to fulfil its legislative function.*
2) *The Lords acts as a more effective legislative chamber than the Commons.*
3) *Parliament often prioritises efficiency over quality when passing legislation.*

Parliamentary paintball is reserved for settling the most heated debates...

It can sometimes feel as though legislation going through the parliamentary process just keeps bouncing from one House to the other, but this back-and-forth is very important. Even if the amendments suggested by the Lords are not accepted by the Commons, the scrutiny that legislation is put under helps to make sure that each bill works effectively when it is passed.

UK Government — Parliament

Parliamentary Scrutiny

Parliament has a crucial role in scrutinising the work of the executive branch and holding ministers to account. In a similar way, I always scrutinise everything my brother gives to me — I'm still not over the time he put nutmeg on my pancakes.

Prime Minister's Questions is a visible form of parliamentary scrutiny

- **Prime Minister's Questions** (PMQs) offers a **weekly** chance for **high-profile** scrutiny in the House of Commons. It receives more **media coverage** than any other regular event in the parliamentary timetable.
- PMQs is supposed to last for half an hour, but most sessions run for **roughly 45 minutes**. It follows a **set format**:

  1. The **leader** of the **largest opposition party** asks **six questions** directly to the **prime minister**.
  2. The **leader** of the **second-largest opposition party** asks **two questions**.
  3. Leaders of **smaller opposition parties** ask questions on a **rota**.
  4. The rest of the session consists of questions asked by **backbench MPs** from **all parties**.

It's important for a prime minister to perform well at PMQs

1) PMQs is **notoriously tricky** — after leaving office, **Tony Blair** compared the event to "*being led to the execution table*".
2) **Strong** performances at PMQs help to **boost the popularity** of the **PM** and other **party leaders** among their own **parties** and the **electorate**, but **weak** performances can pile pressure on leaders.
3) Prime ministers are expected to answer knowledgeably on a **wide range of policy areas**. Questions are **not published in advance**, meaning that prime ministers have to prepare answers on **many possible topics**:

> During one PMQs in September 2023, **Rishi Sunak** answered questions on policy areas including London's **Ultra Low Emission Zone**, **school buildings**, the **furlough scheme** (during the COVID-19 pandemic) and **mortgage rates**.

PMQs often fails to produce meaningful debate despite its high profile

- PMQs is sometimes referred to as an example of '**Punch and Judy politics**'. This means that the participants are more interested in **insulting** and **mocking** each other than in serious debates about policy.

  > Research has shown that of all modern prime ministers, **David Cameron** was the **most inclined** to **mock** his opponent during PMQs. In **2015**, **62%** of his replies to Ed Miliband, the Labour leader at the time, included a **personal insult**.

- **Planted** or **unthreatening questions** have become **increasingly common** in recent years. A planted question is when **backbenchers** are encouraged by the **government whips** to ask about **unthreatening** or **helpful topics**.

  > In the **first PMQs** after details of the **Partygate scandal** (see page 86) became public, **Conservative backbencher** Alicia Kearns asked Boris Johnson about the discovery of an **ichthyosaur skeleton** in her constituency.

There are several other ways Parliament can scrutinise the executive branch

Every government department has a question time in the House of Commons

1) These are **less well attended** than PMQs, but the debate is usually **more serious** and **detailed**.
2) **Departmental questions** allow **shadow ministers** and **backbenchers** to **scrutinise** the government's **policies** and **record** on specific areas.
3) The questions are **monitored by the Speaker** to ensure that they are relevant.

> When **Suella Braverman** was **Home Secretary** in 2022-23, she was frequently asked questions about the Conservative government's record on **migration**, the **Rwanda plan** (see page 19) and **small boat crossings**.

Suella Braverman answering questions in the Commons

Parliamentary Scrutiny

Any MP can ask an urgent question in the House of Commons

- **Urgent questions** are usually asked following a **crisis** or **major event**.
- They are directed at the appropriate **minister** or to the **prime minister**. Prime ministers sometimes choose to send ministers to answer urgent questions **on their behalf**.
- The number of urgent questions asked in the Commons has **increased** in recent years. **Boris Johnson's government** faced **224 urgent questions** in **two-and-a-half years** after the 2019 general election. By contrast, there were only **28 urgent questions** to ministers in **Tony Blair's government** from **1998-2001**.

> In October 2022, Liz Truss was criticised for sending Penny Mordaunt, the Leader of the House of Commons, to answer an urgent question on the mini-budget.

Select committees can summon ministers and special advisers

1) **Select committees** are **cross-party** groups of **backbench MPs** who are **elected** by fellow MPs to **scrutinise** a particular **area of policy**, e.g. the **Treasury Select Committee** scrutinises **economic policy**.
2) Since the **Wright reforms** of **2010**, select committee **chairs** have also been **elected**. This has led to many **senior MPs** becoming select committee chairs, sometimes after careers as ministers.
3) **Ministers** and **special advisers** can be asked to **answer questions** at **select committee meetings**. For example:

Home Secretary **Amber Rudd** was questioned by the **Home Affairs Select Committee** about the **Windrush scandal** in **2018**. She **resigned** after she was accused of **misleading** the committee.

In **2021**, **Matt Hancock** was summoned to give evidence to the **Health and Social Care Select Committee** about his handling of the **COVID-19 pandemic**.

The highest-profile committee is the Liaison Committee

- The **Liaison Committee** meets for roughly an hour and a half, **two or three times** a **year**, to question the **prime minister** on every aspect of **government policy**.
- **Boris Johnson** was subject to particularly testing questioning on the **COVID-19 pandemic** and the UK's preparations for the **Russian invasion of Ukraine**. He also attracted controversy by **postponing** three scheduled Liaison Committee meetings.
- Prime ministers are asked questions on a **wide range** of topics. In December 2023, **Rishi Sunak** faced questions on policy areas including **Israel-Gaza**, **asylum claims**, **foreign aid**, **high-speed rail** and **energy bills**.

> The Liaison Committee consists of the chairs of every other select committee, so it possesses huge amounts of experience and expertise across the full range of policy areas.

The House of Commons can pass a motion of no confidence in the executive branch

1) This is when the Commons votes on whether it **still has confidence** in the **executive branch**. It is the **ultimate method** of holding the **executive branch** to account.
2) If the motion passes, a **general election** is **automatically called** unless the government chooses to resign.

- The **last successful** vote of no confidence was in **1979**, when **James Callaghan's Labour government** was brought down by **Margaret Thatcher's confidence vote**. Thatcher then won a **majority of 43** in the **election** that followed.
- **Theresa May survived** a confidence vote in **January 2019**. But she **resigned months later** once it became clear that she **no longer** had enough **support** among her own **backbench MPs**.

The quality of scrutiny can suffer when the government has a majority

1) It is **rare** for **prime ministers** with a **majority** to be **defeated** in the Commons (see p.84 for statistics). This means that legislation is **debated** but **not often amended** by the whole chamber.
2) **Public bill committees** are temporarily formed to **scrutinise** a **particular bill** as it passes through the Commons. They can **amend legislation**, but have **limited power** in reality:

- These committees reflect the **make-up** of the **Commons**, so a majority government will also have a **majority** on every **public bill committee**.
- Members are chosen by the **party whips** (see p.75), so they are usually made up of MPs with **reputations for loyalty**, rather than expertise.

> Dr Sarah Wollaston (MP for Totnes 2010-2019) was never chosen to sit on public bill committees scrutinising health legislation. Despite having worked as a GP for over two decades, her reputation for being prepared to rebel meant that she wasn't considered suitable.

Parliamentary Scrutiny

The Commons tends to be **more powerful** in scrutinising **minority governments**

- **THERESA MAY** was **undefeated** in the Commons during her **first year** in government (2016-17), when she had a **slim majority**.
- However, after **losing her majority** in the 2017 general election, she **lost 33 votes** in the Commons.
- May also suffered a **record defeat** in the Commons (by 230 votes) in the first vote on her **Brexit deal**.

- **BORIS JOHNSON** suffered **six defeats** in his **first week** as PM in the House of Commons.
- He then **lost control** of the **parliamentary timetable** after MPs supported the Benn Act in September 2019. This allowed **backbench MPs** to **schedule votes**, which is usually the executive's responsibility.

Scrutiny tends to be **more consistent** in the **House of Lords**...

- Since the **House of Lords Act (1999)**, **no party** has had an **overall majority** in the **Lords**. This means that **bills** must achieve **cross-party support**, or enough support from **crossbench peers** (see p.72), to be approved by the Lords. As a result, prime ministers tend to suffer far **more legislative defeats** in the **Lords** than in the Commons (see p.84).
- The Lords has **more time** to consider bills, so the **scrutiny** is usually **more detailed**. The Lords took **8 months** to pass the **Domestic Abuse Act (2021)** compared to **4 months** for the **Commons**.
- Many peers have **significant expertise** that can add to the **quality of scrutiny** in the Lords.

> A debate on the Illegal Migration Bill in 2023 involved Baroness Chakrabarti (barrister and human rights campaigner), Lord Kerr (former Supreme Court judge) and Baroness Butler-Sloss (former Lord Justice of Appeal).

...but the Lords' **powers** to scrutinise are **limited**

The Lords **cannot block**, **amend** or **delay** **financial legislation** (see p.60), so the executive branch receives **very little** parliamentary **scrutiny** of its **Budget** and other **financial statements**. Every Budget has passed **unamended** since **1979**.

The Lords has **no power** over **military interventions**, e.g. invasions, air strikes and drone strikes. The prime minister can use their **prerogative powers** to make **military** decisions **without consulting** the Lords or the Commons (see p.84), so Parliament's role in **scrutinising** these can be **very limited**.

It's **not** just the executive branch who can be **scrutinised** by **Parliament**

1) **Parliamentary privilege** allows Parliament to hold **public figures** to account.
2) It enables **MPs** and **peers** to **speak freely** when naming well-known **figures** who have been accused of **wrongdoing**.

Quick Questions

1) How many times a year does the Liaison Committee meet?
2) Which Home Secretary had to resign after misleading a select committee?
3) Which Act that gave backbenchers control of the parliamentary timetable did MPs support in September 2019?
4) How many Commons defeats did Theresa May suffer during her majority government? How many did she suffer during her minority government?
5) How many times was Boris Johnson defeated during his first week in the Commons?

Exam Practice

For Edexcel students: Evaluate the view that Parliament succeeds in providing scrutiny and holding the executive to account. [30]

For AQA students: Explain and analyse three ways in which Parliament scrutinises the work of the executive branch. [9]

Like yelling stuff? Shake your fist a lot? Join us on the crossbench...

Phew — that's three more pages done and dusted. There's plenty of information to digest here and some of it might take a little while to properly sink in. If you're still unsure about any of it, take a break for a bit and then read these pages again.

UK Government — Parliament

Parliament's Representative Function

And you thought Parliament wouldn't have any more functions... but don't worry, you're nearly at the end of the section. These last two pages are all about how well Parliament represents the people of the UK, with some juicy concepts thrown in.

Parliament is at the heart of the UK's representative democracy

1) Because its members are **elected**, the **House of Commons** is responsible for fulfilling most of **Parliament's representative duties**.
2) All **650 MPs** represent a **local constituency**. As of 2023, most constituencies should have between **roughly 69 000** and **77 000 adults** who are **eligible to vote**.
3) Most MPs hold **weekly surgeries** in their constituencies, allowing **constituents** to ask for their **help** and to **air grievances**.

surgery
Meetings that MPs hold with their constituents.

Kavya began to suspect she'd come to the wrong place to complain about potholes

There are two models of representation that MPs can choose to follow...

1 Trustee model
This is when MPs make **decisions** based on their **own opinions**. It is sometimes known as the **Burkean model** because it was first articulated by Edmund Burke (see page 44).

2 Delegate model
This is when MPs make **decisions** based on their **constituents' judgements**. It is also known as the **mandate model**.

...and there are two ways to judge how representative Parliament is

1 Social (descriptive) representation
This is when you look at how well Parliament **reflects** the **social make-up** of the **United Kingdom** — in terms of **gender, sexual orientation, race, class, wealth, disability, levels of education**, etc.

2 Political (substantive) representation
This is when you look at how far **MPs** and **peers'** voting decisions and behaviour **reflect** the **political views** and **best interests** of the public.

Social representation has improved in some ways but remains poor in others

How social representation has improved

- ✓ In **2024**, **women** made up **41%** of the **House of Commons** — until **2005**, **under 20%** of MPs were female.
- ✓ Following the **2019 election**, Parliament became the legislature with the **highest number** (**45**) of LGBTQI+ representatives in the **world**. In **2024**, this number increased to **64**.
- ✓ The **2024 election** also resulted in **14%** of MPs coming from **ethnic minority backgrounds** within the UK — until **2001**, this statistic was **under 2%**.

How social representation remains poor

- ✗ In 2019, only **6%** of **peers** were from ethnic **minority backgrounds**, compared with just over **18%** of the **population** of **England and Wales** in 2021, **3.4%** in **Northern Ireland** and just under **13%** in **Scotland** in 2022.
- ✗ **87%** of MPs elected in 2019 were **graduates**, but it's estimated that only **around 54%** of the UK population had an **undergraduate degree** in **2023**.
- ✗ **23%** of **MPs** elected in **2024** attended **independent schools**, compared with **7%** of the **population**.

Be careful about questioning the importance of social representation in an essay. You may feel that Parliament doesn't need to reflect exactly the demographics of the UK's population, but evidence from polls suggests that the overwhelming majority of voters believe that politicians are detached from the reality experienced by most constituents.

Parliament's Representative Function

There are **different views** on how **politically representative** Parliament is

Arguments that Parliament is effective at providing political representation

- ✓ The UK is unusual in having **over 200 members** of its legislature with **no party affiliation** — these are **crossbench** and **non-affiliated peers**, as well as a handful of **independent MPs**. This **reduces** the extent to which **partisanship** dominates political representation.
- ✓ Parliament is the **second-largest legislature** in the world, which means that there's plenty of **scope** for **minority interests** to be **represented**.
- ✓ Parliament has **enacted** the results of **every referendum** ever held in the UK. This includes the **2016 Brexit referendum**, despite the fact that **three-quarters of MPs** had supported Remain (see p.41).

Brian had to have a cross-bench peer at Andre's outrageous texts

Arguments that Parliament is not effective at providing political representation

- ✗ As of 2023, The **House of Lords** still contained **92 hereditary peers**, who are the only members of any democratic legislature in the **world** to have **inherited** their positions. Some people argue that this makes Parliament **outdated**.
- ✗ **Hereditary peers** were **60% more likely** than **life peers** to mention their own **business interests** when contributing to **Lords debates** between **2016** and **2021**.
- ✗ Between **2019** and **2024**, at least **20 MPs** were **suspended** from the **House of Commons**, suspended by their **party**, or chose to **resign** their seats following **allegations** of **misconduct**. Some argue that too many MPs **fail** to uphold **expected standards**.
- ✗ There have been a number of high-profile **lobbying scandals** (see page 12) in recent years, suggesting that some MPs and peers prioritise their **own financial interests**.

Mentioning lobbying in an essay on whether Parliament is fulfilling its representative function would make a great synoptic link.

Revision Task

For Edexcel students: Evaluate the view that the House of Commons provides more effective representation than the House of Lords. [30]

For AQA students: 'The House of Commons provides more effective representation than the House of Lords.' Analyse and evaluate this statement. [25]

Imagine that you are answering one of the exam questions above. Choose the **best examples** from the previous pages or from your own knowledge to **support** the arguments below.

1) The House of Lords is less socially representative than the House of Commons.
2) The unelected nature of the House of Lords can make it more effective in providing political representation than the House of Commons.
3) MPs often place their own parties' interests above their constituents' interests.

Essay Plan

For Edexcel students: Evaluate the view that Parliament fails to fulfil its functions adequately. [30]

For AQA students: 'Parliament fails to fulfil its functions adequately.' Analyse and evaluate this statement. [25]

Using the grid on p.298, **plan** an answer to one of the essay questions above.

What's the most common question in a parliament of owls? Whoo? Whoo?

Parliament has more functions than a GCSE maths exam. Anyway... being able to name the different functions of Parliament is important, but you also need to be able to explain what they are and how effectively Parliament manages to fulfil them.

UK Government — Parliament

Prime Minister and the Executive

You'll definitely need to be able to rattle off the powers of the prime minister and the factors that limit their power.

The prime minister is the head of the **executive branch**

The executive branch is often just referred to as 'the government'.

The **executive branch** is made up of a number of **different elements**:

1) PRIME MINISTER — **Head** of the executive branch.

2) THE CABINET — Made up of the **heads of each government department** (e.g. the Home Secretary, the Chancellor, the Education Secretary) and other **senior ministers** appointed by the prime minister.

3) JUNIOR MINISTERS AND AIDES — They work **within** each **government department**.

4) CIVIL SERVANTS — Unelected, impartial **policy experts**.

The executive has **several roles** in running the country

FORMULATING POLICY

Power: Proposing legislation

The **executive** proposes **primary legislation**, in the form of **bills**, to Parliament. If the executive has a **large majority** in the **House of Commons**, passing legislation there tends to be **fairly easy**. But if they lead either a **slim majority** or **minority government**, it can be **very difficult** to **pass new laws** through the Commons.

The **House of Lords doesn't** contain a **majority** for **any party**, so passing legislation through the **upper chamber** can be **much harder** (see p.80).

The executive can wield significant power through **secondary legislation**, which allows them to **re-interpret** the meaning of **laws** that have been passed by **previous Parliaments**.

For example, **the executive** was able to introduce **new regulations** on **sick pay, maternity leave** and **universal credit** during the COVID-19 pandemic **without** passing **new legislation**.

UK Foreign Secretary Lord Cameron with US Secretary of State Antony Blinken in 2023

INTERNATIONAL RELATIONS

Power: Negotiating and signing treaties and trade agreements

The **executive** can shape the UK's **foreign** and **economic policies** by agreeing **international treaties** and **trade deals** without needing to consult **Parliament**. However, Brexit was an **exception** (see case studies on page 86).

The **Foreign Secretary** has a **key role** to play in diplomacy and will often carry out **overseas visits** on behalf of the PM.

MILITARY DEFENCE

Powers:
- **Deployment of troops and declaration of war**
- **Ordering military action, such as air and drone strikes**

Prime ministers have the power to **deploy troops** and **declare war** — though **recent prime ministers** have usually opted to hold a **vote** in the Commons (see p.85).

The new Foreign Secretary was a big hit with the Cabinet

Chancellor Jeremy Hunt on his way to present the Spring Budget in 2023

SETTING THE ANNUAL BUDGET

The **executive** proposes at least one **formal budget** to the **House of Commons** each year.

This budget is often then **updated** through **Spring** and **Autumn Statements**.

The budget is **set** and **presented** by the **Chancellor of the Exchequer**, one of the **highest ranking ministers** in the executive.

Prime Minister and the Executive

Some of the PM's powers are called **prerogative powers**

1) **Prerogative powers** (sometimes called the **royal prerogative**) are the powers that the prime minister has inherited from the **monarch**. They include **patronage**, **negotiating treaties** and **trade agreements**, **troop deployment** and **dissolving Parliament**.

2) Prerogative powers can be exercised **without scrutiny** or **permission** from Parliament. They give the PM a significant amount of **unchecked power** over the political system. For example, **Theresa May** was able to **launch air strikes** in Syria in 2018 **without holding a vote** in the House of Commons.

3) However, prime ministers still need to pass **most policies** through **Parliament's legislative process** (see p.76).

patronage
The power to appoint and dismiss ministers, and recommend appointments to the House of Lords. Mass changes to the membership of cabinet are known as reshuffles.

The prime minister can control the timing of general elections by dissolving Parliament. Usually, they attempt to time the election for when their party is more likely to win, although a general election must be held at least every five years.

The extent of the prime minister's **power** depends on whether they have a **majority**

Because of **first-past-the-post** and the **fusion of powers** in the UK (see p.70), the prime minister usually has a **majority** in the House of Commons. But there have been **notable exceptions** in recent years:

1) David Cameron led a **coalition government** between the Conservatives and the Liberal Democrats from **2010-2015**.
2) Theresa May (2017-19) and Boris Johnson (2019) each led **minority governments**.

majority government
When a single party has more than half the total number of MPs (650) in the House of Commons. This means the government can win most votes without needing support from other parties.

minority government
When the largest party in the House of Commons has fewer than 326 MPs. This means that it will need some support from MPs representing other parties in order to win votes, making it very difficult to pass legislation.

coalition government
When a government is formed by two or more parties in order to exercise a majority in the House of Commons. This usually involves the sharing of ministerial jobs — from 2010-2015, five Liberal Democrats were given Cabinet positions by David Cameron.

The number of **defeats in Parliament** gives an indication of a PM's power

This table shows the number of **parliamentary defeats** in the Commons and the Lords for each prime minister since 1979.

Prime minister (years in office)	Seats won in general elections (size of majority)	Commons defeats during premiership	Lords defeats during premiership
Margaret Thatcher (1979-1990)	1979: 339 (44) 1983: 397 (144) 1987: 376 (102)	4	156
John Major (1990-1997)	1992: 336 (21)	6	85
Tony Blair (1997-2007)	1997: 418 (179) 2001: 412 (167) 2005: 355 (66)	4	460
Gordon Brown (2007-2010)	—	3	68
David Cameron (2010-2016)	2010: 306 (coalition majority of 74) 2015: 330 (10)	Coalition majority: 7 Conservative majority: 3	160
Theresa May (2016-2019)	2017: 317 (9 short of majority)	33	107
Boris Johnson (2019-2022)	2019: 365 (80)	16	248
Liz Truss (2022)	—	0	2
Rishi Sunak (2022-2024)	—	1	166
Keir Starmer (2024-)	2024: 412 (174)	0*	5*

The increasing frequency of executive defeats in the House of Lords is largely due to the reforms in the House of Lords Act (1999). The Conservatives used to have a majority in the upper chamber, but the 1999 reforms mean that no party has a majority.

What does an MP see when they look in the mirror? A PM...
Don't try and learn all the numbers in the table — just make sure you have some examples up your sleeve to quote in the exam.

*Data correct as of 16th December 2024

Prime Ministerial Power

OK, prime yourself for a lot of case studies. You need to know about one pre-1997 prime minister and one post-1997 prime minister in detail for your exam. Having some key facts about other PMs rattling around your brain will also come in handy.

Prime ministerial **power** is **elastic**

The **power** of any prime minister can **vary over time** and is dependent on a **range of factors**:

- The **size** of their party's **majority** in the House of Commons (if they have a majority at all)
- The state of the **economy**
- **International affairs**
- **Domestic crises**
- **Scandals** involving themselves, their ministers, or backbenchers
- The strength of **opposition** parties
- **Public opinion**
- **Media** coverage

These **case studies** show how prime ministers use their powers and how **Parliament**, the **Cabinet** and the **Supreme Court** can curtail the PM's power:

James Callaghan

- Callaghan had already served as **Chancellor**, **Home Secretary** and **Foreign Secretary** before succeeding Harold Wilson as prime minister in 1976. However, the **circumstances** that he **inherited** made it **difficult** for him to achieve his aims.
- The **economy** was in a state of **long-term decline**, culminating in the **Winter of Discontent** in 1979 (see page 33). Labour also lost its **tiny majority** after one of its MPs **resigned**, leading them to sign a **pact** with the **Liberal Party** in 1977 in an attempt to pass legislation.
- After this pact **collapsed**, Callaghan **struggled** to achieve his **legislative goals**, suffering a **defeat** on a **Finance Bill** (a very rare occurrence) in 1978, then **losing** a **confidence vote** in 1979. This led to the **1979 general election**, which was won by Margaret Thatcher's Conservative Party. In all, Callaghan's government was **defeated 34 times** in **three years** in the House of Commons.

Margaret Thatcher

- Thatcher carried out a ruthless **reshuffle** in September 1981, sacking or demoting prominent One Nation **'wet'** cabinet ministers. She replaced them with more right-wing **'dry'** allies. Unsurprisingly, she faced much less opposition from within her cabinet after that, allowing her to speed up her **supply-side reforms**.
- But Thatcher's **relationship** with **Conservative MPs** was ultimately her **downfall**. She forced through the **poll tax** despite backbench and Cabinet **opposition**, and her policy on **Europe** led to the **Cabinet revolt** that brought about her **resignation** in 1990.

Gloria tried hard to assure the PM that she would dry off soon

Tony Blair

- After Labour's **landslide victory** in 1997, Tony Blair enjoyed a period of **unparalleled executive dominance** in the Commons. His government remained **undefeated** for its first 8 years (until 2005). But, during the same time period, Blair suffered **over 300 defeats** in the Lords. Nevertheless, during his 10 years as PM, a **new law** was passed **every 3 hours** on average, which remains a record.
- **Blair** could have used his **prerogative powers** to deploy British **troops** in **Iraq** in 2003 without holding a parliamentary vote. He'd done this in **Afghanistan** in **2001**, but he chose to seek the **House of Commons' approval** because the invasion was so **controversial**. He **won** the vote **comfortably** (by 412-149) and the military campaign began a day later. The Iraq War later became even more controversial though, due to **allegations** that Blair's public **justification** for the invasion didn't represent the **whole truth**.
- After 10 years in power, Blair **resigned** as prime minister in **2007**, amid speculation about a **leadership challenge** from his Chancellor, **Gordon Brown** (see p.89). Blair was one of the **most powerful** prime ministers ever, but his relationship with Brown shows that even the most dominant PMs **face checks** from their **Cabinet**.

> Gordon Brown succeeded Blair as prime minister, but spent most of his premiership having to deal with the global financial crisis.

Prime Ministerial Power

David Cameron

- David Cameron's **Conservatives** formed a **coalition government** with Nick Clegg's **Liberal Democrats** from **2010-2015**. Cameron successfully held the coalition together and implemented his economic programme of **austerity** with Chancellor George Osborne. He was able to dominate most negotiations with Clegg, but a Conservative **backbench rebellion** in 2012 **prevented** him from passing their plan for **House of Lords reform** through the Commons. Cameron was also **defeated** in the House of Commons over his plan to launch **air strikes** against the **Syrian government** in 2013.
- Against the polls' expectations, the **Conservatives** won a **majority of 10** in the **2015 election**. Cameron faced **no significant legislative defeats** in the House of Commons from **2015-16**. But his premiership came crashing down when the British public voted to **leave** the EU in the **2016 Brexit referendum**, despite Cameron having campaigned for the UK to remain in the EU. He **resigned** the following day.

Theresa May

- Theresa May's **first year** as prime minister (2016-2017) was **relatively successful** — her government was **undefeated** in the House of Commons and the **economy** was showing signs of **growth**.
- In 2018 she exercised her prerogative powers to authorise **air strikes** in Syria **without holding a vote** in the House of Commons.
- Passing **Brexit legislation** through a **divided House of Commons** was always going to prove **tricky** for May. However, the **Tories' poor performance** in the **2017 snap election** called by May meant that May had to form a **minority government** to stay in power. This gave huge **influence** to Conservative **backbenchers**. Following this, May **failed three times** to pass her Brexit deal. She also narrowly survived a **vote of no confidence** in 2019 and suffered a **record number of defeats** in the House of Commons before she was forced to **resign** by Conservative rebels.

Boris Johnson

- Johnson also tried to pass **Brexit legislation** through the **House of Commons** after he became prime minister in July 2019. When it became clear this was going to be difficult, he decided to push the limits of his power by **proroguing** (suspending) **Parliament**, claiming it would give him time to draft new Brexit legislation. While prorogued, Parliament would be **unable** to debate a Brexit deal in the lead up to the **deadline**. Normally, prime ministers only **prorogue** Parliament to end a standard **parliamentary session** (basically like the end of a school year) in preparation for a **general election**.
- The **Supreme Court** ruled in September 2019 that Johnson had acted **beyond his power**, and declared the prorogation **null and void**. Parliament started sitting again that afternoon and soon held a **vote** on Johnson's deal. He gained more support than May had managed, but he was still comfortably **defeated**. In an unprecedented move, Johnson reacted by **expelling** the **21 backbench rebels** from the Conservative Party.
- Once Johnson had secured a **large majority** for the Conservatives in **December 2019**, he **passed** his flagship Brexit legislation within a month. But he soon found himself having to lead the UK's response to the **COVID-19 pandemic**. Although many **criticised** Johnson for his handling of the pandemic, he successfully consolidated the government's power by passing the **Coronavirus Act (2020)**. This granted him and his ministers the ability to make big changes to **policy** and **spending plans** (like implementing **lockdowns** and the **furlough** scheme) **without** first **consulting** the House of Commons or the House of Lords.
- However, just as the UK began to **emerge** from the worst of the pandemic, a number of **crises** weakened Johnson, including allegations that he had attended **lockdown-breaking parties** in **No. 10**. After it emerged that he had **failed to dismiss** a **minister** accused of **sexual assault**, more than **50 Tory ministers resigned** from the government. Johnson announced his **resignation as PM** in July 2022.

Liz Truss

Liz Truss took over from Johnson in **September 2022**, but lasted only **44 days** before **resigning**. Despite taking over at a time of economic turmoil, she and her **Chancellor**, **Kwasi Kwarteng**, unveiled the most **significant tax cuts** in modern British history in their **mini-budget**. The **value** of the **pound dropped** instantly and Tory **backbenchers turned on Truss**. She attempted to preserve her position by firing Kwarteng, but only a week later it became clear that a **majority** of Tory MPs wanted her **out of No. 10**.

Prime Ministerial Power

Rishi Sunak

- Sunak initially focused on **stabilising the economy**, but he soon began to prioritise **reducing illegal migration**. His attempt to drive through the **Rwanda plan** (see page 19) failed when the **Supreme Court** declared it **unlawful** in December 2023. After several months of parliamentary ping pong, Sunak eventually **succeeded** in passing the **Safety of Rwanda Act (2024)**. This effectively **overruled** the **Supreme Court's decision** by declaring that Rwanda is a **safe country** for migrants.
- Inflation gradually began to fall, but Sunak and his party continued to **trail** Keir Starmer's **Labour Party** in the **polls** throughout 2023. Sunak's government suffered its **first Commons defeat** in December 2023 in a vote on **compensation** for **victims** of the **infected blood scandal**.
- Throughout 2023 and 2024, there were **rumours** of **attempted plots** by **Conservative MPs** to **remove** Sunak, particularly after the party **lost seats** in **by-elections** and **performed poorly** in the **local** and **mayoral elections** in May 2024.
- Sunak used his **prerogative power** to call a snap **general election** in May 2024, hoping that the **improving economic outlook** and taking Labour by **surprise** could help him to **retain** the **Conservatives' majority**. Significant **campaigning errors** and the **collapse** of the Conservatives' vote in previously **safe seats** that were taken by Labour and the Liberal Democrats meant that Sunak's party instead suffered its **worst-ever general election defeat**.

Quick Questions

1) How large was Tony Blair's Commons majority in 1997?
2) With which party did the Conservatives form a coalition in 2010?
3) What is the name of the powers inherited by the prime minister from the monarch?
4) Which chamber inflicts more defeats on the government: the House of Commons or the House of Lords?
5) On average, how many laws were passed each day during Blair's government?
6) What's the formal name for the prime minister's power of appointment?
7) 'The prime minister has to hold a vote in Parliament before deploying British troops overseas.' True or false?
8) How many rebellious Tory MPs did Boris Johnson expel from the party in September 2019?
9) Which act gave the Johnson government emergency powers during the COVID-19 pandemic?
10) For how many days was Liz Truss PM before she resigned?

What'll last longer — this lettuce or your revision session?

Revision Task

Test your understanding of the Prime Minister and the Executive so far by defining the key terms below:

1) *Minority government*
2) *Coalition government*
3) *Prerogative powers*
4) *Chancellor of the Exchequer*
5) *The Cabinet*
6) *Civil servants*
7) *Ministers*
8) *Budget*
9) *Confidence vote*

Exam Practice

For Edexcel students: Evaluate the view that prime ministers are usually able to achieve most of their aims. [30]

For AQA students: Explain and analyse three ways in which prime ministers possess power over the other branches of government. [9]

Boris may have taken his role as 'Party Leader' a little too literally...

There's certainly been a lot of churn in No. 10 in recent years — just goes to show how quickly a PM's power can drain away. Examiners like to see a good mix of historic and up-to-date examples, so memorise as many as you can from these three pages.

UK Government — Prime Minister and the Executive

Prime Minister and the Cabinet

Nope, we're not rummaging through their cupboards — we're digging into how the PM interacts with their senior ministers.

The prime minister is the head of the Cabinet

Rishi Sunak chairing a Cabinet meeting

1) The Cabinet consists of the most **senior government ministers**.
2) Because of the power of **patronage** (see p.84), the prime minister can **appoint** and **dismiss** Cabinet ministers. There are **various reasons** why the PM would want to **hire or fire** certain ministers. Here are a few **examples** from some Cabinet **reshuffles** in the years 2014 to 2023:

Year	Minister (job title in brackets)	Hired or Fired?	Reason
2014	**Michael Gove** (Education Secretary)	Fired	Gove had spent four years **reforming** the **education system**, but David Cameron decided that his **poor relationship** with **teaching unions** made him a **liability** with the 2015 general election looming.
2016	**Boris Johnson** (Foreign Secretary)	Hired	After Johnson had led the **Leave campaign** to victory in the **Brexit referendum**, Theresa May decided that it was best to keep her most likely **challenger** as **close** as possible.
2018	**Dominic Raab** (Brexit Secretary)	Hired	Prominent Brexiteer David Davis **resigned** after the **Chequers summit** (see p.89), so May decided to **replace him** with another **Leave supporter**.
2021	**Gavin Williamson** (Education Secretary)	Fired	Williamson had faced lots of **criticism** for his handling of **GCSE** and **A-Level exams** during the **pandemic**.
2022	**Suella Braverman** (Home Secretary)	Hired	Braverman **supported** Rishi Sunak's **leadership campaign** and was **rewarded** with a return to the role she had **resigned** from just **six days earlier** (see p.92).
2023	**James Cleverly** (Home Secretary)	Hired	After Sunak fired Braverman, he appointed James Cleverly, previously the **Foreign Secretary**, to replace her. Cleverly was seen as a more **centrist** (and **less divisive**) figure, who Sunak hoped would be a **more effective** standard-bearer for the Rwanda plan.

Two main theories describe the prime minister's relationship with their Cabinet

1 Theory of Cabinet Government

This theory suggests that the prime minister must **discuss** and **agree policy** with the whole **Cabinet** before making **decisions**.

2 Theory of Presidential Government

Influenced by the way **US presidents** make decisions, this theory suggests that the prime minister **discusses and agrees policy** with small groups of **senior advisers** and ministers. These decisions are then **presented** to the **Cabinet without the opportunity** to change the prime minister's mind.

It's not you, it's me

Prime Minister and the Cabinet

Some prime ministers act **more presidentially**...

1) According to the **theory of Cabinet Government**, all **policy decisions** are supposed to be **agreed** by the **whole Cabinet**.
2) Prime ministers with a **large Commons majority** can usually act **more presidentially**, **dictating policy** with a few senior advisers and ministers. Here are some examples:

THE POLL TAX (1990)
Margaret Thatcher imposed a **new** and **controversial tax** known as the **poll tax** — she did this **without Cabinet approval** in what turned out to be the **final year** of her **premiership**. Because it was a **flat-rate tax** that **didn't differ** based on people's **income**, it was **particularly unpopular** with the **One Nation** faction of the Conservative Party.

THE IRAQ WAR (2003)
Tony Blair made the decision to **join the invasion of Iraq** with Alastair Campbell, his **Director of Communications**, and other **senior advisers**. Cabinet ministers **complained** that they hadn't been consulted before the decision was made public.

LOCKDOWN (2020)
Boris Johnson decided to implement a **lockdown** in March 2020 during a meeting with Chris Whitty (Chief Medical Officer) and Patrick Vallance (Chief Scientific Adviser). **Cabinet ministers** were **informed later that day**, shortly before Johnson announced the decision on television.

CANCELLATION OF GCSE & A-LEVEL EXAMS (2021)
Gavin Williamson, the Education Secretary, **wasn't present** in the meeting when Johnson and his advisers decided to **cancel** public **exams** for the **second year running**.

...while others are **influenced** more by their **Cabinet ministers**

When prime ministers **don't have** a large Commons majority, or **face significant opposition** to their leadership, they tend to have a more **collaborative approach**:

The Quad (2010-2015) — Every policy decision during the **Conservative-Lib Dem coalition** government had to be **agreed** by the **four members** of a committee known as **The Quad**. This comprised David Cameron (prime minister) and George Osborne (Chancellor) as the two most **senior Conservatives**, and Nick Clegg (deputy prime minister) and Danny Alexander (Chief Secretary to the Treasury) as the two **leading Lib Dems**.

The Gaukward Squad (2019) — **Weakened** by two record **Commons defeats** over her Brexit deal (see p.86), Theresa May was **forced** to extend the **deadline** for leaving the EU after three Cabinet ministers (David Gauke, Amber Rudd and Claire Perry) **threatened to resign**.

Jeremy Hunt takes over (2022) — Liz Truss **replaced** Kwasi Kwarteng with Jeremy Hunt as **Chancellor** in October 2022 (see p.86). One of Hunt's **conditions** for taking the job was that he should **have control** over his own policy decisions, meaning that Truss had to accept his **swift reversal** of Kwarteng's **tax cuts** — a crucial part of her **leadership campaign**.

Jeremy Hunt

ECHR (2024) — When Rishi Sunak considered **leaving** the **European Convention on Human Rights** to reduce **legal challenges** to government policies, it was reported that he didn't go ahead after discussions at Cabinet revealed **significant opposition** (from up to a dozen ministers) to the proposal.

> The Chequers summit of July 2018 is an example of a PM without a majority not taking a collaborative approach. Theresa May summoned the entire Cabinet to Chequers, the PM's country house, to present her Brexit deal to them. This was a heavily divided minority government, but ministers were unable to propose amendments to the deal. This led to the resignation of David Davis and Boris Johnson, the two most senior Brexiteers in the Cabinet.

A prime minister needs to **take the Cabinet seriously**, even with a **large majority**

Unlike in the US (see p.180), the **UK Cabinet** often includes the prime minister's **biggest rivals**.

Tony Blair appointed Gordon Brown as his Chancellor of the Exchequer

1) Blair and Brown had **reached an agreement** in 1994 that Brown **wouldn't run** for the leadership of the Labour Party if Blair **agreed** to give him **control of economic policy**.
2) But their **relationship soured** during their time in government. Brown was **accused** of actively **briefing against** Blair in the **press**, while Brown felt that Blair had **failed** to keep his **promise** of **stepping down** after **two terms** as prime minister.
3) This **bad blood** meant that Brown increasingly **shut Blair out** of discussions on **economic and welfare policy**.
4) In the end, Blair **agreed** to **step down** in 2007 to ward off the **threat** of a **leadership challenge** from Brown.

Gordon Brown

Prime Minister and the Cabinet

Boris Johnson's downfall was triggered by the resignation of two senior ministers

1) In July 2022, Johnson **appointed Chris Pincher**, who had been accused of **sexual assault**, to a government position. **Rishi Sunak** (the then Chancellor) and **Sajid Javid** (Health Secretary) both **resigned** in **protest** at Johnson's decision.
2) Their resignations were made public in the hour before the **6 o'clock television news**, maximising public attention on their decision.
3) Over the days that followed, **nearly 60 ministers resigned** from Johnson's government, making his position **untenable**.
4) Eventually, **Johnson resigned**, and it was no surprise when both **Sunak** and **Javid** ran in the **leadership contest** to replace him.

Rishi Sunak

Sajid Javid

Margaret Thatcher's resignation was triggered by the resignation of her deputy PM

Geoffrey Howe

1) After resigning in November 1990, Thatcher's deputy prime minister, **Geoffrey Howe**, made an **embarrassing speech** just before PMQs. In this speech he **criticised** Thatcher's **policy on Europe** and **mocked** her **leadership style**.
2) Another former Cabinet minister, **Michael Heseltine**, then **challenged** Thatcher for the **leadership** of the **Conservative Party**.
3) **Thatcher won**, but **not** by a **big enough margin**, and a majority of her **Cabinet** then advised her to step down.

Quick Questions

1) Why did David Cameron fire Michael Gove in 2014?
2) Who did Jeremy Hunt replace as Chancellor in October 2022?
3) Name one of the advisers with whom Boris Johnson made the decision to implement a lockdown in March 2020.
4) Who resigned alongside Rishi Sunak from Johnson's Cabinet in June 2022?
5) What was the name given to the four-person decision-making body used by David Cameron during his coalition government from 2010-2015?
6) Where did Theresa May hold a Brexit summit in September 2018?
7) Name three members of the Gaukward Squad.

Psst... here's a hint for Q6

Still going strong?

Exam Practice

For Edexcel students: Evaluate the view that prime ministers are usually able to dominate their cabinet. [30]

For AQA students: 'Prime ministers are usually able to dominate their cabinet.' Analyse and evaluate this statement. [25]

Use the sentence frames on pages 299-300 to practise **explaining** why the following pieces of information are significant to one of the questions above:

1) *Rishi Sunak decided to re-appoint Jeremy Hunt, Liz Truss's second Chancellor, to run the Treasury, because he felt that the economy would benefit from stability and consistency.*
2) *As his relationship with Tony Blair deteriorated, Gordon Brown refused to share key details of his annual budget announcements with the prime minister, meaning that Blair only found out about some provisions when they were announced in the House of Commons.*
3) *Theresa May appointed three Brexit-supporting Conservative MPs to the role of Brexit Secretary, despite realising that they might disagree with her vision for leaving the European Union.*
4) *The number of special advisers working in No. 10 has increased significantly in recent years. In 1998, there were only 8 special advisers to the PM, but there were 43 by 2022.*

Keep your friends close, but your enemies closer...

Managing their relationship with the Cabinet can be a tricky job for a prime minister. Colleagues who were allies when they were appointed to Cabinet might turn against them if public opinion shifts, or if they think they could do a better job as leader.

UK Government — Prime Minister and the Executive

Collective and Individual Ministerial Responsibility

The next three pages are all about when government ministers choose to resign — or often, when they're forced to...

There are **two conventions** that govern the **conduct of ministers**

1) Collective ministerial responsibility (CMR) — This convention states that every government minister should **publicly support** every aspect of government policy, even on matters that don't relate to the work of their department. If they **criticise** a government policy in public, or if they feel **unable to speak supportively** about a decision, they are expected to **resign**.

2) Individual ministerial responsibility (IMR) — This convention states that individual ministers are responsible for their **own conduct and performance**, and for the **work of their departments**. It is **outlined** in the **Ministerial Code**. If a minister (or member of their department for whom they are responsible) fails to meet **expected standards**, they should **resign**.

Conventions are not legally binding (see p.60). However, there are political consequences for the government if they're not observed.

Collective ministerial responsibilty is **not** always **observed**

Case Studies

Here are some examples of where the convention of **CMR** has and has not been observed:

✓ When CMR has been observed

Geoffrey Howe felt that he could no longer support **Thatcher's policy on Europe**, and so he **resigned** from his position as **deputy prime minister** (see case study on previous page).

Iain Duncan Smith spent the first four years of the coalition government implementing welfare reforms as **Work and Pensions Secretary**. However, his relationship with **George Osborne**, the Chancellor, deteriorated following a series of disagreements about government spending. In 2014, he resigned in protest at Osborne's decision to **cut benefits payments**.

David Davis and Boris Johnson resigned after the **Chequers Summit** (see p.89) in September 2018, complaining that May had made **too many concessions to the EU**.

Jo Johnson (Boris's younger brother) resigned from his position as a minister in the departments of **Business** and **Education** in September 2019. He said that he had been torn "**between family loyalty and the national interest**" in the wake of the decision to **prorogue Parliament** (see p.86).

Robert Jenrick resigned as **Immigration Minister** in November 2023 after months of **tension** between himself and Rishi Sunak over the government's **immigration policy**. Jenrick's resignation letter complained that Sunak's approach to the **Rwanda plan** was "*a triumph of hope over experience.*"

✗ When CMR has not been observed

Michael Gove played a leading role in the **Leave campaign** during the **Brexit referendum** in 2016, **directly opposing** PM David Cameron's position. Cameron had agreed to **suspend collective responsibility** (as had been the case during the AV referendum). Their disagreement reached boiling point when Gove challenged Cameron to a **head-to-head TV debate** two weeks before the vote.

Boris Johnson was appointed as **Foreign Secretary** by Theresa May in a bid to ensure his loyalty after the Brexit referendum. May soon regretted this, when Johnson used his *Telegraph* column to outline his '**Ten steps for a successful Brexit**', which included some proposals that directly **contradicted her policy**. Weakened by Tory divisions over Brexit and fearing that Johnson might challenge her for the party leadership, May allowed him to continue in his post **without sanction**.

Penny Mordaunt was **International Development Secretary** during Liz Truss's premiership. She made it clear that she **disagreed** with Truss's decision **not** to **increase benefits in line with inflation**. Weakened by the ill-fated **mini-budget** (see p.86), Truss **didn't punish** Mordaunt.

Collective and Individual Ministerial Responsibility

❓ Ambiguous case for CMR

In 2003, **Clare Short**, the then **International Development Secretary**, was one of the first **prominent critics** of the **Iraq War**. She complained that Tony Blair had made the decision to invade **without consulting his Cabinet**. In her resignation statement, she argued that *"there is no collective responsibility because there is no collective"*.

Individual ministerial responsibility isn't always observed either

There have been lots of interesting cases of ministers **resigning**, or **not resigning**, when they've **fallen foul of IMR**.

✓ When IMR has been observed

Edwina Currie claimed as **Health Secretary** in 1988 that **British eggs** were infected with **salmonella**. This claim increased public fears over the disease, which led to a **60% fall** in **British egg sales** and the **slaughter** of **four million hens**. Later there was **mass outrage** when it appeared that her claim had been **misleading**, and she had not meant to suggest that **all** British eggs were **unsafe**. Currie **resigned** from her ministerial post, returning to the backbenches with a new nickname: **'Eggwina'**. In 2001, it was revealed that there was in fact a **significant** salmonella outbreak when Currie made her claim.

Priti Patel resigned from her role as **International Development Secretary** in Theresa May's Cabinet in 2017 after it emerged that she'd held **secret meetings** with **Israeli government officials** while supposedly in the country on holiday.

Amber Rudd was **Home Secretary** under Theresa May. She was found to have **misled** a House of Commons **Select Committee** over the **Windrush scandal** (see p.79) in 2018. Rudd had been given **incorrect information** by civil servants, but she still observed the convention of **IMR** and **resigned**.

Matt Hancock resigned as **Health Secretary** in 2021 after pictures were released that showed him **breaking** his own **social distancing guidelines** while having an **affair** with a colleague.

Suella Braverman resigned in October 2022, five weeks after her appointment as Liz Truss's **Home Secretary**, after she admitted sharing **sensitive information** using her **private email address**. In a swift change of fortunes, she was **re-appointed** by Sunak to the same position only six days later.

Gavin Williamson was appointed by Rishi Sunak as **Minister Without Portfolio** in 2022 after helping him win support among Conservative MPs in the leadership election. Williamson lasted just over a **fortnight** before he resigned over claims that he had **bullied colleagues** during his time as **Chief Whip** under Theresa May.

Louise Haigh resigned as **Transport Secretary** in **2024** after it emerged that she had been found **guilty** of **fraud** before becoming an MP. The story became especially embarrassing for **Keir Starmer** when it was **alleged** that he had **known** about the conviction before deciding to appoint Haigh to the **Cabinet**.

> Rishi Sunak signalled that he was likely to take IMR more seriously than Johnson had (see next page) when he sacked Nadhim Zahawi as Chairman of the Conservative Party in 2023. During his spell as Chancellor under Johnson, Zahawi had been involved in a £5 m dispute with HMRC (a government agency that he oversaw) over an unpaid tax bill.

Collective and Individual Ministerial Responsibility

✗ When IMR has not been observed

Chris Grayling, nicknamed '**Failing Grayling**' by the media, served in various Cabinet posts under Cameron and May. Grayling didn't resign from any of his ministerial positions, despite the embarrassment of awarding a **£13.8 m ferry contract** to a company that neither owned nor constructed ferries, chaos over **railway timetabling changes** and an unpopular decision to **stop prisoners receiving books** in the post. After he left the Cabinet when Johnson became prime minister in 2019, *The Guardian* estimated that Grayling had **wasted over £3 bn of taxpayers' money** during his 9 years in government.

Priti Patel was brought back into the Cabinet as **Home Secretary** by Boris Johnson in 2019, but was embroiled in allegations of **bullying civil servants** in the Home Office. She **refused to resign** and Johnson chose not to dismiss her, even after an investigation found that she had **broken the Ministerial Code**.

Gavin Williamson was appointed to the Cabinet as **Education Secretary** by Boris Johnson in 2019. Williamson faced **calls to resign** for his poor handling of **education** during the **COVID-19 pandemic**. This included a **failed attempt** to **distribute laptops** for remote lessons and the embarrassment of having to revert to **teacher-assessed grades** for GCSEs and A-Levels in **2020**. Despite widespread criticism, Williamson **refused to resign** and remained in his post until September 2021.

Boris Johnson tended not to strongly enforce IMR as PM, as the case studies involving Williamson and Patel above demonstrate. He **refused to resign** as prime minister in early 2022, despite allegations that he had **misled Parliament** over the **Partygate** scandal (see p.86).

Patel and Williamson are both excellent case studies in essays on ministerial responsibility because they were expected to resign under Theresa May and Rishi Sunak respectively, but not under Boris Johnson.

Quick Questions

1) Define collective ministerial responsibility.
2) Define individual ministerial responsibility.
3) Give an example of when collective ministerial responsibility has been formally suspended.
4) Give an example of collective ministerial responsibility being upheld.
5) Given an example of collective ministerial responsibility being ignored.
6) How much taxpayers' money did Chris Grayling allegedly waste during his ministerial career? Explain why this is significant.
7) How did the application of IMR differ between the premierships of Theresa May and Boris Johnson?

Ah sweet victory

Exam Practice

For Edexcel students: Evaluate the view that the conventions of collective and individual ministerial responsibility are no longer consistently upheld. [30]

For AQA students: 'The conventions of collective and individual responsibility are no longer consistently upheld.' Analyse and evaluate this statement. [25]

Practise your **evaluation** skills by writing a conclusion to one of the essay questions above.

You might want to consider the following factors:
- the prime minister's leadership style
- the type of government (majority, minority or coalition)
- the amount of pressure (e.g. due to scandals, policy failures or economic crisis) on the PM at that moment in time.

CGP tried to make me resign once...

...in vain. I simply refused, gluing my hands to my desk in defiance. All the bosses could do was shake their heads in despair. Five years later, I'm still here. Of course, productivity has taken a little bit of a dip, now I'm having to type with my nose...

UK Government — Prime Minister and the Executive

Does the PM Have Too Much Power?

You saw earlier in this section all the different powers that the prime minster has at their disposal, but what if that's all a bit much? Not all PMs manage to wield these powers effectively — it depends on a few different factors...

Some believe that the prime minister can wield **too much power**...

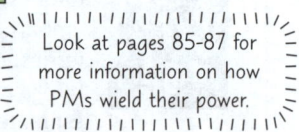
Look at pages 85-87 for more information on how PMs wield their power.

1) Most prime ministers command a **majority** in the **House of Commons**, giving them control over the **legislative process** in that chamber.

2) **Whips** help prime ministers to control their own party's **backbenchers** (see page 75). In recent decades, Margaret Thatcher, Tony Blair, Gordon Brown, Theresa May, Boris Johnson and Rishi Sunak have all enjoyed **undefeated periods** lasting **at least a year** in the House of Commons.

3) The **House of Lords** is **limited** in its ability to check the prime minister's agenda. For example, Sunak's government managed to pass the **Safety of Rwanda Act (2024)** unamended by the Lords.

4) The **power of patronage** means that the PM has significant control over the makeup of their **Cabinet**. This allows them to appoint **allies** to **key ministerial posts** — David Cameron did this when appointing **George Osborne** as Chancellor, as did **Rishi Sunak** when appointing **Oliver Dowden** as deputy prime minister.

5) **Prerogative powers** give the PM the ability to **bypass** Parliament on many important aspects of decision-making. In recent years, both **May** and **Sunak** have launched **air strikes** without first holding **votes** in Parliament.

Prime Minister Rishi Sunak at a press conference for the Rwanda plan in April 2024

6) **Supreme Court rulings** can be overridden by **Acts of Parliament**, allowing a prime minister with a majority to **overcome judicial checks** (see p.100). **Brown** did this with the **Terrorist Asset-Freezing Act (2010)**, which **overruled** the Supreme Court's ruling in **HM Treasury v Ahmed** earlier that year. The **Safety of Rwanda Act (2024)** also overruled a Supreme Court ruling.

7) The UK's **uncodified Constitution** can be adapted to **increase** executive power. During the COVID-19 pandemic, the **Coronavirus Act (2020)** allowed the executive to implement many policies **without debates** or **votes** in **Parliament**.

...but others argue that all prime ministers face **significant checks and balances**

1) All prime ministers can be **checked** by their own **Cabinets**, which usually contain their closest **political rivals** as well as **allies**. Thatcher, Johnson and Blair (to a lesser extent) were forced to resign by pressure from their Cabinet.

2) The **UK's news media** has a reputation for being **critical** of politicians. All prime ministers can expect to face intense **media scrutiny** of their government's **performance** and **conduct** (see page 43).

3) The **Supreme Court** has frequently **ruled against** high-profile **executive policies** under different prime ministers in recent years (see pages 98-99), including:

- **Gordon Brown's** government — **counter-terrorism** measures
- **Theresa May's** government — plans for the **executive** to **control** the **Brexit process**
- **Boris Johnson's** government — the **prorogation** of **Parliament**
- **Rishi Sunak's** government — the **Rwanda plan**

4) The House of Lords may lack the Commons' power but it is far **more likely** to inflict legislative **defeats** on the prime minister.

Discussing the impact of the media in checking prime ministerial power would make a great synoptic link in an essay.

Alesha faced significant checks on her balance

Does the PM Have Too Much Power?

Some prime ministers are **extremely limited** in their power

James Callaghan suffered **34 Commons defeats** in three years.

His Labour Party **lost** the **1979 general election** after his government had been **defeated** in a **motion of no confidence** in the Commons.

John Major

John Major and **Gordon Brown** both struggled to **assert their authority** as a result of **economic crises**.

Under **Major** in 1992, the UK was forced to **leave** the **Exchange Rate Mechanism** (the ERM), an international economic agreement, causing major embarrassment and **deepening** the **recession** the economy was suffering from.

Under **Brown**, the UK suffered from **mass unemployment** and **bank failures** during the 2008 **global financial crisis**.

Gordon Brown

After the **Conservatives** lost their Commons majority in 2017, **Theresa May** suffered **33 Commons defeats** over the next two years.

She was unable to pass her **Brexit deal** due to **opposition** from within the Conservative Party and from the DUP, with whom she had negotiated a confidence and supply deal. As a result, she was forced to **resign**.

Liz Truss had to abandon her tax-cutting, neo-liberal economic agenda and was then brought down by a **backbench revolt**.

She served as PM for only **44 days** before announcing her **resignation**.

Quick Questions

1) Which Act of Parliament overruled the Supreme Court's ruling that Rwanda was not a safe country for asylum seekers?
2) What is the role of party whips?
3) What impact did the Coronavirus Act (2020) have on Boris Johnson's power?
4) Which chamber of Parliament inflicts more defeats on the prime minister?
5) What did the Supreme Court rule in HM Treasury v Ahmed (2010)?
6) During which prime minister's premiership was the UK forced to leave the Exchange Rate Mechanism?
7) Which prime minister's government lost a confidence vote in 1979?

Revision Task

As we have seen, prime ministerial power is **elastic**, meaning that it can **grow or get reduced** depending on **various factors**.

Practise your **analysis** and **evaluation** skills by explaining whether each of the factors below would be likely to lead to a growth or reduction in the power of the prime minister.

1) Minority government
2) Economic growth
3) Landslide election victory

Make sure that you justify your answers — this is important for earning AO3 marks in an exam.

Essay Plan

For Edexcel students: Evaluate the view that the prime minister possesses too much power. [30]

For AQA students: 'The prime minister possesses too much power.' Analyse and evaluate this statement. [25]

Using the grid on p.298, **plan** an answer to one of the questions above.

I'd estimate the prime minister's power at around 100 watts...

As with a lot of essays on UK Government topics, the key to a successful answer is to consider circumstances in which prime ministers are more or less likely to possess great (and potentially too much) power. Remember to include synoptic links too.

UK Government — Prime Minister and the Executive

The Executive and Parliament

Join me on a journey back to November 5th, 1605. A stash of gunpowder is piled high beneath the Houses of Parliament. Guy Fawkes stands among... Oh, hang on, that's executing Parliament, not executive and Parliament. My bad.

With a **large majority** the executive can **dominate** in the **Commons**

1) With a **majority government**, the executive doesn't need the **support** of **opposition MPs** for bills to pass through the **Commons** if every MP of the governing party votes for the legislation.

2) When there are **backbench rebellions**, they are not usually big enough to **prevent** a bill from passing. For example, Tony Blair suffered a **record** number of **backbench rebellions**, but his majorities were so large from 1997-2005 that he was **undefeated** in the Commons.

3) Because the executive controls the **Commons timetable**, it can **decide which bills** to consider and **how much time** to allocate for debate.

4) **Public bill committees** reflect the make-up of the House of Commons. This allows the executive to **reject** the vast majority of **opposition amendments** that are proposed at committee stage (see page 75).

You can use the case studies on p.85-87 to provide additional support to these arguments.

Remember that the PM's prerogative powers mean that Parliament has no power over many important aspects of policy (p. 84).

Because of the executive's control over the legislative process, Parliament has been described as a 'policy-influencing legislature'. By contrast, the US Congress (see p.166) is regarded as a 'policy-making legislature'.

The **Commons** can more easily **check executive power** in **minority** governments

1) Here are some examples of the **executive** being **defeated** while in a **minority government**:

- The Commons **rejected** Theresa May's Brexit deal **three times** in 2019.
- Later in 2019, Remain-supporting **backbenchers** took **control** of the Commons timetable to **prevent a no-deal Brexit** (see page 80).

- Boris Johnson **lost six votes** in the House of Commons during his first week as prime minister.
- Johnson was referred to the **Commons' Privileges Committee** over the Partygate allegations in 2022, which contributed to his **resignation** (see page 86).

The statistics in the table on page 84 can give some insight into recent prime ministers' relationships with Parliament.

2) There tend to be more **backbench rebellions** in **coalition governments**, even if the coalition is a **majority government**. E.g. Cameron's coalition government was defeated on House of Lords reform (2012) and air strikes in Syria (2013).

The executive **rarely dominates** in the **House of Lords**

1) Because there is **no single-party majority** in the Lords, the executive needs to secure support from **opposition peers** and **crossbenchers** in order to pass legislation.

2) **Peers** in the **Lords** tend to be more **independent-minded** than **MPs** in the **Commons**, and they are at **no risk** of **losing their seat** in the Lords if they **go against** the party line.

The House of Lords can check the executive...

1) In 2021-2022, the Johnson government **lost 128 votes** in the **Lords**, compared with just **one** in the House of Commons.
2) Under Rishi Sunak, the Illegal Migration Bill was **unamended** by the Commons in 2023, but the Lords suggested **28 amendments**.

...but there are limits on its power

1) **The Parliament Acts (1911 and 1949)** (see p.60) and the **Salisbury Convention** (see p.70) **limit** the House of Lords' power.
2) The executive can pass legislation **without peers' consent** if it has been delayed for a year by the Lords. This happened in **2004**, when the **Hunting Act** was **passed** without support from the House of Lords.
3) The **executive** can use this power as a **bargaining chip** in Parliament.

The latest fashion trends dominate the Haus of Kommons...

The executive has a big influence over Parliament, especially in the Commons, but there's no guarantee that it will always come out on top. Make sure you know what powers the executive holds in Parliament, as well as how its power can be checked.

The Supreme Court

When it comes to legal matters, the Supreme Court truly does reign supreme. It's the highest court of appeal in the UK. But is it the most appealing page of this section? Read on, drink it all in and then you can hand down your verdict.

The Supreme Court opened in 2009 after the Constitutional Reform Act (2005)

Lords of Appeal in Ordinary:
- The Supreme Court **replaced** the Lords of Appeal in Ordinary (also called the Law Lords) as the **highest court of appeal** in the UK.
- The **Law Lords** were **senior judges** who were **appointed** as members of the **House of Lords**.
- Other peers had no power to make **judicial decisions**, but the **fusion** of the **legislative** and **judicial** branches made the UK **unusual** among democracies, and there were **concerns** over the **executive's role** in appointing judges.

Hehe I'm the best

The Supreme Court:
- The Supreme Court is made up of 12 judges, who are appointed by **independent selection panels**.
- As a court of appeal, it hears cases that have **already been ruled** upon by **lower courts** (such as the High Court, the Court of Appeal or courts in the devolved nations).
- The cases heard in the Supreme Court are often considered to be of **constitutional importance** (see pages 98-99 for case studies).

The judiciary has two core principles

- The Constitutional Reform Act (2005) **separated** the judiciary from the **other two branches** of government.
- This separation **strengthened** the two core principles of **judicial neutrality** and **judicial independence**.

1) Judicial Neutrality

The principle that judges should be **politically neutral** and that their rulings should be based on **existing law alone**.

This is different in the United States, where Supreme Court judges' political views are well known (and usually major factors in their nominations by the president — see page 193).

2) Judicial Independence

The principle that judges should not be **influenced** by other branches of **government** or by factors **outside** the political system when making decisions or choosing which cases to hear.

The judiciary has more authority to challenge the executive branch

Since the Supreme Court opened, it has made several high-profile rulings **against** the executive branch. For example:

- It ruled that Boris Johnson's attempted **prorogation** of Parliament was **unlawful** in 2019.
- It has also ruled against the executive's approach to **Brexit**, **immigration** and **criminal justice** (see p.98-99).

Quick Questions

1) Who served as the highest court of appeal in the UK before the Supreme Court was created?
2) How many judges are appointed to the Supreme Court?
3) Name the two branches of government the judiciary is split from.
4) Name the two core principles of the judiciary.

When a first date goes really well — call that a supreme court...

As the Supreme Court is the highest court in the land, it often has to rule on contentious or controversial topics. This is why it's so important that it maintains its judicial independence and judicial neutrality — there's more about this on page 101.

UK Government — Relations Between the Branches

The Impact of the Supreme Court

Even though the Supreme Court is a relatively new addition to the UK's judiciary, it's already had a significant political impact...

The Supreme Court has **two types** of **judicial review power**

1) It can rule that the executive branch has **acted unlawfully**

- These rulings are known as *ultra vires*, which means '**beyond the powers**' in Latin.
- *Ultra vires* rulings are **binding**, meaning that the executive should **immediately stop** the policy that has been declared **unlawful**.
- Because Parliament is sovereign in the UK's political system, *ultra vires* rulings **cannot** relate to **statute law** that has been passed by Parliament (see page 100).

Humphrey wasn't expecting the ruling to be that binding

2) It can also issue **declarations of incompatibility** with the Human Rights Act (1998)

- These rulings are made when the Supreme Court declares that an existing statute law is **incompatible** with the **Human Rights Act (1998)**.
- Unlike *ultra vires* rulings, declarations of incompatibility are **recommendations** and not binding decisions.
- Laws that are declared incompatible can **remain in place**. Usually, either the declaration will be **appealed** (so the court **reconsiders** if the law is truly incompatible), or legislation will be **adjusted** to **remove** the **incompatibility**.

The Supreme Court has made several **high-profile rulings**

Case Studies

Supreme Court cases that involve the Crown have an 'R' at the start of their name.

R (AAA and others) v. Home Secretary (2023)

- The Supreme Court ruled that the Conservative government's plan to **deport asylum seekers** to Rwanda was **unlawful**. This dealt a major blow to the Sunak government as it had identified the Rwanda strategy as a key part of its 'Stop the Boats' campaign.
- The Supreme Court's justification was that Rwanda's **asylum processing record** was **not reliable** enough to guarantee that vulnerable claimants would not be sent back to their country of origin. In the judges' opinion, this meant the policy broke the UK's **obligations** under **international law**.

Parliament overruled the Supreme Court's decision by passing the Safety of Rwanda Act (2024), but no deportations took place before Labour came to power and scrapped the policy.

Nicola Sturgeon, Scottish FM in 2022

Scottish independence referendum ruling (2022)

The Supreme Court ruled that the **Scottish Parliament** did **not** have the **authority** to call a **second Scottish independence referendum**. This ruling **prevented** the SNP government in Scotland from attempting to hold a referendum without the UK government's **consent**. The judges' justification was that, due to **parliamentary sovereignty**, only Parliament has the authority to call a referendum in the UK.

R (Begum) v. Home Secretary (2021)

Shamima Begum, a woman from East London, left the UK in 2015 to join the Islamic State terrorist group. The Supreme Court ruled **in favour** of the government's view that she should **not** be allowed to **return** to the UK to appeal against the loss of her **British citizenship**.

R (Friends of the Earth and others) v. Heathrow Airport Limited (2020)

- Supreme Court judges ruled that a **third runway** at Heathrow Airport would **not** break the UK's obligations under the **Paris Climate Agreement**. This **disappointed** the environmental groups who had attempted to block a third runway at Heathrow (such as Friends of the Earth and Plan B).
- As well as being a victory for Heathrow Airport Limited (the company that owns the airport) the ruling **upheld** the Conservative government's policy by stating that ministers had taken appropriate account of **environmental factors**.

The Impact of the Supreme Court

R (Miller) v. Prime Minister (2019)

- Boris Johnson's attempt to **prorogue** (suspend) Parliament was ruled **unlawful** by the Supreme Court. The judges found that the prorogation unnecessarily **prevented Parliament** from carrying out its **duties**, including being involved in **discussions** around a **Brexit deal** in the weeks leading up to the **deadline** for a deal. The judges justified their decision by explaining that the prime minister can **only** prorogue Parliament for **two reasons** — to **call a general election** or to **end a parliamentary session**.
- As a result, Johnson had to **change** his **Brexit strategy** by calling a general election (see p.38). This was probably the **highest-profile example** of the judiciary checking the executive in the UK's political history.

The judges ruled that the prime minister's prerogative powers are 'judiciable', which means that courts can rule on them in the future.

R (Steinfeld and Keidan) v. Secretary of State for International Development (2018)

The judges ruled that the **Civil Partnership Act (2004)** was **incompatible** with the **Human Rights Act (1998)** as civil partnerships were **only** available to **same-sex couples**. Following this ruling, Parliament amended the original Act to allow **all couples** to enter into civil partnerships.

R (Kiarie) v. Home Secretary (2017)

The Supreme Court ruled that the May government's **'deport first, appeal later'** policy was **unlawful**. This meant the Home Office had to **stop** denying foreign nationals who had been convicted in the UK the **right to appeal** their deportation before they were forced to leave the UK. This decision **split opinion**:

- Human rights campaigners felt that it successfully restored a **fundamental democratic right**.
- Others felt it **prioritised** the **individual rights** of convicted criminals over the **collective rights** of society as a whole.

R (Miller) v. Secretary of State for Exiting the European Union (2017)

Gina Miller

- Until the prorogation ruling in 2019, this was probably the most **famous** Supreme Court case. The judges ruled **against** the May government's plan to trigger **Article 50**, the process by which countries leave the European Union, without first **consulting Parliament**. This set a **precedent** that May, and later Johnson, needed to win votes in Parliament at **each stage** of the Brexit process.
- Some saw the ruling as an important affirmation of **parliamentary sovereignty** (see page 106). But others regarded it as an **illegitimate intervention** by unelected judges.

HM Treasury v. Ahmed (2010)

The Supreme Court ruled that the Brown government's policy of **freezing** the **financial assets** of terror suspects was **unlawful**. In response, the Brown government used its **Commons majority** to pass the **Terrorist Asset-Freezing Act (2010)**, which gave the **Treasury** the power to freeze financial assets. Because **statute law** takes precedence over **common law**, this Act could go **against** the Supreme Court's ruling.

Quick Questions

1) What are *ultra vires* rulings?
2) With which Act can statue law be declared incompatible?
3) What happens after a declaration of incompatibility?

Exam Practice

For students studying...

Edexcel: Evaluate the view that the Supreme Court has had a positive impact on the UK's political system. [30]

AQA: Explain and analyse three ways in which the Supreme Court has had political influence [9]

I lost my Soupreme Court case about banning tiny pasta...

...much to the relief of the prime minestrone. Make sure you learn these cases that have come before the Supreme Court and how it ruled. They'll be useful in illustrating how the Supreme Court interacts with Parliament and the executive.

The Executive and the Judiciary

The decisions that the courts make can have big implications on politics. So who the most powerful judges are can be of significant interest to the executive. Just like I have significant interest in the judges of the village marrow growing contest...

The **judiciary** has become a **major check** on the **power** of the **executive branch**

1) The courts are able to issue *ultra vires* **rulings** (see p.98), which have become much more **high profile** in recent years.
2) The rulings on Article 50, prorogation and Rwanda have all served as **significant brakes** on the power of the executive, **frustrating** key aspects of government policy (see pages 98-99).

Executive influence was **reduced** by the Constitutional Reform Act (2005)

1) The **Lord Chancellor** (a Cabinet minister) used to oversee **senior judicial appointments** on behalf of the prime minister.
2) Since the Constitutional Reform Act, Supreme Court appointments are now overseen by **independent selection panels** that form for each vacancy that arises.
3) All other judges are appointed by groups that are **separate** from both the executive and Parliament. For England and Wales, this is the **Judicial Appointments Commission**.

The **executive** can still **sidestep** some court decisions...

1) Because the executive usually has a majority in the House of Commons, it can use **Parliament's sovereignty** to its advantage by passing statute law that **overrides** court rulings.
2) This happened in 2010, when the Brown government **passed** the **Terrorist Asset-Freezing Act** to override the Supreme Court's ruling in HM Treasury v Ahmed.
3) In 2024, Parliament passed the **Safety of Rwanda Act** under the Sunak government. This **contradicted** the **Supreme Court's 2023 ruling** that Rwanda was not a safe country for refugees, which had **delayed** the **implementation** of the Conservatives' Rwanda plan.

...and its **influence** over the **appointments process** has not been removed entirely

Sir Brian Leveson

1) In 2017, the then Lord Chancellor, Liz Truss, **attracted controversy** when she **persuaded** the Judicial Appointments Commission to change the **upper age limit** for the **Lord Chief Justice** position — the **highest-ranking** judge beneath the Supreme Court.
2) This change was seen by many as a deliberate attempt to **prevent** the nomination of Sir Brian Leveson, an outspoken critic of the government who had been touted for the role.
3) Under the **Constitutional Reform Act**, the Lord Chancellor can still **veto** Supreme Court nominations, although this power has not yet been used.

Exam Practice

For Edexcel students: Evaluate the view that the judiciary now has sufficient power and independence to check the executive branch. [30]

For AQA students: 'The judiciary now has sufficient power and independence to check the executive branch.' Analyse and evaluate this statement. [25]

Practise your analysis skills by **explaining** the significance of these examples to one of the questions above. You can use the sentence frames on pages 299-300 for guidance.

1) After HM Treasury v. Ahmed (2010), the Brown government passed the Terrorist Asset-Freezing Act, giving the Treasury the power to freeze terror suspects' assets.
2) In 2017, Liz Truss persuaded the Judicial Appointments Committee to change the age limit for the Lord Chief Justice position, effectively ruling out Sir Brian Leveson, who was a leading contender for the role.

Booking a haircut with your bestie — that's an appointment co-mission...

With the judiciary having the potential power to go against the executive's plans, it's not surprising that the relationship between them is so important. A lot rides on whether the actions and intentions of the executive are legally sound.

UK Government — Relations Between the Branches

Judicial Independence and Neutrality

The Supreme Court has to uphold the principles of judicial independence and neutrality to do its job properly. The question of whether or not the Supreme Court is doing this effectively can be a real point of conflict in politics. Read on to find out more...

Some think that the **Supreme Court** is **not upholding** its **core principles**...

Some people argue that the Supreme Court's increasingly **politicised** role harms its ability to uphold its core principles of **judicial independence** and **judicial neutrality** (see p.97). For example:

1. **Conservative commentators** and politicians have criticised what they perceive to be the Court's **'liberal agenda'** following its decisions on Brexit, prorogation and immigration (see p.98-99).

2. **Environmental campaigners** felt that the Court unfairly sided with **corporate** and **government** interests in its Heathrow Airport ruling in 2020.

3. In their **2019 manifesto**, the **Conservative Party** called for **reforms** to judicial review to prevent the Supreme Court from being used as a tool to 'conduct politics'.

...others say the judges' **training** and **rulings** show that the core principles are **upheld**

1) The **contentious nature** of Supreme Court cases guarantees that some people will always be **unhappy** with its rulings. However, judges receive **extensive training** in independence and neutrality throughout their careers.
2) Cases are usually heard by five, seven or nine judges — this **reduces** the influence of individual judges.
3) The most **controversial** rulings on Brexit and prorogation were decided by **11 judges**.
4) The Supreme Court **doesn't** just rule **in favour** of the executive — the government won just 3 out of 11 cases in 2020, but won 15 of 18 in 2022.
5) Supreme Court **judges** are **appointed** by an **independent selection panel**. This should make it **less likely** that judges with a reputation for making **politically motivated** rulings would be nominated to the highest court in the UK.

Members of the press waiting outside the Supreme Court during the legal case R (Miller) v. Prime Minister

The Supreme Court's **lack of diversity** is seen as a barrier to its neutrality

1) The Supreme Court does not reflect the **diversity** of the UK population.
   - 10 of the 12 Supreme Court judges are **white men**.
   - There has **never** been a Supreme Court judge of colour.
2) The Supreme Court also **reflects** a **lack of diversity** among **senior lawyers** in the UK.
3) Critics of the Supreme Court argue that this **lack of diversity** produces rulings that uphold **elite interests**, such as their ruling on the **development** of the **third runway** at **Heathrow Airport** (see page 98). Despite this, the Supreme Court has frequently ruled **against** elite interests:

> In one of its earliest cases in 2010, the Supreme Court ruled that MPs accused of **expenses fraud** should face **criminal** trials, rather than being subject to questioning in Parliament alone. This eventually led to three MPs being **jailed**.

> The **Rwanda ruling** saw the Supreme Court uphold the rights of **asylum seekers**, finding against one of the executive's highest-profile policies.

The gender composition of the Supreme Court will likely change in the future. Across all posts overseen by the Judicial Appointments Commission in 2021-22, women accounted for 49% of applications and 48% of recommendations.

I never eat the middle of an apple, it's one of my core principles...

It's all because of a nightmare I had about a tree growing out of my stomach... Anyway, enough about frightening fruit. When looking at judicial independence and neutrality, be sure to consider the evidence on both sides and any other factors at play.

Parliament and the Judiciary

Relationships can be tricky to navigate, so here's a quick guide to the relationship between Parliament and the judiciary.

Some believe the Supreme Court has **undermined parliamentary sovereignty**...

1) When **controversial** policies are announced by the executive or by one of the devolved administrations, **speculation** now tends to focus on whether it will be subject to **judicial review**, rather than on how **Parliament** will respond.
2) Declarations of **incompatibility** with the Human Rights Act (1998) put **political pressure** on Parliament to amend statute law.

> In your exam, don't write that the Supreme Court can declare laws or policies 'unconstitutional' in the UK. This is the case in the USA, but parliamentary sovereignty in the UK means that no law can be considered unconstitutional.

The Supreme Court

...but others point to **rulings** that have **supported Parliament**

1) The Supreme Court has consistently **defended parliamentary sovereignty** against attempts by the executive to **marginalise** Parliament's influence (see p.98-99).
2) In R (Miller) v Secretary of State for Exiting the European Union (2017), the Supreme Court ruled that the **devolved legislatures** in Scotland, Wales and Northern Ireland should have **no role** in beginning the **Brexit process**. This **reaffirmed** the sovereignty of Parliament in Westminster.

Parliament retains the ability to **overrule** or **ignore** some Supreme Court decisions

1) **Statute law** takes precedence over **all other** sources of the Constitution (see p.60), including common law rulings made by the courts.
2) This allowed the **Brown government** to pass the Terrorist Asset-Freezing Act (2010), which **overrode** the Supreme Court's ruling in HM Treasury v. Ahmed.
3) Declarations of incompatibility are only **advisory mechanisms**, not binding rulings. Parliament may then **choose** to amend statute law.
4) **Only** 17 of 34 declarations of incompatibility between 2009 and 2024 have led to **legislative change**.

> Parliament's ability to make or unmake any law is known as its 'omnicompetence'.

Quick Questions

1) Which act led to the creation of the Supreme Court?
2) In which year did the Supreme Court open?
3) What is meant by judicial neutrality?
4) What is meant by judicial independence?
5) How did the Supreme Court justify its ruling against the executive's Rwanda plan in 2023?
6) Which type of rights (individual or collective) did the Supreme Court prioritise in R (Kiarie) v. Home Secretary (2017)?
7) Which pressure group challenged the construction of a third runway at Heathrow in 2020?

Essay Plan

For Edexcel students: Evaluate the view that the Supreme Court possesses sufficient checks over the executive, but not over Parliament. [30]

For AQA students: 'The Supreme Court possesses sufficient checks over the executive, but not over Parliament.' Analyse and evaluate this statement. [25]

Use the grid on page 298 to **plan** an answer to one of the questions above.

> You need to make sure that you balance looking at the Supreme Court's relationship with both the executive and Parliament across your answer. You could choose to agree with one part of the question, but not the other part, although there's no need to do so.

Introducing two hot new political drag stars: Paula Ment and Judy Sherry...

Parliamentary sovereignty is a key point of contention when it comes to how the branches of government interact — as you'll see on pages 106-107. Keep it in mind when you look at whether different branches have too much or too little power.

The European Union

The European Union has had a major effect on UK politics, from the time it was founding member, right up until the contentious decision to leave. A lot of the EU's guiding principles have helped to shape UK policy and laws.

The **European Union** was founded in **1993** by 12 original members

1) The **founding members** were: Belgium, Denmark, France, Germany, Greece, Ireland, Italy, Luxembourg, the Netherlands, Portugal, Spain and the UK.
2) Before the EU was founded, its members were part of several **separate European organisations**:

The EU flag

- The **European Coal and Steel Community**.
  Formed in **1950**, it created a **common market** for **coal** and **steel** between Belgium, France, Italy, Luxembourg, the Netherlands and West Germany.
- The **European Economic Community**.
  Formed in **1957**, it aimed to produce a **common market** and **customs union** between the same countries as the European Coal and Steel Community.
- The **European Atomic Energy Community**.
  Formed in **1957**, it created a specialist market for **nuclear power** in Europe.
- In **1967**, the **Merger Treaty combined** these three communities into a **single body**. It is seen by some as a precursor to the EU.

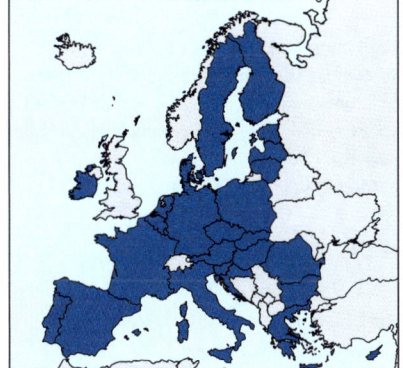

A map of Europe, showing EU member states shaded in dark blue

3) The **UK** formally **left** the EU on 31 January 2020.
4) As of 2024, there were **27 member states**, with a combined population of around **450 million people**.

The **EU** has several **core aims**

- **Establish a common internal market** — in return for **free trade** within the EU, every member state has to follow the same **economic** and **social regulations**.
- **Establish an economic and monetary union** — 20 member states now use the **euro** as their currency.
- **Ensure a safe and affordable supply of food for EU member states** — the EU provides **support** to **farmers** and **agriculture** to ensure food is produced **efficiently** and **affordably**. It also sets **strong regulations** on **food standards**.
- **Promote the values and interests of EU member states across the world** — the EU operates as a **trade bloc**, which means that it negotiates trade agreements as a **single entity**. Individual countries within the EU are **not allowed** to reach their own agreements with non-EU members.
- **Promote peace, equality and environmental action** — the EU is founded on the idea that states whose economies are **interdependent** are more likely to be able to **remain peaceful** and drive **political** and **social change** through **collective action**.

> The UK and Denmark were the only original member states to opt out of adopting the euro. Both countries managed to insert clauses in the Maastricht Treaty (which set up the EU) that enabled them to do this.

These aims are underpinned by **four freedoms of movement**

1) FREE MOVEMENT OF GOODS
This allows **products**, including food, clothing and medical supplies, to be **transported** between EU member states **without** checks.

2) FREE MOVEMENT OF CAPITAL
This allows **money** to be **transferred** between accounts in different EU member states **without** additional charges.

3) FREE MOVEMENT OF SERVICES
This allows **any business** based in a member state to operate **across** the EU.

4) FREE MOVEMENT OF PEOPLE
This allows **anyone** with a **passport** or **residency** in one EU state to **live**, **work** and **travel** across all member states.

> Find out more about the structure and role of EU institutions on page 290.

> The free movement of people was one of the key aspects of EU membership that was debated during the 2016 Brexit referendum. Pro-EU campaigners felt that it gave UK citizens greater economic freedom and helped businesses to fill vacancies. But supporters of Brexit argued that it prevented the UK from being able to control immigration.

UK Government — Relations Between the Branches

The European Union

Some believe that the EU has developed successfully...

Closer integration

In just over 30 years, the EU has **grown** from 12 to 27 member states. Its **legal framework** was strengthened by the signing of the **Lisbon Treaty** in 2007, which included a **binding bill of rights** that applies across all member states.

European Court of Justice

Justice

The European Court of Justice (ECJ) has helped to **clarify** EU law when **disputes** have arisen between member states. This has helped to boost the aim of **integration**.

Be careful not to confuse the European Court of Justice with the European Court of Human Rights. The ECJ is part of the European Union, whereas the ECtHR is not. This means that the ECtHR still has authority over the UK after Brexit, while the ECJ does not.

Foreign policy collaboration

The EU aims to **maintain peace** and strengthen **international security**. During times of conflict, its states have worked together to provide **military** and **humanitarian aid**.

The EU has provided nearly €100 bn in military and humanitarian aid to Ukraine since the Russian invasion in 2022.

Economic growth and solidarity

The EU estimates that between its creation and 2022, the **single market** has added between **3%** and **6%** on average to its member states' **GDP**. It also estimates that there was a **1.4% increase** in **employment** between 1992 and 2006. During **financial crises**, the stronger EU member states have acted to **support** those with weaker economies.

...but others argue that its success has been limited

Lack of democracy

Although the European Parliament is **elected**, it has much **less power** than the **European Commission** and the **Council of Ministers**. The **members** of these bodies aren't **directly elected** into them, but are **appointed** from elected representatives of member states.

Since the Lisbon Treaty, the Council of Ministers has used qualified majority voting to reach decisions — this means that 55% of member states and member states representing at least 65% of the total EU population must support the decision.

Trade deals

Critics of the EU argue that it **stops** member states from signing more **beneficial trade deals** with countries elsewhere in the world.

Immigration

The **free movement of people** has often created **controversy** among EU member states. This was particularly evident in 2015, when EU states **failed** to reach a **collective agreement** on how to handle the Syrian refugee crisis.

Growth of anti-EU sentiment

As well as Brexit, there has been a clear **rise** in **anti-EU sentiment** across Europe in recent years. Explicitly anti-EU parties have significantly **increased** their **share of the vote** in the Netherlands, Italy, France and Germany.

What do cows sound like in Brussels? "MEUUUUUU"

What do you call a root vegetable from Brussels? The European Onion...

The UK isn't a member of the European Union anymore, but the time when it was a member of the EU has had a large influence on its politics. Many current UK laws and policies were first put in place to bring things in line with EU standards.

UK Government — Relations Between the Branches

The Impact of the European Union

I'm sure you've had enough of it from the past decade of newspaper headlines and current affairs programming, but it's time to discuss the effect the EU has on the UK. I'm afraid the budget didn't stretch to a celeb presenter or satirical puppets...

The **EU's critics** believe that it **restricted** the UK's **freedom**

Politics
EU law took **precedence** over UK law. This meant that Parliament had to **accept regulations** that hadn't been **debated** or **voted** upon in the House of Commons or the House of Lords.

Economics
The EU is a **trade bloc**. As a member, the UK could **not** sign its own **trade agreements** with **non-EU countries**, even with countries it had long-standing ties with.

Immigration
Many **Brexiteers** believe that membership of the EU led to **excessive levels** of legal migration. They believe this put pressure on **public services** such as education and the NHS.

The **EU's supporters** feel the UK was **strengthened** by being part of the EU

Economics
The EU accounts for roughly **14%** of the world's **GDP**, giving it significant **leverage** in negotiating **trade deals**. By comparison, the UK represents nearly 3% of the world's GDP.

Migration
EU membership gave UK nationals the ability to **live** and **work anywhere in the EU** without restrictions. By 2016, the year of the referendum, over a **million UK nationals** were living and working in other EU countries. This offered UK nationals greater **economic** and **social opportunities**.

Labour & Immigration
The **free movement of people** meant that UK-based employers could **fill labour shortages** with workers from other EU member states. For instance, in 2016, an estimated 99% of **seasonal agricultural workers** in the UK were from elsewhere in the EU.

Brexit means that the **EU** now has a much **smaller impact** on the **UK**

1) **Statute law** (passed by Parliament) is once again the **supreme source** of the UK Constitution, meaning that Parliament can choose to **repeal** EU regulations.
2) But the UK does still have to maintain a '**level playing field**' with the **EU**. As part of the Brexit deal reached by Boris Johnson, the UK and the EU need to **maintain fair competition** on matters such as **labour laws** and **environmental standards**.
3) In practice, this means that if the UK sought to gain a **competitive advantage** by changing its laws in these areas, the EU would be able to **impose tariffs** or other **trade penalties** against the UK.

Quick Questions

1) Which treaty created the European Union?
2) In which year did the UK leave the EU?
3) Along with the UK, which other original EU member state opted out of adopting the euro?
4) What are the Four Freedoms?
5) What percentage of the world's GDP comes from the EU?

The UK went through a bit of a Brexitstential crisis...
Loads of European countries, not just the UK, are still debating the various benefits and drawbacks to being a member state of the EU. Make sure to prepare well for your exams by working on your knowledge of all the key arguments.

UK Government — Relations Between the Branches

Is Parliament Sovereign?

Changes in the political set-up of the UK have had considerable effects on just how sovereign Parliament can be said to be...

Parliament is meant to be sovereign in the UK's political system

- **Parliamentary sovereignty** means that Parliament can **make** or **unmake** any law and that **statute law** takes precedence over **all other sources** of the Constitution (see page 60).
- There are **two ways** of analysing parliamentary sovereignty:
  1) **LEGAL SOVEREIGNTY** — the **theoretical** location of sovereignty under the **law**. Because Parliament can theoretically **make** or **unmake** any law that it chooses, it can be said to **retain** legal sovereignty. E.g. even though Parliament **couldn't pass laws** on matters **controlled** by the EU while the UK was a member state, it still had the **power** to **withdraw** the UK's membership, as it did in 2020.
  2) **POLITICAL SOVEREIGNTY** — the **practical** location of sovereignty in **day-to-day political terms**. Because the **political reality** is that Parliament simply wouldn't be able to make or unmake any law that it chooses, it can be said to have **lost** some of its political sovereignty. E.g. while **legal sovereignty** suggests that Parliament could, in **theory**, **reverse** a major constitutional change like **devolution**, the **politics** involved would make doing so **nearly impossible**.

There are many occasions when parliamentary sovereignty has been challenged

The European Communities Act (1972)

1) The **European Communities Act (1972)** saw the UK join the **European Economic Community**, which later became the **European Union** in 1993.
2) This meant that **European law took precedence** over UK law, threatening the principle that Parliament was the **ultimate source** of legal and political authority. For example, while the UK was a member of the European Union, Parliament was not able to **legislate** to end freedom of movement (see page 103).
3) The higher status of European law was **affirmed** in a famous court case called **R (Factortame Ltd) v. Secretary of State for Transport (1990)**. The Law Lords (see page 97) ruled **against the executive** by concluding that the UK could not **restrict access** to its waters for European fishing companies.

> The EU operates on the principle of pooled sovereignty. This means that countries agree to give up some of their sovereignty as part of their membership.

The Human Rights Act (1998)

1) The **Human Rights Act (1998)** gave the judiciary the power to issue **declarations of incompatibility**.
2) These declarations mean that judges find that an act passed by Parliament **does not comply** with the Human Rights Act.
3) Although these are **not binding**, they do place **political pressure** on Parliament to change the law.

The Devolution Acts in 1998

1) The **Devolution Acts** in 1998 meant that Parliament was **no longer responsible** for passing **all** laws.
2) Areas of policy like **healthcare** and **education** have been **devolved** to **Scotland**, **Wales** and **Northern Ireland** ever since.
3) The **Scottish** and **Welsh** Parliaments have since gained **greater powers** over **taxation** and other policy areas (see page 64).

The Constitutional Reform Act (2005)

The **Constitutional Reform Act (2005)** removed Parliament's judicial role by creating an independent **Supreme Court** (see page 97).

Coronavirus Act (2020)

1) By passing the **Coronavirus Act (2020)**, Parliament temporarily **gave up** its sovereignty to the **executive** during the COVID-19 pandemic.
2) The **executive** was able to make **decisions** such as imposing lockdowns and closing schools **without** holding votes in Parliament.

Referendums

1) **Harold Wilson's** decision to hold a **referendum** on the UK's membership of the **European Economic Community** in 1975 (see p.5) set a **precedent** that has since been followed by Tony Blair and David Cameron.
2) In the twenty years from 1997 to 2017, there were **7 public votes** on the Good Friday Agreement, devolution, electoral reform, Scottish independence and Brexit.
3) Some commentators believe that the **increasing frequency of referendums** has strengthened **popular sovereignty** at the expense of **parliamentary sovereignty**. Some argue that sovereignty really lies with the **public** and that Parliament is **mandated** to carry out the **will of the people** if it has been expressed through a referendum.
4) Referendum results are **not legally binding**, but there is a **political expectation** that they will be followed.
5) There may now be an **expectation** that major constitutional changes need to be **approved through referendums**.

Is Parliament Sovereign?

Parliament has also **asserted** its **political sovereignty**...

> Technically, political sovereignty resides with the electorate, who then delegate it to Parliament following elections to the Commons.

Devolved governments:

Parliament **overrode** the **Sewel Convention** (which says Parliament **shouldn't intervene** in devolved matters) to pass the **Internal Market Act (2020)**. This act saw Parliament impose **UK-wide regulations** in areas such as **agriculture** that are supposed to be **devolved** to the **Scottish Parliament**, the **Senedd** and the **Northern Ireland Assembly**.

Parliamentary approval:

MPs **took control** of the Brexit process and **both chambers** of Parliament had to **approve** the terms of the UK's deal with the EU.

"Any deals that need ratifying?"

Immigration:

1) As a member state of the EU, the UK had to follow the **principles of freedom of movement** (see page 103).
2) Since Brexit, Parliament can once again **pass laws on migration** from within the EU, such as the **Nationality and Borders Act (2022)**.

Trade deals:

1) The UK was **unable** to sign its own **trade deals** while a member of the EU.
2) Since Brexit, Parliament is able to **ratify trade agreements** that the executive has signed with **foreign countries**.
3) For example, Parliament approved the UK's new **trade deal with Australia** in 2023.

...and Parliament **retains** its **legal sovereignty**

1) If it chose to do so, Parliament could **repeal constitutional reforms** like devolution.
2) The **balance of power** between Parliament and the devolved legislatures has been **reaffirmed** by the Scottish government's failed attempts to hold a second independence referendum (see page 98).
3) The **emergency powers** given to the executive in the **Coronavirus Act (2020)** have now **expired**. Parliament could have chosen to **amend** or **repeal** the law at **any stage**.

> Ending devolution is highly unlikely. Devolution has a popular mandate in Scotland, and the Scotland Act (2016) requires any attempt to remove devolved powers to be ratified by a referendum (see page 64).

Quick Questions

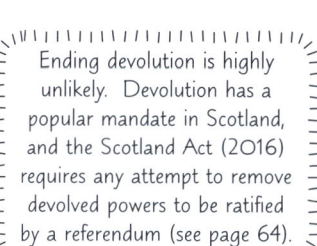

1) On what issue did Harold Wilson hold a referendum on in 1975?
2) What is the difference between legal sovereignty and political sovereignty?
3) What does the 'level playing field' mean in the context of Brexit?
4) Give an example of a policy introduced under the Coronavirus Act (2020).
5) Identify a country with which the UK has signed a post-Brexit trade deal.

Exam Practice

For Edexcel students: Evaluate the view that Parliament remains sovereign in theory, but not in practice. [30]

For AQA students: Explain and analyse three ways in which Parliament exercises sovereignty. [9]

The Commons had no sovereign tea so I nipped to the Lords for Earl Grey...

Challenges to its sovereignty aren't great for Parliament, but they're not entirely negative. Policies like devolution are popular because they make sure that policies which affect local areas are made by politicians who are invested in those places.

UK Government — Relations Between the Branches

Anarchism

I've risen up and overthrown the state of this page — but did I act alone?
Am I a collectivist anarchist or an individualist anarchist? You may never know. But once you've read this section, hopefully you'll have a good idea of the difference between them. So without further ado, let's take a deep breath and dive in.

Anarchism is an ideology that seeks to remove the power of the state

1) The word anarchism comes from a Greek word meaning '**without a ruler**'. Anarchism is often referred to as a **utopian ideology** because it imagines what an **ideal existence** might look like.
2) Its critics believe that the **societies** and **economies** proposed by anarchists are **so unrealistic** that they are **unachievable**.

There are two main strands of anarchism

Collectivist Anarchism

1) **Collectivist anarchists** believe that **state power** can only be **removed** through **collective action**.
2) They believe an **anarchist society** would be based on the principles of **collectivism**, including **common ownership** and **equality of outcome**.
3) This strand can be broken down into **three sub-strands**. Each has distinct views on how anarchism should be **achieved** and the **principles** on which an **anarchist society** and **economy** would be based.

Anarcho-communism
- **Anarcho-communism** is influenced by the ideas of **Marx** and **Engels** (see p.55-56). It calls for a **violent overthrow** of the **state** and **capitalism**.
- Once **workers** have realised the **oppression** that they have suffered under both of these forces, they will establish a **new society** based on the principle of **equality of outcome**.

Key Thinkers: Mikhail Bakunin (1814-1876), Peter Kropotkin (1842-1921), Emma Goldman (1869-1940)

Mutualism
- **Mutualism** is a sub-strand of collectivist anarchism that seeks to **abolish** most forms of **private property** by encouraging **altruism**.
- It aims to **dismantle** the **state's influence** by **peaceful** means.

Under mutualism, small-scale private possessions would still be allowed, because they are not seen as instruments of capitalist or state exploitation.

Key Term — altruism: The idea that humans can act charitably, looking after the interests of others by making decisions that they might not directly benefit from themselves.

Key Thinker: Pierre-Joseph Proudhon (1809-1865)

Anarcho-syndicalism
- **Anarcho-syndicalism** is a sub-strand of collectivist anarchism that emphasises the role that **trade unions** can play in representing **workers' rights** and contributing to the **fall** of the **state and capitalism**.
- Anarcho-syndicalists see **strike action**, rather than violent revolution, as the main way of **achieving anarchism**.

Rudolf Rocker (1873-1958) isn't listed as a key thinker on the specification, but his ideas are influential in anarcho-syndicalism

Mikhail Bakunin is also considered to be a key thinker of the anarcho-syndicalist movement on the AQA specification.

Anarchism

Individualist Anarchism

1) **Individualist anarchists** argue that **individuals** can **remove state power** on their own, without collective action.
2) Anarchists of this strand believe that **individuals** would then continue to form the **basis** of **anarchist societies**, with **no need** for collective action or ownership.
3) Individualist anarchism contains **two sub-strands**:

Egoism
- **Egoism** is the idea that **individuals** should pursue their **own interests** above **everything else**.
- Individualist anarchists believe that this will lead to a **more prosperous** and **fulfilled society**, removing any **need** for dependence on a **state**.

Anarcho-capitalism
- **Anarcho-capitalists** see **capitalism** as the **best economic system** for allowing **individuals** to **flourish** and pursue their **own interests**.
- Anarcho-capitalists view **private property** as the **ultimate goal** of individuals.
- Anarcho-capitalism encourages individuals to **free themselves** from the **limiting influence** of the **state**, including through **refusing** to **pay taxes**.

Key Thinker

Max Stirner (1806-1856)
There are no known photos of Stirner — the best we have is this portrait, drawn by Engels

Stirner is best described as an egoist, although his ideas did influence anarcho-capitalism.

Anarchist thinkers have a **very optimistic** view of **human nature...**

1) Anarchists see humans as **highly capable** and **inherently rational** creatures.
2) They believe humans are capable of making the **best decisions** about their **own lives**, **without** any need for a **power structure** above them.

...and a **very negative** view of the impact of the **state** on **society** and the **economy**

1) **Collectivist** and **individualist anarchists** believe that the **state** is an **unnecessary** and **burdensome** influence on society.
2) They believe that the state **prevents** humans from achieving their **full potential**.

They **all** seek a society **without state power** but **disagree** over how to **achieve** it

COLLECTIVIST ANARCHISM:
1) **Collectivist anarchists** see humans as **inherently collaborative** creatures.
2) They believe people can achieve anarchism through **collective action**, whether **violent** or **peaceful**.

INDIVIDUALIST ANARCHISM:
1) **Individualist anarchists** believe that humans should harness their **selfish instincts** to **remove** themselves from **state authority**.
2) They believe that **maximising competition** is the **most sustainable** way of **eliminating political power**.

"You were right Benji, collective action *is* the key to overcoming tyranny..."

Yep, definitely in the spirit of anarchism for this one. Rule book out the window. Intros as endings and endings as intros. Can you think of anything wilder than that? I certainly can't. That's why they call me the bad boy of educational publishing...

Collectivist Anarchism

You might think the world is in a right old state. Well, what if we all banded together and got rid of the state completely?

Collectivist anarchists believe **political power** always leads to **oppression**

1) **Collectivist anarchists** see all **power** as **inherently corrupting**, meaning that those in power will only ever **pursue their own interests**.
2) **Mikhail Bakunin** believed that even *"the most ardent revolutionary"* would become a dictator *"within a year"* if they held the **absolute power** of the state.
3) Anarcho-syndicalist **Rudolf Rocker** said that *"Power operates only destructively"*, a **negative view** of political power that is held by all collectivist anarchists.
4) Collectivist anarchists believe that **governments**, as well as being **unavoidably corrupt**, exercise power **without authority**.
5) Mutualist **Pierre-Joseph Proudhon** wrote:

> *"To be governed is to be watched, inspected, spied upon, directed ... by creatures who have neither the right nor the wisdom nor the virtue to do so."*

6) Many collectivist anarchists instead support a version of **direct democracy** in which **citizens** are **actively** and **frequently** involved in **political decision-making**.

They believe the **state** must be **overthrown** by **co-ordinated**, **collective** action

1) Because the **state** has so much **power**, and its **members** gain so much from their **privileged position**, collectivist anarchists argue that **direct action** is necessary to overturn its authority.
2) **Emma Goldman** stated that:

> *"No real social change has ever been brought about without a revolution."*

Key Terms

direct action
A term for acts of resistance and protest, usually carried out by workers' groups and other collective organisations. It can include violent acts such as assassinations and damage to private property, as well as peaceful ones like demonstrations and strikes.

They see the **state** and **capitalism** as **obstacles** to **fairness**, **liberty**, and **equality**

1) Collectivist anarchists see **capitalism** as an instrument of **state power**. This is because it **enriches** a small number of **powerful people** while **limiting** the **liberty** and **autonomy** of most **workers**, who are reliant on their **wages** but unable to improve their **position** in society.
2) Collectivist anarchists believe this puts those without power in a situation comparable to **slavery**. Anarcho-communist **Peter Kropotkin** wrote: *"It is futile to speak of liberty as long as economic slavery exists."*
3) As a result, collectivist anarchists argue that the **state** and **capitalism** must be **abolished**, or else one will just **replace** or **recreate** the other.
4) **Mikhail Bakunin**, another anarcho-communist thinker, believed that *"liberty without socialism is privilege, injustice"* and that *"socialism without liberty is slavery and brutality."*

Collectivists also argue that the **law** fails to uphold **true liberty**

1) Because of their views on the **corrupting nature of power**, collectivist anarchists believe that **laws** created by those in power will **never** benefit the **working classes**.
2) This belief is central to the **intellectual justification** that **Kropotkin**, **Goldman** and **Bakunin** made for **disobeying** the law through acts of **violent resistance**.
3) Because they questioned the law's **authority** and its **capacity** to act in the **interests** of ordinary people, they argued that **breaking the law** is the **only** way of achieving **liberty for all**.

Non-core Political Ideas — Anarchism

Collectivist Anarchism

Collectivist beliefs about **human nature** affect their views on **society** and **property**

Society and self-interest

1) Collectivists believe that humans are naturally **sociable** and **cooperative** beings, who are motivated **more** by **altruism** than **self-interest**.
2) Like **revolutionary socialists** (see page 55), collectivist anarchists think that humans have been **alienated** from their **true nature** by **capitalism** and the **state**.
3) As part of his theory of **human sociability**, **Bakunin rejected** the idea that **competition** and **self-interest** can help to liberate individuals. He believed that an individual can only experience true freedom *"when all human beings, men and women, are equally free."*
4) This is a key **difference** between **collectivist** and **individualist anarchism**, whose thinkers encourage the pursuit of **self-interest** as part of their theory of **egoism** (p.109).
5) **Kropotkin** also rejected the need for competition, writing: *"Don't compete! — competition is always injurious to the species."*

Key Terms

human sociability
The collectivist idea that humans are at their best when they are connected to, and collaborating with, other individuals.

Although Goldman was a collectivist anarchist, her ideas share some similarities with the individualist anarchist Max Stirner (see p.113). She wrote about the need for individuals to educate themselves and develop their capacity for self-expression. She argued that people only have as much freedom *"as they have the intelligence to want and the courage to take."*

Private property

1) Their beliefs about **equality**, **co-operation** and **sociability** lead collectivist anarchists to **oppose** the concept of **private property**.
2) They believe in the principle of **collectivisation** — the idea that **private property** should be **abolished** and **collective labour** established.
3) **Kropotkin** expressed the principle of collectivisation by writing that *"All belongs to all."*

They **disagree** over whether **violence** is necessary to **overthrow the state**

Bakunin
- **Bakunin** developed an idea called **propaganda by the deed**. This expressed his call for anarchists to **take action** (including the use of **violence**) to **overthrow** **capitalism** and the **state**.
- His **justification** was that because the **state**, **capitalism** and the **legal system** were all **designed** to uphold each other's interests, only **radical acts** could help to **weaken** and ultimately **overthrow** them.
- **Bakunin** believed that these acts would help to **rally support** behind the anarchist cause by **increasing** workers' **awareness** of their oppression.

Bakunin referred to deeds as *"the most popular, the most potent, and the most irresistible form of propaganda."*

Goldman
- **Goldman** agreed that **breaking the law** was **essential** to achieve anarchism. She wrote: *"No great idea in its beginning can ever be within the law"*.
- She used Friedrich Nietzsche's concept of the **state** as a **"cold monster"** that is **incapable** of acting **morally** or in the **interests** of its citizens.
- **Goldman** felt that **political participation**, e.g. voting in elections, had **failed** to make a difference to **ordinary people's lives**.
- She saw **violence** as a **tactical solution**, as an alternative to political participation, to **enable anarchism**.

All anarchists believe that the state has a coercive relationship with individuals.

Proudhon
- In contrast to Goldman, **Proudhon** believed that the best way of achieving anarchism would be a **peaceful rejection** of the state.
- He thought this would be **inevitable** if the principles of **mutualism** could be established.

Rocker
- **Rocker** also believed the state should be overcome by **peaceful** forms of **collective action**, such as **strikes**, rather than more violent means.
- He **condemned** the plot of fellow anarchists to set off a **bomb** during the Lord Mayor's show in London in **1909**, **disapproving** of the use of **violence** to **advance** the **anarchist movement**.

Non-core Political Ideas — Anarchism

Collectivist Anarchism

Mutual aid is an economic system focused on altruism and collective interests

1) **Proudhon** believed that if economic problems could be *"solved in such a way that individual and collective interests are identical"*, then the result would be *"a state of total liberty or anarchy."*
2) Proudhon proposed an alternative system of **co-operatives** where **negotiation** is based on **collective**, rather than **individual** interests. People would offer their **goods** and **services** to **one another** in a form of **mutually beneficial exchange**.
3) This **principle** that **society** and the **economy** should be based on **altruism** (see p.108) is called **mutual aid**.

Kropotkin — **Kropotkin**, an **anarcho-communist**, shared a similar level of faith in **mutual aid**. He made what he described as a **'scientific'** case for mutual aid. This drew on Charles Darwin's theory of **natural selection** to argue that **societies** characterised by **collaboration** were more likely to **succeed**.

The idea of mutual aid has been adopted by many collectivist anarchists.

Mutualists want to abolish exploitative private property

1) **Mutualists** believe that abolishing **exploitative** forms of **private property** is the key to dismantling the **negative impact** of **capitalism**.
2) Because it is the **only** system that **truly liberates** every member of society, **Proudhon** believed that **anarchy** is the **most orderly** form of society.
3) His great faith in **human nature** meant that he saw anarchy as the **only rational outcome** that **every member** of society would **support** once they had witnessed **mutualism** in action.

Some sub-strands see labour and wages as the source of oppression

1) **Anarcho-communists** and **anarcho-syndicalists** believe that the **labour market** and the **wage system** also need to be **abolished**.

Anarcho-communism
Goldman, **Kropotkin** and **Bakunin** all saw **wages** as a form of **slavery** that forced workers to undertake **labour** for **much less** than the work's true **value**.

Anarcho-syndicalism
Rudolf Rocker, an anarcho-syndicalist, proposed that the labour market and the wage system could be brought down by **mass union-led strikes**, which he called **solidarity**.

Anarcho-syndicalist ideas influenced the Solidarity movement that formed the basis of Polish opposition to the Soviet Union in the 1980s.

2) **Proudhon**, a **mutualist**, instead proposed the creation of a **People's Bank** that would issue **fair wages**, eventually **replacing** the state.

Quick Questions

1) Which anarchist thinker believed that a scientific case could be made for mutual aid?
2) What is the difference between anarcho-communism and anarcho-syndicalism?
3) Which anarchist thinker described the state as a 'cold monster', and what does this label mean?
4) What did Bakunin mean by the idea of propaganda by the deed?
5) Which anarchist thinkers advocate violence, and which prefer peaceful means?
6) Why do some regard anarchism as a utopian ideology?

Revision Task

Test your knowledge of collectivist anarchism by **defining** the following key terms and concepts:
- Mutual aid
- Direct action
- Solidarity
- Human sociability

I'm a big collectivist — I have a full set of shiny Kropotkins...
Collectivist anarchist ideas are pretty varied, but a core idea is that we need each other to liberate ourselves from oppression.

Individualist Anarchism

When we broke up, my ex said I thought the universe revolved around me... Perhaps I'm an individualist anarchist after all.

Individualist anarchists also have a lot of faith in human nature

1) **Max Stirner** argued that **individuals** are so **rational** that they can live **autonomously**, without the **influence** of the **state** or the **protection** of **collective organisations**.
2) In **Stirner's** view, individuals form the **moral centre** of their own universes, meaning that they should be able to **define** their own **purpose** and make their own **decisions**.

Like collectivist anarchists, individualists see the state as an immoral and illegitimate authority that removes humans' autonomy and liberty.

- Individualists' **optimism** leads them to believe that individuals can **reject the state** through their own **insurrection**, rather than through collective revolution.
- **Stirner** wrote: *"Whoever will be free must make himself free"*. He believed that while **revolution** aimed to **collectively** form new **arrangements** for **society**, **insurrection** would allow **individuals** to **arrange themselves**.
- His concept of **insurrection** encourages individuals to **free themselves** from **state influence**, such as **taxation** and the **legal system**, in pursuit of **liberty**.

Key Terms — **insurrection**: Acts of individual resistance against an established power (e.g. the state).

Stirner argued that self-interest should be at the heart of an anarchist society

1) **Stirner** was **deeply suspicious** of **collectivist ideas** because of his views on **individuals** as their own **moral centre**.
2) In a **radical departure** from collectivist anarchists' views on **human sociability** (see p.111), Stirner argued that individuals should be allowed to **exploit one another** while pursuing their own **gain** — this is the basis of his theory of **egoism**.
3) He wrote: *"We have only one relation to each other, that of usableness"*.
4) However, the **end goal** of Stirner's philosophy is the establishment of **unions of egoists** — **voluntary groups** that **enable** individuals to pursue their own **goals** in an **orderly way**.

Although his ideas are based on very different assumptions about human nature, Stirner's vision of unions of egoists shares some similarities with the mutual aid proposed by collectivist anarchists like Kropotkin and Proudhon.

Individualist anarchists value private property and accept some inequality...

1) **Stirner** saw **property ownership** as **crucial** to **freeing** individuals from **state power**. He wrote that *"my power is my property"* and saw a person's private property as an extension of the **self**.
2) Because individualist anarchists **embrace private property**, they also **accept inequality** of both **outcome** and **opportunity**.
3) As such, they have a **less egalitarian** view of **society** and the **economy**.
4) Stirner **opposed** any **collectivist solution** to social and economic issues: *"the people's good fortune is my misfortune!"*

...but they disagree over the role of capitalism

Egoists
- Although he recognised the **value of property**, Stirner **rejected capitalism**, which he saw as another form of **authority** that **coerces** individuals into pursuing interests **other** than their own.
- He described capitalism as *"machine-like labour"* that *"amounts to the same thing as slavery"*.

Anarcho-capitalists
- **Anarcho-capitalists** share similar assumptions about **human nature** to Stirner, but are **in favour** of **capitalism**.
- They believe that without the **overarching interference** of the **state**, **capitalism** will be the **best** way of **maximising** individuals' **autonomy** and **liberty**.

Essay Plan

For Edexcel students: To what extent do individualist anarchists depart from the ideas of collectivist anarchists? [24]

For AQA students: 'Individualist anarchists have very few ideas in common with collectivist anarchists.' Analyse and evaluate this statement with reference to the anarchist thinkers that you have studied. [25]

Using the grid on p.298, **plan** an answer to one of the essay questions above.

I've heard arachno-capitalists make a lot of money on the web...

This Stirner quote neatly sums up how he was different to collectivists: *"We do not aspire to communal life but to a life apart"*.

Non-core Political Ideas — Anarchism

Comparing Anarchist Ideas

Right, you know the deal by now. Here's a lovely page of all the overlap and disagreements. Get a copy pinned on your wall.

A-Co = Anarcho-communist, Mut = Mutualist, A-Sy = Anarcho-syndicalist, Ego = Egoist, A-Ca = Anarcho-capitalist.

Human Nature

	Collectivist Anarchists			Individualist Anarchists	
	A-Co	Mut	A-Sy	Ego	A-Ca
Humans are **rational**, **capable** creatures who can **live autonomously without** the need for any form of **government**, **state** or **political power**. Human **rationality** means that they can **co-exist** in peace **without** the need for a **legal system**. Human nature has been **corrupted** by **state power**.	✓	✓	✓	✓	✓
Humans are naturally **sociable** and **co-operative**.	✓	✓	✓		
Humans are **inherently competitive** beings.				✓	✓

State

	A-Co	Mut	A-Sy	Ego	A-Ca
The state has **no legitimate authority** over human beings. The state's **interference** with **property** is a **deliberate attempt** to **limit** its subjects' **freedom** and **autonomy**. All forms of **political power** should be **rejected**.	✓	✓	✓	✓	✓
The state can **only be overthrown** by **collective action**. The **state** and **capitalism** exist as **interdependent forms of oppression**. The state will **ultimately** be **replaced** by mutual aid co-operatives.	✓	✓	✓		
The state can **only be overthrown** by a revolution that **breaks the existing legal system**. Acts of **violence** can be **justified** to overthrow the **state** and **capitalism**.	✓				
The **power** of the state can be **weakened** by **union-led mass strike** action, known as **solidarity**.			✓		
The **state** can be **rejected**, and ultimately **dissolved**, by **peaceful means**.		✓			
Individual acts of **insurrection** are enough to **reject** the state. The state will **ultimately** be **replaced** by **voluntary unions of egoists**.				✓	✓

Society

	A-Co	Mut	A-Sy	Ego	A-Ca
An **ideal**, **utopian** society would be one **without** any form of **political power**, including a **legal system**. A **stateless society** would **maximise liberty** and **autonomy**. **Education** is **important** to help people to **understand** the extent of their **oppression by the state**.	✓	✓	✓	✓	✓
An anarchist society should be made up of **co-operative organisations** based on the **principle** of **mutual aid**. There is a **scientific basis** for arguing that societies based on **mutual aid** are more likely to be **successful**. Anarchism will help to achieve **true equality of outcome** and **opportunity** in society.	✓	✓	✓		
An anarchist society should be based on the **principle of egoism**. Individuals **owe nothing** to each other.				✓	✓

Economy

	A-Co	Mut	A-Sy	Ego	A-Ca
The state has **no legitimate claim** to **private property**, which makes **taxation** and other **economic interventions** forms of **theft**.	✓	✓	✓	✓	✓
Capitalism is an **additional form of oppression** that, along with the state, **prevents** individuals from enjoying **free** and **autonomous** lives. **Paid employment** is a form of **slavery**.	✓	✓	✓	✓	
Private property must be **abolished**. As well as abolishing private property, people must **overthrow** both the **wage system** and the **labour market** if **capitalism** is to be **dismantled**.	✓	✓	✓		
Abolishing private property will be **enough** to achieve **equality of outcome** and the **dissolution** of both the **state** and **capitalism**.		✓			
Collective organisations and **systemic economic change** aren't needed — instead, **individuals** can **liberate themselves** by **refusing to comply** with the state's **economic interventions**, including **taxation**. **Private property** ownership is at the **heart** of individuals' ability to **resist** the **state**.				✓	✓
Once the **state** has been **rejected**, **capitalism** will be returned to its **true status** as an economic system that **liberates**, rather than **enslaves**, **individuals**.					✓

I think some 0f tHe LeT┤e®s in +hIs Tip may be IndiViduaList An@r©h1sts...

OK, this one's a little complicated. But, be honest, did you really expect things to be clear-cut when dealing with anarchists?

Non-core Political Ideas — Anarchism

Non-core Political Ideas — Ecologism

Ecologism

Unlike the eco cycle on my dishwasher, I promise this section won't take 4 hours to get through. However, there's plenty to get through, so try to find a comfy spot to sit or curl up in and let's get cracking. Ooh, a good ol' cuppa might be a good idea too.

Ecologism aims to **re-balance** the relationship between **humans** and the **environment**

1) **Ecology** is the **study** of the **relationships** between **living beings** (including humans) and their **natural environment**.
2) **Ecologism** is the **application** of the insights gained from studying these relationships to **political**, **social** and **economic issues**.

Ecologism has **three** main strands

Deep Green Ecology
- **Deep green ecology** (also called '**the dark green movement**') wants the **state**, **society** and **economy** to be built around **ecocentrism** (see next page).
- Deep green ecology places the **natural world** at the heart of all decisions. It requires a **radical re-assessment** of **capitalism**, the **law** and **human culture**.

Key Thinkers:
Aldo Leopold (1887-1948)   Rachel Carson (1907-1964)   E. F. Schumacher (1911-1977)

Social Ecology
- **Social ecology** is underpinned by the view that **humans' abuse** of the **environment** is **interconnected** with other forms of **social injustice**.
- Social ecology is a **broad ideological movement** containing **three sub-strands**:

    1) **Eco-anarchism** — a sub-strand of social ecology that regards the **self-serving ineffectiveness** of the **state** as the **major obstacle** to **sustainability**.
    2) **Eco-socialism** — a sub-strand of social ecology that blames **environmental degradation** on **capitalism**.
    3) **Eco-feminism** — a sub-strand of social ecology that sees **environmental problems** as the result of **male desires** for **consumption**, **growth** and **profit**.

Social ecology is on the Edexcel specification, but it doesn't feature in AQA. It's still a good idea to know about its key ideas and its similarities and differences with the other strands.

Key Thinkers:
Murray Bookchin (1921-2006)   Carolyn Merchant (b. 1936)

Murray Bookchin was an eco-anarchist and eco-socialist thinker, while Carolyn Merchant is an eco-feminist thinker.

Shallow Green Ecology
- **Shallow green ecology** (also known as '**the light green movement**') is based on the **key idea** that **gradual efforts** to **improve conservation** are the way forward.
- Shallow green thinkers believe this can achieve the **level of sustainability** needed to **restore** a **positive relationship** between **humans** and the **environment**.
- Rather than overhauling the **state** and **economy**, they argue that **governments**, **businesses**, **voluntary organisations** and **individuals** should **collaborate** to find **solutions** to **environmental problems**.

Jonathon Porritt (b. 1950) isn't a named key thinker on the spec, but his ideas illustrate this strand

Ecologism

Ecologism critiques mechanistic views of the world

1) Mechanistic views see the world as a **machine** that exists to **serve the purposes** and **interests** of **humans**.

2) Ecologists from **all three strands** believe that humans have placed **too much emphasis** on their own **short-term interests** when considering their **relationship** with the **natural world**.

3) Ecologism **criticises** the **anthropocentric** nature of the mechanistic theory.

Followers of the mechanistic theory believe that the component parts of the world-machine aren't intrinsically linked together. So one component of the machine (such as the environment) can be damaged without causing harm to other components, such as humanity. This idea gained popularity in the 17th and 18th centuries during the Enlightenment period, which placed humans at the moral centre of the universe.

ANTHROPOCENTRISM is a term used by ecologists to describe decision-making processes that place the interests of humans above the interests of other living beings and the environment.

4) **Holism** is an **alternative** to anthropocentrism.

HOLISM is the belief that the natural world should be viewed as an interconnected whole, where humanity is an equally important component as other living beings. Supporters of holism believe that political and economic decisions should seek to balance these interests to preserve biodiversity.

biodiversity
The number and variety of living organisms that exist in a particular place.

Key Terms

5) **Deep green ecologists** and **social ecologists** believe that humanity's **abuse** of the environment requires a more **radical** approach to **replace** anthropocentrism — **ecocentrism**.

ECOCENTRISM is the idea that environmental interests should be placed above humanity's interests when making political and economic decisions.

Ecologists seek to improve environmental consciousness

1) Through **improving** people's **environmental consciousness**, ecologists hope to **restore** the **intrinsic relationship** between **humankind** and **nature**.

2) All ecologists promote the idea of **environmental ethics**. In doing so, they question the **authority** of the **state** and **human society** to **dominate nature**.

Evgeni's attempts to improve environmental consciousness were off to a strong start

They disagree over how to achieve sustainability

1) **Deep green ecologists** and **social ecologists** argue that **traditional economics** cannot achieve **sustainability** and call for **radical, post-materialist** changes to the **economy** and **society**.

Post-materialism
The belief that humans need to move beyond the desire to acquire and consume material goods.

2) **Shallow green ecologists** advocate **green capitalism**, which they regard as a more **realistic** and **efficient** way of achieving **sustainability**.

Green capitalism
An economic idea that seeks to harness the power of capitalism for environmental purposes.

My shirt keeps getting mysterious marks on it — it's sus-stain-able...

As you can see, I was so inspired by these ecological ideas that I had a go at rewilding the bottom of that last page. Why not leave the book open in the sunshine and see if it attracts any beasties? Maybe you'll end up radicalising some ladybirds...

Deep Green Ecology

Personally I would have liked them to be a little more specific on the shade of green for the name of this movement. Perhaps something a bit more evocative? Emerald ecology sounds really classy, but alas, deep green ecology is what's stuck.

Deep green ecologists **reject** the idea that **nature** exists for **humankind**

- A **core belief** among deep green ecologists is **biocentric equality** — that **all living things** have **equal value**.
- As a result, they argue that **humankind** must live in a state of **harmony** and **respect** with the **natural world**.
- Because nature is **interconnected**, all **human action**s have **consequences** for the **environment**. This means that humanity needs to **re-consider** every aspect of its **social**, **political** and **economic existence** if it is to **end** its **abuse** of the **environment**.

> **ALDO LEOPOLD** emphasised how humans must be in **harmony** with **all** of **nature** by comparing it to a person — *"you cannot cherish his right hand and chop off his left"*. This belief illustrates the deep green ecologist view that nature is **fundamentally interconnected**.

They believe humans have been **alienated** by **traditional economics**...

1) According to deep green ecologists, it is an **inbuilt impulse** (as well as a **rational method** of **self-preservation**) for humans to **love** and **sustain** the **natural world**.
2) However, they believe that **traditional capitalist economics** has **tricked** humanity into thinking that **destroying the natural world** is **necessary** to gain a **higher standard** of living.
3) Because **traditional capitalist economics** promotes **consumerism**, humans have begun to **consume** and **exploit** the natural world. Humans also **forget** that their **survival** depends on the **health** of the **natural world**.

...and that **existing political, economic** and **social structures** can't help

- Deep green ecologists believe that **efforts** to protect the environment **within existing political, economic and social structures** are **bound to fail**.
- All deep green ecologists believe that the **extent** of humans' **destruction** of the environment means that **fundamental, wide-ranging change is essential**.

E. F. Schumacher
1) **Schumacher** proposed the adoption of **Buddhist economics** to replace the **materialistic consumerism** created by traditional capitalism.
2) Rather than attempting to **innovate** to make human life more **convenient**, Buddhist economics focuses on encouraging humanity to live **within its means** and only to consume the **minimum** that is **necessary for survival**.
3) Schumacher wrote *"Any intelligent fool can make things bigger, more complex, and more violent"*. He believed it was **brave** and **innovative** to make things **smaller**, **simpler** and **less violent**.

Schumacher criticised the dominance of urban interests in modern life, calling for a re-balancing in favour of rural interests.

Aldo Leopold
Leopold argued that **conservation** could **never** succeed under the existing **economic system**. He believed there would be too many vested **corporate** and **government interests** that would **oppose** the level of action **necessary** to restore **biodiversity**.

Leopold argued **industrialism** should be replaced by 'the land ethic'

1) Based on the idea of **biocentric equality**, 'the land ethic' re-positions humankind as an **equal partner** of the environment, rather than as a **destructive consumer**.
2) **Leopold** wrote that the land ethic changes humanity's status *"from conqueror of the land-community to plain member and citizen of it"*.
3) In practical terms, Leopold argued the land ethic **requires humankind** to play an **active role** in **wilderness protection** and **wildlife management**.

Leopold referred to society as a biotic community made up of all living things.

Non-core Political Ideas — Ecologism

Deep Green Ecology

Rachel Carson wanted the state and citizens to help achieve environmentalism

Carson believed that a combination of **tightening regulations** and **grassroots activism** could allow the aims of **environmentalism** to be achieved.

Key Terms
environmentalism — A political ideology whose primary aim is the preservation of the environment.

Regulations
1) In particular, Carson called on the state to **outlaw** the use of **pesticides** in agriculture. She wrote about how the attempt to *"control a few unwanted species"* had *"contaminated the entire environment"*, as **other species** were **harmed** by the use of pesticides.
2) Because **pesticides kill insects** that form part of the **Earth's biodiversity**, and have **knock-on effects** on other species, she considered their impact **comparable to murder**. Carson believed that there wouldn't be *"peace among men whose hearts delight in killing any living creature"*.
3) She campaigned for the creation of **environmental protection agencies** to oversee the **sustainable management** of resources.
4) Her belief that *"In nature, nothing exists alone"* illustrates the deep green ecologist view that nature is **fundamentally interconnected**.

Katya had really embraced deep green ecology

Grassroots Activism
Carson saw the **state** as part of the **problem** of **environmental destruction**. Because of this, she believed that **grassroots activism** by ordinary citizens was **necessary** to put **pressure** on the **political** and **economic** systems to **change**.

Schumacher focused on using technology to engineer sustainability

1) Rather than aiming to **generate profits** and **maximise financial efficiency**, Schumacher believed that **technology** should be designed in ways that **promote** the **health**, **beauty** and **permanence** of both humans and the natural world.
2) He believed that if **individuals** had **access** to appropriate **technology**, they would be **empowered** to **live sustainably** and **healthily**, without needing to **rely** on **large corporations**.
3) Schumacher questioned the **assumption** that **sustainable global development** should involve the **transfer** of **technology** and **economic models** from **developed** countries to **less developed** countries.
4) Instead, he argued that **less developed** countries should **create** their own **models of development** that are **more localised** and **less urbanised**.

Quick Questions

1) Which ecologist thinker advocated Buddhist economics, and how does this differ from traditional capitalism?
2) What is meant by the term biocentric equality?
3) What is the difference between anthropocentrism and ecocentrism?

Revision Task

Practise your **analysis** skills by explaining why deep green ecologists hold the following views:
1) *Technology can provide sustainability*   2) *Pesticides are unjust*
3) *Buddhist economics is preferable to traditional capitalism*

With names like Car-son and Schumacher, you'd think this was Silverstone...
I think it's safe to assume neither would have been a huge fan of motorsports though, what with the emissions and all. But I hope you haven't just raced through all the information on these pages — take a pit stop and make sure it's all sunk in.

Non-core Political Ideas — Ecologism

Social Ecology

Social ecology and all its sub-strands are concerned with the intersections between environmental issues and social oppression. So, shall we dive into the details? See what I did there? So, shall, social? Eh? I crack me up.

Social ecologists think **environmental damage** is linked to **oppressive power**

Social ecology is based on the **belief** that humankind's **destruction** of the natural world is **connected** with other **oppressive power relationships** in society.

Murray Bookchin
1) Bookchin saw **environmental degradation** as a form of **social oppression** like those based on **economic**, **ethnic**, **cultural** and **gender conflicts**.
2) Bookchin argued that people who are most **severely affected** by **ecological problems** are the **victims of these conflicts**.
3) The **corporations** and **governments** in countries that have **traditionally** caused the **worst ecological damage** are often **controlled** by the **most powerful groups** in society. As a result of this, Bookchin argued in his **eco-anarchist** and **eco-socialist analysis** that they have **worked** to **free** themselves of the **consequences** of climate change.

Carolyn Merchant
1) Similarly, **Merchant's eco-feminism** drew a **parallel** between **gender oppression** (see page 123) and the **mistreatment** of the **environment**.
2) Merchant wrote about how **men** consider **women** and nature as **psychological** and **recreational resources**. This means that men **exploit** women and nature in **similar ways**, using them as **sources of pleasure** and **enjoyment**.

They **reject** the idea that **capitalism** can serve **environmental interests**

Bookchin
1) Because it is an **economic system** based on the **principle of growth**, **Bookchin** described **capitalism** as *"inherently anti-ecological"*.
2) He believed it was **impossible** to make capitalism **benefit the environment**, stating *"attempts to 'green' capitalism, to make it 'ecological', are doomed by the very nature of the system as a system of endless growth."*
3) **Bookchin** believed that capitalism **distorts** humans' **judgement**.
4) He wrote about how *"needs are tailored by the mass media to create a public demand for utterly useless commodities"*, which makes people think that they need to **acquire** and **consume** material goods to feel **fulfilled**.

> This rejection of capitalism represents a clear difference between social ecology and shallow green ecology, whose thinkers promote the idea of green capitalism (see page 116).

Inspired by her favourite social ecologist, Julie took a break from revision

Merchant
1) Merchant agreed with Bookchin, taking issue with *"the costs of competition, aggression and domination"* produced by capitalism.
2) She argued that democracy and capitalism have directly **depended** on the **exploitation** of **natural resources** such as **metals**, **soils**, **grasses** and **timber**.

They believe **society** needs **re-structuring** to **protect** the **environment**

1) Like **deep green ecologists**, **social ecologists** propose a **radical re-structuring** of **society**, the **economy** and the **state** to **save** Earth from **environmental degradation**.
2) In place of the **destructive influence** of **capitalism**, **Bookchin** and **Merchant** argued that **lessons** should be learned from **ecology**.
3) Where **capitalism** promotes **competition**, they believed that **ecology** points us towards societies based on **interdependence** and **co-existence**.

> **Bookchin** advocated for **environmental communalism** — a blend of **eco-anarchism** and **eco-socialism** in which people live in **small**, **collaborative communities** based on the **shared principles** of **equality** and **conservation**.

Non-core Political Ideas — Ecologism

Social Ecology

> Both **Merchant** and **Bookchin** were **suspicious** of **traditional democracy**

1) Merchant expressed a **moral concern** with **participatory** (**traditional**) **democracy** because it **prioritises** short-term **human interests** over longer-term issues of **sustainability**.

2) In place of traditional democracy, **Bookchin** favoured **libertarian municipalism** (or **face-to-face assembly democracy**). This is made up of **localised, non-hierarchical discussion forums** that aim to **build consensus** and a sense of **common purpose**.

> Social ecologists are also committed to **biocentric equality**

Bookchin and Merchant **rejected anthropocentrism** (see p.116) and wanted to **restore** humankind's **equal status** with other forms of life.

Biocentric equality is the belief that all living things are equal (see p.117).

Merchant's environmental ethics gives "**non-human nature**" forms the role of "**free autonomous agents**" whose **welfare** should be at the **heart** of **political decision-making**.

Bookchin rejected the existence of **hierarchies**, stating "*there are no hierarchies in nature*". He believed **human hierarchical thinking** had **imposed** these ideas on the **natural world**.

> Social ecologists believe **humans** are **capable** of protecting the environment

1) Although **highly sceptical** of the **state** and the **existing economic system**, social ecologists are **optimistic** about humans' **capacity** to create a **better** and **more sustainable society**.
2) Like other ecologist thinkers, both **Merchant** and **Bookchin** considered **humankind** to be a **highly rational** and **capable** species.
3) **Bookchin** believed that humans should use their **unique capabilities** as a species to "*create our own world*". He warned that we must not follow "*mindless customs and destructive prejudices*", and instead use **reason** and **collaboration** to create a better way of living.

Quick Questions

1) What is the core belief of social ecology?
2) Why did Carolyn Merchant reject participatory democracy as the only method of political decision-making?
3) What is meant by 'biocentric equality'?
4) Which thinker supported libertarian municipalism?
5) What role did Merchant say that 'non-human nature' should play in society?
6) Summarise social ecologists' views on human nature in one sentence.
7) Why did Bookchin criticise social and economic hierarchies?

Exam Practice

Practise your **analysis** skills by identifying and explaining one agreement AND one disagreement between deep green ecologists and social ecologists in the following areas:

1) *Human nature*   2) *The state*   3) *Society*   4) *The economy*

Top Tip for Politicians #542: Write your manifestos on recycled paper...
Though if you want to court the social ecologist vote, the ideas will need to be a bit more radical, and certainly not recycled. As Bookchin said, we don't want to mindlessly replicate what's been done before. Maybe take a leaf out of his book...

Non-core Political Ideas — Ecologism

Shallow Green Ecology

Aaah, shallow green ecology, the local swimming baths to deep green ecology's wild oceans... Similar, but nowhere near as radical.

Shallow green ecologists agree **our treatment** of the **Earth** risks **mass extinction**

- Like **deep green** and **social ecologists**, **shallow green ecologists** call for **humans** to learn to **live in harmony** with the **Earth** on a **sustainable** basis.
- They also blame **consumerism** for **encouraging** the **destruction** of the **natural world**.
- **Jonathon Porritt** has stated that consumerism is *"more powerful than any religion"* and has spread all over the globe.

They argue existing structures of **the state** and **capitalism** can **deliver sustainability**

1) **Shallow green ecologists** advocate **green capitalism** (p.116) as a **solution** to the **environmental crisis**.

   - Because **the state** has **control** over its country's **institutions**, the **capacity to influence market conditions** and **diplomatic links** overseas, shallow green ecologists argue that it can be a **helpful tool** for **advancing** the **environmental agenda**.
   - They believe that if the state **introduces** the right **regulations**, and if **consumers** begin to **demand higher standards** of **environmental ethics**, **corporations** will begin to see that **sustainability** aligns with their own **self-interest**.

   The work of shallow green ecologist Kate Raworth has influenced efforts to promote urban sustainability through subsidised cycling and public transportation networks in cities such as Amsterdam. Raworth has argued that state interventions in society and the economy should preserve a balance between ecological aims and social welfare.

2) Shallow green ecologists therefore want to **utilise** the **profit motive**. This is the idea that companies' **desire for profit** produces **market conditions** where companies attempt to **compete** over things like **price** and **quality**.

   Porritt has been an influential figure in the development of the Green Party in the UK. This illustrates his belief that ecologists need to work with, rather than seek to overthrow, conventional political institutions.

3) **Porritt** has argued that the **profit motive** will **encompass sustainability**. This is based on his belief that once **unlimited growth** stops providing **improvements** to people's **quality of life**, businesses will use **sustainability** as a **selling point**. He said that *"sustainability is going to become one of the key characteristics with which places want to be associated."*
4) Like **Schumacher**, Porritt has called for a **decentralised state** that **empowers individuals** and **local communities** to **take action** on climate change.

Shallow green ecologists take a **pragmatic view** of **sustainability**

- They believe **sustainability** must become a **popular goal** among **the public** and **political figures**.
- Porritt has argued that **ecologists** should make a **positive case** for **sustainability**, rather than **warning** of **impending environmental disaster** as deep green and social ecologists might.
- As a result, **shallow green ecologists** place **less emphasis** on achieving **biocentric equality** than deep green and social ecologists.
- Instead, they aim to **move towards sustainability** through **gradual, targeted actions** by the **state** and **incremental changes** to **social** and **economic** norms.
- They also state that **individuals' actions** can help to tackle the **climate crisis**.
- Porritt has called for individuals to take *"responsibility for their total environmental footprint"*, including making tough decisions like *"how many children they think are appropriate"* when starting a family.

Exam Practice

For Edexcel students: To what extent do ecologists share a common view of society? [24]
For AQA students: 'Ecologists disagree more than they agree on the theme of society.' Analyse and evaluate this statement with reference to the anarchist thinkers that you have studied. [25]
Write an **introduction** to one of the essay questions above. You can use the sentence frames on pages 299-300.

How do you water your house plants? Just Porritt on...
OK, I didn't dig very deep for that gag, but this is a page on shallow green ecology after all. I made a pragmatic choice of joke.

Comparing Ecologist Ideas

Alright, you've made it through the dense forest of information of the main section. Now let's bring it all together...

Human Nature

Idea	Deep Green	Shallow Green	Social
Humans are **rational**, **capable** creatures who have the **capacity** to **live sustainably**. Human nature has been **corrupted** by **consumerism**, **distancing** humankind from its **innate co-existence** with the **natural world**.	✓	✓	✓
Humans have **no greater value** than non-human life forms. Humans are just **one part** of an **enormous**, **highly diverse biotic community**.	✓	✓	
Human nature needs to undergo a **radical transformation** from the **anthropocentric** to the **ecocentric**.	✓		
The **competitive nature** of humanity has led to the establishment of a **hierarchy**, **unequal class** and **gender relationships**, and environmental exploitation.			✓
Humans simply need to **reconnect** with their **natural urge** to **protect** the environment. This will allow them to **oversee systems** that serve both their **social** and **economic** interests and the interests of **sustainability**.			✓

State

Idea	Deep Green	Shallow Green	Social
The **state** has been **partly responsible** for **failures** to achieve **sustainability**.	✓	✓	✓
The state is a **perpetrator** of environmental **degradation**. It needs to be **replaced** by a **radical new system** of government that can **safeguard** the interests of the **natural world**. Any **attempts** at conservation within the **existing political** and **economic system** will inevitably **fail**. **Environmental ethics** should **replace** anthropocentric legal systems. The use of **pesticides** should be **outlawed**.	✓	✓	
Traditional forms of **participatory democracy** are **immoral** because they **prioritise** short-term **human interests** at the **expense** of the **natural world**. The **centralised state** should be **replaced** by **libertarian municipalism**.		✓	
Participatory democracy should be used as a **means** for achieving ecologists' goals.			✓

Society

Idea	Deep Green	Shallow Green	Social
Local communities should be empowered to **deliver sustainability**, actively **protect wildernesses** and **uphold biodiversity**. **Mechanistic world views** need to be **challenged** through **education** and **campaigning**. **Nature** does not exist for the **convenience** of humankind.	✓	✓	✓
Society should be **characterised** by the principles of **biocentric equality**, **holism** and **the land ethic**. Society should **learn lessons** from **ecology** and be based on **co-existence**, rather than **competition**.	✓	✓	
Inflicting **environmental damage** is a form of **social oppression**. Men from **dominant social groups** treat **women** and **nature** in a similarly **exploitative manner**.			✓
Individual members of society have the power to **enact meaningful environmental change** through their own **behaviour** and **campaigning**.			✓

Economy

Idea	Deep Green	Shallow Green	Social
Consumerism and **materialism** have played a significant part in **destroying** the **environment**. **Unregulated capitalism** is **incompatible** with **sustainability**. An **ecologist economy** would be **far less focused** on **growth** and **acquisition**.	✓	✓	✓
Its reliance on **growth** and **materialism** means that **capitalism** can **never** deliver **sustainability**. The **economy** should be based on the **principle** that humans should **consume** only the **bare minimum** that is **necessary** for their **survival**.	✓	✓	
Capitalism should be replaced with **communalism**. **Large companies'** dominance of technology has **prevented** individuals from living in a natural state of **self-sufficiency**. **Democratising** access to appropriate technologies will **reduce** the need for a **market economy**. **Social hierarchies** have allowed **dominant groups** to gain **disproportionate rewards** from **capitalism** while **destroying** the **environment** in the process.		✓	
With the right **regulations** in place, and a significant amount **of social pressure**, **green capitalism** is possible.			✓

Green all the green on this green, I can barely green of anything green...
Don't leave this page open on a lawn — you may never find the book again. That'll certainly put a dampener on your revision.

Non-core Political Ideas — Ecologism

Feminism

You're almost done with the non-core Political ideas. It's time to buckle in and tackle these seven pages on feminism.

There are **four main strands** of feminism

Liberal Feminism

- **Liberal feminism** is based on the liberal principles of **formal equality**, **rights** and the **rational** power of the individual.
- Liberal feminism seeks to **elevate women** to an **equal status** with men in **society** and the **economy**.

Key Thinker — Charlotte Perkins Gilman (1860-1935)

The liberal key thinkers Mary Wollstonecraft and Betty Friedan are also important liberal feminist thinkers. More of their ideas are covered on pages 50 and 52.

Charlotte Perkins Gilman has also been described as a socialist feminist.

Socialist Feminism

- **Socialist feminism** is based on the belief that the oppression of women is **interconnected** with **capitalist oppression** of the **working classes**.
- Socialist feminists see **economic change** as necessary for **women's liberation**.

Key Thinkers — Simone de Beauvoir (1908-1986) and Sheila Rowbotham (b. 1943)

Radical Feminism

Radical feminism is based on the view that **women's oppression** is so **deep-rooted** in society that only a **radical overhaul** will be able to **liberate** them from **gender inequality**.

Key Thinker — Kate Millett (1934-2017)

Post-modern Feminism

- **Post-modern feminism** places great importance on the idea of **intersectionality**.
- **Post-modern feminists** believe that women experience oppression **differently** based on aspects of their **identity**. Oppression due to **sexuality**, **race** and **class** (as well as **other social categories**) **overlap** with **gender-based** oppression.
- Because of this, they believe that attempts to resolve these issues will require **solutions** that **tackle multiple forms** of **oppression** at once.

Key Thinker — bell hooks (1952-2021)

bell hooks' given name was Gloria Jean Watkins. bell hooks is a pen name that is always written in lower case.

Key Terms

intersectionality
The idea that oppression is often based on multiple social categories, such as gender, race and class.

gender
A social categorisation based on characteristics associated with masculinity and femininity. Ideas about gender vary over time and across societies.

sex
The biological characteristics associated with males and females.

Feminist thinkers can also be divided into **two** categories

1) **EQUALITY FEMINISTS** believe that women and men are **essentially the same** in terms of their **true nature**.
2) They believe that **differences** exist because of **social structures** (e.g. **gender stereotypes**) and **economic structures** (e.g. **unequal pay**).
3) They believe that if these structures can be **reformed** so that there is **formal equality** and **equality of opportunity**, women will be able to **reach** their **potential**.

Charlotte Perkins Gilman and Simone de Beauvoir are both equality feminists.

1) **DIFFERENCE FEMINISTS** believe that women and men have **fundamentally different natures**. They believe that while **men** are **inherently competitive** and **power-seeking**, **women** are more **co-operative**.
2) They believe **society** and the **economy** should therefore **change** to **reflect** these **differences**, allowing **women** to create a **different path** to **men**.
3) Difference feminists believe in **essentialism**. This is the belief that the **biological differences** between women and men explain their **different characters**.

Difference feminists are sometimes described as 'cultural feminists'. Their ideas tend to include the belief that women need to establish a feminine culture that challenges the dominance of masculine traits in many cultural aspects.

Feminism

Feminism has gone through eras called 'waves'

Feminism has had several 'waves', which represent **stages** in the ideology's **development**. The waves were:
- **FIRST WAVE (19th Century to mid 20th Century)** — **Charlotte Perkins Gilman** was part of this wave. It focused primarily on **legal** and **political equality**.
- **SECOND WAVE (1960s-1980s)** — **Simone de Beauvoir**, **Kate Millett** and **Sheila Rowbotham** were part of this wave. It focused on **extending** these **rights** to women's **private lives**.
- **THIRD WAVE (1990s onwards)** — **bell hooks** was part of this wave. It focused on providing **alternative perspectives** on the **experiences** of **different groups of women**.

Feminists have a common goal of ending patriarchy but disagree on how to do it

Liberal feminism
- **Liberal feminists** believe in women's **ability** to **improve their own position** through **education** and **campaigning**. **Charlotte Perkins Gilman** believed that the **state's role** should be to **help** women's liberation through **gradual legislative change** that will lead to **political** and **legal equality**.
- **Liberal feminists** are **more accepting of capitalism** than other strands. Like with the state, they believe that **reforms** to the **workplace** and **economic regulation** will be **enough** to allow women to enjoy the same **opportunities** as men.

Socialist feminism
Socialist feminists believe that **women's liberation** depends on **dismantling capitalism**, which they consider to be one of the **root causes** of **patriarchy**.

Radical and post-modern feminism
Radical and **post-modern feminists** see the **state** as an **instrument of patriarchy**. They believe that the state won't be able to **reflect women's interests** unless it is **radically overhauled**.

Key Terms

patriarchy
A system where men hold the power. It is used to refer to political, social and economic structures that are dominated by, and reflect the interests of, men. It literally translates from Greek as 'rule of the father'.

Not that kind of instrument

They also disagree over the type of change that is needed to liberate women

Liberal feminism
Liberal feminists believe that **legal** and **economic changes** in the **public sphere** will also **improve women's position** in the **private sphere** by putting them on an **equal footing** with men.

Radical and post-modern feminism
Radical and **post-modern feminists** believe that a **revolution** in both the **private sphere** and **public sphere** is necessary.

Radical feminists' views on the private sphere are often summed up by the quotation "***the personal is political***", which was popularised by a 1969 essay written by Carol Hanisch.

The idea that existing social and economic structures can be improved by reform and legislative change, rather than revolution, is called reformism.

Key Terms

private sphere
The parts of society where relationships are private, such as home and family life. Feminists argue that women's influence has traditionally been confined to this sphere.

public sphere
The parts of society where relationships are public, such as the workplace, the law and the media. Feminists argue that men have traditionally dominated this sphere.

Revision Task

Test your knowledge of feminism by **defining** the following key terms and concepts:
- Public sphere
- Private sphere
- Sex
- Gender
- Essentialism
- Patriarchy

Equality feminists, difference feminists — feels like I'm in a maths lesson...

Before moving on with the rest of this section, make sure that you've got a handle on the core ideas within feminism. A handy way of doing this is jotting down a few notes from this page and referring back to them as you go through the rest of the section.

Liberal Feminism

As you've probably realised by now, liberal ideas often influence other ideologies. Feminism is no different. So all that there's left to do is get a lovely hot cuppa tea and a biscuit or two before settling in to tackle this page.

Liberal feminists believe that women are equally capable and as rational as men

1) **Charlotte Perkins Gilman** wrote: *"There is no female mind. The brain is not an organ of sex."*
2) Perkins Gilman was a supporter of **Reform Darwinism**, the idea that Charles Darwin's **theory of evolution** had **overlooked** the **rational capabilities** of **female** animals. This theory **emphasised** female animals' ability to **choose** the **best-suited mate** that they can find as a **driver of evolution**.

They believe gender stereotypes prevent women from fulfilling their potential

MARY WOLLSTONECRAFT wrote that men seemed to view women as a second, lesser species, considering *"females rather as women than human creatures"*. She believed this dehumanisation reduced women to *"alluring objects"*.

1) **PERKINS GILMAN** described **society** as *"sick"* because it **forced** women to **fit** into **fixed ideas** about their **role**, especially in **domestic life**, where they were expected to be **mothers** rather than have their own **careers** and **interests**.
2) She believed that women needed to **overturn** the *"androcentric culture"* that men had developed, **rejecting** the **societal pressure** that they faced and instead pursuing their own **individual interests**.

Key Terms — androcentric culture: Where the views and interests of men are placed at the centre of a society's culture. This leads to the marginalisation of other genders.

They want to end misogyny with legislation and social change in the public sphere

Elections and legislation
- **Wollstonecraft** called for **women** to have their own **political representatives**, and **Perkins Gilman** was a prominent member of the **suffrage movement** in the USA.
- **Betty Friedan** campaigned for the state to **legislate** on **equal pay**, **maternity pay** and **abortion rights**.

> Liberal feminists call for changes to the economy, particularly in terms of women's opportunities to access the same employment as men. However, they share other liberals' belief that capitalism is the most efficient and effective economic system (p.49).

Education
- **Wollstonecraft** criticised the *"neglected education of my fellow creatures"*, which she believed was *"the grand source"* of women's **oppression**. She argued that because *"intellect will always govern"*, men would continue to trap women in *"slavish dependence"* until the two sexes received an **equal education**.
- Instead of calling for the **state** to provide **education**, Wollstonecraft and Perkins Gilman both believed that the **responsibility** should lie with **society** and **women themselves**.

Culture
- **Friedan** believed women should benefit from **positive discrimination** to help establish **true political** and **economic equality**.
- Friedan called for *"cultural channels"* such as the **media** to reflect **women's interests** and **true nature** by **focusing less** on their roles as **mothers**, **wives** and **daughters**.

Key Terms — positive discrimination: actions and policies that give an advantage to traditionally disadvantaged groups over other groups.

But they recognise that women also face discrimination in the private sphere

1) For **PERKINS GILMAN**, **sex** and **domestic economics** were **linked** — because **men dominated** the **labour market** when she was writing, **women** were **forced** into playing **passive**, **domestic roles**. She wrote: *"The labor of women in the house ... enables men to produce more wealth than they otherwise could"*.
2) **BETTY FRIEDAN** explored the **problems** faced by her generation of **highly-educated suburban women** who had **given up their careers** to become **housewives** in her book *The Feminine Mystique*. She wrote about how they were *"afraid to ask"* if domestic duties were all there was to life.

> In her famous short story *The Yellow Wallpaper*, Perkins Gilman compared women's plight to a form of imprisonment.

Non-core Political Ideas — Feminism

Socialist Feminism and Radical Feminism

Many feminists criticise capitalist economics as they see it as being completely dominated by men. Read on to find out more.

Socialist feminists see capitalism as a patriarchal economic system

SIMONE DE BEAUVOIR believed that the **economic inequalities** and **class differences** produced by **capitalism** prevented people, and women especially, from being free to **discover** their **true selves**.

SHEILA ROWBOTHAM used Marx's concept of a *"reserve army of labour"* to outline the **injustice** faced by women who worked either for **no pay** or for **low pay** in **domestic** roles or roles considered **unskilled**.

They aim to tackle the overlapping issues of class and gender oppression together

1) **De Beauvoir** criticised the *"double burden"* of **domestic responsibilities** and **low-paid work** that many **working-class women** face.
2) For **Rowbotham**, working-class women had been **prevented** from playing a **full part** in the **feminist movement** because they had been **tied down** by their **domestic duties**. She felt this left working-class women with *"neither the education nor encouragement nor leisure"* to be able to help push for **changes** in the world.
3) Once the **principles of socialism** have been established, socialist feminists believe that women will enjoy **full political** and **economic equality**. Rowbotham wrote about her end goal of *"a truly democratic society"* where every person is able to *"be brave, responsible, thinking and diligent"* and use their skills to help create a free and fair society.

Socialist feminists are divided over how their goals should be achieved

Socialist Society

1) **Rowbotham** argued that **women's liberation** is **dependent** on the establishment of a **socialist society** and **economy**, and so socialism must be achieved **before** women's true freedom could be.
2) However, **de Beauvoir** believed that it would **first** be necessary to **improve** women's rights and status under the **current system**. She wrote of how women must *"fight for the situation now"* in order for *"our dreams of socialism to come true"*.

The Family

1) **Rowbotham** was concerned with the **impact of family life** on women. She believed that **oppressed working-class men** saw the **domination** of their **wives** and **daughters** as one of their few **outlets of power** in a capitalist society.
2) **De Beauvoir didn't** believe that the **family** was an **inherently patriarchal institution**, but stressed that women should **only** enter into **marriage** and **motherhood** if those were roles that they had **actively chosen** for themselves.

Simone de Beauvoir placed more emphasis on individual women

1) As a **leading thinker** in the **existentialist movement**, de Beauvoir was focused on the capacity of **individual women** to enact change.
2) The **central belief** of the existentialist movement is that **individuals** have the **ability** to **define** the meaning of their **own existence**.
3) She criticised society's **expectation** that **women** had to **justify** their **existence** through their **relationships** with others.
4) De Beauvoir **distinguished** between **sex** and **gender**. She believed that women are inevitably affected by their biological sex, stating *"no woman can claim without bad faith to be situated beyond her sex"*. However, she believed that **gender differences** were mythical **social constructs**, writing *"one is not born, but rather becomes, a woman."*
5) She believed that **patriarchal societies** had **relegated women** to a state of *"otherness"*, where **men** are seen as the **norm**, while **women** are regarded as *"the second sex"*, a **deviation** from this norm.
6) One of de Beauvoir's key concepts was *"rapport à soi"* (self-rapport). This concept urged women to **understand**, **value** and **love** themselves, as this would allow them to live a **free** and **fulfilled** life. She encouraged women to embrace their **independence** and **refuse** *"the passivity man means to impose on her"*.

Non-core Political Ideas — Feminism

Socialist Feminism and Radical Feminism

Sheila Rowbotham considered society from a more collectivist viewpoint

1) Influenced by **Karl Marx's** ideas about a **workers' revolution** (see page 55), **Rowbotham** argued that **liberation** couldn't be achieved by **individual women** because the **forces of oppression** were **structural**.
2) She believed that women would need to "*organise in large numbers*" in order to "*become a political force*".
3) Like **bell hooks** (see page 128), **Rowbotham** criticised the **middle- and upper-class** leaders of the **feminist movement** who had **failed** to **achieve liberation** for **working-class women**.

Radical feminism rejects the belief that women can be liberated by gradual reforms

Kate Millett called for a **revolution** in the **public** and **private spheres**.

Sex and relationships

- Millett was opposed to the idea of the **traditional family**, where **women** are forced to play **secondary, submissive roles** in relation to their **fathers, brothers** and **husbands**. She believed that **undoing** the traditional family was **essential** if women were truly to be **liberated** from **oppression**.
- Millett argued that there needed to be a **revolution** in how **society** viewed **sex**. She called for an **embrace of same-sex relationships** that would make women **less reliant** on men, and for an **end** to the **sexist attitudes** that **repressed** women's **freedom** to make their own **sexual choices**.

Carmen had undergone a revolution in her private sphere

Art and culture

- Millett advanced a theory of **cultural feminism**, which stated that **women** needed to **overthrow** their **sexist portrayal** in **art** and **literature**, where they were often depicted as **reliant** on **male approval** and **attention**.
- Millett's *Sexual Politics* aimed to dismantle the **patriarchal idea** that the **differences** between men and women should be seen as **inequalities**.
- Instead, as a **difference feminist** (see page 123), she argued that **gender differences** should be **celebrated** and that women needed to **construct** a **society** and **culture** that **rewarded their characteristics**, rather than **male** ones.
- She believed that, due to the **differences** in how they were viewed **socially**, **male** and **female** were "*two cultures*" and that their "*life experiences are utterly different*". She described the **patriarchal culture** created by men as "*alien*" to women, relegating them to the position of "*subjects*" living under **male rule**.

Sexual Politics was a work of literary criticism in which Millett critiqued the portrayal of women by four prominent male authors: D. H. Lawrence, Norman Mailer, Henry Miller and Jean Genet.

Capitalism

Like **de Beauvoir** and **Rowbotham**, Millett saw **capitalism** as an **instrument of patriarchy**. However, her analysis **focused** more on the **economic power structures** that men had created to **prevent** middle- and upper-class women from **competing** with them in the **labour market**: "*the toil of working-class women ... fails to threaten the patriarchy financially or psychologically*".

Revision Task

Practise your analysis skills by **identifying** and **explaining** the similarities or differences between socialist feminists and liberal feminists on these themes:

1) *Capitalism* 2) *Equality* 3) *Society* 4) *The role of the state*

How do you turn wheat into flour in a feminist way? Millett...

It's worth remembering that the treatment of working-class women is a big issue for a few feminist thinkers. The belief that liberal feminism failed to properly consider their interests and needs has helped to start a few new feminist movements.

Non-core Political Ideas — Feminism

Post-modern Feminism

Post-modern feminism is all about fixing the overlapping ways that women face oppression. This page looks at the sorts of oppression which post-modern feminists are focused on, and how they think they can be fixed.

Post-modern feminism aims to tackle intersectional oppression

1) Despite the progress made by feminism, **women of colour** and **lower-class** women have not had access to the **same opportunities** as other women, particularly in **education** and the **workforce**.
2) **bell hooks** believed that this was because the **white, middle- and upper-class leaders** of the **feminist movement** had **failed** to consider **women of colour** and those **lower down** on the **economic scale**. She wrote about how these leaders of the movement had "*appropriated feminism to serve their own ends*".
3) She therefore believed that **solutions** to feminist issues needed to be **intersectional** (see p.123), tackling the **overlapping power structures** and **inequalities** created in societies **run** by **white, privileged men**.

bell hooks' frustration with previous feminists was summed up by the title of one of her best-known books: Ain't I a Woman?

Society and culture

bell hooks argued that **affirmative action** was necessary to address the **historic inequalities** faced by **women of colour**. She called for women to **free themselves** from the **limits** placed on them by patriarchy.

Key Terms

affirmative action
An American term for positive discrimination. It typically refers to policies that actively promote the interests of social groups who have historically been marginalised and under-represented in areas such as higher education, politics and the workplace.

Selfhood and community

- Drawing on **de Beauvoir's** idea of "*rapport à soi*" (see p.126), **bell hooks** argued that women needed to **learn** to **love themselves**, rather than measuring themselves against **male** — and **white** — **expectations**. She wrote that "*learning to love our female selves is where our search for love must begin*", emphasising that love for oneself cannot be **lost** in the same way as the love of others.
- As part of this process, she believed women needed to "*unlearn self-hatred*" and "*no longer see ourselves and our bodies as the property of men*".
- hooks also believed women need to **collaborate** with each other, and **reject** the **jealousy** and **fear** that they had been **socialised** to experience.

"What, me? Oh you big flirt"

Quick Questions

1) Which feminist thinker is associated with the concept of the 'reserve army of labour'?
2) Distinguish between difference feminism and equality feminism.
3) What did Simone de Beauvoir mean by 'otherness'?
4) What is an 'androcentric culture'?
5) Explain the main aspects of Kate Millett's theory of sexual politics.
6) To which feminist strand does Charlotte Perkins Gilman belong?
7) What does intersectionality mean?

Exam Practice

For Edexcel students: To what extent do feminists share the view that the personal is political? [24]

For AQA students: 'Feminists believe that the personal is political.' Analyse and evaluate this statement with reference to the feminist thinkers that you have studied. [25]

Write a **conclusion** to one of the questions above. You can use the sentence frames on pages 299-300.

Top Tip for Politicians #379: Remember to love yourself (but not too much)...

Anyone else get distracted by their reflection in shop windows? Ah...just me then. Anyway, make sure you've got to grips with the intersectional nature of post-modern feminist views before moving on to the lovely comparisons tables on the next page.

Non-core Political Ideas — Feminism

Comparing Feminist Ideas

Here's another handy page that summarises all the points of agreement and disagreement for this non-core political idea.

Human Nature

	Liberal	Socialist	Radical	Post-modern
Women are equally as capable as men, if not more so. Women possess the same natural rights as men, by virtue of being human.	✓	✓	✓	✓
Individual women are capable of improving their position in society without revolutionary changes to the political system or social order.	✓			
Women's nature and identities are intersectional — influenced by categories such as race, class, sexuality and disability as well as by sex and gender.				✓

State

	Liberal	Socialist	Radical	Post-modern
While the state is dominated by men, its decisions will continue to reflect male interests and reinforce patriarchy.	✓	✓	✓	✓
The state needs to intervene in both the public and private spheres.		✓	✓	✓
Patriarchy's grip on the state is so absolute that the state needs to be overthrown and reconstructed in a new form that will benefit women.		✓	✓	
The state should oversee gradual legislative change to allow women to experience both formal equality and equality of opportunity. Careful intervention by the state in the public sphere will improve women's experiences in the private sphere.	✓			
The state should pursue policies of affirmative action that correct historic injustices, particularly towards working-class women of colour.				✓

Society

	Liberal	Socialist	Radical	Post-modern
Society is patriarchal. Family responsibilities can prevent women from achieving their full potential. Women should be free to express their own identity in society, rather than conforming to patriarchal expectations and stereotypes. Education is crucial to women's ability to reach their full potential. Women's progress is hindered by sexist social attitudes reflected in the media, art and literature.	✓	✓	✓	✓
If women have the same economic opportunities as men, it's possible for them to have equal relationships in the private sphere.	✓			
A sexual revolution is necessary to liberate women from the influence of patriarchy. The traditional family should be dismantled.			✓	

Economy

	Liberal	Socialist	Radical	Post-modern
Men have constructed an economy that reflects their interests and talents more than women's. Women's economic status affects how much freedom they have in the private sphere.	✓	✓	✓	✓
Only major structural changes will give all women the opportunity to thrive economically.		✓	✓	✓
It's possible for women to enjoy equality of opportunity and to compete equally with men in a capitalist economic system.	✓			
Socialism is the only economic system that will allow women economic equality with men.		✓		
Women's marginalised economic position should be tackled at the same time as other economic inequalities, including those based on race, class and disability.				✓

I'm reading a book set in a world with no gravity. I can't put it down...

Phew — that's another summary page done and dusted. If you're struggling to remember all the similarities and differences between the strands, doing a quick comparison between these tables and page 123 might just help all this stay in your brain.

Non-core Political Ideas — Feminism

Multiculturalism

For its supporters, multiculturalism is a bit like a multi-vitamin for society — full of key ingredients for staying healthy and thriving, that you might not be getting enough of otherwise. Not quite as easy to just buy from the pharmacy though.

Multiculturalists value cultural diversity

1) **Multiculturalists** believe that cultural diversity **strengthens societies**.
2) They emphasise the **importance** of a **range of perspectives** for **social progress**.
3) For multiculturalists, **immigration** offers an **opportunity** for the **exchange of ideas**, with **positive consequences** for **politics**, **society** and the **economy**.
4) To enjoy the **advantages** of cultural diversity, multiculturalists stress the need for **tolerance**.

Multiculturalism consists of three main strands

Liberal Multiculturalism
- **Liberal multiculturalism** is based on the belief that **liberal values** offer the **best framework** for **achieving multiculturalism**.
- These liberal values are: **human rights**, **equality of opportunity**, **freedom**, **tolerance**, a **neutral** and **limited government** and **political representation**.

Key Thinkers:

Isaiah Berlin (1909-1997)   Will Kymlicka (b. 1962)

Cosmopolitan Multiculturalism
- **Cosmopolitan multiculturalism** focuses more on an **individual's right** to **choose** their own **culture** than on **group identities**.
- Cosmopolitan multiculturalists believe that the **most important group** to which individuals belong is the **unifying community of humanity**.

Jeremy Waldron (b. 1953)

There are no key thinkers for cosmopolitan multiculturalism on the specification, but Jeremy Waldron is an important figure in the strand who you can mention in your answers.

Pluralist Multiculturalism
- **Pluralist multiculturalists**, while **supportive of liberal values**, do **not** believe that they are **sufficient** on their own **to guarantee multiculturalism**.
- Instead, they believe that **groups** (especially those with **minority status**) require **formalised recognition** to ensure that they can **express** their **identities** without fear of **discrimination**.
- This recognition may take the form of **positive discrimination** (see page 125) where groups have suffered from **historic inequalities**.

Key Thinkers:

Charles Taylor (b. 1931)   Bhikhu Parekh (b. 1935)   Tariq Modood (b. 1952)

Multiculturalists emphasise the importance of rights and recognition...

1) All three strands agree that **legal protections** are **necessary** to uphold the **rights** of all **individuals** and **groups** in society.
2) In societies containing **ethnonationalist movements** or **marginalised indigenous populations**, multiculturalists believe that official **recognition** is an **essential** way of **respecting** their **cultural identity**.

ethnonationalism
A nationalist movement whose identity is rooted in ethnicity, e.g. that of the Kurdish people.

...but disagree over whether there should be any limits to diversity

1) **Liberal multiculturalists** believe that **all members of society** should be expected to respect values such as **equality**.
2) **Pluralist** and **cosmopolitan multiculturalists** argue that there **shouldn't** be any **requirements** for cultures to **conform** to the values of other cultures.

Multiculturalism

There are different ideas about which model of integration will be most successful

1) Integration is the process by which **individuals** and **groups** become **part** of a **new culture** or **society**.
2) **Tariq Modood**, a pluralist multiculturalist, discusses **four models** of **integration**:

1 Assimilation

- **Assimilation** is the idea that **immigrant groups** should **learn** and **absorb** the **cultural values** of the **society** they have **joined**.
- This is generally **supported** by **conservative critics** of multiculturalism, but **liberal multiculturalists** also **support** a degree of **assimilation** with **liberal values**.

2 Cosmopolitan integration

- **Cosmopolitan integration** is the idea that **individuals** are free to **integrate** in societies **as they see fit**.
- As the name suggests, this is the **model favoured** by **cosmopolitan multiculturalists**.

3 Multicultural integration

- **Multicultural integration** is a model founded on the idea that **individuals** and **groups** should be able to **retain** elements of their **own culture** (such as **customs**, **beliefs** and **language**) while **integrating** into a **new** one.
- This is supported by **pluralist multiculturalists** and by most **liberal multiculturalists**.

4 Individualist integration

- **Supporters** of this model **emphasise** the need to **assimilate**, but they are willing to consider **adjustments** on an **individual basis**, rather than applying adjustments to **groups** of people.
- This is the **preferred model** of integration for some **liberals** like **Trevor Phillips** and **Louise Casey**.

The alternative to integration is segregation

Segregation is the idea that **immigrant groups** should have their **own communities** where they are able to **maintain** their own **cultural norms**.

Linked with **far-right** and **far-left critiques** of multiculturalism, as well as with **exclusive nationalism** (see page 138), this model suggests that it is **either not possible** or **not desirable** for immigrants to **assimilate** or **integrate** into cultures other than their own.

> Segregation isn't a multiculturalist idea — it goes against some core principles of multiculturalism. But it's important to know about this contrasting idea to help understand multiculturalism.

Multiculturalism has been criticised from conservative and liberal perspectives

CONSERVATIVE CRITICISM:
- Conservatives such as **Samuel Huntington** (1927-2008) believe that the **opposing values** and **belief systems** held by **different cultures** inevitably create **social tension** that leads to **disorder**.
- As a result, many **conservative critics** of multiculturalism **advocate assimilation**.

LIBERAL CRITICISM:
- Liberals such as **Trevor Phillips** and **Louise Casey** believe that, in order to sustain **social cohesion**, a **balance** needs to be struck between **diversity** and **assimilation**.
- In practice, this would mean that the **state safeguards certain rights**, such as freedom of religion and belief, but **encourages integration** through schemes such as **citizenship tests** that require **competent language skills**.

Ralph and Monica weren't sure if they'd successfully assimilated with their dogs, or the wallpaper...

Cheese brought my friends together — we were into-grating...

It's a nice hobby and someone has to know what all the different holes on a box-grater are for. Fittingly for the multiculturalism chapter, we've used them to make dishes from all over the world. And, from my experience, that makes for a very tasty meal.

Liberal Multiculturalism

We're back to our pal liberalism — just keeps popping up everywhere, doesn't it? Let's see how it's influenced multiculturalism.

Liberal multiculturalists apply liberal values to cultural differences

1) **Liberal multiculturalists** believe that **maximising individual liberty** and **group rights** is the key to achieving the goal of a **multicultural society**.
2) This is based on an **optimistic view** of **human nature**.
3) They place a **high value** on an **individual's right** to **discover** and **choose** their own **identity**.
4) Liberal multiculturalists are committed to the concept of **formal equality** (see page 49).

Berlin: **Isaiah Berlin** argued **against** attempts to **enforce cultural norms** on individuals (as happens under the **assimilation model** of integration), which he regards as **degrading**. He believed decisions about a person's life should depend only on themselves, not on *"external forces of whatever kind."*

Kymlicka: **Will Kymlicka** focused on the **rights of minorities** and **marginalised groups** to express their **cultural identities**.

> Berlin helped develop the ideas of positive and negative liberty (p.51). In Berlin's vision of liberal multiculturalism, negative liberty would take the form of legal protections provided by the state, and positive liberty would be driven by individuals creating an open and tolerant society.

Liberal multiculturalists emphasise the importance of cultural tolerance

1) Because of their belief in the **power of individuals**, liberal multiculturalists consider **tolerance** to be a **moral** and **rational** act.
2) **Berlin** advanced a theory of **value pluralism** — the idea that there should be **no hierarchy** between different **ways of living**. As a result, the **freedom**, **rights** and **identity** of one group **shouldn't** be **at the expense** of the **freedom**, **rights** and **identity** of other groups.
3) Berlin argued that *"freedom for the wolves has often meant death to the sheep."*
4) He believed that **liberalism** is a **precondition** for **value pluralism**.
5) He saw liberalism as **culturally neutral**, because it focuses on **maximising liberty**, rather than trying to **mould society** in an **ideological** way. Therefore he thought it was particularly well suited to allowing **many cultures** to **thrive** under a **pluralist framework**.

> Liberal multiculturalists are influenced by John Locke's views on religious tolerance and by John Stuart Mill's harm principle (p.50).

> Berlin's critics argue that his belief that liberalism is a precondition for multiculturalism undermines the idea of value pluralism (see next page).

They see cultural expression as fundamental to human nature

Berlin:
- Berlin **questioned** the idea that **human nature** is **fixed** and the same **regardless** of **cultural conditions**, believing that this leads to **dangerous attempts** to **engineer societies**.
- Instead, he felt that **individuals** have the **right to discover** and **express** their **identities**.
- Berlin believed all people should be interested in their own and other cultures, writing *"only barbarians are not curious"*.

Kymlicka: **Kymlicka** believed that culture could give people an *"anchor for their self-identification and the safety of effortless secure belonging."*

Kymlicka advocated for the right to recognition and group differentiated rights

1) In common with **modern liberals** like **John Rawls** (see page 52), **Kymlicka** believed that **disadvantaged groups** and **individuals** may require **different treatment** if they are to enjoy **equality of opportunity**.
2) Instead of all groups and individuals receiving **universal rights**, Kymlicka called for **group differentiated rights** — the idea that rights can be **applied differently** to each group, depending on their **circumstances**, in order to achieve a **just outcome**. This would require a more **interventionist approach** by the **state**.
3) Kymlicka hoped that multiculturalism will create societies that are *"multi-ethnic, multi-religious, multi-faith and multi-national"* based on the common principles of **freedom**, **democracy** and **mutual respect**.
4) Kymlicka warned against *"benign neglect"* by states that merely **uphold negative liberty** through **legal rights** like **freedom of expression** and **assembly**. He argued that this allows **minority** and **marginalised groups** to enjoy liberty **only** in the **private sphere** (see page 124).
5) Instead, he argued that groups deserve **public recognition**, including **meaningful political representation** for all groups and **self-determination** for some.

> Kymlicka has advocated for formal recognition and self-government for three minority groups in Canada — the French-speaking Quebecois, and the indigenous First Nations and Inuit peoples.

Non-core Political Ideas — Multiculturalism

Pluralist and Cosmopolitan Multiculturalism

Pluralist multiculturalism is not as simple as sticking an 's' on the end of everything and calling it a day. Plurals aren't even that simple in English. Nope, both pluralists and cosmopolitans are about giving individuals more control over how they integrate.

Pluralist multiculturalists think individuals should choose how to integrate

Modood
- **Tariq Modood** extended **Berlin's** concept of **value pluralism** to include **models of integration** (see p.131). He argued that the **different models** do not have any greater or lesser **value**.
- As a result, **individuals** and **groups** should not just be free to **express** their own **identities**, but also to **choose** their **preferred model of integration**.

Taylor
- **Charles Taylor** agreed, celebrating the *"unique"* character of each individual and warning against expectations of *"external conformity"*.
- Taylor believed that *"our acquisition of rich human languages of expression"* is what allows people to fully **understand** themselves and form their own **identities**.

Like liberal multiculturalists, pluralist multiculturalists have an optimistic view of human nature that emphasises individuals' rationality and ability to define their own identity.

They reject Berlin's idea that liberalism is a precondition for multiculturalism

Parekh
Bhikhu Parekh dismissed the **universalist** claims of some liberals that **liberalism** is the best framework for **guaranteeing multiculturalism**.

Key Terms — universalism
The notion that there is one set of ideas and principles with which all rational individuals will agree.

Taylor
1) **Taylor** warned that **universalism** can cause attempts by **dominant groups** to create *"an image of inferiority in the subjugated"*.
2) This led **Taylor** to argue that **liberalism** cannot claim to be a *'neutral'* doctrine because its **ideas** are used in **disagreements** between **cultures**.

Critics of John Rawls' theory of justice (p.52) regard it as a universalist doctrine. This is because he concluded that, when placed behind a veil of ignorance, all rational individuals would agree with the principles of equality of opportunity and the difference principle.

Taylor advanced a theory known as the politics of recognition

1) **Taylor** went further than **Will Kymlicka** in acknowledging the need for **minorities** and **marginalised groups** to have their rights **recognised** by the **state** and **society**.
2) **Kymlicka** stressed the need for **formal recognition** and the **entitlement** to **self-determination** for some **cultural communities**. **Taylor's politics of recognition** focuses on achieving what he called *"due recognition"* — the end of **social norms** that suggest that some cultures are **superior** or **inferior** to others.
3) To attain the goal of *"due recognition"*, **Taylor** argued for the **equalisation** of **all rights** under a framework that recognises the **unique situation** of every **individual** and **group**. He called this the *"politics of difference"*.
4) **Taylor** emphasised the **importance** of maintaining **the dignity of human life** through what he described as a *"benevolent formula for mutual existence"*. This would mean **individuals** and **groups** do not merely **acknowledge** each other's **existence** and **rights**, but treat each other with **kindness** and **respect**.
5) This includes **actively** seeking to **improve** the **economic prospects** of **marginalised** and **minority** groups.
6) Taylor **opposed** the **individualist model** of integration (see page 131) on the basis that it makes **immigrants** feel that their own culture is **inferior**. He warned that it could make **newcomers** to a society feel that **existing groups** were saying *"we really don't want to have you guys here at all."*

Like Kymlicka, Taylor was born in Canada. Though both acknowledged the need to treat distinct groups in Canadian society differently, Taylor disagreed with Kymlicka's view that immigrant communities should be regarded as having opted into the culture that they had joined.

Bhikhu Parekh argued that all cultures should be criticised and praised

- For Parekh, **multiculturalism thrives** when there is a *"civilised dialogue"* between cultures. He argued that this will lead to a **deep diversity**, in which cultures **learn from one another**, welcoming each other's **insights** and **criticisms**.
- Parekh believed that all cultures *"have their share of unacceptable practices"* that need to be *"exposed and fought."*

Non-core Political Ideas — Multiculturalism

Pluralist and Cosmopolitan Multiculturalism

Modood argued multiculturalism must evolve to capture ever-changing identities

1) **Modood**, a British Muslim, **wrote extensively** about the **decline of racism** in Britain in the **1990s**, and then the **rise of Islamophobia** in **Britain** and other **western countries** following the **9/11 terror attacks** in 2001. His view that multiculturalism needs to **evolve constantly** was **influenced** by these **shifts**.

2) Modood defined the **purpose** of multiculturalism as creating *"a new, ongoing 'We'"*.
3) Like **liberal multiculturalists** and other **pluralist multiculturalists**, Modood **challenged** the **cosmopolitan multiculturalist idea** that groups require **no** special public recognition (see below).

4) He believed that, because society is a collective, integration should focus on welcoming new communities, as well as individuals, *"into relations of equal respect"*. To achieve this, he argued that **customs** and **institutions** must be **adapted** to allow cultures to **coexist** and form new **communities**.
5) This belief led **Modood** to **criticise** the **approaches to multiculturalism** taken by countries such as **Germany** and **France** on the basis that they have **failed to recognise** the **marginalised status** of **non-majority groups**.

France has had a long-held public doctrine of secular assimilation known as 'laïcité'. This doctrine has been used to justify bans on wearing religious symbols such as crucifixes, and garments like Islamic headscarves.

6) Because **public attitudes** and **identities** are constantly in a **state of flux**, Modood believed that multicultural ideas of **citizenship** also need to **evolve constantly**.
7) He argued that **evolving concepts** of **citizenship** and **welcoming strong cultural identities** will ultimately create **more united** societies than those that **ignore** or attempt to **reduce differences**.

Cosmopolitan multiculturalists are focused on the individual

1) **Cosmopolitan multiculturalists** believe that the **most effective** way of celebrating **diversity** is **not** to **grant recognition** or offer **different treatment** to any individuals or groups.
2) They believe **unequal treatment** would cause **tension** between people and so **undermine** the multiculturalist cause. They think people from **all cultural backgrounds** will be able to **integrate successfully** so long as they have **equality** in the **public sphere**.
3) Cosmopolitan multiculturalists are strongly committed to the **importance of choice** and **individual autonomy**.
4) This leads them to **oppose** any attempts to **treat individuals** as though they belong to **coherent collectives**.
5) **Jeremy Waldron** believed that a cosmopolitan multiculturalist should **refuse** to define himself *"by his location or his ancestry or his citizenship or his language"*, even if they have **lived** in the **same place** for **all** their **life**.

The International Space Station — home to cosmonaut multiculturalists

Quick Questions

1) What did Parekh mean by a 'civilised dialogue'?
2) How do cosmopolitan multiculturalists differ from pluralist multiculturalists?
3) How did Taylor criticise liberalism?

Revision Task

Test your knowledge of multiculturalism by defining the following key terms and concepts:
- Cosmopolitan multiculturalism
- Pluralist multiculturalism
- Universalism
- Liberal multiculturalism
- Group differentiated rights

Univers-alist, Cosmo-politan, it's all getting a bit astronomical...

Hopefully all this information hasn't left you seeing stars. When it comes to the strands of multiculturalism, the sticking points tend to be how (and how much) people should assimilate and integrate, and also how much state recognition is necessary.

Criticisms of Multiculturalism

Like any political movement, multiculturalism has its fair share of critics, all coming from different corners of the political spectrum. A big concern is the ways in which different cultural values can come into conflict with one another.

Some **liberals** think **multiculturalism** can **weaken tolerance** and **social stability**

1) **Many forms** of **multiculturalism** allow individuals and groups to **define their own relationship** to their **national culture**. For this reason, some **liberal critics** believe that multicultural ideas can **generate resentment** by **over-emphasising cultural differences**.

2) Some liberal critics are **particularly concerned** with **poorly defined approaches** to multiculturalism that **lack consistent application** by the **state**.

> Criticisms of multiculturalism are not on the AQA specification, but they are on Edexcel's. You could refer to the ideas below in essays for either exam board, but they should only be used to complement the ideas of the three multiculturalist strands and the key thinkers covered on the previous pages.

Trevor Phillips warned that countries that **"flirt"** with multiculturalism are **"sleepwalking to a catastrophe"**.

> Phillips adopted this position following the 9/11 and 7/7 terror attacks, arguing that a failure to integrate had contributed to the increased threat of terrorism.

Louise Casey, another liberal critic, believed that the **best solution** to this problem of ill-defined approaches to multiculturalism is an **individualist integration strategy**. This would have the state **require** aspiring citizens to take part in **common acts** such as **oaths of allegiance** and **attend compulsory language classes**.

Some **conservatives** regard **multiculturalism** as **an impossible aim**

- The **conservative** theorist **Samuel Huntington** was an influential neoconservative thinker. He argued that **multiculturalism** will **inevitably** lead to a **clash of civilisations** because cultures are based on such starkly **different values**.
- He believed that multiculturalism **denies** the concept of **'one nation'** and **breaks** society into **small communities**.

> Huntington's opposition to multiculturalism was influenced by the core conservative values of a desire for order and stability, as well as the desire to maintain traditional values (see page 44).

Some **feminists** argue **multiculturalism** lets **intolerant belief systems thrive**

- Feminist critics like **Marie Macey** state that **value pluralism** (see page 132) fails to recognise that **some cultures** do not **adequately safeguard** the **rights** and **identities** of **women**. For example, cultures based around **fundamentalist religious belief**.
- These critics believe that multiculturalism will **empower conservative communities** and ultimately **restrict social progress** for many **marginalised groups**.

Revision Task

Practise your analysis skills by **identifying** and **explaining** the similarities or differences between multiculturalist thinkers on the following themes:

1) Integration   2) Equality   3) The role of the state   4) Diversity in society

Exam Practice

For Edexcel students: To what extent do multiculturalists accept the importance of a shared set of values in society? [24]

For AQA students: 'Multiculturalists reject the importance of shared values in society.' Analyse and evaluate this statement with reference to the multiculturalist thinkers that you have studied. [25]

Practise your **evaluation** skills by writing a **conclusion** to one of the questions above. You can use the sentence frames on pages 299-300.

Every morning me and my colleagues recite the CGP oath of allegiance...

Top secret, I'm afraid. Anyway, as I said up top, this page is particularly important for Edexcel students, but even if you're doing AQA, it's still really useful to know the criticisms for any political ideology. It may just push your essays to the next level.

Non-core Political Ideas — Multiculturalism

Comparing Multiculturalist Ideas

You know it, you love it, it's the comparison page. Here's multiple key points about multiculturalism for you to mull over...

Human Nature

	Liberal	Pluralist	Cosmopolitan
Identity is a **critical aspect** of **human nature**.	✓	✓	✓
Ignoring the **collective identities** of some groups **undermines** their ability to experience **equality of opportunity**. **Culture** has a **major impact** on the **identities** of individuals and groups.	✓	✓	
Individuals' identities are **not shaped** by the **groups** they **belong** to. **Individuals** are entirely **free to choose** their own **identities**.			✓

State

	Liberal	Pluralist	Cosmopolitan
The state has a **responsibility** to **unify multicultural communities**. All individuals and groups have the **right** to **formal equality**. All individuals and groups should be granted **formal equality** by the **state**.	✓	✓	✓
Formal equality alone is **not enough** to ensure **true pluralism**. As well as formal equality, some groups may need **different treatment** (group differentiated rights) to allow for **equality of opportunity**. Certain groups, like **ethnonationalist** and **indigenous** communities, have a **right to self-determination**. The state's **primary contribution** to **multiculturalism** should be to provide **public recognition** for **cultural groups**.	✓	✓	
A **liberal state** is **best placed** to deliver multiculturalism. **Liberalism** provides the most robust political framework for **protecting** the **rights** of **minorities** and **marginalised** individuals and groups.	✓		
Every **individual** and **group** has the **right** to **choose** their own preferred **model of integration**. **Positive discrimination** may be necessary to achieve **meaningful equality of opportunity** for some groups. Because **economic circumstances** can **shape collective identities**, often in a **negative** way, the state should **actively seek** to provide **economic opportunities** for marginalised and minority groups. **Universalist** claims by liberal multiculturalists are **misplaced** because **liberalism** is **not** a **culturally neutral** ideology.		✓	
There is **no need** for any group to receive **special treatment** in terms of **rights**. **Equality** in the public sphere is **enough** for people of **all cultural backgrounds** to **integrate**. Moves to provide **unequal treatment** will create **discord** and ultimately **undermine** the **multiculturalist cause**.			✓

Society

	Liberal	Pluralist	Cosmopolitan
Multicultural societies are **stronger** and **richer** than **monocultural** societies. Society should be **characterised** by the principles of **tolerance** and **unity** through **diversity**. Integration is **preferable** to **segregation**.	✓	✓	✓
Societies **do not** have to be **fully integrated**. Individuals and groups should be able to **retain elements** of their **own culture** (such as **customs, beliefs** and **language**) while integrating into a new one. In certain circumstances (such as with **national minority groups** and **indigenous communities**), a degree of **separation** is **desirable** to recognise important **cultural differences**. At times, it is **necessary** for the **state** to **intervene** to **protect** elements of **marginalised** and **minority cultures**, rather than encouraging **all groups** to integrate to the **same extent**.	✓	✓	
Economic migrants should **integrate** into **most aspects** of their **new country's culture** because they have made an **active decision** to live there.	✓		
Every **individual** and **group** has the **right** to **choose** their own preferred **model of integration**. No model of integration has any **greater** or **lesser** value. Because **economic circumstances** can **negatively influence** collective identities, **societies** should provide economic opportunities for **marginalised** and **minority communities**.		✓	
Society is made up of a collection of **autonomous individuals** who define their own **cultural identities**. Individuals are **free to integrate** into societies **as they see fit**, but they **shouldn't expect special recognition** or **protection** for their own cultures.			✓

Exam Practice

For Edexcel students: To what extent do multiculturalists share a common view on the principle of rights? [24]

For AQA students: 'Multiculturalists are all committed to the same conception of rights.' Analyse and evaluate this statement with reference to the multiculturalist thinkers that you have studied. [25]

Using the grid on p.298, **plan** an answer to one of the essay questions above.

I eat two types of yoghurt to ensure I'm getting a multicultural breakfast...

Little microorganism joke for you there. Pun intended. But enough jokes, with that you've reached the end of the section on multiculturalism. Just one more non-core political idea to get your head around and it also has a lot to say about identity.

Non-core Political Ideas — Multiculturalism

Nationalism

Right, time for the last section on non-core political ideas. This one is all about nationalism. Nationalism is a set of ideas that argues the case for nationhood — the status of being a nation and having some sort of national identity.

Nationalist thinkers can be split into four strands

These are the strands used by Edexcel but they can also be used in AQA answers.

As well as the five key thinkers on this page you can refer to the ideas of nationalist politicians as evidence in your essays. Just remember that you need to mention at least two of the key thinkers in your exam answers.

Liberal Nationalism

- **Liberal nationalism** applies liberal ideas about **freedom** and **tolerance** to the question of **nationhood**.
- As a result, its thinkers want a world of **autonomous nation states** and often **support** the right to **self-determination** for minority groups and regional movements.
- In line with **social contract theory** (see p.50), liberal nationalists believe that the **consent** of the **people** is crucial to **legitimising** a nation's existence.

Key Thinkers:
Jean-Jacques Rousseau (1712-1778)   Giuseppe Mazzini (1805-1872)

Contemporary politicians
- Nicola Sturgeon (Scottish nationalist)
- Carles Puigdemont (Catalan nationalist)

Key Terms — nation state: A nation that has been able to develop its own state, including institutions such as a government, a legislature, a judiciary and a military.

Conservative Nationalism

- **Conservative nationalism** is influenced by conservative ideas on the need for **tradition**, **order** and **stability** in society.
- This strand stresses the need to create a sense of **cohesion** and **unity** within society.
- Conservative nationalists tend to support attempts by the state to **strengthen national identity** and often **reject** the right to **self-determination** for minority groups or regional movements.

Key Thinker:
Johann Gottfried von Herder (1744-1803)

Contemporary politicians
- Donald Trump (USA)
- Narendra Modi (India)

Expansionist Nationalism

- **Expansionist nationalism** is based on a **rejection** of the liberal idea that **all nations** have a **right** to **self-determination**.
- As its name suggests, its thinkers make intellectual justifications for **expanding** the boundaries of **existing nations**, including by **military invasion**. It is heavily linked to **chauvinism**.

Key Thinker:
Charles Maurras (1868-1952)

Contemporary politicians
- Vladimir Putin (Russia)
- Xi Jinping (China)

Key Terms — chauvinism: The belief that certain groups are superior to others, and therefore deserve preferential treatment by the state.

Post-colonial Nationalism

- **Post-colonial nationalism** rejects **colonial rule** and seeks to have **governance** returned to **indigenous populations**. It became especially prominent after the Second World War.
- Post-colonial nationalists are often influenced by **socialist ideas** about the need to **end exploitation** and **replace** the **capitalist state** with one that aims for **greater social** and **economic equality**.

Key Thinker:
Marcus Garvey (1887-1940)

Contemporary politicians
- Oscar Temaru, former president of French Polynesia
- Paul Néaoutyine, a pro-independence leader in New Caledonia

---

AQA refer to 'minority nationalism' and 'state nationalism'. Minority nationalism is described as a strand made up of thinkers and politicians campaigning for a minority group's right to form their own nation or change their status in an existing nation. State nationalism is described as a strand made up of thinkers and politicians who support the use of state power to expand national identity and strength.

Nationalism and Internationalism

Nope, internationalism is not all about going abroad and spending time on the beach. Instead internationalists disagree with a lot of what nationalists believe in. Here's a lovely page that will tell you a bit more about the differences between the two.

Nationalists tend to be either **inclusive & progressive** or **exclusive & regressive**

← **EXCLUSIVE**   **INCLUSIVE** →

EXCLUSIVE nationalists believe:
- **Only** members of **certain groups** can belong to a nation.
- People from **different cultural**, **ethnic** or **religious** groups **cannot** have the same role in the nation as those from the groups whose identity **aligns** with the **national identity**.
- It's important for citizens to have shared **cultural traits** such as **language**, **beliefs** and **values**.

INCLUSIVE nationalists believe:
- **Nations** can contain people from **different cultural**, **ethnic** and **religious** groups.
- **Consent** is a more **important basis** for nationhood than **arbitrary notions** of **group identity**.
- Inclusive nationalists tend to share similar ideas to **multiculturalists** (p.130).

← **REGRESSIVE**   **PROGRESSIVE** →

REGRESSIVE nationalists believe **traditions** and **fixed cultural identities** underpin nationhood.

PROGRESSIVE nationalists believe **national identity** is bound to **change** over time.

EXCLUSIVE, REGRESSIVE nationalist thinkers:

 von Herder
 Maurras
 Garvey

INCLUSIVE, PROGRESSIVE nationalist thinkers:

 Rousseau
 Mazzini

Internationalists reject the idea that nation states should **define** the **world order**

- **Internationalists** are in many ways the **opposite** of **nationalists**.
- Internationalists argue that **supranational institutions** and **international agreements** are more likely to create **peace** and **stability** than states acting entirely **independently**.
- They believe that **conflict** is the **inevitable consequence** of nation states being free to **pursue** their **own interests** and **defend** their own **cultures** without **regulation**.
- There are **two main strands** of internationalists:

Key Terms
supranational Sitting above individual nations in a hierarchy of power.

1 Liberal Internationalists

Liberal internationalists argue that supranational institutions like the **United Nations** and the **European Union** are **necessary** to **regulate** the behaviour of **states**.

They also emphasise the importance of **trade agreements** and **shared values** that help to **align** nations' **economic** and **political interests**, making conflict **irrational**.

A key part of liberal internationalism is a belief known as democratic peace theory, which is based on the idea that democratic countries do not go to war with each other.

2 Socialist Internationalists

Socialist internationalists reject the idea that **patriotism** is an important aspect of **human identity**.

They believe that **nations** are **bourgeois constructs** designed to **compel** the **proletariat** (see page 55) into **accepting** life under **oppressive capitalist regimes**.

Blimey, there's almost as many flavours of nationalism as there are crisps...

Nationalism is a very broad ideology, so it's useful to classify thinkers in lots of different ways. Nationalist thinkers can range right across the political spectrum, but the one thing that links them is the belief that a nation should be able to define itself.

Non-core Political Ideas — Nationalism

Liberal Nationalism

I mean, just look at all the other political ideas sections — surely you're not surprised to see a liberal strand? This form of nationalism is focused on a nation's role in self-expression and the right of a nation and its peoples to self-determination.

Liberal nationalists think belonging to a nation is essential to human freedom

Rousseau

Rousseau's vision of the **social contract** (see p.50) saw **nation states** as guarantors of **rights** and **liberty**. **Nation states** provide **protection** for their **people**, in return for the **consent** of their **people** that allows the nation state to exist.

Mazzini

1) Mazzini held similar views, arguing that because nation states were the **only** entities that could **formalise** the **protection** of **rights**, human **freedom** rested on the **ability** of people to **consent** to live in an **existing nation** or to **create** their **own** based on a **separate national identity**.

2) Mazzini believed that humans can only **express themselves** through their **nations**. He believed that a person's **country** provided them not only with **rights** and **protection**, but also with core components of their **identity**, such as their **name**, **faith** and **voice**.

They believe people must consent to nationhood and decide how it is governed

The liberal nationalist idea that each **nation** should **decide** how it is **governed** is called **self-determination**.

> The idea of self-determination was central to US President Woodrow Wilson's Fourteen Points at the Paris Peace Conference that followed the First World War. Although many of Wilson's aims were rejected, the Conference did lead to the creation of new countries such as Poland, Hungary and Austria.

Rousseau
- Rousseau developed a concept called the **general will**. This is the belief that **individuals** in a **community** would always **seek** the **good of society** as a whole and so people could be **trusted** to exercise **power**. It has been used to **legitimise** the idea of **democratic government**.
- Rousseau wrote at a time when many **European countries** were making concerted attempts to **grow** their **empires** through **foreign conquest**. He criticised **imperialism** on the basis that it imposed **power structures** on citizens who hadn't had a chance to **choose** their government, which went against his principle of the **general will**.
- Rousseau rejected the idea of **rulers** being **chosen by God** (a popular idea in the medieval and early modern periods) or ruling simply by their own **ability** to **maintain power**. Rousseau's theory of **civic nationalism** requires the **active participation** of **citizens** in **choosing rulers** and **expressing** their **views** on **political decisions**. He argued that this would **continually update** a nation state's **legitimacy**.

José was ready to actively participate, under the orders of General Will

Mazzini argued that nations should be progressive and inclusive entities

1) Like Rousseau, **Mazzini** argued that **tradition** can **limit** individual freedom, and that nation states should be based on **progressive ideas**. He warned people against being **complacent** with the way things had been done in the **past**, writing that: *"The world is advancing. Advance with it."*

2) As part of his **progressive theory of nationalism**, Mazzini argued that **governments** have a **duty** to **improve** their treatment of citizens.

3) In turn, he believed this would help to **strengthen national identity** and **civic pride**, ensuring that people would see **joining** and being **welcomed** into **nations** as an **attractive concept**. He believed that the **reputation** of a nation benefited far more from *"removing its faults than on boasting of its qualities."*

Non-core Political Ideas — Nationalism

Liberal Nationalism

Liberal nationalists apply liberal ideas to their analysis of nations

1) Based on the **liberal** view of **human nature** as **rational**, **moral** and **capable**, liberal nationalists believe that **citizens**, and the **nations** that they **form**, will possess these **traits** in their **political behaviour**.
2) Liberal nationalists generally believe that nation states should focus on **maximising** the **freedom** and **rights** of **individuals**. Nation states should also put in place measures to **stop** their own **authority** from having **harmful effects**.

Rousseau
- Because of his faith in **civic nationalism**, Rousseau believed that **citizens** needed to play an **active role** in **government** by **choosing rulers** and publicly **expressing** their **political views** in **open debate**, rather than placing faith in **representatives**.
- He believed a government should act as "**an intermediary body established between the subjects and the sovereign for their mutual communication**". A government should also be responsible for enacting the **law** and **maintaining civil** and **political freedom** for the people.

Rousseau and Mazzini held different views on representative democracy

Rousseau
1) While Rousseau's views on **human nature** were generally **optimistic**, he also asserted that humans are **imperfect**, which led him to question whether they can **effectively represent** each other's **interests**. He believed that only a "**nation of Gods**" would be able to successfully "**govern itself democratically**" and that **people** could not achieve a **truly democratic** government.
2) Rousseau's critique of **representative democracy** was also based on the logic that electing representatives **undermines** the **active civic engagement** that he saw as **necessary** for a **functioning nation state**.
3) As a result, he compared **representative democracy** to a form of **slavery**, in which **citizens** are **compelled** to follow the **wishes** of their **masters**, the **elected representatives**.

*Instead of relying on representative democracy, Rousseau argued that "**sovereignty of the people**" was a far better guarantor of freedom and civic nationalism.*

Mazzini
1) By contrast, Mazzini had **greater faith** in **representatives** installed by the people, making the case for **republicanism** as a replacement for **dictatorship**.
2) However, like Rousseau, Mazzini stressed the need for the **state** to be **created by**, and continue to **pursue** the **interests** of, its **citizens**. He believed **nations** and **revolutions** must be **driven** by the **people**, writing "**no nation deserves freedom or can long retain it**" if its **people** had not **fought** for it.
3) He wrote of the need for **citizens** to engage in a mix of "**thought and action**" to **sustain** the nation state.

Key Terms — republicanism
Support for the creation or maintenance of a 'republic'. A republic is a nation governed only by rulers who are chosen by their citizens, rather than having inherited their title (as is the case in nations that are monarchies or principalities).

Quick Questions
1) What is the difference between inclusive nationalism and exclusive nationalism?
2) What is the difference between progressive nationalism and regressive nationalism?
3) Which nationalist thinker developed the idea of the general will?

Revision Task
Test your knowledge of nationalism by **defining** the following key terms and concepts:
- Nation state
- Republicanism
- General will
- Social contract
- Self-determination
- Civic nationalism
- Chauvinism

Last June we covered the town hall in rainbows — now *that's* civic pride...
For liberal nationalists, the nation is tightly tied up in its citizens. The nation shapes its citizens' identities and culture, and works to improve their lives. And in return, its citizens should play an active part in how the nation is created and run.

Conservative and Expansionist Nationalism

Where liberal nationalists are more open to their national identity changing with time, conservative nationalists focus on maintaining traditional practices and identities. Meanwhile, expansionists would like to impose their identity on the world...

Conservative and expansionist nationalists share ideas about national loyalty

1) Both **conservative** and **expansionist nationalists** believe that a citizen's **loyalty** to their **nation** is based on **emotion** rather than **reason**.
2) **Johann Gottfried von Herder** rejected the liberal idea of using **rationalist principles** to justify national loyalty, stating *"I am not here to think, but to be, feel, live!"*

They believe that nation states should be more exclusive and regressive

Maurras

- Maurras' **integral nationalism** focused on the idea that the **state** should **avoid** liberal ideas of **progress**, **liberty** and **tolerance**.
- Instead, Maurras believed that the **state** should **promote** the **interests** of its core social groups. He wrote extensively about how he felt that the **French state** should **actively persecute minority groups** such as Protestants, Jews, Freemasons and foreigners. He argued that this would help to create a more **homogenous** sense of **national pride** and **identity**.
- Maurras was particularly **critical** of the **1789 French Revolution**, which he argued had *"handed over power"* to the groups *"who do the least work and the most damage"* by **overthrowing** the ruling **elite**.

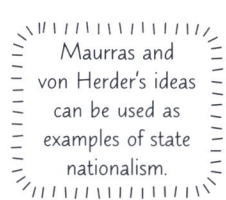
Maurras and von Herder's ideas can be used as examples of state nationalism.

von Herder

- It was von Herder's belief that humans would gain **more fulfilment** from knowing the *"limited activity"* of their **own cultures** as **fully** as possible than by trying to understand *"the shadow of the whole species"*.
- He **dismissed** the liberal argument (see page 130) that **multicultural societies** were a form of **progress** that would help humans to **advance** as a species.

Maurras rejected the idea that citizens should play an active role in government

1) Because of his **pessimistic** view of **human nature**, Maurras argued that the **majority** of people are not **wise** enough to make sound **political decisions**. He wrote:

   "For monarchy to work, one man must be wise. For democracy to work, a majority of the people must be wise. Which is more likely?"

2) Instead of focusing on the **state's obligation** to **individuals**, as liberals do, Maurras emphasised **individuals' obligation** to **submit** themselves to the **nation state**.

Von Herder believed the state should ultimately aim to become dispensable

1) Von Herder asserted that **strong government** was necessary while **citizens** were developing an **understanding** of their **national culture** — otherwise, the **social bonds** would not be tight enough to ensure **peace** or **stability**.
2) Once citizens' cultural knowledge had **improved**, von Herder argued that they would start to become **less reliant** on the **state**. He wrote:

   "The most noble end of government is to become dispensable, so that everyone must govern himself."

3) Von Herder wrote of how continual renewal by each generation could prevent societies from becoming a *"stagnant marsh"*, which was his way of describing nations that **failed to progress** and became stuck in their ways.

Non-core Political Ideas — Nationalism

Conservative and Expansionist Nationalism

Conservatives and **expansionists** have different ideas about a **nation's** focus

Conservative nationalism

For conservative nationalists, the focus of a nation state should be on protecting its own culture.

Von Herder's cultural nationalism emphasises the importance of shared language and cultural traditions as component parts of patriotism.

He developed a concept called the Volksgeist — the spirit of the people. Politically, this means that a nation is bound together by its shared culture.

As well as language and traditions such as festivals and celebrations, von Herder regarded the institutions of the state (such as the military, police force and judiciary) as essential elements of the Volksgeist.

patriotism
A feeling of national pride.

Key Terms

On her way to the loo, Monica happened to find the spirits of the people enjoying a late-night boogie

Expansionist nationalism

Expansionist nationalists think the state's primary focus should be to pursue militarism and chauvinism (see page 137).

As well as helping to provide security, Maurras believed that militarism helps a nation state to expand its influence.

Maurras' philosophy justified imperialism and colonialism on the basis that nation states are only obliged to pursue their own interests, rather than consider the rights of other nations and cultures. This was based on the chauvinistic belief that some nations and groups are superior to others.

militarism
An ideology based on military strength to support an expansionist state.

Key Terms

Quick Questions

1) What do conservative and expansionist nationalists believe loyalty to a nation should be based on?
2) What did Johann Gottfried von Herder mean by the concept of Volksgeist?
3) How did Maurras justify imperialism?
4) Why did Maurras support militarism?
5) Who believed that the state should aim to make itself dispensable? Why did they believe this?

Revision Task

Practise your **analysis skills** by identifying and explaining a similarity or a difference between the views of liberal, conservative and expansionist nationalists on the following themes:

1) The role of the nation state
2) The role of citizens in the political system
3) Imperialism
4) Whether a nationalist society should be inclusive or exclusive

I think I did my driving lessons in a Volksgeist...

Conservative nationalists and expansionist nationalists tend to have exclusionary views on who can or should be part of a nation. For conservatives this is often rooted in protecting traditions, while expansionists view certain groups of people as superior.

Post-colonial Nationalism

As the name suggests, in the aftermath of colonialism, many groups are trying to reassert their nationhood...

Post-colonial nationalists believe colonies have a right to self-determination

- **Marcus Garvey** developed a theory of **pan-African nationalism** that called for an **end** to the **colonisation** of Africa by European countries.
- Garvey believed that, once they were **freed** from the **oppressive relationship** with their **colonisers**, the people of African nations would be able to realise their **true potential**. He wrote: *"the Black skin is not a badge of shame, but rather a glorious symbol of national greatness."*

Garvey's ideas can be used as an example of minority nationalism.

Many post-colonial nationalist movements focus on independence

- Post-colonial nationalist movements have also developed in **French overseas territories** such as **New Caledonia**, **French Polynesia** and **Guadeloupe**. These territories are **governed** by **France**, although they have some **autonomy** over their own **political systems**. They all have **independence movements** that promote pride in aspects of their **indigenous** and **pre-colonial culture**, such as **language**, **music** and **dress**.
- Although most of the **UK's** former colonies are now **independent**, post-colonial nationalism remains strong in a number of them. For example, following a referendum, **Barbados** became a **republic** in **2021**, **removing** Queen Elizabeth II as its **head of state** in favour of a **president** who is **elected** by the **national legislature**.

Marcus Garvey argued for racial separation to solve historical inequality

1) Garvey believed that the **oppressive**, **exploitative** relationship into which white Europeans had **compelled black Africans** through **colonisation** and **slavery** meant that they **couldn't co-exist** in a way that would allow black Africans to **thrive**.
2) As a result, he argued that **black nationalism** should aim to create **separate** communities **free** from **white influence**. He believed that the **educational**, **industrial** and **political success** of black Africans would need to be *"based upon the protection of a nation founded by ourselves."* He argued this new nation should be formed in Africa.

He called for a black revolution to overturn the racist world order

- Garvey emphasised that black Africans needed to *"strike the blow"* for their own **liberty**, rather than **relying** on **white kindness** that would never materialise.
- Garvey argued that **self-education** would be crucial to **black flourishing**, writing that *"intelligence rules the world"*, and urging his fellow black Africans to **free themselves** from *"mental slavery"*.

Like other nationalists, Garvey believed that culture is central to identity

1) Garvey argued for the need for black Africans to **re-connect** with their **true cultural identity**.
2) He believed this was necessary because they had been **compelled** to live in **alien conditions**, either as a result of the **slave trade** or because their **lands** had been **colonised** by **European countries**. He wrote:

"A people without the knowledge of their past history, origin and culture is like a tree without roots."

Garvey was influenced by the socialist thinking of Karl Marx (see page 55-56). His ideas about education and cultural understanding are similar to Marx's concept of class consciousness.

Exam Practice

For Edexcel students: To what extent do nationalists agree on the role of the state? [24]
For AQA students: 'All nationalists agree on the role of the state in society.' Analyse and evaluate this statement with reference to the nationalist thinkers that you have studied. [25]

Practise your **evaluation** skills by writing a **conclusion** to one of the questions above. You can use the sentence frames on pages 299-300.

Not to be confused with The Caterpillar Uprising, led by Marcus Larvae...

Garvey was a controversial figure — criticised for his racial separatism, but also recognised as an advocate of black pride.

Comparing Nationalist Ideas

Right, it's comparison time. Let's get stuck in to seeing where all those different nationalist strands agree and disagree...

Human Nature

Idea	Liberal	Conservative	Expansionist	Post-colonial
Nationality is an **important component** of human nature. Humans are **inherently social** beings, whose desire for a sense of **collective identity** is satisfied by belonging to a **nation**.	✓	✓	✓	✓
Humans' sense of **national identity** is based more on **emotion** than on **rationality**.		✓	✓	✓
Race is an **important component** of human nature, forming the **basis of nationhood**.			✓	✓
It is **rational** for individuals to **organise** themselves into **nations**. Humans are **defined more** by what they have in **common** than by their **differences**. Humans are **fundamentally equal beings** who should enjoy **equal rights** regardless of their **nationality** or **race**.	✓			
Some humans are **superior** to others (**chauvinism**) based on e.g. their **race**.			✓	

State

Idea	Liberal	Conservative	Expansionist	Post-colonial
The **nation** and the **state** should be **bound together** in an **institution** called the **nation-state**. The nation-state is the **most effective** unit of **political organisation**.	✓	✓	✓	✓
Nation-states should base their conduct on **regressive principles**, trying to **maintain** or **return** a sense of **national identity**. Nation-states should **not** aim to be **inclusive**. Nation-states should **actively seek** to **defend** and **promote** their own cultures.		✓	✓	✓
Nation-states should pursue **chauvinist** policies that **prioritise** the **interests** of their **core social groups**.			✓	✓
All nations have a right to **self-determination**, allowing them to **form** their own **nation-states** that are **free** from **imperial** control.	✓			✓
The nation-state's **only obligation** is to **defend** and **pursue** its **own interests**, including by **imperialism** and **colonialism**.			✓	
Historically oppressed groups need their own **separate** nation-states, **free** from **white influence**.				✓

Society

Idea	Liberal	Conservative	Expansionist	Post-colonial
Culture is an **important component** of national identity.	✓	✓	✓	✓
Because **race** helps to **shape** human nature, **racial separation** will help to **produce harmonious societies**.			✓	✓
National identity is a **fluid concept** that should **evolve** frequently, based on the principles of **progressivism** and **inclusion**. Societies comprising **multiple social groups** can be **harmonious** and **stable**.	✓			
Colonisers and other **historically dominant** social groups have an inherently **exploitative relationship** with their subjects. Societies need to be **fundamentally re-structured** to allow **historically oppressed groups** to flourish.				✓

Economy

Idea	Liberal	Conservative	Expansionist	Post-colonial
Nation states should prioritise their own economies instead of seeking to help others.		✓	✓	
Capitalism has been used by colonial powers as a method of preventing the flourishing of independent, post-colonial nations.				✓
Free trade between nation states will **help** to **promote peace**.	✓			

Do national anthems count as country music? Asking for a friend...

Well that's all the core and non-core political ideas out the way. Great job ploughing through some pretty intense and sometimes complicated theories. I think all that's left to do is lie on your back, close your eyes and have a lovely, long nap.

Non-core Political Ideas — Nationalism

Comparative Theories

As its title suggests, this page is all about the theories you'll need to apply when comparing the US and UK. In fact, in a rare turn of events, most of these theories make it quite clear from their name what they're talking about. Except maybe rational...

There are **three comparative theories** you need to know

The three theories below help to **explain** the **similarities and differences** between the US and UK's **political systems**.

1) **Structural** theory

1) As the name suggests, structural theory relates to **structural similarities and differences** between different **political systems**.
2) Structural theory can be used when comparing **constitutions**, the **powers** given to the respective **legislative, executive** and **judicial branches**, the **relationships** between the **branches of government**, and **legal frameworks**. For example:
   - A structural **similarity** between the US and the UK would be that both have **bicameral legislatures** in which **both chambers** have to **approve** the same version of a bill.
   - A structural **difference** would be that the **UK** has a **partly elected legislature**, while the **House of Representatives** and the **Senate** in the **US** are **fully elected**.

Structural differences

2) **Cultural** theory

1) Cultural theory relates to similarities and differences between two countries' **political and social cultures**, e.g. their **histories**, **traditions** and the **influence of different groups**.
2) Cultural theory can help to compare the **role of religion** in politics and society, the **development of conventions**, the **influence of political parties** and their **internal factions**, **interest groups** and **groups of voters**. For example:
   - A cultural **similarity** between the US and the UK would be that both countries have **long-established** traditions of **democracy**.
   - A cultural **difference** would be that the **Religious Right** has a much **more significant influence** on politics in **government** in the **US** than any religious group does in the **UK**.

Cultural differences

3) **Rational** theory

1) Rational theory relates to similarities and differences between the **influence and behaviour of individuals** within two political systems.
2) Rational theory can be used when comparing the **roles** of **president** and **prime minister**, members of the two countries' **Cabinets**, **party leaderships**, **whips** and **judges**. For example:
   - A rational **similarity** between the US and the UK is that both legislative branches contain **whips** who try to use the **personal motivations** of representatives as a way of **persuading** them to **vote** in a certain way.
   - A rational **difference** is that, in the **US**, judges' political philosophies are **openly discussed** and **known** by members of the **public**. By contrast, judges in the **UK** are **expected** to keep their **political views private** under the concept of **judicial neutrality**.

Ratio-nal differences

Use rashernal theory when comparing bacon butties...

Whenever you're comparing the politics of the US and the UK, you'll need to keep these theories in mind. It might help to draw some tables or diagrams to sort each point of comparison into structural, cultural and rational similarities and differences.

The US Constitution

Ah the US Constitution — no, it's not about how well the American body can withstand various extreme conditions. It is, in fact, a single, written document that is fundamental to US politics. Understanding it will really help you follow the rest.

The US has a **codified constitution** that was written in **1787**

- The **Constitution** was written by a group of people called the **framers**, representatives of **twelve** of the **thirteen original states** who gathered in Philadelphia in 1787.
- At the **Philadelphia Convention**, the states agreed on the main **principles** that should underpin the newly **independent** political system. These principles included having an **elected president** who would run the **executive branch** of government.
- Because it is **codified**, the US Constitution is all contained in a **single document**. The **original** version was just over **4500** words, although later **amendments** mean that it is **now** over **7500** words.

> There has always been some tension between the states that make up the US. At the Philadelphia Convention, only 12 of the original 13 states were represented because Rhode Island refused to send a representative, worried that the writing of a national constitution might threaten its independent identity.

The Constitution has **three main aims**...

1 Prevent tyrannical rule

One of the main reasons for the **American War of Independence** was that the **British government** had treated the **American colonies** as resources, imposing **taxation** on them without offering **political representation** in return. The framers' chief concern was to **prevent** their newly independent country from falling under a similar form of **authoritarian rule**.

2 Preserve states' identities

Each of the **states**, which had been governed as **separate colonies** under British rule, had distinct **social** and **political** identities. Although they decided to create a **central government** to provide **security** and administrative **efficiency**, they all wanted to maintain a level of **autonomy** over their own affairs.

3 Protect individual rights

Many of the framers subscribed to the Enlightenment ideas of **classical liberals** such as **John Locke** (see p.50), who asserted that every human has **natural rights** to **life**, **liberty** and **property**. In reality, the framers (some of whom were **slave owners** themselves) did **not** create a political system that **guaranteed** these rights for **all** people. All **white men** were given a degree of **equal protection** by the **original Constitution**, and subsequent **amendments** have since built on its protections by **extending rights** to other groups.

...and is based on **four key principles**

1 Federalism

The principle that political power is **shared** between a **central** (**federal**) government and **regional** (**state**) governments.

2 Limited government

Influenced by the **classical liberal** ideas of **Locke**, this principle expresses the belief that **government** should exist to uphold the **rule of law** and **citizens' rights**. The government **shouldn't** have wide-ranging powers that **interfere** with **individual freedom**.

3 Bipartisanship

The principle that the **people's representatives** should work **together** to achieve **constructive compromises**, rather than working **against** one another and **preventing** legislative progress. The framers didn't expect that political parties would be created in the US, however they soon began to emerge at both **federal** and **state levels**.

4 Separation of powers

The principle that the **three branches** of **government** (see p.148-149) are **physically separate**, with **different** (but **overlapping**) roles. Importantly, this means that **no single person** can have a role in **more than one** branch of government at a time. Because each branch is separate, they should be able to provide **effective checks** and **balances** on each other, thereby fulfilling the framers' aim of **preventing tyrannical rule**.

> This contrasts with the UK, where government ministers are also members of Parliament.

The US Constitution

The US Constitution contains a mixture of enumerated and implied powers

ENUMERATED POWERS — These are powers that are clearly **provided** to a **specific person** or **branch** of federal government. For example, **Article I, Section 7** of the Constitution gives the **president** the power to **veto** legislation passed by **Congress**.

IMPLIED POWERS — These are powers that are **suggested** by the **Constitution** or its **amendments**. For example, Article II appoints the president as **commander-in-chief** of the **Army** and **Navy** of the United States, but it doesn't specifically say that this allows the president to order **military action**.

Amelia wasn't sure about this method of testing her enumerated powers

The strict amendments process makes the Constitution entrenched

1) The US had fought a war of **independence** against the British, so they wanted to **ensure** that their newfound **rights** couldn't easily be **taken away**.

2) This led them to create a **strict amendments process** (outlined in **Article V** of the Constitution) that ensures that any **changes** have **broad support**.

3) Most amendments have been made using the following process (see p.159 for more details):
   - Amendment **proposed** in Congress. In order to pass this stage, it must secure support from **two-thirds** of the members of the **House of Representatives** and **two-thirds** of **senators**.
   - Once successfully proposed, the amendment must be ratified by **three-quarters** of **state legislatures**.

There's a more detailed look at amendments to the Constitution on page 159.

The only amendment not to follow this process is the 21st amendment, which repealed the prohibition of alcohol in 1933. This amendment was proposed by Congress, but ratified by a mechanism called a state ratifying convention, where citizens attending meetings in three-quarters of the states had to give their approval.

4) The amendments process makes the US Constitution **entrenched**. This means that it **cannot** be **amended** in the same way as **ordinary laws** that do not form part of the Constitution.

The US Constitution is sovereign, taking precedence over any law passed by Congress or by one of the states.

Quick Questions

1) In which year was the US Constitution originally written?
2) How many states attended the Philadelphia Convention?
3) What are the three main aims of the Constitution?
4) Give an example of an enumerated power.
5) Give an example of an implied power.
6) Which institution is responsible for proposing constitutional amendments?

Revision Task

Test your knowledge of the US Constitution by **defining** the following key terms and concepts:
- *Enumerated powers*
- *Entrenchment*
- *Implied powers*
- *Federalism*
- *Philadelphia Convention*
- *Separation of powers*

I was scammed by a dishonest goblin — darn him and his imp-lied powers...

It's difficult to overstate just how important the Constitution is to politics in the United States. It gives political power to institutions, guarantees many human rights and has been a major factor in various adventure films over the years. Truly an icon.

US Politics — The Constitution and Federalism

Interpreting the US Constitution

The Constitution is very important, but that doesn't mean it's easy to understand. Like any document made by people, it's not perfect, and it requires a fair bit of thinking to work out exactly what powers it grants and how best to apply them.

The US Constitution can be both **specific** and **vague**

1) Many of the **enumerated powers** are **specific** and **clear** enough that they remain in place to this day, without being **contested**.
2) For example, the president is given the power to **nominate Supreme Court judges**, and the **Senate** is given the power to **ratify** these appointments.
3) In other areas, though, the Constitution is **vague**. There is **no list** of the **powers** that each **state** possesses, leading to **debate** and **confusion** between them and the **federal government**. Instead, **the 10th amendment**, the '**reserved powers clause**', simply says that any powers **not delegated** to the **federal government** are **reserved** by the **states**.
4) The role of the **Supreme Court** is also **vague**. Article III contains no mention of the Court's role in **interpreting** the Constitution during future **disagreements**, but nor does the Constitution give this power to either of the other two **branches of government**.

> Article I, Section 8, Clause 18 of the Constitution, known as the 'Necessary and Proper Clause' or the 'Elastic Clause', grants Congress a wide-ranging, vague power to do whatever it deems to be "***necessary and proper***" to fulfil its duties. This clause has been used by Congress to create federal departments like the Department of Homeland Security, which opened in 2003 as part of the response to the 9/11 terror attacks.

This means the **roles** of each **branch** of government have **changed** over time

1) There are **three branches** of the US government — the **legislative** branch (**Congress**), the **executive** branch (the **Presidency**) and the **judicial** branch (the **Supreme Court**).
2) Their powers have **changed** compared to the **original Constitution**.

> Knowing the examples on these pages will prove handy when you revise the Congress, Presidency and Supreme Court sections. They're all about the power relationship between these branches.

The Legislative Branch — **Congress**

CONSTITUTIONAL ROLE

The framers intended Congress to be the **most powerful** branch of the government. As such, it receives the **most specific** and **clear** grants of **power** in the original **Constitution**, including:

- setting the **annual federal budget**
- **voting on legislation** before it gets sent to the president
- **proposing** constitutional **amendments**
- providing '**advice and consent**' (essentially **scrutiny** and **ratification**) for executive **appointments** and **treaties**.

INCREASED POWERS

- Congress has gained power in some areas, notably over the **states** due to the vagueness of the '**interstate commerce clause**' (see page 156).
- It has increased its ability to **regulate commerce**, including gun sales. For example, Congress introduced a **ban** on **assault weapons** across the United States in **1994**.

> In order to pass this legislation, President Bill Clinton negotiated a sunset clause that meant the law elapsed ten years later.

DECREASED AND LESSER USED POWERS

- Congress has **retreated** from using some of its powers frequently.
- Despite **Article I, Section 8** giving Congress **the power to declare war**, it hasn't formally done so since 1942. The **executive branch** has tended to assume greater control over **foreign policy**.
- Similarly, although Congress still **ratifies formal treaties** that have been **negotiated** by the president with foreign countries and international organisations, such agreements are becoming **increasingly rare**. It is now more common for **presidents** to sign **trade deals** or **executive agreements**, which do not require **congressional approval**. For example, Congress was **not** able to **vote** on **Barack Obama's** deal with Iran in 2015 (see page 188) or on **Donald Trump's** decision to recognise Jerusalem as the official capital of Israel in 2020.

The Executive Branch — **The Presidency**

CONSTITUTIONAL ROLE

- The president receives **more** specific powers from the Constitution than the **judicial branch**, but **fewer** than **Congress**.
- As outlined in **Article II**, presidents continue to **negotiate treaties**, **propose legislation**, submit the **annual budget** to Congress, **nominate judges** and **ambassadors** and **veto** legislation that has been **passed** by both the **House of Representatives** and the **Senate**.

US Politics — The Constitution and Federalism

Interpreting the US Constitution

INCREASED POWERS

The interpretation of the president's **'commander-in-chief'** role has changed over time, partly as a result of the **changing** nature of **warfare**.

- **Congress** made formal **declarations of war** in both world wars.
- Since the Second World War, **presidents** have consistently made **military decisions** without seeking **congressional approval** in advance.
- Wars in **Korea**, **Vietnam**, **Iraq** (twice) and **Afghanistan** (among others) have all taken place **without** formal **congressional declarations of war**.
- Most military interventions now take the form of **targeted raids**, **air strikes** and **drone strikes** — none of which require congressional approval.

> You can use this information about increasing presidential power in your essays on US Presidents.

> Presidents have been able to order high-profile assassinations. Al-Qaeda leader Osama Bin Laden was killed by a Navy Seal operation authorised by Barack Obama in 2011, and Iranian General Qasem Soleimani was killed by a drone strike ordered by Donald Trump in 2020.

In **domestic policy**, presidents have also gained the **power** to issue **executive orders**. These are declarations **building** on existing legislation that can **significantly change** the **interpretation** and **enforcement** of the law. Importantly, they are **not** subject to **congressional approval** — they don't need to be **voted** on before they become **law**.

- **Donald Trump** used an **executive order** to **ban** citizens from seven **Muslim-majority countries** from **entering** the **United States** in one of his first acts as president in **2017**.
- **Joe Biden** issued **17 executive orders** on his **first day** in office in 2021. These included **re-joining** the World Health Organisation and introducing **compulsory mask wearing** on federal property to help control the spread of **COVID-19**.

In **foreign policy**, presidents are also able to make **executive agreements**. These are agreements between the **executive branch** and **foreign leaders**. Like executive orders, they **don't** need **congressional approval** to be **enacted**. Executive agreements have enabled presidents to make **progress** in **foreign affairs** and make **diplomatic decisions** despite the **hyperpartisan** nature of **Congress**.

- **Obama** re-established the **US embassy** in **Cuba** and **eased sanctions** on **Iran** using executive agreements.
- **Trump** used an executive agreement to **re-locate** the **US embassy** in **Israel** from Tel Aviv to **Jerusalem**.
- **Biden** used an executive agreement to sign the **Aukus military pact** with **Australia** and the **UK**.

The Judicial Branch — **The Supreme Court**

CONSTITUTIONAL ROLE

- **Article III** of the Constitution outlines **very few specific powers** or **roles** for the judicial branch, but it did create the **Supreme Court** as an **arbitrator** in **disagreements** between **states**.
- This **vagueness** has allowed the Supreme Court to assume a **much greater role** in the **political system** than the framers might have **imagined**.

INCREASED POWERS

- In a landmark case called **Marbury v. Madison** in **1803**, the Supreme Court essentially appointed itself as the **guardian** of the **Constitution**. It ruled that it had the power to **interpret the Constitution** in cases where its **provisions** were **disputed** by two or more parties. This power is called **judicial review**.
- Since then, the Supreme Court has made **high-profile** (and often **controversial**) rulings on **constitutional**, **political**, **social** and **economic** issues (see p.194-195). Some of the most **important** Supreme Court cases include **Brown v. Board of Education (1954)**, **Roe v. Wade (1973)** and **Dobbs v. Jackson Women's Health Organization (2022)**.

There is **debate** over how the **Constitution** should be **interpreted**

Some believe that the Constitution should be interpreted literally

- **Originalists**, or **strict constructionists**, believe that the **Constitution** should be interpreted **strictly** in line with its **original wording**. They are usually **conservatives**, on the **right** of the American **political spectrum**.
- **Politicians** and **judges** who interpret the Constitution **literally** tend to **support gun ownership** rights, **oppose** the legalisation of **abortion** and **support states' rights** against attempts by the federal government to increase its power.

Others see it as a living document that should be interpreted flexibly

Loose constructionists believe that the Constitution's **original provisions** should be interpreted **loosely** to allow **social progress**. People with this view tend to be **liberals**, on the **left** of the American **political spectrum**.

US Politics — The Constitution and Federalism

Checks and Balances

After the American War of Independence had finished, the framers really didn't want to end up creating another overbearing government system. And so they made sure to fill the Constitution with plenty of checks on power.

Checks and balances put limits on the powers of the different branches

1) The **framers** of the Constitution were **determined** that the US would never experience the kind of **rule** that the original thirteen colonies had experienced when they were **governed** by **Britain**, which they considered **tyrannical**.

2) To fulfil their aim of creating a **limited government**, they designed a system of **checks** and **balances** that was influenced by the French political theorist **Baron de Montesquieu**.

3) Montesquieu's theory relied on a **separation of powers** between the different **branches** of **government**, preventing any **individual** from being able to exercise **control** over more than one branch.

4) The framers wanted **Congress** to be at the heart of the system of checks and balances, giving it particular **responsibility** for **limiting** the power of the **president**, who they saw as **inferior** to Congress.

5) Because it would contain the **highest number** of people, they were confident that **power** would be **dispersed** throughout Congress, rather than **concentrated** in the hands of a **small number** of individuals.

Mittens knew the perils of being involved with too many branches

Although physically separate, the branches have overlapping roles and responsibilities

Legislation: The **president** can **propose legislation** (including the **federal budget**), or ask a member of **Congress** to do so on their **behalf**, but all bills need to be **approved** by a **majority** in both the **House of Representatives** and the **Senate**. Once this happens, the president can choose to **sign** the bill into **law** or **veto** it (send it back to Congress). A **presidential veto** can be **overridden** if **two thirds** of **both chambers** of Congress **vote against** it. The bill **automatically** becomes **law** if the **veto** is **overridden**.

Foreign policy: The president's **commander-in-chief** role **overlaps** with Congress's power to **declare war** (see p.148). The president can also **negotiate treaties** and **nominate ambassadors**, but in both cases these need to be **ratified** by the **Senate**.

Appointments: The president can also **nominate judges** and **members** of their own **executive branch**. As with ambassadors, these appointments need to be **ratified** by the **Senate**.

Congress is able to hold the executive branch to account

Impeachment

If the **president** is suspected of having committed what the Constitution calls a '**high crime** or **misdemeanour**', the **House of Representatives** can vote to **impeach** them. They are then placed on **trial** by the **Senate** — if found guilty, they can be **removed from office**. Although the House impeachment vote requires only a **simple majority** (over **half** of the chamber), the Senate vote requires a **supermajority** of **two-thirds** of those present to **convict** and **remove** the president from office. **Bill Clinton** and **Donald Trump** (twice) were **impeached** by the **House**, but no president has ever been **convicted** by the **Senate**.

Subpoena power

Congressional committees can issue **subpoenas** (legally-binding **summons**) to members of the **executive branch**, asking them to **testify** in investigations.

Although subpoenas are legally binding, there have been notable instances of members of the executive branch failing to comply with them in recent years. Donald Trump ignored subpoenas over alleged Russian interference in the 2016 presidential election. Biden's Secretary of State, Antony Blinken, refused to comply with subpoenas requesting documents relating to the withdrawal of US troops from Afghanistan in 2021.

Checks and Balances

Federalism provides a less formalised system of checks and balances

1) The **10th amendment** reserves all powers **not delegated** to the **federal government** to the **states**, which means the **presidency** and **Congress** are **limited** in their ability to **intervene** in states' affairs.

2) The **vagueness** of the 10th amendment means that the **federal-state relationship** is constantly in a state of **flux** (see page 156), but the states **retain control** over the following **areas of policy**, providing further checks and balances on the federal government:

- Criminal justice
- Drug policy
- Abortion
- Healthcare
- Education
- State taxation

US political parties have influenced how the checks and balances work

1) Although the framers didn't envisage **political parties** forming in Congress, the reality is that the **Republicans** and the **Democrats** have **dominated** federal and state politics for well **over a century**.

2) In recent decades, the two parties have held **increasingly different** policy profiles, with the Democrats drifting to the **left** of the political spectrum and the Republicans moving to the **right**. This process is known as **polarisation**.

3) These policy differences have often been reflected in **disagreements** in **Congress**, where members of the **House** and the **Senate** have increasingly voted **along party lines**. This process is known as **hyperpartisanship**.

The makeup of Congress can affect the chances of legislation passing

- A **united government** is formed when the president's party has a **majority** in both the **House of Representatives** and the **Senate**.
- **United governments** were very **common** from the **mid-nineteenth** century to the **mid-twentieth** century. This enabled some presidents like **Franklin Roosevelt** and **Lyndon Johnson** to pass **legislation** through Congress **without** facing particularly **strong** checks and balances.
- A **divided government** is formed when at least **one chamber** of Congress is controlled by the **other party**.
- Between 1967 and 2024, there were **37 years** of **divided government**, compared with only **20 years** of **united government**.
- During Obama's divided government, Congress consistently **refused** to pass his **gun control proposals**, despite events such as the **Sandy Hook** mass shooting in **2012**.

No period of united government has lasted more than four years since 1968.

Some believe the checks and balances are highly effective

✓ The **executive** and **judicial appointments** processes in the US are far **more rigorous** than in many other political systems.

✓ **Nominees** are subjected to hours of **detailed, high-profile public scrutiny** of their **suitability** to hold a position.

- In 2022, **Ketanji Brown Jackson**, Biden's nominee for the Supreme Court, faced over **20 hours** of **questioning** by the **Senate Judiciary Committee** before the Senate ratified her appointment.

✓ Sometimes, this detailed scrutiny **reveals** that nominees are not of the **required standard** in terms of their **policy knowledge** or **past conduct**.

- In **1987**, Ronald Reagan's nominee for the Supreme Court, **Robert Bork**, was **rejected** by the **Senate** after his **confirmation hearing** brought attention to his **previous rulings** on civil rights issues.

- In **2017**, Donald Trump's nominee for the **Secretary of Labor** position, **Andrew Puzder**, **withdrew** when it became clear that senators would **refuse** to ratify his appointment. A **media investigation** had found that his family had **employed** a cleaner **illegally**.

Natalia found that her balance was also highly effective

The rigorous process that executive and judicial nominees undergo in the US contrasts greatly with the UK, where Cabinet appointments receive no formal scrutiny whatsoever, and assessments for judicial positions take place in private. Checks and balances in the US and the UK are compared in more detail on page 161.

Checks and Balances

Some argue they are **too weak**

✘ **Presidents** are now able to make **all major military decisions without** facing any **constitutional checks** and **balances**.

✘ **Executive orders** can't be checked by **Congress** (although they can by the **Supreme Court**), and **executive agreements** can't be checked by **either** of the other **branches of government**.

✘ In 2020, the **Republican-controlled Senate** rushed through **Amy Coney Barrett's** appointment to the **Supreme Court** in just **30 days** so that she would be **confirmed** before the **presidential election** between Trump and Biden. However, she did still face nearly **20 hours** of questioning by the **Judiciary Committee**.

Amy Coney Barrett

Others argue they are **too strong**

✘ In recent years, Congress has suffered from **legislative gridlock** (p.175), meaning that **very few** laws were passed. This was mainly as a result of **hyperpartisanship**. Between **1983** and **1993**, Congress passed an average of **5%** of bills into law, but between **2013** and **2023**, just **2%** of bills became law.

✘ Despite the framers envisaging **Congress** as the **most important** branch of government, the **Supreme Court's** power of **judicial review** means that it can **declare** that **laws** passed by Congress are **unconstitutional**. In **1995**, the Court ruled in **US v. Lopez** that Congress's **Gun Free School Zones Act** violated the '**interstate commerce clause**'.

✘ In **contrast** to the Republicans' **swift confirmation** of **Coney Barrett** in **2020**, the Republican-controlled Senate **refused** to hold a **hearing** when **Obama** tried to nominate **Merrick Garland** to the **Supreme Court** in **2016**.

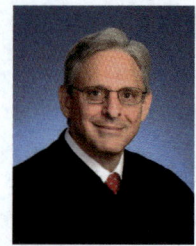
Merrick Garland

Quick Questions

1) What is Congress's subpoena power?
2) What is meant by polarisation?
3) What is meant by hyperpartisanship?
4) How many years of united government were there in the US between 1967 and 2024?
5) How many years of divided government were there in the US between 1967 and 2024?
6) For how many hours was Ketanji Brown Jackson questioned by the Senate Judiciary Committee in 2022?

Exam Practice

For Edexcel students: Evaluate the view that the constitutional system of checks and balances has become ineffective in the USA. [30]

For AQA students: Explain and analyse three ways in which checks and balances operate in the USA. [9]

Hyperpartisanship — when both left and right have had too much sugar...

The Constitution was especially focused on preventing the state, or any particular member of it, from having too much power. As you've seen though, some people aren't sold on its effectiveness, especially with how the political landscape has changed.

US Politics — The Constitution and Federalism

Bipartisanship

All aboard the bipartisanship, where we all put aside our differences and come to a compromise for the good of the country. Or, at least, that was the framers' ideal. However, as time has gone on, this noble idea seems less and less achievable.

The Constitution was written with an **aim** to promote **consensus** and **compromise**

1) As well as being inspired by the desire for **limited government**, the framers designed the systems of **checks and balances** and the **separation of powers** with the rationale that different states and factions would need to **work together** in order to make **progress**.
2) This is the case in the **legislative process** (see page 169), where the **House of Representatives** and the **Senate** have broadly **equal** powers.
3) Because of the president's **veto** power, almost all **bills** are passed with the **support** of the **executive branch**, as well as a **majority** in both **congressional chambers**.
4) The framers also required **supermajorities** in some instances, such as the **constitutional amendments** process (**two-thirds** in **both** chambers of Congress, and then **three-quarters** of the **states**) and the process of **overriding** a presidential veto.
5) Since **political parties** have become a constant feature of the American political system, some argue that these measures work to promote **bipartisanship**, rather than allowing one party to operate on its own.

Key Terms — bipartisanship: When members of both major parties, the Republicans and the Democrats, agree to work together, often to achieve a compromise.

Although Congress can override a presidential veto if two-thirds of both chambers support doing so, this is relatively rare. None of Biden's vetoes were overridden from 2021-2024, and Trump and Obama only had one veto overridden each. Throughout US political history, only 4% of presidential vetoes have been overridden.

There have been some **notable** instances of **bipartisanship** in **recent years**

- Congress passed the **BIPARTISAN INFRASTRUCTURE LAW** in **2021**. This was a **$1.2 tn** spending package aimed at improving **national transportation networks** drawn up by the Biden administration, which had support from both **Republicans** and **Democrats**.
- The House of Representatives voted **228-206** in favour, and the Senate approved the bill by **69-30**. **13 House Republicans** and **19 Senate Republicans** supported the law, and their votes allowed the bill to pass.

In **2018**, the **FIRST STEP ACT** (a **sentencing** and **prison reform** bill) passed through the House with a vote of **360-59**, and through the Senate **87-12**.

Despite this, the first Trump presidency was not known for its bipartisanship (see p.189).

Bipartisanship is particularly prominent in times of **crisis**

There has been plenty of **partisan disagreement** on US **support** for **Ukraine** since the **Russian invasion** in 2022. However, there was **bipartisan support** for the **Additional Ukraine Supplemental Appropriations Act (2022)**, which passed the House of Representatives by **368-57**, and the Senate by **86-11**.

During the **COVID-19 pandemic**, Congress passed two significant bipartisan **stimulus** and **support** packages — the **CARES Act (2020)**, a **$2.2 tn** deal while Donald Trump was president, and the **American Rescue Plan Act (2021)**, a **$1.9 tn** deal signed by Joe Biden.

Donald Trump during a COVID-19 response teleconference in 2020

George W. Bush addressing the nation on September 11th 2001

Similarly, there was **broad bipartisan agreement** over George W. Bush's initial response to the **9/11** terror attacks in 2001. Congress passed a bill creating the new **Department of Homeland Security** by **295-132** in the House of Representatives and by **90-9** in the Senate.

US Politics — The Constitution and Federalism

Bipartisanship

US government and politics is usually hyperpartisan

1) For most of the twentieth century, the **Senate** prided itself on being the **less partisan** of the two chambers (see page 168). However, its **confirmation hearings** for appointments to the **judicial** and **executive branches** have become **highly partisan**.

> In 2016, Senate Republicans **refused** to **consider** Obama's **nominee** to the Supreme Court, **Merrick Garland** (see p.152).

> The **last four** appointments to the Supreme Court have been made with a total of **just eight senators** voting against party lines.

2) Only **one president**, **Andrew Johnson** (in 1868), was **impeached** in the first **200 years** of the United States' history. However, there were **three impeachments** between 1998 and 2021 — **Bill Clinton** in **1998** and **Donald Trump** twice (in **2019** and **2021**).

Some argue that the **requirement** for **convicting** a president and **removing** them from office (**two-thirds in the Senate**) is now **too difficult** in this era of hyperpartisanship. For example, in **2021** Donald Trump was tried over his alleged role in inciting the **January 6th riots**. **57 senators** who voted to remove him from office were still **nine short of the required total**.

3) The use of the **filibuster** for **partisan purposes** has been **increasingly common** in the **Senate** in recent years. Filibusters **prevented** Trump from passing his **replacement** for Obamacare and Biden from passing landmark bills on **abortion** and **voting rights**.

4) **Obama**, **Trump** and **Biden** all failed to pass **significant gun control reforms** due to hyperpartisan **opposition** to their plans.

5) Probably the best example of hyperpartisanship in action, although still rare, is a **federal government shutdown**, which occurs when **Congress** and the **president** cannot agree on the **annual budget**.

> There was **one** shutdown during the **Obama** presidency (in **2013**), and **two** during the first **Trump** presidency (the first in **2018** and another in **2018-19**).

Key Terms

filibuster
A rule that allows a senator to prevent a bill from being passed by talking for the entirety of its allotted time for debate. The only way of preventing a filibuster is by senators issuing a cloture motion (a motion which must be approved by three-fifths of senators and will immediately pass the bill).

Phil was worried he'd bust a vocal chord if he kept going much longer

Revision Task

Practise your **writing skills** by choosing an example to support each of the following points. Then explain the significance of the examples below to a question on whether the US Constitution is fit for purpose.

1) Bipartisan co-operation tends to be more common during crises.
2) Hyperpartisanship has prevented legislative progress in some important areas of policy.
3) The Senate now experiences similar levels of hyperpartisanship to the House of Representatives.

Top Tip for Politicians #732: Be willing to compromise...

The ideals of bipartisanship are all well and good, but it runs into trouble as political positions drift further apart. When two sides of an issue are so staunchly opposed, it's not always easy or effective to compromise. And so the clash continues...

Federalism

The Constitution established the US political system as one built on federalism — where power is shared between a central government and individual states. However, the extent to which states can govern themselves is a big point of contention.

Federalism can either be co-operative or coercive

CO-OPERATIVE FEDERALISM — When the **relationship** between the **federal government** and **state governments** is relatively **consensual**, and any **changes** to the **power dynamic** between the two are **agreed** in **advance**.

COERCIVE FEDERALISM — When the **federal government** uses **acts of Congress** and **executive orders** to **impose** changes to its relationship with the states **against** their **will**.

Some argue that the growth of the federal government has eroded state power

1) The framers of the Constitution did not envisage a **large**, **expansive** federal government. There were just **three executive departments** during George Washington's presidency.
2) There are now **15 executive departments**, many of which have **responsibility** over areas of **policy** that were once the **responsibility** of each individual **state**, such as **education**, **healthcare** and **employment**.
3) **Federal spending** has **risen** hugely as a result, which has **expanded** the **reach** of the **federal government**. In **2023**, **federal subsidies** for **health insurance** reached an estimated **$1.8 tn**.
4) Increasingly, the federal government uses **categorical grants** — **funding** mechanisms that **specify** exactly how **states** should **spend** the money that they are given.
5) The number of **federal programmes tripled** across **all policy areas** between the 1980s and 2024.

There has also been an increasing uniformity of rights across the United States

1) Until **1865**, states were able to decide whether they **maintained slavery**, but slavery was **abolished** across the **entire United States** when the **13th amendment** was ratified.

2) For the **next century**, many **southern states** maintained a system called **segregation**, which in practice meant that **African Americans** continued to possess **far fewer rights** and lived in much **worse conditions** than **white** Americans. This was eventually **abolished** when **Lyndon Johnson** signed the **Civil Rights Act** in **1964**.

These reforms were major steps forward in the United States' protection of rights, but they did reduce the extent to which the states had control over their own legal systems and cultures.

3) **Marriage rights** have also become more **uniform** — the **Obergefell v. Hodges** Supreme Court ruling in **2015** forced **all states** to recognise and allow **same-sex marriages**.

Supreme Court rulings can return policy power to the states

Dobbs v. Jackson Women's Health Organization (2022)
Case Study
- In one of the most **high-profile** and **controversial** rulings in its history, the Supreme Court **overturned** its decision from **Roe v. Wade (1973)**. The **Roe v. Wade** ruling had upheld the **constitutionality** of **abortion** and therefore required **all states** to **offer access** to abortion.
- The **Dobbs ruling** means that **states** can now once again set their **own laws** on **abortion**.
- In the aftermath of this ruling, many **states** have **banned** or **severely restricted access** to abortions.
- Liberal states like **Connecticut** and **Colorado** continue to uphold the **same level** of **abortion access** that they had **before** the Dobbs ruling.

The number of states with restrictions on abortion access has been changing regularly, so it's a good idea to keep track of the news.

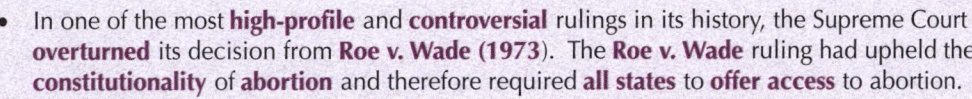

Federalism

The 10th amendment and interstate commerce clause let states retain power

1) The **10th amendment**, also known as the '**reserved powers clause**', establishes that any powers **not explicitly** given to the **federal government** are held by the **states**.

2) The '**interstate commerce clause**' is part of the **Constitution** that is generally interpreted as allowing **Congress** to **regulate trade between states**, but **not** commercial activity **within states**.

3) These have each allowed **states** to **retain** some **power** over how they are **run**. For example, on matters such as:

Drugs

States can still set their own policy on the **legal status** of **drugs**. By **2024**, **32** of the 50 states had legalised the **recreational use of marijuana**, while **Oregon** chose to **decriminalise** the possession of small amounts of marijuana as early as **1973**.

> Technically, marijuana is illegal in federal law under an act of Congress from 1937, but the federal government has not enforced this in recent decades.

Many of these states have **legalised drugs** through the use of another **reserved power** — **direct democracy**. Although direct democracy has not been used at a **federal level** in the US, **states** can choose whether, and how, to hold their own **public votes**.

> Propositions are the closest equivalent to referendums that take place in the US. They only take place at state level, allowing citizens to express their views on social and political issues. In California, 11 propositions were voted on in 2024.

Healthcare

Since the **NFIB v. Sebelius** Supreme Court ruling in **2012**, states have been able to **opt out** of some **federal healthcare subsidies**. **10 states** have chosen not to adopt the expansion to **Medicaid** introduced by Barack Obama's **Patient Protection and Affordable Care Act (2010)**.

During the **COVID-19** pandemic, **states** were able to decide whether they implemented **lockdowns**, **mask mandates** and **social distancing** measures.

Gun ownership

Although the **2nd amendment** means that **all states** have to allow **gun ownership**, they have very different levels of **regulation**. For instance, **New York** has much **stricter laws** on the **documentation** people need to own guns and on carrying them in **public places** than **Kentucky**, where gun laws are very **loose**.

> Congress tried to enforce gun-free school zones across all 50 states in 1994, but the Supreme Court ruled that this violated the 'interstate commerce clause' in US v Lopez (1995).

Death penalty

27 states still retain the **death penalty** for the most serious **crimes**.

Taxation

While all US citizens are subject to **federal taxation**, states can choose the level of **state taxation** they impose on their **residents**, if any at all. For example, **Texas** has **no state income tax**, whereas **California's** highest income tax bracket is over **12%**.

Quick Questions

1) Identify a law that has passed with bipartisan support in recent years.
2) How many votes have been cast across party lines during the past four Supreme Court confirmation processes?
3) What is the difference between coercive federalism and co-operative federalism?
4) Which Supreme Court ruling required all states to offer same-sex marriages?
5) Which previous Supreme Court ruling was overturned by Dobbs v. Jackson Women's Health Organization (2022)?
6) How many states have legalised the recreational use of marijuana?
7) How many states retain the death penalty?

Exam Practice

For Edexcel students: Evaluate the view that the principle of federalism is no longer effectively upheld in the USA. [30]

For AQA students: Explain and analyse three ways in which federalism has changed in the USA. [9]

The tents amendment allows camping across the United States...

OK, I fib, there is no tents amendment. But the 10th amendment ensures states have the ability to set their own laws and policies, giving them all powers not explicitly given to the federal government. There's more on amendments on page 159.

US Politics — The Constitution and Federalism

Democracy in the United States

The US has quite a reputation for its democracy. But is it deserved? Well, dig into these pages and see what you think...

The **US Constitution** is seen as the **first modern democratic constitution**

1) The original Constitution **established** principles of **representative government** and **separation of power**, setting a **democratic precedent** unmatched in the late eighteenth century.
2) The **amendments process** was designed to ensure that **changes** to the **Constitution** would have **indirect democratic consent** by requiring the approval of **Congress** and **state legislatures**. The **elected Congress** and the **amendments process** are both **cornerstones** of American **democracy**.
3) The Constitution's system of **checks and balances** ensures **no single branch of government** can **dominate**, **protecting** democratic governance.

Its **amendments** have **reinforced democracy** in the US

1st amendment (ratified in 1791)
This guaranteed the **fundamental freedoms** of **speech**, **religion** and **assembly**. It was introduced just **four years** after the Constitution as part of the **Bill of Rights**.

12th amendment (ratified in 1804)
This established the **process** for electing the **president** (see p.205-206).

15th amendment (ratified in 1870)
One of the **Reconstruction amendments** (passed after the Civil War), this extended **suffrage** to some **former slaves**.

"I heard there was even more ratifying to be done..."

While the 15th amendment gave the right to vote to all men, regardless of their race, colour or past status as a slave, it wasn't universally applied across all states. It wasn't until the Voting Rights Act of 1965 that all people of colour had their right to vote protected and enforced across the whole of the US.

17th amendment (ratified in 1913)
This established **direct Senate elections**, meaning that the people of each state could now vote for each of their two senators **every six years**.

19th amendment (ratified in 1920)
This extended **suffrage** to **all women** over the age of **21** (at the time, this was also the voting age for men).

23rd amendment (ratified in 1961)
This gave residents of **Washington D.C.** the right to **vote** in **presidential** elections.

26th amendment (ratified in 1971)
This **lowered** the voting age in **federal** (**presidential** and **congressional**) elections to **18**.

The original Constitution **prioritised** the rights of **free white men**

1) Of the **55 constitutional framers** who attended the **Philadelphia Convention** in 1787, an estimated **25 owned slaves**, and **all** were **men**.
2) The **document** that they produced **reflected** their **status**. **Slavery** was accounted for in the original **Constitution** through the **three-fifths compromise**. This section of the Constitution had states agree to the principle that **three** out of every **five slaves** would be **counted** when calculating a state's **total population** for **representation** and **taxation** purposes.

US Politics — The Constitution and Federalism

Democracy in the United States

The **Electoral College** has been criticised for being **undemocratic**

1) The **Electoral College** (see page 208) contains **538 electors** who are technically **responsible** for choosing the **president**.

2) This system was originally designed as an **alternative** to **direct democratic elections**, although this **changed** with the ratification of the **12th amendment** in **1804**.

3) Each **state** has a certain **number** of **electors** depending on the size of its **population**. For example, in the **2024 presidential election**, **California** (the **most populous** state) had **54** electoral college votes, while **Wyoming** (the **least populous** state) had **three**.

4) Because votes in **48** of the **50 states** are awarded on a **winner-takes-all** basis, the Electoral College encourages **presidential campaigns** to focus on a small number of 'vote rich' **swing states**, such as **Pennsylvania**, **Michigan** and **Wisconsin**. States that are considered **solidly Republican** or **Democrat** receive much **less attention** during campaigning.

Mahogany chests containing the Electoral College votes for the 2020 US presidential election

5) Convention dictates that **electors** will base their **vote** on the **preferences** of the **state** that they **represent**. However there are occasionally '**rogue**' or '**faithless**' electors who cast their **vote** based on their **own views**. There were **seven** faithless votes in **2016**, six of which were cast for people who **hadn't** even **stood** for the **presidency**.

> Unlike in the UK and many other democratic political systems, the US has no national-level direct democracy, although many states choose to hold their own public votes (see page 156).

6) The **disproportionate nature** of the Electoral College can mean that a candidate is elected president **without winning** the **popular vote** across the United States. This happened in **2016**, when **Donald Trump** was elected president despite **Hillary Clinton** winning the popular vote. It also happened in **2000**, when **George W. Bush** became president despite **Al Gore** winning the popular vote.

Critics of the Electoral College, such as members of the **National Popular Vote** campaign (see p.209), argue that this is **undemocratic** and **fails to produce** a solid **mandate** for the president.

Quick Questions

1) Which group of people were granted suffrage by the original US Constitution?
2) Which amendment outlines the process for electing the president?
3) Who did the 23rd amendment give the right to vote to?
4) Which amendment lowered the voting age to 18?
5) How many electors are there in the Electoral College?
6) What is a 'rogue/faithless elector'?

Exam Practice

For Edexcel students: Evaluate the view that the US Constitution's greatest flaw is its weak provisions for democracy. [30]

For AQA students: Explain and analyse three criticisms of the extent of democracy in the US Constitution. [9]

Despite its name, you can't get a Politics A-Level from the Electoral College...

But you can sure get a minor headache from trying to make sense of it. And that's why it's super important that you understand how the Electoral College works and the role it plays in US politics. Blimey, anyone got some painkillers?...

Amendments to the US Constitution

I'm sure you've heard a few Americans talk about their first amendment rights, or the right to bear arms. Well, those are all down to amendments to the US Constitution. Actually getting those amendments made can be pretty tricky though...

The **US Constitution** has only been formally **amended 27 times**

1) The **first 10 amendments** to the Constitution are known as the **Bill of Rights**.
2) They were ratified in **1791**, only **four years** after the Constitution had been written.
3) The Bill of Rights contains some of the **most famous** amendments, including:

   1ST AMENDMENT — grants the **fundamental rights** of **freedom of speech**, **freedom of religion** and **freedom of assembly**.

   2ND AMENDMENT — outlines the **right to bear arms**.

   The 2nd amendment is one of the most controversial aspects of the US Constitution.

   5TH AMENDMENT — guarantees **due process** (the **right** to a **free** and **fair trial**) and **protects** citizens from **incriminating themselves** when giving **testimony**.

   10TH AMENDMENT — known as the '**reserved powers clause**', this reserves powers **not** given to the **federal government** for the **states**.

4) Since the Bill of Rights, the Constitution has only been amended **17 times**, most recently in **1992**. Here are some of the most **significant** amendments:

Hugh embraced the right to bare arms

   12TH AMENDMENT — outlined the **procedure** for **electing** the **president** and the **vice president**.

   13TH, 14TH AND 15TH AMENDMENTS — known as the **Reconstruction amendments**, these were ratified after the **Civil War**. They **abolished slavery**, **granted citizenship** to **former slaves** and gave some former slaves the **right to vote**.

   19TH AMENDMENT — ratified in 1920, it extended **suffrage** to **women**.

   22ND AMENDMENT — This **limited** future **presidents** to serving **two elected terms**. It was introduced after the **long presidency** of **Franklin D. Roosevelt**, who was **elected four times** and served from **1933** to **1945**.

Some think the **complexity** of the **amendments process** is a **good** thing

1) Some believe that the **complex amendments process** is an **effective** way of **protecting rights** and ensuring **limited government**.
2) **Amendments** require support from **two-thirds** of both the **House of Representatives** and the **Senate** to be **proposed**. They need support from **three-quarters** of the **states** to be **ratified**. This makes it **very difficult** for **rights** detailed in the Constitution to be **taken away**.
3) The **executive branch** has **no role** in the amendments process, which provides a further **safeguard** against **tyrannical rule**.

An amendment that makes it through Congress remains on the books until it is ratified by three-quarters of states.

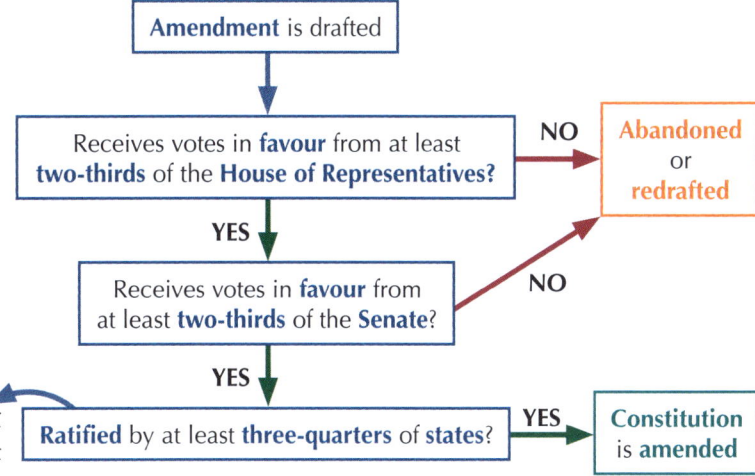

US Politics — The Constitution and Federalism

Amendments to the US Constitution

Others argue the Constitution's **rigidity** prevents **updates** to **rights protections**

Many **liberals** argue that the **2nd amendment** has become **outdated**, but the **complexity** of the **amendment process** means that there is **no prospect** of it being **changed** in the foreseeable future.

- When the 2nd amendment was ratified in **1791**, **the right to bear arms** was considered an **important defence** against **foreign armies** and a potentially **tyrannical federal government**. It was also an important requirement for **hunting**.
- There were **over 600 mass shootings each year** from **2020-2023**. Many of these involved **semi-automatic** or **automatic assault weapons** — guns that are much **more powerful** than the guns available in 1791.

Despite being **popular** among the American people, some **proposed amendments** have **never** been **ratified**.

The **Equal Rights Amendment**, which prohibits **sexual discrimination**, was first proposed in **1923**. However, it is currently only ratified by **33 states**. As this is **five fewer** than the **required number** (**38**), it has not been enacted.

Although 38 states have ratified the Equal Rights Amendment, five states have withdrawn their ratification since 1972, which is why it hasn't been enacted.

Most **constitutional 'amendments'** now come from **Supreme Court rulings**

1) The **most significant** Supreme Court **rulings** are known as **informal amendments** to the Constitution.

See page 194-195 for details of the key Supreme Court cases that have updated the Constitution's rights protection.

2) The **Supreme Court's rulings** on matters like **campaign finance**, **abortion**, **healthcare**, **segregation** and **gun rights** have had just as **significant** an **impact** on US **politics** and **society** as many of the **formal** amendments.

3) The Supreme Court's **role** in **informally amending** the Constitution is **controversial**. Many accuse the Court of having **expanded** its own role **beyond** the framers' intention, while others feel that it enjoys **inappropriate levels of power** given the **politicised** nature of the **appointments** process.

Quick Questions

1) Which amendment to the Constitution extended suffrage to women?
2) Which amendment to the Constitution provides the procedure for electing the president and vice president?
3) Briefly describe what needs to happen for the Constitution to be amended.
4) Why has the Equal Rights Amendment not been enacted?
5) Which body's rulings can act as informal amendments to the Constitution?

Essay Plan

For Edexcel students: Evaluate the view that the US Constitution is outdated and ineffective. [30]

For AQA students: 'The US Constitution is outdated and ineffective.' Analyse and evaluate this statement. [25]

Using the grid on p.298, **plan** an answer to one of the essay questions above.

Top Tip for Politicians #755: Fix your bad breath with amendmints...
The Constitution is so revered in the US that it's not too surprising that changing it is tricky and controversial. Make sure you know the details of the amendments process — and the loopholes that allow the Supreme Court to work around it.

Comparing the US and UK Constitutions

Surprise surprise, the UK also has a constitution. It has some pretty important differences to its US counterpart though...

The **US Constitution** is **codified** but the **UK Constitution isn't**

The **US CONSTITUTION** is **sovereign** and **entrenched** because it is **codified**.

- This means the **original articles** and subsequent **amendments** that make up the US Constitution serve as the **highest form** of **law** in the United States. It **takes precedence** over **all** other laws passed at **federal** and **state** levels.
- For example, the ratification of the **13th amendment** in 1865 meant that **slavery** was **abolished** across **every state**, regardless of **previous laws** that had been passed.
- The strict **amendments process** means that the Constitution tends not to **change** very often. There have only been **27 amendments** since the **Philadelphia Convention** in **1787**, and **no** formal amendments since **1992**.

Because of the differences in the 'location of sovereignty' in the US and the UK, another key difference between the two constitutions is the extent to which they are upheld and updated by their respective judicial branches. There's more on this on p.201-202.

The **UK CONSTITUTION** is **not sovereign** and **unentrenched** because it is **uncodified**.

- Because **Parliament** is **sovereign**, there is no entrenched or higher law in the UK. **Statute law** passed by Parliament **takes precedence** over the **other sources** of the Constitution (such as **common law** and **conventions**), but it can be **amended** or **repealed** at **any time** without going through a **separate** amendments process.
- As a result, the **UK Constitution** is more flexible and gets **amended** far more **frequently**. Since the 27th amendment to the US Constitution was ratified in 1992, the UK Constitution has undergone **major changes**, including to the following areas:

  - Introduction of **devolution**
  - Introduction of the **Human Rights Act**
  - Creation of the **UK Supreme Court**
  - **Introduction** (and subsequent **repeal**) of the **Fixed-Term Parliaments Act**
  - **Brexit**

These reforms are all covered in more detail on p.62-64.

Remember to refer to the UK Constitution as uncodified, rather than unwritten. Most of its sources are in fact written down, but they are not contained in a single, authoritative document.

Chloe's attempt to codify the UK Constitution was off to a slow start

They provide **different levels** of **checks** on the **government**

US Constitution	UK Constitution
The **US Constitution** provides a much **stronger** system of **checks** and **balances**, designed to ensure **limited government**.	The **UK Constitution** contains far **fewer** checks on the **legislative** and **executive** branches. The **fusion of powers** gives the executive branch much greater **influence** over **Parliament** in the **UK** than the **president** has over **Congress** in the **US**.
The framers wanted to prevent the US from experiencing **tyrannical rule** (see p.150), so the **executive branch** is particularly well **checked** by **Congress**. Since **Marbury v. Madison (1803)**, the **judicial branch** has been able to check the executive branch as well.	By convention, the **prime minister** is the **leader of the largest party** in the House of Commons. As a result, they tend to have an **inbuilt majority** in that chamber. Prime ministers with **large majorities** in the House of Commons (e.g. **Tony Blair** from **1997-2007** and **Boris Johnson** after the **2019** election) tend to face **few obstacles** when implementing their **legislative agenda** (see p.96).
The **president** has **very little influence** over the passage of **legislation** through **Congress**. **Presidential appointments** to the **Cabinet** and the **Supreme Court** receive extremely **rigorous scrutiny** in Congress (see p.172).	While the **prime minister** no longer has a **direct role** in **judicial appointments** in the UK, their appointments to **Cabinet** and other **executive branch positions** receive **no formal scrutiny** at all.
The **symmetrical** nature of **bicameralism** (see p.167) in the US further increases the **strength** of checks and balances. In legislative terms, the **House of Representatives** and the **Senate** have **broadly equal powers**, meaning that bills face very **detailed scrutiny** in both chambers.	The **asymmetrical** nature of **bicameralism** in the UK further **weakens** the constitutional **checks** and **balances** on the executive branch. The **House of Lords** is **less powerful** than the **Commons**, and because it has no **elected mandate**, prime ministers are usually able to get their way if there is a lengthy **disagreement** between the **Commons** and the **Lords** (see p.77).

US Politics — The Constitution and Federalism

Comparing the US and UK Constitutions

Both Constitutions are a mix of specific and vague about political issues

	The Constitution is specific regarding...	The Constitution is vague regarding...
US Constitution	• Amendments process — outlined in Article V • Legislative process — outlined in Article I • Electoral process • Suffrage	• Division of power between national and state governments (federalism) — 10th amendment ('reserved powers clause') • Power over trade ('interstate commerce clause') • Scale of Congress's powers ('necessary and proper clause') • Role of the Supreme Court • Checks and balances between the president and Congress in foreign policy
UK Constitution	• Human rights — outlined in the Human Rights Act (1998) • Legislative process — outlined in Erskine May's *Parliamentary Practice* • Devolution • Suffrage	• Constitutional status of referendums • Conventions, e.g. the role of Parliament in authorising military interventions • Checks on the PM's prerogative powers

The UK Constitution has arguably become more similar to its US counterpart

1) Since 1997, there have been moves to **codify** aspects of the UK Constitution, particularly in relation to **rights protection**. The **Human Rights Act (1998)** and the **Equality Act (2010)** have brought **greater clarity** than existed previously.

2) Since the passage of the **Constitutional Reform Act (2005)**, which established the **UK Supreme Court**, the **judiciary** has had a **greater role** in making decisions of **constitutional significance**.

Devolution has moved the UK to an arrangement known as quasi-federalism

Scotland, Wales, Northern Ireland and some parts of England all have some form of **devolved legislature** (see p.66-68). Some of the devolved legislatures now have similar levels of **power** to **state legislatures** in the **US**:

- Since the **Scotland Act (2016)**, the Scottish Parliament has been able to amend **income tax** and **corporation tax** in Scotland as much as it chooses. Under the US Constitution, **all 50 states have this power**, allowing **California** to impose a highest level of income tax of **12%** and **Texas** to have **no state income tax** at all.
- Similarly, both US states and UK devolved legislatures have **primary legislative power** over areas of policy like **healthcare**, **education** and **policing**.

Key Terms
quasi-federalism
A constitutional arrangement where multiple locations of political power exist, but do not technically have permanent status due to parliamentary sovereignty.

Devolution is **asymmetrical** in the UK, while federalism is **symmetrical** in the US. This means that the **devolved bodies** in the **UK** have **unequal** levels of power, while the 50 **states** in the **US** all have **equal power** over their own political systems.

Exam Practice

For Edexcel students: Examine the differences between the features of the US and UK Constitutions. [12]

For AQA students: 'The UK Constitution provides a more effective framework for government than the US Constitution.' Analyse and evaluate this statement. [25]

I don't know why you'd want to cod-ify anything. The smell alone...
Mercifully, a codified constitution is nothing to do with the nation's favourite chippy order. Remember, a codified constitution is all contained in a single, authoritative document, while an uncodified one is spread across multiple different sources.

US Politics — The Constitution and Federalism

Analysing the US and UK Constitutions

Well that's the constitutions fully compared — time to look into exactly why they have those similarities and differences...

There are **structural** and **cultural similarities** between the constitutions...

Structural Similarities

1. **Both** constitutions provide **powers** to **three main branches** of **government**:

   The **legislative branch** — **Congress** in the US and **Parliament** in the UK.
   The **executive branch** — led by the **president** in the US and by the **prime minister** in the UK.
   The **judicial branch** — led by each country's **Supreme Court**.

2. Since the **Constitutional Reform Act (2005)**, which established the UK Supreme Court, **both constitutions** have created a **separation of powers** between the **judicial** branch and the **other** two branches of government.

   - In the **UK**, this means that **nobody** can serve as a **judge** at the same time as serving as a **member of Parliament** or as a **minister** in the **executive branch**. Supreme Court **judges** do **not** take up their seats in the **House of Lords** until after their **retirement**.
   - As part of the total **separation of powers** in the US, **nobody** can sit in **more than one** branch at any given time.

3. Both constitutions contain a blend of **specificity** and **vagueness** about the **political structures** that they create:

   - In the US and the UK, there are very **specific provisions** about the **legislative process** (outlined in **Article I** of the **US Constitution** and in Erskine May's *Parliamentary Practice*).
   - There is a **shared vagueness** concerning control over **military decision making**. This has allowed the **president** and the **prime minister** to assume **more power** as the nature of **warfare** has shifted from **ground wars** to **air** and **drone strikes**:
     1) In the US, **Congress** has not issued a formal **declaration of war** since 1942, despite **Article I, Section 8** of the Constitution granting this power. **Air** and **drone strikes** routinely take place **without** any **congressional approval**.
     2) Similarly, the **convention** established by **Tony Blair** (and then followed by **David Cameron**) that the **House of Commons** should give **prior consent** for **military action** has been **ignored** in recent years. **Theresa May** ignored it when ordering air strikes in **Syria** in **2018**, as did **Rishi Sunak** when targeting **Houthi** rebels in **Yemen** in **2024**.

Cultural Similarities

1. **Both constitutions** create **democratic political systems** in which **voters** are able to choose their **representatives**.

2. In both cases, **democracy** has been **strengthened** through **constitutional amendments**:

   In the **UK**, the **Reform Acts** and the **Representation of the People Acts** have extended **suffrage** and **lowered** the **voting age** (p.6). In the **US**, this has happened through the **15th, 19th, 23rd** and **26th amendments** (p.157).

3. Both constitutions are **overseen** (although to differing extents) by extremely **powerful** groups of **judges** who sit in the respective countries' **Supreme Courts**.

   - In the **US**, Supreme Court judges routinely exercise power by declaring **acts** of **Congress**, the **presidency** and the **states** as **constitutional** or **unconstitutional**.
   - In **2022**, **conservative** justices on the US Supreme Court **overturned** the landmark **Roe v. Wade (1973)** (see p.155) decision by upholding the **constitutionality** of **state-level abortion bans**.
   - In **2023**, **all five** sitting judges on the **UK Supreme Court** unanimously ruled that **Rwanda** should **not** be regarded as a **safe country** for **refugees**, thereby delaying one of **Rishi Sunak's** best-known policies.

Analysing the US and UK Constitutions

Cultural Similarities (continued)

 Both constitutions **underpin** their respective countries' cultures of **rights protection**:

- The US Constitution's **protection** of **free speech** and **assembly** (through the **1st amendment**) helps **pressure groups** and other **organisations** to campaign for **rights**. For example, during the **Civil Rights era**, activists like **Martin Luther King Jr.** and organisations like the **NAACP** successfully campaigned for an **end** to **segregation**.
- Similarly, the **UK Constitution** has created a **rights culture** through **statute law** such as the **Human Rights Act (1998)** and the **Freedom of Information Act (2000)**. These acts allow **pressure groups** and **campaigners** to **challenge** government decisions in the **courts** and through **Freedom of Information requests**. For example, the pressure groups **Plan B** and **Friends of the Earth** have **collaborated** to mount **legal challenges** to the government's plan to build a **third runway** at Heathrow Airport.

"I didn't think the pressure group would be so literal..."

...and **structural** and **cultural differences**

Structural Differences

1. The **US Constitution** is a **codified**, **entrenched document** that can only formally be **amended** with **supermajorities** in both chambers of **Congress** (two-thirds) and across the **state legislatures** (three-quarters). The **uncodified UK Constitution** is much more **flexible**, containing a range of **written** and **unwritten sources**. **Amendment** can be relatively **straightforward** — **statute law** can be amended with **simple majorities** (50% + 1 vote) in the **House of Commons** and the **House of Lords**.

2. While the **US Constitution** creates a **symmetrical** form of **federalism**, recent reforms to the **UK Constitution** have established an **asymmetrical** form of **devolution**.

   - Under the **10th amendment** and the **interstate commerce clause**, the **states** are given the same level of **power** as each other, largely because state **representatives** made up the **framers** of the original Constitution.
   - In practice, this means that in the US, **larger** and **more populous** states like **California** and **Texas** have exactly the **same** level of **control** over their own **political systems** as **smaller**, **less populous** states like **Wyoming** and **Vermont**. For example, each state has **equal control** over its own **income tax** and **corporation tax** thresholds.
   - By contrast, the **Scottish Parliament** has **more power** than the **Senedd** (the **Welsh Parliament**), which in turn has **more power** than the **Northern Ireland Assembly**. The **devolved** bodies in **regions** of **England** have **less power** than any of these **national** devolved bodies (see p.68).
   - While the **Scottish Parliament** can vary **income tax** in Scotland as much as it chooses, the **Senedd** can only **increase** or **decrease** it by up to **10%**. The **Northern Ireland Assembly** and the **regional** devolved bodies in England have **no power** over **income tax**, which is set by the **UK Parliament** in Westminster.

3. There remains a **fusion of powers** between the **executive** and **legislative** branches in the **UK**, while the **US Constitution** outlines a strict **separation of powers** between all three branches:

   - While **UK government ministers** like the **Chancellor of the Exchequer** and the **Foreign Secretary** are also members of **Parliament**, members of **Cabinet** in the **US** are **not allowed** to sit in **Congress**.
   - This typically gives the **UK executive branch** much more **influence** over **Parliament** than the **US executive branch** has over **Congress**, because the **prime minister's** party usually has an inbuilt **majority** in the **House of Commons**.
   - By contrast, **divided government** is more **common** than **united government** in the **US**. Unlike the **prime minister**, who benefits from the **payroll vote**, the **president** cannot **rely** on members of their **executive branch** to help with the passage of **legislation**.

Analysing the US and UK Constitutions

Cultural Differences

1 The different **amendments processes** give different levels of **power** to certain **groups**:

- In the **US**, members of **state legislatures** have **significant power** because of the requirement for **three-quarters** of the states to **ratify** each **amendment** that has been proposed by **Congress**.
- For example, the **Equal Rights Amendment** was proposed by **Congress** in **1923**, but **conservative** state legislatures have consistently **refused** to ratify it.
- In the **UK**, the **devolved legislatures** have **no power** to **influence amendments** to the Constitution because **Parliament** remains **sovereign**.
- This has become apparent since **2016**, when the **Brexit referendum** led to renewed calls for a **second referendum** on Scottish independence. Despite attempts by the **Scottish Parliament** to call a **second referendum**, this power continues to lie with the **UK Parliament** in Westminster. This power was confirmed by a **Supreme Court** ruling in **2022**.

2 Although rulings from both **Supreme Courts** do **update** their respective **constitutions** (through the **informal** amendments process in the **US** and through **common law** rulings in the **UK**), the **judges** on the **US Supreme Court** are a far **more powerful** group than their **UK** counterparts.

- Since **Marbury v. Madison (1803)**, US Supreme Court judges have effectively become **guardians** of the **US Constitution**. They are able to rule on the **constitutionality** (or **unconstitutionality**) of any act of Congress, executive orders or state-level laws and policies.
- In the **UK**, judges are able to issue *ultra vires* rulings and declarations of incompatibility, but they do not have the power to **overrule Parliament**, which is **sovereign** in the **UK** system.

3 Another major **cultural difference** created by the two constitutions lies in the extent to which the political views of **Supreme Court judges** are publicly known:

- In the **US**, most **judges** are known to be either **liberal** or **conservative**, with **Democrat** presidents typically nominating **liberal justices** and **Republican** presidents typically nominating **conservative justices**.
- In the **UK**, the **political views** of judges are **not known** by the public, and Supreme Court judges have a much **lower profile** than their US counterparts.

Quick Questions

1) How many times has the US Constitution been amended?
2) Give an example of a convention that forms part of the UK Constitution.
3) Which constitutional reform introduced a partial separation of powers in the UK?
4) Give one cultural difference between the role of Supreme Court Judges in the US and UK.

Exam Practice

For Edexcel students: Examine the differences between the nature of the US and UK constitutions. [12]

For AQA students: Explain and analyse three ways in which structural theory could be used to study checks and balances in the US and the UK. [9]

Exam Practice

For Edexcel students: Analyse the impact of the US and UK constitutions on their respective political systems. [12]

For AQA students: Explain and analyse three ways in which cultural theory could be used to study the impact of the US and UK constitutions on their respective political systems. [9]

The constituent parts of the constitutions have some consistencies...

Be sure to learn those structural and cultural comparisons, so you can back up your points when analysing US and UK politics.

Congress

Time to tackle Congress — the branch of the US government responsible for passing laws and representing the people.

Congress is the **legislative branch** of the **US federal government**

1) **Congress** was granted its power by **Article I** of the **Constitution**. It was **intended** by the framers to be the **most powerful** and **significant branch** of **government**.
2) Congress has **two chambers**: the **House of Representatives** and the **Senate**.
3) The **bicameral system** was **proposed** by the representatives from Connecticut at the **Philadelphia Convention** in **1787**. The agreement they reached is called the **Connecticut Compromise**.
4) This system was designed to **satisfy** the interests of **all states**, regardless of the **size** of their **population**. In the House of Representatives, states are allocated **members** according to the **size** of their **population**, whereas **representation** in the Senate is **equal** for each state.

Jefferson thought his branch was pretty significant

The House of Representatives
- There are **435 members** of the House of Representatives.
- Each representative is elected by a **congressional district**.
- **States** are **divided** into a certain **number** of congressional districts depending on the **size** of their **population**, although all states have **at least one representative**. **California**, the **most populous** state, elected **52 members** of the House in the **2024** election.
- The **leader** of the **largest party** in the House of Representatives is usually the **House Speaker**. The House Speaker is responsible for **scheduling** and **chairing debates**, and **deciding** which **legislation** the House **votes on**.

The Senate
- There are **100 senators** in the Senate — **two senators** for **each state**.
- **Senators** are elected for **six-year terms**.
- The **leader** of the **largest party** in the Senate is usually the **Senate Majority Leader**. The Senate Majority Leader is responsible for **scheduling debates** and **controlling** which **legislation** senators **vote on**.

5) **Congressional elections** take place **every two years**. One occurs at the **same time** as the **presidential election**. The other takes place **halfway through** the **four-year presidential term** — these elections are known as **mid-terms**.
6) Since **1845**, Congress has **mandated** that **federal elections** should take place on the **Tuesday after** the **first Monday in November**, i.e. the **first Tuesday** to fall **between 2nd November** and **8th November**.
7) During each congressional election, the **entire House of Representatives** and **one third of the Senate** are **re-elected**.

Congress has **three main functions**

1) PASSING LEGISLATION

All **bills** need to be **approved** by **both** the **House of Representatives** and the **Senate** before they are **signed into law** by the **president**. If the president chooses to **veto** the bill, Congress can **still pass it** if **two-thirds** of both the **House** and the **Senate** vote to **override** the president's veto.

Congress is also responsible for **proposing amendments** to the **US Constitution**. A **two-thirds majority** is needed before the amendment **passes** to the **states** for ratification.

2) APPLYING OVERSIGHT

Congress is an **essential part** of the **constitutional system** of **checks** and **balances**, which is designed to **prevent** the **president** and other members of the **federal government** from becoming **too powerful**.

As well as **scrutinising legislation**, congressional committees **analyse policy** and **spending**, conduct **investigations** into **controversies** and **crises**, and **vote** to **confirm** or **block presidential appointments** and **treaties**.

3) PROVIDING REPRESENTATION

The **bicameral system** was designed to **represent** both the **US people** (primarily through the **House of Representatives**) and the **states** (primarily through **the Senate**). Congressional representation can be divided into **two broad categories**:

- **Political (substantive) representation** — the extent to which **members** of Congress **vote** and **act** in a way that **represents** the **views** and **interests** of the **US public as a whole** and their **constituents in particular**.
- **Social (demographic) representation** — the extent to which the **make-up** of Congress **reflects** the make-up of the **US population** in terms of **race**, **socio-economic status**, **sex**, **sexuality**, etc.

When things are positive in Congress it turns into Pro-gress...

In most states, congressional districts are referred to by numbers, e.g. New York's 14th district. In the least populous states that only have one member of the House (e.g. Wyoming), the district is referred to as the state's 'at-large' congressional district.

The House of Representatives and the Senate

*Just like Parliament has two houses, Congress has two chambers. The House of Representatives represents the people of the US, while the Senate represents the states. If you get them muddled up, just remember that **people** live in the **House**...*

Both chambers of Congress have significant roles in the US political system

1) **Unlike** the **UK**, where the **House of Commons** has **more power** than the **House of Lords**, the **two chambers** of Congress were intended to have **broadly equal powers** — this is known as **symmetrical bicameralism.**
2) The **comparable power** of the **House of Representatives** and the **Senate** strengthens **checks and balances** significantly. In order to achieve their **legislative priorities**, **presidents** have to **persuade** both chambers, which are often **controlled** by **different parties**, to **approve** the **same version** of a **bill**.
3) Because they are both **fully elected chambers**, the House and the Senate possess their own **democratic mandates** that they can use to **challenge** or **support** the **president**.

The House and the Senate have some concurrent powers

1) Both chambers are equally responsible for **passing legislation**, **proposing constitutional amendments**, and **overriding presidential vetoes**. Unlike in the UK, there is **no mechanism** that allows **one chamber** to **overrule** or **ignore** the **other**.
2) The **House** and the **Senate** can both establish **investigations**, which usually focus on **alleged misconduct** or **poor performance** by members of the **executive branch**.
3) Both chambers need to vote **in favour** of a **formal declaration of war** — although this hasn't happened since the Second World War.

Key Terms
concurrent powers
Powers that are shared by both the House of Representatives and the Senate.

There are some differences in the House and the Senate's powers

THE HOUSE OF REPRESENTATIVES:
1) **Only** the **House** can initiate **money bills** (legislation relating to **taxation** and **public spending**) — although these still need to be **approved** by the **Senate** as part of Congress's **power of the purse**.
2) The **House** can vote to **impeach** members of the **executive branch**, including the **president**.

THE SENATE:
1) The **Senate** is responsible for placing an impeached individual on **trial**. If **two-thirds of senators** vote in **favour**, the individual can be **removed from office**.
2) The **Senate** has **exclusive power** to **confirm presidential appointments** to the **judiciary**, including the **Supreme Court**, and to the **executive branch**.
3) The **Senate** is also **solely responsible** for **scrutinising** and voting to **ratify** or **block treaties** that the president has negotiated.

Key Terms
exclusive powers
Powers held by either the House of Representatives or by the Senate, but not by both chambers.

Senators have more individual power than representatives

1) There are only **100 senators**, compared with **435** members of the **House**, so their **power** is **more concentrated**.
2) Because **only a third** of senators are ever up for **re-election** at the same time, there are usually **tighter majorities** in the **Senate** than in the **House of Representatives**.
3) Since **1980**, **neither party** has had **more** than **58 senators**, and there have been **three 50-50 splits**. These **slim majorities** in recent decades have given **individual senators** (especially those towards the **centre** of the **political spectrum**) even more power.
4) In recent years, **centrist senators** (such as Republicans **Susan Collins**, **Lisa Murkowski** and **Mitt Romney** and Democrats **Joe Manchin** and **Kirsten Sinema**) have often held the **balance of power**, effectively able to **decide** whether **legislation passes** and whether **appointments** are **confirmed**. As a result, these **moderate senators** tend to have a lot of **influence** and **leverage**, and parties may seek out senators with moderate views to take advantage of this.

The importance of individual Senate seats can be shown by the record levels of spending on the Senate election in Georgia in 2022. This election would decide whether the Democrats would have an outright majority in the upper chamber. The two candidates, Democrat Raphael Warnock and Republican Herschel Walker, were estimated to have raised nearly $300 million combined.

US Politics — Congress

The House of Representatives and the Senate

Committees are extremely powerful in both chambers

1) There are roughly **200 committees** and **sub-committees** in Congress.
2) Their **responsibilities** range from providing **oversight** on particular **policy areas** (e.g. the House Energy and Commerce Committee) to **confirming presidential appointments**.
3) **Nominees** for **senior positions** in the **executive branch** and the **judiciary** face **questioning** and a **vote** from the relevant **Senate committee** before the nomination is **debated** and **voted on** by the **whole chamber**.
4) Committees also tend to provide the most significant **scrutiny of bills** as they move through the **legislative process** (see next page).
5) Only around **4%** of **bills** make it to the point of being **debated** and **voted** on by the **whole House** or **Senate** chamber — most are **rejected** at **committee stage**.
6) Members of committees have the opportunity to **earmark** bills as they pass through the committee stage — this allows them to **introduce provisions** that align with their **political agenda** or the **interests** of their **constituents** (see page 170).

"Umm, I think you earmarked the wrong Bill..."

The House of Representatives has traditionally been the more partisan chamber

1) Because Representatives are elected by **congressional districts**, which have an average electorate of **760 000**, most do not need to **appeal** to the **same number of voters** as **senators**.
2) The short **two-year terms** in the House of Representatives are also seen as a factor that **encourages partisanship**. Representatives will often want to be able to point to **specific achievements** in **passing** or **blocking legislation** when they seek **re-election**.
3) By contrast, the **six-year Senate terms** are supposed to **encourage longer term thinking** by giving senators more time to make an **impact** rather than facing the constant **pressure** of seeking **re-election**.

Because congressional districts are much smaller, they tend not to have the ideological diversity that a whole state would have.

The Senate has become more partisan and polarised in recent years

1) Under majority leaders **Harry Reid (Democrat: 2007-2015)** and **Mitch McConnell (Republican: 2015-2021)**, the **Senate** increasingly **resembled** the **House** in terms of the **tactics** employed by each party and the level of **party discipline** in **voting** on legislation and appointments.
2) From **2009-2021**, senators voted **with their party 64%** of the time, compared with **56%** of the time from **1996-2008**.
3) **Reid** took the so-called 'nuclear option' of **abolishing** the **filibuster** (see p.154) for **appointments** to the **executive branch** in **2013**. McConnell then **abolished** the **filibuster** for **judicial appointments** in **2017**.
4) This means that **appointments** now only need to be **approved** by just over **half** of the senators. Previously, they needed to secure **60 votes** in order to **bypass** a **possible filibuster**. In practice, this allows **appointments** to be made with the **support** of **only one party** when the **president's party** also **controls** the **Senate**.

According to the Pew Research Center, an independent think tank, there were fewer than 30 moderates (centrists) across the House and the Senate by 2022, compared with more than 160 in 1972.

Quick Questions

1) Which article of the Constitution grants powers to Congress?
2) Which state has the most members of the House?
3) How many senators are there?
4) What is meant by concurrent powers?
5) Identify an exclusive power of the House of Representatives.
6) Define symmetrical bicameralism.
7) Who was the Senate Majority Leader when the filibuster was abolished for judicial appointments?

I can talk forever about my favourite steak dish — call me the fillet-buster...
While they've been used effectively by both political parties, filibusters are a controversial political tactic. Some feel it's unfair that a single politician could prevent a motion that there's majority support for, even if that majority is less than 60%.

US Politics — Congress

Congress's Legislative Function

Right, it's time for Congress to lay down the law. And to do that, they first need to draft a bill, then form a committee, then...

The **legislative process** is designed to provide **high levels** of **scrutiny**

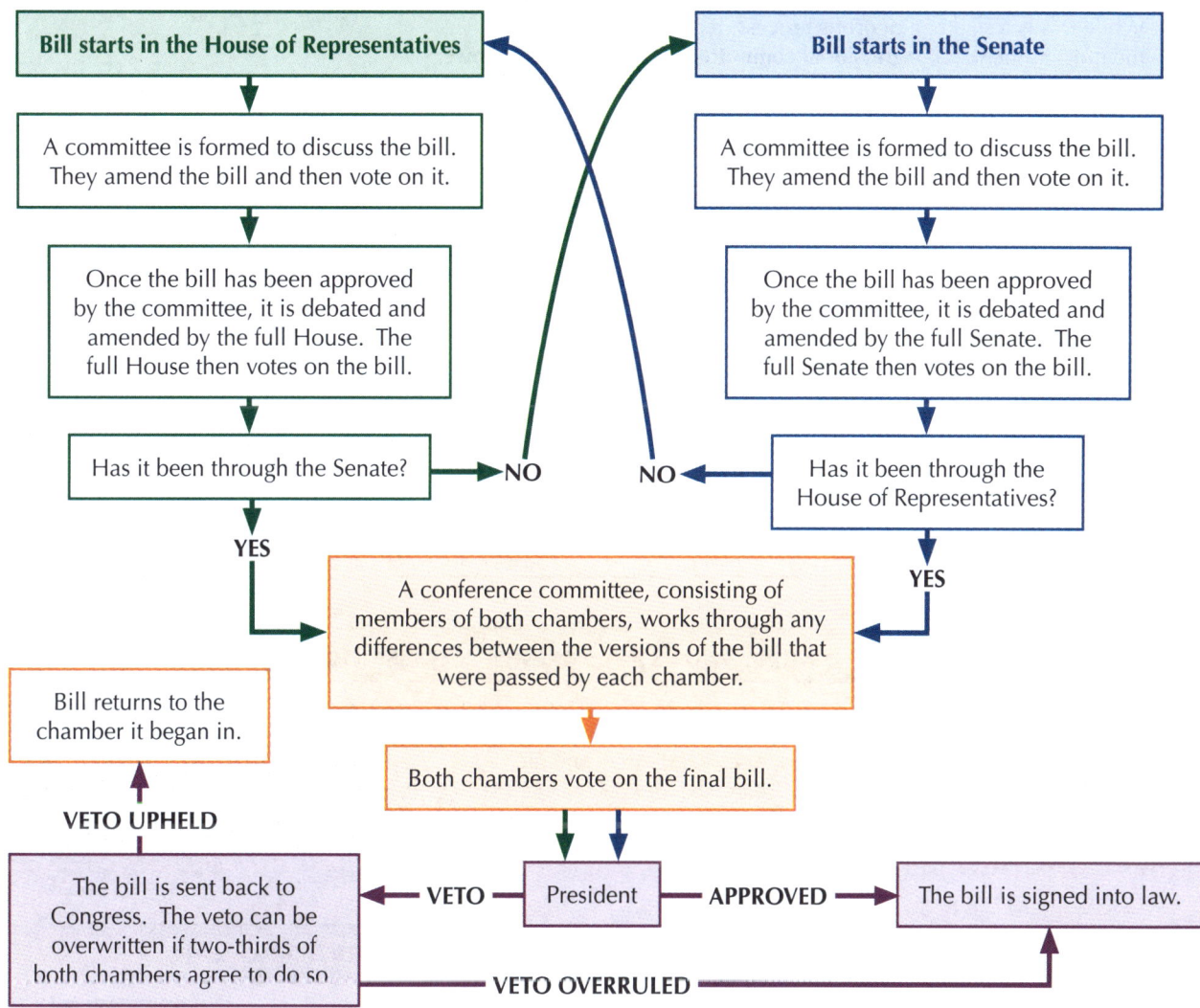

- The process **promotes compromise**. Because the House of Representatives and the Senate **both** have to **agree** on the **same version** of a bill, and because **both chambers** have **equal democratic legitimacy**, it is **impossible** for a bill to be **rushed through** without significant **scrutiny**.
- The existence of the **filibuster** in the Senate **increases** the **difficulty** of **passing legislation** — a **cloture motion,** which ends a filibuster, requires **60 votes** (three-fifths of the Senate). In practice, this means that **most bills** require some **bipartisan support** if they are to pass.

Once a year, the Senate Majority Leader can use budget reconciliation to pass a spending package without the possibility of a filibuster. In practice, this means that the package needs only 51 votes (or 50 if the vice president is from the majority party) to pass. Under Trump, Mitch McConnell used this strategy to pass the Tax Cuts and Jobs Act (2017), and Chuck Schumer did the same with Joe Biden's American Rescue Plan Act (2021).

Congress's **critics** argue that **passing legislation** has now become **too difficult**

1) Between **1983** and **1993**, Congress passed an average of **5%** of bills into law. Between **2013** and **2023**, though, just **2%** of bills became law.
2) All recent presidents have **failed** to pass at least **one major legislative priority** through Congress. **Barack Obama** couldn't pass his **Assault Weapons Ban Bill, Donald Trump** failed to **replace Obamacare** (as a direct result of a **filibuster** by Democrat senators) and **Joe Biden abandoned** attempts to pass a **federal law upholding abortion rights** (which were initially prompted due to the **Dobbs v Jackson Women's Health Organization (2022)** Supreme Court ruling — see p.155).

The Broken Branch (2006) by Thomas Mann and Norman Ornstein argued that Congress was failing to fulfil its functions. Since 2006, Congress's legislative productivity has fallen to an all-time low.

US Politics — Congress

Congress's Legislative Function

Some feel Congress is too dominated by special interests

1) In recent years, committees have only allowed **4%** of legislation to pass through to be **debated** and **voted on** in the **full House** or **Senate chamber**.
2) While this is a sign of a **rigorous process**, it also gives members of the most **influential congressional committees** huge amounts of **power**.
3) Members of committees are in the best position to **mark up** (**amend**) bills in ways that will **boost** either their **congressional district** or **home state**, or for **partisan purposes**.

> While many members of Congress mark up their bills in a way that fulfils their role as representatives, the power that some of them possess over legislation is inconsistent with the framers' desire to prevent concentrations of power.

Susan Collins, a Republican, was a member of **four** separate **Senate committees** in the 118th Congress. She **successfully amended** bills to **fund projects** in her home state of **Maine** that totalled over **$575 million**.

Chuck Schumer, a Democrat senator for New York, made **59 earmarks** worth nearly **$80 million** to New York State during the passage of the **Inflation Reduction Act (2022)**. He was up for **re-election** during the mid-term elections later **that year**.

4) **Critics** of Congress believe that the **legislative process** gives **interest groups**, including **corporations**, **too much influence** over law-making. Many members of **influential committees** receive **campaign donations** from **companies** in the **sectors** that they **regulate**:

During her **2022** mid-term election campaign, **Cathy McMorris Rodgers** (a Republican from Washington State) received nearly **$300 000** in campaign donations from **oil** and **gas** companies. She was a member of the powerful **House Energy and Commerce Committee**, which she went on to **chair** after being re-elected.

Congress has been able to deal with some crises by passing legislation quickly

During the **global financial crisis**, Congress passed Obama's **American Recovery and Reinvestment Act (2009)**, an economic stimulus package, **within a month** of Obama becoming president. Although **no House Republicans** voted for the act, **three Republican senators** (**Susan Collins**, **Olympia Snowe** and **Arlen Specter**) did.

Congress passed **two major stimulus measures** — the **CARES Act (2020)** under Trump and the **American Rescue Plan Act (2021)** under Biden — to address the **economic impact** of the **COVID-19 pandemic** (see p.153).

There have been several other high-profile laws passed in recent years

1) The **Tax Cuts and Jobs Act (2017)**, passed in the first year of the Trump presidency, was the most **significant** set of **tax reforms** since the 1980s.
2) Also under Trump, Congress passed the **First Step Act (2018)**, a **criminal justice** reform act, with **bipartisan votes** in the **House** and the **Senate**.
3) Under Biden, Congress passed the **Bipartisan Infrastructure Law (2021)**, a **$1.2 trillion** package designed to **improve** the US's **transportation networks**, and the **Bipartisan Safer Communities Act (2022)**, the first **major gun control reform** since 1994.

President Joe Biden signing the Bipartisan Safer Communities Act (2022)

Quick Questions

1) Who signs bills into law?
2) How many votes are needed to pass a cloture motion?
3) What percentage of bills does Congress pass each year?
4) Which committee did Cathy McMorris Rodgers become chair of following her re-election in 2022?
5) What were the names of the laws passed under Donald Trump and Joe Biden to address the economic harm caused by the COVID-19 pandemic?
6) Name two other laws passed during the Biden presidency.
7) Under which president were the Tax Cuts and Jobs Act and the First Step Act passed?

My leg-is-late-ive function was why I kept losing at Sports Day...
Familiarise yourself with that diagram on page 169. Have a go at comparing it with the Parliamentary process on page 76.

US Politics — Congress

Congressional Oversight

From vetting appointments to the executive branch and Supreme Court, to scrutinising spending and foreign policy, Congress plays a big role in making sure that the other branches of government are staffed and run correctly. It's a busy life eh?

Congress provides **oversight** of the **federal budget**

1) Congress's **power of the purse** means that it **approves** all **federal spending**. The **president** and the rest of the **executive branch** can only **spend money** that has been **signed off** by **Congress**.

2) In most years, this leads to **lengthy negotiations** between the **president**, the House of Representatives and the **Senate**, who **all** have to **agree** on the **federal budget**.

> **Joe Biden** had to accept **several compromises** when attempting to agree his **final budget** as president in **2024**, including **removing** a provision that would have **restricted** US **investments** in China.

3) Once budgets have been agreed, Congress continues to **monitor spending** through the House and Senate **Appropriations Committees**. The committees **regulate federal spending** and **allocate** what they deem to be **appropriate amounts** of funding needed to implement other legislation.

> In **June 2024**, the House Appropriations Committee allocated over **$185 million** for spending on **labour**, **health** and **education**.

Some see government shutdowns as an example of Congress being prepared to take radical action to enforce checks and balances on the executive branch, while others regard them as a sign that Congress has become a dysfunctional branch of government.

4) When the **House** and the **Senate can't** reach an **agreement** with the **president** over the **federal budget**, and previous **funding agreements** have **run out**, there is a **federal government shutdown**.

> This happened **once** during **Barack Obama's** presidency, when the House **disagreed** with his planned **spending** on his **Obamacare** health reforms. It happened **twice** during **Trump's** presidency, when **neither** the **House** nor the **Senate** was prepared to **sign off** on his proposed spending on the **border wall**.

Both the House and the Senate attempted to pass laws that would prevent Trump from diverting the funds to construct the wall, but he used his presidential veto to block them.

5) Presidents can attempt to **re-allocate funds** to fit with their priorities. In **2019**, Trump declared a **state of national emergency on the US's southern border with Mexico**. This was intended to **divert money** approved by Congress for dealing with **natural disasters** to fund the construction of the wall, but the move was **blocked by federal court rulings**.

Both chambers can carry out **investigations** into the executive branch's performance

1) The **House Oversight Committee** can create **investigatory sub-committees** that focus on **analysing** specific aspects of the **executive branch's performance**.

2) In recent years, **sub-committees** have been formed to **investigate** the handling of the **COVID-19 pandemic** and the **withdrawal of US troops** from **Afghanistan**.

3) Evidence suggests that **congressional committees' oversight** of the executive branch tends to be **more intense** when there is **divided government**.
   - During **divided government** in the **1990s**, House committees devoted over **140 hours** to **investigating** whether **Bill Clinton** had used official White House Christmas cards to approach possible **campaign donors**.
   - However, during **united government** in the **2000s**, they spent only **12 hours** investigating the **Abu Ghraib prison scandal** (see page 186).

Research by the Brookings Institution, a think tank, found that House committees spent under 25% of their time overseeing the executive branch from 2021 to 2023 (during a period of united government), having spent over 35% of their time doing so from 2019 to 2021 (during a period of divided government).

The **Senate** oversees **treaties** that have been **negotiated** by the **president**

1) The **Senate Foreign Relations Committee** scrutinises every **treaty** negotiated by the **president** in detail before recommending to the **full Senate chamber** that the treaty should either be **approved** or **rejected**.

2) A **vote** is then held on the treaty. **Two-thirds** of the **full Senate** must vote **in favour** of a treaty before it can become **legally binding**. In 2018, the Senate ratified the **United States-Mexico-Canada trade agreement** by a margin of **89-10**.

3) If a proposed treaty **fails** to achieve **two-thirds support** in the Senate, it is effectively **null and void**. For example, only **61 senators** voted to approve the **UN Disability Rights Treaty** in 2012.

US Politics — Congress

Congressional Oversight

The Senate also oversees nominations to the executive and judicial branches

1) **Confirmation hearings** are an important part of the **constitutional system** of **checks** and **balances**. They provide a **public forum** for scrutinising the **suitability** of **presidential nominees**.

2) When the nominee is **not** considered **controversial** and receives the **support** of the **majority of senators**, the confirmation hearings may only last a **few hours**:

   > **Joe Biden's nominee** for the **Secretary of Defense** position, Lloyd Austin, was questioned for **just under four hours** in **2021** before being **confirmed** by a margin of **93-2**.

   In the UK, Cabinet appointments don't receive any parliamentary scrutiny because they fall under the prime minister's prerogative powers.

3) The confirmation process can be much **more challenging** when the Senate is **divided** over the nominee's **suitability** for the post:

   > In **2017**, Vice President **Mike Pence** had to cast a tie-breaking vote to confirm **Betsy DeVos** as Donald Trump's **Secretary of Education**. **Democrats** had staged a **24-hour filibuster** the day before in an attempt to **block** DeVos's nomination, arguing that she **lacked** the **necessary knowledge** of the education sector.

4) Senate **opposition** sometimes leads to **nominees** choosing to **withdraw** before their confirmation hearings:

   > - **Andrew Puzder**, Trump's nominee for the **Secretary of Labor** post, **withdrew** in **2017** after **senators** made it clear they **wouldn't** be willing to confirm him (as he had **employed** someone who had **entered** the **US illegally**).
   > - **Sarah Bloom Raskin**, Biden's nominee to become **Vice Chair of the Federal Reserve**, ruled herself **out** of the confirmation process in **2022** after conservative Democrat **Joe Manchin** publicly **stated** that he **wouldn't vote in favour** of her appointment because of her views on the **environment**.

5) **Supreme Court nominees** usually receive **more scrutiny**:

   > - In **2018**, **Brett Kavanaugh** faced over **39 hours of questioning** from the **Senate Judiciary Committee**, which called witnesses to **investigate** allegations that he had committed **sexual assault** as a college student.
   > - In **2020**, Democrats argued that **Amy Coney Barrett's nomination** had been **rushed** through by **Trump** and **Senate Republicans**, who wanted to confirm her place on the Supreme Court **before** the **presidential election**. She was confirmed **27 days after** her nomination, the **second-shortest** period of all the serving Supreme Court justices, but she did still take part in nearly **20 hours** of **questioning** by the Senate Judiciary Committee.

   Between 1789 and 1965, the Senate confirmed 106 nominees to the Supreme Court, and only three of these (under 3%) were confirmed by a margin of fewer than 10 votes. Since 1965, there have been 22 confirmations, but four of these (over 18%) were confirmed by a margin of fewer than 10 votes. This is in part due to increasing hyperpartisanship in the Senate.

Congressional oversight of foreign policy has weakened over time

1) Mostly because of the **difficulty** of securing a **two-thirds Senate majority** in the current **hyperpartisan** era, presidents are increasingly opting to sign **executive agreements** (which do **not require** any **congressional oversight**) instead of **full treaties**.

2) **No treaties** were negotiated or ratified during the **Biden presidency**, and only **one** (the **United States-Mexico-Canada agreement**) during the **2017-21 Trump presidency**.

3) **Biden** negotiated the **Aukus deal** with **Australia** and the **UK** as an **executive agreement**, while **Trump** used **executive orders** to pull the US **out** of the **World Health Organisation** and the **North American Free Trade Alliance (NAFTA)**.

I was able to enact this tree-T without a word from Congress

4) The growth of the president's **commander-in-chief power** (see page 149) has also **marginalised Congress's role** in overseeing **military policy**. Air and **drone strikes** can be conducted **without** any **congressional approval** and Congress has **not issued** a formal declaration of war since the Second World War.

Congress can still hold the executive branch to account over foreign policy

1) As well as holding **investigations** into **foreign policy controversies**, Congress's **power of the purse** means that it retains **oversight** of **spending** on foreign policy.

2) Congress has approved **incremental funding packages** supporting **Ukraine's** response to the **Russian invasion**. It has also been able to **influence** the Biden administration's response to the **Israel-Hamas war**, for example by supporting bills that continue to provide **military aid** to Israel.

3) Under the **War Powers Resolution** of **1973**, Congress must be **notified** within **48 hours** of **armed forces** being **deployed** to military action. The president must seek **congressional approval** if they are **deployed overseas** for **more than 60 days**.

Congressional Oversight

Congress **scrutinises** the **conduct** of the **executive** and **judicial branches**

1) If there are **suspicions** that a **member** of the **executive** or **judicial branch** has **behaved improperly**, congressional committees can issue **subpoenas** requesting **access** to **documents** or **summoning** an **individual** to **testify** in person.

> In **2024**, the **State Department** granted the **House Foreign Affairs Committee** access to **74 pages** of **documentation** relating to its handling of the **withdrawal** of **US troops** from **Afghanistan** — although **Republicans** on the committee **argued** that this was **insufficient**.

2) As with other forms of congressional oversight, **subpoenas** have become **partisan tools** in recent years:

> In **2016**, **Democrats** accused **Republicans** of deliberately **undermining Hillary Clinton's presidential election campaign** during their **investigation** over whether she had **improperly** used her **private email account** while serving as Obama's **Secretary of State**.

> In **2019**, **Republicans** accused **Democrats** of using their **subpoena powers** for partisan purposes when **investigating Trump's tax returns**.

3) If a **majority** in the **House of Representatives** believes that the **president**, another member of the **executive branch** or a member of the **judicial branch** has committed a **'high crime or misdemeanour'**, they can vote to **impeach** them. **Bill Clinton** (see p.188) and **Donald Trump** (see p.189) were both **impeached** over acts committed while **president**.

> In **2010**, the Senate found **District Judge G. Thomas Porteous Jr.** from Louisiana **guilty** of **lying under oath**, permanently **barring** him from serving as a **judge** again.

> In **2024**, articles of **impeachment** against **two** serving **Supreme Court judges**, **Clarence Thomas** and **Samuel Alito**, were introduced by **Alexandra Ocasio-Cortez**, a left-wing Democrat Representative.

Congress helps to **oversee** the **behaviour** of **corporations**

1) In **2024**, the **Senate Committee on Health, Education, Labor, and Pensions** conducted **investigations** into **high prescription drug costs** and issued a **subpoena** to the former **CEO** of **Steward Health Care**, a medical corporation that had gone bankrupt.
2) In recent years, Congress has **conducted hearings** into the **conduct** of **major corporations** such as **Facebook**, **X** and **TikTok**.
3) The investigation into **TikTok** led to a **bill** being **signed** into law in **2024** that would **ban** the social media platform in the **US** unless it was **sold** by its **Chinese owners**, **Bytedance**.

> Although Congress provides some effective oversight of corporations, critics argue that the campaign finance system and lobbying culture give corporations and other interest groups too much influence over congressional decisions — see p.210.

Revision Task

 Shhh...

For Edexcel students: Evaluate the view that congressional oversight of the executive branch has become insufficient. [30]

For AQA students: 'Congressional oversight of the executive branch has become insufficient.' Analyse and evaluate this statement. [25]

Imagine that you are answering one of the exam questions above. Choose the **best examples** from the previous pages or from your own knowledge to **support** these arguments.
1) *The Senate's oversight is becoming more partisan.*
2) *Congress can still provide meaningful foreign policy oversight.*
3) *Congressional oversight of the federal budget can sometimes be too strong.*
4) *The Senate has more significant oversight powers than the House of Representatives.*

I scrutinise the branches in my garden for signs of that darn squirrel....

Dodgy politicians beware: Congress has the power to interrogate appointees and investigate members of the executive and judicial branches. These are crucial checks and balances, although some people question how effective they are.

Representation and Political Parties

Hmmm, representation and parties you say? Get the balloons out — it's time to get festive. Oh that's not what this is about?

The **House** represents **citizens** and the **Senate** represents the **states**

1) The **congressional district model** ensures that **all areas** of the United States receive a **similar level** of **representation** in the **House of Representatives**.
2) The **framers' decision** to give each **state two senators**, regardless of the size of their population, means that **smaller, less populous states** such as **Wyoming** and **Vermont** wield as much **power** in the Senate as much **larger, more populous states** like **California** and **Texas**.
3) **Senators** may represent the **political** and **economic interests** of their **home state** by serving on **committees** overseeing areas of **policy** that are particularly important to their **constituents**.

> The largest district by population size in 2020 was Delaware's at-large district (with over 980 000 people) and the smallest was Rhode Island's 1st district (with 545 000 people).

> **West Virginia's** economy is heavily reliant on coal. One of West Virginia's senators, **Joe Manchin**, served on the **Senate Energy Committee** from 2010 to 2024.

4) **Representatives** and **senators** can each **mark up legislation** so that it **benefits** their **district** or **state**.

> In **2023**, **Chuck Fleischmann**, **Representative** for **Tennessee's 3rd district**, successfully marked up over **$270 million** of spending for his district.

> While some celebrate this practice as effective representation, others find it unfair and inefficient. The phrase 'pork barrel politics' is used by critics to describe inserting unnecessary spending provisions into legislation in the hope of boosting a Representative's chances of re-election.

> In **2023**, **Susan Collins**, **Senator** for **Maine**, successfully introduced **funding** for projects in her home state that totalled over **$575 million**.

> In part because of the influence of its Republican senator Mitch McConnell, the then-Senate Majority Leader, Kentucky received the third-highest federal funding of any state from 2014 to 2018.

Congressional elections help to fulfil the branch's **representative function**

1) **Supporters** of the **congressional election system** believe that the fact that the **House** is **re-elected** every **two years** ensures that it offers **responsive representation** by **frequently refreshing** its members' **mandates**.
2) In combination with **state legislatures**, **governors** and **elected city mayors**, congressional elections ensure that **US citizens** receive **many different layers** of **representation** at a **federal** and **local** level.
3) By **contrast** with the **UK**, where the **House of Lords** is **unelected**, Congress has **greater democratic legitimacy** because **both** the **House of Representatives** and the **Senate** are **fully elected**.

Critics argue congressional elections don't provide a **fair chance** of **representation**

1) The **winner-takes-all**, **disproportionate** nature of first-past-the-post means that **third parties** are very **unlikely** to be **elected** to Congress. While a small number of **independent** candidates have been **elected** (e.g. **Bernie Sanders** and **Angus King** in the **Senate**), **no senators** or **representatives** from **political parties** other than the **Republicans** and **Democrats** have been elected since the **1970s**.
2) The **frequency** of **congressional elections** means that the US has what is often described as a '**constant campaign**', which requires **Representatives** in particular to **raise** vast sums of **money** on a **regular basis**. This is said to **benefit** those who are **wealthy** or **well connected** to networks of donors (see page 210).
3) Since **Citizens United v. Federal Election Commission (2010)**, when the **Supreme Court** ruled that **campaign donations** are an **extension** of **free speech**, there have effectively been **no spending limits** on **presidential** or **congressional election campaigns**. Critics argue that this **benefits** candidates who belong to the **socio-economic elite**.
4) Along with the **greater media attention** and **higher profiles** enjoyed by existing members of Congress, these factors contribute to the **incumbency advantage**. This is a theory that suggests that those **already serving** in the **House** or the **Senate** are **more likely** to be **re-elected** than those seeking to be elected from the **outside**.

- In **2022**, **all 28 incumbent senators** seeking **re-election** were **successful**, as were **94%** of **Representatives**.
- On average, **incumbents** in **2022 Senate races** raised over **10 times** as much as their challengers

5) The **democratic legitimacy** of **congressional districts** also suffers from **gerrymandering** — the practice of **re-drawing the boundaries** of a **constituency** in a way that is likely to **benefit one party**.
6) Research by the **Brennan Center for Justice**, a think tank, suggests that **only 14%** of congressional districts were **competitive** in the **2022 mid-term elections**. This was due to the **combined effect** of **gerrymandering**, **first-past-the-post** and increasing **geographical polarisation**.

Representation and Political Parties

Both chambers have **strengths** and **weaknesses** in **social representation**

Strengths
- ✓ At the time, the **118th Congress** (2023-2025) was the most **ethnically diverse** to date — **28%** of **representatives** and **12%** of **senators** were from **ethnic minority backgrounds**.
- ✓ **13 members** of the **118th Congress** identified as **LGBTQI+**, compared with only **4** in **2011-12**.
- ✓ **29%** of **Representatives** of the **118th Congress** were **women** — the **highest proportion** there had yet been in either chamber.

Weaknesses
- ✗ Only **25%** of **Senators** in **2024** were **female**.
- ✗ **White Americans** account for under **60%** of the **US population**, but made up **75%** of the **118th Congress**.
- ✗ **3%** of the **118th Congress** were **born outside the US**, compared with **over 13%** of the **US population**.
- ✗ **51%** of the **118th Congress** were estimated to have assets **worth over $1 million**, compared with **under 10%** of the **US population**.

Political parties play a central role in both the House and the Senate

1) Almost as soon as the **new political system** had been created after the **Philadelphia Convention** in **1787**, **parties** began to play a **significant role**.
2) Since the **1850s**, the **Democratic Party** and the **Republican Party** have been the **two dominant parties** across the **US**, including in **Congress**.
3) The US has one of the most consistent **two-party systems** in the world — **every elected member** of both the **House** and the **Senate** since the **1970s** has been a **Democrat**, a **Republican** or an **independent** (though there have been few of these).
4) There are **caucuses** of **like-minded representatives** and **senators** within both the **Republican** and **Democratic parties**.
5) While the **Senate** used to be regarded as a **less partisan** chamber than the **House**, there is evidence of **rising levels** of **partisanship** in **both chambers** of Congress.

> By 2024, there were four independent senators — Bernie Sanders, Angus King, Kyrsten Sinema, and Joe Manchin. They all 'caucus' with the Democrats, which means that they usually vote with the party.

caucus
A group of legislators who share interests and have common legislative goals. (Key Terms)

- From **2009** to **2021**, senators were **loyal** to their **party** on **64%** of votes, compared with **56%** from **1996** to **2008**.
- This appears to be influenced by the **narrow majorities** in both chambers. In **2021**, when there was a **50-50 split** in the **Senate**, **Democrats** voted **unanimously** on **87% of votes** where there was an **official party line**.
- The **House** remains **highly partisan** — in the three years from **2019** to **2021**, **Democrats** voted **with their party 96%** of the time.

> Whips generally have less power in Congress than in the House of Commons in the UK (see p.75) because they cannot promise future ministerial positions or threaten to remove the representative from their party.

6) The frequency of **divided government** has also increased the **significance** of **parties** in Congress. As it is much **more common** for the **president's party** to **not** be in **control** of **both** the **House of Representatives** and the **Senate**, they are usually **forced** to **negotiate** with the **opposition party** in order to **pass legislation**.

Divisions between Republicans and Democrats can lead to gridlock in Congress

1) As well as growing levels of **partisanship**, Congress has seen rising levels of **polarisation** in recent years. This means that there are now **more** members of Congress who are considered to be on the **far left** or the **far right** of the ideological spectrum.

- According to the Pew Research Center, **House Republicans** have become **25% more conservative** since the early 1970s, while **Senate Republicans** have become **28% more conservative**.
- **House Democrats** have become **7% more liberal**, and **Senate Democrats** have become **6% more liberal**.

2) Unsurprisingly, this has led to **more disagreements** between the parties in Congress — in recent years, they have been **starkly divided** over **social issues** such as **abortion**, **immigration** and **gun control**.
3) This has led to **gridlock** in many areas of policy. Congress has only passed **one law** on **abortion** in its history (the **Partial-Birth Abortion Ban (2003)**), while Democrats have repeatedly **failed to ban assault weapons** (a major policy on their party platform) since a previous ban **elapsed in 2004**.
4) Gridlock resulting from **partisan disagreements** has also been seen in the **frequency** of **shutdowns** — there were **three** in the decade from **2013** to **2023**, compared with **none** in the **previous decade**.

US Politics — Congress

Representation and Political Parties

Divisions **within** the parties can also cause **gridlock**

As the **two dominant parties** have become **more polarised**, the potential for **disagreements** between the **remaining centrists** and those on the **ideological left** or **right** has **increased**. Because of the **narrow majorities** that have tended to be produced by elections to both the **House** and the **Senate**, **small groups of centrists** (and sometimes **individual senators**) have been able to **prevent legislation from passing**.

In **2013**, Obama's attempt to pass an **assault weapons ban failed** after **opposition** from **conservative Blue Dog Democrats** in the House.	In **2018**, Trump's attempt to pass the **American Health Care Act failed** after it was **rejected** by **three** centrist Republican senators: **Susan Collins**, **Lisa Murkowski** and **John McCain**.	In **2021**, Biden was forced to **abandon** many of the **environmental aspects** of his **Build Back Better plan** after **Joe Manchin**, a **conservative Democrat senator**, **refused** to vote for them.

Some **members of Congress** are willing to **work across party lines**

In **2021**, Congress passed the **Bipartisan Infrastructure Law**, a **$1.2 trillion** spending package aimed at **improving** national **transportation networks** with support from **both Republicans** and **Democrats**. The **House of Representatives** voted **228-206** in favour, with support from **13 Republicans**, and the **Senate** approved the bill by **69-30**, with support from **19 Republicans**.	In **2022**, Congress passed the first major gun control law since 1994 — the **Bipartisan Safer Communities Act**. It passed by **65-33** in the **Senate**, where **15 Republicans** voted in **favour** alongside **all 50 Democrats**, and by **234-193** in the **Senate**, where **14 Republicans** voted in **favour** alongside **all 220 Democrats**.

Both of these laws were passed with **support** from members of the **Bipartisan Problem Solvers Caucus**, a **centrist group** of **representatives** and **senators** who **collaborate across party lines** to pass legislation.

Levels of **partisanship** generally **reduce** during **crises**

1) After the 9/11 terror attacks in **2001**, Congress passed a bill creating the new **Department of Homeland Security** by **295-132** in the **House** and **90-9** in the **Senate**.
2) Congress passed **two major bipartisan measures** during the **COVID-19 pandemic**: the **CARES Act (2020)**, a **$2.2 trillion** deal under Trump, and the **American Rescue Plan Act (2021)**, a **$1.9 trillion** deal under Biden.
3) Following **Russia's invasion** of **Ukraine**, there was **bipartisan support** for the **Additional Ukraine Supplemental Appropriations Act (2022)** — the law was approved in the **House** by a margin of **368-57** and in the **Senate** by **86-11**.

Quick Questions

1) How many members does the House of Representatives have?
2) On which Senate committee did Joe Manchin serve from 2010 to 2024?
3) State what is meant by: a) the incumbency advantage   b) gerrymandering
4) What percentage of the House of Representatives was female in 2024?
5) What percentage of the 118th Congress was estimated to have assets worth over $1 million?
6) Give an example of when division within a party has caused legislation to fail to pass through Congress.

Gerry's mandarins

Exam Practice

For students studying...

Edexcel: Evaluate the view that the role of political parties undermines Congress's ability to execute its functions. [30]

AQA: 'The role of political parties undermines Congress's ability to execute its functions.' Analyse and evaluate this statement. [25]

Write a **conclusion** to one of the essay questions above.

I got fired from my job at the pizzeria due to high levels of parmesanship...
Remember to consider how the two-party system may affect what perspectives get represented in the House and the Senate.

Comparing Congress and Parliament

You may have noticed I've been dropping subtle hints about the similarities between Congress and Parliament. This is why.

Congress and Parliament have the same core functions

Legislation

Both are **law-making bodies** with reasonably **similar legislative processes**. In each system:

- the **same version** of a **bill** must be **agreed** by **both chambers** (although the **House of Commons** can, after a year, pass a bill that has been **delayed** by the **House of Lords**)
- **committee systems** are used for **legislative scrutiny** and **amendments** (see p.76 and p.169).

Oversight and Scrutiny

- Both are the primary means of **scrutinising** and **overseeing** the work of the **executive branch**.
- **Committees** in both Congress and Parliament can subject members of the **Cabinet** to hours of **detailed questioning** about their **policy records** and **decision-making** during crises.
- The strongest form of **congressional oversight** is to **impeach** and then **remove** members of the **executive branch** from office if found **guilty** of **high crimes** or **misdemeanours**. The equivalent in the House of Commons is to pass a **vote of no confidence** in the **government**, triggering a **general election** if successful.

Representation

- Both Congress and Parliament are the **most significant** democratic representative bodies in their respective **political systems**.
- The **first-past-the-post** system is used to **elect** the **House of Commons** and for **congressional elections** to both the **House of Representatives** and the **Senate**.
- The **congressional districts** in the **House of Representatives** are similar to local **constituencies** in the **House of Commons** — both have **one member per seat**.
- Although the levels of social (descriptive) **representation** in both Congress and Parliament have **improved** in recent years, **both** are still **unrepresentative** in terms of **sex**, **race** and **socio-economic status**. The **Senate** and the **House of Lords** are the **least** socially representative chambers in their respective systems in terms of **sex** — in **2024**, **75%** of **senators** and over **70%** of **peers** were **male**.
- Both tend to be **dominated** by **two main parties** — in **2024**, all **535** members of Congress **caucused** with either the **Republicans** or the **Democrats**. Following the **2024 general election**, **80%** of **MPs** represented either **Labour** or the **Conservative Party**.

While the Lords' unelected nature harms its democratic legitimacy, it helps to protect the upper chamber from partisanship. Over 200 peers (roughly a quarter of the chamber) have no party affiliation. Peers who do have party affiliations tend to vote much more independently than their counterparts in the House of Commons, the House of Representatives and the Senate.

Congress and Parliament execute these functions in different ways

Legislation

- Legislation tends to receive much more **detailed** and **lengthy scrutiny** in Congress than in Parliament (which is often **dominated** by the **executive branch**).
- While **public bill committees** in Parliament very **rarely** make **substantial** amendments to legislation, around **96%** of bills **fail** to make it **past** the **committee stage** in Congress.
- The **president** has **very little control** over the **legislative process** in the **US**, whereas **prime ministers** with a **majority** in the **House of Commons** can usually **ensure** that their **legislative priorities** are **passed** by Parliament.

Oversight and Scrutiny

- Because the **legislative** and **executive branches** are **fused** in the **UK**, Parliament provides more **direct** and **regular** oversight of the **executive branch**.
- The **prime minister** faces cross-party **questioning** for around 45 minutes **every week** in Prime Minister's **Questions**, while **government ministers** in each department face detailed **questions** on a regular basis in both the **House of Commons** and the **House of Lords**. During times of **crisis** or **controversy**, ministers can be **summoned** to either House to face **urgent** questions. The prime minister also faces **several hours** of **questioning** from **MPs** who are policy **experts** two or three times a year during meetings of the **Liaison Committee**.
- By contrast, the **president** never has to face **routine questioning** in either chamber of Congress, and members of their **executive branch** are **only questioned** by Congress during **confirmation hearings** or **special investigations**.
- However, Congress provides much stronger **scrutiny** of **executive** appointments. Parliament has **no ability** to consider **ministerial** appointments in the UK, where the prime minister can use their **prerogative powers** to make appointments as they see fit.

US Politics — Congress

Comparing Congress and Parliament

Representation

- Both chambers of **Congress** are **fully elected**, but the **House of Lords** is **unelected**, containing a **mix** of **appointed life peers**, **bishops** and **hereditary peers**.
- Members of the **House of Lords** do **not** represent **geographical areas**, while members of **Congress** either represent **congressional districts** (in the House of Representatives) or **states** (in the Senate).
- The **House of Commons** is by far the **most representative** of the legislatures in terms of **ethnicity** and **sexuality** — following the **2024** general election, **13.8%** of MPs have **ethnic minority backgrounds**, compared with **14%** of the **UK population**, and it had the **highest proportion** of **openly** LGBTQI+ representatives of any **legislature** in the **world**.
- There is a **broader spread** of **party representation** in **Parliament** (**20% of MPs** elected in **2024** did not represent either the Labour or the Conservative parties) than in **Congress**, where there are **no third-party** representatives.

Committees play an important role in both Congress and Parliament

1) In terms of their role in **overseeing** the work of the **executive branch**, **congressional committees** and House of Commons **select committees** play similar roles. Both are made up of **representatives** who develop **relevant policy expertise**, which enables them to subject members of the **executive branch** to **detailed questioning**.

2) The **legislative scrutiny** provided by **congressional committees** can be compared with the **committee stage** in the **House of Lords**. In both legislative processes, this stage involves **line-by-line scrutiny** of **bills** by **representatives** with significant levels of **policy expertise**.

I wouldn't want to be scrutinised by this public bill committee

3) But committees have a much **more significant legislative role** in the **US** than in the **UK**.

4) **Congressional committees** make **significant amendments** to legislation and **prevent** most bills from passing through to the full House or Senate chamber. In contrast, **public bill committees** in the **House of Commons** provide **relatively weak scrutiny** — their members are chosen by **party whips**, with an **inbuilt majority** for the **governing party**. This has resulted in **under 1% of opposition amendments** at this stage being **successful** in recent years.

Power is split more evenly across Congress's chambers than Parliament

In legislative terms, the **House of Representatives** and the **Senate** have broadly **equal powers**. **Both** need to **agree** on the **same final version of a bill** before it is sent to the **president**, and **both** have the **same ability** to **amend**, **block** or **delay money bills** (although all money bills **begin** in the House of Representatives).

Parliament has a system of asymmetrical bicameralism, where the **House of Commons** has **more power** than the **House of Lords**. Since the **Parliament Act (1911)**, the House of Lords has been **unable** to **amend**, **block** or **delay money bills**, while the **Parliament Act (1949)** means that the **House of Lords** can **only delay** other bills for the **duration** of a **parliamentary session** (usually **one year**). Under the **Salisbury Convention**, the House of Lords is expected **not** to **prevent** the passage of **bills** that had been included in the **governing party's** most recent **general election manifesto**.

Parliament is sovereign but Congress is not

Because the **US Constitution** is **codified**, it has **sovereign status** in the nation's **legal system** — this means that **laws** passed by **Congress** have to be **consistent** with the **existing provisions** in the **Constitution**. If the **US Supreme Court** rules that an act of Congress is **unconstitutional**, it is **immediately struck down** and can no longer be **applied**. This happened with the **Gun Free School Zones Act (1990)** after the Supreme Court's ruling in **US v. Lopez (1995)**. In **Biden v. Nebraska (2023)**, the Supreme Court **prevented** Congress from cancelling **$10 000** worth of **student debt** for many **lower-** and **middle-income US citizens**.

Parliament has **sovereign status** in the UK's Constitution, giving it the ability to **pass**, **amend** or **repeal any law** that it chooses. The **UK Supreme Court** can only issue advisory **declarations of incompatibility**, where it **recommends** that **Parliament** consider **changing** an **existing law** to make it **compatible** with the **Human Rights Act (1998)**. Parliament can choose to **ignore** these if it wishes.

I gathered a Committea to scrutinise my hot beverage options...

As with the other comparison pages in the US Politics section, you should use the rational, structural and cultural comparative theories to help analyse and explain the similarities and differences between the US and UK. Look at page 145 for a refresher.

The Executive Branch

The executive branches of the US and the UK are quite like branches of a tree. Their functions are similar, but their structures and strengths are not. And they make very different cabinets. Hmm, that analogy might have got away from me...

The **president** is the **elected head** of the **US executive branch**

The **hierarchy** of the **US executive branch** looks like this:

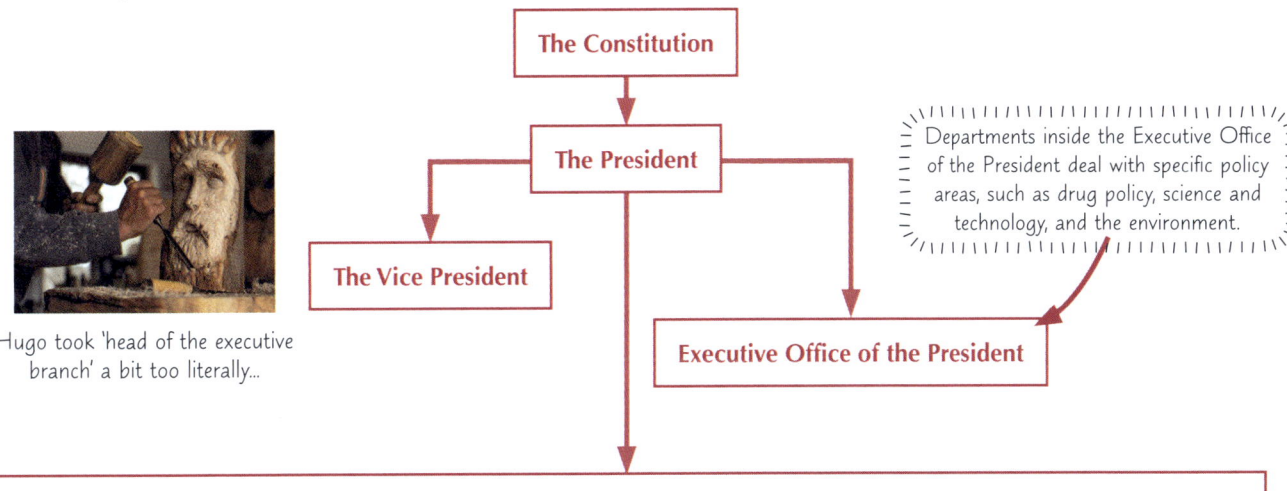

Departments inside the Executive Office of the President deal with specific policy areas, such as drug policy, science and technology, and the environment.

Hugo took 'head of the executive branch' a bit too literally...

Examples of **executive departments** include:
- The State Department
- Department of Defense
- Department of the Treasury
- Department of Homeland Security
- Department of Education
- Department of Labor

There are 15 executive departments in total — there are more examples on the next page.

The **vice president** has **three** main **constitutional powers**

1) President of the Senate

- This is often a **ceremonial power**, rather than a consequential one. The **vice president** now tends to **delegate** the **chairing** of Senate **debates** to another member of their **party**.
- However, being president of the Senate does allow the **vice president** to exercise **significant influence** when **neither party** has a comfortable **majority** in the Senate.
- If there is a **tied vote** in the Senate, the **vice president** casts the **deciding vote**. This power tends to be **rarely used**, due to Senate composition.
  1) **Joe Biden**, as vice president under Barack Obama, never used this power in his **eight years** in office because there were **no tied votes** in the Senate.
  2) **Mike Pence**, Donald Trump's vice president, only cast **13 tie-breaking votes**.
  3) But **Kamala Harris**, Biden's vice president, cast **33 tie-breaking votes** in her **first two years** (**2021-2023**).

Lyndon B. Johnson became president in 1963 following the assassination of John F. Kennedy

2) Counting and announcing Electoral College votes

- A much **less significant** power, the vice president **confirms** the **results** of the **presidential election** by announcing the results of the **Electoral College vote**.
- Despite reportedly facing **pressure** from **Trump** to **refuse** to ratify the **2020 presidential election result**, **Pence** confirmed Trump's **defeat** when he announced the **Electoral College votes** in **January 2021**.

3) Succeeding and deputising for the president

- If the president **resigns**, **dies** or is **removed from office** following **impeachment**, the **vice president** instantly **succeeds** them.
- This most recently happened in **1974**, when **Gerald Ford** became **president** after **Richard Nixon resigned** over the **Watergate scandal** (see page 186).

The Executive Branch

The **head** of each **executive department** sits in the **Cabinet**

1) The **first president**, George Washington, oversaw **three** executive departments:
   - the **State Department** (the equivalent of the **Foreign Office** in the **UK**)
   - the **Department of War**
   - the **Department of the Treasury**
2) Since then, other departments such as the **Department of Education**, the **Department of Veterans' Affairs** and the **Department of Health and Human Services** have been created.
3) The most **recently** formed department is the **Department of Homeland Security**, which was created as part of the response to the **9/11 terror attacks** (see p.182).
4) The president **nominates** the **head** of each department, but every appointment to the Cabinet must be **ratified** by the **Senate** as part of the constitutional system of **checks** and **balances**.

> Unlike its UK equivalent, the US Cabinet does not meet frequently and its members are not considered natural successors to the president (although they are in the line of succession if the president and vice president die in office). Donald Trump waited nearly six months before holding his first full Cabinet meeting, while Joe Biden didn't hold one until his third month as president.

The **Executive Office of the President** was created in **1939**

- The **Executive Office of the President** (**EXOP**) was created to **help** the president **run** the **executive branch** and **direct legislative affairs** in **Congress**.
- The EXOP is a collective term for a number of different **bodies**, which have representatives in the **West Wing** of the **White House**. It is often regarded as being **more important** than the **Cabinet**, whose departments are **scattered** across **Washington D.C.** and **Virginia**.
- The EXOP is led by the **Chief of Staff**, who is one of the president's **closest advisers**, overseeing the **president's diary** and **day-to-day political strategy**.
- The EXOP includes the following offices, all of which exist with the purpose of **improving** the president's **ability** to **govern**:

> The EXOP is not accounted for in the original Constitution. Originally, the president was expected to manage many aspects of governing personally, but as politics became more complex, presidents began to hire more advisers and aides. The EXOP was created in 1939 to create a formal office for these political workers.

White House Office — this office consists of the president's **senior political advisors**, as well as a number of **West Wing staff**. It helps to **oversee** the president's **policy aims** and **political agenda**.

Office of Legislative Affairs — oversees many aspects of the president's **relationship** with **Congress**, especially the **bargaining process** that takes place when attempting to **pass** most pieces of **legislation**.

National Security Council (NSC) — provides a **forum** for **discussing national security**, **military** and **foreign policy**. NSC meetings are often where the president reaches **major decisions** over **military interventions** such as **air** and **drone strikes**.

Office of Management and Budget — oversees the **planning** and **implementation** of the **federal budget**.

From her perch on the Executive Branch, Clarissa shows off her West Wing

Quick Questions

1) Name six executive departments of the US executive branch.
2) What are the three main constitutional powers of the vice president?
3) What is the purpose of the Executive Office of the President?
4) Describe the role of the Chief of Staff in US government.
5) Explain the roles of these offices: Office of Legislative Affairs, the NSC and the Office of Management and Budget.

The vice president can exert their *grip* on the Senate...

Remember, due to the US Constitution, the heads of the US Cabinet can't also have roles in Congress (see p.146). This is a big difference to the UK, where Cabinet ministers are directly involved in either the House of Commons or House of Lords.

Presidential Powers

Prepare to plough through some pages all about presidential powers. Some formal, some informal, the president's powers have changed a lot over time (see page 148-149) and can increase and decrease depending on what's going on politically.

The Constitution grants the president a range of formal and informal powers

Formal Powers

Also known as **enumerated powers** (see page 147), these powers are **clearly delegated** to the president by the **Constitution**. They include:

- **Signing** legislation
- **Vetoing** legislation
- Negotiating **treaties**
- Granting **pardons** and **reprieves**
- Nominating **ambassadors**
- Nominating **federal judges** (including **Supreme Court judges**)
- Nominating **members** of the **executive branch**

Informal Powers

Also known as **implied powers** (see page 147), these are powers that the president has **inherited** or **developed** as a result of their **constitutional roles**. They are also powers associated with **roles** that have **developed** since the Constitution was written. They include:

- Ordering **military action** as part of their constitutional role as **commander-in-chief** of the **US armed forces**
- Issuing **executive orders**
- Signing **executive agreements**
- Issuing **signing statements**, in which they can **emphasise** particular aspects of **legislation** with which they **agree** or **disagree**
- The **power to persuade**

> This theory was developed by presidential scholar Richard Neustadt in the 1960s. It refers to the president's informal power to achieve their aims by making public statements on policy and by convincing members of Congress and state governors to act in accordance with their wishes.

Key Terms

presidential pardon
When the president declares that someone who has previously been convicted of an offence is forgiven, thereby clearing their criminal record and ending any sentence they are serving.

presidential reprieve
When the president declares that someone who has previously been convicted of an offence should have their sentence shortened or ended.

executive order
A declaration made by the president that builds on existing legislation, but usually introduces a new interpretation that was not outlined in the original text of the law passed by Congress. Unlike new laws, executive orders are not subject to any congressional scrutiny, although they can be declared unconstitutional by the Supreme Court.

executive agreement
An agreement signed by the president or another senior member of the executive branch and a foreign leader or group of foreign leaders. Unlike treaties, executive agreements do not need to be ratified by the Senate.

The extent of the president's power depends on political factors

1) When the **president's party** controls **both** chambers of **Congress** (**united government**), they are much more **likely** to be able to **achieve** their **domestic aims**.

2) When the **other party** controls **either** the House of Representatives or the Senate (or **both**) it is much **harder** for them to **pass legislation** and **make appointments**. This often means that they either need to **compromise** or **abandon** some of their priorities:

- **Barack Obama abandoned** plans to **nominate** a **Supreme Court judge** in **2016** after **Senate Republicans refused** to hold a hearing (see p.152).
- **Obama**, **Trump** and **Biden** all reluctantly accepted that they would be **unable** to **pass** their intended legislation on **gun control** due to **opposition** in **Congress**.

> Although it fell well short of the ban on assault weapons that he had originally proposed, Biden did succeed in passing the first federal gun control law since 1994 when he signed the Bipartisan Safer Communities Act (2022) into law. This introduced tougher background checks and made it harder to obtain licences for selling guns.

3) Presidents tend to be **more powerful** just after an **election victory**, because they have usually been elected with a **clear mandate** to enact their **legislative agenda**. This is known as their **honeymoon period**.

4) By contrast, their power tends to **decline** as their **term** nears its **end** — especially towards the **end** of a **second term**, at which point they are **prevented** from seeking **re-election** by the **22nd amendment** (see page 159). During these periods, presidents are described as **lame ducks**.

"I'm still powerful, I swear!"

US Politics — The Presidency

Presidential Powers

Times of crisis can have a big effect on presidential power

Crises often lead to a **short-term boost** in power, especially when there is a clear need for **decisive leadership**.

- ✓ In the **immediate aftermath** of the 9/11 terror attacks, **George W. Bush** succeeded in passing **all** his **major priorities** through **Congress**. These included gaining **authorisation** for wars in **Afghanistan** and **Iraq**, creating the new **Department of Homeland Security** and **increasing** the powers of **law enforcement agencies**.
- ✓ **Donald Trump** possessed more power during the early stages of the **COVID-19 pandemic**. He made a number of **major unilateral decisions** such as **leaving** the World Health Organisation and ordering **Operation Warp Speed**, a federal programme to oversee **vaccine procurement** and **distribution**.

However, crises can also **reduce** the president's **power** and **popularity** if they are seen to be **responsible** for them, or considered to be **handling them poorly**.

- ✗ **Trump's approval ratings fell** as public opinion began to turn against him over his handling of the **COVID-19 pandemic**. This, along with the **economic downturn** caused by the pandemic, was seen as a **key factor** in his **defeat** to **Joe Biden** in the **2020 presidential election**.
- ✗ **Joe Biden's popularity** and **poll ratings declined** as a result of his perceived **failings** in dealing with the **Israel-Hamas war**. A **ceasefire** that he predicted would happen "*within days*" never came about, and he **confused** the conflict with the **Ukraine war** in a media **interview**.

The extent of the president's power also depends on economic factors

1) **Economic circumstances** can either lead to a **growth** or a **reduction** in **presidential power**.
2) Presidents whose period in office coincides with **economic growth** will usually be more **popular** (and therefore more likely to be **re-elected**) than presidents who govern during **economic crises**.
3) **Jimmy Carter**, **George H. W. Bush** and **Donald Trump** all **lost re-election attempts** in the middle of **economic crises**.
4) If a president has been **elected** on the promise of **dealing** with an **existing economic crisis**, they tend to be **successful** in passing their **early measures** through **Congress**. **Obama** oversaw the passage of the **American Recovery and Reinvestment Act (2009)**, while **Joe Biden** passed the **American Rescue Plan Act (2021)**.

> In these circumstances, the presidential powers of persuasion become particularly important. The president needs to persuade Congress, foreign leaders, the electorate and the media (and others) that they are taking the right approach.

There is debate over whether the president has too much or too little power

Too much power

1) Some argue that the president now has **more power** than the **framers** of the **US Constitution intended**.
2) Two of the framers' **primary aims** were to **prevent tyrannical rule** and ensure a **limited government**, but the **president** now has **significant, unchecked power** in both **foreign** and **domestic policy**.
3) Some presidents have also chosen to **erode states' identities** through **coercive federalism** (see page 155).

Too little power

1) Some believe that the president does **not** have **enough power** in some areas.
2) Because of rising **hyperpartisanship** during the **confirmation** processes for presidential **nominations** to the **Supreme Court** and **executive branch positions**, many posts are left **empty** for long periods.
   - There were **only 8 Supreme Court judges** for most of **2016**.
   - There was an **Acting Secretary of Labor** from **March 2023** to **January 2025** because Republican senators voted **against** holding a **confirmation hearing** for Biden's nominee, **Julie Su**.
3) The **difficulty** of passing legislation through **Congress** has sometimes affected presidents' ability to **respond** to crises. There has only been **one** major federal **gun control law** passed since **1994**, the **Bipartisan Safer Communities Act (2022)**, despite an average of more than 600 mass shootings each year from 2020 to 2023.

The extent of my power depends on how much cake I've eaten...

Times of crisis can be a double-edged sword for a president. Delivering a clear plan and taking action can boost their powers and approval rating. But if they're seen struggling to deal with the issue, it can put their presidency in danger (see p.171).

Congressional Checks on Presidential Power

As you saw in the Constitution section (p.146-165), the framers were keen to make sure that there were plenty of checks and balances on presidential power. The last thing they wanted was a leader without accountability who could become a tyrant.

Congress provides significant checks on the president's power in domestic policy

1) The **House of Representatives** and the **Senate** need to **approve** the **same version** of a **bill** before it goes to the **president**, who can decide either to **sign** or **veto** it (see page 169).
2) **Divided governments** have been much **more common** in recent years. Presidents have rarely been able to **rely** on passing legislation through **party loyalty alone**, which tends to be much **weaker** in the US than in the UK (see page 226).
3) Passing legislation through the **Senate** is complicated further by the fact that **most bills** require support from **60 senators** to overcome a possible **filibuster**. This means that **support** from some senators in **both parties** is usually needed.
4) **Barack Obama**, **Donald Trump** and **Joe Biden** all **failed** to achieve at least one of their **major domestic policy aims** as a result of **gridlock** in Congress:

   - **Obama** failed to implement **stricter gun control** measures.
   - **Trump** failed to **replace** the **Obamacare** health reforms and to **build** most of the wall that he had promised on the **US border** with **Mexico**.
   - **Biden** failed to pass a federal law **guaranteeing abortion rights** in all 50 states.

Anja's power of the purse was sadly lacking

5) Congress also has the **power of the purse**, allowing it to **amend** or **refuse to pass** the president's proposal for the **federal budget**.
6) **Barack Obama** faced one **government shutdown** (in **2013**) and **Donald Trump** faced two (in **2018** and **2018-19**), when Congress refused to pass their respective budgets.
7) More commonly, Congress can **force** the president to **change** their **priorities** through the **threat** of a **shutdown**. **Joe Biden** narrowly **avoided** a shutdown in **2024** by signing the **American Relief Act (2025)**, a **slimmed down** version of the original bill that involved several **compromises** between Democrats and Republicans.

The Senate has to confirm presidential appointments

- The **Senate** is able to **reject appointments** made by the **president** if they feel the nominee is **unsuitable** for the role. For example, the Senate rejected Ronald Reagan's **Supreme Court nominee Robert Bork** in **1987**.
- Sometimes, senators will **publicly declare** that they are **unwilling** to **confirm** an appointment, leading the nominee to **withdraw** before they have been rejected. This happened to **Andrew Puzder**, Trump's appointee to the **Secretary of Labor** position in **2017**
- Even when the Senate does **confirm** a **presidential appointment**, they will hold **many hours** of **hearings** that provide **significant scrutiny** of the nominee's **suitability** for the post and **ability** to deal with **pressure**.

The president can evade some checks, but is limited by the Constitution

1) The president can issue **executive orders** if they realise they're **unlikely** to be able to **pass legislation** through **Congress**:

   - In **2016**, **Obama** passed an executive order **strengthening background checks** and making it **harder** for **guns** to be **sold** over the **internet**.
   - In the aftermath of **Dobbs v Jackson Women's Health Organization (2022)** (see p.155), **Biden** issued an executive order **strengthening access** to **contraception** and **family-planning services**, in **2023**.
   - In **2024**, **Biden** issued an **executive order** that would **temporarily prevent asylum requests** once the number of daily arrivals on the US's border with Mexico **exceeded 2500**.

2) However, **executive orders** are limited in their scope and can be easily **repealed** by the **next president**. Executive orders **cannot** commit new **federal funding** to a policy (see page 171) and are subject to possible **judicial review**.
3) The president can choose to make **recess appointments** if they feel that their nominee is **unlikely** to be **confirmed** by the **Senate**. These take place during a **congressional holiday**, when the Senate is not sitting. As a result, appointments made during this time are **not** subject to **scrutiny** and **approval** from the **Senate**.

> Obama made 32 recess appointments during his presidency, but the Supreme Court ruled that he had exceeded his constitutional power by making such extensive use of this power. Neither Trump nor Biden attempted any recess appointments.

Congressional Checks on Presidential Power

Congressional checks on foreign policy are less significant

- The president's broad **commander-in-chief powers** means that they can order **military actions** such as **air strikes**, **drone strikes**, **assassinations** and even **ground invasions** without **congressional approval**.
- In **2024**, **Biden** issued an **executive order** that would **temporarily prevent asylum requests** once the number of daily arrivals on the US's border with Mexico **exceeded 2500**.
- Presidents can also choose to **limit congressional checks** on their **diplomatic policy** by signing **executive agreements** instead of **formal treaties**. Formal treaties are subject to **confirmation** by the **Senate**, but executive agreements aren't.
- Presidents in their **second term**, or approaching the **end** of their **first term**, will often shift their focus to **foreign policy**. This is because they are **more likely** to be able to achieve relatively **quick victories overseas** than by going through the **bargaining** process with **Congress**.

The idea that the president has more power in foreign than domestic policy was developed by presidential scholar Aaron Wildavsky. His 'two presidencies thesis' argues that foreign and domestic policy are so different that they should be regarded as two separate presidencies.

Two of Bill Clinton's major successes in his second term were his involvement in the Balkans conflict and in the Good Friday Agreement (see page 188)

Congress is still able to influence the president's military and diplomatic decisions

1) Under the **War Powers Resolution (1973)**, the president must notify **Congress** within **48 hours** of committing forces to **military action** and must then seek **congressional approval** if armed forces are **deployed overseas** for more than **60 days**.
2) Congress's **power of the purse** means that it can influence **spending** on **foreign policy**.

   - In **2007**, **Democrats** in Congress limited **George W. Bush's** control over the **Iraq war** by making continued **funding** for the war **dependent** on a programme of **troop withdrawals**.
   - In **2022-2024**, **Joe Biden** had to seek **congressional approval** for sending **aid** to **Ukraine**.

3) When presidents do choose to sign **formal treaties** with foreign countries, they require the **approval** of **two-thirds** of the **Senate** before they come into force. **Obama** was frustrated by this requirement when the **UN Disability Rights Treaty** was only approved by **61** senators in **2012**.

Congress holds the president to account with subpoenas and impeachment

1) Members of the executive branch can be **summoned** to give **evidence** in front of **congressional committees** under Congress's **subpoena powers**.
2) **Bill Clinton** was impeached in **1998** on charges of **obstructing Congress** and **perjury** over an **affair** with a White House intern, **Monica Lewinsky**.
3) **Trump** was impeached **twice** — first in **2020**, for allegedly offering an **illegal deal** to the then-president of Ukraine, and then over his alleged role in inciting the **January 6th Capitol riots** in **2021**.

Essay Plan

For Edexcel students: Evaluate the view that Congress possesses insufficient power to provide adequate checks on the executive branch. [30]

For AQA students: 'Congress possesses insufficient power to provide adequate checks on the executive branch.' Analyse and evaluate this statement. [25]

Using the grid on p.298, **plan** an answer to one of the essay questions above.

US ambassadors to Central Europe? They're the congressional Czechs...

Ultimately, the president depends on the House of Representatives and the Senate to approve their policies in order to pass and fund them. Even though the president has power, they won't get very far if they can't get Congress to play ball.

Judicial Checks on Presidential Power

The Supreme Court's role as 'guardians' of the Constitution can be a significant check on a president carrying out their aims.

The **Supreme Court** can rule that **laws** or **executive orders** are **unconstitutional**

Domestic policy is likely to face checks from the Supreme Court as part of its **judicial review** power.
This allows it to declare **any act of Congress** or **presidential decision** (including **executive orders**) unconstitutional:

President	Supreme Court Rulings
Bill Clinton	**Bill Clinton's** efforts to control **gun violence** were **restricted** by the Supreme Court's **US v. Lopez (1995)** ruling that the imposition of **gun-free school zones** in all 50 states was **unconstitutional**.
George W. Bush	In **Rasul v. Bush (2004)**, the Supreme Court **overruled George W. Bush's** policy of **indefinitely detaining terror suspects** at Guantanamo Bay without offering them a **trial**.
Barack Obama	**Barack Obama's** landmark **healthcare reform**, passed into law as the **Patient Protection and Affordable Care Act (2010)**, was checked by the Supreme Court's ruling in **NFIB v. Sebelius (2012)**. It ruled that the legislation's attempt to make **healthcare insurance** a **legal obligation** was **unconstitutional**. This has allowed **10 states** to **opt out** of the **Medicaid expansion** that the reform provided.
Donald Trump	**Donald Trump** had to **add** several non-Muslim majority **countries** to his **travel ban** so that it would be **upheld** by the Supreme Court in **Trump v. Hawaii (2018)**.
Joe Biden	In **NFIB v. Department of Labor (2022)**, the Supreme Court ruled against **Joe Biden's executive order** requiring **employees** in **medium** and **large companies** to **wear masks** or receive a **COVID-19 vaccine**. **Biden v. Nebraska (2023)** saw another significant check on Biden's power. The Supreme Court **ruled against** his plan to cancel **$10 000** of many **middle-income** and **lower-income** Americans' **student debts** as part of the broad **HEROES Act**.

Supreme Court rulings may support or go against a president's aims

Biden described the Supreme Court's **anti-abortion ruling** in **Dobbs v Jackson Women's Health Organization (2022)** as an *"exercise in raw political power"*. He subsequently **supported** Democrats' failed **attempts** to pass the first-ever **federal abortion law** through **Congress** as a **challenge** to the Dobbs ruling.

- Although **Trump** himself had nominated **three** of the **nine judges**, the Supreme Court **ended** his efforts to **challenge** the **result** of the **2020 presidential election** in **Trump v. United States (2020)**.
- But, four months before the **2024 presidential election**, the Supreme Court delivered an important **victory** for **Trump** (and a **blow** to **Democrats**). It ruled in **Trump v. United States (2024)** that he was **immune** from **federal prosecution** for **official acts** carried out when he was **president**.

The **strength** of Supreme Court checks **varies** depending on its **composition**

1) The president does have some **influence** over the **make-up** of the Supreme Court.
2) In his four years as president from **2017** to **2021**, **Trump** made **three appointments** to the Supreme Court: **Neil Gorsuch**, **Brett Kavanaugh** and **Amy Coney Barrett**. All three judges are **conservatives** and hold views on issues such as **abortion**, **gun rights** and **federalism** that fit with Trump's **ideology**.
3) In his eight years as president from **2009** to **2017**, **Obama** appointed **two** Supreme Court judges: **Sonia Sotomayor** and **Elena Kagan**. Both are **liberals** who share Obama's **ideology** on issues such as **abortion**, **same-sex marriage** and **gun control**.
4) Due to the **conservative majority** on the Supreme Court, **Biden** arguably faced more **stringent checks** from the **judicial branch** than **Trump** did during his first presidency.

> Amy Coney Barrett's appointment secured a 6-3 conservative majority on the Supreme Court (see p.193). This is the biggest majority for either conservatives or liberals since the Warren Court of the 1950s and 1960s.

My preferred Supreme Court makeup is a bold red lip and smokey eyes...
Being a Supreme Court judge is a lifelong position, so a lot of importance is placed on who is nominated to sit on the court.

US Politics — The Presidency

Imperial and Imperilled Presidencies

"What on earth are imperial and imperilled presidencies?", I hear you cry. It's all to do with the power presidents can exert.

Some **presidents** were **so powerful** they were said to have **imperial presidencies**

George W. Bush

The need for **decisive action** after the **9/11 terror attack** gave **Bush** more **power** than any other 21st century president to date:

- Bush passed the **Patriot Act (2001)**, a major **counter-terrorism law**, **six weeks** after the 9/11 attacks by margins of **357-66** in the **House of Representatives** and **98-1** in the **Senate**.
- Bush also **oversaw** the invasions of **Afghanistan** (in **2001**) and **Iraq** (in **2003**) and the creation of the **Department of Homeland Security** in **2002**. Although all these decisions were **scrutinised** and **voted on** by **Congress**, Bush faced very little **opposition** from either his own party, the **Republicans**, or the **Democrats**.
- The **Bush administration** continued to **benefit** from **united government** when the **Iraq war** started to become more **controversial**. The **Abu Ghraib** scandal, which centred on **allegations** that **US military personnel** had **tortured** and **mistreated** Iraqi **prisoners of war**, received only **12 hours** of **questioning** in the Republican-controlled **House of Representatives** in **2004-05**.

imperial presidency
A term coined by presidential scholar Arthur Schlesinger to describe presidencies where the president's power is comparable to an emperor. In practice, this means they can dominate proceedings with Congress and act unilaterally (on their own) in many aspects of domestic and foreign policy.

By contrast, House Republicans had devoted over 140 hours of questioning a decade earlier to investigate whether Democratic president Bill Clinton had used his Christmas card list to find potential campaign donors.

Ronald Reagan

Ronald Reagan was considered by some commentators to have been an **imperial president**, especially with respect to his **foreign policy**:

- In 1986, it emerged that Reagan had sanctioned **illegal trade** with **Iran**. He had also given **funding** to a **Nicaraguan rebel group** known as the **Contras** as part of an effort to **minimise** the **international influence** of the **Soviet Union**. This was known as the **Iran-Contra scandal**.
- Reagan received **very limited scrutiny** from Congress over this **scandal** and wasn't even **summoned** to give **evidence** to the committees that were established to **investigate** the affair.

Presidents who **lacked power** can be said to have **imperilled presidencies**

Gerald Ford

After the **Watergate scandal**, vice president **Gerald Ford** succeeded **Richard Nixon** as president. One of Ford's **first acts** was to **pardon** Nixon, **preventing** his former boss from facing **prosecution**.

Ford then **struggled** to **distance** himself from the **controversy** of the scandal, and **lost** the **1976 presidential election** to **Jimmy Carter** against a backdrop of a **struggling economy**.

Ford is one of **only five US presidents** who **never won** a **presidential election**.

imperilled presidency
When a president possesses so little power that they are regarded as being in danger of only serving one term due to their weakness or of having to resign from office due to a scandal.

Watergate scandal
President Richard Nixon ordered a break-in at the Watergate Hotel in Washington D.C., the campaign headquarters for his Democratic rival during the 1972 presidential election. The scandal led to Nixon's resignation from office.

Joe Biden

Although he **began** his presidency in **favourable circumstances** with **united government** and a **strong mandate** (from **winning** both the **popular vote** and the **Electoral College Vote** in **2020**), **Joe Biden** arguably **ended** his time in the White House as an **imperilled president**.

Concerns over Biden's **mental fitness** for office **increased** after a **poor performance** in the first televised **debate** between him and **Donald Trump** in **2024**. This eventually led to his decision **not to run for re-election**. Once this **decision** had been made, he was essentially a **lame duck president** (see page 181), with an **approval rating** of **only 36%** in **July 2024**.

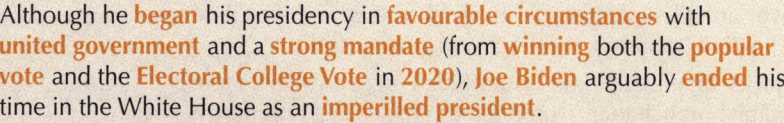

Imperial and Imperilled Presidencies

Most presidencies contain a **mix** of **imperial** and **imperilled** moments

Richard Nixon

Until his resignation, **Nixon** was perhaps the ultimate **imperial president**. He oversaw **major changes** to the **US's foreign policy** in **Vietnam** and **China** with very **limited oversight** from Congress.

But Nixon's presidency became **imperilled** and **ended abruptly** as a result of **media investigations**, **congressional pressure** and the Supreme Court's decision in **United States v. Nixon (1974)** that required Nixon to hand over the **tapes** that **incriminated** him in the **Watergate scandal**.

Barack Obama

Obama's presidency saw a record **563 drone strikes**, including **more** in his **first year** as president than **George W. Bush** had ordered during his **entire 8-year presidency**. Obama also ordered the **assassination** of **Osama bin Laden**, former leader of **Al-Qaeda**, in **2011**.

However, Obama **struggled** to pass **significant domestic legislation** after losing **control** of the **House of Representatives** in the **2010 mid-terms**, and the **Senate** in the **2014 mid-terms**. In particular, he **failed** to pass his **Assault Weapons Ban Bill** through Congress.

Donald Trump (2017-2021)

Trump acted **imperially** in many ways. In **2019**, he attempted to **divert money** intended for **natural disaster relief** to fund the **construction** of his **border wall project**, although he was **blocked from doing so by Congress**. In addition, he used **executive orders** to implement his **travel ban** and to declare that the **US** would **leave** the **World Health Organisation**.

However, Trump was also **imperilled** by the **two impeachments** that he faced. The **second**, in **2021**, saw the **Senate** come the closest to convicting a president since the 19th century.

Revision Task

Practise applying the theories of presidential power by **identifying** and **explaining** which one is most relevant to each of the points below.

1) *Joe Biden's presidency was overshadowed by questions over his mental fitness.*
2) *George W. Bush oversaw the response to 9/11 with minimal interference from Congress.*
3) *Barack Obama struggled to pass significant domestic legislation after losing control of the chambers of Congress.*
4) *Donald Trump is the only president in history to have been impeached twice.*

Essay Plan

For students studying...

Edexcel: Evaluate the view that the power of the president has grown to such an extent that they can now be described as imperial. [30]

AQA: 'The power of the president has grown to such an extent that they can now be described as imperial.' Analyse and evaluate this statement. [25]

For this exam question, you should also make use of Aaron Wildavsky's two presidencies thesis (see page 184).

Using the grid on p.298, **plan** an answer to one of the essay questions above.

Whose bright idea was it to use words as similar as imperial and imperilled?

That makes it especially important to read these pages and your exam questions carefully. You don't want to mix up an imperial and an imperilled presidency. Learning these case studies will help you support your points in the exam too.

US Politics — The Presidency

Judging the Effectiveness of Presidents

Presidents are just as flawed as the rest of us, but unfortunately for them, their ups and downs will be on the record forever.

There are a few ways to judge how **effective** a **presidency** was

Presidents are often judged based on things like their **election performance**, whether they achieved their **aims** and the extent to which they have achieved **long-lasting legacies**.

Bill Clinton

- 👍 Oversaw **economic recovery**, aided by the '**dotcom boom**' of new **online businesses**. It helped deliver a **budget surplus** (the US made more money than it spent) by the end of his presidency.
- 👍 Helped to broker the **Good Friday Agreement** peace deal in Northern Ireland, as well as participating in peace talks which **ended** a long **civil war** in the **Balkans**.
- 👍 Comfortably **re-elected** in the **1996** presidential election, becoming the first **Democrat** to be re-elected since **Franklin D. Roosevelt** in **1944**.
- 👎 In **1998**, he became only the **second** president in **history** to be **impeached** by the **House of Representatives**, facing counts of **perjury** and **obstructing Congress** over his **affair** with a White House intern, **Monica Lewinsky**. He was **acquitted** by the **Senate**, meaning that he **remained** president until **2001**.
- 👎 Spent much of his presidency accepting **compromises over policy** with **Republicans**. For example, he accepted a **ten-year sunset clause** on the **assault weapons ban** that he signed into law in **1994**, meaning that the ban was **lifted automatically** in **2004**.
- 👎 Blamed by some for **failing** to deal with **Al-Qaeda**, the terrorist group responsible for the **9/11 attacks**, before they became too **strong**.

> Oddly, Clinton received his highest approval ratings during the impeachment, as many voters felt that he was impeached for partisan reasons. This earned him the nickname Teflon Bill.

George W. Bush

- 👍 Developed a **clear** and **decisive** response to the **9/11 attacks**. For a **brief period** in late **2001**, this made him the **most popular president** since nationwide approval ratings were introduced in the 1930s, with support from **90%** of Americans.
- 👍 Having **narrowly** won the **2000 presidential election** (see page 208), he was more **convincingly re-elected** in **2004**, winning **286 electoral college votes** to John Kerry's **251**.
- 👍 Passed **significant domestic legislation**, including the **Economic Growth and Tax Relief Reconciliation Act (2001)** and the **Jobs and Growth Tax Relief Reconciliation Act (2003)**, both **tax-cutting** measures, and the **No Child Left Behind Act (2001)**, a major **education** reform.
- 👎 The '**war on terror**' arguably **failed** to achieve any of its **long-term aims**. The **Taliban** returned to power in **Afghanistan** in **2021**, and terrorist groups such as **Al-Qaeda** and **ISIS continue** to operate in Iraq.
- 👎 Criticised for **failing** to co-ordinate a **swift** and **effective response** to **Hurricane Katrina** in **2005**, which left over a **million** residents of New Orleans **homeless** or living in **damaged accommodation**.
- 👎 By **November 2008**, he had become the **least popular president** since approval ratings began, with support from only **25%** of Americans.

Barack Obama

- 👍 Oversaw **economic recovery** from the **worst recession** since the **Great Depression** of the **1930s**.
- 👍 Passed the **most significant reform** to **healthcare** since the **1960s** — the **Patient Protection and Affordable Care Act (2010)**, known by many as **Obamacare**.
- 👍 Won a **second term** in the **2012** presidential election. He devoted much of his energy in this period to **international affairs**, agreeing **ground-breaking deals** with **Cuba** and **Iran**, and signing the **Paris Agreement** (see page 268).
- 👎 **Failed** to legislate on **gun control**, which he described as the "*greatest frustration*" of his presidency.
- 👎 Criticised by many for **failing** to **protect Iraq** from **terrorism** following the **withdrawal** of most **US troops** in **2011**.
- 👎 **Disagreements** with **Congress** over his plans for the **federal budget** led to a **government shutdown** in **2013**, the first since the mid-1990s.

Judging the Effectiveness of Presidents

Donald Trump (2017-2021)

👍 Passed the **Tax Cuts and Jobs Act (2017)**, one of the most significant **tax-cutting laws** in recent US history.

👍 Presided over **high levels** of **economic growth** (until the onset of the **COVID-19 pandemic** in early **2020**).

👍 Successfully appointed **three Supreme Court judges** in his four-year term, weighting the court in **favour** of **conservatives**.

👎 **Lost** the **2020 presidential election** to Joe Biden, and **lost** over **60 court cases** that he filed **challenging** the result.

👎 Became the **only president** to be **impeached twice**, and came very **close** to being **removed from office** during his **Senate trial** in **January 2021**.

👎 Criticised for **failing** to achieve either of his **two main campaign pledges** from the **2016** presidential election: constructing a **wall** on the **US's border** with **Mexico** and **repealing Obamacare**.

Joe Biden

👍 **Persuaded** centrist members of **Congress** to help him pass the **American Rescue Plan Act (2021)** and the **Bipartisan Infrastructure Law (2021)**, two of the major parts of his **Build Back Better** plan to help stimulate the US's **economic recovery** after COVID-19.

👍 Passed the **Bipartisan Safer Communities Act (2022)**, the first major **gun control reform** since **1994**.

👍 **Strengthened** the US's **relationship** with fellow **NATO member states**, helping to co-ordinate their **response** to the **Russian invasion** of **Ukraine** in **2022**.

👎 Criticised for **failing** to oversee an orderly **withdrawal** of **US troops** from **Afghanistan** in **2021** — within **months**, the country had been **overtaken** by the **Taliban** once again.

👎 Faced persistent **questions** over his **mental fitness** for the job. These intensified after a **poor performance** in the first televised **debate** of the **2024 presidential election campaign**, and after he mistakenly introduced **Ukraine's President Zelensky** as his arch-rival **President Putin** of **Russia**.

👎 As a result of these criticisms, in **July 2024**, he **withdrew** his candidacy from the **2024 presidential election**. He was **replaced** by his vice president **Kamala Harris**.

Quick Questions

1) Which president helped to broker the Good Friday Agreement?
2) Who did George W. Bush defeat in the 2004 presidential election?
3) Identify one of Barack Obama's domestic policy achievements.
4) How many Supreme Court justices did Donald Trump appoint?
5) Who is the only president to have been impeached twice?
6) Why was the Bipartisan Safer Communities Act (2022) so significant?
7) Identify one of Joe Biden's foreign policy failings.

Melissa had crafted the perfect ensemble for the impeachment hearings

Essay Plan

For students studying...

Edexcel: Evaluate the view that presidents since 1992 have tended to be unable to achieve most of their aims. [30]
AQA: 'Presidents since 1992 have tended to be unable to achieve most of their aims.'
Analyse and evaluate this statement. [25]

Using the grid on p.298, **plan** an answer to one of the essay questions above.

Cue the theme music, it's time for CSI*: Washington D.C.

Remember, when you're evaluating these things in the exam, you need to equally analyse the positive and negative periods of a president's time in office. Keep those three key criteria of elections, aims and legacy in mind when making your judgement.

*Case Study Investigation

Comparing the US President and UK PM

The US and the UK have had a long history of working with, and against, each other. So it might not come as a surprise to you that there are plenty of comparisons to be made between the president and the PM. Crack on to see more...

Both **president** and **PM** have significant **power** over **foreign policy**

1) The president and prime minister can **deploy troops** on **overseas missions**, order **air** and **drone strikes** and **initiate troop withdrawals** without needing to **consult** their respective **legislative branches** in advance. For example:

   - In **2021**, **Biden** and **Boris Johnson** agreed to **bring forward** the **withdrawal** of US and UK **troops** from **Afghanistan**, without needing to seek the **consent** of **Congress** or **Parliament**.
   - Both **Joe Biden** and **Rishi Sunak** ordered air strikes on the **Houthi rebels** in **Yemen** in **2023** without first holding **debates** or **votes** in **Congress** or **Parliament**.

2) In the US, this power comes from the president's **commander-in-chief** role. In the UK, the prime minister has inherited these powers from the monarch as part of the **royal prerogative** (see page 84).

The **prime minister** generally has **more power** over **domestic policy**

1 The **prime minister** is, by convention, the **leader** of the **largest party** in the **House of Commons**. Due to the **fusion of powers** between the **executive** and **legislative** branches in the **UK**, prime ministers tend to possess an **inbuilt majority** in the **Commons**.

2 This typically enables the prime minister to **succeed** in **passing legislation** through **Parliament**, where they are also able to **control** the **timetable** and the **scrutiny** that legislation receives in **public bill committees** (see page 79). For example, **Tony Blair** spent **eight years undefeated** in the **House of Commons** from **1997** to **2005**, while **Rishi Sunak** lost only **one** vote from **November 2022** to **July 2024**.

3 By contrast, the **separation of powers** in the **US** means that the president is much **less likely** to be able to pass legislation through **Congress**. When they do manage to do so, they usually have to make **significant compromises**.

> Similarities and differences that stem from the powers set out in the US and the UK's constitutions can be explained by looking at their political structures (see page 145).

4 **All** recent presidents have **failed** to pass **major legislative priorities** through **Congress** — **Barack Obama** on **gun control**, **Donald Trump** on a **border wall** and **healthcare reform** and **Joe Biden** on **abortion**.

5 Gun control, healthcare and abortion are all areas of **broad, cross-party consensus** in the UK, but they create **major divisions** between and within the **Republican** and **Democratic** parties in the **US**. As a result, **presidents** are much **more likely** to face **difficulties** making changes in these **policy areas** than **prime ministers** would be.

> These differences come from the social and political cultures of the US and the UK — see page 145.

6 Because of Congress's **power of the purse**, the president is much **more likely** to face **difficulties** in implementing their **economic policy** than prime ministers. **Obama** and **Trump** (twice) both experienced **government shutdowns** and **Biden** was forced to **compromise** with Congress in order to pass his final budget as president in **2024** (see page 171).

7 In the UK, the **annual budget** tends to be **passed unamended** through the **Commons**, while the **Lords cannot** amend **financial bills** (at least since 1911 — see page 60). The **Commons** has only **rejected** one **finance bill** since 1978 (under **Theresa May** in **2019**).

US Politics — The Presidency

Comparing the US President and UK PM

The **president** is **less accountable** to **Congress** than the **PM** is to **parliament**...

1) While the **president** can be **impeached** and **summoned** for **questioning** under Congress's **subpoena powers**, they do **not** frequently **respond** to **questions** in either the **House of Representatives** or the **Senate**.
2) The annual **State of the Union** address sees the **president** address **both chambers** of **Congress**, but there is **no opportunity** for **questioning**. This makes the event more of a **publicity exercise** for the president.
3) By contrast, the **prime minister** faces **weekly** parliamentary **scrutiny** at **Prime Minister's Questions**, and has to answer questions from **policy experts** on the **Liaison Committee two** to **three** times **per year** (see p.79).
4) The **executive branch** can also face a **vote of no confidence** from the **House of Commons**, which will prompt a **general election** if the government **loses** the vote. **Jim Callaghan's** Labour government was the last government to **lose** a vote of no confidence, in **1979**. There is **no direct equivalent** in the **US**, although the **Senate** can **remove** the **president**, or **members** of the executive branch, from **office** following **impeachment** by the **House of Representatives**.

...**except** when dealing with **appointments** and **treaties**

US president
- The president's **nominations** to **executive branch positions**, including members of the **Cabinet** and **ambassadors**, are subject to **confirmation** by the **Senate**. This is part of the constitutional system of **checks and balances**.
- This means that the **Senate** can choose to **reject** presidential nominations, or **refuse** to hold **hearings**. Biden's nominees for the **Secretary of Labor** and **Secretary of Housing and Urban Development** positions were left **vacant** from **March 2023** and **March 2024** until the **end** of his presidency.
- The **Senate** has to ratify **any treaties** agreed by the **president** before they come into effect. In **2012**, the Senate **failed** to pass the **UN Disability Rights Treaty**, signed by **Obama**, by the **required two-thirds majority**.

UK prime minister
- The **prime minister** can appoint **any** member of Parliament to their **Cabinet** without any **scrutiny** from **Parliament**. **Rishi Sunak** made **David Cameron** his **Foreign Secretary** in **2023**, appointing him to the **House of Lords** and the **Cabinet** at the same time, without any chance of this being **blocked** by Parliament.
- The **prime minister** can **negotiate** and **sign** most **treaties without** needing the **approval** of **Parliament** (the **Brexit deal** was an **exception**).

Ambassadorial appointments are also part of the prime minister's prerogative powers. Boris Johnson appointed Karen Pierce as the UK's ambassador to the US in 2020.

The **president** is **more likely** to be checked by the **judiciary** than the **PM** is

US president

The **US Supreme Court** can, as part of its **judicial review powers** (see page 149), declare **any law** or presidential decision **unconstitutional**. **Biden**, **Trump** and **Obama** all faced **Supreme Court decisions** that went against their aims and policies (see page 185).

UK prime minister

Prime ministers have faced **increasing checks** from the **UK Supreme Court** in recent years. **Theresa May**, **Boris Johnson** and **Rishi Sunak** all suffered **high-profile legal defeats** (see pages 98-99).

However, **parliamentary sovereignty** and the UK's **uncodified Constitution** mean that the **UK Supreme Court** can **only** rule that the prime minister has acted beyond their powers (*ultra vires*). The prime minister can **overrule** Supreme Court decisions by passing **statute law** through Parliament, as **Sunak** did with the **Safety of Rwanda Act (2024)**.

Exam Practice

Have a look at page 145 for more about comparative theories.

For Edexcel students: Analyse the extent to which the US president and the UK prime minister are accountable to their legislative branches. In your answer, you must consider the relevance of at least one comparative theory. [12]

For AQA students: Explain and analyse three ways in which structural theory could be used to compare the powers of the US president and the UK prime minister. [9]

The president is a morning person but the PM is a night owl...
Everything between noon and midnight is pm time after all. Be sure to look at the similarities between the president and the PM from both a structural angle (e.g. political systems, constitutions) and a cultural one (e.g. social norms and priorities).

US Politics — The Presidency

The US Supreme Court

Ever since the Constitution was first written and enacted in 1787, the US has had a Supreme Court. It's a pretty big deal.

The **Supreme Court** is the **highest court** in the **United States**

1) Most **cases** that the **Supreme Court** considers are **appeals**, where it **reviews a ruling** that's already been made by a **circuit court**, a **district court** or a **state-level Supreme Court**.
2) In most instances, the Supreme Court **decides** which cases it will hear — of the estimated **8000 cases** that are **filed** to the Court each year, it holds **hearings** on around **70 to 80**.

> If the Court chooses not to hear a case, the decision of the highest court to hear it already will remain in place. This means that the Court can sometimes have a significant influence without even making a ruling.

3) Supreme Court rulings are based on a **legal principle** called *stare decisis* — this means that the Court should, where possible, **justify** its decision based on **precedents** established by **previous rulings**.

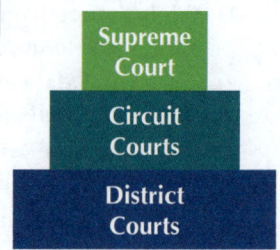

The hierarchy of courts in the US Federal Court System

Supreme Court **justices** are **nominated** by the **president**

1) The Supreme Court has **nine** justices (judges) — one **Chief Justice** and eight **Associate Justices**.
2) When a **vacancy** arises due to the **retirement** or **death** of a justice, the **president** can **nominate anyone** of their choosing to fill the place on the Court.
3) If the **Chief Justice** retires or dies, the president can choose either to **nominate** a **new justice** to replace them, or to **elevate** one of the **Associate Justices** to the position.

> When **William Rehnquist** died in **2005**, **George W. Bush** nominated **John Roberts**, previously a **federal judge**, to replace him as **Chief Justice**.

Technically, Supreme Court nominees don't actually need to have a legal background, but in practice they tend to be experienced judges or law professors.

4) In recent decades, it has become the norm for presidents to choose justices based on their **judicial philosophy** — the **role** they think the **law** should play in **society** and how they **interpret** it.

- **Supreme Court appointments** are one of the best ways in which a **president** can have a **long-lasting legacy**. So a justice's **ideological leanings**, alongside their **legal experience**, are **key factors** influencing a president's **selection decisions**.
- **Democrat** presidents therefore nominate **liberal** justices, who tend to have a **loose constructionist** ideology (see p.149). This is based on the belief that the **Constitution** is a **living document** that should frequently be **re-interpreted** and **updated**.
- **Republican** presidents nominate **conservative** justices, who tend to have a **strict constructionist**, **originalist** ideology (see p.149). This is based on the belief that the **original wording** and **intentions** of the **Constitution** should be **preserved**.

Mark would regret choosing a barbed wire fence to demonstrate his ideological leaning

The **Senate** must **confirm** Supreme Court **nominations**

1) Once a **nomination** has been made, the **Senate Judiciary Committee** usually schedules **several days'** worth of **hearings**. The nominee is **questioned** on their **background**, **experience**, **character** and **judicial philosophy**.
2) After the **hearings** have **finished**, the **Committee** holds a **vote** on whether to **recommend** the nominee to the **full Senate chamber**.
3) **All 100 members** of the Senate can then **vote** to **confirm** or **refuse** the nomination. Although they can choose to **ignore** the **Committee's recommendation**, the full chamber **usually** votes in the **same way**.
4) Since **1987**, when **Robert Bork's** nomination was **rejected** by the Senate over his record on **civil rights**, the Senate has confirmed **every Supreme Court nominee** except **Merrick Garland**, who was nominated by **Barack Obama** in **2016**.

> Senate Majority Leader **Mitch McConnell**, a **Republican**, **refused** to hold **hearings** or a **vote** on Garland's nomination. He argued that **Obama** shouldn't be able to make a **Supreme Court appointment** because he was **leaving office** later that year.

See page 172 for more about judicial appointments.

5) This reflects rising levels of **partisanship** in the confirmation process. While Bork's replacement, **Anthony Kennedy**, was confirmed **97-0** by the Senate in **1988**, the **past seven nominees** have all been confirmed by **fewer than 70** senators.

The US Supreme Court

Justices sit on the Supreme Court for life or until retirement

- In recent years, **Antonin Scalia (1986-2016)** and **Ruth Bader Ginsburg (1993-2020)** served on the court until their **deaths**.
- **John Paul Stevens**, who was nominated by **Gerald Ford** in **1975**, served until his **retirement** in **2010**.
- When **George W. Bush** nominated **John Roberts** as **Chief Justice** in **2005**, he was **50** years old. This meant that he could, health permitting, lead the Court for **several decades**.

> Supreme Court justices (and judges in lower federal courts) can be impeached by the House of Representatives and then removed from office if they are found guilty by the Senate. Only one Supreme Court justice has ever been impeached (Samuel Chase in 1805).

The balance of liberal and conservative justices has changed in recent years

1) Historically, **the Supreme Court** has been **balanced** between **conservative** and **liberal justices**.
2) Until the **death** of **Ruth Bader Ginsburg** (a long-serving **liberal justice**) in **2020**, the Supreme Court had been balanced **5-4** in favour of **conservative, Republican-appointed** justices for **nearly 20 years**.
3) Throughout much of this period, **Anthony Kennedy**, who had been appointed by **Republican** president **Ronald Reagan**, acted as a **swing justice**, tipping the balance in favour of the conservative or the liberal justices in 5-4 split decisions like **Obergefell v. Hodges (2015)**, **Citizens United v. FEC (2010)** and **D.C. v. Heller (2008)**.
4) However, since **2020**, the Supreme Court has had a **6-3 conservative majority**.

Key Terms — swing justice: *A judge who is more politically centrist and may vote in either direction. They can be the deciding factor in how a case is ruled.*

Justice	Nominated by (year of confirmation)	Judicial philosophy
Clarence Thomas	George H.W. Bush (1991)	Conservative
John Roberts (Chief Justice)	George W. Bush (2005)	Conservative
Samuel Alito	George W. Bush (2006)	Conservative
Sonia Sotomayor	Barack Obama (2009)	Liberal

Justice	Nominated by (year of confirmation)	Judicial philosophy
Elena Kagan	Barack Obama (2010)	Liberal
Neil Gorsuch	Donald Trump (2017)	Conservative
Brett Kavanaugh	Donald Trump (2018)	Conservative
Amy Coney Barrett	Donald Trump (2020)	Conservative
Ketanji Brown Jackson	Joe Biden (2022)	Liberal

> Until the balance was tipped in 2020, John Roberts often served as a swing justice (see p.198).

The Supreme Court's main constitutional role is to clarify federal law

1) Because each **state** has its own **legal system**, there can often be **contradictions** between **federal** and **state law**. The **Supreme Court** can **clarify** how these laws should be **applied**, based on **previous rulings** and the **Constitution's provisions**.
2) **Individuals** and **organisations** (such as **campaign groups**, **corporations** and **religious bodies**) can **appeal against** a **federal** or **state law**. Here, the **Supreme Court** acts as an **arbiter**, ruling on how the Constitution's provisions and previous rulings should be **applied** to the **dispute**.
3) The areas of **vagueness in the Constitution** (see p.148-149), and the evolution of **US politics** and **society** since **1787**, mean that there are often **disputes** over how the **framers' intentions** should be **interpreted** in the **present day**.

I needed a swing justice to judge my Charleston dance contest...
The Supreme Court really lives up to its name. Its powers over constitutionality mean it has a huge influence on legislation.

US Politics — US Supreme Court and Civil Rights

Notable Supreme Court Rulings

The US Supreme Court's rulings have wide-reaching implications. Read on to find out about some particularly juicy ones...

The Supreme Court has **significant influence** over **US politics**

The Supreme Court has made **major rulings** on **wide-ranging areas** of **politics**. For example:

Supreme Court Case	Description
Brown v. Board of Education of Topeka (1954)	The Court **overruled** its **previous decision** in **Plessy v. Ferguson (1896)**, which had upheld **racial segregation**. As a result of this landmark ruling, the practice of **preventing African Americans** from accessing the **same public services** as **white Americans** was **outlawed**.
Roe v. Wade (1973)	The Court ruled that the **Constitution's protection of privacy** should **extend** to **abortion rights**. This meant that women **across the United States** could **access** an **abortion**, although **interpretations** of the ruling **differed** between **states**.
United States v. Nixon (1974)	In one of its most **famous rulings**, the Court paved the way for **Richard Nixon's resignation** as president when it **ordered** him to **hand over** the **tapes** that **incriminated** him in the **Watergate scandal**.
United States v. Lopez (1995)	The Court ruled that the **Gun-Free School Zones Act (1990) violated** the **Commerce Clause** from **Article I** of the **Constitution** by indirectly **preventing** the **sale of firearms** in **gun-free zones** around schools. The Court outlined its view that **Congress** can legitimately **regulate commerce between states**, but **not within** them.
Rasul v. Bush (2004)	The Court ruled that **terror suspects detained** by the Bush administration had the **right** to a **fair trial**. Although this ruling was a blow to Bush's counter-terror policies, most of the inmates in Guantanamo Bay, the US's highest-level detention centre, never received a trial.
D.C. v. Heller (2008)	The Court found that the **2nd amendment's 'right to bear arms'** covers **individual gun ownership**. As a result, this ruled that the **District of Columbia's handgun ban** was **unconstitutional**.
Citizens United v. Federal Election Commission (FEC) (2010)	Based on its interpretation that the **1st amendment's freedom of speech** should **extend** to **political donations**, the Court ruled that **limits** to the **amount** that **individuals** or **groups** could **donate** were **unconstitutional**.
National Federation of Independent Business (NFIB) v. Sebelius (2012)	The Court **upheld parts** of the **Patient Protection and Affordable Care Act (2010)**, known as **Obamacare**, but **declared** that its **requirement** for **states** to **comply** with its attempt to **expand Medicaid** was an **unconstitutional** violation of their rights.
Shelby County v. Holder (2013)	The Court **struck down** two sections of the **Voting Rights Act (1965)** that **prohibited** certain **congressional districts** from **changing** their **election procedures** without **authorisation**. This decision meant many districts then **introduced** measures that are alleged to be designed to **suppress voters** from certain **underrepresented racial groups**.
Obergefell v. Hodges (2015)	The Court **upheld** the **constitutionality** of **same-sex marriage**, meaning that **all 50 states** had to **allow** same-sex marriages.
Department of Homeland Security v. Regents of the University of California (2020)	The Court ruled that the **Trump administration's** plan to **abolish** an **Obama-era immigration policy** called **Deferred Action Against Childhood Arrivals (DACA)** was **unconstitutional**. DACA gave **immunity** against **deportation** to millions of Americans who had arrived in the US **illegally** as **children**.

Notable Supreme Court Rulings

Supreme Court Case	Description
Roman Catholic Diocese of Brooklyn v. Cuomo (2020)	The Court ruled against then-**New York Governor Andrew Cuomo's** policy of **restricting** the **number of people** who could gather for **religious services** during the **COVID-19 pandemic**.
National Federation of Independent Business (NFIB) v. Department of Labor (2022)	The Court ruled **against** an **executive order** by **Joe Biden** that would have **required employees** in medium and large companies to **wear masks** or **receive a COVID-19 vaccine**.
Dobbs v. Jackson Women's Health Organization (2022)	In one of the most **high-profile decisions** in its history, the Court **overturned** its previous ruling in **Roe v. Wade (1973)**. Its decision meant that **conservative states** could **implement total** or **partial bans** on **abortion**.
New York State Pistol and Rifle Association v. Bruen (2022)	The Court ruled that **New York state's requirement** that individuals wishing to carry **firearms in public** needed to **demonstrate** a **special need** for **self-protection** was **unconstitutional**.
Trump v. Thompson (2022)	The Court ruled that **Donald Trump** could **not block** the **release** of **White House documents** relating to the **January 6th riots** on Capitol Hill. As well as strengthening legal challenges against the former president, this ruling could have consequences for future presidents by adding to the precedent from United States v. Nixon (1974) that executive privilege doesn't extend to official White House documents.
Biden v. Nebraska (2023)	The Court ruled **against Biden's plan** to **cancel** a portion of **college debt** for many **lower-** or **middle-income Americans** (up to **$10 000** per person).
SFFA v. Harvard (2023)	The Court ruled that the use of **affirmative action policies** in **college admissions** was **unconstitutional**.
Trump v. United States (2024)	The Court ruled that **Donald Trump** was **immune** from **federal prosecution** for **official acts** he carried out while he was **president**.
Moyle v. United States (2024)	While choosing **not** to make its **own ruling**, the Supreme Court **restored** a previous **Circuit Court decision** that **Idaho's planned ban** on **emergency abortions** was **unconstitutional**.
United States v. Rahimi (2024)	The Court **upheld** the **constitutionality** of **temporary firearms bans** for **individuals** deemed to be a **physical threat to others**.
Garland v. Cargill (2024)	The Court ruled that a **federal ban** on **'bump stocks'**, gun attachments that **aid rapid fire**, was **unconstitutional**.

This ban was implemented during the first Trump presidency, but it was also supported by Biden, who was president at the time of the ruling.

Quick Questions

1) What was the ruling in Roe v. Wade (1973)? Which Supreme Court ruling overturned this ruling?
2) In which case did the Supreme Court consider the constitutionality of Obamacare?
3) What was the ruling in Department of Homeland Security v. Regents of the University of California (2020)?
4) Which Supreme Court ruling prevented limits on religious worship during the COVID-19 pandemic?
5) What did the Supreme Court decide in New York State Pistol and Rifle Association v. Bruen (2022)?

Supreme Court rulings are like your email password. They're case sensitive...
As you read through the rest of this section, it's a good idea to keep flicking back to these pages for a refresher. These rulings are key examples of the power and influence that the Supreme Court has over the law and US politics as a whole.

Influence of the Supreme Court

The US Supreme Court is able to check the power of the executive branch, the legislative branch and state governments when they overstep their constitutional roles. And, unlike its UK counterpart, its rulings are binding. No wriggling out of it.

Supreme Court rulings can show judicial activism or judicial restraint

Judicial activism

- This is a way of **operating** as a **judge** which seeks to **actively expand** the **interpretation** of the **law** to **promote** a **social cause**.
- **Supporters** of judicial activism argue that courts should consider the **broader societal implications** of their **decisions**, rather than only basing rulings on **existing legal precedent**.
- Examples of judicial activism in **Supreme Court rulings** include: **Brown v. Board of Education of Topeka (1954)**, **Roe v. Wade (1973)** and **Obergefell v. Hodges (2015)**.

Judicial restraint

- This is a way of **operating** as a **judge** which **focuses** on **existing legal precedents**, often **resisting** attempts to **expand** the **law**.
- **Supporters** of judicial restraint in the Supreme Court prefer this approach because it usually **defers** to the **decisions** of the **executive branch** and **state-level courts**. These bodies are **directly accountable** to the **electorate**, unlike Supreme Court judges.
- Examples of judicial restraint in **Supreme Court rulings** include: **Rasul v. Bush (2004)**, **NFIB v. Department of Labor (2022)** and **Biden v. Nebraska (2023)**.

1) There's often **debate** over whether **specific rulings** are examples of **judicial activism** or **judicial restraint**.
2) In both cases, **critics** of the **Supreme Court** argue that it is wielding **excessive influence** and acting in an overly **political** manner, either by **allowing** or **preventing reforms** from taking place.
3) Supporters of **judicial activism** tend to have a **loose constructionist** judicial philosophy, believing that the **Supreme Court** should **interpret** the **Constitution** as a **living document** that ought to **adapt** as the **needs** and **opinions** of **American society** evolve.
4) Meanwhile, supporters of **judicial restraint** typically have a **strict constructionist** judicial philosophy, believing that the Supreme Court's job is to **protect** the **original Constitution** from being **changed** beyond the **framers' intentions**.

The Supreme Court is able to check the power of other government branches

1) Since **Marbury v. Madison (1804)** (see page 149), the Supreme Court has had a **significant role** in **checking** the other two **branches of government**.
2) The Supreme Court frequently checks the power of the **executive branch**, as in the following cases (see pages 194-195):

- **United States v. Nixon (1974)**
- **NFIB v. Sebelius (2012)**
- **NFIB v. Department of Labor (2022)**
- **Trump v. Thompson (2022)**
- **Biden v. Nebraska (2023)**
- **Garland v. Cargill (2024)**

3) The Supreme Court **refused** to hear Trump's **challenge** to the **validity** of the **2020 presidential election results**. The Court's supporters point to this as an example of its **effectiveness**: a **third** of its members had been **nominated by Trump**, and **two-thirds** by **Republican** presidents, but they **refused** to show him **preferential treatment**.
4) The Supreme Court's status as the **guardian** of the **US Constitution** means that it can also strike down **acts of Congress** and **state laws** as **unconstitutional**:

- **Fletcher v. Peck (1810)** — the Court ruled that it was **unconstitutional** for **Georgia** to **repeal** the **Yazoo Land Act (1795)** and so **invalidate** the **sales** of the **land** covered by the act (even though the **passing** of the act was **influenced** by **bribery**). This was the **first time** the **Supreme Court ruled** the **actions** of a **state legislature** as **unconstitutional**.
- **FEC v. Ted Cruz for Senate (2021)** — the Court ruled **against** a **section** of the **Bipartisan Campaign Finance Reform Act (2002)**, overturning the **$250 000 limit** on **reimbursing** candidates' **personal loans** to their campaigns from post-election **campaign donations**.

> See pages 194-195 for a number of additional examples of cases where the Supreme Court ruled on the constitutionality of policies and practices.

US Politics — US Supreme Court and Civil Rights

Influence of the Supreme Court

The Supreme Court has always been able to **check** the **power** of the **states**

Although the Supreme Court often **protects** the **states** from **federal government overreach**, it also frequently **rules against** their attempts to **challenge** or **extend federal law**.

The following **Supreme Court rulings** checked the power of **states**:
- **Brown v. Board of Education of Topeka (1954)**
- **Gonzales v. Raich (2005)** — the Court ruled **against medical exemptions** for **marijuana use** in **14 states**, including California.
- **Roman Catholic Diocese of Brooklyn v. Cuomo (2020)**
- **New York State Pistol and Rifle Association v. Bruen (2022)**

See p.194-195 for more on some of these cases.

Since 2009, federal prosecutors have been instructed by the executive branch not to enforce the federal ban on marijuana use. In 2023, Joe Biden issued a presidential proclamation pardoning people who had previously been convicted of marijuana possession under federal law.

The **cases heard** by the Supreme Court are **determined** by **the Rule of Four**

1) The Supreme Court's judges **choose** which **cases** they hear, accepting only **70-80** from **over 7000** petitions **each year**.
2) Deciding which cases to hear is based on a principle called the **Rule of Four**, which states that **at least four** of the Court's nine **judges** need to **agree** that a case is **worth hearing**.
3) The **Rule of Four** has received more **attention** in recent years since the **balance** of the Supreme Court tipped to a **6-3 conservative majority** following the confirmation of **Amy Coney Barrett** in **2020**.

Some argue the Supreme Court is an **effective** way of **protecting** the **framers' aims**

✓ Across its many rulings in recent decades, the Supreme Court has managed to strike a **balance** between allowing the interpretation of **individual rights** to **progress** while also maintaining **states' ability** to **preserve** their own **legal** and **political cultures**.

✓ The Court's rulings frequently **prevent abuses of power**, which was perhaps the framers' **most important aim** when writing the **Constitution**.

✓ Sometimes, the Court allows the **states** to **regain power** from the **federal government**. At other times, its rulings **prevent** the **federal government** from **encroaching** on issues that it deems to be under **states' jurisdiction**.

Naomi's job was to judge the aim of the frame

Some believe that its **influence** has grown **stronger** than the **framers intended**

✗ The Supreme Court has been described as an **imperial judiciary** because it has granted itself **more power**, through rulings such as **Marbury v. Madison (1804)**.

✗ While there are **significant checks** and **balances** on **Congress**, the **Presidency**, and the **states**, there are very **few** checks and balances on the **Supreme Court**. While **judges** can be **impeached**, this has **not** happened to a Supreme Court judge for **over 200 years**.

✗ The Court's power is made more **controversial** by the **politicisation** of the **appointments process**. It has become clear that **presidents** choose **nominees** based on whether their **judicial philosophy aligns** with their **own**. The **Senate confirmation process** is now guided by which **party** is in **control** of the chamber.

The abolition of the filibuster for Supreme Court appointments in 2017 means that, in practice, Supreme Court justices can be confirmed by just one party during times of united government.

Essay Plan

For Edexcel students: Evaluate the view that the Supreme Court's most significant impact on public policy has been through judicial activism. [30]

For AQA students: 'The Supreme Court's most significant impact on public policy has been through judicial activism.' Analyse and evaluate this statement. [25]

Using the grid on p.298, **plan** an answer to one of the essay questions above.

My US political commentary alter-ego is called Uncle Stitutional...

As you can see, the Supreme Court's decisions carry a lot of weight, and not everyone is happy with how much power it has. Think about how the case examples on p.194-195 could serve as evidence for and against the strength of the Supreme Court.

Is the Supreme Court Political or Judicial?

As the appointment of judges becomes more partisan, some fear that the Supreme Court has drifted from its intended role.

Some believe that the **Supreme Court** has become a **politicised body**...

1) The **appointments process** is now **highly partisan** at every stage — **presidents** nominate **justices** based on their **judicial philosophy**, and the **Senate's confirmation** is **conditional** on the **majority party's support**.
2) Between **1789** and **1965**, the average time between **nomination** and **confirmation** was **13 days**, but this increased to **54** days from **1965** to **2020**. This suggests that the **process** has become **more rigorous**, but also **more contested** between the parties.
3) As a result of **Mitch McConnell's** refusal to hold hearings for **Merrick Garland** in **2016** (see p.152), **Clarence Thomas** was the **only judge** on the Supreme Court during the **Trump** and **Biden presidencies** who was **confirmed** by a Senate not controlled by the **same party** as the **president**.

Some believe that this statistic represents the positive growth of scrutiny, rather than a negative trend of increased partisanship.

> Critics of the appointments process believe that it allows interest groups an excessive level of influence. All six conservative members of the Supreme Court are members of the Federalist Society, a right-wing judicial pressure group.

Justices have often voted **along ideological lines** in recent **controversial rulings**

1) In **2023-24**, several **conservative justices** frequently **voted** as a **bloc** (group).
   - In the **15** highest profile cases, **Brett Kavanaugh** and **John Roberts** both voted with the conservative majority **14 times**, while **Samuel Alito** and **Amy Coney Barrett** did so **13 times**.
   - Liberal justices **Elena Kagan** and **Sonia Sotomayor**, both appointed by Barack Obama, voted together on **all 15** of the highest-profile cases in **2023-24**.
2) Here are some examples of **bloc voting** in recent years:

Trump v. Hawaii (2018) — 5-4
(all five conservatives in favour; all four liberals against)

Dobbs v. Jackson Women's Health Organization (2022) — 6-3
(all six conservatives in favour; all three liberals against)

SFFA v. Harvard (2023) — 6-2
(all six conservatives in favour; both liberals against)

Ketanji Brown Jackson did not take part in this case because she had served on a board of former Harvard students.

Trump v. United States (2024) — 6-3
(all six conservatives in favour; all three liberals against)

City of Grants Pass v. Johnson (2024) — 6-3
(all six conservatives in favour; all three liberals against)

In this high-profile case, the Court ruled that presidents had absolute immunity for acts committed while in office. This prevented several criminal prosecutions of Trump for his alleged role in inciting the 2021 Capitol Hill riots.

...others argue it remains a **judicial body** that considers **cases** on their **merit**

1) It remains **rare** for decisions to be made along **ideological lines**:
   - In **2023-24**, roughly **50%** of the Court's cases were decided **unanimously**.
   - Only **8%** of cases were decided along **exact ideological lines**.
   - **90%** of decisions had **at least one liberal justice** in the **majority**.
2) **John Roberts** has occasionally acted as a **swing justice**.
   - In **2019-20**, Roberts sided with the **majority** in **52** of **53** cases.
   - He sided with the **liberal justices** in **June Medical Services v. Russo (2020)**, an **abortion** ruling, and in **Department of Homeland Security v. Regents of the University of California (2020)** (see p.194).

The Court has reached contrasting rulings on gun control and abortion in recent years.

> From 1988 to 2018, Anthony Kennedy was regarded as a swing justice. Despite having been nominated by Reagan, a Republican president, Kennedy often sided with liberal justices in rulings on social issues such as same-sex marriage and abortion.

I lift gavels at the gym to make sure I have a judicial body...
Many believe the Supreme Court should have a balance of liberal and conservative judges. In recent years, some have accused Republicans of attempting to 'stack the court', by appointing justices that will weight the balance in favour of their ideology.

Civil Rights and Racial Equality in the US

The US has a complicated history with civil rights, so it's no surprise that it's a major point of contention in politics.

There are many **disagreements** over the **scope** of **civil rights**

1) Some Americans believe that the **emphasis** should be placed on **individual rights** — the rights of people to **act freely**, **without** fear of **interference** from the **government** or **other individuals**.
2) Others think individual rights should be **balanced** against **collective rights** (see p.13) — the rights not to experience **discrimination**, **violence** or other **restrictions** on their **freedom**.
3) There is also significant disagreement over which **type of freedom** is most important:
   - **Negative freedoms** (see p.51) — generally **protected** by **legal measures**, e.g. constitutional rights and legislation.
   - **Positive freedoms** (see p.51) — generally offered by **access to services**, e.g. education and healthcare.
4) There's also debate whether civil rights should aim for **equality** or **equity**. Supporters of equity will usually be open to **affirmative action** (see p.128).
5) **Liberals** often have a **broader definition** of civil rights than **conservatives**. Many liberals argue that civil rights should extend to **positive freedoms**, while conservatives tend to consider these **individual responsibilities**, rather than civil rights.

Key Terms — equity: *The belief that some individuals and groups may require different treatments to address historical or current inequalities.*

The **US Constitution protects** many civil rights

Key Terms — habeas corpus: *A legal principle stating that prisoners have the right to a hearing to determine whether their detention is lawful.*

Article I, Section 9 states that *habeas corpus* will **not** be **suspended** unless it **benefits public safety** during a **rebellion** or **invasion**.

Article III, Section 2 outlines the right to **trial by jury** in **all criminal cases**, and requires that the **trial** be **held** in the **state** where the **crime** was **committed**.

The **amendments** also **guarantee** a range of **civil rights**:
- **1st amendment** — freedoms of **speech**, **assembly** and **religion**
- **2nd amendment** — the **right to bear arms**
- **5th amendment** — guarantees **due process** (the right to a **free** and **fair trial**) and **protects** citizens from **incriminating themselves** when testifying.
- **13th, 14th, 15th amendments** — **abolished slavery** and **extended citizenship** and **voting rights** to **all male Americans**, regardless of race. The **14th amendment** also contains an **Equal Protection Clause**, which **guarantees equal legal protections** for all Americans, and a **Due Process Clause**, which includes the **right to privacy**.
- **19th amendment** — extended **voting rights** to **women** over the age of **21**.

Interestingly, given that protecting individual rights was one of their key aims, the framers included very few provisions for safeguarding rights when they wrote the Constitution in 1787. By 1791, the Bill of Rights had added much greater detail and specificity.

The voting age for men and women was later lowered to 18 by the 26th amendment in 1971.

Civil rights have evolved over time

The **right to bear arms** was relatively **uncontroversial** when the **2nd amendment** was written. However, it has been more **hotly debated** as **technology** has **developed**:
- When the **Bill of Rights** was ratified in **1791**, the most advanced guns were **duelling pistols**. **Modern assault weapons** can fire **hundreds of rounds per minute**.
- **Gun-related violence** has become a **major problem** in US society, responsible for almost **49 000 deaths in 2021**.
- This has sparked **debate** between groups such as the **National Rifle Association (NRA)** (which argues that the right to bear arms is a **fundamental civil right** that should **not** be **amended** in any way) and **Everytown** (which campaigns for **gun control measures** that **outlaw assault weapons** and make it more **difficult** to obtain a **licence** for other guns).
- While the **NRA emphasises** the **importance** of the **individual rights** (see p.13) of **US citizens** to **own guns**, **Everytown** believes that the **collective rights** of **victims** of **gun-related violence** should be taken into account.
- Many **liberals** believe that the Supreme Court unjustifiably extended the Constitution in its rulings on **gun rights** in **D.C. v. Heller (2008)** and **New York State Pistol and Rifle Association v. Bruen (2022)** — see pages 194-195.

In many cases, there is a debate over whether rights should be uniform across all states, or whether states should be able to determine their own rights culture.

US Politics — US Supreme Court and Civil Rights

Civil Rights and Racial Equality in the US

When the Constitution and the Bill of Rights were written, there were **no national debates** over **social issues** such as **abortion** or **same-sex marriage**. But these have become **key issues** since the **mid-20th** century:

- The **abortion debate** is broadly **split** into **two** camps — **pro-life** campaigners, who believe that **foetuses** have the right to life, and **pro-choice** campaigners, who emphasise the **right of women** to **choose** whether they **give birth**.
- **Supporters** of **same-sex marriage** argue that the **principle of equality** means that **all citizens** have the **right to marry**, regardless of their **sexuality**. But **opponents** often **cite** certain **religious beliefs**, arguing that the **1st amendment's freedom of religion** is **harmed** by the expectation that **all states** must offer **same-sex marriage**. As a result, many **conservatives** argue that the Supreme Court unjustifiably extended the Constitution in its ruling on **Obergefell v. Hodges (2015)** — see page 194.

Throughout US history, there have been **questions** over how **effectively** the **Constitution** and the **political system** that it created manage to advance **racial equality**:

- As **many** of the **framers** were either **slave owners** or **financial beneficiaries** of the **slave trade**, the original **Constitution** did **not prohibit slavery**. Slavery was **abolished** after the **Civil War** ended in **1865**, but the system of **racial segregation** that replaced it in many states continued for another **100 years**.
- **Native American communities** have long been **marginalised** by the US political system. Congress had existed for nearly **180 years** before it passed its first law on **Native American rights**, which **aren't mentioned** at all in the **original Constitution** or its **amendments**. Native Americans were only granted citizenship rights in 1924.
- Many Americans believe that **affirmative action policies** are **necessary** to combat continuing **racial inequalities**, but others argue that this is a **breach** of the Constitution's **principle of equality**.

> The original Constitution outlined the three-fifths compromise: the principle that, when determining the size of a state's population, an enslaved person should count for three-fifths of a free person — see p.157.

The Supreme Court has used judicial review to protect and extend civil rights

- The Supreme Court's rulings **extended civil rights** in cases such as **Brown v. Board of Education of Topeka (1954)**, **Roe v. Wade (1973)** and **Obergefell v. Hodges (2015)**.
- The Supreme Court's rulings have acted to **protect civil rights** in cases including **Roman Catholic Diocese of Brooklyn v. Cuomo (2020)** (see page 195) and **Kennedy v. Bremerton School District (2022)**. In this case, the Court ruled in **favour** of a high school American Football coach's **1st amendment** right to **pray** during his team's games.

> The Dobbs v. Jackson Women's Health Organization (2022) ruling is one of the most divisive civil rights decisions in the Supreme Court's history. While liberals argue that it failed to protect women's civil rights by removing the constitutional right to an abortion, conservatives believe that it restores the rights of unborn children, which they believe were infringed by the Roe v. Wade (1973) ruling.

Some believe it has not done enough to protect civil rights in recent years

1) Rulings such as **SFFA v. Harvard (2023)** (see p.195) have **removed** existing **civil rights policies**, while others such as **City of Grants Pass v. Johnson (2024)** (which **upheld** the **constitutionality** of **bans** on **homeless** people **sleeping outside**) have **failed** to **extend** them.
2) There are also concerns about **voting rights**, as in cases such as **Shelby County v. Holder (2013)** (see p.194) and **Alexander v. South Carolina Conference of the NAACP (2024)**. This ruling upheld the **constitutionality** of **gerrymandering** (see p.174) by the **South Carolina** state legislature. This changed boundary strengthened **Republicans'** chance of **winning** the state's **1st congressional district** by **moving** the votes of tens of thousands of **African Americans** to another **district**.

Essay Plan

For Edexcel students: Evaluate the view that the Supreme Court makes up for the ineffectiveness of the Constitution and Congress in terms of protecting civil rights and racial equality in the US. [30]

For AQA students: 'The Supreme Court makes up for the ineffectiveness of the Constitution and Congress in terms of protecting civil rights and racial equality in the US.' Analyse and evaluate this statement. [25]

Using the grid on p.298, **plan** an answer to one of the essay questions above.

It's pasta night at the Supreme Court — they're serving Ra v. Oli...

The role of the Supreme Court in protecting and expanding civil rights often leads to its most controversial cases and rulings.

Comparing the US and UK Supreme Courts

They may have the same name, and a similar function, but the US and UK Supreme Courts operate quite differently...

The US Supreme Court has **more** significant **judicial review powers** than the UK's

- Since **Marbury v. Madison (1804)**, the **US SUPREME COURT** has been able to declare any **act** of **Congress**, the **presidency**, or the **states unconstitutional**. This effectively makes it the **guardian of the Constitution**.
- Because the **US Constitution** is **sovereign**, the Court's **judicial review power** has **no limit**, allowing it to issue **binding rulings** which **all** other **branches** and **levels** of **government** have to **comply** with.

- By contrast, **parliamentary sovereignty** means that the **UK SUPREME COURT cannot** issue binding rulings that **overrule statute law** that was **passed** by **Parliament**.
- However, it can still make *ultra vires* rulings, in which it can **declare** that the **executive** has acted **beyond its power**.
- Since the **Human Rights Act (1998)**, UK courts have been able to issue **declarations of incompatibility** — **non-binding rulings** that recommend Parliament **reviews existing laws** based on their **inconsistency** with the rights outlined in the Act.

Its **checks** and **balances** on the **legislative branch** are **stronger** than the UK's

The **US Supreme Court** has made high-profile rulings that have **struck down** aspects of **laws** already passed or under consideration by **Congress**. Examples of these include (see page 194-195):

- **United States v. Lopez (1995)**
- **Shelby County v. Holder (2013)**
- **Garland v. Cargill (2024)**

> Because of constitutional sovereignty in the US, Congress can't overrule Supreme Court rulings.

- This contrasts with the **UK judiciary's** relationship with **Parliament**. For example, **17** of **34 declarations of incompatibility** in the UK have led to **legislative change** since **1998**.
- Parliament can also choose to **overrule** UK Supreme Court **rulings**, as it did when passing the **Safety of Rwanda Act (2024)**. This **overruled** the Supreme Court's assessment in **R (AAA and others) v. Home Secretary (2023)** that **Rwanda** was **not** a **safe** country for asylum seekers to be deported to due to the **risk** that some would be **sent back** to the countries where they had **faced persecution**.

Both Supreme Courts **prevent excessive executive power** and **expand civil rights**

1) The **US Supreme Court** has provided many **high-profile checks** on **executive power**, requiring presidents to act **within** the **Constitution** through its decisions. Examples of this include: **United States v. Nixon (1974)**, **Rasul v. Bush (2004)** and **Biden v. Nebraska (2023)**.

> See pages 194-195 for more cases.

2) Similarly, the **UK Supreme Court** has issued numerous *ultra vires* rulings that have **stopped** the **executive branch** from **acting unlawfully**:
   - **R (Miller) v. Secretary of State for Exiting the European Union (2017)** — the Court ruled that Theresa May's government couldn't begin the process of **leaving the EU** without **Parliamentary consent**.
   - **R (Miller) v. The Prime Minister (2019)** — the Court **reversed** Boris Johnson's attempt to **prorogue Parliament** by ruling that it had been an **unlawful** use of his **prerogative powers**.
3) In checking executive power, both Supreme Courts can have a **significant influence** on **public policy**:
   - In **NFIB v. Department of Labor (2022)**, the **US Supreme Court** ruled that Joe Biden's **vaccine workplace mandate** was **unconstitutional**.
   - Similarly, in **R (AAA and others) v. Home Secretary (2023)**, the **UK Supreme Court** dealt a blow to the Conservative government's **immigration policy** by declaring that **Rwanda** was an **unsafe** country for **deportations**.
4) Both courts have recently helped to **extend civil rights** around **marriage** and **partnerships**:
   - The US Supreme Court's ruling in **Obergefell v. Hodges (2015)** allowed **same-sex marriage** to be legalised **throughout** the US.
   - The UK Supreme Court's ruling in **R (Steinfeld and Keidan) v. Secretary of State for International Development (2018)** (see p.99) prompted Parliament to **amend legislation** to allow **all people** to enter into **civil partnerships**.

US Politics — US Supreme Court and Civil Rights

Comparing the US and UK Supreme Courts

Both Supreme Courts clarify the limits of de-centralised power

Although there are **differences** between their **de-centralisation of power** (**federalism** in the **US** vs **devolution** in the **UK**), both **constitutions** contain areas of **vagueness** (see p.162) that the Supreme Courts have attempted to **clarify**:

- In its rulings on a **second Scottish independence referendum** (in 2022) and in **R (Miller) v. Secretary of State for Exiting the European Union (2017)**, the UK Supreme Court clarified the **inferiority** of the **devolved legislatures** to the **Parliament** in Westminster. It **re-affirmed** the principle that **only Parliament** can call a **referendum** in the UK, and ruled that the **devolved legislatures** didn't need to be **consulted** over the **Brexit** process.
- Similarly, the US Supreme Court clarified states' rights on **gun control** in its **D.C. v. Heller (2008)** and **New York State Pistol and Rifle Association v. Bruen (2022)** rulings. These affirmed the **right to bear arms** as an **individual right**.

Appointments to the US Supreme Court are much more politicised than in the UK

1) Since the **Constitutional Reform Act (2005)** (see p.63), the UK has mirrored the US in having a **judiciary** that is **independent** from their respective **legislative** and **executive** branches. The **US judiciary** has been **separate** and **independent** from **Congress** and the **Presidency** ever since the **Constitution** came into effect in **1789**.

2) Both **executive branches** previously had **significant roles** in **appointing** the most **senior judges**. While the **president** continues to **nominate Supreme Court** and **federal judges** in the **US**, the **prime minister** no longer has **direct involvement** in **judicial appointments** in the **UK**.

3) While the **US Senate** is responsible for **confirming** the **appointments** of **Supreme Court** and **federal judges**, the **UK Parliament** plays **no role** in confirming **judicial nominees**. UK Supreme Court judges are **appointed** by ad hoc, **independent selection panels** and all **other judges** are **appointed** by the **Judicial Appointments Commission**.

4) The differing **appointments processes** influence the extent to which the two Supreme Courts can be considered **neutral**. While judges' **political views** are **not** made **public** in the **UK**, they are well known in the US, and Supreme Court judges are often appointed for their political outlook.

Leanne wished she had a whole senate to confirm her appointments

Both courts have made divisive decisions in recent years

The contrasting **political cultures** of the **US** and **UK** have an impact on the **types of case** that their **Supreme Courts** hear. The UK Supreme Court **rarely** has to deal with the kind of highly divisive **social issues** (such as **abortion** and **gun rights**) that the **US** Supreme Court rules on.

However, there are parallels between the levels of **political controversy** caused by recent rulings by both courts.
- The **Dobbs v. Jackson Women's Health Organization (2022)** ruling on **abortion** received a similarly **hostile response** in the liberal media as the UK Supreme Court's **two Brexit rulings** had received in the conservative media.

Both courts have also been **accused** of **failing** to protect **environmental rights** in recent years:
- In **R (Friends of the Earth) v. Heathrow Airport Ltd (2020)**, the UK Supreme Court ruled that the government's plan to build a **third runway** at Heathrow Airport was **legal**, **dismissing** the legal **challenge** of **environmentalists**.
- Similarly, in **Ohio v. Environmental Protection Agency (2024)**, the US Supreme Court **limited** the extent to which the **federal Environmental Protection Agency** could **regulate pollution** caused by the states. This meant that corporations involved in the **production** and use of fossil fuels **haven't been restricted** as much as they would have been if the **Environmental Protection Agency** had won the case.

Exam Practice

For students studying...

Edexcel: Examine the differences between the extent of the Supreme Court's power in the US and the UK. [12]
AQA: Explain and analyse three ways in which the Supreme Court's power differs in the US and the UK. [9]

AO2 Analysis

How does a Supreme Court cool down on a hot day? With just ice...
There's lots to consider when comparing the Supreme Courts. Take a look back at pages 95-97 for a refresher on the UK's.

US Politics — US Supreme Court and Civil Rights

Comparing Rights Protections in the US & UK

You've made it to the final two pages of this section — all that's left to do is compare the levels of rights protections of the US and the UK. After that, I reckon you've earned yourself a study break. I'll have a tea please, black and two sugars. Ta.

Both the **US** and the **UK constitutions** have mechanisms for **protecting rights**

1) Although the **US Constitution** is **codified**, and the **UK Constitution** is **uncodified** (see p.161), they both contain **definitive lists** of the **rights** that belong to **every citizen**.
2) The **Bill of Rights**, as well as the **13th, 14th, 15th**, and **19th amendments**, all protect rights in the **US**, while the **Human Rights Act (1998)** and the **Equality Act (2010)** do so in the **UK**.
3) In the US and the UK, the **Supreme Court** has **judicial review powers** that it can use to **protect** and **extend rights**.

Both political systems have some **tension** between **individual** and **collective rights**

Campaign groups and **politicians** often **disagree** over whether **individual** or **collective rights** should be **prioritised** in issues such as **immigration** and **policing**:

> In the **US**, **conservatives** often **argue** that the **collective rights** of existing US citizens should be **prioritised** over the **individual rights** of those wishing to **enter the US**, whether legally or illegally. In **Trump v. Hawaii (2018)**, the US Supreme Court **supported** this argument, upholding Donald Trump's **travel ban** (see p.185).

> In **R (Kiarie) v. Home Secretary (2017)**, however, some argue that the **UK** Supreme Court **prioritised** the **individual rights** of **foreign nationals** convicted of committing crimes, ruling that the Home Office's '**deport first, appeal later**' policy was **beyond** its **legal authority** (see p.99).

There is **less consensus** over how **rights** should be **defined** in the US than in the UK

Some **social issues**, such as **gun ownership**, **abortion** and **marriage rights**, remain **highly polarised** in the **US**, but have a **broad consensus** in the **UK**. The differences here are due to the respective **cultural backgrounds** of the US and the UK — see page 145 for more.

	US	UK
Gun ownership	Disputes over the meaning of the **2nd amendment**, and the extent to which the **states** should be able to **control** their own **gun laws**, continue to be extremely **controversial** in the **US**. This is demonstrated in Supreme Court cases such as **D.C. v. Heller (2008)** and **New York State Pistol and Rifle Association v. Bruen (2022)**, and in the **failures** of Obama, Trump and Biden to **pass** their intended **gun control measures** through **Congress**.	**All handguns** have been **banned** in the **UK** since the **Firearms (Amendment) Act (1997)**, which followed the **Dunblane Massacre**. The **major parties** all continue to **support** this ban.
Abortion	As a result of **Dobbs v. Jackson Women's Health Organization (2022)**, abortion laws **vary** from **illegality** from the **point of conception** in **conservative states** such as Oklahoma and **Texas** to **legality** until the **25th week of pregnancy** in **liberal states** such as **Massachusetts** and **New York**.	Since **2020**, all four constituent nations of the **UK** have **legalised** abortion. In **England, Wales** and **Scotland** abortions are legal up to **24 weeks of pregnancy**, while they are legal up to **12 weeks of pregnancy** in **Northern Ireland**.
Marriage rights	The US Supreme Court's **Obergefell v. Hodges (2015)** ruling forced **all states** to **legalise same-sex marriage**, but **over 30** continue to **ban** the practice either in their **state constitutions** or **state laws**. If the Supreme Court ever **reversed** the Obergefell ruling, the **majority** of states would **not allow** same-sex marriage.	The **Marriage (Same-Sex Couples) Act (2013)** passed through Parliament with **relative ease** and **same-sex marriage** has been **supported** by **all major UK parties** ever since.

Comparing Rights Protections in the US & UK

The US Supreme Court has more power over rights than its UK counterpart

- Since **Marbury v. Madison (1804)**, the **US Supreme Court** has been able to **rule** that any **act** of **Congress**, the **presidency** or the **states** is **unconstitutional**. This occurred in rulings such as **D.C. v. Heller (2008)** and **Shelby County v. Holder (2013)** — see pages 194-195 for more examples.
- This extends to **rights cases**, meaning that it effectively exercises its **sovereignty** when there are **disputes** over **rights** between **different branches** or **levels** of **government**. For example, the **Obergefell v. Hodges (2015)** ruling **universalised** the **right** to **same-sex marriage** across **all 50 states**. See p.200 for more on how the **Supreme Court's rulings** have **influenced civil rights**.

Try as she might, Saskia the squirrel couldn't escape the disagreement between branches

- By contrast, the **UK Supreme Court** can issue **declarations of incompatibility** recommending that **Parliament reviews** existing laws' **compatibility** with the **Human Rights Act (1998)**. However, these can be **ignored** and the **executive branch** can also use **Parliament** to **overrule** the Supreme Court's *ultra vires* rulings on rights cases — see page 100.
- In the **US**, the executive would be **unable** to act in a similar way. A **constitutional amendment** (which needs to be **proposed** by **two-thirds** of both **Congress** and the **Senate**, and then **ratified** by **three-quarters** of the **states**) would be the **only way** of **overruling** the **Supreme Court**, but the **executive** has **no formal role** in the **amendments process**.

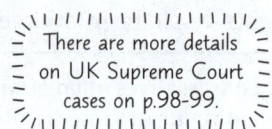

There are more details on UK Supreme Court cases on p.98-99.

Quick Questions

1) Define *habeas corpus*.
2) In which US Supreme Court cases has the right to bear arms been defined as an individual right?
3) Give two examples of US Supreme Court rulings that have protected religious freedoms.
4) Which US Supreme Court case ruled that affirmative action in college admissions was unconstitutional?
5) Outline how Supreme Court justices are appointed in the US and UK.
6) How does the political culture regarding abortion differ in the US compared to the UK?
7) Why are the UK Supreme Court's declarations of incompatibility less powerful that the US Supreme Court's rulings of unconstitutionality?

Essay Plan

For students studying...

Edexcel: Analyse the extent to which the US and the UK Supreme Courts protect rights effectively in their respective political systems. In your answer, you must consider the relevance of at least one comparative theory. [30]

Have a look at page 145 for more on rational, structural and cultural comparative theories.

AQA: 'Rights are less effectively protected in the UK than in the US.' Analyse and evaluate this statement. [25]

Using the grid on p.298, **plan** an answer to one of the essay questions above.

Exam Practice

For students studying...

Edexcel: Examine the similarities between the ways in which rights are protected in the US and the UK. [12]

AQA: Explain and analyse three ways in which cultural theory can be used to compare rights protection in the US and the UK. [9]

C'est mon droit d'écrire ce Top Tip en français...
Hé, oui, hein! Pourquoi pas, au nom de dieu! Je vais... OK, can't keep that up any longer. Running out of vocab. Also, CGP might exercise the right to fire my derrière... Anyway, I'm off for a brew and a biscuit before doing the next section.

Presidential Elections

Unsurprisingly, a LOT goes into getting a presidential candidate to the point where they're one of the boxes in a polling booth.

US presidential elections have seven stages

1 The invisible primary

> According to the US Constitution, a presidential candidate must be a natural born citizen of the USA, be at least 35 years old and have lived in the USA for at least 14 years.

1) This stage **begins** when the **first candidate** declares their **intention** to **run** for the **presidency**, and lasts **until** the **Iowa caucuses**.
2) During this period, the candidates **focus** on **raising** as much **money** as they can, **campaigning** in **key states** and **improving** their **national name recognition** and **awareness** of their **policies**.
3) The parties hold **televised debates** between their **nomination candidates**. In **2016**, there were so many **Republican candidates** that the party had to organise **two separate debates** on the **same evening**.
4) **Many** candidates **fail** to make it through the invisible primary and **pull out** of the race. This may be due to many factors, e.g. a **lack of money**, **poor support** or the effect of a **scandal**.
5) Although the invisible primary is **important** in setting the **tone** for a presidential campaign, **many front-runners** during this stage have **failed** to win their **party's nomination**.
   - In **2016**, **Donald Trump** trailed **Ted Cruz** in the polls **throughout** the invisible primary, but later on went to secure the **Republican nomination** comfortably.

Ted Cruz

2 Primaries and caucuses

1) Beginning in **Iowa** and **New Hampshire**, voters in **all 50 states** have the chance to select the **major parties' presidential candidates**.
2) Most states hold **primaries** — straightforward **elections** in which **voters** fill out a **ballot paper** to express their **preference**. A few states (e.g. Iowa) hold **caucuses**. These are meetings where **voters** express their preference for a candidate by physically **gathering** in a **designated area**.
3) Candidates **compete** for party **delegates**, whose **votes** at the **national nominating convention** help to **decide** the party's **final selection** of their presidential nominee. In **some states**, delegates are awarded on a **winner-takes-all basis**, but others states award them **proportionately**.
4) **After** the **Iowa caucuses** and the **New Hampshire primary**, the biggest day in this stage is **Super Tuesday** (the **first Tuesday in March** of an election year) when many states hold their **primaries** or **caucuses** on the **same day**.
5) After this point, **over 20 states** have indicated their **preference** for the Republican and Democratic **nominations**, meaning that **one candidate** from **each party** usually has a clear sense of momentum.
   - In **2020**, **Joe Biden** was **expected** to **pull out** of the Democratic nomination race after **poor performances** in **Iowa** and **New Hampshire**, but he emerged as a **surprise front-runner** when he won **nine states** on Super Tuesday.
6) To pay for **national media campaigns** and **targeted campaigns** at **state level**, candidates need to continue **raising money** throughout this period.
   - Despite **winning** the **Iowa** caucuses in **2020**, **Pete Buttigieg struggled** to raise enough money to **compete** with well-funded opponents like **Joe Biden** and **Michael Bloomberg**. This meant that he **dropped out** of the Democratic nomination race **before Super Tuesday**.

> Primaries can be open or closed. Open primaries allow anyone eligible to vote in a presidential election to vote for their preferred candidate. Closed primaries only allow registered supporters of that party to vote for their preferred candidate.

Key Terms — delegates
Nominated representatives of the fifty state parties. More populous states have more delegates, so their primary or caucus results have a larger bearing on the nomination than less populous states.

Pete Buttigieg

3 Running mate selection

1) Once a party's nominee has been **confirmed**, the **successful candidate** chooses their **vice-presidential candidate** — known as their **running mate**.
2) When the president is running for **re-election**, this is usually the **incumbent vice president**. Candidates hoping to become president will typically choose someone who will **balance their ticket** and **improve** their **chances** of **winning** in crucial **battleground states**.
   - In **2024**, Kamala Harris chose **Tim Walz**, the **governor of Minnesota**, in the hope that he would help her to target **white midwestern** and **rural voters** in **key states** like **Ohio**, **Michigan** and **Wisconsin**.
   - **Donald Trump** chose **J. D. Vance**, a senator from **Ohio**, for similar reasons, in addition to him being **well known** with voters **across the US**.

> Presidents running for re-election can choose to replace their vice president with a different running mate. Roosevelt replaced John Nance Garner with Henry Wallace for the 1940 presidential election, then replaced him with Harry Truman for 1944's.

Key Terms — balanced ticket
The idea that, between them, a presidential candidate and their running mate should balance each other in terms of their age, experience, ideology, regional background and appeal to voters.

Presidential Elections

4 | National nominating conventions (NNCs)

NNCs are also known as National Patry Conventions.

1) This stage is when the **delegates cast votes** to **confirm** their party's **presidential nominees**, and the party sets its **platform** and **policies** on **key issues**.
2) **Most NNCs** take place when there is **only one candidate remaining**. As a result, their informal purpose has become **generating media attention** designed to **boost** the **party's polling figures**.
   - However, as a candidate's polling figures usually **improve** during their party's NNC, the **overall significance** of polling figures on the outcome of the presidential election tends to be **limited**. For example, in **2020**, **Trump** gained a **slim lead** in the polls **over Biden** after the **Republican National Convention**, but then **lost** both the **popular vote** and the **Electoral College** in the **election**.
3) The other informal purpose for both parties at NNCs is presenting a **united front** and **avoiding** any sense that there are remaining **internal divisions** left over from the primaries and caucuses.
   - In **2024**, the **Democratic National Convention** was designed to **promote Kamala Harris** to a wider audience. **Supportive speeches** were made by figures such as **Barack** and **Michelle Obama**, **Joe Biden** and **Oprah Winfrey**.

5 | Presidential election campaign

The first televised debate of the 2024 campaign contributed to Joe Biden's decision to withdraw — see page 189.

1) This is when the **Democratic** and **Republican** presidential **nominees** formally face off in a **head-to-head campaign**.
2) There have been **televised debates** between the **two nominees** in every presidential election since **1960**, when **John F. Kennedy** outperformed **Richard Nixon**. Since **1976**, there has also been a **vice-presidential debate** between the two running mates.
3) Occasionally, there are **third party** or **independent candidates** who threaten to **harm the chances** of the two main parties, but **none** have taken part in a **televised presidential debate** since **Ross Perot** in **1992**.
4) For the rest of the campaign, candidates tend to **focus** on **targeting swing voters** in **key battleground states** and **undermining** their **opponent** through **attack adverts** on television, social media, radio and billboards.
5) In the **three months** leading up to the **2024** presidential election, **Trump**, **Vance**, **Harris** and **Walz** made **over 200 visits** to just **seven key swing states**: **Michigan**, **North Carolina**, **Georgia**, **Pennsylvania**, **Arizona**, **Nevada** and **Wisconsin**.

6 | Election day and count

1) The **Constitution** gives **Congress** the power to **schedule federal elections**. Since **1875**, **Congress** has specified that the **presidential election** should take place **every four years** on the first **Tuesday after 2nd November**.
2) Voters in **all 50 states** can either **register their vote in person** at a polling station or submit **postal votes** in advance. **Results** are announced at **different times** the next day, depending on **time zones**, **population density** and other factors.
3) There have been two particularly **controversial counts** in recent decades:
   - In **2000**, electronic counting machines **broke** in **Florida**, the state that ended up deciding the outcome of the presidential election. **George W. Bush** was eventually declared the winner after the **Supreme Court ruled against** a statewide **recount** in **Bush v. Gore (2000)**.
   - In **2020**, Donald Trump's campaign **claimed** that **thousands of postal votes** for him had been **discarded** by **pro-Biden officials**, but **61 of the 62 lawsuits** that the Trump campaign filed **challenging** the results were dismissed.

7 | Electoral College

1) Devised by the framers of the Constitution as a **safeguard** against **authoritarian rule**, the **Electoral College** is the final stage of the **presidential election process**.
2) **Each state** is allocated a certain number of **Electoral College Votes** (**ECVs**) equal to the state's **number of House representatives** plus its **number of senators** (which is **two** for each state). In the **2024** presidential election, **California** had **54 ECVs**, while **Wyoming** had **three**.
3) Each state decides how its **ECVs** are **awarded**. **Most states** award their **ECVs** on a **winner-takes-all basis**, meaning that the **candidate** that wins the **most votes** in the **state** receives **all** their **ECVs**, but **Maine** and **Nebraska** use a **different method** (see page 209). A candidate needs a **minimum** of **270 ECVs** to be **elected** as president.
4) The Electoral College can be the **deciding factor** in presidential elections. In **2000** and **2016**, the **candidate** who was **elected** president **won** the **most ECVs**, but did **not win** the **popular vote** — see p.208.
5) Although the **results** of the **Electoral College** are usually known **within a couple of days** of the election, they are **not formally certified** until **January**, when the **vice president** announces the results in **Congress**.

Presidential Elections

US presidential elections are the longest in the world

1) From the moment that **Hillary Clinton** announced her **intention** to run for the **presidency** in **April 2015**, the 2016 presidential election campaign began and **lasted nearly 19 months**.
2) After his **loss** in the **2020 presidential election**, **Donald Trump** signalled his intention in **January 2021** to **win back** the presidency in the **2024** election. This meant that the **invisible primary** for the **2024 election** essentially **lasted three years**.

Committees connected to Trump's campaign continued to raise money throughout 2021, 2022 and 2023.

The election process requires candidates to raise vast sums of money

1) In the **2020 presidential election**, candidates spent **over $4 billion**, with the **Biden** and **Trump** campaigns spending nearly **$2 billion combined**.
2) This makes it very **difficult** for **outsider candidates** without access to **existing networks of donors** to mount a **realistic challenge** for the presidency (see page 210).
3) In **2024**, Kamala Harris's campaign and affiliated **super PACs** (see page 210) spent **over $1.6 billion** compared with **Trump's $1 billion**. **Green Party** candidate **Jill Stein** (who raised just over **$2 million**) and **independent** candidate **Cornel West** (who raised just over **$1 million**) struggled to **compete**, and **neither** came close to winning any **ECVs**.

Incumbent presidents have an advantage in the election process

1) It is **very rare** for **incumbent presidents** to be **challenged** for their party's **nomination**, so they usually **advance through** the **first four stages** of the process with relative **ease**.
2) This means they can **save** the vast **majority** of their **campaign finance** for the **election campaign** and they **don't** usually face **attacks** from members of their **own party**. These attacks **will** be part of the **process** for the **opposition** though, **exposing weaknesses** in their candidates' **experience** and **personality** long **before** the presidential election campaign.

There are supporters and critics of the election process

Angelica was no stranger to an intense spotlight

SUPPORTERS of the process argue that it is a good test of candidates' **suitability**.
- Throughout the various stages of the process, **candidates** need to **withstand** extremely **high levels of scrutiny** over their **character**, **public speaking**, **policies** and **professional record**.
- In some ways, this **mirrors** the kind of **intense spotlight** that would be placed on them if they were to be elected as **president**.

CRITICS believe that election process is **undemocratic**.
- The **large amounts of money** required for a **presidential campaign** significantly **limits** the **diversity** of **people** who are able to put themselves forward as **candidates**.
- **Iowa** and **New Hampshire**, the two states that receive the most **attention** during the **primaries** and **caucuses**, don't tend to attract **representative electorates**. Both states have less diverse populations than the **US average**, which critics argue entrenches the **advantage** that **white candidates** possess in the process.
- **Opponents** of the **Electoral College** argue that it **distorts** the **influence** of a **small number of states**, which can lead to a candidate being **elected without** winning the popular vote. This is hugely **controversial** (see page 208).

Quick Questions

1) What is the invisible primary? Who led the 2016 Republican nomination polls after the invisible primary?
2) What is the difference between a primary and a caucus?
3) What is Super Tuesday?
4) Who won the Democrats' Iowa caucuses in 2020?
5) When did the first televised presidential debate take place?
6) What was the total amount spent by presidential candidates in 2020?

Since pulling out of the election race, Joe's just been Biden his time...

Running for president is quite an involved and intense process, and it starts years before an election takes place. Make sure you know the seven stages — making flash cards for each stage with their key milestones might help you remember them.

The Electoral College

In presidential elections, it's not always as simple as 'whoever gets the most votes wins'. The votes that ultimately decide the results of an election come from the Electoral College. And those don't always perfectly align with the popular vote.

The **Electoral College** ensures **all states** have **influence** over the **election**

1) The **Electoral College** is composed of **electors** (**senior state political figures** and **national political figures**) all of whom possess **one ECV** (Electoral College vote — see page 206). **Every state** has at least three ECVs, giving them **influence** over the **outcome** of **presidential elections**.

   For each state: number of ECVs = number of house representatives + number of senators.

2) **Advocates** of the Electoral College believe that this contributes **positively** to the US' **representative democracy** and helps to **achieve** the framers' key **aim** of **preserving states' identities**.

Some states have **much greater influence** than others

1) The **winner-takes-all** nature of the Electoral College in **48 of the 50 states** means that campaign attention is focused on a small number of **vote-rich battleground states** that are seen as **crucial** to determining the **election's outcome**.

2) **Critics** of the Electoral College believe that it **harms** the US' **representative democracy** by **discouraging** candidates from **addressing** the **concerns** of voters in **non-battleground states**.

3) They also feel it **reduces** the **influence** of **votes** in historically **safe 'blue'** (**Democrat**) or **'red'** (**Republican**) states. For example, **California** is a **blue state** that has voted for the **Democrat candidate** in **every presidential election** since **1992**. In the **2020 presidential election**, over 6 million Californians voted for **Trump**, but their votes **weren't** ever likely to have an **impact** on the **outcome** of the race.

4) During the **2020** presidential election, **33 states** hosted **no official campaign events**, while **75%** of official campaign events took place in **six swing states**: **Georgia**, **Michigan**, **Pennsylvania**, **Nevada**, **Arizona** and **Wisconsin**.

5) **Pre-election analysis** in **2024** suggested that **80%** of Americans lived in **spectator states** (**non-battleground states**).

6) In **2024**, **seven** key **swing states** (those listed above plus **North Carolina**) hosted **94%** of **official campaign events**, despite containing just **18%** of the **US population**.

7) In **2000**, the Electoral College meant that the **presidential election** was effectively **decided by 537 votes** in **Florida**, where **George W. Bush** beat **Al Gore** by this tiny margin to secure the **presidency**.

Key Terms

vote-rich
A term used to describe more populous states with a high number of Electoral College Votes.

Technically, it is possible to win the Electoral College vote by winning a majority of the popular vote in just 12 states.

The Electoral College can produce **disproportionate results**

1) There have been **five presidential elections** in which the **winner** of the Electoral College **has not** won the **popular vote**. For example:

   - In **2000**, **George W. Bush** was **elected** president after winning **271 ECVs** — just **one more** than the **lowest number needed** to become president. However, **Al Gore** won **over 500 000** more votes than Bush overall.
   - In **2016**, **Donald Trump** was elected **president**, having won **304 ECVs** compared to **Hillary Clinton's 227**. However, **Clinton** won **51%** of the **popular vote** with **nearly 3 million more** total votes than Trump.

   Defenders of the Electoral College point out that Trump won 30 of the 50 states in 2016.

2) On other occasions, the Electoral College has **distorted** the **electoral mandate** of presidents who did win the **popular vote**.

   - In **1984**, **Ronald Reagan** won **59%** of the popular vote, but **98%** of ECVs.
   - In **1992**, Bill Clinton won **43%** of the popular vote, but **69%** of ECVs.

   Electors are supposed to cast their ECV based on their state's popular vote (except in Maine and Nebraska), but there are sometimes faithless electors who vote for a different candidate as a protest (see page 158). There were seven faithless votes in 2016, six of which were cast for people who hadn't even stood for the presidency.

3) The Electoral College also **entrenches** the US' **two-party system** by only **rewarding concentrated support**.

   - **No third party** or **independent** candidate has won a **single ECV** since the controversial pro-segregationist **George Wallace** won 46 (winning the **popular vote** in **five southern states**) in **1968**.
   - **Ross Perot** won **19%** of the popular vote in **1992**, but his dispersed support meant that he **didn't** win any ECVs.

The Electoral College

Critics of the Electoral College would like it replaced with a different system

Proposed **alternative systems** include:

The congressional district method

This is already used in **Maine** and **Nebraska**. This system would **require** presidential candidates to win a **majority** across the United States' **435 congressional districts**.

Direct national election

This is already used in **many presidential elections worldwide**. A direct national election would **abolish** the **Electoral College** completely and **automatically elect** the **candidate** who wins the **most votes**.

National popular vote

This system theoretically **preserves** the **Electoral College**, but **states** would **have** to cast **all** their **votes** for the **candidate** who wins the **national popular vote**, meaning that the **influence** of **individual states** would be **reduced**.

Since April 2024, 17 states and the District of Columbia have passed laws pledging to adopt the national popular vote. This means that they would award all their ECVs to whichever candidate wins the national popular vote, rather than the candidate who wins their state's vote. None of these states will adopt the method until enough states have voted to do so — there need to be 270 Electoral College votes to ensure the ECV result matches the popular vote's result.

Supporters believe the Electoral College system is the best option

1) **Supporters** of the Electoral College argue that it **best preserves** the **framers' intentions** and **state identities**, by **balancing** the level of **influence** of the **most** and **least populous states**.

2) They also find notable **issues** with the proposed **alternatives**:

   ✗ The **congressional district method** suffers from the problem of **gerrymandering** (see page 174). Many regard this as a **partisan** and **undemocratic tool** that can be used to **suppress** certain groups of **voters**.

   ✗ In a **direct national election** without an Electoral College, **less populous states** such as Wyoming and Vermont would have very **little influence** over the **election**. As a result, **campaigning** would likely **focus** mostly on more **densely populated urban areas**.

   ✗ Similarly, the **national popular vote** method essentially **removes the role of states** in presidential elections.

Quick Questions

1) How many states hosted no official campaign events in 2020?
2) Name three battleground states from the 2024 presidential election.
3) Which state essentially decided the outcome of the 2000 presidential election?
4) Who won the popular vote in the 2016 presidential election?
5) How many ECVs did Ross Perot win in 1992?
6) Identify one alternative to the Electoral College.
7) Which states already use the congressional district method?

Essay Plan

For Edexcel students: Evaluate the view that the Electoral College has a harmful impact on US presidential elections. [30]

For AQA students: 'The Electoral College has a harmful impact on US presidential elections.' Analyse and evaluate this statement. [25]

Using the grid on p.298, **plan** an answer to one of the essay questions above.

A novel way to spoil your ballot — make an electoral collage...

Please don't actually do this, it'd be far too messy. A big criticism of the Electoral College is that it concentrates candidates' attentions around a few swing states. This can lead to people in 'safe' red or blue states feeling neglected by the campaign.

US Politics — Democracy and Participation

Campaign Finance and Election Performance

There are many factors that affect how likely a candidate is to be elected as president — background, personality, etc...
But one of the undeniable ones is money. How much a candidate needs and how they raise it can be difficult to determine.

Citizens United v. FEC (2010) removed limits on political donations

1) The Supreme Court's ruling that **political donations** represent a form of **free speech** (see p.194) meant that they are **protected** under the **1st amendment** (see p.159).
2) The Court's ruling involved **declaring** that **sections** of the **Bipartisan Campaign Reform Act (2002)**, sometimes referred to as the **McCain-Feingold reforms**, were **unconstitutional**.
3) Although the **reforms** still apply to **spending** by official campaigns and **political parties**, the Citizens United ruling has led to the creation of **political action committees** (**PACs**) and **super political action committees** (**super PACs**).
4) **PACs** and **super PACs** are **legally independent** from candidates' **campaigns** and from **political parties**, but they are able to spend **unlimited sums of money** on behalf of their **preferred candidates** and party.
5) In **2020**, the **highest-spending** super PACs were the **Senate Leadership Fund**, which spent nearly **$295 million** attempting to maintain the **Republicans' Senate majority**, and the **Senate Majority PAC**, which spent around **$230 million** attempting to **win back** the chamber for the **Democrats**.

- **Citizens United v. FEC (2010)** has led to **large increases** in the amount of **money** available to **campaigns**. **Total campaign spending** has increased from under **$2 billion** in the **2004** presidential and congressional elections to over **$14 billion** in the **2020** elections.
- Much of this money is spent on **advertising** — either **in favour** of a candidate or **attacking** their opponent.
- In the **2024** election, **$72 million** was spent on advertising in **under three months** during the **primary season**.

The Citizens United ruling also had a significant impact at state level. In California in 2022, more than $550 million was spent on a proposition to legalize sports betting on Native American lands.

There are a number of concerns over the existing campaign finance system

1) Since **Citizens United**, **corporations** have been able to spend **unlimited amounts of money** on **political campaigns**, which potentially gives them opportunities to **increase** their **influence** over **elected politicians**.

   - In **2020**, more than **two-thirds** of Congress received **donations** from **pharmaceutical companies**. It has been alleged that this **high volume** of **political donations** from pharmaceutical companies has helped to **limit federal regulation** of that industry in recent years.
   - Some also suggest that the **influence** of pharmaceutical companies has made it **harder to tackle** problems such as the **high cost** of **prescription drugs** and the **opioid epidemic**.

2) Those who **oppose** the current **campaign finance system** believe that it gives an **advantage** to **wealthy, well-connected candidates** who can either **self-fund** their campaigns or access **large donations** through their **social networks**. In **2024**, 51% of **representatives** and **senators** were estimated to have assets worth **over $1 million**, compared with **under 10%** of the **US population**.

3) Beyond just presidential elections, **spending** and **donations** from **corporations** can have a **big effect** on **propositions** (laws that are voted on by the public, see page 156):

   In **2020** in **California**, **Proposition 22**, a **state proposition** concerning **workers' rights**, attracted over **$200 million** in spending from big corporations such as **Uber** and **DoorDash**. **Unions** who **opposed** the proposition were only able to spend around **$15 million** and the proposition passed in a major **victory** for the **corporations**.

US Politics — Democracy and Participation

Campaign Finance and Election Performance

Some argue that donor influence is overstated

- **Hillary Clinton** spent more than **double** the amount that **Donald Trump** spent in the **2016 presidential election**, but **Trump** still **won**. Trump's campaign was **boosted** by his **strategy** of **dominating media coverage** by making deliberately **controversial statements** in **public appearances** and on **Twitter** (now **X**).
- In **2024**, **Kamala Harris' campaign** and affiliated **super PACs** spent **over $600 million more** than **Donald Trump's**, but **Trump** comfortably **won** both the **popular vote** and the **Electoral College**.
- Candidates **don't** need to rely completely on taking **donations** from **large corporations** and **wealthy individuals**. For example, during **Barack Obama's** successful **2008** primary campaign, **90%** of his donors gave **less than $100 each**.

This strategy gave Trump an estimated $2 billion's worth of additional media coverage during the 2016 campaign.

Various factors can affect the electability of a candidate

Policies and Campaign Slogans

In **1992**, **Bill Clinton** built his campaign on the promise of **fiscal responsibility** and **deficit reduction**. This helped him to **attack** incumbent president **George H. W. Bush's economic record** and to **calm** some **voters' fears** that the **Democrats** couldn't be **trusted** on **economic issues**. The election is best remembered for the **campaign slogan** *"It's the economy, stupid"*, devised by **Clinton's** strategist, **Jim Carville**.

Barack Obama's positive messages of **'Yes, We Can'** and **'Change We Can Believe In'** fitted with the **public desire** for change in the **2008** presidential election.

Donald Trump's policy priorities in **2016** (constructing a **wall** on the **US southern border** with **Mexico** and replacing **Obamacare**) and his **'America First'** campaign slogan helped him to win the crucial **swing states of Arizona**, **Ohio** and **Pennsylvania**.

Bruno's campaign slogan was a little too simple, but he liked it

Economic Circumstances

- Incumbent President **George H.W. Bush** had **approval ratings of 90%** after the **successful US involvement** in the **Gulf War** in **1991**, but an **economic recession** led to a **net approval rating** of **–64%** by August **1992**.
- **Bush's** position was also **harmed** by his decision to **increase** some **taxes** as part of a **compromise** with congressional **Democrats** in **1990**. This went **against** his **promises** during the **1988 election campaign**, where he had memorably declared: **"Read my lips — no new taxes."**

When predicting Bill Clinton's victory in the upcoming 1996 presidential election, economist Douglas Hibbs wrote that since the Second World War, US elections could be seen as "a sequence of referendums on the White House party's economic record."

- The **global financial crisis** that developed in the lead up to the **2008 election** benefited **Obama's** campaign.
- Although incumbent president **George W. Bush** wasn't standing, the **economic circumstances** gave weight to Obama's calls for **economic** and **social change**.
- Polls suggest that **voters trusted him** to tackle the **crisis** more than they did **John McCain**, the **Republican candidate**, by a margin of **51%** to **39%**.

Signs of **positive economic growth** meant **Trump** began **2020** with an approval rating of **49%**. But the recession caused by the **COVID-19** pandemic **reduced public support** to a low of **38%** during the election campaign. This benefitted **Joe Biden's** campaign, as Trump had planned to position the **economy** as the **key aspect** of his **campaign strategy**.

Economic growth or **recovery** can **benefit** some **incumbent** presidents in their **re-election campaigns**. This occurred with **Bill Clinton** in **1996**, **George W. Bush** in **2004** and **Barack Obama** in **2012**.

US Politics — Democracy and Participation

Campaign Finance and Election Performance

Candidate Personality

Obama used his personality to good effect in the **2008 election campaign**, gaining huge amounts of **media attention** over his **public speaking performances**.

Trump's personality also helped him to gain **media attention**, with him gaining an estimated **$2 billion** of free **publicity** during the **2016 election campaign**, despite being **divisive** among voters.

Many argued that **Joe Biden's dependable personality** gave him a **competitive advantage** over **Trump** in the **2020 election**, who was seen as more **unpredictable** by many voters.

In some presidential elections, the candidate's choice of running mate can improve or harm their chances of winning the election. In 1992, George H. W. Bush suffered from the unpopularity of Dan Quayle, his vice president, who had made headlines after misspelling 'potato' on a visit to a children's spelling competition. In 2008, John McCain's poll figures initially improved after he chose Sarah Palin as his running mate, but she was then responsible for a series of high-profile gaffes, which included failing to name any newspapers that she read.

Domestic and International Factors

- While they stand very **little chance** of winning any **Electoral College** votes (see page 208), **third party** or **independent candidates** can have a significant **spoiler effect** on the **outcome** of **presidential elections**.
- **Independent** candidate **Ross Perot** won **19%** of the **popular vote** in **1992**, inadvertently helping **Bill Clinton** by **splitting** the **right-wing vote** with **George H. W. Bush**.
- In **2000**, **Green Party** candidate **Ralph Nader** won over **97 000** votes in **Florida**, which benefited **George W. Bush**, whose **margin of victory** over **Al Gore** in the state was **only 537** votes.

- Although **public opinion** was starting to **turn against him** by the time of his **re-election attempt**, **George W. Bush** benefited from the **continuing popularity** of his **war on terror** in **2004**.
- Among the **51%** of voters who **approved** of the decision to go to **war** in Iraq, **85%** voted for Bush. Among the **45%** who **disapproved**, **87%** voted for his Democratic opponent, **John Kerry**.
- By **2008**, pledging to **end the war** in Iraq was seen as a **vote-winner** for **Barack Obama**.

In addition to the **economic crisis** created by **COVID-19**, **Trump's** broader **handling** of the **pandemic** also **harmed** his **re-election attempt in 2020**. He attracted criticism for **withdrawing** from the **World Health Organisation**, for **claiming** that **household disinfectant** could be used as a **vaccine** and for **refusing** to implement **social distancing measures** during the campaign. By contrast, **Joe Biden** pledged to **introduce stricter measures** to deal with the pandemic, including **mask and vaccine mandates**.

In 2020, 76% of Americans felt that Trump hadn't taken the risks of contracting COVID-19 seriously enough.

Exam Practice

For students studying...

Edexcel: Evaluate the view that presidential elections tend to be won by candidates with the most popular policies. [30]
AQA: 'Presidential elections tend to be won by the candidate with the most popular policies.' Analyse and evaluate this statement. [25]

Practise your **evaluation skills** by writing **one** sentence outlining how persuasive you find each of the arguments below:

1) *Money is the main variable underlying all other factors that influence the outcome of presidential elections.*
2) *A presidential candidate's personality is irrelevant if the economic circumstances in which an election is held do not work in their favour.*
3) *Incumbent presidents are more likely to be re-elected than to lose a presidential election.*
4) *Candidates with popular policies can overcome any domestic and international circumstances to win elections.*

AO3 Evaluation

Surely having a sweet personality makes for an ideal presidential candy-date?
Donations play a big role in political campaigns — they can have a huge influence on the result and any resulting policies.

US Politics — Democracy and Participation

Comparing US and UK Elections

Get the International Space Station on the phone for these pages, you're looking at both sides of the Atlantic at once. That's right, it's another comparison between the US and UK. This time, it's all about elections and election campaigns.

Elections in the US are more regular than in the UK

The **US Constitution** delegates the **timings** and **frequency** of **federal elections** to **Congress**, which has fixed the system as:

- **Presidential elections** take place **every four years** (as mandated by the **Constitution**).
- All **435 representatives** of the **congressional districts** (the **House of Representatives**) get **re-elected** every **two years**.
- A **third** of the **Senate** is **re-elected** every **two years**, with senators serving **six-year terms**.

By convention, **general elections** need to happen at least **every five years** in the **UK**, but they are often held **more frequently**:

- There were **five general elections** between **2010** and **2024**.
- All **650 seats** in the **House of Commons** are **re-elected during** a general election.

Since the 22nd amendment was ratified in 1951, presidents have been limited to two elected terms in office. There is no limit on elected terms in office for prime ministers.

Elections produce different mandates in the US and UK

1) The **presidential system** in the **US** means that the **president** has a **direct, personal mandate**. However, because of the **Electoral College**, they **don't** need to have **won** the **popular vote**.
2) There is **no direct election** for the **prime minister** in the **UK**:
   - Under the **parliamentary system**, the **prime minister** is usually the **leader** of the **largest party** in the **House of Commons**.
   - This means that they do not have a **personal mandate** from the general public as a whole. They only have one from their **local constituents** (who elected them as their **MP**) and from their **party members** (who have elected them as **party leader**).

Campaign finance regulation is much stricter in the UK

- Since the **US Supreme Court's** ruling in **Citizens United v. FEC (2010)**, there has been **no limit** on **donations** to **super PACs**.
- This has led to a large **increase** in **spending** on **presidential** and **congressional election campaigns**. Over **$14 billion** was spent during the **2020** cycle, including nearly **$500 million** on the **Georgia Senate races** alone.
- In the **US**, the **Citizens United ruling** means that **campaign spending** in **state-level proposition and initiative campaigns** is subject to the same **loose regulations** as presidential and congressional elections.

- By contrast, the **Political Parties, Elections, and Referendums Act (2000)** imposes a **spending limit** on parties of **£30 000** per constituency in **UK general elections**.
- The whole **2024** UK general election campaign saw over **£15 million** donated to parties.
- **Spending** on **direct democracy** is also more **limited** in the UK. The **Electoral Commission** sets **limits** for each campaign's **spending** in **referendum campaigns**. For example, the **Remain** and **Leave campaigns** in the **2016 referendum** on the UK's membership of the **EU** were only allowed to spend **£7 million** each. The **Leave campaign** was **fined** over **£61 000** for **exceeding** its **spending limit**.

UK general election campaigns are becoming similar to US election campaigns

1) The US has held **debates** between the **Democratic and Republican presidential candidates** since **1960**.
2) Since **2010**, there have been **televised debates** during every **UK general election campaign**. In **2024**, broadcasters presented these as **presidential-style contests**, referring to the **debates** between **Rishi Sunak** and **Keir Starmer** as 'prime ministerial debates' and 'the battle for No. 10'.
3) **UK election strategists** have begun to **borrow campaigning tactics** from the US, such as **attack advertisements**, which have played a **prominent role** in **US elections** for several decades. For example, in **2019**, the **Conservatives** purchased a **domain name** designed to **look like** information on the **Labour manifesto** and used the **website** to **attack Jeremy Corbyn** and the **Labour Party's policies**. In 2023, **Labour** published a **controversial poster** claiming that **Rishi Sunak** didn't believe that adults **convicted** of **sexually assaulting children** should go to prison.

US Politics — Democracy and Participation

Comparing US and UK Elections

Both countries use electoral systems that produce disproportionate results

US presidential elections rely on the Electoral College, which mostly operates on a winner-takes-all system, while UK general elections use a constituency-based form of first-past-the-post. Both these systems mean that parties with concentrated support tend to be rewarded, while those with dispersed support struggle.

> In 1992, Bill Clinton won 43% of the popular vote, but 69% of Electoral College Votes (ECVs), while Ross Perot won 19% of the vote, but no ECVs.

> In the 2024 general election, the Labour Party won 34% of the popular vote, but 63% of seats in the House of Commons, while Reform UK won 14% of the vote, but 0.7% of seats in the Commons.

The extent of two-party dominance is greater in US elections than in the UK

- All 435 members of the House of Representatives represented the Republican or Democrat parties following the US elections in 2024.
- By contrast, 18% of MPs represented parties other than Labour or the Conservatives following the 2024 general election in the UK.

Direct democracy is used differently in the US and the UK

"OK everyone, make sure you have signal for the recall election"

1) Direct democracy is used more frequently in the US. The UK has only held 13 referendums in its history, but in 2020, there were 12 propositions in California alone.
2) Unlike the UK, direct democracy has never been used in the US at a federal level. However, 26 states use propositions or initiatives, while 19 states allow recall elections.

> - The threshold for recall elections in the US differs from state to state.
> - In 2003, Arnold Schwarzenegger was elected Governor of California after Gray Davis, the previous governor, was recalled by voters who blamed him for energy and economic crises.
> - Since Parliament passed the Recall of MPs Act (2015), constituents have been able to recall their local MP, triggering a by-election if 10% of the voters in the constituency sign a petition.
> - In 2019, Fiona Onasanya, MP for Peterborough, was recalled after being convicted of perjury.

3) US states can choose whether, and how, they use direct democracy, while referendums can only be called by the UK Parliament, and not by the devolved legislatures (see Scottish independence ruling on page 98).

Exam Practice

For students studying...
Edexcel: Examine the differences between campaign finance in the US and the UK. [12]
AQA: Explain and analyse three ways in which campaign finance differs between the US and the UK. [9]

Exam Practice

For students studying...
Edexcel: Analyse the similarities between the controversies surrounding campaign finance and party funding in the US and the UK. In your answer, you must consider the relevance of at least one comparative theory. [12]
AQA: 'The similarities between elections in the US and the UK are more significant than the differences.' Analyse and evaluate this statement. [25]

My friends don't all get on, so my birthdays have a two-party system...
Remember that, when it comes to comparing US and UK politics, you can look at things from a rational, structural or cultural perspective (see page 145). You'll need to be able to analyse similarities and differences based on each of these perspectives.

Interest Groups in the US

Interest groups are bodies outside the electoral system that seek to influence policy and political decisions in favour of their interests. Isn't that interesting? No? Well I have bad news about the next few pages then. But maybe it'll surprise you.

Interest groups in the US can be divided into three categories

1 Single-issue interest groups

These organisations are defined by their belief in a **single cause** or **representation** of a **single section** of American society. They have a **narrow focus** on the **specific policy areas** that are most **relevant** to their purpose. Prominent examples include the **National Rifle Association** (**NRA**), which campaigns to uphold **gun ownership rights**, and **Planned Parenthood**, a **healthcare** and **sex education** body that **supports** the **right to abortion**.

2 Professional interest groups

These organisations represent an **industry** or **collection of industries**. They attempt to **influence policy** in a way that **furthers** the **corporate interests** of their **sector**. Examples include **United Auto Workers** and the **Pharmaceutical Research and Manufacturers of America**.

3 Policy interest groups

Sometimes known as **think tanks**, these organisations formulate **policy proposals**, **scrutinise** existing **policy** and attempt to **influence** the **political process**. Some policy groups, like the **Bipartisan Policy Center**, are **non-partisan**, but others hold distinct **ideological positions**, such as the conservative **Heritage Foundation** and the liberal **Roosevelt Foundation**.

The US political system encourages the activity of interest groups

1) The **separation of powers** and **federalism** both **increase** the number of **access points** that interest groups can use to have their views heard. As well as the **535 members of Congress**, interest groups can form **relationships** with thousands of **executive branch officials**, and with members of the 50 **state legislatures**. All of these people have the **power** to determine wide-ranging aspects of their state's **legal**, **political** and **economic systems**.

2) The **1st amendment's** protection of **free speech** and **assembly** has often been used to **safeguard interest group activity**, such as with the Supreme Court case **Citizens United v. FEC (2010)** (see page 194).

3) The **frequent federal elections** and **loose regulation** of **campaign finance** gives interest groups the opportunity to **donate** large sums of **money** to **political campaigns** in the hope that this will secure **future influence** or **favourable policy-making**.

4) The Supreme Court's broad power of **judicial review** incentivises interest groups' attempts to **support** or **challenge policies** introduced at **federal** or **state** level. If they believe that a future ruling **benefits** or **harms** their interests, they can either **sponsor** a case themselves (as **Citizens United** did) or submit an *amicus curae* brief.

Key Terms

amicus curae brief
A written submission to a court in which an individual or group sets out legal arguments and recommendations relating to a specific case.

Some interest groups are consistently powerful...

Groups that are either **extremely wealthy**, or whose **interests align** with both the **Republicans'** and **Democrats' policy positions**, can achieve a level of **influence** that **isn't dependent** on which **party** is in **power**.

- **Pharmaceutical companies** such as **Pfizer** and **AstraZeneca** have **large profits**, which means that they can **donate money** to both **Democratic** and **Republican candidates**.
- In the **2020** election cycle, **pharmaceutical** and **health companies** donated **millions** of dollars to both the **Biden** and **Trump** campaigns.

- The **American-Israeli Public Affairs Committee** (**AIPAC**), which aims to **maintain** close links between the **US** and **Israel**, has retained **influence** irrespective of the party in power.
- The **US** has provided over $2.5 billion in **annual military aid** to **Israel** throughout five presidencies **since 1999**. Since **2019**, the **US federal budget** has included a **minimum** of **$3.8 billion** each year for **military aid** to **Israel**.

US Politics — Democracy and Participation

Interest Groups in the US

...others have a **stronger relationship** with **one** of the **two main parties**

Republican
- The **Federalist Society** — a **conservative judicial group** whose membership includes all six **Republican-nominated** Supreme Court judges.
- **Koch Industries** — an **oil and gas conglomerate** owned by the billionaire **Koch brothers**. **Koch Industries** donated **tens of millions** of dollars to **Republican candidates** in the **2024** election cycle.
- **National Rifle Association** — a **conservative group** that **supports** the **rights** and **interests** of **gun owners**, campaigning **against efforts** to **limit ownership rights** or **restrict sales**.

Democrat
- **Everytown** — founded by **Michael Bloomberg**, a billionaire **Democrat supporter**, Everytown campaigns for **tighter gun control measures** at **federal** and **state level**.
- **Sierra Club** — an **environmental** pressure group that campaigns for **renewable energy** and regulation to **reduce carbon emissions**.
- **Planned Parenthood** — a **liberal healthcare organisation** and campaign group that provides **advice** on **birth control**, as well as carrying out **abortions** and **campaigning** for a **woman's right to choose** whether they give birth.

Some argue interest groups **positively contribute** to the US' **pluralist democracy**

1) Some interest groups produce **election scorecards** that summarise how different candidates' **policy positions align** with the group's aims. Some argue this **aids democracy** by helping to **educate voters** and **improve turnout**.

   - The **League of Conservation Voters**, an **environmental** campaign group, produces a '**Dirty Dozen**' list of **twelve candidates** in each election whose **policy positions** they consider **harmful** to the **environment**.
   - The **NRA** gives school-report-style **grades** for **candidates** based on their **record** and **beliefs** on **gun ownership**.

2) By organising **protests** and other forms of **direct action**, interest groups encourage **informal political participation** and provide opportunities for people to express their **1st amendment** rights of **free speech** and **assembly**.

   - In **2017**, **3-4 million** people took part in the **Women's March**, a protest **against Trump's presidency**.
   - After the death of **George Floyd** in **2020**, **over 15 million people** took part in **Black Lives Matter protests** across the US.

Crowds at the 2017 Women's March in Washington D.C.

3) Interest groups can provide important **scrutiny** that helps to **improve policy-making** and **educate the public**:

   - The independent **Brookings Institution** produces **reports investigating** aspects of the US' **economy**, **trade** and **foreign policy**.
   - The conservative **Heritage Foundation** scrutinises every area of **federal government policy**, producing its own **recommendations** that are often adopted by **Republican** politicians.

4) By submitting *amicus curae* briefs to the Supreme Court, interest groups **represent** the **views** and **interests** of **diverse groups**. This helps to ensure that **many opinions** and **perspectives** are **considered** by judges.

   Over **140** *amicus curae* **briefs** were submitted to the Supreme Court during its hearing of **Dobbs v. Jackson Women's Health Organization (2022)**. These included submissions by **religious organisations**, state-based campaign pro-life and **pro-choice groups**, and **medical associations**.

5) While the role of **corporations** in **US politics** is **controversial**, their **supporters** argue that they represent an **essential part** of the **economy**. They also argue that their **ability** to **represent** their **views** and **interests** ultimately **benefits** the **wider population** by **improving employment rates** and **productivity**.

Interest Groups in the US

Some argue interest groups also **help** to **protect rights**...

Interest groups have been involved in many **landmark Supreme Court rulings** that have **protected** or **extended rights**. For example:

- Conservative interest group **Citizens United** brought the case **Citizens United v. FEC (2010)** (see p.210) to the Court over limits on **political donations** and won.
- The **National Federation of Independent Businesses** (**NFIB**) won **two** major Supreme Court cases in recent decades — **NFIB v. Sebelius (2012)** (see p.194) and **NFIB v. Department of Labor (2022)** (see p.195).
- The **NAACP** (a **civil rights** interest group) was instrumental in the **Brown v. Board of Education of Topeka (1954)** case that led to the **end** of **segregated schooling**.
- In **Planned Parenthood v. Casey (1990)**, the **pro-choice** interest group successfully **overturned** an **abortion ban** in Pennsylvania. The Supreme Court **upheld** its earlier ruling in **Roe v. Wade (1973)** that **abortion rights** were **protected** by the **right to privacy** in the **14th amendment**.

As with many court rulings on rights, some believe that the Supreme Court's decisions in these cases didn't lead to better rights protection. In every ruling, though, the Supreme Court did listen to concerns raised by interest groups on behalf of some sections of US society.

...others argue that the **most powerful** interest groups **promote elitism**

1) Since the **limit** on **political donations** was **removed** by the **Citizens United ruling** (see page 194), **corporations** and other **interest groups** have been able to **spend huge amounts** of money on **political campaigns**. For examples, **businesses** were able to vastly **outspend** the **unions** who **opposed Proposition 22** in **California** in **2020**, enabling it to **pass** (see page 210).

2) Some interest groups offer **opportunities** for **political influence** that are only available to the **wealthy**. As a result, their **interests** may be **better represented** in politics than those of less wealthy people.

Some feel interest groups may **encourage disorder** or **undermine democracy**

- The **Proud Boys**, a **far-right, exclusively male militant organisation**, was **heavily involved** in the **January 6th riots** on **Capitol Hill** in **2021**. The **insurrection** led to over **100 police casualties**, including **one death**.
- **Six** members of **Operation Save America**, an **anti-abortion campaign group**, were found **guilty** of having used **force** to **intimidate women** outside an **abortion clinic** in **Tennessee** in **2021**.
- While **most Black Lives Matter protesters** in 2020 were **peaceful** and **law-abiding**, over **10 000** were **arrested**, including **hundreds** on **burglary** and **looting** charges.
- Many liberals blame the **National Rifle Association** (**NRA**) for helping to **prevent tighter** gun control measures. Despite polls suggesting that nearly **two-thirds** of Americans **support** stricter gun laws, and over **40 000 gun-related deaths** in the **US** in 2023, the **NRA** has **successfully campaigned against** a **federal assault weapons ban** since 2004.

Essay Plan

For Edexcel students: Evaluate the view that interest groups have a positive impact on democracy in the US. [30]

For AQA students: 'Interest groups have a positive impact on democracy in the US.' Analyse and evaluate this statement. [25]

Using the grid on p.298, **plan** an answer to one of the essay questions above.

I campaign for longer lie-ins as part of an into-rest group...
With big political decisions occurring at both state and federal levels, it's important to consider the influence of interest groups whenever you're analysing US politics. Their actions can have a huge effect on both politicians and the opinions of the public.

US Politics — Democracy and Participation

Comparing Interest Groups in the US and UK

Interest groups act in almost every political system, but how they operate and what they achieve can differ significantly.

Interest groups employ **similar methods** in the **US** and the **UK**

Direct action

Interest groups in both countries organise **direct action** such as **protests**, **sit-ins** and **publicity-seeking stunts**:

- In **2017**, **3-4 million** people participated in the **Women's March** in **Washington D.C.** in **protest** of **Donald Trump's** presidency.
- An estimated **1 million people** marched in **London** as part of the **anti-Brexit People's Vote protest** campaign.
- In the **UK**, **protest groups** such as **Just Stop Oil** and **Extinction Rebellion** have pursued a strategy of **disrupting roads**, **sports matches** and **airports** to **raise awareness** of their cause.
- In **2020**, **over 15 million** people took part in **Black Lives Matter protests** across the **US** following the death of **George Floyd**. **Tens of thousands** joined **similar protests** in the **UK**.
- In **2023**, **Greenpeace** covered then-prime minister **Rishi Sunak's** family home in Yorkshire in **oil-black fabric**.

Lobbying

Well-funded interest groups in both countries use **lobbying** as a method of **directly engaging** with **political decision makers**:

- **Koch Industries** regularly engages in lobbying activities as part of its efforts to **influence** the **regulation** of **fossil fuel industries**.
- **AIPAC** has successfully lobbied members of Congress from both parties to **maintain high levels** of **US military aid** to **Israel**.
- In the UK, the **Betting and Gaming Council** has **lobbied against** tighter regulations in the industry.
- **Greensill Capital** paid **David Cameron** an estimated **$10 million** to lobby on its behalf, including when it was attempting to take part in a **government loan scheme** during the **COVID-19 pandemic**.

"Sorry I'm late folks, I could only find red fabric..."

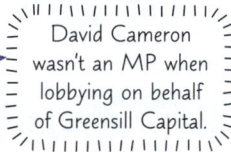

David Cameron wasn't an MP when lobbying on behalf of Greensill Capital.

Electioneering

Electioneering describes attempting to **influence** the **outcome** of an **election** by making **campaign donations** or **participating** in the **campaign**. Interest groups in the US and the UK engage in **electioneering**:

- In the US **2022 mid-terms**, **Cathy McMorris Rodgers** received nearly **$300 000** in campaign donations from **oil and gas companies**.
- **Lord Bamford**, the chair of **JCB**, donated nearly **£3 million** to the **Conservative Party's** election fund during **Boris Johnson's** time as **prime minister**.
- In the US, bodies like the **League of Conservation Voters** and the **NRA** produce **reports** on **election candidates** that analyse how **well**, or **poorly**, their **policies align** with the **group's ideals** (see page 216).
- Similarly, in the UK, **Greenpeace** ranks parties' **manifestos** based on their **environmental provisions**. The **Best for Britain** campaign has an **online tool** that **advises voters** on the best way of **voting tactically** to **prevent** a Conservative victory in their constituency.

Legal challenges

Both countries' systems of **judicial review** allow interest groups to **pursue** their **agenda** through **court cases**:

- The **National Federation of Independent Businesses (NFIB)** won **two high profile Supreme Court challenges** in recent decades, **NFIB v. Sebelius (2012)** and **NFIB v. Department of Labor (2022)**.
- In **R. (Friends of the Earth and others) v. Heathrow Airport Limited (2020)**, **environmental** interest groups **challenged** the construction of a **third runway** at **Heathrow Airport** (see page 98).

Comparing Interest Groups in the US and UK

Interest groups have **more opportunities** to **lobby** and **influence US elections**

1) Since **Citizens United v. FEC (2010)**, **US** interest groups have been able to make **unlimited campaign donations** via **super PACs** — see page 210 for details about **recent political donations**.
2) **Critics of lobbying** in the US describe it as having **revolving door syndrome**. This describes how people frequently move between jobs in **Congress**, the **executive branch** and **lobbying firms**. Almost **half** of the **former members** of the 115th **Congress (2017-19)** were working in **lobbying** by **2024**.
3) **Lobbying** is also **boosted** by the **influence** of **congressional committees**. Nearly **half** of the **House Committee on Transportation and Infrastructure** received **donations** from the **rail company Norfolk Southern** in 2022.
4) The **federal system** also creates more **access points** for interest groups in the **US** than the **devolved system** in the **UK**. Because **all 50 states** can **pass laws** on policy areas including **taxation**, **workers' rights** and **healthcare**, interest groups can have a **significant impact** at **state level**. For example, **Proposition 22** in 2020 in California — see page 210.

1) In the **UK**, there are **tighter regulations** on **lobbying** and **campaign donations**:
   - The **Political Parties, Elections, and Referendums Act (2000)** introduced a spending limit on parties of **£30 000 per constituency** in UK general elections.
   - The **whole UK general election campaign** in **2019** saw just over **£30 million** donated to parties. **62%** of this total came from **individuals**.
   - Under the **Transparency of Lobbying, Non-party Campaigning and Trade Union Administration Act (2014)**, interest groups and other **third parties** can only spend up to **£319 800** on **campaigning** in **England**, with **lower limits** set for **Scotland**, **Wales** and **Northern Ireland**.
2) While **lobbying** does happen at a **devolved level** in the UK, it's **less embedded** into the **political culture**. This is partly because the **devolved legislatures** have **less autonomy** than their **state equivalents** in the US.

Lobbyist influence in the UK appears to have grown in recent years

1) In **2020**, **Hanbury Strategy**, a **lobbying firm** who had worked with clients including **Deliveroo** and **GlaxoSmithKline**, was asked to hire **special advisers** to work in **No.10**.
2) A **fifth** of the **Conservative MPs newly elected in 2019** had worked in **lobbying** or **public relations**.
3) **34** of the **new Labour MPs elected in 2024** had worked in **public affairs**, an industry that **includes** many **lobbying firms**.
4) The number of **registered lobbyists in Scotland** increased from **under 500 in 2018** to **nearly 1300 in 2023**.

Dave had come to regret his time in public affairs

Exam Practice

For Edexcel students: Analyse the ways in which interest groups are more influential in the US than in the UK. In your answer, you must consider the relevance of at least one comparative theory. [12]

For AQA students: 'Interest groups have a more significant impact in the US than in the UK.' Analyse and evaluate this statement. [25]

See page 145 for more on comparative theories.

Exam Practice

For Edexcel students: Examine the similar methods employed by interest groups in the US and the UK. [12]

For AQA students: Explain and analyse three ways in which the methods used by interest groups in the US and the UK are similar. [9]

Turns out, lobbying is not just hanging around a hotel reception...

The politics of the US can be pretty darn influential, even all the way across the Atlantic. The increasing role of lobbyists in UK politics really shows how some features of US politics have started to become part of other countries' political systems.

US Politics — Democracy and Participation

The Democratic and Republican Parties

The US is well-known for its two-party system, so it's only right we dig a little deeper into each of those two parties.

There are **three** main **Democratic Party factions** in **Congress**

1) Progressive Caucus

The most **left-wing**, **liberal** faction. Members of the Progressive Caucus support **higher levels** of **federal government intervention** in the **economy** than any other grouping in Congress. They are **socially liberal** and they tend to prefer **soft power** to hard power in **foreign policy**.

2) New Democrat Coalition

The **New Democrats** are considered the **pragmatic** faction. They are often prepared to **compromise** on **social issues** and tend to be **more supportive** of **foreign interventions**. It used to be the **largest** Democratic Party **caucus**, but it's now **on par** with the **Progressive Caucus**.

3) Blue Dog Democrats

The **Blue Dogs** are the most **conservative** Democratic faction. Most of their members represent **conservative congressional districts**, and they tend to have **less liberal** views on issues like **abortion**, **gun control** and **climate change** than members of the other factions. It is the **smallest caucus** in the Democratic Party, with only **11 members** elected in the **2022 House mid-terms**.

Most Democrats now support **progressive economic** and **social policies**

1) Under **Joe Biden**, the Democrats either **reversed** many of the **tax-cutting measures** from Donald Trump's **Tax Cuts and Jobs Act (2017)** or allowed them to **expire**.

2) Democrats in the Senate **unanimously** voted for Biden's **Bipartisan Infrastructure Law (2021)**, which included **$7.5 billion** for **electric vehicle charging points** and **$65 billion** for **green energy transmission**.

3) Following the **Dobbs v. Jackson Women's Health Organization (2022)** Supreme Court ruling, both the **Progressive Caucus** and the **New Democrat Coalition** have **supported** the passage of a **federal law protecting abortion rights**.

4) All Democrats in both the House and the Senate voted to pass the **Respect for Marriage Act (2022)**, which affirmed the **rights** of **same-sex couples** to **marry** under federal law, and the **Bipartisan Safer Communities Act (2022)**, which **tightened** the **background checks** carried out on people applying for **gun licences**.

Same-sex marriage had been legal in all 50 states since Obergefell v. Hodges (2015), but Congress had never previously passed a law in support of it.

Conservative Democrats still have some **influence** in Congress

1) **Henry Cuellar**, one of the most **prominent Blue Dogs** in the **House of Representatives**, **voted against** fellow **Democrats'** attempt to pass a **federal abortion law** in 2022.

2) Although they both became **independents** towards the **end** of their time in the **Senate**, **Joe Manchin** and **Kyrsten Sinema** continued to **caucus** with **Democrats** until **standing down** in **2025**. Both **opposed** Biden's attempt to use **federal stimulus packages** to enact parts of the **Green New Deal**, a **legislative package** proposed by **progressive Democrats**.

3) **31 House Democrats** belong to the **bipartisan Problem Solvers Caucus**, which attempts to **work across party lines** to strike **compromises** that enable legislation to **pass**.

*There are no binding national party manifestos in the US, meaning that each state party can formulate their own policy platforms. Political scientist Nelson Polsby described the US as a "**100 party system**" because of the policy variations between state parties.*

The **Democratic Party** remains **split** over **foreign policy issues**

1) The **most left wing members** of the **Progressive Caucus** (informally referred to as **The Squad**) are much **less supportive** of **Israel's actions in Gaza** than many other Democrats.

Representative **Rashida Tlaib** described Israel's actions as "**genocide**", a label that **centrist Democrats** have **rejected**. Tlaib and **Cori Bush** attempted to introduce an **amendment** to a **foreign affairs bill** in **2024** that would have **prevented military aid** to **Israel** until there was a **ceasefire** and **hostages** held by both sides had been **released**.

2) When the **House of Representatives** voted on providing **additional funding** for Israel in April 2024, 173 **Democrats** voted in **favour** and 37 **against**.

3) In **2022, 50 congressional Democrats**, including Senators **Bernie Sanders** and **Elizabeth Warren** and Representatives **Alexandria Ocasio-Cortez** and **Ilhan Omar**, wrote a letter to **Biden** expressing their **concern** over the number of **civilian casualties** caused by **US drone strikes**.

US Politics — Democracy and Participation

The Democratic and Republican Parties

Democrat **voters** tend to be **young, diverse, urban** and **college-educated**

The groups of people who vote for a party can be described as their '**coalition of voters**'. You can find out about a party's coalition of voters by looking at the **demographics** of people that **voted for them** in **previous elections**.

> According to exit poll data, the following groups voted **Democrat** in the **2020 presidential elections**, the **2022 mid-terms** and the **2024 presidential election**:
> - the **majority** of voters **under 30**
> - the **overwhelming majority** of **black** voters
>
>   **92%** of black voters voted for Joe Biden in 2020, and **85%** voted for Harris in 2024
> - the **majority** of **urban** voters
> - the majority of voters with **postgraduate degrees**

There are **three** main **Republican Party factions** in **Congress**

1 | Republican Study Committee

The **largest Republican faction**. The Republican Study Committee's members tend to be **fiscally** and **socially conservative**. They have often **supported foreign policy interventions** that they consider to **advance** the **national interests** of the **US**.

2 | Freedom Caucus

The **most conservative** Republican faction. **Dedicated supporters** of **gun rights**, **pro-life abortion laws** and **low** levels of **federal spending**, its members tend to hold **isolationist views** on **foreign policy**. The Freedom Caucus was **instrumental** in **overthrowing Republican speakers John Boehner** in **2015** and **Kevin McCarthy** in **2023**.

3 | Main Street Caucus

The **most moderate** Republican faction, the Main Street Caucus' members are **more prepared** than their colleagues in other factions to **compromise** with **Democrats**, particularly when passing **bipartisan economic packages**.

During the Obama presidency, Democrats occasionally allied with a small Republican faction called the Liberty Caucus, made up of libertarians who wanted to limit the role of the federal government in every area of policy. The faction's founder, Justin Amash, supported same-sex marriage, and defected from the Republicans to the Libertarian Party in 2020, before leaving Congress in 2020. Since then, the Liberty Caucus has lost influence and prominence.

Although they're not technically members of the Main Street Caucus, senators Susan Collins (Maine) and Lisa Murkowski (Alaska) both hold similar ideological views.

Most Republicans are **fiscally** and **socially conservative**

1) **227 House Republicans** and **51 Republican Senators** voted to pass the **Tax Cuts and Jobs Act (2017)**, **reducing income tax** in **most brackets** and introducing a new flat **corporation tax rate** of **21%**, down from a **previous high** of **39%**.
2) **No Republicans** in the **House** or the **Senate** voted for Joe Biden's **$1.9 trillion American Rescue Plan Act (2021)**. Later that year, **200 House Republicans** voted **against** Biden's **$1.2 trillion Bipartisan Infrastructure Law**.
3) In **2022**, **169 House Republicans** voted **against** the **Respect for Marriage Act (2022)**, the first act **supporting same-sex marriage** to pass through **Congress**.
4) In **2023**, **House Republicans** voted to **resume** the **construction** of the **border wall** that had begun during Donald Trump's presidency.
5) **193 House Republicans** and **35 Republican senators** voted against the **Bipartisan Safer Communities Act (2023)** (see page 176), which introduced **tougher background checks** for **gun licence applicants**.
6) From **2022-2024**, **Senate Republicans blocked** attempts by Democrats to pass a bill establishing a **federal right to abortion**. When the **Ensuring Access to Abortion Act** passed through the **House** in 2022, only **three** Republicans **supported** it.

The 13 House Republicans who voted against the act didn't oppose the principle of cutting taxes, but wanted the act to ensure that every person in the US received a tax cut.

US Politics — Democracy and Participation

The Democratic and Republican Parties

A small number of centrist Republicans remain in Congress

1) During the **Biden presidency**, several **high-profile** pieces of **legislation** were **passed** with **support** from **moderate Republicans**:

   - **Bipartisan Infrastructure Law (2021)** — approved by **13** House Republicans and **19** Republican Senators.
   - **Bipartisan Safer Communities Act (2022)** — approved by **14** House Republicans and **15** Republican Senators.
   - **Respect for Marriage Act (2022)** — approved by **39** House Republicans and **12** Republican Senators.

In 2024, 31 House Republicans were members of the bipartisan Problem Solvers Caucus, along with the same number of House Democrats.

Like the Democrats, the Republicans' policies vary between different state parties. Republicans in conservative states like Oklahoma and Texas have introduced total abortion bans, while others support partial bans. Chris Sununu, Republican governor of New Hampshire, has argued that abortion should remain legal in his state.

2) During **Trump's presidency** from **2017-2021**, a **small number** of **moderate Republican Senators** worked with **Democrats** to **defeat** his **replacement** for **Obamacare** and to **limit funding** for the **border wall**.

The Republican Party is divided on foreign policy

1) In **2022**, **18 House Republicans** and **1 senator** voted **against** allowing **Finland** and **Sweden** to join **NATO**.
2) In April 2024, **112 House Republicans** voted **against** providing **additional aid** to **Ukraine**, with **101** voting **in favour**. **Marjorie Taylor Greene**, a prominent member of the **Freedom Caucus**, called for the **removal of Mike Johnson** as **Speaker** after he **allowed the vote** to happen.

Republican voters are more likely to be white, rural and non-college educated

According to exit poll data, the following groups voted **Republican** in the **2020 presidential elections**, the **2022 mid-terms** and the **2024 presidential election**:

- the **majority** of **white male** voters
- the **majority** of **rural** voters
- the majority of **white** voters **without a college degree**

66% of white voters without a college degree voted for **Donald Trump** in **2024**. This figure has remained **stable** — **65%** in 2020 and **66%** in 2022.

Quick Questions

1) Name the three categories of interest group.
2) Give one example of electioneering carried out by an interest group in the US.
3) Why are there more opportunities for interest groups in the US political system?
4) What are the three main factions of the Democratic and Republican parties?
5) Briefly describe the coalition of voters for the Democratic and Republican parties.

Exam Practice

For Edexcel students: Evaluate the view that the Republicans and Democrats now have distinct positions on every area of policy. [30]

For AQA students: 'The Republicans and Democrats now have distinct positions on every area of policy.' Analyse and evaluate this statement. [25]

Practise your **evaluation skills** by writing a **conclusion** to one of the questions above.

Caucus — when a crow swears at you because the bird feeders are empty...

The stark divisions in US politics don't stop at the two main parties — there's considerable tension within each party too. But it's not all bad news. Sometimes, this leads to constructive compromise and groups from each party working together.

Comparing US and UK Party Policies

It's time to take a leaf out of your judgey friend's book (you know the one) and compare parties. First we'll be swinging to the left (Labour and Democrats) and then to the right (Conservative and Republican). Oh, and make sure you've RSVP'd.

The **Democrats** and **Labour** share **progressive economic** and **social policies**

1) Both parties aim to transition towards **net zero carbon emissions** through **public investment**:

   - **Democrats unanimously supported** Joe Biden's **Bipartisan Infrastructure Law (2021)**. It included **$7.5 billion** in federal funding for **electric vehicle charging points** and **$65 billion** for **green energy transmission**.
   - **Labour's 2024 manifesto** included the pledge to create **Great British Energy**, a **state-owned green energy company**, alongside the commitment to borrow **£17.5 billion** to fund **green investment**.

2) Both parties **support** the principle of **re-distributive taxation**. This aims to **improve economic** and **social equality** by **taxing higher earners** at a **higher rate** and then **re-investing** this money in **public services**.

   - **Biden** either **reversed** many of the **tax-cutting measures** from Trump's **Tax Cuts and Jobs Act (2017)** or allowed them to **expire**.
   - At **state level**, Democrat-controlled **California** has the **highest rates** of **income** and **corporation tax** in the **US**.
   - In **2024, Labour** attempted to **fund** the **recruitment** of **6500 new teachers** by imposing **Value Added Tax** (a flat **20% tax**) on **independent school fees**.

3) The **Democrats** and **Labour** also share **similar views** on the rights of **same-sex couples**, **abortion** and **gun control**.

Democrats and Labour have **similar foreign policies**

1) **Keir Starmer** has expressed his **support** for the **Aukus** deal, a **military co-operation agreement** negotiated by **Biden**, **Rishi Sunak** and the **Australian prime minister Anthony Albanese**.
2) On his first day as **president** in **January 2021**, Biden signed an **executive order** re-joining the **World Health Organisation (WHO)**, which **Trump** had **left** due to **disagreements** over the **COVID-19 pandemic**. **Labour supports** the UK's continuing **membership** of the **WHO**.
3) Both parties are prepared to **support international allies** in **conflicts**. The **Democrats** and **Labour** are both **in favour** of maintaining military aid to Ukraine.

Democrats and Labour **differ** over **healthcare** and **education**

Healthcare

- **Labour** has supported **universal, free-to-access public healthcare** since the establishment of the **National Health Service** (**NHS**) in **1948**.
- However, the **Democrats** have **focused** their efforts on **expanding private medical insurance**. A **small number** of **left-wing Democrats** support **universal healthcare**, but **neither Barack Obama** nor **Joe Biden** attempted to pass this through **Congress**.

Student debt

- The **Democrats** have taken a **more interventionist** stance on the issue of **college debt**. Biden planned to cancel **$10 000** worth of many Americans' **college debt** through the **HEROES Act**.
- In contrast, **Labour dropped** a previous pledge to **reduce student loan payments** from their **2024 manifesto**.

Private schooling

- Although the **Democrats** and **Labour agree** on the **principle** of **re-distributive taxation**, the **Democrats** have **never attempted** to levy **tax** on **private education** in the US.
- By contrast, the introduction of **VAT** on **independent school fees** was one of **Labour's major policies** in their **2024 manifesto**.

US Politics — Democracy and Participation

Comparing US and UK Party Policies

Republicans and the Conservatives are both committed to tax and spending cuts

1) Both parties have introduced **significant tax cuts** during their time in government:

   - Under **Trump, Republicans** in **Congress unanimously supported** the **Tax Cuts and Jobs Act (2017)**, which **reduced** most **income tax brackets** and introduced a **new flat rate** of **21% corporation tax**.
   - **Liz Truss's** government planned to **abolish** the **additional rate of income tax (45%)** for the **highest bracket of earners** (although she **resigned** before this could be implemented).
   - Under **Rishi Sunak**, the Conservatives introduced **two cuts** to **National Insurance** in **2023**.

2) Both parties have **opposed** centralised efforts to achieve **net zero** through **high levels** of **public spending**:

   - **200 House Republicans** voted **against** Biden's **Bipartisan Infrastructure Law** in **2021**.
   - In their **2024 manifesto**, the **Conservatives** placed a greater **emphasis** on **lowering energy bills** than on making the **transition** to **green energy**, promising that bills would be **lower** for each year of the new Parliament than they had been in **2023**.

Both parties contain advocates of isolationism and reducing immigration

1) The **right wing** of each party is **strongly opposed** to **high net migration**:

   - One of **Trump's major policies** in the **2016**, **2020** and **2024** elections was to **build a wall** on the **US' southern border** with **Mexico**. In **2023**, **House Republicans** voted to **re-start** the **construction** of this **border wall**.
   - The **Trump administration** attempted to **cancel DACA**, Obama's policy of **deferring** the **deportation** of people who had come to the US **illegally** as **children** (see page 194).
   - From **2022** to **2024**, the main **immigration policy** of the **Conservative government** was the implementation of a deal to **deport illegal migrants** to **Rwanda**.
   - In **2023**, then-Home Secretary **Suella Braverman** argued that **migrant labour** *"harms the UK's national character"*.

2) Both parties have supported efforts to **re-affirm national sovereignty**. There are some similarities between the **Republicans'** 'America First' approach and the **Conservatives'** support for **Brexit**:

   - Under **Trump**, the US **withdrew** from **international agreements** and **organisations** such as the **Paris climate agreement**, the **Iran nuclear deal** and the **WHO**.
   - Although the **Conservatives** remained **supportive** of these **agreements** and **organisations** throughout their time in government, their decision to pursue a **hard Brexit** was based on a similar belief in the **importance** of **national sovereignty**.

The Conservatives are generally more socially liberal than the Republicans

1) Most **Conservatives** now **support same-sex marriage**, **pro-choice laws** on abortion and **maintaining** the UK's **strict gun laws**.
2) In contrast **Republicans** tend to **oppose same-sex marriage**, hold **pro-life** views on abortion and **oppose** any attempts to **limit** 2nd amendment **gun ownership rights** (see page 221).

Exam Practice

For students studying...

Edexcel: Analyse the differences between the policies of the Democratic Party and the Labour Party. In your answer, you must consider the relevance of at least one comparative theory. [12]

AQA: Explain and analyse three ways in which cultural theory can be used to compare the policy profiles of the Democratic Party and the Labour Party. [9]

My party policy is to have *at least* three different flavours of crisps on offer...

The comparisons on these pages are based on either the shared views of the parties or the cultural norms in each country. This might be ringing bells for you about cultural comparative theory — have a flick back to page 145 if you need a recap.

Comparing US and UK Party Unity

In my experience, party unity is only truly achieved when you play that one song that gets everyone dancing. Unfortunately, the power of pop can't do the same for political parties, no matter how catchy it is. So put down the guitar and get reading.

The **Democrats** and **Labour** have **divisions** between their **left wing** and **centre**

1) The **Democrats** and **Labour** both have **internal divisions** over **economic policy** between **supporters** of **interventionist economics** and **advocates** of a more **neo-liberal approach**:

   > **Left-wing Democrats** including **Alexandria Ocasio-Cortez** have expressed **support** for a **70% tax rate** for **billionaires**. Members of the **New Democrat Coalition** and **Blue Dogs support** maintaining the **highest rate** of **federal income tax** at **37%**.

   > **Left-wing Labour MPs** such as **John McDonnell support** the **re-nationalisation of industry**. However, **Keir Starmer dropped** Labour's previous **commitments** to **nationalise** the **water**, **broadband** and **energy** sectors from their **2024 election manifesto**.

2) The most **left-wing** members of the **Democrats' Progressive Caucus** are **critical** of **Israel's actions** in **Gaza**. Many **centrist** Democrats have consistently **voted to maintain** US support for Israel. **Labour** has also been **divided** over the **Israel-Hamas War**.

   - **Rashida Tlaib** described Israel's actions as *"genocide"*, a label that **centrist** Democrats have **rejected**. Similarly, left-wing **Labour MP Kate Osamor** used a **Holocaust Memorial Day message** in **2024** to describe **Israel's response** to **Hamas'** 7th October attack as **genocide**. This resulted in her being **suspended** from the **Labour party**.
   - **56 Labour MPs** voted **against** the **party whip** in November **2023** when they voted to **demand** an **immediate ceasefire**.

The **right wing** and **centre** of the **Conservatives** and **Republicans** are also **divided**

On **immigration**, the **right wing** of the **Conservative Party** has **clashed** with the **centre** over the **Rwanda plan** and **legal migration**:

- **Lord Clarke**, a prominent **One Nation conservative** who previously served as a **government minister**, **voted against** the **Safety of Rwanda Act** in **2024**. He argued that its attempt to **overrule** the Supreme Court's ruling in **R (AAA and others) v. Home Secretary (2023)** made it *"a step too far"*.
- By contrast, **right-wing MP Suella Braverman**, who helped to **devise** the **Rwanda plan** as **Home Secretary** under Boris Johnson and Rishi Sunak, **argued** that the **UK** should **leave** the **European Convention on Human Rights** to ensure that the **policy** could be **implemented**.

"These flipping politicians, they're always winging it..."

There have been **similar divisions** over **immigration** in the **Republican Party**:

- **Centrist Republican Senators Mitt Romney**, **Susan Collins** and **Lisa Murkowski** voted **against Donald Trump's** attempts to **divert emergency funds** to **construct** the **border wall** in 2019.
- In **2023**, **conservative House Republicans** voted to **re-commence** the **construction** of the **wall**.

Both parties have been **divided** over **foreign aid**:

- In April **2024**, **112 House Republicans** voted **against** providing **further aid** to **Ukraine**, **Israel** and **Taiwan**. **101** House Republicans voted in **favour**.
- In **2021**, **24 Conservative MPs** (including **Theresa May** and **Jeremy Hunt**) voted **against** the **Johnson government's** plan to **reduce** the **UK's foreign aid spending** from **0.7%** of GDP to **0.5%**.

Comparing US and UK Party Unity

Internal party divisions are arguably more significant in the US

1) In the **US**, there are **no binding national manifestos**, so **each candidate** and **state party** can formulate their **own policy platforms**. In contrast, **every candidate** in **UK general elections** is expected to **support** their **party's manifesto**.

2) The **fusion of powers** in the **UK** generally gives **government whips more power** than their equivalents in the **US**. **Rebellions** can be **prevented** through the **promise** of a **future promotion** to a **ministerial position** and **over 100 MPs** are **bound** by **collective responsibility** (see page 91) to **vote with the government**.

3) By contrast, the **separation of powers** in the **US** means that party whips **can't promise promotions** to the **Cabinet** as a way of ensuring **loyalty**.

4) **Social issues** tend to be **more divisive** in the **US** than in the **UK**. While there are **major internal divisions** over **abortion**, **gun control** and **healthcare** in the **US**, these are all areas of **relative consensus** within (and between) **UK parties**.

5) Because there are **only two parties** represented at a **national level**, the **US** has a **tradition** of **big tent parties** that contain a very **broad range** of **ideological views**:

> The Safety of Rwanda Act (2024) (see p.87) is a great example of the power of party whips in the House of Commons. Despite rumours of a major rebellion from centrist Conservative MPs, only 11 MPs ended up voting against the bill. Most of these were right-wing MPs like Suella Braverman and Robert Jenrick, who felt that it didn't go far enough in asserting the UK's sovereignty over the European Court of Human Rights.

- In recent years, the **House Democratic Party** has included **conservative Blue Dog Democrats** like **Henry Cuellar** and **left-wing progressives** such as **Alexandria Ocasio-Cortez**.
- In the **Senate**, **climate change sceptic Joe Manchin** has sat alongside **Green New Deal supporters** like **Elizabeth Warren**.
- While **Labour** and the **Conservatives** do include a **range** of **ideological views**, the fact that the **party leaderships** have much **more power** over **candidate selection** means that they can act to **reduce divisions**.
- In **2019**, **all Conservative candidates** were required to **support Boris Johnson's Brexit deal**, while **most new Labour candidates** in **2024** were **centrists** whose **ideology aligned** with **Keir Starmer's**.
- The **relative success** of parties such as the **Liberal Democrats**, the **SNP** and **Reform UK** also means that politicians **across the ideological spectrum** are likely to find a **party** that **aligns** with their positions.

> In March 2024, right-wing MP Lee Anderson defected from the Conservative Party to become Reform UK's first representative in the House of Commons. He was re-elected as a Reform UK MP in the general election later that year.

US-style caucuses have emerged in the UK in recent years

1) In the **Labour Party**, there has been **tension** between the **Momentum faction**, made up of **left-wing MPs** who supported **Jeremy Corbyn's leadership** (such as **John McDonnell** and **Rebecca Long-Bailey**) and the **centrist Progress faction** (whose prominent members include **Alison McGovern** and **Wes Streeting**).

2) Several **right-wing factions** emerged in the **Conservative Party** during **Theresa May** and **Boris Johnson's** leadership:

- The European Research Group, a pro-Brexit faction, gained prominence when refusing to support May's deal with the European Union.
- During the COVID-19 pandemic, the Covid Recovery Group was formed to campaign for an end to lockdowns and social distancing measures.

> Steve Baker, a prominent right-wing MP until the 2024 general election, was a leading member of both the European Research Group and Covid Recovery Group. He also set up the Net Zero Scrutiny Group, which aimed to control the government's spending on green initiatives.

3) **Centrist Conservative MPs** formed the **One Nation Caucus** in **2019**.

Revision Task

Practise your **analysis skills** by explaining **why** the following similarities and differences exist between parties in the US and the UK.

1) *There are fewer internal party divisions on social policy in the UK than in the US.*
2) *Parties in both the US and the UK contain factions of like-minded representatives.*
3) *In the UK, party leaders and whips have more influence over their representatives' voting.*

Party division: ensuring everyone gets an equal number of cocktail sausages...

While many internal party divisions are cultural, the fact they cause less disruption in the UK than in the US is partly structural. Party whips in the UK give incentives for party unity — or threaten anyone who falls out of line... I'm looking at you, Brenda.

Comparing US and UK Party Systems

While both the US and UK have reputations as being two party systems, it's not quite so simple in the UK, especially for the devolved legislatures. So you'd better grab a whole bunch of balloons as we dive into this page — two isn't going to cut it.

Both the US and the UK have two-party systems at a national level

1) **All 435 members** of the **House of Representatives** represented either the **Republican** or **Democrat parties** in **2024**.
2) Only **18%** of **MPs** represented parties **other than Labour** or **the Conservatives** following the **2024 UK general election**.
3) The major parties are **boosted** by the **disproportionate** nature of the **electoral system** in both countries:

> - In **1992**, **Bill Clinton** won **43%** of the **popular vote**, but **69%** of **ECVs** (Electoral College Votes).
> - In the **2024 general election**, the **Labour Party** won **34%** of the popular vote, but **63%** of seats in the **House of Commons**, while **Reform UK** won **14%** of the vote, but **0.7%** of seats.

The degree of national two-party dominance is much greater in the US

1) **Every president** since **Ulysses S. Grant** in **1869** has been a **Republican** or a **Democrat**.
2) **No third party** or **independent candidate** has won a single **ECV** since **George Wallace** won **46** in **1968** (meaning the **Republicans** and the **Democrats** have won the past **7490 ECVs**).

The **UK's parliamentary system** allows **other parties** to play occasional roles in **government**, which **wouldn't** be **possible** under the **US'** system of **directly electing** the **president**.

- From **2010-2015**, the **Liberal Democrats** served in a **coalition government** with the **Conservatives**.
- From **2017-2019**, the **Democratic Unionist Party** (**DUP**) were in a **confidence and supply** agreement with the **Conservatives**.

The UK now has a multi-party system at devolved level

1) The **Scottish National Party** (**SNP**) has been **in government** in Scotland since **2007**. From **2021-2024**, the **Scottish Green Party** had **two ministers** in the **Scottish Cabinet**.
2) **Labour**, the **Conservatives** and the **Liberal Democrats** don't stand for election in **Northern Ireland**. **Sinn Féin** and the **Democratic Unionist Party** (**DUP**) are the two **largest parties** there, but the **Alliance**, the **Ulster Unionist Party** (**UUP**) and the **Social Democratic and Labour Party** (**SDLP**) have all had ministers in the **Northern Ireland Executive** in recent years.

Johan had begun to realise that his multi-party days were behind him

The Republicans and the Democrats also dominate state politics

1) **All 50 state governors** serving in **2024** were **Republicans** or **Democrats**.
2) There have only been **two exceptions** in recent decades:
   - **Jesse Ventura**, **Reform Party Governor of Minnesota** from **1999-2003**.
   - Former Republican **Wally Hickel** was re-elected as the **Governor of Alaska** representing the **Alaskan Independence Party** in **1990**.
3) In **2024**, only **106** of the **7575** members of **state legislatures** across the US were **third party** or **independent** candidate representatives.

Exam Practice

For Edexcel students: Examine the similarities between the performance of third parties and independent candidates in the US and the UK. [12]

For AQA students: Explain and analyse three similarities between the performance of third parties and independent candidates in the US and the UK. [9]

Fine, you've got me, I've finally run out of party jokes (and snacks)...

The prevalence of independence movements in the UK compared to the US can be explained through cultural differences. The influence of third party candidates is more structural, as it's linked to how UK Parliament and elections work.

Global Politics — The State and Globalisation

State and Nation State

There's a lot to learn when it comes to globalisation, but don't get yourself into a state — you'll be a pro after these pages.

A **state** and a **nation** are **not the same**

State — A **unit of political authority** that is classed as an **actor** in the **international system**. It has **absolute power** over its **territory** and **population**, and has **sovereign equality** with **other states** in the international system.

Key Terms — sovereign equality: The principle that all states are equal and should be treated as equals in the international community.

Nation — A **group of people** who share **common ties** of **culture**, **language** or **history**. There can be **many different nations** within a state.

Some nations have never achieved statehood, e.g. the Kurds.

When the **United Nations** was formed in **1945** it had **51 members**. By 2024, there were **193 members**.
- Many of these nations **gained** their **independence** from **colonial powers** (e.g. **Nigeria** from the **British Empire**).
- Others **became independent** after **breaking away** from **multi-national states** (e.g. **Croatia** from **Yugoslavia**).

Not all units of **territory** are classed as a **state**

There are **four principles** for determining whether or not a **territory** qualifies as a **state**:

1) **PERMANENT POPULATION** — To be a **state**, a **territory** must have a **stable population** located in a **particular area**.
2) **DEFINED TERRITORY** — A state must have **territory** that it **controls** within a **clearly defined border**.
3) **EFFECTIVE GOVERNMENT** — A state needs a **functioning government** that can **effectively govern** the **territory** it controls.
4) **DIPLOMATIC RELATIONS** — A state will be able to carry out **diplomatic relations** with **other states**, e.g. by having **foreign embassies** and **diplomats** to represent its interests.

These principles are based on the Montevideo Convention of 1933.

Gibraltar is an example of a territory that isn't a state. It meets the principles of having a permanent population, a defined territory and an effective government, but it does not have diplomatic relations with existing states.

Although **not** a principle of the Montevideo Convention, **recognition** is also seen as an important factor. While **recognition** as a **state** is not a condition of **statehood**, states **can't** carry out **diplomatic relations** without recognition.

- **Kosovo** is an **aspiring state** that is **recognised** by approximately 100 UN member states but has **not yet** been recognised by the **whole** international community.
- However, recognition can **change** over time. The **last country** to become a **state** was **South Sudan**. It became independent from Sudan in **2011** following a **referendum**, and was then accepted as a member of the **United Nations**.

The **nation state** is a fairly **modern idea**

A **nation state** is a **state** where the population shares a **common culture**, **history** and **language**. The **people** of a nation state generally belong to the **same ethnic group**. For example, as of 2024:
- **Japan** has a population of around 123 million with around 98% described as ethnically Japanese.
- **South Korea** is a highly homogeneous society of around 52 million people.
- **Tunisia** has a population of around 12 million that is almost exclusively made up of Arabs (98%).

Quick Questions

1) How many member states are there in the United Nations?
2) What can a state not enter into with other states if it doesn't have recognition?
3) Which state became a member of the United Nations in 2011?
4) Give two examples of territories that are not considered to be states.

So territories and nation states can be states but states aren't always nations...
What's so confusing about that? The truth is, defining a state is a complicated process. There's no straightforward way to identify a state, and sometimes even the international community can't agree on which nations and territories are states.

Sovereignty

If you thought sovereign power was about living it up in palaces and putting on fancy crowns, think again. Sovereignty is a pretty important concept to get your head around. If only there was a handy revision guide lying around that explains it...

There are **different strands** of **national sovereignty**

NATIONAL SOVEREIGNTY is when a state has **absolute power** over the subjects and citizens **within its territory**.

You need to know the difference between the strands of national sovereignty, so make sure you understand what each one involves.

INTERNAL SOVEREIGNTY

The ability to wield absolute power **within a state**. For example, the **UK Parliament's** ability to exercise supreme power with **no other body** or **person** being able to **overrule** its laws.

EXTERNAL SOVEREIGNTY

The ability to **act independently** on the **international stage**, so that **all states** are **equal** in theory. This means a state can **decide** its own **foreign policy** without **interference** by **other states** or **intergovernmental organisations** (IGOs).

- It's argued that the modern-day concept of **independent sovereign states** was created by the **Treaty of Westphalia** (also known as the Peace of Westphalia) in 1648.
- The Treaty was an important **turning point** in **European** and **world history** because it allowed **state rulers** to practise the **religion** of their choice **without interference** from other **states**.

Some argue that **states** have **lost sovereignty** in **recent years**...

1) Those who argue that there has been a **loss** of **state sovereignty** believe in the existence of the **post-sovereign state**, where **power** has **shifted away** from the **state**.
2) They argue that the **system** of **independent states** created after the Treaty of Westphalia, where **each state** has its **own national sovereignty**, has become **increasingly redundant**.
3) There are several **factors** that have affected **state sovereignty**:

Globalisation
The growing **interconnectedness** of the **world** in **trade**, **finance** and **production** means that states have **less independence** than in the past.

Climate Change
Climate change is a **global issue** — states **need** to **work collectively** through **treaties** like the **Paris Agreement**, which was adopted in 2015.

Human Rights
The creation of **international courts** and **tribunals**, such as the **International Criminal Court** (ICC), means that **member states** are expected to allow their **citizens** to be **tried** by these courts.

Military Intervention
There has been a **growing trend** towards using **military intervention** for **humanitarian reasons**, e.g. in Iraq and Libya. This **ignores** the **wishes** of the **sovereign states** that experience these interventions.

IGOs
Hundreds of IGOs, such as the **International Monetary Fund** (**IMF**), have been created since the **end of the Second World War**. This has led to **certain decisions** being made at this level **instead** of at the **state level**. For example, the World Trade Organisation (WTO) imposes **trade tariffs** to help create **stability** in world trade.

Regionalism
The **growth** across the world of **regional organisations**, such as the **African Union** and the **EU**, has led to some **decision-making** being **transferred** from **states** to a **regional body**.

Moussa Faki Mahamat, Chairperson of the African Union Commission, with US Secretary of State Antony Blinken in 2023

Global Politics — The State and Globalisation

Sovereignty

...but national sovereignty remains important

1) Some argue that states are still the **main actors** in **international affairs** and that the **decline** of the **state** is **exaggerated**.
2) Here are some **key arguments** for the **continued importance** of **national sovereignty** in the **international system**:

Argument	Evidence for continued importance of national sovereignty
The principle of non-interference	• A **key element** of the **Treaty of Westphalia** in 1648 was the principle that states **should not interfere** in the **affairs** of **other states**. • This allowed them to exercise **absolute power** within **their borders** and have **independence of action** in the **international arena**.
Military forces	• Most **armed forces** are still under the **sovereign control** of the **state**. For example, the **British** army, navy and air force were **never incorporated** into a combined **EU military force**. • States that have **nuclear weapons** carefully **guard** their **control** over them.
Citizenship	• The power to decide who is and who is not a **citizen** remains firmly in the control of the **governments** of **sovereign states**. For example, **Shamima Begum** was a British citizen who **left the UK** to join the **Islamic State** in Syria when she was 15. The **UK government** stripped her of her **citizenship** on **security grounds** in 2019.
National borders	• Large amounts of **time** and **resources** are committed to **policing national borders**. For example, **Sunak's government** had a policy of **reducing** the number of **migrants** reaching Britain in '**small boats**'. • States have also committed significant resources to **defending national borders** from **invasion** by other states, e.g. Ukraine defending itself against Russia's 2022 invasion.
Intergovernmentalism	• **IGOs** such as the **United Nations** follow the principle of **intergovernmentalism**, which gives **member states** the power to **veto** (block) **resolutions**. For example, Russia and China **vetoed** a US-sponsored draft of a resolution that called for an **immediate** and **sustained ceasefire** in **Gaza** in March 2024. • Intergovernmentalism **limits** the **power** that **IGOs** have over their **member states**. • If states don't like the **policies** of an **IGO**, then they have the power of **withdrawing** from the IGO. For example, **Brexit**, when the UK **left the EU** in 2020.
Lack of a world government	• States remain **important actors** because there has never been a **world government**. It can still be argued that there is nothing '**above**' the state. • A **powerful state** may be able to act on the international stage **without fear** of any serious **consequences**, even when their actions are denounced as **illegal**. E.g. The **US-led invasion of Iraq** in 2003 and **Russia's invasion of Ukraine** in 2022.

world government
The idea of a supranational body that has legislative and executive authority over states. It would make decisions in areas of global importance (e.g. climate change, nuclear weapons).

Did somebody say supernatural? No? Oh, I'll just go then...

Despite the emergence of various international organisations, there is some evidence that the state is still regarded as a more significant factor in the lives of its citizens. For example, participation in national elections within the EU is far higher than in those for the European Parliament.

Quick Questions

1) What is meant by national sovereignty?
2) Which treaty led to the acceptance of the principle of non-interference?
3) Name three ways that national sovereignty is being eroded.
4) Name three ways that national sovereignty remains important.

What do you call a cuppa at the palace? Sovereign-tea...

Having sovereignty doesn't guarantee absolute independence. There are lots of factors linked to globalisation that affect how far a state can exercise its sovereignty, especially when it comes to global issues that can't easily be solved by a single state.

Globalisation

Next up on this magical tour of important concepts in global politics — globalisation. Are you excited? I'm excited.

Globalisation is about the **world** becoming more **interconnected**

1) The world can increasingly be seen as one 'global village' rather than a collection of separate states.

2) **Events** and **actions** that happen in one part of the world can have **significant consequences** in other parts of the world, effectively **shrinking** the world.

There are **three main forms** of globalisation

1) **Economic** Globalisation

- The **production of goods** (such as cars and computers) is **internationalised**, and **service industries** (such as financial services) now **operate across continents**.
- The **financial sector** is particularly globalised because of the amount of **capital** being **invested** internationally and **currencies** being **exchanged** every day. This has been made easier by the **revolution** in **technology**, which allows **trillions of dollars** to be traded **electronically**.
- The **cost** of **exporting goods** has been **greatly reduced**, causing **trade volumes** to **massively increase**.
- **Business** and **enterprise** are increasingly **globalised**:

    1) An example of this is the development of **transnational corporations** (TNCs) such as **Shell** and **Apple**.
    2) This is also illustrated by the creation of **Intergovernmental Organisations** (IGOs), such as the **International Monetary Fund** (IMF), **World Bank** and **World Trade Organisation** (WTO).
    3) These IGOs follow the **Washington Consensus** — a term first used by the economist **John Williamson** in 1989. This aims to **liberalise trade** by promoting **deregulation** (the relaxation of rules and removal of barriers) and **policies** of **low taxation**.
    4) **Trade rules** are now **enforced globally** and only a few states (e.g. North Korea) are **outside** the **reach** of these IGOs.

- **Economies** across the world are **interconnected** — the impact of the **2007/8 Credit Crunch** was felt across the **entire globe**, showing how far economic interconnectedness has developed.
- The importance of pursuing policies that are supported by **global financial markets** was illustrated by the fall of the **Truss government** in the UK in 2022. It was the government's proposal of **unfunded tax cuts** to stimulate the economy that **spooked** the markets, ultimately leading to Truss's resignation.

2) **Political** Globalisation

Key Terms — non-state actors: *Organisations or individuals who have political influence on the world stage but aren't tied to any one state.*

- Since 1945 there has been a **huge expansion** in the number of **IGOs**, such as the **ICC**, **UN** or **EU**, and **Non-Governmental Organisations** (NGOs), such as **non-state actors** like Greenpeace and Amnesty International.
- Global **institutions** such as the **ICC** and **UN** have had a large impact on global politics, e.g. the **ICC** has **prosecuted** war criminals. At the 2015 UN Climate Change Conference, **nations** from around the world signed the **2015 Paris Agreement** to put measures in place to tackle **climate change**.

> The increase in IGOs is another factor that has affected sovereignty. More decision-making has been transferred from individual states to regional or global bodies. Decisions in these institutions are made using either intergovernmental methods (where the state still has a veto) or supranational methods (where the state does not have a veto). Both of these methods diminish state sovereignty.

Former UK Prime Minister Gordon Brown

- **Political ideas** such as **democracy**, **international law** and **human rights** have become more **widely accepted** around the world in recent decades. This means that states are **more likely** to **adopt** or **stick to** these norms of international behaviour.

> The **advance** of political globalisation has been said to have created a form of **global governance** where **global issues** are now **effectively** managed at the **regional** and **global level** rather than at **state level**. Former UK prime minister **Gordon Brown** observed during the 2008 **global financial crisis** that *"global problems require global solutions"*.

Globalisation

3) Cultural Globalisation

- Some have argued that there are now fewer **cultural differences** between **states**. They say this has led to the formation of a **homogeneous global monoculture**, which Benjamin Barber called "**McWorld**".
- In this global monoculture, people **increasingly** view the **same** content and have the same style of clothes, brands, music, phones and material aspirations as people in **other parts of the world**.

> One example of this is the **appeal** of **English Premier League football**, which is watched by over **one billion people** worldwide each week.

- **Tourism** has **increased** enormously in recent decades as **foreign travel** has become **more affordable**.
- The **growth** of **migration** has meant that over a quarter of a billion people no longer live in the country where they were born.
- Developments in **technology** mean that **media** can be **instantly transmitted** to people all over the world. This has enabled **cultural influences** such as news, advertising and celebrity culture to be spread **across the world**.

Cultural globalisation is also known as 'Coca-Colonisation'.

Boris found the perfect beach towel for his trip to the Med

Some describe cultural globalisation as '**Americanisation**' or '**Westernisation**'. They argue that the **driving force** behind this **cultural assimilation** has been the **appeal** of the '**American Way**', the **popularity** of the **English language** and the **dominance** of the **Western world**.

American chain restaurants in the city of Shenzhen, China

An alternative view is that '**hybridisation**' is taking place. This is where **different cultures** are **blended together** rather than **one culture** being overly **dominant**.

Key Terms

cultural assimilation
When the values, behaviours and beliefs of one group are adopted by another group.

American Way
A set of values that presents Americans as go-getting, free, individualistic people living in a land of opportunity where anything is possible with hard work.

Quick Questions

1) What are the three main forms of globalisation?
2) Give a definition for the term 'economic globalisation'.
3) Name three organisations that help promote economic globalisation.
4) Which organisations have helped to promote political globalisation?
5) Name three political ideas that have become more widespread as part of political globalisation.
6) Explain what is meant by 'global monoculture'.
7) What does 'Americanisation' mean?
8) How is 'hybridisation' different from 'Americanisation'?

Exam Practice

Evaluate the view that cultural globalisation has had a greater impact on the world than any other form of globalisation. [30]

Make sure you consider the impact of each type of globalisation in your answer. It's a good idea to make judgements about the impact of each factor you discuss before coming to your final conclusion.

[Joke outsourced to Antarctica — allow 2-3 working years for delivery]...
There are lots of different factors driving globalisation and they're often interconnected. Don't just think of the three main types of globalisation (economic, political and cultural) as separate processes — think about how they fuel one another too.

Impact of Globalisation on the State System

As well as having economic, political and global effects, globalisation has changed the way states interact with each other.

Globalisation has affected the **state system** in **different ways**

There is **increasing interconnectedness** and **interdependence** between states

1) States have become more **interconnected** and **interdependent** because:
   - **Communication** and **transportation** has become **quicker** and **cheaper**.
   - There's been an **increase** in **migration**.
2) Since the end of the **Cold War** and the **democratisation** of countries in **Eastern Europe** and parts of **South America**, the extent of globalisation has changed:
   - **Widening of globalisation** — the **number** of **states** experiencing globalisation has **greatly increased**.
   - **Deepening of globalisation** — globalisation has become **more intense** and is affecting more and **more areas** of people's lives.

There are **more challenges** to **state control**

Globalisation has **challenged** the **authority** of **states** over the **control** of their **citizens**. For example:
- The **creation** of the **ICC** and **War Crimes Tribunals** has **limited** the **power** of states to **resist demands** for their citizens to **face trial** at **The Hague** (where the ICC is based).
- The repeated **failed attempts** to **extradite** Wikileaks founder **Julian Assange** from the UK to face trial in the USA illustrated the increasingly **global nature of justice** and how states can **challenge** the **sovereign control** of other states.

Globalisation has prompted **changes** to **international law**

1) There has been some **pressure** to **develop international law** to manage the **widening** and **deepening** of globalisation.
2) **Global rules** have been established about **trade**, and the **WTO** was created in **1995** to manage these rules. The **2015 Paris Agreement** was established to address **environmental concerns**.
3) Changes to **international law** have been made in an attempt to **keep up** with the **rapid development** of **globalisation**, but these have sometimes **failed**. For example, in the 2007/8 Credit Crunch, the **investment decisions** of **large financial institutions** caused the **global economy** to enter a period of **deep recession**. Global capital markets **lacked effective global regulation** to **prevent** this.

Globalisation has affected the **frequency** of **forcible interventions**

Forcible interventions are when a **state** takes **military action** against another state. Forcible interventions can be for **humanitarian reasons** (e.g. Somalia in 1992) or **non-humanitarian reasons** (e.g. Afghanistan in 2001, where the military action was primarily to defeat Al-Qaeda).

Globalisation initially brought about an increase in humanitarian interventions:
- The **Holocaust** during the **Second World War** caused a massive **shift** in **global opinion** about **rights protection**. Growing **awareness** of **human rights abuses** meant that states felt the need to **ignore traditional state sovereignty** and instead act to **protect** the **citizens** of a state from its **own rulers**.
- For example, in **Libya** in **2011**, the **UN Security Council** permitted **NATO** to use "**all necessary means**" to protect its people from **persecution** by Colonel Gaddafi.

More recently, the desire of the international community to intervene has declined:
- The **disruption** caused by **humanitarian interventions** has caused states to be **more reluctant** to **take military action** to protect civilians — e.g. in Syria in 2013 or Myanmar in 2017.
- **Non-humanitarian interventions** have also been **impacted** by globalisation. States that were initially drawn into **international disputes** are now less so — they fear the **economic** and **political disruption** caused by these interventions, e.g. the consequences following the invasion of Iraq in 2003.

Top Tip for Politicians #892: Be careful when using social media... Ed Balls...
Remember that globalisation is an ongoing process — changes in globalisation could lead to further changes in the state system.

Global Politics — The State and Globalisation

Debate on the Impact of Globalisation

Unsurprisingly, there's lots of debate over the extent of the effects of globalisation. Hyperglobalisers, transformationalists and globalisation sceptics (don't look at me, I didn't name them) have all got a finger or two in the globalisation pie.

There is **no consensus** on the **impact** of **globalisation**

HYPERGLOBALISERS say the impact of globalisation on **states** and the **state system** has been **huge**:

1) States are **no longer able** to **effectively** exercise **independent power** in the international system.
2) Globalisation has made **state borders** more '**porous**' and **open** to the operation of global market forces, ideas and cultural influences. This has turned states into '**post-sovereign states**' that can **no longer resist** them.
3) States have become **interdependent** and are **no longer** the **key actors** in the international system.
4) States are at the **mercy** of **TNCs** and **IGOs** who decide where to **invest** or **provide aid** or **assistance**.

TRANSFORMATIONALISTS say globalisation **hasn't** had the impact that **hyperglobalisers** suggest, but it has still had a **significant impact** on **global politics**:

1) Globalisation has been a **challenge** but **also** an **opportunity** embraced by many states. For example, **China** and **India** have **taken advantage** of the **globalised economy** and **gained significant power** in the international system.
2) **Smaller states** gain **influence** by **collaborating** in organisations like the EU and UN. **International collaboration** allows them to have **more influence** over issues like the **environment**, **trade** or **human rights** than if they act alone.

GLOBALISATION SCEPTICS say the impact of globalisation has been **greatly exaggerated**:

1) **States** are **still** the **key actors** in the international system.
2) **State sovereignty** means there are **limits** on the operation of **IGOs** such as the UN or the EU.
3) **Power politics** means that states are still able to act **independently** in the international system.
4) Some states (Russia, the USA, the UK, France and China) can use their **veto** in the **UN Security Council**, and they can even decide to use **military action** outside the control of the UN (e.g. in Iraq in 2003).

There's also a debate between **realist** and **liberal** views

	Key Beliefs	Views on Globalisation
REALISTS	• States are the **key actors** in the state system and are motivated by their **own national interest**. • The state system is a **reflection** of **human nature** which is naturally **greedy** and **selfish**. • **War** and **conflict** are **inevitable** in the state system. • States must **defend** themselves from **external threats** — **survival** in a hostile world is the **main concern**.	• The **impact** of globalisation has been **exaggerated**. • States will **always** be the **key actors** in the **international system**. • **International organisations** should only be **tolerated** if they are in the **national interest** of a state. • **IGOs** will eventually **decay** and **collapse** due to **member states** pursuing their own interests. • The realities of **power politics** will always eventually **reassert themselves**.
LIBERALS	• States have the **potential** to be **co-operative** and to **work together** for **mutual advantage**. • **Human beings** are **not greedy** by nature and have the **ability** to work **with others** for **common purposes**. • **War** is **not inevitable** because states can create **international organisations** that **promote co-operation**. • **Organisations** like the UN and EU can work to **reduce** the **chance** of **conflict** and **war**.	• Globalisation has had a **significant effect** on the **international system**. However, **liberals** are more **optimistic** about the **impact** of globalisation. • There are **enormous advantages** gained from **increased trade** and **international co-operation**. • States have become **more interdependent** and **wealthier** because of **economic globalisation**. • **Political globalisation** promotes **peace**. There are far **more IGOs** and **NGOs** than **ever before**. This has helped to **spread political ideas** that contribute to peace, such as **democracy** and **human rights**.

The UK exiting the EU and the failure of the UN to prevent numerous conflicts demonstrates this.

Debate on the Impact of Globalisation

There's also debate over the **impact** of **globalisation** on **contemporary issues**

Impact on **poverty**

POSITIVE IMPACT

- ✓ **Johan Norberg** has written about the benefits of globalisation. He argues that **capitalism** and **trade** have **cut** the number of people in **poverty** by billions, and that the **competition** and **innovation** that accompany them drive up **efficiency** and **standards**.
- ✓ The effect has been to benefit people around the world and help many countries that suffered great **poverty** a few decades ago (like China and India) to **rapidly industrialise** and **enrich** many people.

Ajay Banga, elected president of the World Bank after being nominated by the Biden administration in 2023

NEGATIVE IMPACT

- ✗ **John Pilger** argued that globalisation has **favoured** the **rich** and **strong** states, which **control** 'global economic agents', such as the **IMF** and **World Bank**.
- ✗ **Between-country** and **within-country inequality** have greatly **expanded** since the 1980s when the **Washington Consensus** opened up many **poorer** countries to **free-market capitalism**.
- ✗ The **gap** between the **richest** and **poorest** in the world has **grown**. The impact of globalisation on **reducing** poverty has **not** been **consistent** worldwide.

Impact on **conflict**

POSITIVE IMPACT

- ✓ **Complex interdependence** means that states are far **less** likely to **use military force** as it will **disrupt** their own **economies**.
- ✓ The **democratic peace thesis** states that democratisation **prevents** war because, unlike in authoritarian regimes, democratic rulers are **directly accountable** to their **electorate**.
- ✓ **Democratic zones of peace** have developed, meaning that the use of **military force** in areas like Western Europe, North America and South America has become very unlikely.

Key Terms

complex interdependence
A theory developed by Nye and Keohane in the 1970s which argues that states are increasingly dependent on one another.

NEGATIVE IMPACT

- ✗ **Military force** is an ever-present **feature** of **global politics**. **Arms manufacturers** continue to **thrive** and there are many **ongoing conflicts**. Though there hasn't been a **world war** since 1945, over **200 separate conflicts** have since taken place.
- ✗ Globalisation causes **more tension** as people suffer the effects of **environmental degradation** and the impact of **economic** and **cultural globalisation**.
- ✗ **Samuel Huntington** argued that globalisation brings different **civilisations** and **cultures** into **contact** and **conflict** with each other.

Impact on **human rights**

POSITIVE IMPACT

- ✓ The adoption of the **Universal Declaration of Human Rights** by the UN General Assembly in **1948** has led to it setting **universal standards**.
- ✓ **War crime tribunals** were set up in the 1990s, and the **International Criminal Court** was established in 2002 as a **permanent court** to try war criminals. **State leaders** such as Slobodan Milosevic and Charles Taylor were **prosecuted**.
- ✓ The **International Court of Justice** (ICJ) rules on **disputes** between countries where **human rights issues** are at stake.
- ✓ NGOs like **Amnesty International** and **Human Rights Watch** have campaigned against states **abusing** their own citizens.

NEGATIVE IMPACT

- ✗ **Economic needs** have often been **prioritised** over **human rights**, especially where there is high **demand** for **cheap oil** and **consumer goods** from **authoritarian regimes** such as Saudi Arabia and China. Workers are often exploited and their rights neglected when **trade deals** are signed.
- ✗ Human rights are **not** universally accepted, and some **states** have been **reluctant** to **support interventions**. This is made worse if the **country** committing the abuse is a **permanent** member of the **UN Security Council** and has a **veto** on the Council's attempts to take action.

For example, Abu Ghraib prison in 2003, the persecution of the Uighur minority in China or the atrocities by invading Russian forces in Ukraine in 2022.

Debate on the Impact of Globalisation

Impact on the **environment**

POSITIVE IMPACT

- ✓ **International accords** like the **2015 Paris Agreement** lay out a way for humanity to **control** and **address** the 'collective dilemma' of **climate change**. Some argue that **action** by **individual** states would be **futile**, but **collective** action that involves the **majority** of **states** would have a **significant impact**.
- ✓ **NGOs** such as **Greenpeace** and **Friends of the Earth**, as well as the campaigning of activists like **Greta Thunberg**, have **raised** the **profile** of the issue **worldwide**.
- ✓ Globalisation can help with **future progress** on environmental issues — e.g. **collaborating** on **new forms** of **technology** (such as **carbon capture**) and **coordinated international action** on **climate change** could have an impact.

Greta Thunberg addressing MEPs during a meeting of the European Parliament's environment committee

NEGATIVE IMPACT

- ✗ Globalisation has led to **increased** trade and far **greater global demand** for **consumer goods** such as cars and electronic devices.
- ✗ The **manufacture** and **use** of these goods contributes to **higher levels** of **carbon emissions** as well as the **increased** use of Earth's **resources**.
- ✗ The **increase** in **global travel** and high **global demand** for **vehicles** has also contributed to the use of **non-renewable** energy sources and **higher emissions** of greenhouse gases into the **atmosphere**.
- ✗ **Habitat destruction** and **land use** for the **production** of **goods** has also had a significant impact on global **biodiversity**.
- ✗ The **spread** of **Western** consumer culture also leads to **higher volumes** of **waste**, resulting in **unprecedented** levels of **pollution** in **water** and on **land**.

Invest in a Flysla™ today — the only car with built-in air purifying technology that reverses climate change
What do you mean this isn't real? I saw it online...

Quick Questions

1) Which perspective believes that globalisation has had the greatest impact on global politics: hyperglobalisers, globalisation sceptics or transformationalists?
2) Who is more positive about the effects of globalisation on poverty: Johan Norberg or John Pilger? Explain why.
3) What is meant by 'complex interdependence'?
4) What was Samuel Huntington's main argument about civilisation and culture?
5) Which agreement has been the most far-reaching in terms of the environment?

Revision Task

Test your knowledge by identifying which of the following are **liberal beliefs** and which are **realist beliefs**:

- States will always be the key actors in the international system.
- Globalisation is a positive force that leads to many benefits.
- International organisations are inevitably doomed to failure.
- International organisations can help states to cooperate and prosper.

Have a look back at page 234 if you need a reminder about liberal and realist beliefs.

Essay Plan

Evaluate the extent to which the impact of globalisation has been exaggerated.   [30]

Using the grid on p.298, **plan** an answer to the essay question above.

It's a good idea to use lots of relevant examples when discussing the economic, cultural and political factors behind globalisation, as well as mentioning different perspectives on globalisation.

What's all this globe nonsense? Everyone knows Earth is flat*...

Globalisation is a very important concept in global politics, so make sure you understand it and can explain the key arguments about its impact on the state system. Have another read through these pages until you're confident you know them inside out.

*The view expressed here bears no relation to scientific reality

Global Governance and the UN

As you saw in the last section, we live in an increasingly globalised world. But if the globe is one big community, how can we keep everyone on the same page and working together? Well, that's where global governance comes in.

There's a **difference** between **global governance** and **world government**

Global governance

Global governance is where states **work together** on matters of **mutual concern**.

- It results in **sovereignty** being **partially eroded** in areas where global governance is undertaken.
- It consists of a range of **IGOs**, **NGOs** and **treaties** which have a **significant impact** on states and the states system.
- **Political** and **economic** global governance exist in the world today through **institutions** such as the **UN**, **NATO**, **WTO**, **IMF** and the **World Bank**.
- Global governance emerged with the creation of **IGOs** in the **nineteenth century**. This followed the **international anarchy** of previous centuries where no such organisations existed above the state.

World government

World government (see p.230) is where one central authority has a **monopoly** over the legitimate **use of force**.

- It results in a **significant loss** of **sovereignty** as important matters (such as the use of **armed forces**) would be **controlled** by the world government.
- Whereas global governance involves **multi-level** and **multi-institution** decision-making, **world government** has only one **central authority**.

The **United Nations** is the leading institution of **political global governance**

1) The **UN** provides an important global **forum** at times of crisis.
2) It was created at the end of the **Second World War** in **1945** with the aim of **preventing** conflict on a **global scale** happening **again**.
   - In the space of **thirty years**, two world wars had killed over **70 million people** and left much of **Europe** devastated.
   - The victorious **allies** decided to create a **new organisation** that would not make the same **mistakes** as its predecessor, the **League of Nations**.
3) The **founding treaty** of the **UN** is the **UN Charter**. This document was signed by the **original 51 members** on 26 June 1945.

Key Terms — League of Nations
A body created after WWI following the Treaty of Versailles in 1919. Despite early successes in maintaining the peace, the absence of key global actors such as the USA meant that its ability to deal with crises was limited.

The UN was founded with four main aims that continue to this day

1 Maintaining international peace and security:
The UN should be a **forum** for **resolving conflicts** and **preventing wars**.

2 Upholding international law:
Helping to enforce the rule of law should **reduce conflict** between states.

The UN headquarters in New York City, USA

3 Promoting social and economic development:
The **Wall Street Crash** of **1929** and subsequent **Great Depression** of the 1930s had helped to foster **extremism** and **nationalism**. It was hoped this could be **avoided** in future by **promoting development** through the creation of the **World Bank** and **IMF**.

4 Protection of human rights:
In **1948**, the UN created the **Universal Declaration of Human Rights** which was intended to **prevent** a **recurrence** of the **Holocaust** that took place in the **Second World War**.

Global Governance and the UN

The UN has had **successes** and **failures**

1) The **longevity** and **universality** of the UN suggests that it has been **successful**.
2) However, the UN may **fail** to enact its **decisions**. The UN is **not** a **world government**, but a collection of **independent sovereign states**. Its **member states** are free to **ignore** the UN's decisions if they **disagree** with them.
3) Its other successes and failures can be looked at in terms of its **founding aims**:

Peace and security

Success: ✓ The UN has helped **prevent** the recurrence of another **world war**.

Failure: ✗ There have been **over 200 conflicts** worldwide since 1945, with **millions** of people **dying** as a result.

International law

Success: ✓ The **International Court of Justice (ICJ)** has successfully promoted the **rule of law** globally over the last **eight decades**.

Failure: ✗ **International law** has not been **respected** in conflicts such as:
- the **Iraq War** in 2003
- the **Russian invasion of Ukraine** in 2022

Social and economic development

Success: ✓ **Most** people today are far **better off** than those who lived in 1945, with **billions** of people **no longer living in poverty**.

Failure: ✗ **Huge inequalities** in the **standard of living** remain.
✗ **Famine**, **child mortality** and **low life expectancy** are still **problems** in many regions around the world.

Human rights

Success: ✓ The **1948 Universal Declaration of Human Rights** paved the way for the body of international **human rights law** we have today.

Failure: ✗ **Human rights abuses** have persisted, e.g.:
- the **1994 Rwandan genocide**
- the **mistreatment** of detainees at **Guantanamo Bay** after 2001

Quick Questions

1) What is the founding treaty of the United Nations?
2) How many original members were there of the United Nations?
3) How many conflicts have occurred since 1945?

Exam Practice

Examine the ways in which the United Nations achieves its main aims. [12]

And I thought the United Nations was an international football fan club...

Ever since the First World War, there have been attempts to create an organisation of countries that will work to help prevent a conflict of that scale from happening again. And the one that's stood the test of time so far is the United Nations.

Global Governance — Political and Economic

Role and Significance of the UN

The UN is a big political body, and just like a human body, it's got some important organs. These are less squelchy though.

The **UN Charter** outlined **six principal organs**

The **UN Charter** also says that the UN should be composed of **sovereign states**. This is reflected in the **composition** of the **Security Council** and the **General Assembly**.

Don't confuse the UN with world government — the preservation of state sovereignty is one of the UN's key principles.

Organ	Description
Security Council (UNSC)	• The **most powerful** part of the UN structure. • There are **5 permanent members** on the Security Council — the **USA**, the **UK**, **Russia**, **France** and **China**. There are a further **10 non-permanent members** that are **elected** by the General Assembly for **two years** at a time. • The Security Council is the **only body** that can pass **binding resolutions** in areas of **international law** such as **military intervention** and **economic sanctions**. For this there needs to be a **two-thirds majority** (9 out of the 15 and **agreement** among the **five permanent members**). **Any P5 member** may **veto** any resolution. • The UNSC can **convene quickly** to deal with any **international issue** or **crisis** that arises. *The 5 permanent members of the UNSC were its founding members. They are known as the P5.*
General Assembly (UNGA)	• The main **forum for discussion** of the UN — but lacks the **power** of the **UNSC**. • It is the main **policymaking** organ of the UN. • It is made up of **representatives** from **all 193** member states (plus **two non-member observer states** — Vatican City and the State of Palestine). • Meets at the **UN headquarters** in New York with the **annual meeting** being held each **September**. • **Resolutions** on designated **important issues** require a **two-thirds majority** to pass while other issues usually require a **simple majority**. Resolutions are **non-binding** in international law. • The UNGA elects the **non-permanent** members of the **UNSC** and, together with the UNSC, is responsible for appointing the **Secretary-General** and **International Court of Justice** (**ICJ**) **judges**. • It also appoints **Economic and Social Council** (**ECOSOC**) **members** and sets the **UN budget**.
Economic and Social Council (ECOSOC)	• Made up of **54 members** who are elected by the **UNGA**. • Promotes **economic**, **social** and **environmental development** among member states of the UN. • Responsible for **coordinating** the work of agencies such as the **WHO** (World Health Organisation), **UNESCO** (Educational, Scientific and Cultural Organisation), the **IMF** and **World Bank**. • Has a range of **programmes**, **commissions** and **funds** such as the **UNDP** (United Nations Development Programme) which **promotes** human **development**.
International Court of Justice (ICJ)	• Successor to the **Permanent Court of International Justice** that was created with the founding of the League of Nations in 1920. It consists of **15 judges** from different member states serving **nine-year terms**. • Adjudicates **international disputes** referred to it by member states. In this way the ICJ **upholds international law**. It has presided over **nearly 200 cases** brought before it since 1945. The ICJ is able to deliver both **legally binding** and **non-legally binding rulings**. • Provides **advisory opinions** on legal questions submitted by **authorised agencies**.
The Secretariat	• The **civil service** of the UN — it **carries out** the decisions of the various **institutions** of the UN and provides their **staff**. **190** of the UN's member states are **represented** among its **staff**. • Led by the **Secretary-General** (**Antonio Guterres** since 2017), who is appointed for **five years**. Someone may serve in the position of Secretary General for a maximum of **two consecutive terms**. • The **make-up** of the Secretariat reflects the **diversity** of the membership of the UN.
Trusteeship Council	• Created to assist the **decolonisation** process after 1945, and to ensure that **newly independent states** were able to manage the **transition** to **full independence**. • The last **trust territory** (out of 11 in total) overseen by the Trusteeship Council was **Palau**, which achieved **independence** in 1994. This left the Trusteeship Council without any **further responsibilities** and so it was **suspended**.

My favourite UN organ is the one the national anthems are played on...

That's a lot of info to take in on those organs. Make sure you know it — we're about to dig even deeper on the following pages.

Global Governance — Political and Economic

Strengths and Weaknesses of the UN

The various organs of the UN have strengths and weaknesses based on their composition, organisation and powers. Understanding these can be helpful for analysing the way that the UN has achieved or fallen short of its goals (p.242-243).

The Security Council can respond quickly but it's not fully representative

Strengths of the UNSC

✓ The **composition** of the UNSC reflected the global power dynamics after the Second World War. Allowing the P5 to have **veto powers** helped to protect their **vital interests** and ensured they **remained members**. The same cannot be said about the **League of Nations** — many states **left** the League during its existence.

✓ The UNSC can **respond rapidly** to crises and pass **binding resolutions** — as it did with **Resolution 1973** against the Libyan government in 2011, sanctioning **military force** to protect the Libyan people from **persecution** by **Muammar al-Gaddafi**.

✓ The UNSC currently reflects **global opinion** by including 10 non-permanent members **elected** from different continents, roughly in **proportion** to the **population** of those regions. This allows major powers such as **India**, **Germany** and **Japan** to often be elected and have their voice heard in the UNSC.

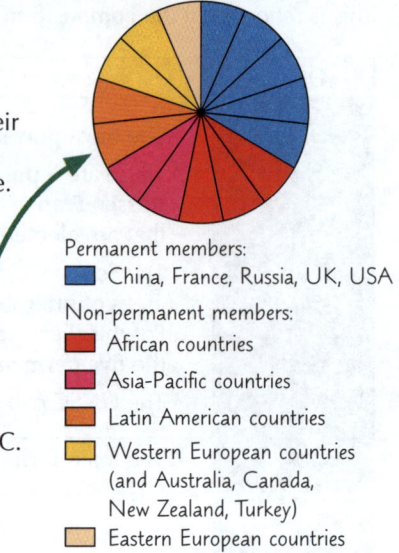

Permanent members:
- China, France, Russia, UK, USA

Non-permanent members:
- African countries
- Asia-Pacific countries
- Latin American countries
- Western European countries (and Australia, Canada, New Zealand, Turkey)
- Eastern European countries

Weaknesses of the UNSC

✗ The **composition** of the UNSC does not **reflect** the world of today — it **preserves** the power of the victors of the Second World War. **P5 members** can **veto** any action taken against them, rendering the UNSC **ineffectual** on matters like the **US/UK** invasion of **Iraq** (2003) or the **Russian** invasion of **Ukraine** (2022).

✗ The UNSC often **fails to agree** on **action** or **avoids** debating **certain issues**. This was the case when the **USA** and **UK** bypassed the UNSC over **Iraq** and when the UNSC failed to act over **Rwanda** (1994) or the civil war in **Syria** (2012).

✗ Some argue the UNSC needs **reform** so that **major powers** such as **Japan**, **India** or **Germany** have a **permanent seat**. The P5 does not include any **African**, **South American** or **Muslim** states. The UNSC is **not democratic** and the inclusion of the **UK** and **France** in the **P5** does not reflect the realities of power today.

The General Assembly is more diverse but may not be as powerful as it seems

Strengths of the UNGA

✓ The UNGA acts as the **global forum** for **discussing** and drawing **attention** to **crises** in the world.

✓ The UNGA is far more **representative** than the **UNSC** as it contains **near-universal** membership. It can reflect the views of **world opinion** — such as approving the granting of **observer status** in the UNGA to the **State of Palestine** in 2012.

✓ The **diversity** of the UNGA membership means that the priorities of the **Global South** (see p.256) are **better represented** than would otherwise be the case if these powers were in the hands of the **UNSC**.

✓ The UNGA has control of the **budget** of the UN and is jointly responsible with the **UNSC** for appointing the **Secretary-General** (the figurehead of the entire UN). These are **key powers** in the running of the UN.

Weaknesses of the UNGA

✗ The UNGA can only make **non-binding resolutions** so lacks the power of the **UNSC**.

✗ The UNGA is **not** as **representative** as it first appears. States are represented by their **governments** (many of which, like **Saudi Arabia** or **China**, are **not democratically elected**) rather than their **people**. There are many **authoritarian states** in the UN.

✗ As the UNGA and UNSC are **jointly** responsible for appointing the **Secretary-General**, the **P5** can use their **veto** powers to block the **appointment** or **renewed appointment** of a candidate. This **reduces** the **influence** that the UNGA has in reality.

> Because of state sovereignty, the UN is only as united as its member states. Disagreements between states often prevent it from taking action.

Global Governance — Political and Economic

Strengths and Weaknesses of the UN

The Economic and Social Council has had great success but may be inefficient

Strengths of the ECOSOC

- ✓ The ECOSOC carries out a wide **range of activities** with its 15 **specialised agencies** and a host of **programmes**, **funds** and **commissions**. These are focused on areas such as **labour rights**, **refugees** and **health**.
- ✓ The ECOSOC supervised the implementation of the **Millennium Development Goals** (**MDGs**), which had a major **global impact** on **development**. Since they were established in 2000, the number of people living in **extreme poverty** has fallen by over **50%**, and **58%** of the **global population** now have access to **safe drinking water** in their **homes**.
- ✓ The **Sustainable Development Goals** (**SDGs**), also overseen by the ECOSOC, **replaced** the MDGs in 2015 and enabled a more **coordinated** global approach to dealing with issues of **sustainability**.
- ✓ The ECOSOC has been able to **reflect** the **concerns** of countries in the **Global South**. The priority for many of these states has been **development**, so ECOSOC has allowed the UN to have greater **inclusivity** than its other principal organs.

*Kelly's development relied on there **not** being goals...*

Weaknesses of the ECOSOC

- ✗ While ECOSOC's **broad scope** enables it to deal with many **global issues** through a range of **agencies**, **programmes**, **funds** and **commissions**, it can be incredibly tough to **coordinate**. This can lead to **duplication** and **inefficiency** as the work of different agencies and programmes **overlap**.
- ✗ Many states **benefiting** from **ECOSOC programmes** are **members** of the **ECOSOC** themselves and suffer from **poor governance** and **corruption**. The **assistance** provided does not necessarily get to those who **need** it due to **governmental inefficiency** or as local officials **misappropriate** funds.
- ✗ ECOSOC's **membership** and the number of agencies it manages have **increased** over time, but **no real change** has been made to its **structure** to accommodate this. This has led to significant **debate** over whether it should be **broadened** further, or **reduced** and **streamlined**.

The International Court of Justice has been influential but its power is limited

Strengths of the ICJ

- ✓ The **decisions** of the ICJ carry significant **moral authority**, leading to a **high** rate of **compliance**. This enables countries to **resolve** disputes **without** the **use of force**.
- ✓ The ICJ has **independently** adjudicated in nearly **200 cases**. The **judges** are appointed from a range of **different states** and are fully **independent** from any **state influence**. This creates **trust** and **acceptance** of its decisions from **UN member states**.
- ✓ The ICJ is able to act in a **wide range** of cases from **border disputes** and **maritime access** to cases involving **human rights**. It is **highly respected**, as the nickname '**World Court**' suggests.

Weaknesses of the ICJ

- ✗ The ICJ deals with **disputes between states** and not cases that involve **individuals** (now dealt with by the **ICC**). Some believe that decisions made by the ICJ can be **influenced** by **geopolitical factors**, often at the **expense** of smaller, **less powerful states**. For example, **Nicaragua v United States (1986)**.
- ✗ **Both parties** involved in a case must **consent** to the court having **jurisdiction** before the case can be heard. The issue of **consent** is a stumbling block **preventing** cases being heard.
- ✗ Just over a **third** of states (**74**) have submitted themselves to be bound by the **optional clause** of the ICJ. Many states **ignore** the rulings of the ICJ as it **lacks enforcement powers**.

Quick Questions

1) Which organ of the United Nations can pass binding resolutions on UN member states?
2) Which organ of the United Nations has been suspended?
3) How many non-permanent members does the Security Council have?

I've not eaten in a while — I'm starting to get UNGA pangs...

UNSC, UNGA, ICJ... sorry, the office cat just walked over my keyboard. Down Brian, down. Anyway, understanding the strengths and weaknesses of all these UN departments will be really impawtant for you in getting through your final exams.

Global Governance — Political and Economic

How the UN Resolves Issues

So we've looked at the UN's aims, it's big important parts, and how they measure up. Now it's time to look at what they actually do to resolve issues. It's a bit more complex than my preferred tactic of 'let's all just have a cuppa and talk it out'.

One of the **main roles** of the UN is to **prevent war**

Initially, the UN envisaged that the use of **collective security** would **preserve peace**, as **aggressive states** would be **deterred** by the **collective action** of UN members if they **invaded** another state.

If a state threatened to **attack** another state, the UNSC could:

- use **non-violent diplomatic measures** under **Chapter VI** of the UN Charter; or
- use **forceful measures** under **Chapter VII** of the UN Charter, including **economic sanctions** or **military action**.

The UNSC was effectively paralysed during the Cold War

- During the **Cold War**, tensions between the **USA** and **USSR prevented agreement** by the UNSC on taking forceful action.
- In response, the UN created a **compromise measure** called **peacekeeping** (not outlined in the **UN Charter**). This allowed the UN to send in **peacekeepers** (dubbed **blue helmets**) to **preserve a ceasefire** as long as the state in question **consented** to UN action.

The UN has a mixed record of success in preventing war

- 👍 Some missions have helped allow **peace** to be brokered and **democratic elections** held, e.g. in **Cambodia** in **1991-3**.
- 👍 The UN **successfully** employed **Chapter VII** measures in liberating **Kuwait** from **Iraqi** forces in **1990-1** and against the **persecution** of the **Libyan people** by their **government**, which was stopped by **military action** in **2011**.
- 👎 Other missions have resulted in **disaster**, such as the '**darkest hour**' of the UN in **Rwanda** in **1994** where the **peacekeeping** contingent was **withdrawn** by the UNSC just as the **genocide** started.
- 👎 The **failure** to take significant **action** over the civil war in **Syria** in **2012** and **inability** of the UN to **prevent** actions by the P5 members in invading **Iraq** in **2003** and **Ukraine** in **2022** underscore the **failings** of the UN.
- 👎 **UN peacekeepers** arrived in **Darfur**, **Sudan** years after the **conflict** began, because the **Sudanese government** did **not consent** to this action from the UN until **2007**. **Consent of the state** is needed before peacekeepers can **intervene**.

As the UN does not have its own army, it is completely dependent on member states providing personnel for its peacekeeping missions.

With my greedy pals I need to use this piece (of cake) keeper...

The UN has had **significant successes** in **reducing poverty**...

1) **Billions** of people have been lifted out of **poverty** since the Second World War.
2) The work of **ECOSOC** and its various **agencies** such as the **WHO** and **programmes** such as **UNDP** (UN Development Programme) have resulted in significant **successes** such as the **eradication** of **smallpox** (1980) and coordinating **action** on **COVID-19** (2020).
3) The creation of **MDGs** and **SDGs** (see previous page) has helped **improve** life chances for many on a range of indices from **child mortality** to primary school **education**.

...but **extreme poverty persists**, especially in Sub-Saharan Africa

1) Some argue that **income and wealth inequality** has significantly widened in recent decades. They believe this is caused by the UN pursuing a **pro-capitalist**, **neo-liberal agenda** through the **IMF**, **World Bank** and **WTO**. Countries like **India**, despite economic growth, have **tens of millions** of people in extreme poverty.
2) **Poor governance** and **corruption** have continued across the world — especially in the **Global South**, such as in **Somalia** and **South Sudan**.
3) **Child mortality** (of children under 15) remains high, with **16 000** children estimated to **die per day** worldwide.

Global Governance — Political and Economic

How the UN Resolves Issues

The UN has tried to defend human rights...

1) The **Universal Declaration of Human Rights** (**UDHR**) was agreed by the **UNGA** in **1948** and has been used to **assess** the degree to which states uphold **human rights**.
2) The UN has agreed numerous **conventions** on **women**, **refugees**, **indigenous people** and **children** to further the **rights** of **marginalised groups**.
3) The **ICJ** has **adjudicated** on cases against **states** regarding human rights, such as the case filed by **Bosnia and Herzegovina** in 1993 alleging **genocidal action** by **Serbia and Montenegro** during the Bosnian war.
4) **War crimes tribunals** were set up over human rights abuses in **Yugoslavia**, **Rwanda** and **Sierra Leone**, leading to **hundreds** of **charges** and **convictions**.
5) The International Criminal Court (**ICC**) was created in **2002** and **125 states** have joined. It can **prosecute** individuals for **war crimes**, **crimes against humanity** and **genocide** — 11 people have been **convicted** so far.

...but it has not ensured their universal protection

1) The existence of **authoritarian regimes** with poor human rights records means that **billions** of people do **not** enjoy the **provisions** of the UDHR.
2) As it is only a **declaration** and not legally binding, **sovereign states** can **continue** to abuse the human rights of their citizens.
3) **Decisions** on human rights made by the **ICJ** can be easily **ignored** as the court is not able to **enforce** its rulings.

Subsidiary agencies like the Human Rights Council (UNHRC) may have dictatorships (such as China) among its members.

> For example, **Israel** built a **security fence** around the **West Bank** in **2004**, arguing it was needed to **prevent** attacks from **Palestinians** and to **increase** Israel's **security**. The ICJ ruled that the construction of the wall was **against international law**. The **General Assembly** adopted a **resolution** advising that Israel **stop construction** of the wall and **remove** parts that had already been built. This has **not** been done.

4) **War crimes tribunals** and the **ICC** have not been used to take legal action against the **USA** and **UK** for **alleged human rights abuses** carried out in **Iraq** or **Afghanistan**. This has led to claims of **selectivity** in the upholding of human rights. It is often **weaker states**, such as those in **Africa**, that have legal action taken against their **citizens** or **leaders** — **not** those from the **great powers** or **superpowers**.

The UN has taken concerted action on the environment since the 1980s

1) The first major success came with the **Montreal Protocol** (1987) that protected the **ozone layer** by the banning of **CFCs** (chlorofluorocarbons), used in **fridges** and **freezers**. The Protocol had a **notable impact** on **reducing** the size of the **holes** in the **ozone layer** above both the North and South Poles.
2) The issue of **global warming** has become the **main focus** for the UN, especially with the creation of the **Intergovernmental Panel on Climate Change** (**IPCC**) in **1988**.

> The **Kyoto Protocol** (**1997**), **Copenhagen Accord** (**2009**) and **Paris Agreement** (**2015**) each laid out plans to tackle the issue. These included setting **emissions targets** for signatories, committing to providing '**climate finance**' for **poorer states** and the aim to **limit the rise in global temperatures** to **1.5 °C** above the **pre-industrial average**.

There have been many criticisms of the UN over the environment

- The UN has been **slow** to respond to the threat of climate change.
- There's been an **upward trend** in global temperatures. For example, **June 2023** to **May 2024** was, at the time, the **hottest 12-month period** on record, averaging more than the Paris target of **1.5 °C** above the pre-industrial average.
- **Sovereignty** has proved a difficult issue. Some states have at times been able to **avoid** having targets set for them (**no developing states**, including **India** and **China**, were given climate targets in the **Kyoto Protocol**) and states can **withdraw** (as the **USA** initially did from the **Paris Agreement**) if they wish to do so.

My Maths teacher always said you could resolve things with trigonometry...
Vectors are far easier than the mess of global politics. There's no simple formula, which makes the UN's job pretty darn tough.

Global Governance — Political and Economic

NATO

Oh no, we're not finished with acronymed organisations yet. First we're looking at one that may be familiar from action films.

The role of NATO has changed over time

1) The **North Atlantic Treaty Organisation** (**NATO**) was formed in **1949** in response to perceived **Soviet expansionism**.
2) NATO originally had **12 members** from **Western Europe** and **North America** but has since expanded to **32 members** by **2024**.
3) There have been **three main stages** in the development of NATO's role.

Stage	Description
1949-1989	• **Lord Ismay**, the first **Secretary General** of NATO, famously explained the role of NATO as *"to keep the Soviet Union out, the Americans in, and the Germans down"*. • The reason for NATO's **formation** in **1949** was **collective security** following the **Berlin Blockade** in **1948/9**. **Article V** stated that an attack on **one** NATO member was to be treated as an attack on **all** members. • NATO concentrated on strengthening its **conventional weapons** and **nuclear deterrence** to **prevent** an attack by the **USSR and its allies** (a group known as the **Warsaw Pact** formed in **1955**). A **nuclear arms race** followed, creating a **'balance of terror'**. This was finally **defused** by the **conciliatory policies** of **Mikhail Gorbachev** (who became **Soviet leader** in **1985**) and the **falling** of the **Berlin Wall** in **1989**. NATO eventually won the **Cold War**. During this period, NATO's role was primarily **military defence**, but also **political** — to **defend states** against the **threat** of **communist expansion**.
1990-2013	• With the **collapse** of the **Soviet Union** there was a possibility that NATO would no longer be **needed**. In response, NATO embarked on **'out of area'** operations to **demonstrate** its continued **relevance**. • NATO **first** used its **military power** in Bosnia in **1994-5**. It conducted **air strikes** to support **UN peacekeepers** against **Bosnian Serb forces** to prevent **ethnic cleansing**. NATO then undertook a mission in **Kosovo** for **similar reasons** in **1999**. • In **2003**, NATO took over **responsibility** for **security operations** in Afghanistan, after the USA and its **allies** had initially **invaded** the region with the aim of **dismantling** the terrorist group **Al-Qaeda**. **Operation Ocean Shield** (2009 to 2016) was undertaken to tackle **piracy** off the coast of **Somalia**. • NATO also **expanded** eastwards, increasing its **membership** enormously to **28 states**, incorporating many former **Warsaw Pact** members and **ex-Soviet states** such as **Estonia** and **Latvia**. During this period, NATO's role seemed to transform into combatting **terrorism**, preventing **human rights abuses**, promoting **regional stability** and conducting **anti-piracy** missions.
2014-present	• In recent times there seems to have been a **reversion** to NATO's **initial role**. • In 2008 **Russia** attacked and invaded neighbouring **Georgia**. In 2014 Russia **annexed Crimea** from Ukraine, while conducting **hybrid warfare** in the east of the country. This was followed by the full-scale Russian **invasion** of **Ukraine** in 2022. • The **failure** of NATO to **prevent** such occurrences and the desire to stop any **future attack** on NATO members has galvanised it into action. In 2024, **Jens Stoltenberg**, the **Secretary General** of NATO, described the formation of an *"alliance of authoritarian powers"*, naming **Russia**, **China**, **North Korea** and **Iran** as the new **threat**. • Despite accusations by President Trump that NATO was *"obsolete"*, **Finland** joined in **2023** and **Sweden** joined in **2024**, and much more emphasis has been placed on **increasing defence spending** by member states to the target of **2%** of GDP. NATO's role seems to have gone back to being **military defence** and **political** in nature.

NATO

NATO has **strengths**...

Expansion
NATO has expanded to **32 member states** and accounts for over **50%** of **global defence spending**.

Flexibility
NATO has proven to be highly **adaptable**. It has **countered** new and old **threats** such as **nuclear warfare**, **terrorism**, **hybrid warfare** and **cyber terrorism**.

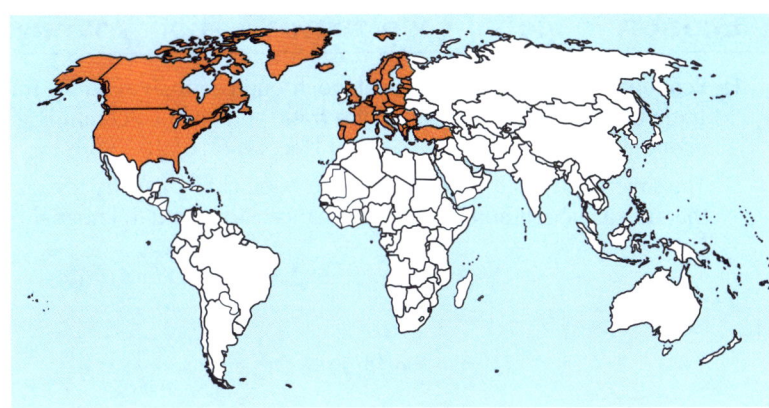

A map showing NATO member states highlighted in orange

Democratisation
NATO **expansion** has also led to **political success**. Many **former communist** and **ex-Soviet** states have been transformed into **stable** multi-party **democracies**. As democracies, they have been able to **join** NATO.

Deterrence
The **nuclear deterrents** possessed by NATO members the **USA**, **UK** and **France** helped to **deter** the **Soviet Union** from using nuclear weapons during the **Cold War**. NATO's **overwhelming military strength** has continued to **protect** it since the fall of the Berlin Wall.

...and **weaknesses**

Over-expansion
NATO expansion has **frightened Russia**, which claims to be **encircled** by NATO expansion. NATO members risk being drawn into a **third World War** in their commitment to **defend** small **new member states**.

Lack of Unity
The **differences** in **defence spending** by NATO member states exposes its **deep divisions**. In 2023, **Poland** spent 3.8% of its GDP on defence but **Luxembourg** only spent 0.72%.

'Free Rider' Problem
Some in the **USA** feel that a few NATO members have become **complacent** and **taken advantage** of **high US defence spending**. The USA has been angered by the fact that many **other NATO members** spend **less than 2%** of their **GDP** on **defence**.

Lack of Success
Afghanistan has been left to the Taliban, **Libya** has become a **failed state** following NATO military action and NATO **deterrents** were **not enough** to prevent **Russia** from **annexing Crimea** and **invading Ukraine**.

Quick Questions

1) What was the first major environmental success of the UN?
2) How many states are members of NATO?
3) How did NATO's role change in the second stage of its development?
4) Which countries joined NATO in 2023 and 2024?

"I'm a huge fan of the strength of neigh-tow"

Exam Practice

Examine the criticisms that have been made of NATO in recent years. [12]

Aaah, November Alpha Tango Oscar. I love their phonetic alphabet...

We use it all the time here at Charlie Golf Papa books. Does make meetings run long though. Anyway, do you think you know all about the changing role of NATO, its successes, its failures and its fancy way of using the alphabet? You do? Bravo...

Global Governance — Political and Economic

Economic Global Governance

Well, that's the organisations in charge of political global governance out of the way — time to tackle the ones in charge of money and trade. Including the incredibly descriptively named World Bank and International Monetary Fund.

Economic global governance is about managing the world's economy

1) **Economic global governance** is done through a range of **IGOs**, **trade agreements** and regional **trade blocs**. The aim is to **liberalise trade** and enable **economic growth** while trying to prevent **economic slumps**, such as the Great Depression of the 1930s.

2) The **sovereignty** of the nation state has been **challenged** by the creation of various **institutions** that **manage** economic global governance. You need to know about these **five**:

   1) the **International Monetary Fund (IMF)**   2) the **World Bank (WB)**

   3) the **World Trade Organisation (WTO)**   4) the **G7**   5) the **G20**

The IMF and the WB date back to the Second World War

The **IMF** and **World Bank** were created at the **Bretton Woods Conference** in **1944**. The **Bretton Woods system** was a **redesign** of the **global economic system** after the Second World War.

- The **Great Depression**, which followed the **Wall Street Crash** of **1929**, was an **economic slump** that lasted more than a decade.
- States had imposed **tariff barriers** on imports to **protect** their industries, leading to a **huge drop** in world **trade** and creating mass **unemployment**.
- This contributed to the outbreak of the Second World War by fuelling **extremism** and **nationalism**. There was a strong desire to **avoid** a **repetition** of this in the future.

The crash on Wall Street, Millom, in 2024 was less catastrophic

The **IMF** and **WB** were tasked with helping to **manage** the **world economic system** but were each given certain **roles** to fulfil (see below and next page). Both institutions have **expanded** and now have near **universality** in terms of **membership**.

The IMF has had four main roles

1) Supervising exchange rates

- Originally, the IMF was responsible for **managing the system of fixed exchange rates** which tied the values of **currencies** to the value of the **US dollar**. The purpose of this system was to provide **stability** for **exchange rates** so that businesses had more **confidence** in being able to **trade** in other **countries**.
- This system was **abandoned** in **1971** and exchange rates have been **free floating** against one another since then. The IMF now plays a **supervisory** role to ensure stability.

The IMF has 191 members, and its headquarters are in Washington D.C.

2) 'Lender of last resort'

- This role involves providing **low-interest** or **no-interest** short-term **loans** to states that are experiencing a **balance of payments crisis**.
- This aims to help the state to recover by **structurally adjusting** their economy so that its **balance of payments** problems are resolved and **debt** reduced. The hope is that providing this assistance **protects** the **global economy** from being '**contaminated**' and dragged into **recession**.
- The **UK** received a **$3.9 billion loan** in **1976** when its government was facing an **economic crisis**. **Greece**, **Ireland**, **Spain** and **Portugal** received loans following the 2007/8 **Credit Crunch**.

Economic Global Governance

3) Surveillance

- Beginning in the **1970s**, this role involves **monitoring trends** in the global economy and **ensuring** that **member states** are carrying out **economically sensible policies** that do not threaten to cause an **economic crisis**.
- For example, in **2022** the IMF warned Prime Minister **Liz Truss** that her proposed **unfunded tax cuts** threatened to **destabilise** the UK's **public finances** and cause higher levels of **inflation**.

4) Technical assistance

Many states lack the **economic expertise** of the **richest** countries. The IMF provides **support** and **advice** over matters such as **economic reform measures** or **tax collection policies**.

The role of the World Bank has changed since it was formed

The **World Bank** was first tasked with helping **reconstruction** in **Western Europe** following the Second World War.

The World Bank has 189 member countries, and its headquarters are in Washington D.C.

Later it concentrated on the **developing world** by providing **low-interest** or **no-interest loans** to fund capital projects to help **improve** their **infrastructure** and **agriculture**.

The focus has since **shifted**, with **less** emphasis on **structural reform** and **more** emphasis on **human and social development**. The World Bank has focused on achieving the **Millennium Development Goals** (MDGs) and the **Sustainable Development Goals** (SDGs), intended to **end extreme poverty**.

Today, the World Bank focuses on issues such as **preventing environmental degradation**, improving **healthcare**, protecting the **rights** of **indigenous people** and promoting **gender equality**. For example, it developed programmes to tackle **HIV**, **TB** and **malaria** and provided **$12 billion** to fund **COVID-19 vaccines** in **78 countries** during the pandemic.

Like the IMF, the World Bank also provides **training** and **advice** to countries to **assist** their **development**. The World Bank makes its **research** on development available to **states** and **NGOs** to learn from.

Quick Questions

1) At which conference were the IMF and World Bank created?
2) Which institution is the 'lender of last resort'?
3) Who received a loan from the IMF in 1976?
4) Which countries received loans from the IMF after the 'Credit Crunch'?
5) What is the name given to the IMF's role of monitoring trends in the global economy and the economic policies of its members?
6) What is the purpose of the loans that the World Bank provides? How does this differ from the loans handed out by the IMF?

The International Monetary Fund is what I call my holiday savings...

Although the IMF and the World Bank started for different reasons, they've ended up playing quite similar roles in global governance. Make sure you understand exactly how they're different, so you don't get them confused during your exams.

Criticisms of the IMF and World Bank

Monitoring and managing the world's economic issues is quite a task, so it's not a surprise that there are many that think the IMF and World Bank aren't doing it quite right. A lot of it boils down to prioritising certain interests and economic models.

Some believe the IMF and World Bank's **voting systems** are **unfair**

1) The **IMF** and **World Bank** give **greater voting power** to the **richest** states as they are the **greatest contributors** to the **lending power** of each organisation.
2) The **structure** of **decision-making** in both institutions means that decisions need to be made with an **85% majority**.
3) **Representatives** of the **USA** account for around **16%** of the **voting power** in each organisation, which means that the USA has an **effective veto**.
4) This has led to **criticism** for a few reasons:

Criticisms
- ✘ The institutions are accused of being **controlled** by the **USA** and their **allies**, with the **Global North** (see page 256) commanding more than **50%** of the **voting power** in both institutions.
- ✘ The institutions are **not** democratic — **developing** countries wield very little **power** in both organisations. This means the institutions reflect the **priorities** of the **richest** states.
- ✘ The **voting rights** of **newly emerging powers**, such as **Brazil**, **China** and **India**, do **not** reflect their growing **importance** in the world economy.

Some believe their **leadership** may lead to **bias**

1) The IMF and World Bank have always had **managing directors** from **developed countries**. The head of the **World Bank** has **always** been from the **USA** and the managing director of the **IMF** has **always** been from **Europe**.
2) The institutions both have their **headquarters** in **Washington D.C.**, leading to **allegations** of **Western bias**.

Some **object** to the **conditions** the IMF and World Bank place on **loans**

The institutions have been accused of adopting the **philosophy** of the **Washington Consensus** (see p.231), where **finance** will **only** be given to the recipient country if they follow the **conditions** laid down in the loan agreement. These conditions formed part of the **Structural Adjustment Programmes**.

Structural Adjustment Programmes (SAPs)

- **SAPs** involved **loans** with **conditions** that required recipient countries to follow **specific** economic policies such as **privatisation**, **public spending cuts** and encouraging **free trade** by reducing tariffs on **imports**.
- These policies aimed to make the recipient country **more competitive** in the **global marketplace** and to attract greater levels of **Foreign Direct Investment** (FDI). This would hopefully **reduce poverty** and stimulate **economic growth**.

In the aftermath of the dinner party, Ola and Kostas reached a washing-up consensus

Criticisms of Loans and SAPs
- ✘ SAPs adopted a **one-size-fits-all** strategy that is not sufficiently **tailored** to the **needs** of the **recipient country**.
- ✘ SAPs **undermined** democracy and **sovereignty** by **forcing** recipient countries to **accept** certain **economic policies**. States like **Greece** had to accept what an **IGO** told them to do.
- ✘ SAPs may do **more harm** than **good**. They often led to sharp **public spending cuts** and **damage** to **public services** such as **health** and **education**, which can **adversely impact** the **poorest** people.
- ✘ SAPs have been accused of being a form of **neocolonialism**, with **powerful** states **controlling** and **exploiting weaker states** and serving the **interests** of **Western TNCs**.
- ✘ Some states that received loans have accumulated **huge debts** and have been weighed down by **interest payments** to the IMF and World Bank, e.g. Jamaica.
- ✘ **Corruption** and **poor governance** in many recipient countries has meant that there has been a **lack of oversight** on whether the money gets to where it needs to.

Global Governance — Political and Economic

Criticisms of the IMF and World Bank

There's debate on the **effectiveness** of the IMF and World Bank

The IMF

The IMF headquarters in Washington D.C.

Successes

- 👍 **Adaptability**, **longevity** and near **universality** of the IMF
- 👍 A record **$140 billion** was distributed to those **in need** in 2022
- 👍 **South Korea** and **India** have benefited greatly from **IMF loans**
- 👍 **Voting rights** are gradually being **amended** to reflect emerging powers
- 👍 **Debt relief** has been granted to many **poor states**
- 👍 IMF has an impact on the **borrowing habits** of states, making them more **self-sufficient**
- 👍 IMF works with **other organisations** and the **EU** to aid members in need (e.g. Greece and Ireland during the 2007/8 Credit Crunch)

Shortcomings

- 👎 **Failed** to **predict** or **prevent** the Credit Crunch or Asian Crisis
- 👎 **Voting rights** do **not** reflect the **economic importance** of the **Global South**, and the **USA** retains an **effective veto**
- 👎 The **Washington Consensus** means that states needing economic help have to adopt **neo-liberal policies** of **privatisation** and **spending cuts** that harm **public services**
- 👎 Loan conditions have often **encouraged** countries to focus on growing **cash crops** to export, but this can **hinder diversification** and make countries **dependent** on only a few types of export
- 👎 IMF loans can be **counter-productive** and actually **harm economies** — e.g. Argentina and Mexico in the 1980s
- 👎 Within-country **inequality** has **grown** and not been reduced

> The Asian Crisis was a financial crisis that occurred in East and Southeast Asia in 1997.

The World Bank

Successes

- 👍 **Adaptability**, **longevity** and near **universality** of the WB
- 👍 **SAPs** were replaced by **Poverty Reduction Strategy Papers** (**PRSPs**)
- 👍 **Loan conditions** are made in **consultation** with recipient states and with **consideration** for local needs
- 👍 **Debt relief** has been granted to many **poor states**

> SAPs were discredited for their neo-liberal, one-size-fits-all approach. PRSPs are more tailor-made to a state's individual needs. However, PRSPs have been criticised for being effectively the same as SAPs in practice.

The World Bank headquarters in Washington D.C.

Shortcomings

- 👎 The WB's policy for avoiding **involuntary resettlement** isn't always effective. For example, groups like the Maasai have been **persecuted** and **evicted** in Tanzania
- 👎 **Large amounts** of **funding** have gone towards **fossil fuel production**
- 👎 **Funding** from the World Bank is **small** compared to what can be provided by **alternative sources** of funding like **China**, **India** and **private investors**

Exam Practice

Examine the criticisms that have been made of the IMF and World Bank. [12]

My big criticism of my bank is that my account is nearly empty...

It's important to consider how the influential figures in an organisation may lead to biases or blindspots. You need to be able to analyse how the structure of a system may affect the judgements that it makes, in both positive and negative ways.

The World Trade Organisation

Another organisation, another acronym. This one deals with managing trade between countries, aiming to make it easier for everyone to enjoy free trade. But whether it's successful, and if its aims are even good for everyone, is a matter of debate.

The **World Trade Organisation (WTO)** was founded in 1995

1) The **WTO** is based in **Geneva**, Switzerland, and originally had **124 members**. Like the IMF and World Bank, the WTO upholds **global economic governance**.
2) At the **Bretton Woods Conference** in **1944**, there was a **failed** attempt to create an **IGO** that managed **global trade**. Instead, the **General Agreement on Tariffs and Trade (GATT)** came into force in **1948** to promote **trade liberalisation** and establish **global trade rules**.
3) **Trade rounds** were held where states would **negotiate** new areas to bring within the **influence** of the **GATT**, to **reduce tariffs** and scrap **subsidies**. The **Uruguay Round** led to the formation of the WTO as an IGO.
4) The latest round, the **Doha Development Round**, began in **2001** but has **stalled** due to **disagreement** over **agricultural subsidies**.
5) **Ngozi Okonjo-Iweala** was elected **Director-General** in **2021**. She is the first **woman** and first **African** to lead the WTO. The leading **decision-making body** of the WTO is the **Ministerial Conference**, which convenes **every two years** and works through **consensus** of its members.

Key Terms

Trade rounds
Negotiations that take place between states to discuss trade rules, tariffs and regulations on a particular issue, e.g. agricultural subsidies or services. It can take many years to reach agreement.

Director-Generals of the WTO can serve two terms. Ngozi Okonjo-Iweala's first term ends in 2025.

Ngozi Okonjo-Iweala

The aim of the **WTO** is to **promote free trade**

- The WTO **promotes free trade** by encouraging members to **reduce tariffs** and **subsidies**. This is in line with **classical development theory** (see p.254) that champions **free market economics** as the driving force behind **economic growth**.
- The WTO uses the **most favoured nation** principle. The **trade benefits** given to the **most favoured** trading member of the WTO must be given to **all members**.
- The WTO acts an **adjudicator** for **trade disputes** between members through its **Dispute Settlement Body (DSB)**.

Here at CGP we use robots as our Dispute Settlement Bodies

The **WTO** has a number of **strengths**...

Growing membership
The WTO has now expanded to **166 members** with many other states, such as **Azerbaijan** and **Uzbekistan**, set to join.

Promoting political stability
Another effect of the expansion of the WTO has been the growing **stability** experienced by **new members**. Former eastern bloc countries have transitioned to **liberal free-market economic systems** and successfully **integrated** into the **international community** with little disruption.

Trade liberalisation
The **impact** of the GATT and WTO has been dramatic. It has led to members being able to **reduce** the **average tariffs** on imports (from 1947 levels), enabling them to **cut subsidies** for nationalised industries. This has helped to **raised standards of living** by increasing **affordability**.

Representative
It is more **representative** than the IMF or World Bank — **two-thirds** of the members are **developing** states.

Comprehensive
Over **98%** of world trade is now under the remit of the WTO.

Resilient
WTO members continued to **trade freely** without resorting to **protectionism** after the 2007/8 Credit Crunch.

Wide range of areas
Nine **trade rounds** have been held so far. These have brought areas such as **legal** and **financial services** and **intellectual property** under the influence of the GATT and WTO.

Global Governance — Political and Economic

The World Trade Organisation

Poverty reduction

Increased levels of **trade** have played a part in lifting **billions** of people out of **poverty** since **1945**.

Economic growth and expansion of trade

The world has been **transformed** since **1945** and **economic growth** has been experienced in all parts of the world. The **value** of **world trade** has **multiplied** around **370-fold** since **1950**.

Resolution of trade disputes

The WTO can act as a **neutral arbiter** in resolving **trade disputes**. Its **rules-based** approach in trade disputes helps **avoid trade wars** or more **serious conflict** between members. Cases involving **Boeing** and **Airbus** and the infamous **Banana Wars** have been heard by the **DSB**.

...and a number of **weaknesses**

Disagreement between WTO members

The **Doha Round** (2001 onwards) has **failed** to reach an **agreement**. There has been a **stalemate** between **developed** and **developing states** on whether there should be **further trade liberalisation**. Developed states use **agricultural subsidies**, such as those provided by the **EU** (via the **CAP**), **USA**, **Japan**, the **UK** and **Canada**. This has seriously **harmed** the ability of developing states to **compete** with these **subsidised agricultural goods**. For example, it is estimated that total agricultural subsidies from the **EU** is around **$50 billion** every year. It has meant that the **future** of the **WTO** is at stake due to the **lack of progress**.

Key Terms

Common Agricultural Policy (CAP)
A policy of subsidies in agriculture used by the EU to keep food prices low and to protect the farming sector. It results in foreign imports (especially from developing states) in agricultural goods being unable to compete.

Mixed results in preventing trade disputes

The WTO has **not always** prevented **trade wars** breaking out. The **Trump administration** imposed **$250 bn** worth of **tariffs** on **Chinese imports** with **China** responding with **$110 bn of tariffs**. There is a fear that **protectionism** may return and jeopardise the **progress** made by the WTO.

Western domination

The **richer states** dominate **decision-making** as they do in the IMF and World Bank.

Lack of democracy

- The WTO is **not democratically accountable** and the **resolution** of **trade disputes** is done in **secret**.
- Decision-making is dominated by the **EU** and **US**.

Protects power over true liberalisation

Some argue that while the WTO presents itself as a **trade liberalisation body**, it actually **upholds** the **power** and **interests** of the **richest** members. It does this by **preventing free trade** in **agriculture** and **textiles**.

Threat to sovereignty

The national **sovereignty** of states is **eroded** by the **WTO** because it is an **IGO** whose **rules** are **enforced** on its members.

Neocolonialist

Some argue that the WTO is an agent of **neocolonialism** like the **IMF** and **World Bank**. The **control** of **trade rules** by the **richer states** allows them to dictate the **terms of trade** in their **favour** and keep **poorer members** in a state of **dependency**.

Focus on trade liberalisation

The WTO's **dedication** to **trade liberalisation** as the **solution** to **economic issues** has caused it to **neglect** other **factors** such as **environmental issues** and **labour rights** which have a significant effect on the economy.

But who's going to help me get a good deal for my shiny trading cards?

I guess this dragon will just have to sit in my collection for now. Anyway, back to the WTO. Free trade faces many similar criticisms to the other international organisations — particularly that it prioritises richer countries over poorer ones.

The G7 and G20

We've moved on from simple acronyms and now we're on to numbers and letters. These aren't fully international, but groups made up of certain countries. Helpfully, the number tells you how many nations are part of the group. Isn't that handy?

The G7 began as the G6

1) The **oil price shock** of **1973** prompted the formation of a new and informal group — the **G6**.
2) The leaders of the **USA**, the **UK**, **France**, **Japan**, **West Germany** and **Italy** first met in Rambouillet in France in **1975** to coordinate a **response** to the **energy crisis**.
3) The G6 then expanded to become the **G7** in **1976** with the inclusion of **Canada**.
4) The G7 comprises the **largest economies** in the **Global North** (see page 256).
5) The G7 expanded to become the **G8** in **1997** with the inclusion of **Russia** — but its membership was **suspended** following its **annexation of Crimea** in 2014.

The G7 tackles political and economic issues

1) Initially the G7 focused on **economic issues**, but this remit has **expanded** to **any** pressing **political** or **economic matter** that they wish to discuss.
2) Unlike the IMF, World Bank and WTO, the G7 is **not** a **permanent organisation** and has **no secretariat** or **headquarters** — it is an **annual meeting** where **leaders** of the **member nations** gather to **discuss political** and **economic issues**.
3) The role of **G7 president** and the **venue** of the summit **rotates annually** between the **member states**.
4) The G7 summits last **three days** and usually end with a shared **official statement** to close proceedings. The leaders of the G7 normally **pledge** to fulfil certain **agreed goals** — but these are simply **declarations of intent** and **not binding** in any way.

Veronica hadn't realised 'bishop to G7' would be such a political move

The G7 has strengths and weaknesses

Strengths of the G7
- Allows global **leaders** from the **richer states** to **discuss** and agree on ways to tackle **urgent matters**.
- **Restricted membership** of like-minded states makes **agreement** more likely.
- Invites representatives from other states to **participate** — the **EU** attends each year and states like **China** and **India** are often invited.
- The G7 leaders can discuss **any issue** they wish, making it a **highly flexible forum**.
- Has had **successes**, such as:
  - The **2005 Gleneagles summit** agreed to **write off** the **$40 billion debt** of **18** poor **countries**.
  - The **2021 Carbis Bay summit** committed members to provide 870 million **COVID-19 vaccines** to poorer nations.

Rishi Sunak and Emmanuel Macron during the 2024 G7 Summit in Italy

Weaknesses of the G7
- **Promises** made by the G7 are **not binding** and can be quickly **forgotten**.
- Sometimes the G7 **fail** to reach an **agreement**.
- No **permanent** organisation or staff to **enforce** the promises made.
- The G7 is very **exclusive**:
  - The G7 does **not** include **major global actors** such as **China**, **India**, **Brazil** or **Russia** as **permanent members** — unlike the G20.
  - Has been accused of being a **club for the rich** representing **over 50%** of **global net wealth** — developing states are not included.
- The G7 doesn't have any permanent organisation and so **lacks** a **permanent structure**. This means there can be a **lack of continuity** in its actions.

Global Governance — Political and Economic

The G7 and G20

The G20 was designed to reflect the changing structure of the global economy

1) In 1999 a new **intergovernmental forum** was created — the **Group of 20** (**G20**). It was formed in **response** to a series of **world economic crises**, such as the **Asian financial crisis** of **1997** and **Russian financial crisis** of **1998**.
2) The G20 focuses on **economic matters**. It is intended to be a **broader** and **less exclusive** group than the **G7** and is considered a **better forum** for dealing with problems of a **global** nature.
3) Its **membership** is comprised of **19 large economies** along with the **EU** and the **AU** (**African Union**, who joined in 2023). It accounts for around **80%** of **global GDP**.
4) The G20 meets **annually** and is attended by the **head of government** or **state** of each member. The **venue** of each summit **rotates** between the **member states**, with the **host** acting as the **chair**.

The G20 has a number of strengths...

1) The range of membership in the G20 means that it is better placed to assume global leadership on economic affairs. It took the lead role in response to the 2007/8 Credit Crunch — coordinating the response with a $692 billion stimulus package. Additionally, the G20 members vowed to avoid protectionism and set up the Financial Stability Board to prevent future crises.

2) Because of its larger membership, it is able to broaden its agenda beyond economics by discussing issues like climate change and the terrorist threats that are significant concerns for non-G7 states.

3) It is more representative than the G7. Inviting Spain, the UN, ASEAN (Association of South East Asian Nations), WTO, IMF and World Bank and others to attend means a diverse range of voices are heard.

4) Provides a voice for developing states and the Global South, which tend to be neglected by organisations such as the G7.

Then UK Prime Minister Rishi Sunak speaking at the G20 conference 2022

...and a number of weaknesses

It can be argued that the **G20** suffers **similar** problems as the **G7**.

1) The G20 doesn't have any power to enforce its promises, so the pledges made in its official statements may not be fulfilled.

2) The G20 doesn't have any permanent organisation. It doesn't have a secretariat or a permanent structure. This may harm its continuity of action from one year to another.

3) G20 membership is exclusive and arbitrary — 174 UN member states are not members, including large economies such as Spain and Poland.

Quick Questions

1) Which IGO performs surveillance on the world economy?
2) For which institutions does the USA effectively wield a veto?
3) Who are the members of the G7?
4) Which institution included the African Union as a member in 2023?

I was gonna have a summit on summat... But I can't remember what...
The G7 and G20 give certain nations a place to discuss urgent issues and work out how they're going to respond. These summits are meant to help them set clear goals and courses of action, but it's up for debate how effective they are.

Economic Development Theories and Poverty

Poverty is one of the biggest economic issues facing the world, so it's a pretty high priority for global governance. Improving economic development is often thought to be one of the main ways to help reduce poverty. The question is, how?

You need to know **three** different **theories of development**

You can use **different theories** of **development** to frame your arguments about how **global economic governance** can deal with the issue of **poverty**.

1) Classical Economic Development Theory

This theory is inspired by the works of **Adam Smith** and **David Ricardo**.

Adam Smith
- In *The Wealth of Nations* (1776), **Smith** argued that growth results from free market **capitalism**, **competition** and **entrepreneurialism**.
- The **profits** made from the **division of labour** and **specialisation** could be **reinvested** in **new technology**, producing a **beneficial cycle** of profit and reinvestment.
- He believed that the **profit motive** would act as an **invisible hand**, allocating resources **efficiently** without the need for **government intervention** (see p.51).

David Ricardo
- **Ricardo** came up with the law of **comparative advantage**. This suggested that states can **benefit** from international trade by **specialising** in producing goods that they can make **most efficiently** and **exporting surpluses** to other states.
- By **specialising** in their **strengths** (e.g. agriculture suited to their climate), states should be able to **increase** their rate of **production**.
- If **every state** does this, rather than trying to make everything they need themselves, then everyone is **better off**.

Classical economic development theory supposes that if states pursue these ideas, their economies will **grow** and **poverty** will **decrease**.

2) Structural Development Theory

As a response to classical economic development theory, **structural development theory** was put forward to argue that **external factors**, such as the **structure** of the **global economy**, can determine whether **development** occurs.

Structural development theory states that **neocolonialism** has created an economic system where **poorer states** produce primary goods for **developed states** and **TNCs**. These poorer states are trapped in this **dependent economic relationship**. As a result, substantial **state intervention** is required to redress this balance.

It has been influenced by thinkers such as **Raul Prebisch** and **Ha-Joon Chang**.

Raul Prebisch
- Writing in the **1940s** about **Chile**, **Raul Prebisch** criticised **classical development theory** as it suggested that **lack of development** was the **fault** of the **poorer states** themselves and not of the **global economic structure**.
- He argued that, **instead of prioritising** trade with **developed states** (especially in **agricultural goods** and **raw materials**), **developing states** should aim to be as **self-sufficient** as possible.
- He suggested that **developing states** should impose **tariff barriers** on **cheap imports** to **protect infant industries** until they were strong enough to **compete** in the **global marketplace**.

Ha-Joon Chang
- Economist **Ha-Joon Chang** carried out **research** into the **effects** that **state interventions**, such as **tariff barriers**, had on countries.
- His **findings** suggested that countries with **greater state intervention** developed **more successfully** than states that were just **exposed** to free market forces.

Global Governance — Political and Economic

Economic Development Theories and Poverty

3) Neoclassical Development Theory

In response to **structural theorists** and **increasing** levels of **state intervention**, **neoclassical development theory** emerged.

- The election of **Margaret Thatcher** as prime minister of the UK in **1979** and **Ronald Reagan** as president of the USA in **1980** meant the ideas of the **New Right** were popularised. These included a **return** to the values of **classical economic theory** in the form of **neoclassical development theory**.
- The perceived **failure** of **state intervention** and **regulation** to promote **growth** in **underdeveloped states** prompted **neoclassical development theorists** to demand the **retreat of the state**. Instead of state intervention, they advocated for **privatisation**, **deregulation**, **reduced public spending** and **trade liberalisation**.
- The **World Bank** adopted these principles in **1980** in what later became known as the **Washington Consensus**. This stated that **market forces**, not the state, **drove development** and the "**dead hand**" of the state needed to be **removed**.

There are **two** broad approaches to **measuring poverty**

1 ORTHODOX MEASUREMENTS OF POVERTY focus on it in purely **economic terms**:

- The **richer** the country is the more **developed** it is, as measured by a country's **GDP per capita**.
- This way of measuring poverty is central in **classical** and **neoclassical development theories**. For the World Bank, people living on **less** than **$2.15 a day** are in extreme poverty. To eliminate poverty, **income** levels need to **increase**. Classical and neoclassical development theories suggest this can be done by following **free market principles**.

However, there are **criticisms** of this approach:

- If the GDP per capita figure increases, the **increases in wealth** may not be **shared equally** by the whole population — it might only benefit the **rich**. So headline GDP figures may suggest that **development** is taking place, but it may also be a sign of greater **inequality**.

"Due to free market principles, no one will mind if I eat this without paying... right?"

2 ALTERNATIVE MEASUREMENTS OF POVERTY use a **broader** set of factors such as **human rights**, **protection** of **indigenous peoples**, **social inclusion** and the **empowerment** of **women**.

- In his book *Development as Freedom* (1999), **Amartya Sen** advocated a broad measure of development. Sen argued that development is related to **freedom** and includes **opportunities** and access to **education**.
- The **Human Development Index** (**HDI**) has been created to better measure poverty. It not only includes GDP but also includes health and education. **Switzerland** ranked as the **most developed** country by this measure in 2022, and **Somalia** the **least**.

One example of an alternative measurement of poverty comes from the **Zapatista Movement** in **Chiapas, Mexico**. Separate from the **Mexican state**, the Zapatista Movement measures **poverty** not just on **income levels**, but by considering the **genuine empowerment**, **gender equality** and **self-governance** of the **indigenous people** in this part of southern Mexico. Communities are **self-sufficient** and **not at all dependent** on **central government assistance** from Mexico City, with their own **health care**, **education** and **agricultural systems**. While from an **orthodox measure** they may appear to be **below** the **poverty line**, this is **not necessarily** the reality for the **people living in** these communities.

Exam Practice

Examine the main arguments of neoclassical development theory and structural development theory. [12]

Neon Classical Development theory involves a lot of fluorescent columns...

It's no wonder poverty is a stubborn problem when there are divided opinions on how to measure it. A country's wealth won't always reflect the wealth of its people, so other factors may need to be considered when judging development and poverty.

Theories on the Causes of Poverty

Just like there are lots of different ideas on how to measure poverty, there are also different thoughts about the root causes of poverty. Some put it down to fundamental inequalities between the different groups in our economic systems.

There are **many theories** on the **causes** of **poverty**

The North-South Divide

In 1980 and 1983 former West German Chancellor **Willy Brandt** produced reports titled the **North-South Divide**.

- These reports examined the **persistence** of poverty and concluded that the world was **divided** between the **Global North** and **Global South**.

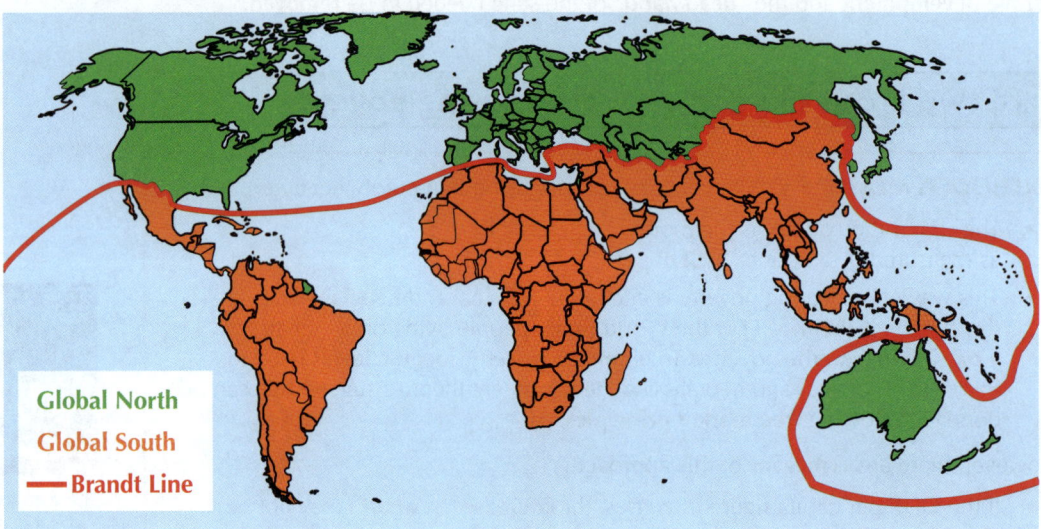

Global North
Global South
—— **Brandt Line**

- The **Global North** was **developed** due to earlier **industrialisation**. The **Global South** was less developed and **poorer**, **exporting** agricultural products and raw materials, which made it **dependent** on the Global North.

- The **Global North** was the source of **aid**, **TNCs** and **foreign direct investment** for the **Global South**, which suffered from **corruption**, **poor human rights** and **instability**.

- Brandt's argument was **supported** by the fact that some of the **richest** states **grew exponentially** from the early **1960s** to the early **2000s**, while some of the **poorest** states experienced **very little growth**.

Criticisms

The **North-South Divide** has been criticised for being **inaccurate** and **out of date**.
- The '**Brandt Line**', which divides the Global North and Global South, running mainly at approximately **30 degrees north** of the equator, seemed **arbitrary**.
- The **inclusion** of states such as **Australia**, **New Zealand** and, by some measures, **Singapore** drew **criticism** as although they are **geographically** located in the **Global South**, they are treated as being part of the **Global North**.
- Many states considered to be **disadvantaged** in the Global South have achieved **exceptional growth** over the last 40 years. **China** now has the **second largest** economy in the world and **India** and the 'Asian Tiger' economies have at times recorded **double-digit growth rates**.
- Meanwhile, many states have performed **poorly** since the demise of the **Eastern Bloc** (in particular **Moldova** and **Ukraine**) but are treated as being part of the **Global North**.
- However, it is true that many states in **Sub-Saharan African** countries appear **trapped** in the situation that Brandt described over 40 years ago.

"I flew all the way to Australia for winter, but I'm still in the Global North?"

Global Governance — Political and Economic

Theories on the Causes of Poverty

Dependency Theory

This theory emerged in the 1940s thanks to the work of **Raul Prebisch** and **Hans Singer**. To **escape dependency** on richer states, **developing states** needed to **protect** themselves from the **cheap exports** of the developed countries and to use **tariffs** to protect their developing industries.

- According to this theory, the **structural imbalances** in the **global economic system** resulted from **colonialism**. These imbalances then continued due to the **neocolonial policies** of the developed states.
- The **developing states** make up the **periphery**, with **resources** and **wealth** flowing to the **developed states**, who make up the **core**. This replicated the situation present during the **colonial era**. As a result, the **periphery** remained **structurally dependent** on the **core**.
- **Dependency Theory** is a **rejection** of the **Modernisation Theory** posed by **Walt Rostow**. Rostow's theory argued that states would **inevitably** become **developed states** if they followed the **five stages of transition** from an **agriculture-based society**.

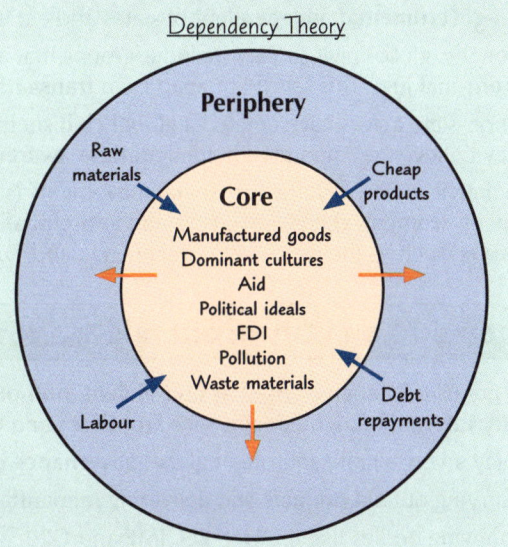

Criticisms

Policies **based** on the **theory** have been criticised for leaving developing states **poorer**. This occurs through actions such as:
- subsidising **inefficient** industries,
- **artificially** making prices **higher** by putting **tariffs** on **foreign imports**,
- placing developing countries in **debt** as they could not afford these measures.

World-Systems Theory (WST)

In 1974 **Immanuel Wallerstein**, a neo-Marxist, developed his explanation for the continuation of poverty. He said that the world was not divided but formed **one single system connected by economic relations**.

- Wallerstein said there were **three types of state**: the **core**, the **semi-periphery** and the **periphery**.
- The development of **capitalism** since the seventeenth century meant that **core** states developed due to extracting **surplus value** from the states in the **periphery**.
- **Semi-periphery states** have some aspects of **industrialisation**, but are not as advanced as the core states. They are **dominated** by the **core states** but **dominate** the **peripheral states**.
- **Free trade** allows **core states** to make use of **cheap labour** and raw materials from **peripheral states** and carry out **economic dumping** of cheap manufactured goods to those **peripheral states**. This leaves the **periphery** at the mercy of **neocolonial control** by the **core** states.
- The **dependency** of **peripheral states** on **economic aid** from **core states** maintains the **subservient position** of peripheral states (e.g. **Mozambique** receiving $300 m from the **World Bank** in **2022**).

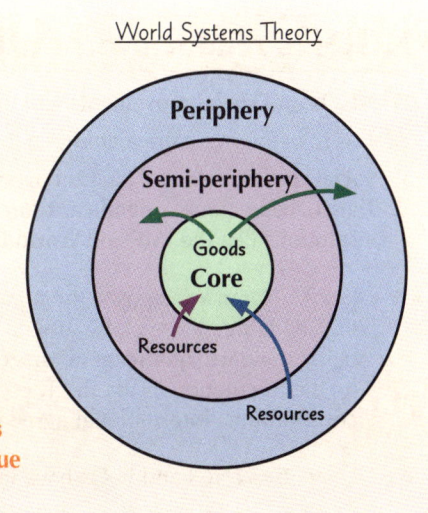

Criticisms

- Some argue **WST** is far too **simplistic** in its view by pigeon-holing countries as being simply **core**, **semi-periphery** or **periphery** states.
- Similarly, some argue that the rise of states like **China** and **India challenges** the view that it is merely **developed** states that are able to reach a **full** stage of development in a **global capitalist system**.

Independent International Bodies

It's not only groups and coalitions of states that can act at an international level. More and more you can see businesses, charities and other organisations working and exerting their influence across the world.

Global civil society describes independent bodies that act internationally

1) **Global civil society** consists of **non-state actors** in the international system that are **non-governmental**, **independent** of states and act **internationally**.
2) Traditionally, global civil society includes groups that are **private**, **self-governing**, **voluntary** and **non-profit-making**. This sets them apart from **transnational corporations** (**TNCs**), which are profit-making.
3) These non-state actors have created a **global civil society** by **campaigning** on issues that they believe are important, helping to **raise awareness** of them globally.
4) A global civil society can include **social movements** (such as the **green** movement, **women's rights** movement and **anti-globalisation** movement) and **NGOs** (such as the Red Cross, Greenpeace and Oxfam).

Unlike IGOs, NGOs are not made up of states.

NGOs tend to be non-profit and work with global governance organisations

1) **NGOs** are usually characterised as **non-violent**, **non-profit** bodies such as **Amnesty International**, **Médecins sans Frontières** and **Greenpeace**.
2) They play a very significant role in **global governance organisations**:
   - by carrying out **aid projects** and delivering **humanitarian** work
   - by **lobbying** bodies like the **UN**, **EU**, **IMF** and **G20**
3) There is **controversy** around the **effectiveness** of NGOs. In her book *Dead Aid* (2009), **Dambisa Moyo** claims that **economic aid** removes the **incentive** to become **self-reliant** while rewarding **corrupt** and **unaccountable** state leaders.

There are now over 8000 NGOs in operation.

TNCs are non-state actors

1) The term **non-state actors** (**NSAs**) is not just restricted to TNCs but incorporates **NGOs**, **religious groups**, **terrorist organisations** and **international criminal gangs**.
2) It has been estimated that there are now **over 75 000** TNCs controlling **over half** of world trade. Examples include Walmart, Apple, Amazon and HUAWEI.
3) It is unclear if the **rise in TNCs** demonstrates that **states** are **declining** in significance. A **quarter** of the TNCs ranked in the Forbes 500 are **state-controlled** and many of the largest economies in the world, such as the USA and China, house the **headquarters** of various TNCs. **China** is home to the **largest number of TNCs** ranked in the Forbes 500 (142), with the USA on 135.

NGOs, social movements and TNCs have significant influence on politics

1) **NGOs** and **social movements** aim to **improve society** globally and have **specific goals** that they want to achieve.
2) This may involve **campaigning** on their chosen issue, **direct action** and publishing **reports** calling for international action.
3) **Social movements** and **NGOs** have **multiplied** in number in recent decades. They have become a **significant force** in **global politics** and work to **persuade** institutions like the **IMF** and **World Bank** to **alter** their **policies**.

> In 1972 **Oran Young** used the phrase '**mixed actor model**' to describe the changing nature of the international system. Instead of **states** being the only **significant actors**, other entities could wield **influence** on the international system. These actors could be **institutions**, **corporations**, **international agreements** or **social movements**.

4) Like NGOs, **TNCs** and **IGOs** have **increased** in numbers.
5) Social movements, NGOs and TNCs have a **significant** (and growing) **influence** on the international system, but there is **controversy** over their impact on **poverty**, **human rights**, **conflict** and the **environment**.

Sandra may have been the lead but Iona knew that she was the most significant actor...

My production of 'UN: The Musical' failed because I hired non-state actors...

While a lot of global governance is carried out by states and the organisations they've formed, it's important to remember that independent organisations are able to exert their influence on a global scale too. Be sure to consider them in your analyses.

Global Governance — Political and Economic

Realism and Liberalism in Global Politics

Realism vs. Liberalism — a heavyweight rivalry for the ages about to get renewed on this page. To learn more about this epic rivalry, have a read through the Global Politics Comparative Theories section on pages 294 to 297. Ding! Ding! Ding!

Realists and liberals have **different ideas** about the **UN**

There are a number of areas of **disagreement** between **realists** and **liberals** over the operation of the **United Nations**.

	Realist views	Liberal views
War	**Realists** argue that the UN's recent **failures** in **Ukraine**, **Sudan**, **Gaza** and **Lebanon** are grounds for **scepticism** over its ability to **resolve conflicts**. They expect that the UN is **doomed** to **fail**, as they see **war** as **inevitable** in the **international system**.	**Liberals** see the UN as a **key mechanism** for **conflict resolution**, citing the **success** of the UN in **preventing** a **third World War** and many successful **peacekeeping operations**.
State sovereignty	**Realists** believe that the UN is **dominated** by **sovereign member states** who uphold the **Westphalian principle** of **non-interference** (see p.230), which **undermines** the UN's capacity to tackle **international issues**.	**Liberals** believe that **cooperation** between **states** can allow **humanitarian interventions** and **peacekeeping** to take place.
Security Council	For **realists**, the existence of the **Security Council** ensures **structural power** has been **retained** by the **P5**, with their **veto** acting as a **convenient protection** of their **interests**.	**Liberals** believe that the **Security Council** acts as a **forum** for **dispute resolution** as well as a **platform** for **intervening** in **common areas** of **concern**.
Reform	**Realists** argue that the **lack of reform** of the UN (especially on **membership** of the **Security Council** — see p.240) reveals that its **primary purpose** is to **defend** the **interests** of the **most powerful states**.	**Liberals** argue that the UN has been **reformed**, with **Security Council membership** increasing from **9** to **15** and the UN **successfully responding** to **new challenges** such as **climate change**.

They are **divided** over other **IGOs** too

Realists and **liberals** are also **deeply divided** over the **existence** of **IGOs** and their **likelihood** for **success**.

- On **Bretton Woods institutions** like the **IMF**, **World Bank** and **WTO**, **realists** argue that they have just helped to **preserve western structural dominance** in **global economics**. **Liberals** argue that these institutions have **successfully** performed the role of **global economic governance**, **averting** a repeat of the **economic disaster** of the **Wall Street Crash** in **1929**.
- **Realists** consider **NATO** to be a **successful organisation**, but, like any alliance, they **expect** that it will **ultimately collapse** due to **growing tensions** and **diverging interests** between its members. **Liberals** view NATO as more of a **political body** than an **alliance** of states, with the **promotion** of **common values** of **democracy** and **human rights** being **instrumental** in its **future success**.
- **Realists** see the **creation** of the **G7** and **G20** as **concentrating power** in the hands of the **richest states**, allowing those states to **dominate** the **global agenda**. **Liberals** see the formation of these organisations as a **recognition** of the **limits** of a **single state** and the need for **greater cooperation** to achieve **common goals**.

They also **differ** on the **nature** of **global politics**

Realists believe that **global politics** is **dictated** by the **demands** of **relative gains** — in an **anarchic world** a state's **relative position** compared to **others** is of **central importance**. This aligns with the **billiard ball model**.

For **liberals**, **absolute gains** are **more important**. The **cobweb model** means that states are **connected closely** to one another and have **mutual interests** that mean the **relative position** of one state compared to others is **not** as **significant** as whether a state is becoming **more prosperous** over time. For this reason, states are **not** in a **destructive struggle** to achieve **hegemony** but can **all develop** and **grow** at **different rates** — **mutual growth** is **beneficial** to **all**.

> **Key Terms**
>
> **billiard ball model**
> *A model of global politics that sees states as independent actors, imagining them as billiard balls of different sizes. The stronger the state, the bigger the ball, and the more likely it is to get its way.*
>
> **cobweb model**
> *A model of international relations that says that states are not independent actors, but are connected by bonds of trade, investment and common interests.*

If you're a realist about the UN, does that make you an unrealist?
The realist/liberal divide comes up a lot in global governance. Keep these differences in mind as you read the other sections.

Global Governance — Political and Economic

The ICJ, ECHR and ECtHR

I hope you like acronyms, because these next few pages are full of them. These ones relate to international law and rights.

International law is meant to bring order and stability between states

International law is a collection of **rules** governing relations **between states**.
It has **evolved** over time to encompass areas as diverse as **trade**, **war**, **maritime law** and **postal services**.

- International law is **uncodified** because it's not contained in a **single document**. It is contained in numerous sources such as **treaties**, **international custom** and **legal writings**.
- **Modern international law** has its roots in the **UN Charter** (see page 239) written in 1945, which created the **International Court of Justice** (**ICJ**) based in **The Hague**. The ICJ is the UN's **judicial organ**.

The International Court of Justice resolves disputes between states

1) The ICJ establishes a **rules-based** approach to international affairs and has **two** main purposes:

   - To give rulings to **settle disputes** in cases brought by member states.
   - To give **non-binding advisory opinions** to UN bodies and agencies that request them.

   Have a look at p.239 and p.241 for more about the ICJ.

2) The legitimacy of the ICJ comes from its **universal membership** (all UN states are involved and may bring cases to it).
3) The ICJ has played an important role in helping to **maintain peace**. It is seen to have **moral authority** and has adjudicated in nearly **200 cases**. Its **rulings** have been largely **accepted**.
4) However, the ICJ has been **criticised** for lacking powers of **enforcement**. It relies on states **submitting** to its authority and its rulings can be **ignored**. Although the **Security Council** can take action to **enforce** ICJ rulings, it has **never** actually done so. The ICJ also relies on **states** bringing cases to the court — it is **reactive**, not **proactive**.
5) Only **74 states** have signed the **Optional Clause** of the ICJ **submitting** to its jurisdiction, with states such as the **USA** and **Israel declining** to sign. For example:

   119 states have not signed the Optional Clause.

   - In **Nicaragua v USA** in **1986** the **USA refused** to acknowledge the jurisdiction of the ICJ when it ruled that the **USA** had **violated international law** by **mining** the ports on the Nicaraguan coast.
   - In **2004**, the advisory opinion of the ICJ was **ignored** when it ruled that a **wall** built by **Israel** along the border of **Palestinian** areas was **illegal**.

The ECHR and the ECtHR provide rights protection in Europe

EUROPEAN CONVENTION ON HUMAN RIGHTS (ECHR)	EUROPEAN COURT OF HUMAN RIGHTS (ECtHR)

• The **ECHR** was created by the **Council of Europe** in **1950**, inspired by the **United Nations Universal Declaration of Human Rights** (**UDHR**). The ECHR is an **international agreement** where states commit themselves to **upholding human rights** within their state. It was hoped this would help **prevent** a repeat of the **Holocaust** and other **human rights abuses** resulting from the rise of **totalitarian regimes**.
• **Rights** contained in the **ECHR** include the **right to life** (Article 2) and the **right to a private life** (Article 8).
• The ECHR has contributed to the spread of the **rule of law** and **democratisation** in Europe, especially in former **Eastern bloc** states.
• There are **restrictions** to the ECHR's **jurisdiction**:
  1) **Belarus** is not a signatory, nor is **Russia** since it was **expelled** from the Council of Europe following its invasion of **Ukraine**.
  2) Some in the **Conservative Party** have wanted the UK to **withdraw** from the ECHR because of its impact on **national sovereignty**.
	• The **ECtHR** was created in 1959 to hear cases brought by **citizens** from member countries who felt that their **human rights** were not being **upheld** in their own **country**.
	• The **majority** of European countries have joined the **Council of Europe**, allowing around **700 million citizens** to bring cases to the **ECtHR**.
	• The creation of the **ECtHR** has meant that **European citizens** have enjoyed a **greater** degree of **protection** of their **human rights** than people in many other parts of the world. Human rights law has continued to **evolve** in areas such as **women's**, **transgender** and **gay rights**. The growth of a **rights-based culture** in the UK has led to **greater compliance** with the rulings of the ECtHR.
	• However, the **ECtHR** lacks the power of **enforcement** to ensure that rights are upheld across Europe — it's **powerless** if states decide to **withdraw**. The power of states to **ignore** its rulings shows the continued importance of **sovereignty**.

Enforcing and Protecting Human Rights

After the many human rights abuses of the first half of the 20th century, it was clear that human rights needed protecting. So the UN got cracking on how to measure human rights abuses, and how to bring the abusers to justice.

The UDHR has set out standards for states to be measured against

1) The **Universal Declaration of Human Rights** was signed by members of the **United Nations** in **1948**. In reaction to the horrors of the **Holocaust** and other **human rights abuses** during the **Second World War**, member states created a document that stated **30 human rights** that people were **entitled** to.
2) The UDHR led to the **development** of further human rights protections:
   - The signing of the **International Covenant on Civil and Political Rights** and **International Covenant on Economic, Social and Cultural Rights** together with the **UDHR** formed the **International Bill of Human Rights** in 1966.
   - The creation of **UN Special Tribunals** and the **ICC** were also direct consequences of the UDHR.
   - Many other **conventions** have been agreed by the **UN General Assembly** aiming to uphold the rights of groups of people, such as for **women**, **children** and **refugees**.
3) However, the UDHR is **not** binding **international law** — it's a **declaration** by the UN General Assembly. States such as **Saudi Arabia** did **not** sign it, and **state sovereignty** means that states can act in **whatever way they wish** in relation to their citizens.

UN Special Tribunals were created to bring individuals to justice

1) After the **Second World War**, the victorious powers brought **leading figures** from **Nazi Germany** and **Imperial Japan** to **trial** at the **Nuremberg Trials** and **Tokyo War Crimes Tribunal**. Many individuals were **executed** or **imprisoned** as a result.
2) The attempt to bring individuals who committed **war crimes** or **crimes against humanity** to **international justice** diminished with the onset of the **Cold War**. The UN became **paralysed** as the superpowers could **not agree** on which state leaders should be **prosecuted**. As **permanent members** of the Security Council, countries like the **USA** and the **USSR** could use their **veto to block proposals** for prosecuting state leaders, resulting in **stalemate**.
3) It wasn't until **1993**, following the end of the **Cold War**, that the first **UN Special Tribunal** was set up. As a result of **ethnic cleansing** carried out in **Yugoslavia**, the UN created the **International Criminal Tribunal for Yugoslavia (ICTY)**.
4) This was followed by two more Special Tribunals — the **International Criminal Tribunal for Rwanda (ICTR)** and the **Special Court for Sierra Leone (SCSL)** — which were created due to the **genocide** and **crimes against humanity** that had been perpetrated in those regions.
5) These tribunals spent over **20 years** collating **evidence** and tracking down **suspects**. It led to **publicity** for the crimes, **accountability** for perpetrators and **justice** for victims.
6) It was hoped that the **conviction** of **state leaders** such as **Charles Taylor** (Liberia) and **Jean Kambanda** (Rwanda) for their crimes would serve as a **deterrent** to others in future.

This wasn't what Carlos expected when he signed up for Cold War reenactment

Criticisms of UN Special Tribunals

UN Special Tribunals have been **criticised** for being **too**...
- ...**geographically specific**: it was only **Yugoslavia**, **Rwanda** and **Sierra Leone** that were the subject of **investigation** in the tribunals. The **jurisdiction** did not extend to any **other part** of the world.
- ...**time-specific**: the tribunals only investigated **human rights abuses** specifically at the times in question. E.g. It only investigated abuses in **1992-5** in **Yugoslavia** and not alleged abuses in **Kosovo** in **1999**.

Allegations were raised of **victors' justice** — that **weaker states** were being **targeted** by Western states to forward their **geopolitical priorities** and that this **undermined** the **legitimacy** of the tribunals.

There were also problems in **bringing suspects to court**:
- It took **over a decade** for **Radovan Karadzic** and **Ratko Mladic** to face trial having remained at large in **Serbia**.
- **Yugoslav** President **Slobodan Milosevic** died before the court could **conclude** its proceedings.

The tribunals involved **huge expenditure** and **coordination**, with **suspects**, **victims**, **witnesses** and **documents** being transported to **The Hague** or **Arusha** in Tanzania for hearings.

Global Governance — Human Rights and Environmental

Enforcing and Protecting Human Rights

The ICC was established as a permanent court for trying individuals

1) While the UN Special Tribunals have had some success, they had a limited remit and were reactive. The Rome Statute of 1998 proposed the creation of the International Criminal Court (ICC) — this was intended to be a permanent, proactive court to uphold human rights universally. The ICC was formed in 2002, after 60 states ratified the Statute. 124 state parties had joined by 2024.

2) The ICC is able to investigate alleged human rights abuses and its Chief Prosecutor (or the UN Security Council) can then issue indictments charging individuals with war crimes, crimes against humanity and genocide. The aim of the organisation is to bring perpetrators to justice and to deter others from committing human rights abuses. The court has convicted 11 people so far.

Criticisms of the ICC

1) The membership of the ICC has grown significantly since 2002, but it still lacks universality. Despite there being 124 members (equating to around 30% of the world's population), there are 69 states that remain outside the jurisdiction of the ICC including the USA, China, Israel, India and Russia. These states have raised concerns about sovereignty (see below).

2) The ICC has also faced allegations of racism as all the people convicted have been from Africa. This has led to Burundi leaving the ICC due to this alleged unfair targeting of weaker states.

3) The ICC has at times been unable to enforce its will:
   - Despite issuing indictments against the former President of Sudan, Omar al-Bashir, on charges of war crimes, genocide and crimes against humanity, no arrest or trial followed. Similarly, Vladimir Putin has not been brought before the court, showing its limited power — especially when dealing with a UN Security Council member.
   - The ICC has also failed to gain cooperation from its various member states who failed to hand over Omar al-Bashir when he was visiting their country, e.g. South Africa.

Human rights and sovereignty can be directly in conflict

1) Since the Treaty of Westphalia in 1648, a key principle of the international system has been non-interference. All states are equal and entitled to absolute authority within their borders and to exert full control over their citizens. A universal notion like human rights (applying to all people equally) goes against this principle.

2) Sovereignty has been a major stumbling block in achieving progress in the field of human rights. States can justifiably argue that they are completely within their rights to pursue whatever policies they wish — as independent states they have complete autonomy. This means that states are not forced to follow the UDHR.

Quick Questions

1) Which international court hears disputes between states?
2) Name one state that has not signed the Universal Declaration of Human Rights.
3) UN Special Tribunals were set up to hear cases involving war crimes committed in which three states?
4) How many states have joined the International Criminal Court?

Exam Practice

Evaluate the extent to which the work of the ICC and ICJ differs. [12]

Practise writing essays or your exams will be a (Treaty of West) failure...

There are a lot of treaties and documents and organisations to learn when it comes to human rights, so make sure you've got them all straight in your head. It might be an idea to rustle up some flashcards to help you match each one to its purpose.

Global Governance — Human Rights and Environmental

Humanitarian Intervention

Despite all the deterrents, human rights abuses still occur. And sometimes other countries decide to step in.

Humanitarian intervention is forcible action to try to improve people's lives

1) The **central argument** for **humanitarian intervention** is that, in certain circumstances, the **international community** must use **military action** to **uphold** the human rights of citizens where they are being **abused** or **not protected** by their own government. However, humanitarian intervention is extremely **controversial**.
2) The **number** of humanitarian interventions **increased** following the **end of the Cold War** as there was **less gridlock** in the UNSC — these interventions had **mixed results**.
3) Although they led to some **short-term achievements**, the **effectiveness** over the **longer term** has been questioned.

	Details of the intervention	Questions of effectiveness
Northern Iraq 1991	• The UN Security Council Resolution 688 declared that Iraq must stop repressing its own civilians. • The USA, UK and France used this as a pretext to establish a no-fly zone (NFZ) in Northern Iraq, following their liberation of Kuwait in 1991. • The aim was to prevent Saddam Hussein's forces targeting fleeing Kurdish civilians with air strikes following the use of poison gas in places such as Halabja in 1988.	• While an NFZ was established, Iraqi ground forces were still able to enter Kurdish regions. • The NFZ lasted for 12 years and, during this time, bombing raids by the USA, UK and France killed an estimated 1400 civilians. • The intervention did not address the root causes of the problem — Saddam Hussein remained in power until 2003.
Somalia 1992	The US government deployed troops to Somalia to support a UN operation to resolve the disputes between fighting warlords and end the civil war.	• Following the killing of 17 troops in Mogadishu, President Clinton withdrew US forces, who were soon followed by the remaining UN forces (although there has been ongoing US activity in Somalia since). • Somalia has largely been left as a failed state, leading to continued civil war and piracy taking place off the Somalian coast.
Kosovo 1999	• NATO launched a 78-day air war in response to the ethnic cleansing of Kosovans in southern Serbia. Hundreds of thousands of Kosovan refugees fled to Albania. • The decision of Slobodan Milosevic to cease military operations in Kosovo led to NATO peacekeepers occupying the region and the repatriation of many of the Kosovan refugees to the area. The NATO peacekeepers (KFOR) jointly keep the peace with the UN peacekeeping force (UNMIK).	• The intervention in Kosovo led to a protracted dispute between Kosovan Muslims and Kosovan Serbs with recriminations on both sides. • The attempt by Kosovo to claim full statehood has also not been universally accepted.
Sierra Leone 2000	• The British government intervened in Sierra Leone to stop militia groups carrying out human rights abuses against its civilian population. • Charles Taylor, President of neighbouring Liberia, was responsible for backing militia fighters that amputated limbs and killed civilians in Sierra Leone. He was convicted at the Special Court for Sierra Leone and given a 50-year sentence.	• The intervention successfully helped to restore order in Sierra Leone, allowing the UN Mission in Sierra Leone to continue its humanitarian and peacekeeping work. • The defeat of militia groups paved the way for democratic elections to be held in the country in 2002. • However, while the intervention helped to secure peace and stability in the short term, it did not address the root causes of the unrest, such as poverty, inequality and corruption.
Libya 2011	• During the Arab Spring of 2010-11, rebel forces opposed to Libyan dictator Colonel Gaddafi seized power in Benghazi. • Consequently, rebel forces around Benghazi maintained their control of the city, in part thanks to NATO air strikes, naval blockades and NFZs, and Gaddafi's forces retreated. • The actions of NATO also allowed humanitarian corridors to be opened up, allowing aid to enter the city. • Eventually, Gaddafi was lynched in Sirte and his regime overthrown by the Libyan people.	• Some states, such as China and Russia, accused the 'alleged' protection of civilians in Libya of being a smokescreen for illegal regime change by Western states. They felt that they had been misled into abstaining on the Security Council vote approving the use of military intervention. • Libya has been left as a failed state and there has been very little action with regard to humanitarian interventions since.

Responsibility to Protect Human Rights

Many feel there is an obligation for others to step in and stop human rights abuses — but this idea isn't so straightforward.

The **Responsibility to Protect (R2P)** gives states a **duty** to **stop** human rights abuses

1) In **2005** the **Responsibility to Protect** was agreed as a principle governing **interventions** by the **UN**.
2) It states that where **countries** are carrying out **abuses** against their **own citizens**, **UN member states** have an **obligation to intervene** and **protect** them.
3) This was the **justification** for the intervention in **Libya** in **2011** when **Colonel Gaddafi's** forces were carrying out **atrocities** against Libyan **citizens**.

Colonel Muammar al-Gaddafi, leader of Libya 1969-2011

The principle of **R2P** raises a number of **problems**

1) It overrides the principle of non-interference

With **R2P**, the principle of **non-interference** (see page 230) would **not stand** in cases where **citizens** of a country were victims of **genocide**, **ethnic cleansing** or other forms of **human rights abuse**.

2) It has often been highly selective

- Some argue that interventions are **more likely** to occur when the **interests** of **Western states** are **threatened** or when the **international community** has not been **divided**. For example, **human rights abuses** in the **Democratic Republic of the Congo**, **Sudan** and **Myanmar** have **not** prompted **Western-led interventions**, but crises in **Bosnia**, **Kosovo** and **Libya** have. Many argue that in **Bosnia** and **Kosovo**, **Western states** were keen to tackle the **worst conflict** and **genocide** since **1945** due to them being in **close proximity** to their states and electorates. Events in **Zimbabwe** or **Sri Lanka** have been further from home and easier to **ignore**.
- The **divisions** in the Security Council have **prevented action**. States such as **Russia** and **China** have been **less keen** to authorise humanitarian intervention, as they value state **sovereignty** and **non-interference** very **highly**.
- Relatively little **media attention** was paid to the **civil war** that broke out in **Sudan** in **2023**, despite the **scale** of the humanitarian crisis rivalling those in **Ukraine** and **Gaza**. Similarly, there was **little coverage** of conflicts in **Yemen**, **Ethiopia**, **Somalia** and **Haiti**. This illustrates how the push for humanitarian interventions has been **selective** in character.

3) It reveals Western hypocrisy

- Despite **vowing** to protect human rights **globally**, there has sometimes been **reluctance** amongst **Western states** to **intervene**. This may be because of the **risk** of such operations for their **incumbent governments**, who may be seeking **re-election** and wish to avoid **negative publicity**.
- Some argue that **Western states** use the argument of **human rights protection** when it **suits** them. For example, **Western states** seemed more keen to discuss the **rights** of the **civilian population** in the case of **Libya** (a strategically vital, **oil-rich** state) than in the case of **Sudan** or **Myanmar**.
- Although claiming to **promote human rights**, Western states have been **accused** of committing numerous **human rights abuses** in **Afghanistan** and **Iraq** following the military invasions in **2001** and **2003**. Some argue this demonstrates their **hypocrisy** when it comes to upholding human rights.

Quick Questions

1) Does the Universal Declaration of Human Rights provide binding international law?
2) Which treaty that strengthened the sovereign independence of states was signed in 1648?
3) What is humanitarian intervention?
4) Give three examples of humanitarian intervention.
5) The principle of Responsibility to Protect contradicts which feature of the Treaty of Westphalia?
6) Give two examples of situations where Western states have failed to intervene to stop human rights abuses.

R2P sounds more like an adorable robot from a sci-fi franchise to me...

Protecting people from human rights abuses on a global scale can be a difficult thing to manage. Whenever a country puts itself in a position of moral superiority over another nation, its own morality and motives are bound to come under scrutiny.

Different Perspectives on Human Rights

When you dig a bit deeper into human rights, you find a lot of different ideas about which rights are worth protecting.

Human rights can be classified into three generations

1) First Generation Rights — civil and political

These rights reflect **individual freedoms** such as the right to **vote**, the right to **life** and **freedom of expression**. They are associated with the rise of **liberalism** in the 17th and 18th centuries, and place **limits** on the power of the **state**.

2) Second Generation Rights — social and economic

These include the rights to **education**, **health care** and **work**. They are associated with the rise of **socialism** in the 20th century and place greater emphasis on the need for **social** and **economic entitlements** to allow people to be **genuinely free**. They require **positive action** by **governments** to ensure **services** are provided by the state.

3) Third Generation Rights — collective (or 'solidarity')

These include the right to **self-determination**, the right to a **healthy environment** and the right to **peace** and **development**. These rights are associated with **decolonisation**, the newly **independent states** that came into being after the Second World War and the desire to have **rights** that applied to **groups** of people rather than **individuals**.

The generations are accepted and enforced to varying degrees

Although the **Universal Declaration of Human Rights** states that human rights are **indivisible** and that the different **generations** of human rights exist, they are **not universally accepted** and **enforced**.

- People on the **right** of the political spectrum tend to accept **First Generation** rights as they place **limitations** on the action of the **state** (**negative rights**).
- People on the **left** of the political spectrum accept and give importance to **Second Generation** rights as they are seen as **positive rights**. They place a **positive obligation** on the **state** to provide **healthcare**, **education** and **social services**. As this requires **taxation-funded spending** by the state, it also results in a degree of **redistribution of wealth**.

There are different perspectives on the concept of human rights

- Some people argue that rather than being **universal**, human rights are a **Western construct** born out of the **liberal values** that are common in the West. The concept of **cultural relativism** argues that the existence of different **cultural traditions** and **diversity** means that you **cannot** have a **universal set** of **human rights**.
- The enormous **cultural diversity** between different regions of the world means that human rights are extremely difficult to enforce. There are **four main perspectives** that are **alternatives** to the prevailing **Western viewpoint**:

  1) ASIAN VALUES — while the **Bangkok Declaration (1993)** supports the UDHR's stance on the **universality** of human rights, it also **emphasises** the importance of **national sovereignty**, **cultural relativism** and that human rights should be considered in the **context** of a country's **historic**, **cultural** and **religious** background.

  2) ISLAMIC VALUES — some countries that pursue **Islamic law** as the basis of their **legal system** (e.g. Saudi Arabia) object to the notion of human rights as it is created by human design rather than being **divinely ordained**. They argue that the teachings of the **Qu'ran** need to be followed rather than any **human-made laws**.

  3) RUSSIAN VALUES — the Western notion of human rights is **criticised** as it is seen as **decadent**. Instead, the **traditional**, **conservative** views of the **Russian Orthodox Church** should be followed.

  4) AFRICAN VALUES — the **African Charter on Human and People's Rights (1986)** was a response to **colonialism** and aims to strike a **balance** between **Third Generation** and **individual rights**. It also acknowledges **cultural relativism**, which allows for **nuanced differences** in values between various **African states**.

Fourth generation of human rights — revision MUST come with snacks...
Remember to consider how and why different people may agree or disagree with protecting different kinds of human rights.

Global Governance — Human Rights and Environmental

Environmental Issues and Climate Change

It's become much clearer as time's gone by that the climate and environment are facing some *gulp* serious problems. It's also become clear that it'll need states to work together in order to start improving things for the environment.

Concern over the **environment** has grown since the **mid-20th century**

1) **Rachel Carson's** book *Silent Spring* (1962) alerted the public to the dangers of the overuse of **pesticides** in agriculture, and its effects on the **environment** (see p.118).
2) By the 1970s, concerns were growing over **pollution** and **acid rain**.
3) The first **United Nations Conference on the Human Environment** took place in Stockholm in 1972.
4) By the 1980s, a **hole in the ozone layer** had appeared over **Antarctica** caused by the release of **CFCs** (chlorofluorocarbons) into the atmosphere. This had potentially dangerous repercussions due to the protective qualities of the **ozone layer** against radiation from the Sun. In 1985 the **Vienna Convention** was created to tackle the problem.
5) The **Montreal Protocol** was signed in 1987. It aimed to phase out **CFCs** that were used in the refrigeration and aerosol industries. The Montreal Protocol was the first truly **universal** treaty on the environment, ratified by **197 states** and the **EU**.
6) In 2003, former UN Secretary-General **Kofi Annan** stated that the Montreal Protocol was "**perhaps the single most successful international agreement to date**".

"There'd better not be any CFCs hiding in here..."

Human-induced climate change is said to require a **global response**

- **Anthropogenic** or **human-induced climate change** is known as a **collective dilemma** — an issue that **cannot** be tackled by one state **alone** but requires **concerted action** internationally or globally.
- In response, the creation of the **Intergovernmental Panel on Climate Change (IPCC)** and the **United Nations Framework Convention on Climate Change (UNFCCC)** marked the first step on the path towards **environmental global governance**.

1) Since the advent of **industrialisation** in the mid-eighteenth century, there has been a **steady increase** in the **global average temperature**.
2) A period of slight **global cooling** appeared to take place between **1940** and the **mid-1970s**, and there were fears over the prospect of a new **ice age** at this time rather than **global warming**.
3) But since the late **1970s** there has been a **discernible acceleration** in the rate of temperature increase, causing the issue to become the **central focus** for **environmentalists**.
4) Estimates suggest that in **2023**, the average temperature had reached a level of **1.45°C** higher than pre-industrial times.
5) The **increase** in production of **greenhouse gases**, such as **carbon dioxide (CO_2)** and **methane**, have been identified as **major causes** of **global warming**. The level of CO_2 found in the **atmosphere** has grown from **280 ppm** in the **pre-industrial** era to **419 ppm** in **2023**.

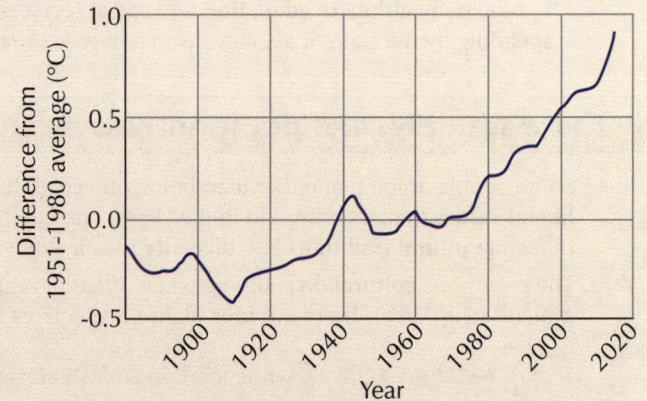
Graph of difference in annual global average temperature from 1900 to 2016 compared to the 1951-1980 average

Exam Practice

Examine the importance of climate change and environmental issues in global politics. [30]
Write an **introduction** to the essay question above. You can use the sentence frames on page 299.

My bouldering partner dumped me — talk about climb-mate change...

Collective dilemmas really help justify the existence of international organisations. Issues of such a large scale need a way for states to come together and take collaborative action to fix them. How successful they have been at this, though, is debatable.

The IPCC, UNFCCC and UN Conferences

Another parade of acronyms to decode in this page. These ones are all for things focused on tackling climate change.

The **IPCC** is a body of the UN and was created in **1988**

1) The **Intergovernmental Panel on Climate Change** (**IPCC**) was created to bring together **scientists** from around the world to **report** on **climate change** and to suggest ways of **tackling** it.
2) The organisation of the IPCC is **intergovernmental** (currently with **195 member states**) to prevent accusations of the body drafting reports that may **favour** certain states over others. Its scientists are drawn from both **developed** and **developing** states, giving it added **legitimacy**. The **UN** ensures that the Panel is **neutral** and produces **objective** reports.

Reports
- The process of compiling reports pools the **scientific talent** and **knowledge** from across the world, making them increasingly **authoritative**. This **expert advice** is used by **states** and other **actors** to shape their **policies** and **actions**.
- The **evidence** that the IPCC finds will determine the **conclusions** in the report. The reports are a **collaboration** between scientists who hold a range of views and so involve a degree of **compromise** over the recommended actions.
  - The **First Assessment Report** by the IPCC was published in **1990** and stated that **human activity** was causing **increased emissions** of **greenhouse gases**.
  - The **Sixth Assessment Report** was produced in **2021-2** and called for "*massive and immediate cuts to greenhouse gases*". The final report, published in **2023**, was a **synthesis** of work done by **three working groups** and involved **hundreds** of scientists.

3) The IPCC was awarded the **Nobel Peace Prize** in **2007** for raising **awareness** about **climate change**. The process of **sharing** and **increasing knowledge** on climate change can be seen as one of its **successes**.

Criticisms
- The IPCC **cannot** force states to **act** on its **advice**, so the IPCC lacks **powers of enforcement**.
- Its various reports have been **criticised** for being **too pessimistic** on climate change and at other times **too optimistic**. **Wide ranges** in projections (e.g. sea level rises ranging from 29 cm to 110 cm) highlight the **uncertainty** about what will happen in the **future** — and therefore **what to do** about it.

The **UNFCCC** was created in **1992**

1) The **United Nations Framework Convention on Climate Change** (**UNFCCC**) was written at the **Rio Earth Summit** in 1992. It was signed by **154 states**, creating a process for future **environmental agreements**.
2) The UNFCCC established "*common but differentiated responsibilities*". For example, it distinguished between **developing states** and **developed states**. As developed states had a **longer history** of being **industrialised**, they have a "*historic responsibility*", as their actions contributed **more** to climate change than developing states.
3) States that have signed the UNFCCC attend a **Conference of the Parties** (**COP**) **every year**. The **reports** of the **IPCC** play an **important role** in informing these conferences. Some notable COPs include the ones held in **Kyoto**, **Copenhagen** and **Paris** (see next page).
4) **Genuine progress** has been made in **global environmental cooperation** since the UNFCCC was created.
   - It had a membership of **198 parties** by **2024**, each of which committed to **reducing greenhouse gas emissions**.
   - The fact that no states have **left** the framework demonstrates the **universality** and **legitimacy** of the Treaty. It has therefore been able to place **pressure** on states to **cooperate** over the issue of climate change.

Criticisms

Critics of the UNFCCC argue that:
- ✘ It has **failed** as states have **not** met their **targets** — **greenhouse gas emissions** have continued to **go up**.
- ✘ It lacks a way to **force** states to keep their commitments, and so it is no substitute for having a **supranational body** that can **compel** states to act in a particular way.
- ✘ **Rivalries** have formed between **developed states** and **developing states**. **Developed** states are set **emission reductions targets** but **developing** states are **not**.
  - **Developed** states argue that this gives **developing** states an **unfair economic advantage** and that the **rapid increase** in **emissions** by those states was **underestimated** by the UNFCCC.
  - **Developing** states argue that **developed** states have been the **historic contributors** to the **rise** in greenhouse gas emissions and so should bear the **costs** of reducing the effect of climate change.

Global Governance — Human Rights and Environmental

The IPCC, UNFCCC and UN Conferences

UN conferences on **climate change** have had **successes** and **failures**

	Successes	Failures
Rio Earth Summit – UN Conference on Environment and Development (1992)	✓ This was the second major summit regarding the **environment** and the **largest** international conference ever assembled at that time (**178 states**). It marked the first time that the issue dominated **global public attention**. ✓ States agreed to the **creation** of the **UNFCCC**, establishing a process of **future action** on **climate change** by annually holding the **Conference of the Parties** (**COP**). **154 states** signed it. ✓ States agreed to **cut emissions**.	✗ The summit **failed** to set **specific goals** for states to achieve. ✗ The lack of **legally binding targets** meant that **developing states** could continue to **industrialise** without restrictions on the emission of **greenhouse gases**. ✗ In particular, the **USA** felt that it gave **developing states an unfair advantage**, as the burden for **cutting emissions** was placed on **developed states**. ✗ The lack of state **accountability** and **monitoring** meant that **emissions** continued to **increase**.
Kyoto Protocol – UN Conference on Climate Change COP 2 (1997)	✓ **192 states** signing the **Kyoto Protocol** was a turning point in global environmental governance. ✓ For the first time **legally binding targets** were agreed for the **37 developed states**. These aimed to **reduce** the amount of **greenhouse gases** that they produced by at least **5.2%** compared to their **1990** level by **2012** (the **EU's** target was **8%** and the **USA's** was **7%**). ✓ A cap and trade **carbon trading system** was created so that states who **exceeded** their **carbon reduction targets** could sell **carbon credits** to those that **failed** to. This **encouraged** states to **exceed targets** and promoted **green technology**. ✓ The **treaty** came into force in **2005** when Russia ratified it.	✗ The ratification in **2005** was seen as **too little too late** given that the Protocol was due to end in **2012**. ✗ **Developing states** were **not** set **binding targets**, which meant that they carried on **industrialising** at **increasing rates**. Some signatories at Kyoto were surprised how **rapidly** these states (such as **China** and **India**) **increased** their **emissions** as a result. Many developed states felt that this meant developing states were gaining an **unfair economic advantage**. ✗ **President Bush withdrew** the **USA** from the **Kyoto Protocol** in **2001**. This was significant as they were responsible for **36%** of **global emissions**. ✗ Critics argued that the cap and trade system allowed **richer states** to **avoid** their **responsibilities**.
Copenhagen Accord – UN Climate Change Conference COP 15 (2009)	✓ The **Copenhagen Conference** tried to create a **successor agreement** to the **Kyoto Protocol**, which was due to expire in 2012. ✓ The **Copenhagen Accord** created a **Green Climate Fund** that would give **$100 billion each year** until 2020 for **green technology** in the **developing** world. ✓ The Accord also included commitments to "**deep cuts to carbon emissions**" and **limiting global warming** to a **maximum** of **2 °C** above the pre-industrial average.	✗ The conference met during the **recession**, so **economic** concerns **dominated**. ✗ **Developed** and **developing** states **clashed** over who was **responsible** for climate change so far, who should pay the **costs** of dealing with **climate change** and whether developing states should now face **legally binding targets**. ✗ The delegates only **took note** of the Accord — **no** new **legally binding targets**, **penalties** for transgressors, details on **monitoring processes** or **specifics** on the **Green Climate Fund** were agreed.
Paris Agreement – UN Climate Change Conference COP 21 (2015)	✓ The **Paris Agreement** was the **first universal legally binding treaty** on climate change. ✓ States set their **own carbon reduction targets** (Nationally Determined Contributions, NDCs), giving them **greater flexibility** and **ownership**. These were to be **reviewed** every **5 years**. ✓ The agreement stated that **temperature increases** should be "**well below**" **2 °C** and ideally only **1.5 °C** above pre-industrial levels. ✓ **Climate finance of $100 billion per year** was promised for **developing states** to move to **green technology** and **adapt** to **climate change**. ✓ The agreement committed to **net zero carbon emissions** by some point between **2050 and 2100**. ✓ **195 states** and the **EU** had ratified it by **2024**.	✗ Concern was expressed over the **level** of the **targets** set by each signatory and the **lack** of **enforcement** mechanisms or **penalties**. The **IPCC** estimated this would result in an **increase** in **global temperatures by 2.7-3.0 °C by 2100**. ✗ Some were sceptical about the **vague promise** of the **$100 billion climate finance**, and about how much **success** states would have in **honouring** their own **emissions targets** (NDCs). ✗ The **vagueness** of achieving net zero emissions somewhere between 2050 and 2100 **decreased confidence** in the **target**. ✗ Under **President Trump**, the **USA withdrew** from the Paris Agreement in **2017**. This was **significant** as the USA was one of the **largest emitters** in the world and **crucial** to successfully **reducing global emissions**. However, **Joe Biden reinstated** the US's participation after he became president.

Competing Views on the Environment

As you might have seen on pages 115-122, people have a lot of strong political views about protecting the environment.

Deep green ecology takes an ecocentric viewpoint

Norwegian philosopher **Arne Næss** coined the term **deep ecology** (also called deep green ecology) in 1972. He believed that:

- Since the Industrial Revolution, **human beings** had placed themselves **above nature** and that was the **root** of their **problems**.
- **Humans** had **no right** to view themselves as being **more important** than any other form of life. Humans were **equal** with **all other living things** on Earth.
- **Environmental problems** could only be **solved** by taking an **ecocentric** viewpoint. This would allow humans to live in **harmony** with other creatures and not view them as being mere **resources**. Other life forms had **intrinsic value** in themselves, and humans should only use other living things to satisfy their **essential** needs.
- **Deep green ecologists** argue that the **current approach** to tackling **climate change** is **flawed** as it seems to be **protecting state interests** and **not** putting the **needs** of the **planet first**. As **humans** are part of the **natural world**, they believe harming **nature** is also harming **ourselves**.

There's more information on deep green ecology on pages 117-118.

Arne Næss (1912-2009)

Næss believed in radical societal change

Næss believed that a **total rethink** of **society** was necessary. His beliefs included that:

- The ideal level of the **global human population** should be around **100 million** to preserve the **ecosystem**.
- **Materialism** and **consumerism** lead to **ruin** and a **richer** life is experienced if humans are **in touch with nature** rather than aiming to own more and more **material goods**.
- There was **no need** for **economic growth**. In fact, the **opposite** was necessary to stop the **greed** of **capitalism** and to **protect** the **environment**.

Shallow green ecology takes a more pragmatic view

1) **Shallow green ecology**, as promoted by **Anthony Weston**, argues that both **economic development** and **ecological protection** can be achieved — they are **not mutually exclusive**. Shallow green ecology is a **reformist** rather than a **radical** theory, aimed at **limiting growth** rather than **reversing** it.

2) Shallow green ecologists believe:
   - **Human ingenuity** and **invention** can be harnessed to develop **green technology**. Carbon dioxide and other **greenhouse gas** emissions **can be cut** without shrinking the global economy if we adopt **eco-friendly** products such as **electric cars**, **heat pumps**, **solar panels** and **wind turbines**.
   - The history of environmental conferences shows it is **possible** to **limit** the **emissions** of **developed** states while allowing the **continuing growth** of **developing** states. **Intergovernmental agreements** (see p.243) can achieve effective **environmental global governance**.

3) Shallow green ecology is more **anthropocentric** (**human-centred**). Other life forms are of **instrumental value** — **resources** for the **benefit of humans** only. Shallow green ecologists promote **sustainable development**.

There's more information on shallow green ecology on page 121.

Brie and Burrata definitely had instrumental value

Sustainable development

- In **1987**, the **Brundtland Commission** sought to **balance** the need for **development and economic growth** in the **Global South** with the need for **global environmental protection**.
- The Commission defined **sustainable development** as meeting **"the need of the present"** without **negatively** affecting **"the ability of future generations to meet their own needs"**.
- Sustainable development would aim to ensure **intergenerational equity** (fairness between generations) as well as **protecting** the interests of **rich** and **poor states**.
- The adoption by the UN of the **Sustainable Development Goals (2015-2030)** demonstrates the importance of sustainable development. These were the successor of the UN's **Millennium Development Goals (2000-2015)**, which had already included sustainable development as the 7th **goal** in **2000**.

For deep green ecologists, radical change is Næss-cessary...
The resistance to radical action is seen by some as a big obstacle to tackling climate change. And speaking of obstacles...

Global Governance — Human Rights and Environmental

Obstacles to International Cooperation

While many of us realise that we need to take global action to ease the damage of climate change, what exactly should be done is a point of contention. Questions over who should shoulder the bulk of the responsibility are hotly debated.

The **tragedy of the commons** is an analogy for how the **environment** is **harmed**

Tragedy of the commons

- Imagine a piece of **common land** that is used by **all farmers** in a village to let their **livestock graze**.
- The **common land** is **not owned** by any of the farmers, so there is **no incentive** for farmers to **stop grazing** more cattle on it. A farmer can gain a **large benefit** from grazing **more cattle** on the land, **without** seeing an **immediate drawback**.
- However, as **more and more** farmers do this, eventually the **capacity of the land** will be **exceeded** and the land will become **over-grazed** and **unable** to **sustain** the livestock of the entire village. This could lead to **famine** and **death**.

Key Terms — tragedy of the commons: Where the self-interested actions of individuals go against the common good and cause a shared resource to be depleted or damaged.

1) In 1968, **Garrett Hardin** (1915-2003) applied the analogy of the **tragedy of the commons** to the environment. In his analogy, parts of the Earth that are not owned by any one individual (such as **oceans**, **the Earth's atmosphere**, **outer space** and **Antarctica**) were the **global commons**.

2) Just as individual farmers would see **no immediate cost** to grazing more cattle, the state sees no immediate cost to having a hundred more **cars** using their **roads**. The state will get all the **benefits** of the hundred extra cars, but they will only experience a **fraction of the drawback** of extra CO_2 emissions being pumped into the atmosphere.

Garrett Hardin summed up his fears as: "Freedom in a commons brings ruin to all".

3) The result is that, just like the **common land**, the **global commons** will become **increasingly polluted** and **exhausted**. This would eventually lead to **tragedy** for **humanity**.

4) There are potential **solutions** to the tragedy of the commons:

Privatise the **global commons**. The **owners** would then have a **clear incentive** to **protect** and **maintain** it.	Use **collective international agreements**. These would put **restrictions** and **protections** in place, but would need to be **approved** by **all parties**.	Put the **global commons** under **communal ownership**. **Rejecting** the idea that **common resources** will inevitably be **exploited**, this would make it a **collective responsibility** to **protect** and **maintain** them. It may **encourage collaboration** with others and **respect** for **nature**.

Self-interest can be another **obstacle** to **international cooperation**

1) While **liberals** believe that states are **willing to cooperate** on **climate change**, **realists** argue that the international system is composed of **states** seeking to **defend** their **interests** and **ensure** their **survival** in a **hostile** and **competitive** world. States are therefore **unlikely** to tackle environmental problems **effectively** in ways that don't immediately **serve** their **own interests**.

2) If a state does agree to **cut its emissions** (as the USA did in the **Paris Agreement**) then it may be **harming** its own **economic self-interest** and **power** and giving an **advantage** to its **competitors**. This was the logic applied by **President Trump** when he **withdrew** the **US** from the agreement in **2017**.

3) It is **very difficult** for states to successfully **reach agreements** on the **environment** due to issues of **trust** and questions of **fairness**. Some states are concerned that other states can become **free riders**. This means a state might **agree** to cut their emissions but fail to keep their word and carry on **industrialising** at the **same rate** as before, relying on **other states** to **compensate** for their **emissions**.

Climate change **doesn't** affect **all areas** of the world **equally**

- Another obstacle to tackling climate change has been the **differential impact** of the problem.
- The most damaging effects of climate change have been concentrated in the **developing world**. For example, **rising temperatures** and **droughts** in **East Africa** and **rising sea levels** threatening **low-lying states** like **Bangladesh** and **islands** in the **Pacific Ocean**.
- Areas that are **less adversely affected** have **less incentive** to act.

Global Governance — Human Rights and Environmental

Obstacles to International Cooperation

It's **not obvious** how to **measure responsibility** for climate change

Per capita vs total output

- **Developing** states may prefer to use the **per capita measure** of emissions. Developed states have **much larger per capita emissions** than developing states.
- **Developed** states could argue that in terms of **total output** of carbon emissions, **China** (**32%** of **global emissions** in 2024) now emits more than **double** the quantity of the **USA** (**13%** in 2024) due to its **huge population**. Some argue it makes little sense targeting states like the USA if their **share** of **total emissions** is **falling** compared to others.

> Per capita emissions are the total emissions of a state divided by its population. The USA, Malta, Belgium, Kuwait, UAE, Brunei and Saudi Arabia have some of the largest per capita emissions.

Historic vs current emissions

- One estimate given at the **Kyoto Conference** stated that **developing** states will not surpass the **total historic emissions** of **developed** states until the mid-22nd century.
- But with the **global population** projected to peak at **11 billion** in the 21st century, it may be necessary to prevent **developing** states with **increasing populations** from causing **environmental damage** (e.g. **Brazil** deforesting the **Amazon rainforest**).

Emissions outsourcing

- **Developing** states claim that a lot of **their emissions** are due to the **activity** of **developed** states.
- This is because many Western **TNCs**, whose **products** are destined for **Western markets** and **consumers**, have **relocated** to countries like **Thailand** and **produce emissions there**.
- This phenomenon is known as **emissions outsourcing**. It's **not obvious** which country is **responsible** for the emissions produced by these companies.

Developing states feel they should be allowed to **catch up** first

1) Many developing states argue that **poverty** poses a far more **real and present danger** to their populations than **environmental problems**. For example, some estimates show that **129 million people** in **India** were living in **extreme poverty** (less than $2.15 per person per day) in **2024**.
2) Asking developing states to place **limits** on their **industrialisation** process means they will be at a **disadvantage**. They will not have experienced the **benefits** described by **Rostow's Modernisation Theory** (see page 257) in the same way as the developed states did.
3) According to **Dependency Theory**, developing states will be condemned to a perpetual state of **subordination** to core (developed) states due to the **environmental restrictions** placed on their **industrialisation**.

There are **different views** about whether the **obstacles** can be **overcome**

REALISTS argue that **action on climate change** is doomed to **fail**. Unless states are **threatened** by climate change's consequences to their **security** or **economy**, there is **no incentive** to act.

LIBERALS argue that the success of the **Montreal Protocol** demonstrates the **potential** for **global environmental governance** and that the same could be achieved in tackling climate change.

Quick Questions

1) Name a leading proponent of deep ecology.
2) Who are human beings co-equal with according to deep ecology?
3) Which commission promoted the concept of sustainable development?
4) Who promoted the idea of the tragedy of the commons?

The tragedy of the commons is what PMs call losing a vote in parliament...

The competing interests of states make unified action on climate change difficult. While developed states are still hurt by the consequences of climate change, developing states often feel the negative effects of both climate change and action against it.

Non-state Actors and Environmentalism

A lot of the driving force for environmental change comes from civilian organisations, rather than from states. But because they don't have the same authority as national officials, they're vulnerable to public and legislative backlash.

Non-state actors have helped build awareness and action on climate change...

Pressure groups and campaigners

1) **Pressure groups** such as **Greenpeace**, **Friends of the Earth** and the **WWF** have had a significant impact at a **national**, **regional** and **global level**.
2) The emergence of **individual campaigners** like Greta Thunberg has also caught the attention of a **global audience**.
3) These **non-state actors** appear regularly at **environmental conferences** and in the **media**. This has helped to increase **awareness**, **publicity** and **education** on the scientific understanding of **environmental issues**.
4) The actions of these non-state actors have **helped** to **create** a growing **global civil society** regarding the environment.

Protest groups

1) **Direct action** of groups like **Just Stop Oil** and **Extinction Rebellion** have played a similar role in keeping the issue in the **public eye**. The **number** and **size** of these **groups** has **increased** and helped the environment to be recognised as one of the **most important global issues** facing the planet.
2) These groups play a **critical role** in holding **nation states** and **companies** to **account**, by **monitoring** them and calling for **greater action**.

The actions of groups such as these have helped to prompt **policy change** on a **national** and **local** level. For example, many states have made moves to **limit** the usage of **petrol** and **diesel vehicles** in the future by introducing **Low Emission Zones** (**LEZs**) and **congestion charges** in an attempt to **reduce** the use of **personal vehicles** and **encourage** the use of **public transport**.

...but they've had mixed results

1) While environmental campaign groups have **helped to raise awareness** of environmental issues, their successes remain fairly **limited** in scope.
2) Groups like **Just Stop Oil** and **Extinction Rebellion** have been **criticised** for some of their **protest methods**. Acts of protest like **throwing soup** at famous artworks, **blocking traffic** on motorways and **disrupting** various **public events** have generated **public anger** towards the groups and may have had a **negative** effect on their campaigns. This disruptive style of protest has led to **new legislation** which gave police **increased powers** to stop and/or arrest **potential protestors**.
3) Environmental campaign groups also have to **compete** for **funding** and **attention** with a number of other organisations and NGOs fighting **other issues**, e.g. **poverty**.

There are questions over the role of TNCs in addressing climate change

1) There are **over 75 000 TNCs** globally, with the majority being based in **developed states**. This gives TNCs **significant influence**, usually aligned with the **interests** of those developed states.
2) Many TNCs have made changes to be **more sustainable** in recent years. Some (e.g. Tesla) have also helped to develop **new green technology**.
3) However, many of these corporations face **criticism** for **flaunting** their **green credentials** while in practice **prioritising profits** over environmental issues.
4) Some argue that **certain sectors** (such as the **oil and gas industry**) have played a **large role** in casting **doubt** over the claims of the **environmental movement**. A number of TNCs have been accused of promoting **scepticism** of the science regarding **climate change** or of being **climate change deniers**.
5) This struggle to **influence global opinion** has had a significant effect on the **success** of the **environmental movement**.

Exam Practice

Evaluate the view that concerted action has been taken on tackling climate change. [30]
Write a **conclusion** to the essay question above.

Next step: outlawing salad dressing...

Oh, that kind of oil, never mind. As with all aspects of global governance, it's important to consider how non-state actors are able to influence change on a global scale. They can have a wide and powerful reach, even if their direct powers are limited.

Hard Power and Soft Power

Just like a boiled egg, when it comes to power, states acting on the global stage have two options before them: hard or soft.

Hard power is the ability to reward and punish

There are **two main forms** of **hard power**:

ECONOMIC POWER — the ability of a state to provide **economic aid** to other states (or withdraw it), to impose **economic sanctions** or to put up **trade barriers** against another state.

MILITARY POWER — this consists of a state's **army**, **navy**, **air force** and new forms of military power such as the ability to wage **cyber warfare**. It includes **surveillance** on rival states — e.g. **espionage** and **satellite technology**. Military power can be used **defensively** (including as a **deterrent**) or **aggressively** (to achieve certain **objectives**).

Key Terms — hard power: The use of the military and economic power to influence the behaviour and interests of other states and political actors.

Demographic power and the possession of natural resources are generally considered to be part of economic power.

Hard power is seen as very important by realists

1) Realists view global politics as **anarchical** — the **absence** of a **global government** can drive states to be **power-seeking** and so states are **constantly concerned** about their **security**.
2) Realists view **hard power** as the **best** way of **preventing** an **attack** by others and for **maintaining** a state's **position** in the **international system**.

> **Examples** of **hard power** being used include:
> - the **Gulf War** of **1990/1** and the **war in Kosovo** in **1998/99**
> - the **US's high level** of **defence spending**
> - the imposition of **economic sanctions** on **Russia** following its **annexation** of **Crimea** in **2014**
> - **threats** made by **Putin** warning the **West** of **Russia's nuclear capability** to **deter** further **escalation** over **Ukraine**.

3) There are **limits** to **hard power** — it can be **counterproductive** as well as **expensive**. The **US interventions** in **Vietnam**, **Afghanistan**, **Iraq** and **Libya** resulted in **high economic and military costs** and **increased anti-US sentiment**. The **costs** of using **hard power** may **outweigh** its **potential gains** in a highly **interdependent world**.

Soft power is achieving political aims through attraction rather than coercion

1) Instead of **spending** large sums of **money** on **armed forces**, providing **economic aid** or **occupying** other **states**, soft power focuses on **diplomacy** and **cultural attraction**.
2) **Supporters** of soft power believe that **shaping the preferences** of others is **far cheaper** and **more efficient** than using hard power.
3) There are **four key elements** of **soft power**:

CULTURAL POWER — the **influence** and **appeal** of a state's **culture**. This can include things such as **film**, **television**, **music**, **social media** and **recognisable brands**. E.g. **Hollywood** and **Disney®** in the **US**.

POLITICAL VALUES — having **clear** and **appealing** political **principles**. E.g. the **US's** 'American dream' and its reputation as 'the **land of the free**'.

FOREIGN POLICY — having good **international relations**, allowing **collaboration** and **cooperation** with **other countries**. E.g. showing strong **support** for **human rights** and **democracy**.

SHARED LANGUAGE — having a **common language** to help easily **spread ideas** and **beliefs**. E.g. the global reach of the **English language** has led to it being a **significant tool** of **soft power** for the **US** and **UK**.

Key Terms — soft power: The capacity to influence the behaviour and interests of others through attraction and persuasion.

Soft power has become increasingly prominent due to increased globalisation

1) **China** began its programme of **Confucius Institutes** in **2004**. They aim to **promote Chinese language** and **culture** and now operate in over **500 locations worldwide**.
2) The **UK** has the **British Council**, a body operating in **over 100 countries** which **promotes** the **English language** and closer **cultural relations** between the **UK** and **other states**. It also has a **highly regarded** news **broadcaster** in the **BBC**.
3) **Qatar**, **France**, **Brazil** and **Russia** have benefited from **hosting sporting events** (e.g. the **Olympics** and football **World Cup**).
4) The **US** and **UK** benefit from having **highly attractive universities** such as **Oxford** and **Harvard**.
5) The **limits** of **soft power** are **clear** in situations where it's **less effective**. **Soft power** has **little use** when confronting **aggressive uses** of **militaristic power**, such as the **Russian invasion** of **Ukraine**.

Hard Power and Soft Power

Some argue that smart power is the best solution

1) At the time of the Iraq War in **2003**, **Joseph Nye** (who had **coined** the term **soft power**) popularised the term **smart power**.
2) He aimed to **counteract** the idea *"that soft power alone could produce effective foreign policy"*, citing the **limitations** of the use of **soft power** in **countering** the development of **North Korea's nuclear weapons programme**.
3) **Smart power** is the **combination** of using **soft power** when **possible** and **hard power** when **necessary**.

> **Barack Obama** made use of **smart power** in his efforts **against** the **Islamic State** group.
> - He used **hard power** in his **increased** use of **unmanned drone strikes** (which attracted **controversy** due to **high numbers** of **civilian casualties**) and the **killing** of **thousands** of **alleged terrorist operatives** in **Pakistan**, **Yemen** and **Somalia**.
> - However, he also employed **soft power** by using **diplomacy** to try to **improve relationships** with **Middle Eastern states** in the wake of years of **US military action** in the region. **Radio broadcasts** and the **internet** were also employed to help **counter Islamic State propaganda** and **influence** in the area. These aimed to **erode support** for the organisation and **weaken** the **resolve** of its members.

Minnie used her smart power to order more tennis balls

Structural power is about the structure of the international system

1) **Structural power** is the term used by **Susan Strange** in her book *States and Markets* (1988) to describe a **state's position** in the **structure** of the **international system**. The **strongest states** have *"the power to decide how things will be done"*.
2) **Structural power** often comes from having a **significant** or **powerful role** in bodies such as the **UN**, the **G7**, the **G20** and other IGOs. For example:

> - After **1945**, the **IMF** and **World Bank** were created through the **Bretton Woods system**, which was dominated by the US and the UK. The US has an effective **veto power** in these institutions — see page 248.
> - Additionally, the US has a **permanent seat** and **veto power** on the **UN Security Council** and is a **founding member** of **NATO**, giving it a **pivotal position** in the **global power structure**.
> - Its capacity to **control** these IGOs allows it to **dominate their agenda**.

> China created the **AIIB (Asian Infrastructure Investment Bank)** in **2016** as an **alternative source** of **finance** for **developed** and **developing states**. **Over 100 states** have **joined**, including the **UK**, **Germany** and **Australia**, demonstrating China's **growing global influence**.

Quick Questions

1) What are the two main forms of hard power?
2) Give two examples of how hard power can be used.
3) What is meant by soft power?
4) What are the four key elements of soft power?
5) What is smart power?

Exam Practice

Evaluate the extent to which soft power has replaced hard power in the international system. [12]

Hard, soft, smart — is this a revision guide or a mattress shop?

It's often quite clear when a state is making use of hard power — it's difficult to miss things like military threats and economic sanctions. Soft power can be a little trickier to spot, as it's all tied up with how a state presents itself to the rest of the world.

Classifications of Power

Alright, it's time to talk about power. And especially — superpowers. But not those kind unfortunately, so I'm afraid you'll have to put your capes away. Although 'emerging powers' is a classic feature of many a comic book origin story...

The way we **classify political power** has **changed** over **time**

Traditionally, states could be classified as **great powers**, **middle powers** and **small powers**. But since the **Second World War**, the term **superpower** has been used as a term to describe the **strongest powers**.

A **superpower** needs to have **global reach**

1) The term **superpower** was coined in **1944** by the American international relations professor **William Fox**. He used the term to describe the **US**, **Soviet Union** and **British Empire**.
2) By the **end** of the **Second World War** and with the onset of the **Cold War**, it became clear that only the **US** and **Soviet Union** would retain this status. The **US** was the **only superpower** after the Cold War ended.
3) A **superpower** needs a **strong military** and **economy**, and crucially, **global reach**. As Fox described, these states have "*great power plus great mobility of power*".
4) This would include:
   - the ability to **deploy military force worldwide**
   - **financial** and **trading links** that are **global** in nature
   - an **ideology** with **global appeal** and an **attractive culture**
   - considerable **political**, **structural** and **soft power**.

When you're working for a superpower, sometimes you just can't help yourself

The **US** is argued to still be a superpower due to:
- it having **over 750 overseas military bases**
- it having the **second largest** arsenal of **nuclear weapons**
- its huge **economic might**
- its attractive **culture** and **political system**
- considerable **structural power**, playing a leading role in the **UNSC**, **IMF** and **NATO**.

Its status as a **superpower** means that US has numerous **allies** and a large **sphere of influence**. Most of these **alliances** were made during the **Cold War**.

Some argue there have been significant **shifts** in global power since **2000**. US power has been **challenged** by the **rise** of **China** and **India** and the **re-emergence** of **Russia**.
- **China** has become the **second largest economy**, with **India** now in **third** place. Some predict that by **2050** the **four leading global economies** will be **China**, **India**, the **US** and **Indonesia**. This would represent a major **shift away** from **Western power** towards **Asia**, with Asia **responsible** for **over half** of **global output**.
- **China's increased military spending** and acquiring of **military bases overseas** has **extended** its **global influence**.
- The **flashpoints** in **Syria**, **Ukraine**, **Gaza** and **Taiwan** have **stretched** the **US's power**.

A **great power** is **one rank below** a **superpower**

1) **Great powers** possess a **large population** and have **great military**, **economic**, **diplomatic**, **cultural** and **structural power**. But they **lack** the same degree of **global reach** that was a characteristic of the **Cold War superpowers**.
2) **China**, the **UK**, **France** and **Russia** are generally viewed as **great powers** because they are **members** of the **UNSC** and **possess nuclear weapons**.
3) Some argue that **Germany**, **Japan**, **India** and **Italy** also qualify as great powers. Others claim these states should be regarded as **middle powers** or **small powers**.

> The term 'great power' was first used towards the end of the Napoleonic Wars in 1814. It referred to the leading powers at the time — France, Great Britain, Austria, Russia and Prussia.

Often the **classification** of **powers** is **not clear-cut**

1) It can be tricky to **define** when a state **stops** being a **great power** and becomes a **superpower** — and vice versa.
2) It's also not always clear which **factors** are **most important** in determining whether a state is a **superpower**. For example, **Japan** in the 1980s was described as an **economic superpower** (though few hold this view today).
3) Some have suggested that the **EU** is also a contender for **superpower status** due to its **economic size**, huge **land mass** (4.1 million km²), **population** (449 million) and significant **soft power** influence globally.
4) However, its **disparate nature** (made up of **independent member states**), lack of **centralised political leadership** and **combined armed forces**, as well as the **loss** of the **UK** following **Brexit**, mean it is generally **not** classed as a **superpower**.

Global Politics — Power and Development

Classifications of Power

Emerging powers include BRICS and MINT

1) **Emerging powers** are states with an **increasingly** significant **economic influence**. They're expected to play a **growing role** on the **international stage** due to their **rapid rates** of **economic growth** (illustrated by their **membership** of the **G20**).
2) **Jim O'Neill** (then Chairman of Goldman Sachs Asset Management) coined the term **BRIC** in **2001**. It originally referred to the emerging powers of **B**razil, **R**ussia, **I**ndia and **C**hina, with **S**outh Africa joining in **2010** to form **BRICS**.
3) In time, this group became an **IGO**. In **2009**, representatives of these countries **met** for their **first summit**. BRICS has met for a diplomatic summit **every year** since.
4) **Egypt**, **Ethiopia**, **Iran** and the **UAE** joined BRICS in 2024.
5) The table below shows how the original **BRICS** states compared to the **US** in the main **measures of power** in 2024.

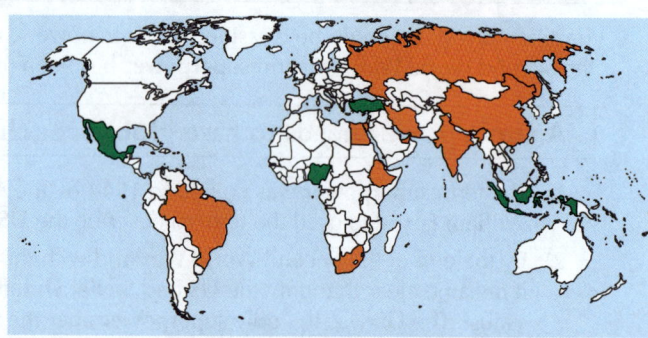

Map showing BRICS countries (orange) and MINT countries (green)

Country	US	China	Russia	India	Brazil	South Africa
Population (million)	342	1430	144	1440	218	61
Land Mass (million km²)	9.4	9.7	17	3.3	8.5	1.2
GDP (trillion $)	28.8	18.5	2.1	3.9	2.3	0.4
Military Spending (million $)	832	227	109	74	25	2.7
Nuclear Warheads	5044	500	5580	172	0	0
Aircraft Carriers	11	2	1	2	1	0
Foreign Military Bases	750+	2	20	14	0	0
Active Armed Forces (million)	1.328	2.035	1.1	1.475	0.366	0.065

6) O'Neill also identified a group he called **MINT**: **M**exico, **I**ndonesia, **N**igeria and **T**urkey. These are all **fast-growing mid-sized economies**.
7) These **emerging powers** are seen to be **challenging** the prevailing **global order**, reflecting a growing **shift in power** from the **Global North** (led by the **US**) to the **Global South**.

See page 256 for more on the Global North and Global South.

Quick Questions

1) What is the defining feature of a superpower?
2) Give four examples of great powers.
3) Why might the EU not be considered a superpower?
4) Which countries make up BRICS?
5) Which countries make up MINT?

Essay Plan

Evaluate the view that the rise of China challenges the US's status as the sole global superpower. [30]
Using the grid on p.298, **plan** an answer to the essay question above.

I never go hiking without a few BRICS of Kendal MINT cake...

Well, if there's one thing that should be clear from these pages, it's that power isn't fixed. You can be a superpower one decade and merely great the next, as a new power emerges. There's more on the impact of these changes on page 282.

Global Politics — Power and Development

Polarity

You've come to the right place if you want clarity on polarity. Just don't expect hilarity before we get into polarity...

There are **three** main **polar models** for **power** in **global politics**

1) Unipolarity (or hegemony)

Unipolarity is where **one power pole** is **dominant** in the **international system** over the other global actors. The **unipolar power** may be dominant in a range of areas, such as the **military**, **economy** and **culture**. A unipolar power may even create a **hegemony** — a situation where the **power** plays a **leadership role** in the global system.

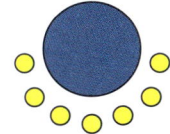

- **Realists** see **benefits** to **unipolarity** as it involves a **concentration of power**.
- **Hegemonic Stability Theory** asserts that a **unipolar power** is often a **benign hegemon**. Because of its **domination** it enjoys enormous **structural power** and can **enforce** the rules of the **system** that it has created, e.g. the **US** and the **Bretton Woods** system. The hegemon can **facilitate liberal trade rules** and **economic cooperation** which others can **benefit** from, while their **own position** in the system is **secure**.
- If there are **disputes** among **subordinate states** then the **unipolar power** can act as the **arbiter** to **resolve** them. It can also act as the **'world's policeman'** to bring any **dissident states** that **defy** the rules back in line. For example, the **US** and its **allies** liberating **Kuwait** from **Iraqi control** in **1991**.

- **Liberals** tend to **dislike unipolarity**. The **concentration of power** in the hands of one state can lead to **resentment** among other states and lead to **arrogance** and **over-confidence** by the hegemon.
- An example of this is the **invasion of Iraq** in **2003** where the **US** and its **allies** acted **unilaterally**, **defying** international law. **Noam Chomsky** has described this behaviour as *"malign or predatory hegemony"* where the **unipolar power** can **ignore global rules** and **attack** its **rivals** without fear of **consequences**.
- When the hegemon's **power decreases**, it may **lash out** to **retain its position** (e.g. the invasions of Afghanistan and Iraq) or **others** may be **emboldened** to **challenge** it (e.g. Russia invading Ukraine or China threatening to retake Taiwan).

2) Bipolarity

Bipolarity is a system where **two evenly-matched dominant power poles** (such as the US and Soviet Union during the Cold War) effectively **neutralise** the threat to **each other**.

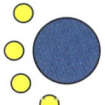 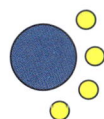

- **Realists** prefer **bipolarity** to unipolarity because they believe it leads to **stable international relations**. Bipolarity produces a **zero-sum game** situation (i.e. **my gain is your loss**) where **neither side** can **allow** the **other** side to **gain** any **advantage**, and the actions of their **opponent** become **highly predictable**.
- **Kenneth Waltz** championed **bipolarity** as the **most stable** polar system. As a **neo-realist**, he believed that the **only check** on **power** is **power itself**.
- With **fewer actors** than in a multipolar system, there is **less scope** for **miscalculation**.
- Each side can manage its **sphere of influence**. This is known as **bipolar discipline**.
- Examples of bipolar systems include:
  1) the stable rivalry between **India** and **Pakistan**.
  2) the **US** and the **Soviet Union** during the **Cold War**. The **balance of terror** between the two superpowers meant there was an effective **deterrent** — **Mutually Assured Destruction**.

- **Liberals** argue that **bipolarity** leads to **arms races**, **war plans** and **heightening tensions**. The **First World War** resulted from **two superpowers** mobilising their **armies** after the assassination of Franz Ferdinand.
- **The Cold War** resulted in **continual proxy wars** that **killed 20 million people** and nearly caused **nuclear war** in **1962** with the **Cuban Missile Crisis**. As former US Defence Secretary **Robert McNamara** admitted in 2003 — *"We lucked out. It was luck that prevented nuclear war."*
- Liberals believe **President Reagan** worsened **tensions** during the **Cold War** by dramatically **increasing US military spending** and declaring the **Soviet Union** as an *"Evil Empire"*. The Soviets were convinced that **NATO's Operation Able Archer** in **1983** was not just a military exercise but preparation for an **all-out attack**. With **nuclear weapons**, it only takes a small **human error** to cause large-scale disaster.

Global Politics — Power and Development

Polarity

3. Multipolarity

Multipolarity is a system that involves **three or more dominant** power poles. The international system called the **Concert of Europe** following the **Congress of Vienna** in **1815** and the **inter-war years** from **1919** to **1939** are examples of **multipolar systems**.

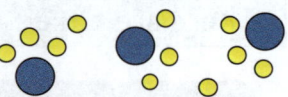

- **Realists** believe that **multipolarity** is the **least stable** polar system and the **most likely** to lead to **war**. It causes **uncertainty** in the international system.
- As there are so **many actors** to consider, **miscalculations** are more likely. **Risk-taking** is also more **tempting**, as states have relatively **similar** levels of **power**.
- States are likely to **shift** allegiances, heightening **suspicion** and **distrust** as there is not the same level of **security** as in a **bipolar system**.
- The **fluidity** in the international system means it is more difficult to establish a **balance of power**.
- Realists attribute the **outbreak** of the Second World War to **multipolarity**. The **rise** of Germany, Italy and Japan **challenged** the established **power** of Britain and France.

- **Liberals** believe that **multipolarity** leads to **equilibrium** and **peace**, and fosters **cooperation** and **multilateralism**.
- All **states** have an **interest** in **preserving** the system and **maintaining** their **position**.
- There is no **zero-sum game**, as **power** is **less concentrated** and more evenly **distributed**.
- An example of **successful** multipolarity is **Britain's** role in Europe during the **1800s**. It would **intervene** in **European** affairs to **protect** the **interests** of Britain, **preventing** the potential **rise** of **states** that may try to **dominate** the continent (e.g. **France**, **Russia** or **Germany**). This **preserved** the multipolar system, resulting in a **long period** of relative **peace**.

Power transition theory refers to changes in polarity

1) **Power transition theory** argues that **war** is **more likely** when states are **rapidly rising** or **declining** in **power**.
2) This is because **states** can easily make **miscalculations** about how **powerful** they are when there is a period of **flux** in the **international system**. Some argue that **Germany's** decision to use **force** in **1914** was a **miscalculation** due to the **uncertainty** caused by **power changes**.

Academics disagree about the world's polarity

Several theories have been **suggested** for what **polar system** followed the **end** of the Cold War:

Hyperpower — Hubert Vedrine

This theory proposes that the **scale** of the **US's power** and **influence** is so **great** that the term **superpower** is **inadequate**, and the US is instead a **hyperpower**. The **invasions** of Afghanistan and Iraq serve as **evidence** of the sheer **power** of the **US**.

The Unipolar Moment — Charles Krauthammer

In **1991**, Krauthammer **dismissed** the view that the world had **returned** to being **multipolar**. Instead, he argued that the **US** was vastly **stronger** than any other **rival**, in a **"unipolar moment"**. He used the US's vast network of foreign **military bases**, system of global **allies** and **structural power** as **evidence** of this.

Limited Unipolarity — John T Rourke

This theory proposes that the **power** of the **US** is **great** but **limited** by its political system and the **interconnected** nature of the **world**. It argues that the **US electorate** do not want to bear the **costs** of **hegemonic power**, so its leaders are **limited** in the **power** they can exert. The US therefore acts as an unenthusiastic policeman — wanting the **status** of a **unipolar power** but not the **costs**.

Back to Bipolarity — Hans Binnendijk

This theory argues that although **power** ebbs and flows over time, the international system will always **return** to **bipolarity**. The **US** may currently act as the **primary** superpower, but in time other **powers** will **grow** and act as a **counter** to it. **China's** rise to economic **supremacy** and greater **assertiveness** in Taiwan and the **South China Sea** were seen as evidence of a future **bipolar system**.

Emerging Multipolarity — Samuel Huntington

This theory argues that although the **US** remained a **superpower** after the **Cold War**, that did **not** mean that the world was **unipolar**. The US **continues** to face **challenges** from other civilisations, e.g. the **Islamic world**, **Russia** and **China**. As **power** shifts, the world will become more **multipolar**.

Nonpolarity — Richard Haass

This theory argues that **polarity** may be a **misleading** model to describe **power relations** in the world. It suggests it is more **accurate** to say that we now are in an age of **nonpolarity** due to the number of **states**, **NGOs**, **IGOs**, **TNCs** and **terrorist groups** that act internationally.

Global Politics — Power and Development

Developments in Global Politics

Liberal ideas of what an economy and government should look like have had a powerful influence on global politics.

The **world's economies** have become **increasingly liberalised**

1) States have **increasingly** engaged in **international trade** since the **Industrial Revolution**.
2) In *The Wealth of Nations* (1776), **Adam Smith** wrote about the advantages of **free trade**, claiming it was of **benefit** to both **trading parties**. **World trade** accounted for **21%** of **global output** in **1913**, compared to **2%** in **1800**.
3) Increased **protectionism** due to the **world wars** and 1929's **Great Depression** led to a sharp **decrease** in **international commerce**. However, the creation of the **Bretton Woods system** in 1944, **decolonisation** after the Second World War and the **collapse** of **Soviet-style communism** caused **economies** across the world to become increasingly **liberalised**.
4) The ideas of the **New Right** in the **1970s** (see page 255) challenged the orthodoxy of **interventionist** strategies and led to **institutions** like the **IMF** and **World Bank** adopting the **Washington Consensus** (see page 231) as their method for **economic development** for developing countries.
5) This philosophy of **economic freedom** has gained **widespread acceptance** in places such as the **East Asian 'tiger'** economies, countries in **transition** in **eastern Europe**, and in **China** since 1978 (despite its communist regime).
6) The creation of the **WTO** in **1995** helped **reduce poverty**, and the value of **exported goods** and **services** as a share of **GDP** grew to **31%** by **2022**.
7) **Liberals** believe that this has promoted **greater democratisation, interdependence** and **cooperation** between states.
   - **Commercial liberalism** means that **peace** and **harmony** is promoted by **international trade** as a **war** would be **too damaging** to a state's own economy (as described by Thomas Friedman's **Dell Theory of Conflict Prevention**).
   - However, some states (e.g. **China** and **Russia**) are **not** yet **completely liberalised** or **fully immersed** in the **global economy**. They use **protectionism** or rely on heavy **state involvement** to support and run their economies.

Liberal democracies have created a **rule of law** international order

1) The **rule of law** is regarded as a cornerstone of **liberal democracy**, ensuring **good governance** and the **protection** of **rights**. This means that the **law** is seen as the ultimate **authority**, that there is **equality** before the law and **no one** is above the law. This enables **order** to exist in these **liberal democracies**.
2) This has influenced **global affairs**, as **states** that **uphold** the rule of law are seen by liberals as **more likely** to **respect** international law. **International agreements** (e.g. **trade rules** in the WTO) must be respected by all **signatories** to uphold **international order**. It is also the **principle** that the **ICJ** uses when **ruling** on **inter-state disputes**.
3) Liberal democracies **working together** have created a rule-based international order — an **international** rule of law.

This can be **contrasted** with the **realist** view. The condition of **international anarchy**, where states are **sovereign** and **independent**, means that states are constantly **competing** with each other to act in their **own interests**. Thomas Hobbes described this as a condition of "***war of all against all***". As a result, **realists** believe that the idea of an **international rule of law** governing relations between states are **incorrect**.

The **number** of **democracies** has **increased** over the last **200 years**

1) **Liberals** believe **democratic states** are **more stable** and **less aggressive** than non-democratic states. They are more likely to **respect international law**, exhibit **greater tolerance** and suffer **less** from **extreme nationalism** or **religious fundamentalism**. They believe that **Immanuel Kant's** concept of **perpetual peace** will result from democratic states' **accountability**, internal **checks and balances** and their **cooperative** nature.
2) **Francis Fukuyama** in *The End of History* (1992) argued that the **liberal democratic** system of government (combining **democratic values**, upholding the **rule of law** and utilising a **liberal economy**) was the end point of **human development**. Fukuyama predicted that a **new** world order would be **established**, championing these **values** and creating a **cooperative** and **peaceful** liberal world order. He argued that **alternatives** to liberal democracy such as **monarchical rule** and **communism** were **doomed** to fail.
3) However, the increasing number of **authoritarian regimes** (e.g. Afghanistan), **illiberal economic practices** such as the use of **protectionist tariffs**, and the frequent **breaches** of international law by some states has **cast** severe **doubt** on the accuracy of Fukuyama's **predictions**. The growing extent of **global inequality** which has seen the **Global North** benefit much more than the **Global South** in the last 40 years also goes **against** Fukuyama's predictions.

I always liked The End of History — it was my last lesson before home time...

One way or another, liberal ideology has had a strong hand in shaping global politics. Have a look back at p.49-53 for more on the basics of liberalism. It may help you see where these policies and structures come from, and why realists may disagree.

States, Governments and Global Politics

Turns out, there are many ways to run a government, and some of them can get global politics into quite a **state**.

There is division over how **types of government** influence **global politics**

Realists believe that **different** systems of government have **little impact** on **global politics**. They believe that because of the **anarchic nature** of global politics, and as **state actors** are motivated by **securing** their **power**, it's **irrelevant** whether the state is **democratic** or **not**.

Liberals believe systems of government have a **huge impact** on global politics. They see **governments** as the **main cause** of **war** and **conflict**. In particular, **non-democratic** states are more likely to be **unstable** and produce **conflict** than **democratic states**, as they are less **responsive** to the **public**.

There are **four main types** of **state**

Whether a state is said to be democratic or non-democratic is open to interpretation. It's best to think of different systems of government as being on a continuum — some will display many features of democracy, some will appear far more authoritarian, and some a mixture of the two.

1 Democratic states

- About **20%** of **countries** are considered to be **fully democratic states** — many are in **Europe**, **North America** and **Australasia**. They hold **free** and **fair elections** and have **accountable governments**.
- These states are liberal democracies. They abide by the principle of the rule of law, **judges** are **independent**, **human rights** are **respected** and there are **checks and balances** on governmental power.

Liberals believe in the **democratic peace thesis**. This is the belief that democratic states tend to **peacefully** resolve disputes. Governments are **constrained** by **public opinion** and their leadership is **elected**. Leaders are also used to **compromise** and **negotiation** as they are part of the **parliamentary process**.

Realists argue that all states (including democratic ones) are **power-seeking** and all states are subject to the condition of **international anarchy**. **Democratic states** have **invaded** many other **countries** (e.g. the US and allies' invasions of Iraq and Afghanistan) and have **huge arms industries**.

2 Semi-democratic states

- A large proportion of states can be described as **semi-democratic**. They may have **democratic features** such as elections and multi-party politics, but also **non-democratic features** such as authoritarian rulers who wish to **maintain** their **power** (e.g. by arresting **political opponents**, committing **electoral fraud** and suppressing **free speech**).
- **Turkey** is an example of a semi-democratic state. It has elections and an **active civil society** but the country's **media** is **tightly controlled**, which **limits** the **press freedom** required for a **full** and **effective** democracy.

Liberals view semi-democratic states as **more stable** and **less aggressive** than **non-democratic** and **autocratic states**, but **more likely** to exhibit **warlike tendencies** than **democratic states**.

3 Non-democratic states

- **Non-democratic states** include all **states** that do **not** have **democratic intentions** (including **autocratic** states). These states are sometimes labelled as being **authoritarian**, although they may still hold **elections** to give the **appearance** of **democratic legitimacy**.
- An **example** of a non-democratic and **increasingly** autocratic state today is **Russia**. Although **claiming** to be **democratic**, it has not allowed **free** and **fair elections**, enabling **Putin** and his **United Russia party** to stay in **power**.
- Some argue that **Mexico pre-2000** was also an example. Although it **claimed** to be **democratic**, the **PRI** (Partido Revolucionario Institucional) held **uninterrupted power** for **71 years**, until **opposition parties** gained **power** in **2000**.

4 Autocratic states

- Around **70%** of the world's **population** are said to live in autocratic states. In autocratic states, **one person**, **party** or **body** has **absolute power**. This means that their **citizens** do **not** have **freedom of speech** and other **human rights**, the **media** and **judiciary** are **controlled** by the **state** and **open dissent** isn't tolerated.
- States like **Afghanistan** and **North Korea** can be said to be **autocratic**. 200 years ago, autocratic **monarchies** dominated Europe, but they have since largely become **democratic states**.

Liberals argue that these states are the **most destabilising** in global politics. Their **leaders** are **not accountable** to their **population** so are **not** constrained by them. These states are often **militaristic**, meaning their **rule** is derived from the use of **force** by the **military**. Because of this, they may have an **aggressive** foreign policy.

Global Politics — Power and Development

States, Governments and Global Politics

There are **two** other **types of state** that cause **instability** in **global politics**

Rogue states

1) Rogue states **don't obey** the **rules** and **customs** of the **international system**. They **defy international law** and act primarily out of **self-interest**. This has a **destabilising effect** on global politics and threatens **international peace**. Rogue states are usually **authoritarian** in nature.
   - **Iran** has been termed a **rogue state**, due to its **sponsorship** of **international terrorism** and **suppression** of its people's **human rights**.
   - **North Korea** is also considered a rogue state as it **threatens** its **neighbours** (**South Korea** and **Japan**) and **tested nuclear weapons** in **2006**, in **defiance** of the **Treaty on Non-Proliferation of Nuclear Weapons (1968)**.
   - At different times **Cuba**, **Iraq**, **Afghanistan**, **Syria** and **Libya** have all been labelled as rogue states.
   - There is some **subjectivity** around the term. **Noam Chomsky** and **William Blum** have argued that the **US** and **Israel** should be called rogue states — they argue that these countries have launched **illegal wars**, **violated international law** and committed **human rights abuses**.

2) It has been suggested that the term 'rogue state' has been used for **propaganda purposes** (like '**Axis of Evil**') to **undermine** the **legitimacy** of a **state** or to **justify economic sanctions** or **military intervention**.

Ewan's choice to go rogue was certainly causing instability

> George W Bush originally used the term 'Axis of Evil' to refer to states such as Iraq, Iran and North Korea for their alleged plans to develop weapons of mass destruction and their pursuit of policies which he deemed to be in direct opposition to American interests.

Failed states

1) Failed states are **unable** to carry out their **core duties** as a **state**, such as ensuring the **safety** of its **citizens**, **securing** their **borders** or **providing** basic **public services**. **Large parts** of failed states become **ungovernable** as their **governments** do **not** have a **monopoly** on the **use of force**, are **not** seen as **legitimate** and **can't uphold** the **rule of law**. This situation is often the result of **civil war**, with **lawlessness** developing from the resulting **power vacuum**.

2) Failed states can bring **disorder** to **neighbouring states**. This **spillover** could involve **ethno-nationalist violence** or the movement of **refugees**. Failed states can also be seen as an opportunity for **criminal gangs**, **extremist groups** and **drug traffickers**.

3) Recent examples of states labelled as **failed states** are **Somalia**, **Sudan**, **South Sudan** and **Syria**.
   - In **Somalia**, **US** and **UN peacekeeping forces** pulled out in **1994/5**, leaving the state to descend into **disorder** and **violence** between **rival warlords** vying for power. **Criminal gangs** engaged in **piracy** from the coastline, while **Al-Shabaab** used Somalia as a base for its **terrorist attack** on the **Westgate** shopping centre in **Nairobi, Kenya** in **2013**.

4) Like 'rogue state', the term 'failed state' has been **criticised** as being a **convenient label** to **justify foreign intervention**.

> Somalia and Sudan topped the Fragile States Index (a scale which measures the likelihood of conflict and instability in states) in 2024.

Quick Questions

1) Why are liberal economies argued to help prevent war?
2) Which type of state do liberals believe is more likely to be peaceful?
3) An autocratic state is ruled by what?
4) State what is meant by: a) a rogue state   b) a failed state

Exam Practice

Examine the impact that rogue states and failed states have on global politics. [12]

A Brogue State — where everyone is forced to wear business-casual...

It's important to consider how states can be given labels in order to justify action against them. Sometimes intervention can be helpful, but if it's not the correct cause of action, or if it ends at the wrong time, it can lead to further problems to arising.

The Impact of Changes in Global Power

Now, you may need to sit down for this, but it turns out changes in power can have a big effect on global politics. Gasp...

Changes in global politics can have worldwide consequences

Global politics is constantly **evolving**, as are the **global issues** that states must address. The **power** of **individual states rises** and **falls**, and this has far-reaching **consequences** for the **world order**.

Conflict

1) **Gradual power changes** in the **international system** can also affect the prospects of **conflict**.
2) One form of power change that can have a significant effect is **hegemonic decline**.
   - More **conflicts** may occur as the **hegemon's power declines** and **new states** aim to **replace** it.
   - It has been argued that the **gradual weakening** of the **US** and its **allies** in the 21st century led to its **rivals** seeking to **assert** their **authority**, e.g. **Russia** invading **Ukraine** and **China** in the **South China Sea**.
3) The **gradual power changes** in the international system could also explain **Obama's** policy of refocusing **US foreign** and **defence policy** on **Asia**, rather than **Europe** (known as the **Pacific Tilt**), and **Trump's trade war** to **counter** the rise of **China**.
4) **Power Transition Theory** argues that **moments of power change** are the **most dangerous** in **world affairs** as **rising powers** seek to **exert** their own **authority** in an **unstable system**. This may lead to **conflict** with the **declining power** or **other states**.

Poverty

While the **US** still plays a **large role** in **tackling global poverty**, the **influence** of **other nations** has started to **increase**:

- **China** and **India** have reduced their **own levels of poverty** and also have **growing influence** in **tackling poverty** in areas such as **Africa**, **Asia** and **Latin America**. For example, **China** has **invested** heavily in **infrastructure programmes** and **trade partnerships** with **Ethiopia**, **Kenya** and **Ecuador**.
- The **Asian Infrastructure Investment Bank** is seen as a **rival** to the **Western-dominated World Bank**.
- **International organisations** such as the **ASEAN** and the **AU** have become **more prominent** in the global fight against poverty. This has helped to **shift** the **balance of power** away from the **US**, its **allies** and the **Bretton Woods institutions** (although they remain **incredibly powerful** in **global economics**).

Human Rights

Changing global power structures can also affect the **promotion** and **protection** of **human rights** across the globe.

- The **US** and its **allies** have led numerous **humanitarian interventions** across the world, intending to promote **democracy** and **liberal values**. However, the **decline** of **Western influence** has meant these **interventions** are **less effective**.
- **Western democracies** have been **accused** of committing **human rights abuses** during these interventions, e.g. in **Afghanistan** and **Iraq**.
- **Human rights abuses** are still **prevalent** across the globe. The **decline** of **Western values** and **soft power** has allowed other states to **ignore international criticism** of its actions and **pursue** their **own rights agendas**. Examples of these include **China's** alleged treatment of **political opponents**, **Afghanistan's** restrictions on **women's rights** and **Russia's** reported **intimidation** of **LGBTQ+** people.
- The **resurgence** in **authoritarian states** also **weakens** the **universal standard of human rights**, with **allegations** of **atrocities**, e.g. the **treatment** of the **Uighur minority** in **China**.

Environment

1) **Environmental global governance** has become **increasingly far-reaching** with the creation of the **IPCC** and **UNFCCC** (see page 267).
2) However, the **lack** of **global unity** witnessed after the **COP21 climate summit** and the subsequent **Paris Agreement** may make it **harder** to **tackle climate change**.
3) Some argue that the **rapid growth** of **emerging powers** has had **disastrous consequences** for the **environment**, e.g. with **China** becoming the **world's largest emitter of CO_2**.
4) However, as its **economy** has **grown**, **China** has also become a **world leader** in **green technology**.

There's more analysis of the effects of global politics on conflict, poverty, human rights and the environment on pages 235-236 and 293. The sections on Global Governance (pages 237-272) look at how each of these issues is tackled on the global stage.

My advice for dealing with power changes is to always have a torch nearby...

As emerging powers become more and more influential, the US's status as the sole superpower looks less and less certain.

Regionalism

Even at this late stage in the book, we've got one more 'ism' that you need to learn about. This time, it's regionalism. It's all about how states can form alliances and organisations in their geographic area to tackle problems collectively.

The **creation** of the **EU** is part of the **development** of **regionalism**

1) **Regionalism** is where **states** within the same **geographical** location **cooperate closely** together, creating a '**world of regions**'. This may be a **loose arrangement** such as the Pacific Islands Forum (**PIF**) or may involve **deep integration** or **pooled sovereignty**, as in the case of the **EU**.

2) Regionalism has been one of the most **significant developments** of the last 100 years and has had a huge **impact** on **global politics**. **Regional organisations** have become very **significant actors** in their own right.

3) The **20th century** witnessed a **huge growth** in the number of **regional organisations** in a series of **waves of regionalism**, such as in the period immediately **after** the **Second World War**, the **1960s** and then again in the **1990s**.

4) It is estimated that there are now over **30 Regional International Organisations** (**RIOs**) and **373 Regional Trade Agreements** (**RTAs**).

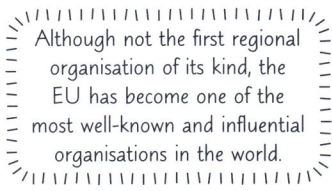
Although not the first regional organisation of its kind, the EU has become one of the most well-known and influential organisations in the world.

Always be prepared for a wave of regionalism

There are **three main types** of **regionalism**

1) Security regionalism

Security regionalism concerns the desire of states to achieve **greater protection** from perceived **threats** to member states.

- **NATO** is viewed as a classic example of security regionalism, forming in **1949** in response to the **perceived threat** of **Soviet expansionism**.
- The creation of the **European Economic Community** (**EEC**, later the **EU**) was intended to **prevent** a **recurrence** of catastrophic **world war** in **Europe** in addition to **economic** reasons.
- The **African Union** (**AU**) has employed **peacekeeping** forces to deal with **security issues** in places like **Sudan**.

2) Political regionalism

There are various **political reasons** for states to form **regional bodies**.

- The **Arab League** was formed in the **Middle East** and **North Africa** in the period after the Second World War. One aim of the Arab League was to **collectively defend** the **interests** of member states and give them a **unified voice** on the **world stage**, as many of them had recently **gained independence**.
- The **Council of Europe** was formed in **1948**. It drafted the **European Convention on Human Rights** in order to **prevent** a **recurrence** of **atrocities** like the **Holocaust** in **Europe**.
- The **Pacific Islands Forum** has **campaigned** on the issue of **climate change** on the **global stage** due to the **threat** of **sea level rise** devastating low-lying countries.

3) Economic regionalism

Economic reasons have been the **most prominent motivation** for regionalism.

1) The **benefits** of **trade** and the idea of **comparative advantage** has meant that states have sought to **increase** their **prosperity** by forming **regional bodies** and creating **Regional Trade Agreements**.
   - The **European Economic Community** was formed with the intention of **promoting** greater **trade** and **interdependence** to generate **wealth** by creating a **customs union**, as well as aiming to prevent war.

2) Economic regionalism was the **main reason** for the waves of **regionalism** in the **1980s** and **1990s**.
   - An example is the **United States-Mexico-Canada Agreement** (**USMCA**), originally called **NAFTA**. It was created to **promote** the **free movement of trade** between the three countries — it was **not** motivated by other **political** or **security concerns**.

3) **Open regionalism** aims to **take advantage** of the **opportunities** provided by **participation** in the **global marketplace** to **increase exports** and **imports**. It aims to act as a **building block** in the process of **globalisation**.
   - An example of this is the **Asia-Pacific Economic Cooperation** (**APEC**), which has **21 member states** including the **USA**, **Japan** and **China**.

Top Tip for Politicians #982: LOA (learn organisation acronyms)...

It might not always be clear exactly what type of regionalism a body is going for, especially as the issues they tackle can be interconnected. For instance, some theories say changes to economic policies can help to improve security — see page 293.

Regionalism, Globalisation and Sovereignty

While regionalism and globalisation both involve states working closer together, they don't necessarily go hand-in-hand.

There are **questions** over **regionalism's role** in **globalisation**

Some people believe that **regionalism** is a **building block** towards **globalisation** while others see it as a **stumbling block**.

Building block

Regional bodies may **facilitate globalisation** by acting as a **stepping stone** for **individual states**.

- Participating in regional organisations may **prepare smaller states** for **cooperation** on a **wider global stage**, e.g. through **regional customs unions**, **economic competition** and **regional market forces**.
- The recent growth in **RTAs** has coincided with **increased global trade**.
- **Large regional bodies** may enable **individual states** to **exert greater structural power** and **influence**. For example, the **representation** of the **EU** at the **World Trade Organisation** has led to **better trade deals** for **EU member states**.

Stumbling block

Regionalism can be used as a **defensive** measure **against globalisation**.

- The **EU** aims to strike a **balance** between **global cooperation** and **protection** of its **member states' interests**. For example, the **Common Agricultural Policy** (**CAP**) subsidises the **agricultural sector** of EU member states, **protecting** the bloc from **cheap imports**.
- Likewise, the **AU** and **Arab League** stand up for their members to **protect** their **regional culture** and **practices** from **outside interference** and **Westernisation**.

The EU is sometimes referred to as 'Fortress Europe', particularly in relation to its economic and trade policies.

Regionalism can have a **significant effect** on **state sovereignty**

1) The **erosion** of **state sovereignty** varies according to the **nature** of the **regional body**.
   - The **EU** has been considered a prime example of an organisation that has had a **significant impact** on **sovereignty**. The **supranational** nature of many of its institutions and the drive towards an **Economic and Monetary Union** (**EMU**) (see page 289) indicate that **decision-making** is increasingly made **by the EU** rather than by its **member states**.
   - Some believe that the EU may be heading towards **political union** if it fulfils its **original aim** of "**ever closer union**". This could eventually create a '**United States of Europe**' comparable to the USA.
2) Other regional organisations have a much **more limited impact** on **state sovereignty** and are **intergovernmental** in nature (see p.289).
   - The **USMCA** is focused on **facilitating trade** between the three signatories.
   - Decisions made by the **AU** and **Arab League** are generally **not binding**. Instead, the organisations seek to **promote cooperation** and **represent** their **members' interests** on the **global stage**.
3) **Political regionalism** is seen by some as a **challenge** to the **Westphalian principle** of **state sovereignty**. As a result, states have been more **reluctant** to adopt **political regionalism**.
4) However, the **growing importance** of **transnational issues** such as **climate change**, **human rights**, **pandemics** and **terrorist threats** may spur **greater levels** of **political regionalism** and **regional cooperation**.

Quick Questions

1) NATO is an example of what form of regionalism?
2) The regionalism wave of the 1980s and 1990s was an example of what form of regionalism?
3) Why can regionalism be seen as a stumbling block to globalisation?
4) Give one way that the AU and Arab League limit their impact on their members state sovereignty.

My little cousin's toys are both building blocks AND stumbling blocks...

I live in fear of stepping on them — just like some states fear that regional bodies will step on their sovereignty. States can be very sceptical of regional bodies if they feel that they are being bound by decisions that are out of their control.

Global Politics — Regionalism and the EU

Significant Regional Bodies

To fully understand how the EU fits into regionalism, it's useful to look at other regional bodies with similar levels of influence. So join me for a trip around the world — through North America, Africa and Asia. Please keep all limbs inside the vehicle.

There are many **significant regional bodies** other than the **EU**

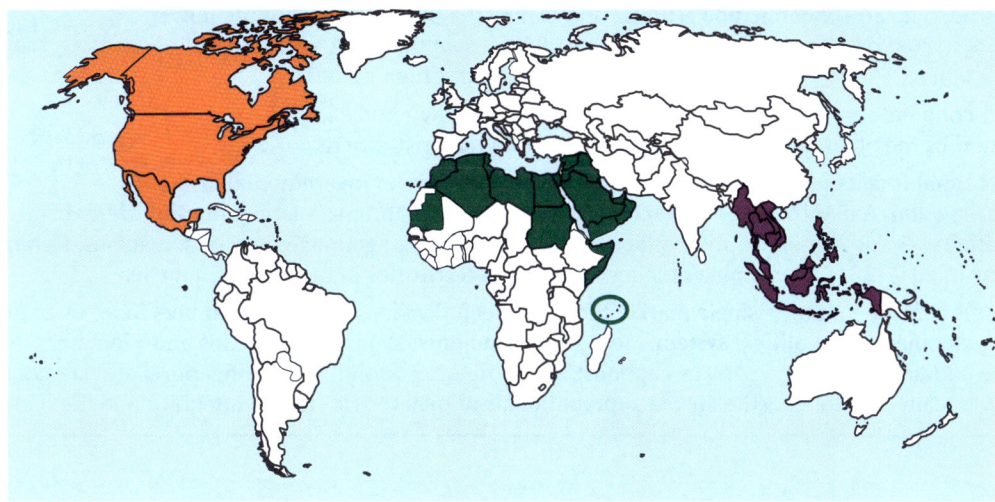

Map of the world showing the member states of the USMCA (orange), the Arab League (green) and ASEAN (purple)

NAFTA/USMCA

- **NAFTA** came into force in **January 1994** to **promote trade** between the three countries in **North America** (the USA, Canada and Mexico). It was primarily an example of **economic regionalism**.
- The hope was that the **free trade area** established between them would bring **economic prosperity** which would result from having **fewer border checks** between its signatories. The agreement was **limited** in nature, and did **not seek** any form **political regionalism** between the three states.
- The **impact** of NAFTA was **significant**, **increasing trade** in **goods** and **services** by **397%** between the three signatories in the period from **1994-2014** and **binding** their **economies** more **tightly together**. One downside was an **accusation** that **manufacturing jobs** were **lost** in the **USA** because of the **cheaper labour** available in **Mexico**.
- Subsequently, **President Trump** initiated the **USMCA** to try and **tackle** this **problem**. Trump aimed to **revise** the **terms** of NAFTA in a more **favourable** way for the **USA**, having said that **NAFTA** was "**perhaps the worst trade deal ever**". However, the **changes** made by **USMCA** are said to have been **small**.

Arab League

- The **Arab League** was created in **1945** to **defend** the **interests** of **Arab states**, many of whom had recently gained **independence** after the **Second World War**.
- Originally, the League was an act of **political regionalism** (aiming to **collectively speak** for the **members** on the **international stage**) and **security regionalism** (aiming to **ensure** that the **sovereignty** of **member states** was not subject to **renewed imperial subjugation** following the **retreat** of the **British** and **French empires**). It was also formed for **cultural** reasons — to **protect** the **shared culture** of **member states** from **Western influence**.
- The League has grown to **22 members** and is run on the basis of **intergovernmentalism** — each member of the **Council of the League** has a **veto**. As the Council only meets **twice a year**, the **scope** for achieving **agreement** within the League is **limited**, which **restricts** its **ability to act**.
- In recent times, the League has **focused** more on **resolving disputes** within the Arab world but has had **limited success** due to its internal **divisions**. Divisions have occurred due to the influence of the **Cold War**, perceived **US imperialism** in the area and struggles over who should be the **dominant state** in the region. It was **divided** over its **response** to the **Iraq War** in **2003** and the **civil war** in **Syria** in **2011**.
- Its decisions are **only binding** for members that **voted for them**, **limiting** the **influence** of the organisation.
- The Arab League has had some **success** in **gaining recognition** for **Palestinian statehood** (**145 UN members** had recognised it by **2024**) and has **enabled** the establishment of a **free trade area** (the **Greater Arab Free Trade Area**, **GAFTA**) with **18 member states**.

Global Politics — Regionalism and the EU

Significant Regional Bodies

ASEAN

- ASEAN was created in **1967** during the **Cold War** and the **Vietnam War**. It originally had **five members** and was primarily formed for **security** reasons, due to **concerns** about the **intentions** of the **Soviet Union** and **Communist China**. By **2024**, ASEAN had **10 members** and its aims had **changed** significantly.
- **ASEAN** has become an **economic powerhouse** and is now the **6th largest economic power** in the world. It created its own **free trade area** in **1992**, formed the **ASEAN Regional Forum** with **Japan** in **1994** and created a **free trade zone** with **China** in **2005**.
- ASEAN still **cooperates** on **security** matters. It has created its own **nuclear free zone** and its members **share intelligence** on **potential terrorist threats**.
- The **ASEAN summit** takes place **twice a year** and operates in an **intergovernmental** fashion. It aims to follow the '**ASEAN Way**' of **protecting state sovereignty** and maintaining **non-interference** in **domestic affairs**. Some argue that this explains its **weak response** to **genocide** carried out against **Rohingya Muslims** in **Myanmar** in **2017-2018** or to **China's** claims to **disputed territories** in the South China Sea.
- While there is a desire to form a **single market** there are **deep divisions** between **members** in terms of their **stage of development** and **political system**. Some are **communist** states (such as **Laos** and **Vietnam**) while others have traditionally been viewed as **capitalist** '**Asian Tiger**' economies (e.g. **Singapore**) and are considered more economically developed. The **lack** of **supranationalism** may **restrict future integration** in the region.

The founding members of ASEAN were Indonesia, Malaysia, the Philippines, Singapore and Thailand.

African Union

- The **African Union** (**AU**) succeeded the **Organisation of African Unity** (**OAU**). Originally, the **purpose** of the **OAU** was to **defend** the newly formed states' **independence** from **colonialism** and uphold **state sovereignty**. It also aimed to end **apartheid** in southern Africa. It gave **Africa** more of a **voice** on the **world stage** and promoted **economic and social development**. The OAU had a **mixed record** of **success** and was dubbed a '**Dictators' Club**' because of the **lack of democracy** and **poor human rights record** of its members.
- Created in **2002**, the **AU** consists of **55 member states** (as of 2024). It **revamped** the **institutions** of the OAU, modelling them on those of the **EU**. A **free trade** area has been created, together with a **Pan-African Parliament** (**PAP**), **Assembly of the African Union**, **African Union Commission** and an **African Court of Justice and Human Rights**.
- It has undertaken **peacekeeping** operations in **Darfur** and **Somalia** in collaboration with the **UN**. The AU also helped to **negotiate** a **deal** to **repatriate** the Chagos Islands to **Mauritius** from **UK** control in **2024**.
- The AU has **increasing influence** on the **world stage**. It **threatened** to **withdraw** its member states **collectively** from the **ICC** after the ICC faced accusations of **racism** in **2013**. Since **2023**, the **AU** has been represented in the **G20** and is a **permanent observer** at the **UN General Assembly**.
- However, the AU lacks the **enforcement powers** to make its resolutions **binding**. Although there is a **desire** to create a **single market**, a **single currency** and **central bank**, there hasn't been significant progress on these initiatives. A number of **member states** have been **suspended** at times from the AU, further **weakening** the **organisation**. As of **2024**, **6 states** have their **membership suspended**.
- Africa faces a **significant number** of **large-scale issues** that affect multiple member states, such as **debt**, **poverty**, **famine**, **HIV/AIDS epidemics** and **conflict**. The difficulty of dealing with these issues may go some way to explaining why the AU has had a **mixed record** of success.

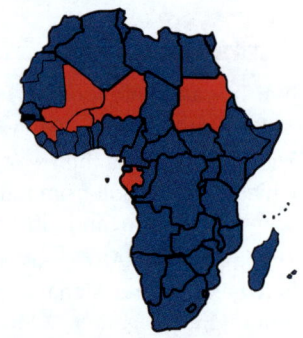

Map of Africa showing the member states of the African Union (blue) and states that had suspended memberships (red) in 2024

Exam Practice

Examine the role and significance of the Arab League and the African Union. [12]

Significant regional bodies can often be found at your local gym...

Make sure you're familiar with these four regional bodies and how they and their regionalism have developed over time. While some have stuck close to their original focus (e.g. USMCA), others have broadened their approach (e.g. ASEAN).

Global Politics — Regionalism and the EU

The Development of the EU

You've already looked at the EU's core aims and principles back on pages 103-104. Now it's time to take a closer look into how the membership, focus and structure of the EU have changed over the years. So EU'd better prepare yourself...

States must fulfil certain criteria to join the EU

1) The **requirements** to **join** the **EU** are known as the **Copenhagen criteria**.
2) They require that **applicants** must be **democratic**, operate on the principle of the **rule of law**, have **respect** for **human rights** and have a **functioning market economy**.
3) A number of countries, such as **Montenegro**, **Serbia**, **Albania** and **Ukraine**, were in the process of **applying** to **join** the **EU** in 2024.

As far as Clarissa was concerned, her country definitely had a functioning market economy

The EEC and then the EU expanded over time

1) The creation of a pan-European IGO was meant to encourage **cooperation** and **trade**, and **reduce nationalism**. It was hoped it would **prevent future wars**, as member states came to **depend** on each other for their **prosperity**.
2) It was also prompted by a desire to protect **liberal democracies** from **communist influence** from the USSR and **aggression** from **fascist states**. Over the years, **former communist states** (like East Germany) and **former fascist states** (like Spain and Portugal) became **liberal democracies** and joined the EU.
3) The **timeline** below shows the states joining the **EEC** (**European Economic Community** — 1957 to 1993), the **EU** (**European Union** — 1993 to present), the **number of member states** in each IGO and some **key events**.

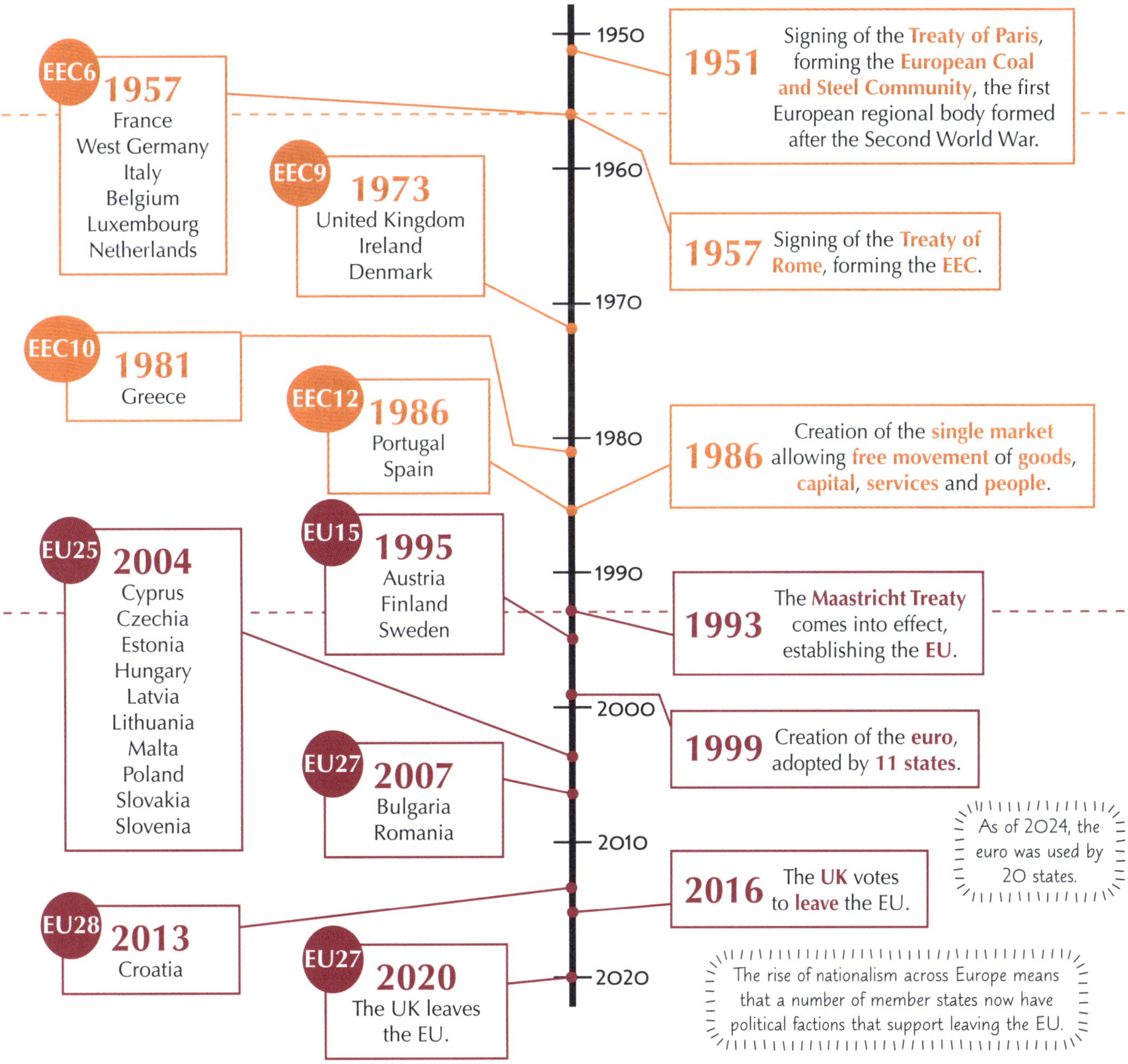

EEC6 1957 — France, West Germany, Italy, Belgium, Luxembourg, Netherlands

EEC9 1973 — United Kingdom, Ireland, Denmark

EEC10 1981 — Greece

EEC12 1986 — Portugal, Spain

EU15 1995 — Austria, Finland, Sweden

EU25 2004 — Cyprus, Czechia, Estonia, Hungary, Latvia, Lithuania, Malta, Poland, Slovakia, Slovenia

EU27 2007 — Bulgaria, Romania

EU28 2013 — Croatia

EU27 2020 — The UK leaves the EU.

1951 Signing of the **Treaty of Paris**, forming the **European Coal and Steel Community**, the first European regional body formed after the Second World War.

1957 Signing of the **Treaty of Rome**, forming the **EEC**.

1986 Creation of the **single market** allowing **free movement** of **goods**, **capital**, **services** and **people**.

1993 The **Maastricht Treaty** comes into effect, establishing the **EU**.

1999 Creation of the **euro**, adopted by **11 states**.

2016 The **UK** votes to **leave** the EU.

As of 2024, the euro was used by 20 states.

The rise of nationalism across Europe means that a number of member states now have political factions that support leaving the EU.

Global Politics — Regionalism and the EU

The Development of the EU

Treaties are used to define the aims and powers of the EU

1) Since the signing of **Treaty of Paris** (1951), which created the **European Coal and Steel Community**, a number of other **treaties** have subsequently been signed, allowing even deeper **integration**.
2) The treaties lay down the **objectives** of the **EU**, set out the **rules** which EU **institutions follow** and determine the **precise powers** that the EU can exercise.

Key Terms — qualified majority voting (QMV): A form of vote used extensively by the Council of Ministers in the EU. For a standard qualified majority decision to pass, at least 55% of member states, representing 65% of the EU population, must vote in favour.

1957 Treaty of Rome	• Established the **EEC**, creating a **common market** and **customs union**. • This led to the **removal** of **tariffs** on goods **between member states** and the adoption of a **common external tariff**. • It also established the **European Atomic Energy Community** (**EURATOM**). • Institutions such as the **European Commission** and the **Council of Ministers** were created and members committed themselves to establishing an "**ever closer union**".
1986 Single European Act	• Created the **single market** (which came into operation in **1993**), allowing the **free movement** of **goods**, **services**, **capital** and **people**. • To **deepen** the level of **integration** between **member states**, it also **reformed** the **institutions** of the **EEC** by extending the policy areas that used **qualified majority voting** in the **Council of Ministers**. This made it **harder** for a **single country** to **veto** a proposal.
1992 Treaty on European Union (or the Maastricht Treaty)	• Created the **European Union** and widened the EU's **areas of cooperation** to **political matters** such as **citizenship**, **justice**, **home affairs** and a **common foreign** and **security policy**. • The **co-decision procedure** was introduced whereby the **Council of Ministers** and **European Parliament** jointly decided on **EU legislation**, giving the **European Parliament** more **power**. • The **Social Chapter** gave **European workers greater rights**. It also prepared the way for **Economic and Monetary Union** and the establishment of a **single currency**. • The principle of **subsidiarity** was recognised. This meant that **decisions** should be made at the **lowest possible level** (e.g. **local** or **national**) and that the **EU** would **only** make **decisions** where this **wasn't** the **most effective measure**.
1997 Treaty of Amsterdam	• **Reformed** EU **institutions** in preparation for **more states joining** the EU. • Further **QMV** was allowed in the **Council of Ministers** and the **powers** of the **European Parliament** were strengthened. • The **Schengen Agreement** was incorporated into **European law**, allowing **passport-free travel** among **all EU countries except** the **UK** and **Ireland**. As of **2024**, **25 EU member states** participate in the Schengen Agreement.
2000 Nice Treaty	• Similar to the Treaty of Amsterdam, the Nice Treaty **reformed** EU **institutions** to **accommodate** the **increase** in **EU member states** to 25.
2007 Lisbon Treaty	• Comprehensively **overhauled** the EU's **institutional structure**, giving the **European Parliament** more **power** and further **extending QMV** in the **Council of Ministers**. • Created a **President of the European Council** and a **High Representative for Foreign Affairs**. Also created the EU's own **diplomatic service** — the **European External Action Service**.

Quick Questions

1) The Treaty of Rome created which organisations?
2) How many states were members of the European Union in 2024?
3) What is the name of the criteria that applicant states have to meet to become a member of the EU?
4) The single market allows the free movement of what?

AO1 Knowledge

When I finish a big revision session, I reward myself with a Nice Treat(y)...
Here's a revision task — recreate the timeline on p.287 on your wall and use sticky notes to place the events in the right order.

Global Politics — Regionalism and the EU

The Euro and Institutions of the EU

Get ready to read the words 'euro' and 'European' so many times that they lose all meaning — if it hasn't happened already...

The **euro** is part of **Economic and Monetary Union**

1) An **Economic and Monetary Union** (**EMU**) is a **trade bloc** where all states in the bloc have a **common market**, a **customs union** (where **free trade** exists within the bloc and each state has the same **external tariffs**) and share the **same currency**.
2) Plans for an **EMU** go back to the aims of the founders of the EEC to form **closer unions** between the member states. In **1986**, the **Single European Act** created what became the **single market** in **1993**.
3) The **Maastricht Treaty** came into effect in 1993, marking the **next stage** of **economic integration**. This Treaty established the process of creating a **single currency** (the **euro**) to replace member states' own national currency. Of the members at the time, only the UK and Denmark **opted out**, with **all remaining member states** committing to **adopting** the **euro**.
4) The **euro** was formally **adopted** by **11 member states** in **1999** (although **notes and coins** weren't in circulation until **2002**). By 2024, **20 member states** had adopted the euro. A number of other member states now **accept** the **euro** as **legal tender** without having adopted it as their state currency.
5) **All new states** that **join** the **EU** are now **required** to pledge to **adopt** the **euro** when they are **ready** to do so. Some fear that this puts **pressure** on states that had **previously opted out** (e.g. Denmark) to also adopt the euro.
6) In order to adopt the euro, states have to fulfil certain **convergence criteria**. These include having **low inflation**, **low interest rates** and a **low level of national debt**.

The euro has **major implications** for **sovereignty**

1) The **more states** that join the **single currency**, the **greater** its **impact** on their **economic policy**.
2) The **European Central Bank** (**ECB**) controls **monetary policy** for the **eurozone**. This means that the level of **interest rates** is **fixed** by the **ECB** rather than **national central banks**.
3) Following the **2010 Greek financial crisis**, the **Fiscal Compact** was agreed in **2012**, which meant that **single currency members** agreed to maintain a **balanced budget**.
4) This **influence** of the EU EMU over member states **economic policy** has prompted some to **speculate** that the EMU could eventually lead to **political union**.

My assistant for the EMU vs emu demonstration seems to have run off...

Benefits of the euro
- It makes **trade easier** by **removing fluctuations** in **exchange rates**.
- **Protects smaller states** in the eurozone from the **exchange rate volatility** they faced in the past.
- The **strength** of the **euro** has **increased** in relation to **other currencies** such as the **British pound** or the **yen**.
- **Member states** can **support** any state that gets into trouble by **pooling resources**. For example, **bailouts** were provided to **Greece** during its **financial crisis**.

Criticisms of the euro
- States **did not stick** to the **guidelines** set out in the **convergence criteria**. This contributed to the **Greek financial crisis**.
- The **level of interest rate** set by the **ECB** has **better suited** the economies of **northern Europe** (e.g. Germany) than economies in the **south** (e.g. Spain).
- The ECB is an **unelected** institution — its huge power adds to the sense of a growing **democratic deficit** in the EU.
- The demand for **balanced budgets** by the **Fiscal Compact** further **reduces** the **sovereignty** of member states.
- Some fear that the **power** that the EU accumulates through the EMU will lead to a **federal superstate**.

The idea of the EU as a federal superstate sees the EU becoming a sovereign state composed from the union of its member states, similar to the USA. Power would then be concentrated in Brussels to decide key issues across the EU.

The EU's institutions can be either **intergovernmental** or **supranational**

Intergovernmental institutions — these allow **individual states** to **veto** decisions. A **single state** with **veto power** can **prevent** a decision from being **enacted** if it **disagrees** with it. As **states** have the **power** to **refuse** the decisions of the other states, intergovernmental institutions are seen to **preserve state sovereignty**.

Supranational institutions — these do **not** give individual states **veto power**. Any decision **agreed** by the **majority** is **passed** and **enacted**, and **all members** of the institution are **bound** by that decision. As states may be bound to **carry out policies** they do **not** fully **agree** with, supranational institutions are seen to **erode state sovereignty**.

Global Politics — Regionalism and the EU

The Euro and Institutions of the EU

There are **6 main institutions** of the **EU** that you need to know about:

The European Council intergovernmental	• The **heads of government** of each **member state** meet **four times a year** at a **European Council** or **summit** to discuss the **future direction** of the **EU**. • States can **veto** any **proposal**.
The European Commission supranational	• The European Commission is made up of **one appointee** from **every member state**. Each appointee heads up their own **policy portfolio**, like **trade** or **transport**. • It **proposes** the **EU budget** and oversees the **implementation** of the EU's **budget** and its **laws**. It is also called the **Guardian of the Treaties**, as it ensures that the decisions outlined in the treaties are **upheld**. • **Commissioners** represent the **collective interest of the EU**, not a single state.
The Council of Ministers supranational and intergovernmental	• **Relevant government ministers** from each member state attend meetings. • Member states can use their **veto** on **important decisions** such as on **foreign policy** and **matters of war**. • The Council of Ministers decides on **less contentious policy issues** by using **QMV** (see p.288). • It also **co-decides** with the **European Parliament** any **legislation** that is **proposed** by the **European Commission**.
The European Parliament supranational	• The only **directly elected** institution of the EU. • It is made up of **720 MEPs** who are **elected every 5 years**. • **No member state** has **enough MEPs** to **veto** legislation.
The European Court of Justice supranational	• The institution that **enforces** EU **law**. • It is made up of **one judge from each member state**, ensuring that EU **law** is applied **uniformly** by **each state**.
European Central Bank supranational	• The institution that controls **monetary policy** for members of the **single currency**. • It determines the level of **interest rates** for **euro** members.

There is debate over the EU's intergovernmentalism and supranationalism

1) There is considerable **uncertainty** about the **future identity** of the **EU**. While some expect it to remain at least **partly intergovernmental**, with member states retaining their **national veto** on key matters, others anticipate that the EU will become a **fully integrated political union**.

2) There are a **number of factors** suggesting a **push towards** a **fully supranational EU**. For example, the desire to establish an **EMU** and its subsequent **development** in the **eurozone**. Additionally, **QMV** is now used for **80%** of **decisions** made in the **Council of Ministers**, **reducing** the range of matters on which a state can use its **veto**.

3) However, the growth of **populist** and **nationalist movements** in countries like **Germany**, **Austria** and **Hungary** may mean that further moves towards **greater EU unity** could be met with **greater resistance**. This **backlash** may be **fuelled in part** by **concerns** over the **alleged loss** of **cultural** and **national identity**. Concerns over **migration** both **within** and **outside** the EU have also influenced their rise.

4) The fact that the **European Parliament** is the EU's only **directly elected institution** has led some to allege that the EU suffers from a **democratic deficit**. However, some states have **allowed their citizens** to **directly vote** on **EU decisions** — for example, **Ireland** held **referendums** on whether to **ratify** the **Lisbon Treaty** in 2008 and 2009.

5) However, **measures** do currently **remain** in place to **protect** the **sovereign interests** of member states. States retain the **veto** for **important matters** in the **Council of Ministers**, are able to negotiate **opt outs** (or even leave the EU entirely) and **state leaders** are able to **steer** the direction of the EU at **summits**.

The EU EMU didn't fly in Britain...
When the United Kingdom decided not to sign up to the common currency (along with Denmark and, later, Sweden), some said the United Kingdom was burying its head in the sand — like an ostrich... not wanting to be an EMU... All very confusing.

The EU as a Global Actor

The lights go down. A hush spreads through the audience. The first lilting notes of music begin to trickle from the speakers as the great red curtains part. A spotlight snaps on and behold, the global actor you've all been waiting for — the EU!

There is debate over the **EU's power** on the **global stage**

1) Some argue that the **EU** has become a **significant global actor**, with some even likening it to a **superpower** (see page 275).
2) The EU has great **significance** in **international affairs**, but the **claim** that the EU is a **superpower** is open to **question** due its **lack** of **unified leadership**, **armed forces** and **global reach** in **military** terms **compared** to the **USA**.
3) The EU has a number of **strengths** that point towards its potential as a **superpower**, but also faces **obstacles** that would bring that status into question.

"Honestly, I expected the global stage to be bigger"

Political power

Strengths and influence
- ✓ The appointment of a **President of the European Council** and **High Representative for Foreign Affairs** in **2009** gave it **central focus** and **leadership**.
- ✓ The EU used its **diplomatic influence** on issues like the **Iranian nuclear programme** and **climate change**.
- ✓ As of 2024, the EU is still attracting **new members**, with **Ukraine**, **Serbia** and **Albania** all hoping to join.

Restrictions and obstacles
- ✗ As it is composed of 27 **separate states**, the EU does **not** speak with a **single voice**.
- ✗ The EU has been **divided** over how to tackle **Russia's war** in **Ukraine**.
- ✗ The **political interests** of EU member states **differ too much** — it **can't** act in a **unified way** like the **USA** can.

Economic power

Strengths and influence
- ✓ It is only **rivalled** by the **USA** in terms of **GDP**.
- ✓ The EU accounted for **16.6%** of world trade (imports and exports) in 2022.
- ✓ It has nearly 450 million citizens and contains the **largest single market** in the **world**.
- ✓ The EU is home to a **huge number** of **TNCs**.

Restrictions and obstacles
- ✗ The **Greek financial crisis** showed the **fragility** of the EU's **economic power**.
- ✗ **Portugal**, **Italy**, **Greece**, **Spain** and **Ireland** have been **bailed out** of financial crises.
- ✗ **Brexit** meant the **fifth largest economy** in the world (and its **67 million people**) **left** the EU.
- ✗ **China** and **USA** have both achieved **higher growth rates** in recent decades, leaving the EU behind.

Structural power

Strengths and influence
- ✓ The EU is **represented** at significant **global institutions** such as the **WTO**, **G7** and **G20**.
- ✓ One EU state, **France**, has a **permanent seat** on the UN Security Council and wields **veto power**.

Restrictions and obstacles
- ✗ It is **not** a **member** of the **UN Security Council** — it only has **observer status** at the **UN**.
- ✗ **Individual** EU **member states** are **represented** and **vote** at the **UN**, but **not** the **EU** itself.
- ✗ The **EU is not** represented at the **IMF** or **World Bank**.

The EU as a Global Actor

Military power

Strengths and influence
- ✓ The EU has **evolved** from being a **primarily economic** entity into a **geopolitical** player.
- ✓ The EU has undertaken **peacekeeping operations** in a number of places — such as the **Democratic Republic of Congo** and **Kosovo**.
- ✓ The EU has created its own **high readiness** military capability.

While the EU doesn't have extensive military power, military power has become less significant with the advent of soft power.

Restrictions and obstacles
- ✗ The fact that there is **no EU army** but **multiple separate forces** severely **weakens** its **military power**.
- ✗ The EU is **not** seen as the **primary source of defence** for its members. **European defence** is largely provided by **NATO**, as evidenced by the **growth** of **NATO** to **32 members** following the Russian invasion of Ukraine in 2022.
- ✗ The EU has had to **rely** on **NATO** and the **USA** to **intervene** in **Bosnia** and **Kosovo**.
- ✗ **Brexit** has **weakened** the EU's **military capability**.
- ✗ It has **not fought any wars** and **lacks global** reach.

Soft power

Strengths and influence
- ✓ The EU's **values** make it an **attractive** regional body that states want to **join**.
- ✓ The EU has provided **global leadership** on issues like **human rights** and **climate change**.
- ✓ The EU pursues **attractive causes**. It provides more **humanitarian aid** (€1.7 billion in 2023) and **development aid** (€70.2 billion in 2021) than the **rest** of the **world combined**.
- ✓ The **criteria** for **joining** the **EU** has meant that new member states have **embraced human rights** and **democracy**.
- ✓ The EU has helped to **promote** and **protect democracy**. The EU Commission claims the EU has carried out around **300 election observer missions** in **75 states** from 2000-2024.

Restrictions and obstacles
- ✗ **Liberal democracy** is being **challenged** by growing **populist** and **nationalist** movements in **many** EU **states** (e.g. Austria and Hungary).
- ✗ The EU's **democratic deficit** (see page 290) **harms** its **appeal**.
- ✗ The EU has appeared **less attractive** due to its **financial crises** and its **relatively poor growth** performance **compared** to its main **rivals** recently.
- ✗ Soft power is **limited** in terms of **utility**. **Soft power** is **no substitute** for **military power** in many situations, such as **military aggression** and **invasions**.

Essay Plan
Evaluate the view that the European Union has become a superpower comparable to the US. [30]
Using the grid on p.298, **plan** an answer to the essay question above.

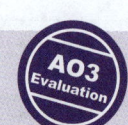

Exam Practice
Examine the extent to which institutions of the EU operate on the basis of intergovernmentalism or supranationalism. [12]

And the COLIN* for Best Global Actor in a Soft Power role goes to...
The EU is undoubtedly influential, but there are still some things holding it back from being as powerful as some other global players. Make sure you can provide evidence for both sides when you're discussing the powers of the EU in your exam.

*legally distinct from an Oscar in every way

Regionalism and Contemporary Issues

One of the big appeals of regionalism is being able to present a united front to tackle large-scale issues. But does it succeed?

Regional bodies can help tackle large-scale concerns

1) Regional bodies may be better at **coordinating concerted action** on **international issues**, such as **poverty** and **the environment**, as they have **fewer members** to manage than **global institutions**.
2) This makes action on international issues **more achievable**, especially if regional bodies act as **building blocks** — an **intermediary stage** in working towards **solutions** to **global issues**.
3) Regional bodies can also exert **more influence** on **international negotiations** than an **individual state** (especially on issues like **climate change**). For example, the **EU** has had considerable **influence** on matters regarding **poverty** through their presence in organisations such as the **WTO**.
4) However, the **increase** in the **number** of **regional bodies** in recent times has **not** resulted in an equivalent **increase** in **solutions** to global problems. Like states, regional bodies often act to pursue the **self-interest** of their **members** and **not all** member states will **positively contribute** to solving these issues.

Conflict

- Some argue that regionalism has had a **positive effect** on **conflict resolution**.
- **Liberal institutionalism** argues that the creation of international organisations **promotes cooperation** and **breaks down barriers** between states, helping to **avoid war**. This is supported by the concept of **commercial liberalism** — the idea that **economic integration** between states in a regional bloc helps **prevent war** between its members, as there would be **too much to lose**. The **EU** is an illustration of these concepts in action.
- Additionally, the **AU** and **EU** have undertaken **peacekeeping** in conflict zones like **Darfur** and **Kosovo**. The EU was also involved in **negotiations** over the **Iranian nuclear programme**.
- However, regional bodies can be **limited** in their **ability** to **intervene** in conflicts — the **EU** and **Arab League** had **little impact** on **stopping conflict** in **Syria**.

Poverty

- Regionalism can help **poverty reduction**.
- Many regional bodies are created for **economic reasons** (such as **USMCA**, **ASEAN** and the **EU**) and have helped to **promote trade** in their regions.
- The creation of the **single market** and the **EMU**, as well as its heavy **investment** in **development aid**, demonstrate the EU's commitment to **improving trade**.
- However, the **protectionist** policies of the EU such as its **common external tariff** and **CAP** make it **harder** for farmers in **developing states** to **compete** fairly with **subsidised** EU producers. **Austerity policies** imposed on **Greece** by the EU after its **financial crisis** made **poverty soar** there.

Human rights

- Regionalism has a **mixed record** on **human rights**.
- Human rights have been **promoted** through the creation of the **European Convention on Human Rights** and the **EU's** commitments to **human rights protection**.
- However, there are **many regional bodies** that **do not share** this **interpretation** of **universal human rights**. For example:
  1) The **Arab League**, **AU** and **ASEAN** have **member states** that have **intolerant laws** on **homosexuality**.
  2) **AU members failed** to **arrest** and **hand over** the ex-Sudanese leader, **Omar al-Bashir**, to the **ICC**.
  3) The **EU** had to **rely on NATO** to **intervene** over **genocide** and **ethnic cleansing** in **Bosnia** and **Kosovo** in the **1990s**.
- But the EU has been very successful in **spreading democracy** and **human rights** by stipulating that any **new members** must **uphold** such values to join it. This has led to a transformation in **rights protection** for people in **eastern Europe**.

Environment

- The **EU** has played a big role in **tackling climate change**. It has provided **global leadership** through **increasing** its use of **renewable energy** and setting **ambitious targets** for **reducing emissions**.
- Regional bodies such as the **Small Islands Developing States** (**SIDS**) and **Pacific Islands Forum** (**PIF**) have been active in **raising awareness** about the **perils** of **climate change**.
- However, many regional bodies see **development** as being **more urgent** than concerns over **climate change**.
- By definition, a **regional body** on its own **cannot solve** all environmental issues. As a **global concern**, it ultimately needs a **global approach** to tackle it.

We're on page 293? No wonder I'm struggling for jokes at this point...

When analysing influence on the global stage in your exam, it's all about these four key issues. So don't you forget 'em.

Global Politics — Regionalism and the EU

Comparative Theories

You might have picked up on a not-so-subtle theme of realism vs liberalism in this section of the book. Well, here, in the final section on Global Politics, we're bringing it all together. Just like a season finale of a beloved sci-fi show. Weeeeee-oooooo...

The main **comparative theories** in **global politics** are **realism** and **liberalism**

Realism

1) **Realism** revolves around the ideas of **power**, **international anarchy** and the **centrality** of the **states**.
2) Realism has its **foundations** in works such as *The Leviathan* (1651) by **Thomas Hobbes** (see p.44).
   - **Hobbes** viewed humans as **selfish**, **greedy** and **untrusting**.
   - He argued that without **strong government** (a Leviathan) humans would exist in a **state of nature** where there was a constant "*war of all against all*" and their lives would be "*nasty, brutish and short*".
   - For realists, **domestic analogy** suggests that in the **absence** of a **global government**, this **state of nature** exists **internationally** as there is **no higher authority** than the state. The resulting **international anarchy** means there is **inevitably** competition and **conflict** between states — states **cannot rely** on **anyone except themselves**.

Key Terms — domestic analogy: The idea that the behaviour of states and the relationship between them can be modelled as the behaviour and relationships between individuals in society.

Liberalism

1) **Liberalism** emphasises the importance of **ideas**, the **natural harmony** between states and the existence of a **range** of **different actors** in the **international system**.
2) The **liberal perspective** developed from thinkers such as **John Locke** (see p.49) and his idea of the **social contract**.
   - **Locke's** view of **human nature** was more **optimistic** than Hobbes', seeing humans as **sociable**, **cooperative** and largely **peaceful**.
   - After the **Second World War** and with the **collapse of communism** in the **1990s**, liberalism challenged the **dominance** of **realism**.
   - For liberals, **domestic analogy** suggests that the **institutions**, **rule of law** and **cooperation** which enable a **state** to operate can also be applied at the **international level** to allow for a **peaceful** and **interdependent global society**.

A showdown for the ages...

The **realist outlook** has several **core ideas**

States and the balance of power
- **States** are the **most important** actors in global politics — all other bodies are **subordinate** to them.
- **Nothing** can be achieved **without power** — and the only **check** on **power** is **power** itself.
- The **Billiard Ball Model** (see page 259) reflects the **centrality** of **states** in **global politics** — each **state** is in **competition** with **all** the **others**, with **no external force** controlling the process.
- The **best** that can be hoped for is a **temporary balance of power** (such as in the **Cold War**).
- **Competition** between states is **fierce**. A state's place in the **global pecking order** is crucial for its survival.

International anarchy and its implications
- **States** exist in a condition of **international anarchy** with **no overarching global government**.
- By nature, **humans** are **egoistical**, **greedy** and **self-interested** — they **crave power**. This **human egoism** translates into **state egoism** — states desire **greater power** in order to **survive**.
- Eventually, as **divisions** grow between states, they will seek to **leave IGOs** to **further** their own **interests** (e.g. **Brexit**).

The security dilemma
As one state **increases** its **military spending**, **other states** will feel **threatened** by this. These states will **respond** by **increasing** their own **defence spending**, resulting in an **arms race**.

The inevitability of war
- Due to **anarchy** and **human nature**, **war** is **inevitable**. The **history** of **humanity** is a **history** of **war**.
- Any period of **peace cannot last** indefinitely — it will always come to an **end** eventually.

Comparative Theories

There are **three core strands** of **realist thought** in **global politics**

OFFENSIVE REALISTS argue that all states are **power-maximisers**. This says that the **object** of the **state** is to **maximise** its **power** in a **dangerous world** to ensure its **survival** and **future success**. As a result, **war** is **commonplace**.

DEFENSIVE REALISTS reject this view and say that states are **security-maximisers**. This argues that **states** try to ensure their **survival** by **prioritising** their **defence** against external threats — but this can **sometimes** lead to **war**.

NEO-REALISTS (or STRUCTURAL REALISTS) reject the **'inside-out'** view that **internal factors** (caused by **human nature** being **evil**) make **states** behave in ways that lead to **conflict**. Instead, they support an **'outside-in'** theory — that the **behaviour** of **states** is determined by **external circumstances**. They believe it is **international anarchy** and the prevailing **system** of **polarity** (see p.277-278) that **shapes** states' **behaviour** on the international stage, **not** any flaw of **human nature**.

The **liberal outlook** has several **core ideas**

Morality and optimism in human nature

- Humans can **rationalise** problems and **rise above** their **base human desires**. **Foreign policy** based on **human rights** and **democracy** can lead to **peace**.
- **Individuals** are capable of **enlightened self-interest** and have the capacity to **cooperate** for **mutual best advantage**. What is **best** for the **collective** may be **best** for a **single state**.
- **War isn't inevitable** and is **irrational** when considered from the **viewpoint** of what is **best** for the **collective**. War is less likely because **humans** are **rational**.

Complex interdependence

- **Joseph Nye** and **Robert Keohane** coined the term **complex interdependence** in **1977** to explain the **lack** of a **major global conflict** since the Second World War. As states have become more **closely connected** (in terms of the **economy**, **human rights**, **immigration**, etc.), states are far **less likely** to use **military force** as it will **disrupt** their own **societies**.
- The **Cobweb model** (see page 259) suggests that states are **linked** and **bound** by **common interest** (like the strands in a cobweb), rather than being **self-contained** and **immune** to **outside influence**.

Possibility of harmony and balance

- Trying to achieve a **balance of power** in the **international system** can ultimately lead to **war**. Instead, pursuing **cooperation** leads to **peace**.
- This **cooperation** can **benefit** and **improve** the **condition** of **all states**, not just one.

Likelihood of global governance

- **IGOs** such as the **UN** provide a level of **global regulation** in **international affairs**.
- States are **cooperative** by **nature** and are interested in dealing with problems **collectively**. **IGOs** are the **best method** for tackling **global issues**.

Impact and growth of international organisations

It isn't just states that play an **important** and **active role** on the global stage — **IGOs**, **NGOs**, **TNCs**, etc, are all of **increasing importance** (see page 258).

There are **four core strands** of **liberal thought** in **global politics**

COMMERCIAL LIBERALS argue that **economic connections** between states **prevent war** breaking out. Increasingly states have **too much to lose** by going to war and **disrupting** their own **supply chain** — especially as the world has become increasingly **globalised**.

REPUBLICAN LIBERALS argue that **democracy promotes peace**. This has prompted the idea of **democratic zones of peace** and **non-democratic zones of conflict**. The **democratic peace thesis** argues that **no two democratic states** have **fought** a **war** against one another.

LIBERAL INSTITUTIONALISTS argue that the **interactions** between **states** through different **IGOs** helps to **prevent war**. States are able to have **closer relations** and **settle disputes** more easily **without** resorting to **violence**. The different channels of **communication** between states help to build **trust** between them.

NEO-LIBERALS acknowledge the **limitations** of the **liberal perspective** and recognise the existence of **anarchy** in global politics. Neo-liberalism **shifts** the focus **away** from **morality** and **ideals**, towards **economic** and **environmental security** matters. However, it maintains the **importance** of creating a **framework** of **international bodies** to aid **cooperation** between states and to help **regulate** global affairs.

Comparative Theories

The society of states is a compromise between realism and liberalism

Hedley Bull tried to find a **compromise** position between the ideas of **liberals** and those of **realists**.

- In *The Anarchical Society* in 1977, he argued that although **states** exist in a situation of **international anarchy** with **no overarching authority**, they also form a **society of states**.
- States have **common interests** that lead them to form an **international community** with **shared norms** of **behaviour**, **rules** and **values**. Their **actions** are governed by the **rules** of **international law**, **diplomacy** and **mutual interests** — not just considerations of **power**.
- This view has been described as **liberal realism**.

Global political events can be evaluated through a liberal or realist lens

The table below summarises the **realist** and **liberal** outlooks on the **topics** covered in the **Global Politics section** of this book.

	Realism	Liberalism
The State and Globalisation	• The **growing number** of **states** in the **international system** supports the **realist** view that the **state** remains of **central importance** in global politics. • The **growing power** of states like **China** and **India**, as well as **unilateral military action** taken by states like **Russia** in recent years, seems to **support** this analysis. • There has been a move back towards **state authority**, especially given the **renewed success** of **Trump** in **2024** and his **America First rhetoric**.	• The continued **globalisation process** in all areas (**economic**, **political** and **cultural**) suggests that the **state** is becoming **less relevant** and that its **power** is being **eroded**. • The **borders** of the **state** continue to become more **permeable** and open to **external influences**. • **Hyperglobalists** may be right — the **world** and the **state** appear to be **changing** drastically due to **globalisation**.
Global Governance — Political and Economic	• Despite the **United Nations** retaining **near universal membership**, it has **struggled** to **manage** the scale of **issues** arising since **2000** (e.g. **9/11** and **conflicts** in **Afghanistan**, **Iraq**, **Ukraine**, **Myanmar**, **Gaza** and **Sudan**). • **Realists** believe **institutions** such as the UN **can't overcome** the inherent **self-interest** of their **member states** and are therefore **ineffective**. • The **expansion** of **NATO** in recent years (including the admission of **Sweden** and **Finland**) indicates that **power politics** is still relevant. This has been **enhanced** by a need to **counter** the **threat** of Russian aggression. • The rise of **China** and its **alternative financial institutions** (e.g. **AIIB**) demonstrates areas where the **Bretton Woods institutions** may act more as **agents** of **US power** than bodies of **global governance**.	• **Global governance** supports the **liberal perspective** of **increasing cooperation** over global issues. • Liberals cite multiple **examples** of **increasing global governance**, such as the formation of the **G20** in **1999** (and its importance in dealing with the 2007/8 **Credit Crunch**), the **increasing membership** of the **WTO** and the continuation of the **IMF** and **World Bank** (with **near universal membership**). • The **UN** has carried out **humanitarian interventions** in places such as **Libya**. • **NATO** has **promoted** the values of **democracy** and **human rights** to an **increasing number** of **states**.
Global Governance — Human Rights and Environmental	• The **continued** existence of **human rights abuses** and **atrocities** also demonstrates the **limitations** of **human rights global governance**. • The **interests** of sovereign states come **before** any **consideration** of universal values. The human rights abuses in **prisons** like **Abu Ghraib** and **Guantanamo Bay**, and the **death tolls** in **Gaza**, **Syria** and **Sudan**, are cited as evidence of this. The **ICC** has had a **limited impact** in this regard. • Realists believe the **failure** of concerted international action on **climate change** was an inevitable **consequence** of an **international system** based on **sovereign states**. • The **continued rise** in CO_2 emissions shows a **reluctance** on the part of **states** to **conform** to **global rules** that may **harm** their **national interest**.	• The issue of **human rights** has continued to attract a lot of **global attention** with the **success** of the **war crimes tribunals** and creation of the **ICC** — which now has **125 members**. • **Huge steps** have been made regarding **environmental global governance** in recent decades at both **national** and **international** levels. • Being a **global issue**, climate change is seen as a prime example of a **liberal cause** — with **progress** being made due to the **Paris Agreement**.

Global Politics — Comparative Theories

Comparative Theories

	Realism	Liberalism
Power and Development	• The continued **global power shifts** from the **Western** world to **China** and **India** demonstrate the **importance** of **military** and **economic power** in the international system. • Realists believe there is an endless process of **competition** between **states**, with global politics appearing **less unipolar** in recent times and **increasingly bipolar** or **multipolar**. • Even **soft power** has become an **increasingly important** battleground for **nations** to exert greater **influence** in global politics. • Despite the growth of different forms of **international cooperation**, realists believe that states **retain** their position as the **primary actors** in international affairs. For example, the **UK leaving** the **EU** and the **US not ratifying** the **Rome Statute**. • Realists believe this shows that the **vision of progress** towards a global **liberal democratic** future **utopia** as predicted by Francis Fukuyama is **wrong**.	• The number of states with **democratic governments** has **increased** over the **last 200 years**. • Liberals see the consolidation of **democratic rule** in **Eastern Europe** as an example of this. • Liberals see continued growth of **'Asian Tiger' economies** in the 21st century as evidence of a **shift away** from protectionist policies. • The rise of **soft power** shows that states cannot as readily resort to **hard power** as they would have done in previous eras. • The more **interconnected** nature of the world, with **growing levels** of **education** and **literacy**, and instantaneous forms of **communication**, means that **attractiveness** has never been so important.
Regionalism and the EU	• The **rise** of **nationalism**, the **departure** of the **UK** from the **EU** and the **success** of **populists** such as **Viktor Orban** and **Georgia Meloni** suggests that **regionalism** is becoming **less popular**. • Realists believe that the **EU** has been **struggling** to tackle these forces because **regional bodies** will only exist as long as they are **aligned** with the **national interest** of their **members**. • Many **regional bodies** have not wished to **exert** the same degree of **power** over their **member states** as the EU. This is intentional — **member states** in the **Arab League** or **USMCA** prioritise their **sovereignty** and do not wish for **deeper integration** beyond **economic** or **political benefits**.	• The **continued growth** of the **EU** and increase in **regional bodies** and **free trade agreements** is evidence that the liberal **global perspective** may be **correct**. • Since **2000**, the **membership** of the **EU** has **increased** from **15** to **27** and the array of **policy areas** that it **legislates** on has **broadened**. • The **world** has never been as **regionally connected** as it is today.

Quick Questions

1) What is the domestic analogy?
2) Why do realists believe war is inevitable?
3) Name and describe the three strands of realist thought in global politics.
4) Why do liberals believe IGOs are the best method for tackling global issues?
5) Name and describe the four strands of liberal thought in global politics.
6) What is meant by the society of states?

To defend against vampires, consider a society of stakes

Revision Task

Practise your **analysis** skills by explaining the central **differences** between realism and liberalism. Use the following key terms and concepts to **contrast** the perspectives presented by the two theories.

- Human nature
- International anarchy
- Power and ideas
- Importance of the state and other actors
- Prospects for peace and war
- The balance of power

Exam Practice

Examine how realists and liberals disagree on human nature and the likelihood of war. [12]

My work in compearative theories has revealed that I just prefer apples...

Phew... that's finally the last proper section of this chunky ol' book done and dusted. I'm exhausted from writing it and you're probably knackered from reading it. I reckon you've earned a break before tackling some exam practice. I'm off for a nap.

Exam Skills

Planning Your Essays

Righty, let's start off the Exam Skills section with some essay plans. Needless to say, make sure you're looking at the right type of essay. For shorter answer questions, you'll just need the Main Paragraph sections of each essay plan.

Edexcel 'Source' Essays / AQA 'Extract' Essays

INTRODUCTION
- **Define criteria** for answering the question
- Discuss the **two-sided argument** (with reference to the source)
- Direct your **answer** to the question (with a brief justification)

*In AQA extract questions, you'll be expected to comment on the **provenance** of the extracts (i.e. who wrote it and where it was published).*

MAIN PARAGRAPHS
- **WEAKER** Argument
  - Quote
  - Example
  - Analysis
- **STRONGER** Argument
  - Quote
  - Example
  - Analysis
- Judgement

For 30-mark source essays (Edexcel) or 25-mark extract essays (AQA), you should usually aim for 3 main paragraphs.

CONCLUSION
- **Answer** the question (with reference to the source)
- Acknowledge the merits of **alternative points of view/factors**
- Assert the **superiority** of your **chosen line of argument**

UK, US and Global Essays

INTRODUCTION
- **Define criteria** for answering the question
- Discuss the **two-sided argument** (with reference to the source)
- Direct your **answer** to the question (with a brief justification)

MAIN PARAGRAPHS
- **WEAKER** Argument **Point 1**
  - Example
- **WEAKER** Argument **Point 2**
  - Example
- **Analysis** of the significance of these examples
- **STRONGER** Argument **Point 1**
  - Example
- **STRONGER** Argument **Point 2**
  - Example
- **Analysis** of the significance of these examples
- Judgement

Aim for 3 main paragraphs for 30-mark essays (Edexcel) or 25-mark essays (AQA). For the comparative essays in AQA Paper 2, aim to make these points comparisons between the UK and the US.

CONCLUSION
- **Answer** the question
- Acknowledge the merits of **alternative points of view/factors**
- Assert the **superiority** of your **chosen line of argument**

Political Ideas Essays

INTRODUCTION
- **Define criteria** for answering the question
- Discuss the **two-sided argument**
- Direct your **answer** to the question (with a brief justification)

Edexcel students — you should use qualifying adverbs like 'largely', 'mostly' and 'partially' in your judgement so you properly address the 'extent' aspect of Political Ideas questions.

MAIN PARAGRAPHS
- **WEAKER** Argument **Point 1**
  - Example of agreement/disagreement between specific strands and thinkers
- **WEAKER** Argument **Point 2**
  - Example of agreement/disagreement between specific stands and thinkers
- **Analysis** of these agreements/disagreements
- **STRONGER** Argument **Point 1**
  - Example of agreement/disagreement between specific strands and thinkers
- **STRONGER** Argument **Point 2**
  - Example of agreement/disagreement between specific strands and thinkers
- **Analysis** of these agreements/disagreements
- Judgement

CONCLUSION
- **Answer** the question
- Acknowledge the merits of **alternative points of view/factors**
- Assert the **superiority** of your **chosen line of argument**

*For **AQA**, one Political Ideas question will also use extracts, so you may need to use elements from the plan above.*

Sentence Frames — Edexcel

Here's a handy collection of sentence frames to help you go about constructing the arguments needed to write a top-notch essay.

30-Mark Source Essays

INTRO
If [use wording of question], there would need to be [criteria]. The source advances a persuasive case for arguing that [weaker argument] due to [...]. However, this is outweighed by the source's more convincing view that [stronger argument] because [...].

MAIN PARAS.

WEAKER Argument
The source offers a plausible, though ultimately flawed, argument that [...] by asserting [...]. This is supported by the fact that [evidence]. This is significant because [...].

→ *STRONGER Argument*
However, the source advances a more convincing argument that [...]. This is a stronger line of argument because [evidence].

→ *JUDGEMENT*
Therefore, it is more persuasive to argue that [...] because [evidence].

CON.
In summary, the source's most convincing line of argument is that [...] due to [...]. It should be acknowledged that the source also makes a plausible case that [...]. Nevertheless, it remains more persuasive to conclude that [...] because [...].

30-Mark UK, US and Global Essays

INTRO
If [use wording of question], there would need to be [criteria]. There is a plausible case for arguing that [weaker argument] due to [...]. However, this is outweighed by the more convincing view that [stronger argument] because [...].

MAIN PARAS.

WEAKER Argument
There is a plausible, though ultimately flawed, argument that [...] by asserting [...]. This is supported by the fact that [evidence]. This is significant because [...].

→ *STRONGER Argument*
However, a more convincing argument is that [...]. This is a stronger line of argument because [evidence].

→ *JUDGEMENT*
Therefore, it is more persuasive to argue that [...] because [evidence].

CON.
In summary, the most convincing line of argument is that [...] due to [...]. However, it should be acknowledged that [...]. Nevertheless, it remains more persuasive to conclude that [...] because [...].

24-Mark Political Ideas Essays

*In questions on political ideas, you'll need to judge the **extent** to which different strands **agree** or **disagree** on a particular idea.*

INTRO
For [ideology] to [use wording of question], there would need to be broad agreement across the strands over [introduce paragraph themes]. It could be argued that [weaker argument] due to [...]. However, this is outweighed by the more persuasive view that [stronger argument] because [...].

MAIN PARAGRAPHS

WEAKER Argument
[Ideology] mostly does/does not present a common view, but there are areas of disagreement/agreement across the strands. For instance, [Strand X] and [Strand Y] agree/disagree over [...]: while [Strand X Thinker A] believes [...], [Strand Y Thinker B] offers the similar/contrasting view that [...]. This is because [explanation of why they are similar/different].

→ *STRONGER Argument*
Nevertheless, it is more convincing to argue that [stronger line of argument] because [justification]. [Strand X Thinker A] and [Strand Y Thinker B] agree/disagree over [...]. These similar/different ideas stem from [...].

→ *JUDGEMENT*
Therefore, the similarities/differences outweigh the differences/similarities because [justification].

CON.
In summary, the most convincing line of argument is that [...] due to [...]. However, it should be acknowledged that [...]. Nevertheless, it remains more persuasive to conclude that [...] because [...].

Exam Skills

Sentence Frames — AQA

This beautiful selection of sentence frames has been designed to help you turn your essays into works of art. Gorgeous.

25-Mark Extract Essays

INTRO: If [use wording of question], there would need to be [criteria]. Extract 1 advances a persuasive case for arguing that [weaker argument] due to [...]. However, this is outweighed by extract 2's more convincing view that [stronger argument] because [...].

MAIN PARAS.

WEAKER Argument
Extract 1 offers a plausible, though ultimately flawed, argument that [...] by asserting [...]. This is supported by the fact that [evidence]. This is significant because [...].

→

STRONGER Argument
However, extract 2 advances a more convincing argument that [...]. This is a stronger line of argument because [evidence].

→

JUDGEMENT
Therefore, it is more persuasive to accept extract 2's argument that [...] because [evidence].

CON. In summary, extract 2's line of argument that [...] due to [...] is most convincing. It should be acknowledged that extract 1 also makes a plausible case that [...]. Nevertheless, it remains more persuasive to conclude that [...] because [...].

25-Mark Comparative Essays

INTRO: If [use wording of question], there would need to be [criteria]. There is a plausible case for arguing that [weaker argument] due to [...]. However, this is outweighed by the more convincing view that [stronger argument] because [...].

MAIN PARAS.

WEAKER Argument
A plausible, though ultimately flawed, case can be made for arguing that [...]. This is demonstrated by [...] illustrating that [...]. A further argument in support of the notion that [...] is [...]. This is exemplified by [...], which means [...].

→

STRONGER Argument
Nevertheless, the more persuasive argument remains that [...]. This is a stronger line of argument because [evidence]. Furthermore, it is also the case that [...], which proves that [...].

→

JUDGEMENT
Therefore, it is more compelling to argue that [...] because [evidence].

CON. In summary, the most convincing line of argument is that [...] due to [...]. However, it should be acknowledged that [...]. Nevertheless, it remains more persuasive to conclude that [...] because [...].

25-Mark Core Political Ideas Essays

*As well as addressing the information in the extracts, you should also talk about how this information relates to **other strands** and **thinkers**.*

INTRO: For [ideology] to [use wording of question], there would need to be broad agreement across the strands over [introduce paragraph themes]. It could be argued that [weaker argument] due to [...]. However, this is outweighed by the more persuasive view that [stronger argument] because [...].

MAIN PARAGRAPHS

WEAKER Argument
The two extracts exemplify areas of (dis)agreement across the strands of [ideology]. For instance, in extract 1 [Strand X Thinker A] writes that [...]. In extract 2 [Strand Y Thinker B] offers the similar/contrasting view that [...]. These ideas are similar/different because [...]. This is representative of broader (dis)agreements between [Strands X and Y] because [...].

→

STRONGER Argument
Nevertheless, it is more convincing to argue that [stronger line of argument] because [justification]. The two extracts also show areas of (dis)agreement across the strands of [ideology]. Extract 1 includes [Strand X Thinker A]'s belief that [...]. This coheres/clashes with [Strand Y Thinker B]'s idea in extract 2 that [...]. These similar/different ideas stem from [...]. Furthermore, they reveal a wider (dis)agreement between [Strands X and Y] over [...].

→

JUDGEMENT
Therefore, the similarities/differences outweigh the differences/similarities because [justification].

CON. In summary, the most convincing line of argument is that [...] due to [...]. However, it should be acknowledged that [...]. Nevertheless, it remains more persuasive to conclude that [...] because [...].

Exam Skills

Helpful Phrases

In addition to those chunky sentence frames, here are a bunch of handy phrases that you can use in your essays. Don't feel you have to use them exactly, but they can be great for highlighting your analysis and helping your writing flow.

Here are some other **helpful phrases** to use in essays

BUILDING an argument
- *This is supported by a wealth of evidence:* [...]
- *There have been several instances of this in recent years:* [...]
- *An example with long-lasting significance is* [...]
- *There are several thinkers who agree over this fundamental principle.* [...]

UNDERMINING an argument
- *This case is undermined by* [...]
- *While this argument is accurate, it does not represent the norm.* [...]
- *However, this tends to be an exception to the more common reality, which is* [...]

Introducing SIMILARITIES
- *These two [thinkers or extracts] do not wholly disagree, because both accept that* [...]
- *Because of their similar views on* [...], *thinkers from both strands also agree over* [...]
- *These similarities are also reflected in agreements over* [...]
- *Similarly,* [...]
- *Furthermore,* [...]

Introducing DIFFERENCES
- *However, there is a divergence of views over* [...]
- *There are profound differences between* [...] *and* [...] *over* [...]
- *This disagreement over* [...] *also leads to wider differences over* [...]
- *By contrast,* [...]
- [...], *whereas* [...]

Introducing EVIDENCE
- *An example of this is* [...]
- *One way of showing this is* [...]
- *This happened most notably when* [...]
- *This judgement is justified by* [...]

Analysing EVIDENCE
- *This highlights that* [...]
- *This is important because* [...]
- *Arguably, this shows that* [...]
- *This may imply that* [...]

EVALUATING sources/extracts
- *Source/Extract* [...] *is right to highlight* [...]
- *Source/Extract* [...] *rightly points out* [...]
- *Source/Extract* [...] *fails to account for* [...]
- *Source/Extract* [...] *doesn't address* [...]

EVALUATING agreement/disagreement
- [...], *the extent of agreement/disagreement is minimal.*
- [...], *the agreements/disagreements are fundamental.*
- [...], *agreements/disagreements are minimal/infrequent.*

TRANSITIONING between arguments
- *Although these arguments are all accurate, there is a more persuasive case that* [...]
- *More often than not, however,* [...]
- *These points notwithstanding, it is more typically the case that* [...]

SYNTHESISING arguments
- *These arguments may not outweigh the opposing side, but they do provide an important layer of nuance.*
- *While the examples of* [...] *and* [...] *are important, it is more often the case that* [...]
- *It is therefore important to take into account both* [...] *and* [...] *in arguing that* [...]

I end all my chats with 'see ya later alligator'. I'm going through a phrase...

Don't panic about learning all these word for word. The important thing is to remember the structure provided by the plans and sentence frames, and to use the right kind of language so it's really clear to the examiner that you know your stuff.

Annotated Essay — Electoral Systems

Time to see those essay plans and sentence frames in action — starting with some UK Politics. Some important things you need to keep in mind are the Assessment Objectives, or AOs. You get AO1 marks for demonstrating your knowledge and understanding of politics. AO2 marks are for analysing political information and scenarios. Finally, AO3 marks are awarded for evaluating political facts, events and viewpoints — this involves making a judgement and coming to a conclusion.

1. Evaluate the view that the advantages of first-past-the-post outweigh the case for using a different electoral system in general elections.

PARAGRAPHS
1) MP-constituency link
2) Party representation
3) Formation of government

*The answer below shows an **introductory paragraph** and then the **first main paragraph** of the essay.*

ANSWER

If first-past-the-post's advantages were to outweigh the case for using a different electoral system in UK general elections, its maintenance of a strong MP-constituency link and reliable track record in creating stable governments would be considered sufficient to outweigh other systems' provision of voter choice and greater proportionality. While first-past-the-post is the system most likely to deliver a majority government, recent evidence suggests that this is no guarantee of stability. Other systems — notably AMS — manage to preserve constituency representation while also delivering stable government, increased voter choice, and a higher degree of proportionality than first-past-the-post. It is therefore more convincing to argue that its advantages are not sufficient to outweigh the case for replacing it in UK general elections. This is due to the fact that AMS combines the advantages of first-past-the-post with the advantages of more proportional systems.

There is a plausible case for arguing that first-past-the-post's advantage of maintaining a strong MP-constituency link outweighs the case for using either STV or AMS in general elections. Because first-past-the-post uses single-member constituencies, representation is direct, clear, and localised — approximately 60-90 000 constituents are represented by one MP, who can become an expert in local matters such as healthcare, education, employment and crime. Many MPs elected under first-past-the-post have strong track records in placing constituency matters above party loyalty or their own career prospects: for instance, Mark Menzies, the Conservative MP for Fylde, has consistently opposed fracking on behalf of his constituents, even though his party leadership has been supportive of the practice. This advantage of first-past-the-post is not present in the same way in proportional systems that use multi-member constituencies: under STV in the Northern Ireland Assembly, there are 5 MLAs for each constituency, which arguably weakens the direct, personal link between representatives and constituents found under first-past-the-post. However, it is more persuasive to argue that this advantage of first-past-the-post does not fully outweigh the case for using a different system in UK general elections. Single-member constituencies can be problematic because the MPs elected often lack a strong mandate from a significant proportion of the electorate: 229 of 650 MPs were elected in 2019 with under 50% of the vote in their constituency, while in 2015, Alasdair McDonell was elected to represent Belfast South with only 24.5% of the vote. By contrast, multi-member constituencies offer a more nuanced form of representation: in Fermanagh and South Tyrone, which Sinn Féin won by a margin of only 57 votes in the 2019 general election, there are three Sinn Féin MLAs, one UUP MLA, and one DUP MLA in the Northern Ireland Assembly. Unlike under first-past-the-post, where only 43% of voters were represented by the outcome, this meant that STV represented over 70% of voters in the constituency. Moreover, AMS, a mixed system, combines the best elements of first-past-the-post with the best elements of proportional systems in terms of constituency representation: while over half of constituencies are elected under first-past-the-post, with single members who offer specialised representation, there are also regional constituencies, like North East Scotland, that are elected under the Party List system. This has allowed voters who support parties with more dispersed support, such as the Scottish Green Party and the Scottish Conservative Party, to be represented, which would be unlikely under a pure first-past-the-post system. Because other systems provide more nuanced representation while retaining localised constituencies, it is therefore more convincing to argue that first-past-the-post's advantage of maintaining a strong MP-constituency link does not outweigh the case for using a different system in UK general elections.

Exam Skills

Annotated Essay — Socialism

1 To what extent do socialists share a common view on the economy?

PARAGRAPHS

1) Views on capitalism

2) Views on the state's role in the economy

*The answer below shows an **introduction**, the **second main paragraph** and the **conclusion**.*

ANSWER

Socialists could be described as sharing a common view on the economy if there were broad agreement between the fundamentalist, revisionist, and Third Way strands over capitalism and the state's role in the economy. All socialists advance critiques of capitalism and share the view that the state has a role to play in providing a form of economic equality. Despite these areas of commonality, there are more significant disagreements between fundamentalists and the Third Way over the moral and economic impact of capitalism, and between all three strands over the level of state intervention required to alleviate capitalism's undesirable features. It is therefore more convincing to argue that socialists largely do not share a common view on the economy.

[...]

In spite of the many differences in their views of the state's role in the economy, socialists do have many views in common; neither revisionists nor fundamentalist socialists support unregulated capitalism, with fundamentalists like Karl Marx and Rosa Luxemburg calling for the state to abolish private property in the pursuit of equality of outcome. Similarly, revisionists such as Anthony Crosland support a mixed economy in which there is a balance between state ownership (as advocated by Marx) and private ownership. Moreover, both revisionist and fundamentalist socialists share a common view that the state has a crucial role to play in achieving economic equality: fundamentalist Marx called for a dictatorship of the proletariat following a violent revolution, which would oversee the structural changes needed to remove the 'chains' imposed by capitalism and begin the move towards equality of outcome. Revisionists Crosland and Beatrice Webb also believed that state intervention was necessary to reform capitalism: the former supported a progressive taxation system to redistribute wealth, while the latter argued that 'the possession of wealth...seems almost invariably to sterilise intelligence'. Despite these commonalities, it remains more convincing to argue that revisionist and fundamentalist socialists have a largely different view on the state's role in the economy: while fundamentalist Marx envisaged a dictatorship of the proletariat, he believed the state would 'wither away' once society had been restored to its natural condition, meaning that there would be no need for any state intervention in the economy. This contrasts with revisionists Webb and Crosland, both of whom revised Marx's beliefs about the state to advance a more permanent view of its role as an enabling, regulatory instrument for achieving socialist goals. While Marx aimed for complete equality of outcome — 'from each according to his abilities, to each according to his needs' — revisionists aim to improve equality of opportunity and reduce material inequalities, with Crosland writing of a society where class differences are 'very much smaller'. Furthermore, the differences are even more pronounced when the views of Third Way thinkers are considered: Giddens believed that a neo-liberal, largely non-interventionist state could achieve his guiding principle of equality of opportunity without any nationalised ownership, using tax yields to fund high-quality public services. This represents a stark difference within socialism, given that fundamentalists hold such strident views on private ownership and material inequality. As there are significant disagreements between the strands over both the means and the ends of the state's role in the economy, the argument that socialists do not in fact share a largely common view of the economy is more compelling.

[...]

The extent of disagreement between socialist strands over capitalism and over the state's role in the economy mean that it is most accurate to argue that socialists largely do not share a common view on the economy. The commonalities that do exist — namely the shared view that capitalism is a flawed economic system that requires some form of regulation or intervention by the state — are outweighed by the more fundamental disagreements. The fact that fundamentalist socialists call for the abolition of capitalism and the institution of private property, while the Third Way seeks to harness capitalism to maximise the growth of private property, provides a clear illustration of socialists' largely divergent views on the economy, which is replicated in further disagreements between all three strands over nationalisation, private ownership, economic equality and taxation.

Exam Skills

Annotated Essay — US Presidency

1. Evaluate the view that US presidents since 1992 have tended to be more imperilled than imperial.

PARAGRAPHS
1) Foreign policy
2) Domestic policy
3) Economic policy

*The answer below shows the **introduction**, the **first main paragraph** and the **conclusion**.*

ANSWER

To argue that presidents since 1992 have been imperilled rather than imperial is to suggest that recent administrations have been primarily characterised by ineffectiveness and weakness in foreign, domestic and economic policy. Proponents of this view would point to Supreme Court rulings on executive action, the strict checks imposed by Congress on the President's economic agenda, the increasingly partisan nature of the Senate's oversight and the increasing frequency of previously rare checks such as impeachment and government shutdown. Conversely, those challenging this view would argue that, in foreign policy especially, recent presidents have been able to act imperially — without experiencing significant checks from Congress or the Supreme Court. Hence it is most convincing to argue that presidents since 1992 have tended to be more imperilled in domestic and economic policy, but more imperial in foreign policy.

As Wildavsky's 'two presidencies' thesis states, the president has a greater chance of acting imperially in foreign policy, where they face fewer congressional checks compared with domestic or economic policy. Nevertheless, it is important to acknowledge that no president can act imperially in foreign policy for the duration of their presidency. During Trump's first presidency, he failed both in his bid to broker a nuclear disarmament agreement with North Korea and in his effort to propose a lasting solution to the Israel-Palestine impasse due to external checks from international forces. Furthermore, Trump's handling of diplomatic relations with Ukraine, which saw him accused of offering a quid pro quo deal in return for information on Hunter Biden, led to his first impeachment, thereby directly imperilling him. Similarly, George W. Bush suffered significant policy failures during his War on Terror: the Abu Ghraib scandal, combined with controversy over the presence of WMD in Iraq, significantly weakened his public approval ratings, which dropped to 23% in 2008, the lowest ever recorded. While it might be inaccurate to describe Bush as imperilled since he faced no realistic threat of being removed from office towards the end of his second term as president, checks and balances in foreign policy meant that he did not leave office as an imperial president. More often than not, though, the limited scope of congressional checks and balances in foreign policy mean that presidents since 1992 have been able to act unilaterally. Biden ordered air strikes in Syria, Afghanistan, Yemen and Iraq, as well as imposing economic sanctions on Russia, without consulting Congress. This creates the impression that he possessed a far greater capacity for imperial actions in foreign policy than in domestic policy, where he was consistently checked by Congress. This reflects a trend experienced by other recent presidents: the authorisation of the use of military force in Iraq, passed by Congress in 2002, has been used 41 times in over 20 countries, effectively giving presidents a blank cheque for ordering military interventions. Obama, Trump and Biden have all made extensive use of executive agreements (most notably with Iran in Obama and Biden's case, and with Israel in Trump's). Executive agreements allow presidents to bypass Congress, instead of signing treaties which are subject to Senate ratification. So while it is important to acknowledge the elastic nature of presidential power, one must conclude that their capacity for unilateral action in foreign policy has made them more imperial in this area than imperilled.

[...]

Overall, it would appear that presidents since 1992 have been more imperilled than imperial in domestic and economic policy due to increased hyperpartisanship in Congress and the frequency of divided government. While presidents such as Obama, Bush and Clinton have had considerable success in domestic and economic policy, this does not justify claims of an 'imperial' presidency: they have simply fulfilled some aspects of their agenda within the limits of the Constitution. However, in terms of foreign policy, presidents since 1992 have been more able to act unilaterally. Hence the view expressed in the question is only partly convincing as presidential power is so elastic in nature that no recent president can be regarded as consistently imperial or imperilled.

Annotated Short Answers — Edexcel & AQA

Edexcel 12-mark questions and AQA 9-mark questions don't need an introduction or a conclusion. You should dive straight into your analysis of the idea posed by the question. There are no AO3 marks available in these questions, so you don't have to make any judgements — you just need to carry out political analysis with evidence to support your points.

For **Edexcel** students

1 Analyse the differing influence of third parties and independent candidates in the US and the UK.

(12 marks)

In your answer, you must consider the relevance of at least one comparative theory.

PARAGRAPHS

1) Performance in national elections
2) Performance in state/devolved elections
3) Influence on policy

*The answer below shows the **first paragraph**.*

PARAGRAPH

Third parties and independent candidates have had more influence in national elections in the UK than in the US, where the two-party system in elections is far more extreme: over 98% of the vote was won by Republicans or Democrats in the 2020 election. In the 2024 UK general election, third parties won 45% of the vote. In the UK, the popular success of third parties has often translated into seats in Parliament: the SNP won 48 seats in the 2019 general election, while the Liberal Democrats won 72 seats in 2024. In the US, by contrast, third-party popular support has rarely translated into seats in Congress or electoral college votes: no candidate outside the Republican or Democrat party since 1968 has won electoral college votes, while all 535 members of the 118th Congress caucused with either the Republicans or the Democrats. Although Ross Perot (an independent) gained 18.9% of the popular vote in the 1992 election, he was unable to gain electoral college votes as his voter base was dispersed across the country. The contrasting success of parties in the US and UK has partly resulted from the broader ideological profile of the major parties in the US. In the past decade, some right-wing voters in the UK have turned to UKIP and Reform UK for their isolationist and anti-immigration foreign policies, winning them popular vote shares of 13% in 2015 and 14% in 2024 respectively. In 2024 especially, this was seen to harm the Conservative Party, which dropped to its lowest-ever share of the popular vote — 24%. In the US, however, these views are embedded within the conservative right of the Republican party, exemplified by representatives like Matt Gaetz and Marjorie Taylor Greene, limiting the ideological space available for the Libertarian Party and the Reform Party. Because these comparisons stem from the differing political and ideological cultures of the US and the UK, they can be analysed using the cultural comparative theory.

Annotations:
- The **comparative theories** you need to apply here are covered on page 145.
- The paragraph begins with a clear and effective **comparison** between the two systems — AO2.
- Summary of **political trend** and **examples** — AO1 and AO2
- Reference to **source** of **difference** — AO2
- **Comparison** and **evidence** — AO1 and AO2.
- Reference to **relevant comparative theory** — AO2

For **AQA** students

1 Explain and analyse three ways in which democracy could be reformed in the UK.

(9 marks)

PARAGRAPHS

1) Compulsory voting
2) Lowering the voting age
3) Extending the vote to prisoners

*The answer below shows the **first paragraph**.*

PARAGRAPH

In order to combat the poor mandates produced by low levels of turnout, the UK could introduce compulsory voting, which is already used in Australia. Turnouts have declined from an average of over 70% until the 1990s to low points of under 60% in 2001 and 2024. This affects the quality of the mandate given to the governing party, contributing to the sense that the UK is suffering from a democratic deficit — in 2024, Labour won the support of just over 20% of all eligible adults. By making voting compulsory, turnouts would likely reach over 90%, meaning that all elected MPs would have a stronger mandate in their local constituency, and ensuring that support for governing parties would be much closer to, or over, 50%. Compulsory voting may also help to improve levels of political understanding and engagement by reducing the scope for apathy.

Annotations:
- Suggestion of **reform** — AO1.
- **Evidence** of flaw in UK democracy — AO1.
- **Explanation** of how reform addresses flaw — AO1 and AO2.

Aaaah comparative theories, my old nemesis, we meet again...

If a 12-mark question specifically just mentions differences, you only need to look at differences, not similarities. The same is true vice versa. If a question doesn't explicitly mention similarities or differences, you can discuss either or both in your answer.

Exam Skills

Annotated Source Essay — Edexcel-style

In the Edexcel exams, there'll be one 30-mark question in each of papers 1 and 2 that uses at least one source. You'll have to use the information presented in the source, in addition to your wider political knowledge, to answer the question.

UK Constitution

1 Source

> Supporters of codifying the UK's Constitution believe that one of the most compelling arguments in favour of codification is that it would bring the UK into line with virtually every other democracy in the modern world. They also point out that codification would add much more clarity than the uncodified Constitution offers. In recent years, there has been great uncertainty over the limits of executive power and over the relationship between Parliament and the devolved legislatures in Scotland, Wales and Northern Ireland.
>
> The uncodified Constitution also contains many unenforceable conventions, which undermine the effectiveness of government by failing to provide clear expectations for how each branch should behave.
>
> Under the current uncodified Constitution, rights can be changed with relative ease by the government of the day, especially if it has a large majority in the House of Commons. Parliamentary sovereignty, a key pillar of the uncodified Constitution, limits the extent to which these rights can be protected by the judiciary.
>
> Meanwhile, opponents of codification believe that the Supreme Court's swift reaction to Boris Johnson's attempt to prorogue Parliament in September 2019 proved the efficiency of the UK's uncodified Constitution, thereby undermining arguments that executive power can only be checked with a codified document. Similarly, the Supreme Court has provided clarity over Parliament's relationship with the devolved legislatures in rulings on Brexit and attempts to hold a second Scottish independence referendum.
>
> Under the uncodified Constitution, Parliament sits supreme, able to make laws as it wishes. The executive governs within the limits of those laws — rather than giving unelected judges the ability to dictate terms to elected politicians in Parliament, the judges simply interpret the law that has been passed by Parliament. Parliamentary sovereignty would no longer be possible under a codified constitution, which would instantly assume the position of the highest form of law in the United Kingdom.

Using the source, evaluate the view that a codified constitution would improve the effectiveness of government in the UK.

(30 marks)

---

*A good way of planning source essays is to **annotate** the source(s) and sort the arguments **in favour** of and **against** the question. You should aim to pick out at least **six quotations**, and then pair these together to form the basis of **three paragraph themes**, like the ones suggested here.*

PARAGRAPHS
1) Protection of rights
2) The location of sovereignty
3) The role of conventions

*The answer below shows an **introduction**, the **third main paragraph** and the **conclusion**.*

ANSWER

If the UK's Constitution were to require codification in order to improve the effectiveness of government, there would be compelling evidence to suggest that writing it into a single, authoritative document would better satisfy the core functions of limiting executive power, protecting rights and providing a framework for effective government. The source presents plausible arguments that the current uncodified and unentrenched nature of the Constitution provides insufficient clarity and allows excessive executive power, at the expense of rights protection. However, its arguments that the codification would threaten parliamentary sovereignty and constitutional flexibility are more convincing because these are two of the greatest strengths in the UK's existing political system.

[...]

*The opening sentence defines the **criteria** that the essay will use as a basis for its **judgement** and shows that you **understand** what **codification** means — AO1 and AO3.*

*This sentence **engages** with the **source**, showing that the essay is basing its **analysis** and **evaluation** on the arguments that it outlines.*

Annotated Source Essay — Edexcel-style

The paragraph opens by quoting the source and signposting its eventual judgement — AO1 and AO3.

Example — AO1.

Example — AO1.

Pointing out that a previous example is a rarity or an exception is a very effective form of analysis, enabling you to make the case that the typical state of affairs is different — AO2.

Judgement of the strength of arguments — AO3.

This sentence acknowledges the merits of the weaker side of the argument — AO3.

The source presents a valid, though ultimately flawed, argument that the UK's Constitution does require codification because 'the uncodified Constitution...contains many unenforceable conventions, which undermine the effectiveness of government by failing to provide clear expectations for how each branch should behave.' The notion that codification is necessary to bring greater clarity to the structure of government holds some weight given the presence of unwritten conventions, which can enable the executive to take advantage of contradictory or opaque elements of constitutional law. For instance, the Sewel Convention, which states that Westminster will not interfere in devolved policy matters, was broken during the passage of the Internal Market Act (2020), which imposed UK-wide regulations on agriculture, supposedly a devolved policy area. This is significant because it shows that, without codification, the presence of unenforceable conventions creates confusion that can be exploited by the executive, at the expense of the integrity of devolved bodies. By absorbing existing conventions into a single, written constitution, codification would certainly help to improve the clarity of the constitutional framework, and therefore the effectiveness of government. However, the source offers a more compelling argument against codification when acknowledging that 'the Supreme Court's swift reaction to Boris Johnson's attempt to prorogue Parliament in September 2019 proved the efficiency of the UK's uncodified Constitution, thereby undermining arguments that executive power can only be checked with a codified document.' This is a stronger line of argument because there is a weight of evidence suggesting that, on the rare occasions when the executive has attempted to exploit constitutional conventions, either the judiciary or Parliament has been able to prevent the exercise of excessive power. In the case of R (Miller) v the Prime Minister (2019), the Supreme Court prevented Boris Johnson from proroguing Parliament — by convention a prerogative power that the PM only uses to call an election or end a parliamentary session — to halt parliamentary scrutiny of the Brexit process. Furthermore, instances of the Sewel Convention being broken are rare, and arguably necessary in order to preserve the UK's internal unity, thereby further weakening the case for codification outlined above. In over twenty-five years of devolved government, the Convention has only been broken on a handful of occasions. Each time, Parliament has made plausible arguments that it has no option but to overrule the devolved bodies. In fact, conventions can often serve as a useful source of constitutional flexibility, and therefore effective government. This was the case when Theresa May chose not to observe a convention established by Tony Blair and David Cameron when ordering air strikes against the Assad regime in 2018. The unenforceable nature of the convention allowed the UK to take swift action against a government that had just used chemical weapons on its own people. Therefore, the fact that conventions are very rarely broken by the executive for nefarious reasons, coupled with their role in allowing a flexible, responsive government, means that the source's arguments against the idea that codification would improve the effectiveness of government are more convincing than its case in favour.

Overall, the source's arguments that a codified constitution would not improve the effectiveness of government in the UK are more convincing than its arguments in favour of this proposed change. Although the source does outline a persuasive case that codification would improve the clarity of the Constitution, with a corresponding improvement in the effectiveness of government, its arguments that codification is required to establish sufficiently clear limits on the power of the executive and to protect rights are undermined by compelling evidence to the contrary. In reality, major change of this kind would threaten parliamentary sovereignty and, in so doing, harm the flexibility and responsiveness that represent the greatest strengths of the UK's Constitution in its present form. Furthermore, the weight of evidence from recent years suggests that there are already sufficiently clear limits on executive power and sufficiently stringent protection of rights, thereby rendering the argument that codification would improve the effectiveness of government a weak one.

Explanation — AO2.

This sentence uses evaluative language to introduce the stronger side of the argument, quoting the source again in doing so — AO1 and AO3.

Explanation — AO2.

The conclusion begins by clearly answering the question and again referencing the source — AO3.

The conclusion finishes by assessing the superiority of the chosen line of argument, outlining a clear set of justifications for reaching this judgement — AO3.

Oh that kind of source? So I didn't need to write my essay in ketchup?

One of the key things to keep in mind when answering these questions is to make sure your response refers back to the source. You might know the topic inside out but if your points aren't related to the source, you'll lose out on most of the marks.

Exam Skills

Annotated Extract Essay — AQA-style

In the AQA exams, there'll be one 25-mark question in each exam paper that makes use of written extracts. Usually there are two extracts and it's important that you can analyse the similarities and differences between the points put forward by each extract. Beyond just what's written, the source of the extract can also affect how reliable or convincing its argument is.

Paper 2 — Government and Politics of the US

1 The executive branch of government: the President

Extract 1

Presidential power is so imbalanced that it's like watching two totally different people — one who never needs to worry about how their actions will be received and one who worries about every tiny detail before proceeding with the utmost caution.

For all the American rhetoric about checks and balances and tyrannical rule, the truth is that presidents do whatever they want in foreign policy. They order air strikes, drone strikes and assassinations. They move embassies, sign trade deals and make sweeping commitments on polarising areas of policy like climate change. And they do all of this without any fear of political reprisals, or even much interest, from Congress.

But in domestic policy, most presidents end up assuming a kind of pathetic persona, beaten into submission by the endless rounds of bargaining and compromise with powerful members of their own party and centrist members of the opposition party and the constant threat of being mocked in the media for failing to implement yet another of the promises that won them the election.

Extract taken from an article published by The Small Street Journal, *a non-partisan magazine based in Washington D.C. Its contributors are anonymous, but many of them are rumoured to work in the White House or in Congress.*

Extract 2

Neither the idea of an imperial presidency nor an imperilled presidency is entirely accurate. Presidents have in their armoury a range of constitutional and extra-constitutional powers that they can use to achieve some of their aims, but there will usually be checks and balances in their way that prevent them from exercising too much power.

In foreign policy, the president tends not to face particularly strong checks from Congress, but media scrutiny is extremely strong, and public opinion often shifts on the popularity or unpopularity of the president's international dealings.

In domestic and economic policy, some recent presidents have occasionally appeared imperilled, prevented from passing the policies that they care about most through a hyper-partisan Congress, and sometimes even unable to agree the federal budget in time to prevent a shutdown.

But these presidents still have tools at their disposal: executive orders and vetoes give them a considerable degree of control over public policy, while the present era of polarisation in Congress makes the threat of being removed from office following an impeachment extremely unlikely.

Extract taken from a book chapter written by Barry Rains, a historian who has been granted access to The White House during five consecutive presidencies.

Analyse, evaluate, and compare the arguments in the above extracts regarding the extent of presidential power.

(25 marks)

When it comes to planning your extract essays, it's a good idea to annotate the extracts. You can leave notes or use different symbols to sort the arguments into groups where the extracts agree with each other, disagree with each other and support or contradict the premise of the question.

Annotated Extract Essay — AQA-style

As this essay is on the same theme as the one on page 304, a lot of the annotations there also apply to this essay.

PARAGRAPHS
1) Foreign policy
2) Domestic policy
3) Economic policy

*The answer below shows the **introduction**, the **first main paragraph** and the **conclusion**.*

As with on p.304, your answer must refer to at least two presidents.

ANSWER

The above extracts mostly disagree over the extent of presidential power. While Extract 1 argues that the president enjoys almost unchecked power in foreign policy but possesses very little power in domestic policy, Extract 2 argues that the contrast between the two areas of policy is not so stark, and that all presidencies are characterised by a blend of unilateral action and checks and balances. They do, however, agree that the president generally faces fewer congressional checks in foreign policy, and more in domestic policy. Because both extracts appear to have been written by people with first-hand, insider knowledge of the US political system, there is no reason to view either as being substantially more credible, although the provenance of Extract 2, as an anonymous extract, is less certain. While both extracts have their merits, Extract 2 ultimately presents a more persuasive account of the extent of presidential power, because it considers the impact of extra-constitutional checks and implied powers to give a fuller representation of the president's status in the US system.

This first sentence clearly addresses the 'analyse' and 'compare' parts of the question. Importantly, it instantly engages with arguments offered in the extracts, instead of stating its writer's own opinion — AO2.

These sentences aren't strictly necessary, but provide a useful introduction and framing of the theory that will be discussed.

This is an important note. There should always be at least one area of agreement between extracts, even when they generally offer very contrasting points of view.

This is an effective evaluation of the two extracts' origins, although the phrase 'less certain' could have been followed with more analysis, e.g. '...making it marginally less credible as an insight into presidential power.'

This final sentence provides a clear and justified answer to the question. Importantly, it echoes the chain of reasoning used in the final sentence of the introduction.

Extract 1 states that 'presidents do whatever they want in foreign policy', arguing that they face fewer congressional checks compared with domestic or economic policy. This view holds plenty of weight: the limited scope of congressional checks and balances in foreign policy mean that presidents often make unilateral decisions in a manner described as 'imperial' by presidential scholar Arthur Schlesinger. As Extract 1 alludes to, Biden ordered air strikes in Syria, Afghanistan, Yemen and Iraq, as well as imposing economic sanctions on Russia, without needing to consult Congress. This reflects a trend demonstrated by other recent presidents: the authorisation of the use of military force in Iraq, passed by Congress in 2002, has been used 41 times in over 20 countries, effectively giving presidents a blank cheque for ordering military interventions. Coupled with Extract 1's argument, this evidence all points towards the conclusion that presidents can control the extent of their power in foreign policy. Extract 2 does agree that presidents face fewer congressional checks in foreign policy — 'in foreign policy, the president tends not to face particularly strong checks from Congress' — but Barry Rains' account of presidential power's extent also acknowledges the fact that 'media scrutiny [of foreign policy] is extremely strong, and public opinion often shifts on the popularity or unpopularity of the president's international dealings.' This perspective can be supported by a wealth of evidence from recent presidencies. George W. Bush suffered significant policy failures during his War on Terror: the Abu Ghraib scandal, combined with controversy over the presence of WMD in Iraq, significantly weakened his public approval ratings, which dropped to 23% in 2008, the lowest ever recorded. This suggests that Extract 1's suggestion that presidents 'do whatever they want in foreign policy' is unrepresentative of reality. It is also worth acknowledging that although congressional checks in foreign policy may not be, as Extract 2 concedes, 'particularly strong', they do still exist. Trump's handling of diplomatic relations with Ukraine, which saw him accused of offering a quid pro quo deal in return for information on Hunter Biden, led to his first impeachment. Furthermore, Biden's Secretary of State, Antony Blinken, has been subject to congressional subpoenas as part of investigations into his handling of the US withdrawal from Afghanistan in 2021. Because Extract 2 provides such a balanced perspective on the extent of presidential power in foreign policy, this is a more persuasive argument regarding presidential power than the comparatively limited analysis offered by Extract 1.

Example — AO1.

Comparison of extracts — AO2.

Example — AO1.

Engagement with extract — AO1.

This is an excellent sentence, using the evidence just presented as the basis for countering a claim addressed earlier in the paragraph.

[...]

Overall, because Extract 2 provides such a balanced perspective on the extent of presidential power in foreign policy, and because it has been written by someone who personally witnessed such decisions being made, it is more convincing to accept the argument it presents — that presidents face checks and balances on their power across foreign, domestic and economic policy, but that congressional checks tend to be weakest in foreign policy. While this coheres with the argument offered in Extract 1 that presidents have more control over the extent of their power in foreign policy, it does not reach such a stark judgement over the gap between the extent of presidential power in foreign, domestic and economic policy. As both extracts agree, some presidents possess such little power to persuade Congress in domestic policy that they can be regarded as imperilled at certain stages of their presidency. Neither extract accounts for the fact that the president can use budget reconciliation measures to implement aspects of the economic agenda, nor do they acknowledge the success enjoyed by some presidents, such as Clinton and Biden, in bargaining with members of the opposition party to pass legislation through a divided Congress.

Evaluates the extract's quality and provenance — AO3.

This sentence acknowledges the merits of the alternative view offered in Extract 1, and identifies once again that the two extracts contain some agreements, while also repeating the essay's justification for considering Extract 2 more convincing.

This final sentence exposes the weaknesses in the extracts — AO3. You should avoid presenting new information in your conclusion, so you should consider these points more fully in the paragraphs on domestic and economic policy.

Exam Skills

Edexcel-style Source Questions (30 marks)

Hello and welcome to the Edexcel essay onslaught. First up, we've got a source essay on UK Politics for you to tackle. So now's your last chance to hop back to pages 3-14 and get some last-minute revision under your belt before diving into some serious practice.

Paper 1 — UK Politics

Democracy and Participation

1 Source

> There are several possible innovations that have been put forward to address declining electoral turnout and public disengagement with politics and elections.
>
> The overall finding of recent research is clear: where compulsory voting legislation is introduced and enforced, it does typically increase turnout to levels above those recorded in countries with optional voting. However, there is also an argument that compulsory voting would merely give the appearance of improving British democracy, rather than actually doing so.
>
> Given the high levels of turnout among 16-18-year-olds in the Scottish independence referendum in 2014 (as well as in recent Scottish Parliament elections), many have also argued that the franchise should be extended to 16- and 17-year-olds. Campaign groups such as the Electoral Reform Society point out that the way people come into contact with politics in their formative years is crucially important for the future of democracy.
>
> When they can vote, 16- and 17-year-olds have higher rates of turnout than 18- to 24-year-olds — with 75% voting and 97% saying they would vote in future elections. They accessed more information from a wider variety of sources than any other age group.
>
> However, where some feel that the voting age should be lowered to 16 — the same age at which you can legally marry, have sex and enter the armed forces in most of the UK — others think that 18 is still too young an age for individuals to start voting in elections. Instead, they argue that people should be given the vote in their twenties, once they have gained some life experience, are paying taxes, and can think independently.
>
> Even simpler reforms, like electronic voting, are not without their issues. In an era of increasingly sophisticated election interference by rogue organisations and foreign governments, there are concerns over whether voters can have confidence in the results of elections where ballots have been cast electronically.

Using the source, evaluate the view that there should be further reforms to voting and suffrage in the UK.

In your response, you must:

- Compare the different opinions in the source
- Consider the view and the alternative view in a balanced way
- Use a balance of knowledge and understanding both arising from the source and beyond the source to help you analyse and evaluate

(30 marks)

Exam Skills

Edexcel-style Source Questions (30 marks)

Ding ding ding, round 1 done, on to round 2. Here's another source essay question, but this one's all about UK Government. Scuttle back to pages 96-107 for a quick refresher. And if you enjoyed answering these questions, you'll absolutely love what's waiting for you on the next few pages...

Paper 2 — UK Government

Relations Between the Branches

1 Source

> Some believe that parliamentary sovereignty has fully returned thanks to Brexit. Parliament can once again make or unmake any law that it chooses, giving the UK control over its borders as well as its international arrangements.
>
> Parliamentary sovereignty is one of our longest-standing constitutional principles, and has been one of the key reasons for the UK's success.
>
> Parliament remains the supreme legal and political authority in the UK: the devolved legislatures sit firmly beneath Parliament in the hierarchy of institutions, as was demonstrated by the Supreme Court's ruling that the Scottish Parliament does not have the power to call a second referendum on Scottish independence.
>
> Any threats to parliamentary sovereignty are only temporary — the nature of Parliament's power means that it can choose to repeal any previous law.
>
> Others disagree, arguing that Brexit failed to have the effect that its supporters desired: sovereignty remains pooled with the European Union as a result of the level playing field trading arrangements included in the European Union (Future Relationship) Act (2021). Under international law, Parliament cannot simply repeal or make unilateral changes to the UK's relationship with the European Union.
>
> They believe that sovereignty is not an absolute concept: even where Parliament has theoretical power to repeal previous reforms such as devolution or the establishment of the Supreme Court, it would be politically unthinkable to do so.
>
> Much of Parliament's power is exercised in practice by the executive branch, which tends to possess a majority in the House of Commons. This was particularly evident during the COVID-19 pandemic, when ministers were able to introduce policies without prior parliamentary scrutiny.

Using the source, evaluate the view that Parliament remains sovereign in theory, but not in practice.

In your response, you must:

- Compare and contrast the different opinions in the source
- Examine and debate these views in a balanced way
- Analyse and evaluate only the information presented in the source

(30 marks)

Edexcel-style Essay Questions (30 marks)

Now for some exam questions without sauces, I mean sources. Sorry, I've just had a plate of chips without any sauce. Awful. Anyway, straight in at the deep end with these **Edexcel-style 30 markers**.

- Remember to make use of the **Essay Plans** and **Sentence Frames** on pages 298-299 for guidance on how to structure your answers.
- Questions **marked with an asterisk** [*] have a full **sample answer** included in the Sample Answers section (starting on p.322).

Paper 1 — UK Politics

Democracy and Participation
1. Evaluate the view that corporations, lobbyists, and think tanks have excessive influence in the UK.
2. Evaluate the view that radical reforms are needed to combat voters' disillusion and apathy in the UK.

Political Parties
3. Evaluate the view that the advent of a multi-party system has improved the quality of democracy and government in the UK.
4. Evaluate the view that media support is the most important factor in a political party's chances of success.

Electoral Systems
5. Evaluate the view that referendums held in the UK since 1997 have had a generally positive impact.
6. Evaluate the view that only proportional electoral systems can deliver adequate levels of democracy.

Voting Behaviour and the Media
7. Evaluate the view that class remains the dominant factor influencing voting behaviour in the UK.
8. Evaluate the view that age is the most important determinant of voting behaviour and turnout in the UK.

Paper 2 – UK Government

In your answer to the questions in Paper 2, you should draw on relevant knowledge and understanding from Component 1: UK Politics.

The Constitution
1. Evaluate the view that the House of Lords will not be fit for purpose until there are substantial reforms to its powers and composition.
2. Evaluate the view that the case for extending devolution in England has been strengthened by the reforms implemented in Scotland, Wales and Northern Ireland since 1997.

Parliament
3. Evaluate the view that the House of Lords more effectively fulfils Parliament's functions than the House of Commons.
4. Evaluate the view that parliamentary scrutiny of the executive is insufficient.

Prime Minister and the Executive
5. *Evaluate the view that the prime minister is able to successfully control the political agenda.
6. Evaluate the view that prime ministers have more control over Parliament than over their own Cabinet.

Relations Between the Branches
7. Evaluate the view that Parliament is sufficiently able to limit the power of the executive.
8. Evaluate the view that the Supreme Court has too much influence over the UK's political system.

Paper 3 – Government and Politics of the USA

The Constitution and Federalism
1. Evaluate the view that the US Constitution is no longer fit for purpose.
2. Evaluate the view that the amendments process to the US Constitution frustrates effective government.

Edexcel-style Essay Questions (30 marks)

Congress

3 Evaluate the view that Congress fails to fulfil its legislative function, but not its functions of oversight and representation.

4 Evaluate the view that the congressional system of checks and balances no longer operates effectively.

The Presidency

5 Evaluate the view that presidents are unable to achieve their aims during divided governments.

6 Evaluate the view that recent presidents have tended to be imperilled, rather than imperial.

US Supreme Court and Civil Rights

7 Evaluate the view that US Supreme Court decisions tend to reflect the loose constructionist ideology.

8 Evaluate the view that the Supreme Court has failed to promote equality.

Democracy and Participation

9 Evaluate the view that the Electoral College should either be reformed or abolished.

10 Evaluate the view that campaign finance laws have a negative impact on US politics and government.

11 Evaluate the view that the Democrats can rely on a more stable coalition of supporters than the Republicans.

12 Evaluate the view that incumbency is the most important factor determining the outcomes of presidential and congressional elections in the US.

Synoptic (cross-topic) questions

13 Evaluate the view that congressional checks on the president are insufficient.

14 Evaluate the view that the Presidency has a bigger impact on US public policy than the Supreme Court or Congress.

15 *Evaluate the view that Congress is more effective than the Supreme Court in protecting civil and constitutional rights.

Paper 3 – Global Politics

The State and Globalisation

1 Evaluate the view that economic globalisation has had a greater impact on global politics than political or cultural globalisation.

2 Evaluate the view that national sovereignty is being eroded by the process of globalisation.

Global Governance — Political and Economic

3 Evaluate the view that NATO has proven to be a more successful organisation than the United Nations.

4 Evaluate the view that economic global governance has had more impact on global politics than political global governance.

Global Governance — Human Rights and Environmental

5 Evaluate the view that human rights are not adequately protected by international courts and humanitarian interventions.

6 Evaluate the view that international summits and agreements on climate change are doomed to failure.

Power and Development

7 Evaluate the view that the rise of China has challenged the status of the USA as a unipolar power.

8 *Evaluate the view that hard power has become more important than soft power in global politics in recent years.

Regionalism and the EU

9 Evaluate the view that economic regionalism has advanced more markedly than political and security regionalism.

10 Evaluate the view that the European Union has now become a significant global actor.

Exam Skills

Edexcel-style Political Ideas Qs (24 marks)

Yes, there are even more questions for you. Here's a page of questions on political ideas. Remember you can use the essay plans and sentence frames on pages 298-299 to help you structure your answers.

Paper 1 – Core Political Ideas

Conservatism

1 *To what extent is there more that unites than divides New Right and One Nation thinkers?

2 To what extent do conservatives accept inequality?

Liberalism

3 To what extent do liberals share a common view on how freedom should be maximised?

4 To what extent do liberals share a united view of human nature?

Socialism

5 To what extent is socialism characterised by the pursuit of equality?

6 To what extent do socialists agree on the economy?

Paper 2 – Non-Core Political Ideas

Anarchism

1 To what extent do anarchists seek to overthrow inequality as much as they seek to overthrow the state?

2 To what extent do anarchists seek collective solutions to the problems that they identify?

Ecologism

3 To what extent do ecologists see capitalism as the major obstacle to implementing their ideas?

4 To what extent are ecologists' ideas based on the common principle of equality?

Feminism

5 To what extent do feminists believe that cultural change is most important for ending patriarchy?

6 To what extent do feminists believe that women have a distinct nature and require a different status in society and the economy?

Multiculturalism

7 To what extent do disagreements between multiculturalists stem from different views on integration?

8 To what extent are there more agreements than disagreements between multiculturalists?

Nationalism

9 To what extent do nationalists share common views on the state?

10 To what extent do nationalists tend to disagree more over small details than over major principles?

Exam Skills

Edexcel-style Exam Questions (12 marks)

And here's the final hurdle for Edexcel students. Just a few 12-mark essays between you and the end of this book. Remember, there's no AO3 marks available for these questions, so they don't need introductions, conclusions or for you to pass judgement. Simply dig into your analysis right away.

'Examine' Questions

1 *Examine the differences between the core features of the US and the UK constitutions.

2 Examine the similarities between the checks and balances in the US and the UK.

3 Examine the similarities between the US federal system and the UK system of devolution.

4 Examine the similarities between the roles of the House of Representatives and the House of Commons.

5 Examine the differences between the Senate and the House of Lords.

6 Examine the similarities between the weaknesses of Congress and Parliament.

7 Examine the ways in which the US president and the UK prime minister can have a similar impact on politics and government.

8 Examine similarities between the executive branches' accountability to the legislature in the US and the UK.

9 Examine the differences between the extent of the Supreme Courts' powers in the US and the UK.

10 Examine the ways in which the extent of judicial independence in the US and the UK is similar.

11 Examine the different natures of the party systems in the US and the UK.

12 Examine the differences between the policy profiles of the Republican and Conservative parties.

13 Examine the ways in which the methods employed by pressure groups in the US and the UK are similar.

'Analyse' Questions

In your answers, you should consider the relevance of at least one comparative theory.

1 Analyse the differences between the US federal system and the UK system of devolution.

2 Analyse the ways in which the separation of powers is similar in the US and the UK.

3 Analyse the extent to which there is an equal relationship between the House of Representative and the Senate compared to between the House of Commons and the House of Lords.

4 Analyse the ways in which the US president can have a greater impact on politics and government than the UK prime minister.

5 *Analyse the similarities between the power of pressure groups in the US and the UK.

6 Analyse the ways in which there are similar criticisms of campaign finance and party funding in the US and the UK.

AQA-style Extract Questions (25 marks)

Your turn now AQA readers, an ensemble of essay questions using extracts for you to tackle. First of all, we've got one on the UK Constitution. Head over to pages 60-69 for some last-minute revision.

Paper 1 — Government and Politics of the UK

1 UK Constitution

Extract 1

Codification would bring the UK into line with virtually every other democracy in the modern world. In recent years, there has been near-constant uncertainty over the limits of executive power, and over the relationship between Parliament and the devolved legislatures in Scotland, Wales and Northern Ireland.

The uncodified Constitution also contains many unenforceable conventions, which undermine the effectiveness of government by failing to provide clear expectations for how each branch should behave. Some are ignored so often that they've become a laughing stock among politicians and constitutional experts — the equivalent of teachers who can never control their classes.

Under the uncodified Constitution, rights can be changed with alarming ease by the government of the day, especially if it has a large majority in the House of Commons. Parliamentary sovereignty, a supposedly sacred pillar of the uncodified Constitution, prevents judges from performing the role that they perform in pretty much every other democracy in the world.

Extract taken from 'Who Are We Kidding?', an article published in 2021 by *The Sunday Distress*, a weekly newspaper that leans to the left of the political spectrum. The article was written by the newspaper's editorial team.

Extract 2

Opponents of codification believe that the Supreme Court's swift reaction to Boris Johnson's attempt to prorogue Parliament in September 2019 proved the efficiency of the UK's uncodified Constitution, thereby undermining arguments that executive power can only be checked with a codified document.

Similarly, the Supreme Court has provided clarity over Parliament's relationship with the devolved legislatures in rulings on Brexit and attempts to hold a second Scottish independence referendum.

Under the uncodified Constitution, Parliament sits supreme, able to make law as it wishes. The executive governs within the limits of those laws — rather than giving unelected judges the ability to dictate terms to elected politicians in Parliament, the judges simply interpret the law that has been passed by Parliament.

Parliamentary sovereignty would no longer be possible under a codified constitution, which would instantly assume the position of the highest form of law in the United Kingdom.

Extract taken from a blog post published in 2024 by a website aimed at A-Level politics students. Uploaded under the headline 'To Codify or Not to Codify? At Least Ask the Question', the post was written by Mr S Mugly, a politics teacher with a large online following.

Analyse, evaluate and compare the arguments in the above extracts regarding the case for codifying the UK's Constitution.

(25 marks)

AQA-style Extract Questions (25 marks)

And with that first extract essay defeated, it's on to a second. This one's all about core political ideas and liberalism in particular. Check out pages 49-53 to refresh your memory before you tackle it.

Paper 3 — Political Ideas
1 Liberalism

Extract 1

The conception of justice which I want to develop may be stated in the form of two principles as follows: first, each person participating in a practice, or affected by it, has an equal right to the most extensive liberty compatible with a like liberty for all; and second, inequalities are arbitrary unless it is reasonable to expect that they will work out for everyone's advantage, and provided the positions and offices to which they attach, or from which they may be gained, are open to all.

[...]

It should be noted that the second principle holds that an inequality is allowed only if there is reason to believe that the practice with the inequality, or resulting in it, will work for the advantage of every party engaging in it. Here it is important to stress that every party must gain from the inequality.

Extract taken from John Rawls' 'Justice as Fairness', in the Philosophical Review vol. 67, no. 2.

Extract 2

The sole end for which mankind are warranted, individually or collectively, in interfering with the liberty of action of any of their number, is self-protection.

[…]

The only purpose for which power can be rightfully exercised over any member of a civilised community, against his will, is to prevent harm to others. His own good, either physical or moral, is not a sufficient warrant. He cannot rightfully be compelled to do or forbear because it will be better for him to do so, because it will make him happier, because, in the opinions of others, to do so would be wise, or even right.

[…]

The only part of the conduct of any one, for which he is amenable to society, is that which concerns others. In the part which merely concerns himself, his independence is, of right, absolute. Over himself, over his own body and mind, the individual is sovereign.

Extract taken from John Stuart Mill's 'On Liberty', which was first published in 1859.

Analyse, evaluate and compare the arguments made in the above extracts about liberal attitudes towards society. In your answer, you should refer to the thinkers you have studied.

(25 marks)

AQA-style Essay Questions (25 marks)

And we're not done. Oh no, far from it. Here's a veritable smorgasbord of **25-mark** essay questions without extracts for the **AQA** specification. That's me done for now — I need to prepare my next snack.

- Remember to make use of the **Essay Plans** on page 298 and **Sentence Frames** on page 300 for guidance on how to structure your answers.
- Questions **marked with an asterisk** [*] have a full **sample answer** included in the Sample Answers section (starting on p.322).

Paper 1 – Government and Politics of the UK

Analyse and evaluate the following statements.

Democracy and Participation
1 'Referendums held in the UK since 1997 have had a generally positive impact.'
2 *'Neither individual nor collective rights are adequately protected or guaranteed in the UK.'
3 'Corporations, lobbyists and think tanks have excessive influence in the UK.'

Political Parties
4 'The Conservatives have retained more of their traditional policy positions than Labour.'
5 'The advent of a multi-party system has improved the quality of democracy and government in the UK.'

Electoral Systems
6 'None of the electoral systems used in the UK are fit for purpose.'

Voting Behaviour and the Media
7 'Class remains the dominant factor influencing voting behaviour in the UK.'
8 'Media support is the most important factor in a political party's chances of success.'

The Constitution
9 'The case for further devolution in England has been strengthened by the reforms implemented in Scotland, Wales and Northern Ireland since 1997.'

Parliament
10 'The House of Lords more effectively fulfils Parliament's functions than the House of Commons.'
11 'There is insufficient parliamentary scrutiny of the executive.'

Prime Minister and the Executive
12 'The prime minister can dominate the UK's political system.'
13 'Prime ministers have more control over Parliament than over their own Cabinet.'

Relations Between the Branches
14 'The Supreme Court has too much influence over the UK's political system.'
15 'The only remaining threat to parliamentary sovereignty is devolution.'

Synoptic (cross-topic) questions
16 'Radical reforms are needed to combat voters' disillusion and apathy in the UK.'
17 'General elections tend to result in significant changes to politics and government in the UK.' In your answer, you should refer to results from at least two different general elections.
18 'Reforms to the House of Lords since 1997 have been less successful than reforms to the judiciary and rights protection.'

AQA-style Essay Questions (25 marks)

Paper 2 – Comparative Politics

Analyse and evaluate the following statements.

The Constitution and Federalism
1. 'Both the US Constitution and the UK Constitution are unfit for purpose.'
2. 'The US Constitution more successfully facilitates democracy than the UK Constitution.'

Congress
3. 'Congress is less effective in fulfilling its legislative function than Parliament, but not more effective in fulfilling its functions of oversight and representation.'
4. 'The congressional system of checks and balances in the US no longer operates as effectively as Parliament's checks on the executive branch in the UK.'

The Presidency
5. 'US presidents are less likely than UK prime ministers to achieve their aims.'
6. 'UK prime ministers have more control over the three branches of government than US presidents.'

US Supreme Court and Human Rights
7. 'The US Supreme Court is both more politicised and less independent than the UK Supreme Court.'
8. 'The US Supreme Court has a more significant impact on public policy than the UK Supreme Court.'
9. 'Rights are insufficiently protected in both the US and the UK.'

Democracy and Participation
10. 'Campaign finance in the UK increasingly resembles the US system.'
11. 'Interest groups have a more positive impact on democracy and government in the US than in the UK.'
12. *'Electoral outcomes and voting behaviour in US federal elections are more predictable than in UK general elections.'
13. 'There are more policy divisions between political parties in the US than in the UK.'

Paper 3 – Political Ideas

Analyse and evaluate the following statements with reference to the thinkers you have studied.

Anarchism
1. 'Anarchists seek to overthrow inequality as much as to overthrow the state.'
2. 'Anarchists mostly seek collective solutions to the problems that they identify.'

Ecologism
3. 'Ecologist thinkers see capitalism as the major obstacle to implementing their ideas.'
4. 'Ecologist ideas are based on the common principle of equality.'

Feminism
5. 'Feminists believe that cultural change is most important for ending patriarchy.'
6. 'Feminists believe that women have a different nature to men and therefore require a different status.'

Multiculturalism
7. 'Disagreements between multiculturalists stem from different views on integration.'
8. 'There are more agreements than disagreements between multiculturalists.'

Nationalism
9. 'Minority nationalists do not share similar views to state nationalists.'
10. 'Nationalist thinkers tend to disagree more over small details than over underlying principles.'

Exam Skills

AQA-style Exam Questions (9 marks)

The final batch of practice for AQA students awaits. Behold, this bumper spread of 9-mark questions. Remember, these answers don't need an introduction or conclusion — just dive straight into the analysis. So without further ado, take a deep breath, have a big stretch and get stuck in.

Paper 1

UK Politics

1. Explain and analyse three forms of political participation in the UK.
2. Explain and analyse three differences between representative and direct democracy in the UK.
3. Explain and analyse three methods employed by pressure groups in the UK.
4. Explain and analyse three criticisms of the role played by corporations, think tanks or lobbyists in the UK.
5. Explain and analyse three policy differences between the Labour Party and the Conservative Party.
6. Explain and analyse three limits on the influence of minor parties in the UK.
7. Explain and analyse three features of referendums in the UK.
8. Explain and analyse three differences between proportional electoral systems and first-past-the-post.

UK Government

9. Explain and analyse three ways in which the UK Constitution has been reformed since 1997.
10. Explain and analyse three differences between the powers of the devolved bodies in the UK.
11. Explain and analyse three arguments in favour of extending devolution in England.
12. Explain and analyse three roles performed by committees in Parliament.
13. Explain and analyse three criticisms of the representation offered by Parliament.
14. Explain and analyse three factors influencing the selection of Cabinet ministers in the UK.
15. Explain and analyse three checks on the power of the prime minister.
16. Explain and analyse three ways in which the power and composition of the UK's judiciary has changed in recent years.
17. Explain and analyse three aims of the European Union.
18. Explain and analyse three ways in which the European Union has impacted politics and policy-making in the UK.
19. Explain and analyse three features of the UK Constitution.

Paper 2

US Politics

1. Explain and analyse three amendments that have been made to the US Constitution.
2. Explain and analyse three ways in which the US Constitution aims to protect rights.
3. Explain and analyse three ways in which members of the House of Representatives and the Senate perform their representative role.
4. Explain and analyse three criticisms of congressional oversight.
5. Explain and analyse three checks on the power of the president.
6. Explain and analyse three ways in which some presidents can act imperially.

AQA-style Exam Questions (9 marks)

7 Explain and analyse three ways in which the US Supreme Court has exercised its power of judicial review.

8 Explain and analyse three criticisms of the US Supreme Court.

9 Explain and analyse three features of the Electoral College.

10 Explain and analyse three strengths of primaries and caucuses in the US.

11 Explain and analyse three constraints on minor party influence in the US.

12 Explain and analyse three policy differences between the Republican Party and the Democratic Party.

13 Explain and analyse three methods used by pressure groups in the US.

14 Explain and analyse three ways in which pressure groups aim to protect rights in the US.

15 Explain and analyse three developments in the protection of civil rights in the US.

16 Explain and analyse three criticisms of the extent to which civil rights have been protected in the US.

Comparative Politics

17 Explain and analyse three differences between the House of Lords and the Senate.

18 Explain and analyse three ways that structural theory could be used to study the features of the US and UK constitutions.

19 Explain and analyse three ways that cultural theory could be used to study the strengths and weaknesses of the US Congress and the UK Parliament.

20 Explain and analyse three ways that structural theory could be used to study the relative independence of the judiciary in the UK and the US.

21 Explain and analyse three ways that rational theory could be used to study the UK prime minister and the US president.

22 Explain and analyse three ways that cultural theory can be used to study internal unity and divisions within political parties in the US and the UK.

23 Explain and analyse three ways that rational theory can be used to study elections, campaign finance and voting behaviour in the US and the UK.

24 Explain and analyse three ways that cultural theory can be used to study the influence of pressure groups in the US and the UK.

25 *Explain and analyse three ways that cultural theory can be used to compare the power of pressure groups in the US and the UK.

Paper 3
Political Ideas

1 Explain and analyse three ways in which conservative thinkers view the economy.

2 Explain and analyse three ways in which conservative thinkers view tradition.

3 *Explain and analyse three ways in which liberal thinkers view the state.

4 Explain and analyse three ways in which liberal thinkers view the concept of rationalism.

5 Explain and analyse three ways in which socialists view society.

6 Explain and analyse three ways in which socialists view revolution.

Exam Skills

Sample Answers

These pages give you some good-quality, sample answers of the exam questions on pages 310-321 marked with an asterisk [*].

> Your answers are **bound to be quite different** from these sample answers. But have a think about **how your answers compare** to these in terms of:
> - how **supporting evidence** for the concepts is worked into the answer (AO1)
> - how the concepts are **analysed** and **explained** — e.g. the connections, similarities and differences (AO2)
> - how the arguments are **evaluated** — e.g. how the relative strengths of different arguments are judged, and what overall conclusions are reached (AO3)
> - how the **sentence frames** on pages 299-300 have been used to **structure** the answers

Edexcel-style Essay Questions (30 marks)

Page 312: Paper 2 — UK Government

5 *Evaluate the view that the prime minister is able to successfully control the political agenda.*

The prime minister's status as the leader of the largest party gives them the ability to control many aspects of the political agenda. This is especially true when they are in possession of a Commons majority and considered an electoral asset to their party. When the prime minister only commands a small majority or a minority government, they are often unable to control their relationship with Parliament, and less able to control the Cabinet agenda. It is also worth acknowledging that very few prime ministers have been able to exert much control over the media narrative about their premiership. That said, it is ultimately more convincing to argue that prime ministers are generally able to control the political agenda due to the prevalence of single-party majority government and the unilateral nature of prerogative powers.

There have been notable instances of prime ministers being unable to successfully control the political agenda due to high-profile defeats in Parliament. After losing her majority in the 2017 general election, Theresa May suffered 33 Commons defeats in two years, losing control over Brexit, the defining policy priority of her premiership, with three high-profile defeats, one by a record margin of 230. Despite leading a majority government through his coalition agreement with the Liberal Democrats, David Cameron was forced to abandon plans to reform the House of Lords following a Tory backbench rebellion in 2012, while Tony Blair was forced to do likewise after a defeat over ID cards in 2005. All prime ministers are subject to scrutiny in the House of Lords, which can reduce their ability to control the political agenda: even during a period of dominance over the Commons, Boris Johnson suffered significant defeats in the Lords over both the Internal Market Bill and the Trade Bill. The former is a particularly significant example because it forced Johnson to re-evaluate the government's intention to break the law over the Northern Ireland Protocol, suggesting that even powerful prime ministers do not have an unmitigated level of control over the political agenda. However, these arguments are outweighed, firstly by the fact that most prime ministers are able to control the political agenda by dominating the House of Commons. The disproportionate nature of first-past-the-post tends to produce a majority government, while the legislative process (with only a simple majority needed at each stage) means that there are rarely significant obstacles to a majority government's attempts to pass its policy priorities into law. With majorities of 179 and 167, Tony Blair spent the first eight years of his premiership undefeated in the Commons, while Keir Starmer did not suffer a legislative defeat in the Commons between winning his 174-seat majority in the 2024 general election and the end of 2024. This control is usually reflected in the PM's relationship with the House of Lords: asymmetrical bicameralism means that the unelected second chamber (which lost its financial privilege in 1911) is often unable to prevent executive control. These limitations mean that all prime ministers, irrespective of whether they have a large Commons majority, are able to control the economic policy agenda, and that peers' opposition to other government legislation will only ever be temporary. After the stand-off over the Trade Bill had lasted several weeks in 2021, where the Lords had pushed for Parliament to have more control over trading and sanctions, the Lords eventually backed down and allowed Johnson to control the agenda. The frequency of majority governments and the weaknesses of the Lords therefore mean that prime ministers are generally able to control the political agenda by dominating Parliament. This argument is strengthened by the fact that those few prime ministers who have been unable to do so have tended, like May and Callaghan, to operate in atypical circumstances of minority government.

There is also a plausible, if ultimately flawed, case for arguing that the prime minister is typically unable to control the political agenda through their relationship with Cabinet. The fact that the prime minister's closest political rivals, and most likely successors, tend to hold Cabinet positions can make it difficult for them to dominate policy decisions and public communications. Again, control is especially unlikely when prime ministers are leading a minority or coalition government. After reluctantly appointing rival Boris Johnson as her Foreign Secretary in 2016, Theresa May was unable to control his challenges to collective responsibility through his high-profile columns in the Daily Telegraph, while David Cameron was forced under the Coalition Agreement to secure the approval of Nick Clegg and Danny Alexander (along with George Osborne, his fellow members of the so-called Quad) for every government policy from 2010 to 2015. Even prime ministers with a large majority often struggle to control the Cabinet agenda. Despite their majorities, both Margaret Thatcher and Boris Johnson were ultimately brought down by resignations and a lack of support from their Cabinets, while Keir Starmer's credibility suffered an early hit when Louise Haigh, his Transport Secretary, resigned in 2024 after it emerged that she had been found guilty of fraud before becoming an MP. These examples illustrate that prime ministers at different stages of their premiership and with differing levels of power often cannot control the political agenda through their relationship with Cabinet. However, it is more persuasive to argue that, despite these instances, the prime minister is typically able to control the most significant elements of their relationship with Cabinet. Prerogative powers allow the prime minister to appoint and dismiss Cabinet ministers without facing any checks and balances from the other branches of government. For example, David Cameron fired Michael Gove as Education Secretary in 2014 after polling indicated that his reputation was harming the overall popularity of the government, while Keir Starmer was able to appoint a Cabinet made up largely of centre-left loyalists such as Wes Streeting, Liz Kendall and Rachel Reeves in 2024. Furthermore, the prime minister usually possesses ultimate decision-making power over policy, allowing them to control many aspects of the political agenda without first seeking Cabinet approval. For example, under Tony Blair's system of 'sofa government', some ministers found out about the decision to hand over control of interest rates to the Bank of England when the policy was announced on television. Insiders from Boris Johnson's government have suggested that the most important decisions were made on exclusive WhatsApp groups containing only a small number of ministers and unelected advisors such as Dominic Cummings, Chris Whitty and Patrick Vallance. While prime ministers may struggle to control the behaviour and performance of their Cabinet, it is therefore usually the case that they control its membership and decision-making, suggesting that, in this area, it is more convincing to argue that they do control the political agenda.

Finally, the prime minister can, at times, succeed in controlling the media narrative about their premiership. It is often the case that prime ministers who are struggling domestically seek to focus on foreign policy for a short-term boost in their popularity. This has been seen frequently in recent years with Rishi Sunak's success in negotiating the Windsor Framework (an amended post-Brexit relationship between the UK and the EU) in 2023 leading to favourable media coverage, and Boris Johnson often visiting Kyiv and hosting President Zelensky, which created a distraction from headlines about the Partygate and PPE scandals. Prime ministers are similarly able to control some of the information flow to the media and the public. For instance, Tony Blair and Alastair Campbell were able to persuade the media that they had strong evidence to justify the invasion of Iraq in 2003, while Boris Johnson explained the reasoning behind his government's decisions in responding to the COVID-19 pandemic at daily televised press conferences. These examples both suggest that the prime minister does have some control over the political agenda, but it is ultimately more

Sample Answers

compelling to argue that the media narrative is an area where prime ministers are not typically able to control most aspects of the agenda. The British press enjoys significant freedom, giving it licence to conduct investigations and produce coverage that shape the political agenda well beyond the prime minister's control. In recent years, The Guardian's coverage of the Windrush scandal and the Daily Mirror's Partygate coverage have dealt significant blows to the authority of Theresa May and Boris Johnson respectively, while Johnson's premiership ended after journalists uncovered that he had known about sexual assault allegations against Chris Pincher before appointing him as a government whip. Increasingly, prime ministers are also unable to control the narrative emerging from social media: Keir Starmer struggled to control the flow of information during the 2024 summer riots, when right-wing conspiracy theorists spread misinformation on X, and Johnson eventually made a policy U-turn after Marcus Rashford's campaign to extend free school meals during holidays gained significant social media traction in 2020. These examples suggest that, despite their best efforts, no prime minister can exert consistent control over the media narrative, which can often have wider implications for their control of the political agenda.

Therefore, while UK prime ministers can generally control the political agenda through their dominance of the House of Commons and their prerogative powers over the Cabinet, their ability to control the media and public perception is more limited. Parliament, particularly the House of Lords, and the increasing power of the media, especially social media, present significant challenges to the prime minister's ability to control the agenda, as can their Cabinet rivals. However, the frequency of majority governments ensures that prime ministers, in most circumstances, remain able to shape much of the political agenda, despite occasional setbacks, such as high-profile defeats or media scandals.

Page 313: Paper 3 — Government and Politics of the USA

15 *Evaluate the view that Congress is more effective than the Supreme Court in protecting civil and constitutional rights.*

Proponents of the view that Congress is more effective than the Supreme Court (SC) in protecting civil and constitutional rights would point to Congress's legislation on voting rights, the SC's inability to be proactive in protecting rights, and the SC's efforts to rule against minority rights in recent years, such as by striking down Deferred Action for Parents of Americans and Lawful Permanent Residents (DAPA). Conversely, those challenging this view would argue that most major advancements in rights have come from the SC, such as same-sex marriage, and that Congress has been reluctant to uphold rights to the same extent. Overall, the most convincing view is that the SC has proven more effective than Congress in protecting minority rights through judicial review, as Congress often defers to the executive. However, Congress has protected voting rights more effectively.

A plausible, if ultimately flawed, case could be made that Congress is more effective than the SC in protecting rights because the SC remains fundamentally limited by its inability to be proactive. The SC must wait for cases to be brought before it and cannot uphold or defend rights entirely of its own volition. For instance, Washington D.C.'s ban on handguns was in operation for decades before it was struck down by the 2008 case District of Columbia v. Heller, suggesting the SC is less able to protect rights due to its reactive nature. Furthermore, the SC's reluctance to enforce its power of judicial review can be detrimental to rights. For example, the SC refused to hear the case Planned Parenthood v. Jegley (2015), effectively allowing abortion rights to be stripped from citizens in Arkansas. By contrast, Congress has arguably proven more effective in protecting civil and constitutional rights by proactively passing legislation. For instance, it upheld collective rights during COVID-19 by passing the CARES Act in March 2020, protecting the collective safety of the people. However, it is far more convincing to argue that the SC is more effective in protecting rights through its power of judicial review. In particular, the SC ruled that President George W. Bush had denied detainees at Guantanamo Bay constitutional rights in cases such as Rasul v. Bush and Boumediene v. Bush.

Conversely, Congress allowed Bush to infringe on rights by deferring to him in the aftermath of 9/11, permitting the establishment of the Department of Homeland Security and military tribunals without significant checks. This deference was influenced by Bush's approval ratings of 90% after 9/11, which allowed him to exercise dominance over Congress. In this way, although the SC cannot be proactive, it has proven more willing than Congress to protect constitutional rights when cases are brought before it, justifying the view that the SC has protected these rights more effectively. However, in terms of upholding minority rights, there is some weight to the view that Congress is more effective than the SC. The SC has been willing to make rulings detrimental to minority rights. For instance, in United States v. Texas (2016), it struck down Obama's DAPA programme, which had protected the rights of immigrants by entitling them to constitutional protections. Furthermore, the SC overturned Roe v. Wade in its landmark Dobbs v. Jackson (2022) ruling, which undermined the rights of women. Congress, by contrast, has not imposed the same level of scrutiny on presidential efforts to protect rights. Nevertheless, it is more compelling to argue that the SC has proven far more effective in protecting civil and constitutional rights. Congress's Defense of Marriage Act failed to protect the constitutional rights of LGBTQI+ couples to marriage, but the SC struck it down in United States v. Windsor and Obergefell v. Hodges (2015), granting the constitutional right to family life to same-sex couples. Moreover, Congress has been unwilling to legislate to protect minority rights, effectively making the SC a quasi-legislative body. Landmark cases such as Brown v. Board of Education struck down Plessy v. Ferguson, protecting the civil rights of Black Americans, while Swann v. Charlotte-Mecklenburg Board of Education promoted racial integration and minority rights. The need for a two-thirds majority in the current era of hyperpartisanship has made formal amendments an unrealistic prospect for engineering social change, highlighting Congress's ineffectiveness in upholding rights. As such, although the SC has occasionally proven ineffective in protecting rights, it is largely convincing to argue that it has been more effective than Congress in areas such as civil rights and abortion.

Finally, there is also a plausible case for arguing that the SC has been more effective than Congress in protecting voting rights. Congress is not entirely effective in protecting voting rights, as it often practises gerrymandering. For instance, in North Carolina during the 2020 election, the Republican-dominated legislature drew a congressional map designed to disenfranchise voters, harming both the constitutional right to vote and civil rights, as minorities were targeted. President Biden lost the state by just 1% of the vote in 2020, yet Republicans gained 8 seats compared to the Democrats' 5, illustrating Congress's failures in protecting voting rights. The SC, by contrast, has historically been more willing to protect voting rights, as demonstrated in the case Shaw v. Reno, where it struck down maps infringing on rights. However, neither branch has proven particularly effective in protecting voting rights. Congress has made efforts, such as the proposed John Lewis Voting Rights Act, which has raised awareness about voting rights and mobilised pressure groups like the NAACP. By contrast, the SC effectively enabled states to systematically remove voting rights through rulings like Shelby County v. Holder (2013), which eliminated the requirement for pre-approval of voting maps. Therefore, while Congress has promoted voting rights through recent legislation, the SC has deferred to states in key cases, making Congress the more effective branch in this area.

On balance, the most convincing view is that the SC has protected civil and constitutional rights more effectively than Congress. Although the SC has ruled against executive efforts to protect rights, its willingness to protect rights against an imperial president like George W. Bush demonstrates its comparative effectiveness. Furthermore, while the SC has occasionally ruled against minority rights, most major advancements in rights in recent years have come from the SC rather than Congress. Neither branch has been particularly effective in protecting voting rights. In conclusion, it is largely unconvincing to suggest that Congress has protected civil and constitutional rights more effectively than the Supreme Court.

Sample Answers

Page 313: Paper 3 — Global Politics

8 *Evaluate the view that hard power has become more important than soft power in global politics in recent years.*

Hard power is coercive power that involves a state or actor being compelled to act in a certain way, usually by another state's military or economic power. Soft power is a concept coined by Joseph Nye in 1990, and describes power based on attraction and persuasion. Soft power has become increasingly significant in international affairs since the end of the Cold War and involves a state or actor being attracted by another state's foreign policy, cultural influence or values. To assess whether hard power has become more important than soft power in recent years, it is necessary to examine the main forms of power in global politics — military, economic and cultural power. It is clear that, despite the numerous incidences of the use of hard power, soft power has become more prevalent than hard power since the end of the Cold War.

Advocates of hard power argue that military force provides the most effective form of power in global politics, and that soft power is limited and can only succeed in certain circumstances. Hard power has frequently been employed in recent years, whether it be the US-led interventions in Afghanistan and Iraq, or the seizure of Crimea by Russia in 2014. Increasingly vast resources are spent on the military and huge stockpiles of nuclear weapons are still possessed by the USA and Russia. The USA has over 750 military bases worldwide, and both China and Russia have been rapidly developing their military capabilities in recent years. Russia invaded Ukraine in 2022 and China has been conducting training exercises off the coast of Taiwan. The former head of NATO, Jens Stoltenberg, has warned of an 'axis of authoritarianism' due to these threats. Despite these arguments for the continued importance of hard power, the frequency of inter-state wars has declined since the end of the Cold War, indicating a reduction in the use of hard power. It can also be argued that the shortcomings of hard power have been revealed by the problems facing Russia and the USA in their military operations in Ukraine, Afghanistan and Iraq, when measured in terms of economic cost and lives lost. Furthermore, military action has not always been effective, as shown by the USA's ultimate withdrawal from Afghanistan, and may have proved counterproductive by eroding the soft power of the US and its allies. An increased use of both soft and hard power led Nye to champion the term 'smart power' — the idea that states can use soft power when possible and hard power only when necessary. This was employed by Obama during his efforts against the Islamic State group, where he used a combination of unmanned drone strikes to kill alleged terrorist operatives, while using diplomatic and cultural tactics to counter Islamic State propaganda and influence in the Middle East. Hence, a 'smarter' form of military power (which is cheaper and arguably more effective) has grown in importance compared with traditional hard military power.

Economic power is an important component of hard power and is thought to be of increasing importance in global politics. One of the key determinants of power is the size of a state's economy. The USA, the European Union and China are all seen as being very important economic actors globally due to the sheer size of their economies. This allows these actors to be the home of many of the leading TNCs in the world and to carry significant weight in global affairs. The fact that the IMF and World Bank follow the Washington Consensus, and that the USA is able to dominate these bodies, illustrates the power the USA has in asserting its policies and priorities. Furthermore, it can be argued that the military power possessed by a state is largely determined by the state's economic power. The use of economic sanctions by the United Nations against states like Iran over its nuclear programme and the trade war between the USA and China during Trump's first term as president shows the continued significance of hard power in international affairs. However, liberals would argue that the increasingly interconnected nature of the global economy means that soft power has become far more important. Military action is used less as a tool of state policy due to the harmful economic repercussions that it can cause. States have become much more economically interconnected in terms of their supply chains, and this may explain states' reluctance to use military force in some circumstances (for example, China refraining from seizing control of Taiwan). As military power has become of less utility in global politics, soft power has become more important. Liberal notions of a cobweb model existing in international relations means that persuasion has become much more prevalent than coercion. The formation and expansion of the EEC/EU since 1957 has illustrated the decline in the significance of hard power and the growing soft power appeal of EU membership. The nature of the global economy has meant that tariffs and trade wars are far less common than in the past, and economic sanctions are of limited use in achieving desired outcomes. Therefore, the globalised nature of international politics means that soft power has become of increasing importance in world affairs in recent years.

A key component of soft power in global politics is culture and diplomatic influence. Cultural power can be observed in the huge influence that the US has on other countries in terms of music, television programmes, cinema and streaming platforms such as Netflix. It is not just in these areas that states can exert cultural power — educational establishments such Harvard and Yale have a significant impact on its overseas students and can instil the values of those states upon them. However, there are limits to the deployment of soft power. Hard power can be deployed immediately, but it takes decades for a state to develop soft power. There is also no guarantee of it being effective, and its success often cannot be measured. China has developed its soft power in recent times by increasing the number of Confucius Institutes across the world and using its diplomatic influence to promote development in Africa and Latin America. But critics of soft power argue that it is dependent on hard power, namely the economic power to finance such huge operations. Moreover, league tables of soft power often seem to simply reflect the hard power of many states, with the USA, China, UK, Germany and France at the top of the rankings. These standings might also reflect the historic legacy of the empires these states built through the use of hard power. Nevertheless, the growing importance of soft power in global politics cannot be denied. In recent decades, technological advances such as the spread of the internet and social media mean there is far more cultural awareness between states. The attractiveness of ideas such as the USA being the 'land of the free' and 'leader of the free world' have an immense impact on global politics. According to Nye, soft power involves shaping the preferences of others so that you do not have to coerce them — they want to emulate you. In a world where it is becoming much more difficult to exert hard power due to its expense and the public opinion backlash it results in, soft power has become an increasingly common and cost-effective tool in international politics.

In conclusion, there has been a shift away from traditional hard power to soft power since the end of the Cold War. Encouraging other states to share one's aspirations and goals is seen as a more effective way of achieving one's aims than invasion and occupation. War has become relatively uncommon, and it may well be that the liberal vision of an interconnected world where states avoid using hard power has become the norm. States are too closely bound by economic ties and international supply chains to resort to hard power unless absolutely necessary (smart power). The allure of joining a regional body like the European Union, or befriending a state like the US, may be a far more powerful force than threats and coercion. States are competing more culturally and diplomatically, building friendships and alliances, and trying to shape the preferences of others through peaceful means.

Sample Answers

Edexcel-style Political Ideas Qs (24 marks)

Page 314: Paper 1 — Core Political Ideas

1   *To what extent is there more that unites than divides New Right and One Nation thinkers?*

   To argue that there is more to unite rather than divide the New Right from One Nation conservatives is to suggest that thinkers from both strands broadly agree on human nature, the state, the economy and society. However, it is more compelling to argue that there is largely more to divide rather than unite, as New Right thinkers are far more optimistic in their beliefs on human nature and reject the idea of a welfare state.

   A plausible, if ultimately flawed, case can be made that there is more to unite the New Right with One Nation conservatives on human nature. All thinkers from both strands believe that human nature is, to some extent, fallible — from Rand's belief in selfishness as an innate and unavoidable feature of human nature, to Macmillan's belief that humans are incapable of self-actualisation without the assistance of a welfare state. As such, both One Nation thinkers and New Right thinkers believe that human nature is flawed, marking an area of unity. However, it is more compelling to argue that One Nation and New Right thinkers are divided over the extent to which humans are rational. New Right thinkers place far more faith in human rationalism. For example, Nozick's idea of self-ownership suggests individuals are capable in themselves of self-actualisation. This contrasts with Disraeli's belief in social obligation, which suggests individuals must rely on others. Moreover, it is difficult to reconcile Rand's notion of 'ethical egoism', where selfishness is a virtue, with Disraeli's 'noblesse oblige' belief that the upper classes have an obligation to be altruistic to the poor, further marking an area where the two strands differ. In this way, although thinkers from both strands believe that humans are fallible, New Right thinkers believe that selfishness is a virtue rather than a vice, and place more faith in the fundamental trait of human rationalism, suggesting there is largely more to divide rather than unite.

   A plausible case can be made that there is more to unite rather than divide the New Right from One Nation conservatives on the state. Thinkers from both strands share a belief that the state should provide law and order in society. For instance, Nozick's 'minarchist state' draws on the Lockean idea of a 'nightwatchman state', which protects individuals, and Rand's strong state also indicates a desire for law and order. Similarly, Disraeli believed that 'the palace is not safe when the cottage is not happy', indicating a desire for the state to mitigate rebellion by ensuring law and order and thus suggesting unity between the strands. However, the more persuasive view remains that there is more division than unity between One Nation and New Right conservatives. One Nation thinkers believe that the state should intervene in the economy, helping individuals to self-actualise through the provision of welfare, as seen in Churchill and Macmillan's broad acceptance of the Beveridge Report's desire for state action to rid society of the Five Giant Evils of want, ignorance, disease, idleness and squalor. Rand and Nozick, by contrast, believed that welfare would create a culture of dependency, and — as a result of their optimism in human nature — placed the emphasis on the individual to self-actualise. Furthermore, whilst Scruton believed that the state should intervene with an aesthetic agenda, to protect natural landscapes, for Disraeli, state intervention was purely pragmatic and to ensure there was not a 'divided Britain' and reduce the threat of uprising, as per his warning that 'the palace is not safe if the cottage is not happy'. Therefore, whilst thinkers from both strands are united in their view that the state should provide law and order, they are largely divided in that Rand and Nozick reject the notion of a welfare state and Scruton ascribes an aesthetic role to the state.

   A partially convincing case can be made that there is more to unite than divide the New Right from One Nation conservatives on society. Thinkers from both strands accept inequality. Scruton believed that homosexuals should not have adoption rights in society and subscribed to capitalism, which entails material inequalities, whilst Disraeli's belief that individuals are endowed with different roles in society suggests acceptance of inequality, indicating unity. Nevertheless, it is more accurate to suggest that New Right and One Nation conservatives are largely divided on society, as New Right thinkers view society as more individualistic. Rand proposed an atomised society, suggesting a belief in individualism, whilst Nozick's 'entitlement theory' presents a highly individualised view of society that suggests no collectivism whatsoever. By contrast, One Nation thinkers such as Disraeli view society as a collective force, hence the name 'One Nation', which suggests there is more to divide than unite New Right and One Nation thinkers. Moreover, whilst Disraeli advocated altruism in society and reforms such as the Factory Act, Rand believed that 'altruism is incompatible with capitalism, with individual rights,' further indicating division rather than unity. As such, although thinkers from both strands unite over aspects of inequality, they are divided on whether society is collective and altruistic, and thus they are divided to a larger extent.

   Overall, while thinkers from both strands are united in their view that the state should provide law and order, they are largely divided in that neo-liberals Rand and Nozick reject the notion of a welfare state, and neo-conservative Scruton ascribes an aesthetic role to the state. Furthermore, although all thinkers believe in human fallibility, Rand held that selfishness was a virtue and the New Right placed more faith in human rationalism, unlike One Nation conservatives. Finally, the strands are largely divided on society, with the New Right treating it as individualistic and rejecting altruism in favour of individualism. There is therefore more to divide rather than unite the New Right from One Nation conservatives.

Edexcel-style Exam Questions (12 marks)

Page 315: 'Examine Questions'

1   *Examine the differences between the core features of the US and the UK constitutions.*

   The US Constitution is codified, meaning that it is contained within a single, authoritative, and entrenched document. By contrast, the UK is rare among democratic nations in maintaining an uncodified constitution, which is derived from multiple sources, some of which — statute law, authoritative works, common law and treaties — are written, and a range of historical conventions that are partially or wholly unwritten. The codified nature of the US Constitution is protected by a stringent amendments process — requiring super majorities in chambers of Congress and among the fifty states — whereas the UK Constitution is far more flexible. Statute law, for instance, can be amended with only a simple majority in both houses of Parliament, while conventions have no legally enshrined status at all, and can be ignored, as was the case in April 2018 when Theresa May launched air strikes in Syria without first consulting Parliament. This explains why the US Constitution has only been amended twenty-seven times since 1787 (most recently in 1992), while the UK Constitution is frequently amended. Some recent examples of this were the passage of the Coronavirus Act (2020), when Parliament granted the executive sweeping emergency powers to impose restrictions designed to limit the spread of COVID-19 without requiring parliamentary scrutiny, and the Public Order Act (2023), when Parliament granted the police the power to arrest protesters on suspicion of plans to cause 'undue' disruption.

   Secondly, the US Constitution is sovereign over the entire nation's political system. This means that its provisions take precedence over laws passed by Congress or at state level. Since Marbury v. Madison (1803), the Supreme Court has effectively exercised the Constitution's sovereignty through its power of judicial review, which allows it to strike down acts of Congress or state laws as unconstitutional. This happened in the case Roman Catholic Diocese of Brooklyn v. Cuomo (2020), when New York State's ban on religious gatherings during the COVID-19 pandemic was ruled incompatible with 1st amendment rights. By contrast, Parliament is sovereign in the UK, which means that statute law takes priority over the other sources of the Constitution. For example, after the Supreme Court's common law ruling in R (AAA and others) v. Home Secretary (2023), Parliament passed a piece of statute law — the Safety of Rwanda Act (2024) — that overruled the Supreme Court's ruling that Rwanda was an unsafe country to use as an alternative centre for processing asylum claims. This difference between the two constitutions stems from the fact that the US Constitution is codified, which automatically confers sovereign status, while the UK has retained its uncodified Constitution, which is based on the 'twin pillars' of parliamentary sovereignty and the rule of law.

Sample Answers

Finally, the US has a federal constitution, which creates centres of political power at a federal level (in Washington D.C.) and at state level (across the fifty constituent states of the US). The US's federal system predominantly stems from Article IV and from the 10th amendment, which outlines that 'all powers not delegated to the federal government are reserved to...the states'. Unlike the US, the UK has traditionally had a unitary constitution, meaning that there is a single location of political power in Westminster, where both Parliament and the executive are based. Even since the introduction of devolution, the Constitution still defers to statute laws passed by Parliament when there are conflicts. For example, when the Scottish Parliament attempted to call a second independence referendum in 2022, the Supreme Court clarified that only the UK Parliament had the authority to pass a law calling a referendum. These differences stem from the fact that the thirteen original states were involved in drafting the US Constitution at the Philadelphia Convention in 1787, whereas the UK Constitution has evolved over time, mostly under the direction of politicians and judges in Westminster.

Page 315: 'Analyse Questions'

5   *Analyse the similarities between the power of pressure groups in the US and the UK.*

Some US and UK groups hold permanent insider status, meaning that they can always influence government. For example, in the UK, the Confederation of British Industry (CBI) has traditionally been seen as a centre of economic influence and expertise, given the importance of its members to the economy, making its support attractive to leaders of all parties. Prominent politicians such as Rishi Sunak, Boris Johnson and Keir Starmer have all given speeches to the CBI in recent years — e.g. during the 2019 general election campaign, all major party leaders spoke at the annual CBI conference. Similarly, in the USA, AIPAC is regarded as a permanent insider, influencing both parties' policies on Israel, in part because of its large donations — in 2024, it gave over $20 million to Democratic candidates, and over $12 million to Republican candidates. AIPAC's influence can be seen by both parties supporting a package of military aid from the US to Israel worth almost $4 billion over 10 years. These similarities can be explained by the fact that, in both political systems, there are certain consensus issues, shown in the examples given above, that are considered equally important by both major parties.

Another similarity between the power of pressure groups in the US and the UK is the presence of groups whose influence fluctuates depending on which party is in government. For example, the Federalist Society in the US has greater influence under a Republican administration. About 90% of Trump's judicial appointments from 2017 to 2021 were members, as well as all three of his Supreme Court nominations, whereas Joe Biden did not nominate any Federalist Society members to judicial positions during his presidency. This is similar to the Centre for Social Justice's influence in shaping Conservative policy in the UK, for instance the introduction of Universal Credit, whereas their influence is now much reduced under the new Labour government, which has closer relationships with centrist think tanks like the Tony Blair Institute for Global Change. These similarities can be explained using cultural comparative theory because they are due to the presence of at least two major parties in each country. This allows the government to change following democratic elections, and creates opportunities for pressure groups whose ideology is aligned with one party alone to have inconsistent influence.

Cultural theory can also be used to compare the power of pressure groups in the US and the UK is through the activities of outsider groups that seek to make use of their democratic rights and both countries' cultural commitment to upholding a free media. In both the US and the UK, there are a range of outsider groups which employ direct action in attempts to raise their profile and apply pressure on elected politicians. This sometimes does lead to changes being made. A prime example of this in the US is the NAACP, which was able to help dismantle segregation in the Civil Rights era, and which continues to use direct action through Moral Monday rallies that highlight continuing inequality and discrimination. Similarly, in the UK, recent years high-profile protests organised by the NFU (against changes to inheritance tax laws) and the Stop

Brexit campaign (calling for a second referendum) have generated significant publicity for their causes. Because both countries have long, well-established democratic political cultures that protect freedoms of speech and assembly, cultural theory can help to explain these comparisons.

AQA-style Essay Questions (25 marks)

Page 318: Paper 1 — Government and Politics of the UK

2   *'Neither individual nor collective rights are adequately protected or guaranteed in the UK.' Analyse and evaluate this statement.*

Overall, it is clear that individual rights are neither protected nor guaranteed, as parliamentary sovereignty and the omnicompetence of statute law means that judicial rulings can be ignored and important laws such as the Human Rights Act (1998) theoretically repealed. However, consistent laws against terrorism as well as against disruptive protests suggest that collective rights are adequately protected, if at the expense of individual rights. Overall, the view in the question is only partly convincing as only individual rights are not adequately protected or guaranteed.

The flexibility of the Constitution has been used to protect and guarantee individual rights at the expense of collective rights in recent years. However, there is some evidence to suggest that individual rights are protected and guaranteed. For example, landmark laws such as the Freedom of Information Act (2000), which has been invoked to uncover scandals such as the MP expenses scandal in the late 2000s, and the Equality Act (2010), which prevents discrimination on the grounds of race, age, disability and sex, have bolstered rights protection. Equally, David Cameron used the flexibility of the Constitution to pass the Marriage (Same-Sex Couples) Act (2013) through Parliament, further pointing to effective individual rights protection. It is also important to note that the flexibility of the Constitution allowed the ECHR to be incorporated into UK law through the HRA (1998), which has protected and guaranteed collective and individual rights. The Supreme Court (SC) can issue declarations of incompatibility with the ECHR to enforce rights protection. Indeed, 20 of 29 declarations of incompatibility became final between 2000 and 2015, suggesting both individual and collective rights are effectively protected. However, it is more convincing to argue that individual rights are neither protected nor securely guaranteed due to parliamentary sovereignty and the omnicompetence of statute law. The government can effectively disregard individual rights protection where it sees fit. For instance, the SC has ruled the blanket ban on prisoners' voting to be incompatible with ECHR. However, the government has since avoided the issue and failed to extend the vote — an indication of ineffective individual rights protection. Whilst politicians such as Dominic Raab have been keen to highlight that collective rights are not effectively protected, emphasising that terrorists such as Abu Qatada were able to remain in the UK, as the judiciary enforced Article 8 of the HRA which protects the right to family life, it is clear that collective rights are sufficiently protected. The Counter-Terrorism and Sentencing Act (2021) is also aimed towards the collective right to safety from terrorism. But it is at the expense of individual rights since the law revived Control Orders, which allow the government to indefinitely hold suspected terrorists under house arrest, even when based on suspicion rather than concrete evidence. Equally, laws such as the Freedom of Information Act have not proven wholly conducive to rights protection — almost two-fifths of requests in 2019 resulted in no information being disclosed. In this way, it is only partly compelling to accept the view in the question that neither individual rights nor collective rights are adequately protected and guaranteed. Parliamentary sovereignty means that rights are not 'guaranteed', as the government could theoretically repeal important laws such as the HRA (1998) whilst passing laws such as the Terrorism Act which infringe on civil liberties. Collective rights, however, seem adequately protected and guaranteed, as recent legislation has demonstrated.

A plausible, if ultimately flawed, case can be made that collective and individual rights are adequately protected and guaranteed through the development of common law. The judiciary has established common law precedent which protects the rights

Sample Answers

of individuals. In KV (Sri Lanka) v Secretary of State for Home Department (2019), for instance, the judiciary ruled that the Home Office had acted unlawfully when attempting to deny asylum to a Sri Lankan man based on the claim that he had organised his own torture. This illustrates that common law through judicial rulings can effectively protect individual rights, and 'guarantees' them through binding rulings. Similarly, the judiciary protected collective rights in 2018 by ruling that Parliament should extend the 2004 Civil Partnerships Act to all citizens, as it was discriminatory for it to be confined to homosexual couples. Common law therefore seems to adequately protect individual rights through these judicial rulings, and guarantees them by setting precedent which future governments and courts usually abide by. Nevertheless, this argument overlooks the fact that common law can be overridden by statute law, with the government again protecting collective rights at the expense of individual rights. For instance, the SC set a common law precedent in HM (Treasury) v Ahmed (2010), which ruled that the Treasury did not lawfully exercise the power to freeze the assets of terror suspects. However, this was effectively overturned through statute law in the same year: the Terrorist Asset Freezing Act (2010) was passed by Brown's government. In a similar example, the Sunak government overturned the SC's protection of individual rights in R (AAA and others) v. Home Secretary (2023) by passing the Safety of Rwanda Act (2024) through Parliament. Parliamentary sovereignty means that statute law cannot be struck down by other bodies. In this way, collective rights do seem adequately protected and guaranteed as the government usually favours the rights of the collective in statute law. However, individual rights are not 'guaranteed' through common law precedent, as this can be overridden by statute law due to the omnicompetence of Parliament. Therefore, it is only partly convincing to argue that neither individual nor collective rights in the UK are adequately protected and guaranteed.

Finally, the actions of civil liberties groups in protecting and guaranteeing rights should also be acknowledged. Pressure groups have certainly proved successful on a local level, bolstering individual rights. For example, Liberty was successful in forcing the BCP Council to amend part of its Public Spaces Protection Order, which had previously allowed for the criminalisation of rough sleepers and beggars — a clear infringement on individual rights. Furthermore, Liberty has also bolstered individual rights in South Wales through a successful judicial review challenge which secured a ban on the use of facial recognition technology, further pointing to effective individual rights protection. Judicial review has also proved a powerful mechanism for groups seeking to protect collective rights. In 2020, for instance, Friends of the Earth and Plan B brought a successful judicial challenge to the Court of Appeals against government plans for a third Heathrow runway, emphasising that Chris Grayling had failed to mention the Climate Change Act (2008) and the Paris Climate Accord (2015) in his assessment of the runway's impact. This protects collective rights in mitigating against the environmental impact of the runway, which would have breached both the 2008 and 2015 laws, although the Supreme Court later overturned the decision in R (Friends of the Earth and others) v. Heathrow Airport Limited (2020). However, it is clear that civil liberties groups remain fundamentally constrained in the extent to which they can protect both individual and collective rights, supporting the view in the question. Indeed, civil liberties groups are often eclipsed and disregarded by the government, particularly when tackling terrorism and terror suspects. Equally, though common law precedent has gone some way in protecting individual rights, it is clear that statute law continues to favour collective rights at the expense of individual rights, as demonstrated in the previous paragraph. Finally, pressure groups cannot hope to 'guarantee' collective or individual rights protection, as they lack direct political influence and their aims must usually align with those of the government if they are to be achievable.

Therefore, the view that neither individual nor collective rights in the UK are adequately protected and guaranteed is partly convincing, as individual rights have been threatened by recent laws, but legislation has continued to bolster collective rights.

Page 319: Paper 2 — Comparative Politics

12 *'Electoral outcomes and voting behaviour in US federal elections are more predictable than in UK general elections.'*
Analyse and evaluate this statement.

If electoral outcomes and voting behaviour were more predictable in US federal elections than in UK general elections, there would be a more consistent dominance by the two main parties in the US, a more stable coalition of voters for each party and elections would be shaped by a more consistent set of salient issues. While there have been significant shifts in voting behaviour in the US in recent years, fuelled most notably by the rise of Donald Trump and the insurgent right wing of the Republican Party, these do not outweigh the extraordinary unpredictability of the outcomes and voting behaviour in the past five UK general elections. In these elections, there have been significant swings in support for each party by certain demographic groups, and the pendulum has swung unpredictably between two-party dominance and multi-party success.

A plausible case can be made for arguing that electoral outcomes have been more predictable in UK general elections than in US federal elections in terms of the parties' overall performance. The outcomes of the past two general elections have been broadly predictable from the early weeks of the campaign: polls reliably suggested in 2019 that Boris Johnson's Conservatives were on course for a majority, while polls indicated a large majority for Keir Starmer's Labour Party for more than a year before the 2024 general election. By contrast, the past three presidential elections have all been too close to call, with Trump's victory in 2016 and Biden's in 2020 representing surprises to many polling companies. In 2024, Trump's margin of victory — by 312 to 226 in the Electoral College, and by 1.5% in the popular vote — was unexpectedly comfortable, while the Harris campaign performed much more poorly in key swing states such as Pennsylvania, Ohio and Georgia than most polls had predicted. This unpredictability has been mirrored in congressional elections, which have delivered swings in party control of the House of Representatives in 2010, 2018 and 2022, and in the Senate in 2014, 2020 and 2024. These examples all suggest that, in terms of the overall performance of the major parties, voting behaviour has become more predictable in UK general elections than in US federal elections. However, it is ultimately more convincing to argue that voting behaviour actually tends to be more predictable in US federal elections, which are consistently dominated by the Republicans and the Democrats, than in UK general elections, where voters' allegiances to the Conservative and Labour parties have shifted frequently in recent years. While the two main parties' share of the popular vote in presidential elections has remained fairly stable 95% in 2016, 98% in 2020, and 98% in 2024 — the opposite has been the case in the UK: in 2017, the Conservatives and Labour shared 82% of the popular vote, which fell to 76% in 2019, and then to a record low of only 57% in 2024. In this time period, Reform UK was created as a successor to the Brexit Party, winning 15% of the popular vote and five seats in the 2024 general election, while the Liberal Democrats have increased their number of seats from 12 to 72. By contrast, there has not been a single third-party member of Congress elected in the 21st century, making two-party dominance much more predictable in the US than in the UK. Therefore, while the overall winning party has at times been easier to predict in UK general elections than in US federal elections, this is outweighed by the significant swings in the margin of victory and in the performance of minor parties in the UK, compared with the stable and predictable maintenance of the two-party system in US federal elections.

A similarly credible case can be advanced that demographic voting behaviour is more predictable in UK general elections than in US federal elections. For example, Labour's coalition of voters relies heavily and predictably on university graduates, around 40% of whom voted for the party in both the 2019 and 2024 general elections. This contrasts with the more volatile and less predictable voting behaviour among college-educated voters in the US — the Democrats' share of the vote among voters with postgraduate degrees fell and among college-educated Hispanic voters it fell by a significant amount between the 2020 and 2024 presidential elections. Similarly, age has become a reliable predictor of voting behaviour in UK general elections, with only a fifth of over 70s (a demographic dominated by the Conservatives) voting Labour in 2024, compared with 14% in 2019. By contrast, the Democrats' share of under 30s'

Sample Answers

votes fell significantly in the 2024 presidential election compared to the 2022 mid-term elections. Nevertheless, the more persuasive argument is that, by most demographic indicators, US federal elections are again more predictable than UK general elections. The Republicans' voter base has been extremely stable and predictable in recent years, winning the support of around 60% of white male voters and around 65% of white voters without a college degree in all three elections. Combined with the Democrats' success in securing over 85% of black voters across the past three federal elections, this suggests that voting behaviour has become more predictable across several demographic indicators than in the UK, where Labour's share of the ethnic minority vote has fallen from around 75% in 2017 to less than 50% in 2024. Furthermore, while age is often said to be the most reliable predictor of voting behaviour in the UK, the Conservatives' support among over 70s fell from around 70% to less than 50% between the 2019 and 2024 general elections, while the Green Party and Reform UK both enjoyed significant success, each increasing their share of the under 30 vote by around 10%. Due to these large, election-defining discrepancies, and to the relatively stable nature of both the Democrats' and the Republicans' voter bases in recent years, it is therefore more persuasive to argue that voting behaviour is more predictable in US federal elections than in UK general elections.

It is therefore important to acknowledge that the overall outcome of federal elections is often more difficult to predict than of UK general elections, but both the broader electoral outcomes and demographic voting behaviour are generally more predictable in US federal elections than in UK general elections. This is due to the continued dominance of the Democrats and the Republicans in the US, which contrasts with the increasing success of traditionally minor parties in the UK, and the emergence of dependable coalitions of voters for each party in the US, compared with much less stable demographic support in the UK. Nevertheless, it must be recognised that, despite the increasing success of minor parties in the UK, it remains entirely predictable that general elections in both countries will be won by one of the two main parties.

AQA-style Exam Questions (9 marks)

Page 321: Paper 2

25 **Explain and analyse three ways that cultural theory can be used to compare the power of pressure groups in the US and the UK.**

The first way in which cultural theory can be used to compare the power of pressure groups in the US and the UK is through the differing reasons why some groups are able to hold insider status. For example, in the UK, the Confederation of British Industry (CBI) has traditionally been seen as a centre of economic influence and expertise, given the importance of its members to the economy, making its support attractive to leaders of all parties. Prominent politicians such as Rishi Sunak, Boris Johnson and Keir Starmer have all given speeches to the CBI in recent years — e.g. during the 2019 general election campaign, all major party leaders spoke at the annual CBI conference. By contrast, pressure groups in the USA often achieve influence through campaign donations. For example, AIPAC is regarded as an insider, influencing both parties' policies on Israel, in part because of its large donations — in 2024, it gave over $20 million to Democratic candidates, and over $12 million to Republican candidates. AIPAC's influence can be seen in the fact that both parties have supported a package of military aid from the US to Israel worth around $4 billion over 10 years, and Kamala Harris and Donald Trump both gave a speech to AIPAC during the 2024 presidential election campaign. The different political cultures of the two countries — the US system treats political donations as an extension of free speech while the UK system has a more regulated fundraising culture — means that cultural theory can underpin these comparisons.

Another way in which cultural theory can be used to compare the power of pressure groups in the US and the UK is through the presence of groups whose influence fluctuates depending on which party is in government. For example, the Federalist Society in the US has greater influence under a Republican administration. About 90% of Trump's judicial appointments from 2017 to 2021 were members, as well as all three of his Supreme Court nominations, whereas Joe Biden did not nominate any Federalist Society members to judicial positions during his presidency. This is similar to the Centre for Social Justice's influence in shaping Conservative policy in the UK, for instance the introduction of Universal Credit, whereas their influence is now much reduced under the new Labour government, which has closer relationships with centrist think tanks like the Tony Blair Institute for Global Change. These similarities can be explained using cultural comparative theory because they are due to the presence of at least two major parties in each country. This allows the government to change following democratic elections, and thus creates opportunities for pressure groups whose ideology is aligned with one party alone to have inconsistent influence.

A final way in which cultural theory can be used to compare the power of pressure groups in the US and the UK is through the activities of outsider groups that seek to make use of their democratic rights and both countries' cultural commitment to upholding a free media. In both the US and the UK, there are a range of outsider groups which employ direct action in attempts to raise their profile and apply pressure on elected politicians. This sometimes does lead to changes being made; the prime example of this in the US is the NAACP, which was able to help dismantle segregation in the Civil Rights era, and which continues to use direct action through Moral Monday rallies that highlight continuing inequality and discrimination. Similarly, in recent years high-profile protests organised by the NFU (against changes to inheritance tax laws) and the Stop Brexit campaign (calling for a second referendum) have generated significant publicity for their cause. Because both countries have long, well-established democratic political cultures that protect freedoms of speech and assembly, cultural theory can help to explain these comparisons.

Page 321: Paper 3

3 **Explain and analyse three ways in which liberal thinkers view the state.**

Most classical liberals believe that a minimal, nightwatchman state is the most likely guarantor of individuals' liberty. Under John Locke's theory of the social contract, individuals agree to give up some of their liberty by following the law, in return for the state's protection of their 'natural rights' to life, liberty, and property. Due to their extreme faith in humans' rationalism, the state's role would not extend beyond ensuring these core ingredients of a free and fulfilling life. Locke's fellow classical liberal, Adam Smith, advanced a similar view of the state as a set of institutions with minimal ambitions and scope through his economic theory, which positions the state in a 'laissez faire' role, in which free market capitalism, rather than the state, serves as the 'invisible hand' that guides society.

By contrast, liberal thinkers such as Mary Wollstonecraft (a classical liberal) and Betty Friedan (a modern liberal) envisage an enlarged role for the state as a guarantor and enabler of women's rights and freedom. Although sharing many of Locke's views about a nightwatchman state, Wollstonecraft argued that the state should extend the franchise to women, and that the state should include female representatives, based on her argument that women have the same potential for rational thought and conduct as men. As a modern liberal who shaped the second wave of feminism, Betty Friedan called for the state to play an active role in passing legislation that would give women the same economic and social status as men, including legislation concerning maternity rights, abortion and equal pay. Hence modern liberals can be seen to differ from classical liberals in that they see a greater role for the state in maximising social justice.

John Rawls, another modern liberal, advances the most interventionist conception of the state among the key thinkers. Building on T. H. Green's distinction between negative and positive freedom, Rawls argues that a just society must be governed by an enabling state. Under this more interventionist vision, the state would seek to achieve two objectives: ensuring equality of opportunity and satisfying the 'difference' principle, which holds that any social or economic inequalities that do exist serve to benefit the least advantaged in society.

Acknowledgements

With thanks to Alamy for the images on pages 9, 11, 13, 18, 20, 23, 25, 27, 28, 29, 49, 66, 70, 78, 100, 108, 115, 123, 137, 138 and 269.

Image of Liz Truss on p.3: Simon Dawson / No10 Downing Street, licensed under the Open Government Licence v3.0. http://www.nationalarchives.gov.uk/doc/open-government-licence/version/3, via Wikimedia Commons

Brexit data on p.4: BBC News, 2016. https://www.bbc.co.uk/news/uk-politics-eu-referendum-35616946

Pages 4, 5, 6, 7, 8, 9, 15,16, 17, 26, 27,28, 30, 57, 62, 63, 68, 81, 86, 105, 177 and 178 contain Parliamentary information licensed under the Open Parliament Licence v3.0. https://www.parliament.uk/site-information/copyright-parliament/open-parliament-licence/

Australian voter turnout data on p.8: © Commonwealth of Australia 2017. https://www.aec.gov.au/elections/federal_elections/voter-turnout.htm

Data on how much each political party spent during the 2017 general election on p.17: Reproduced from the Electoral Commission's webpage on campaign spending: Political parties and non-party campaigners | Electoral Commission 2025 with kind permission from the Electoral Commission.

Pages 19, 28, 64, 66, 67, 68, 72, 79, 83 86, 87, 88, 89, 90, 91, 93, 95, 96, 219, 231, 250 and 252 contain public sector information licensed under the Open Government Licence v3.0. https://www.nationalarchives.gov.uk/doc/open-government-licence/version/3/

Jeremy Corbyn approval ratings data on p.32: YouGov Plc, 2017 © All rights reserved. https://yougov.co.uk/politics/articles/49978-how-britain-voted-in-the-2024-general-election

Social class data on p.34: ONS, licensed under the Open Government Licence v.3.0. https://www.nationalarchives.gov.uk/doc/open-government-licence/version/3/

Voting data on pages 34, 35, 38 and 42: YouGov Plc, © All rights reserved. https://yougov.co.uk/politics/articles/26925-how-britain-voted-2019-general-election https://yougov.co.uk/politics/articles/49978-how-britain-voted-in-the-2024-general-election

Data on proportion of Muslims in different areas on p.35: Focaldata, 2024. https://www.focaldata.com/blog/how-britain-voted-2024

Information about young voter and Muslim turnout at the 2024 election on p.35: IPPR, 2024. https://www.ippr.org/articles/half-of-us

2019 election poll data on p.36: IPSOS, 2019. https://www.ipsos.com/en-uk/how-britain-voted-2019-election

Effect of Bigotgate on opinion polls of Brown on p.36: The Guardian, 2010. https://www.theguardian.com/politics/2010/apr/29/unpublished-sun-poll-brown-bigot

Information about voters leaving Labour in 2019 on p.36: BMG research, 2020. https://www.bmgresearch.co.uk/bmg-independent-labour-policies-popular-but-many-want-change-in-direction/

Polling data about Rishi Sunak leaving D-Day memorial on p.37: The Telegraph, 2024. https://www.telegraph.co.uk/politics/2024/06/07/general-election-latest-news-rishi-sunak-keir-starmer/

Continued relevance of Leave and Remain as aligned demographics data on p.38: YouGov, 2024. © All rights reserved. https://yougov.co.uk/politics/articles/49978-how-britain-voted-in-the-2024-general-election

Details of turnout in Brexit referendum on p.39: 'How Britain voted in the UK referendum'. IPSOS, 2016. https://www.ipsos.com/en-uk/how-britain-voted-2016-eu-referendum

Details of 2022 Conservative polling figures on p.39: The Guardian, 2022. https://www.theguardian.com/politics/2022/oct/16/rees-mogg-coffey-and-hunt-would-lose-seats-in-election-poll-suggests

Details of Truss disapproval rating in 2022 on p.39: YouGov, 2022. © All rights reserved. https://yougov.co.uk/politics/articles/44092-liz-trusss-net-favourability-rating-falls-70

Details of polling indicating likely success of Farage in Clacton on p.39: The Times, 2024. https://www.thetimes.com/uk/article/the-poll-that-could-push-nigel-farage-back-into-politics-7jfm0djzp

Details of decrease in polling gap due to Conservative social care policy 2019 on p.39: The Guardian, 2017. https://www.theguardian.com/politics/ng-interactive/2017/may/08/general-election-2017-poll-tracker-who-is-in-the-lead

Details of polling and results of 1992 election on p.40: BBC News, 2015. https://web.archive.org/web/20200420230626/https:/www.bbc.co.uk/news/uk-31504146

Details of polling and results of 2024 election on p.40: BBC News, 2024. https://www.bbc.co.uk/news/uk-politics-68079726 https://www.bbc.co.uk/news/election/2024/uk/results

Conservative spending on Facebook ads 2017 and 2019 on p.41: BBC News, 2020. https://www.bbc.co.uk/news/uk-politics-54449451

Details of Conservatives YouTube ads 2019 on p.41: The Guardian, 2019. https://www.theguardian.com/politics/2019/dec/12/how-parties-used-facebook-instagram-and-google-ads

Data on 'Labour Connects' on p.41: © Labour, 2025. https://labour.org.uk/resources/digital-resources/

Voting data on p.41: 'How Britain Voted in 1997'. IPSOS, 1997. https://www.ipsos.com/en-uk/how-britain-voted-1997

Details on polling and Sun endorsement 1997 on p.42: The Guardian, 2009. https://www.theguardian.com/news/datablog/2009/oct/05/sun-labour-newspapers-support-elections

Telegraph/Guardian readers voting Conservative/Labour on p.42: YouGov Plc, 2017, © All rights reserved. https://yougov.co.uk/politics/articles/18384-how-britain-voted-2017-general-election

Details on polling in run up to 2024 election for conservative-leaning paper readers on p.42: Best for Britain, 2024. https://www.bestforbritain.org/the_read_wall

Daily Mail and Daily Mirror front page data on p.43: Press Gazette, 2022. https://pressgazette.co.uk/publishers/nationals/daily-mail-partygate-front-pages/

Image of Thomas Hobbes by David Beck on p.44: Scottish National Portrait Gallery No. 188

Image of Edmund Burke by Sir Joshua Reynolds on p.44: National Galleries Scotland. Bequeathed conditionally by Miss E. Drummond to the National Gallery of Ireland; transferred 1969.

Image of Michael Oakeshott on p.44: Library of the London School of Economics and Political Science, via Wikimedia Commons.

Image of Roger Scruton on p.44: Fronteiras do Pensamento, CC BY-SA 2.0. https://creativecommons.org/licenses/by-sa/2.0, via Wikimedia Commons.

Photo of John Stuart Mill on p.49: London Stereoscopic Company, Public domain, via Wikimedia Commons.

Photo of John Rawls on p.49: Published by the Belknap Press of Harvard University Press. Photograph taken by Alec Rawls, John's son.

Photo of Betty Friedan on p.49: Fred Palumbo, World Telegram staff photographer. Restored by Adam Cuerden.

Photo of Beatrice Webb on p.54: Gregorysilva, licensed under CC BY-SA 4.0. https://creativecommons.org/licenses/by-sa/4.0, via Wikimedia Commons

Image on p.54 of Anthony Crosland: © Crown Copyright. Contains public sector information licensed under the Open Government Licence v3.0. https://www.nationalarchives.gov.uk/doc/open-government-licence/version/3/

Image on p.54 of Anthony Giddens: Szusi, licensed under CC BY-SA 3.0. http://creativecommons.org/licenses/by-sa/3.0/, via Wikimedia Commons.

Source for increase in Senedd popularity on p.66: Beaufort Research Ltd., 1,000 adults representative of the Welsh population were interviewed online between 2 and 9 March 2021. https://www.walesonline.co.uk/news/politics/senedd-election-abolish-assembly-wales-20333673

Source for support of Scottish independence between 2018 and 2020 on p.66: YouGov Plc, 2024. © All rights reserved https://yougov.co.uk/politics/articles/50536-scottish-independence-10-years-on

Northern Irish employment data on p.67: © Northern Ireland Assembly Commission 2019.

Image of Boris Bikes on p.67: Tiaa Monto, licensed under CC BY-SA 3.0. https://creativecommons.org/licenses/by/3.0/deed.en

Image on p.67 of Andy Burnham: Rwendland, licensed under CC BY-SA 4.0. https://creativecommons.org/licenses/by-sa/4.0 via Wikimedia Commons

Poll about public support for the creation of an English Parliament on p.68: YouGov Plc, 2023 © All rights reserved. https://yougov.co.uk/topics/politics/trackers/support-for-creation-of-a-new-english-parliament-along-the-lines-of-the-existing-scottish-parliament

Image of Sadiq Khan on p.68: Scottish Government, licensed under CC BY 2.0. https://creativecommons.org/licenses/by/2.0/

Image on p.71 licensed under CC BY 3.0. https://creativecommons.org/licenses/by/3.0/deed.en, via Wikimedia commons

Image of the Archbishop of Canterbury on p.72: Licensed under CC BY 2.0. https://creativecommons.org/licenses/by/2.0

Image of Baroness Lawrence of Clarendon on p.72: Roger Harris, licensed under CC BY 3.0. https://creativecommons.org/licenses/by/3.0, via Wikimedia Commons

Percentage of bills passed into law in 2022-2023 on p.76: Hansard Society, 2023. https://www.hansardsociety.org.uk/blog/what-is-the-state-of-the-governments-legislative-programme-as-parliament

Data about David Cameron's PMQs answers on p.78: University of York, 2019. https://www.york.ac.uk/news-and-events/news/2019/research/david-cameron-rudest-prime-minister-at-pmqs/

Ethnic minority census data on p.81: Office for National Statistics (ONS) — Census 2021, licensed under the Open Government Licence v3.0. https://www.nationalarchives.gov.uk/doc/open-government-licence/version/3/

Percentage of MPs in 2024 that attended independent schools on p.81: Sutton Trust, 2024. https://www.suttontrust.com/our-research/parliamentary-privilege-2024/

Data about peers mentioning business interests on p.82: The Times, 2021. https://www.thetimes.com/article/revealed-the-truth-about-the-house-of-lords-peers-who-are-born-to-rule-nbdvcfrv3

Image of Michael Gove on p.88 and 91: Licensed under CC BY 3.0. https://creativecommons.org/licenses/by/3.0/deed.en

Image of Dominic Raab on p.88: Chris McAndrew, licensed under CC BY 3.0. https://creativecommons.org/licenses/by/3.0, via Wikimedia Commons

Image of Gavin Williamson on p.88 and 93: Richard Townshend, licensed under CC BY 3.0. https://creativecommons.org/licenses/by/3.0, via Wikimedia Commons

Image of Suella Braverman on p.88 and 92: David Woolfall, CC BY 3.0. https://creativecommons.org/licenses/by/3.0, via Wikimedia Commons

Image of James Cleverly on p.88: Richard Townshend, licensed under CC BY 3.0. https://creativecommons.org/licenses/by/3.0, via Wikimedia Commons

Image of Jeremy Hunt on p.89: Chris McAndrew, licensed under CC BY 3.0. https://creativecommons.org/licenses/by/3.0, via Wikimedia Commons

Image of Sajid Javid on p.90: Richard Townshend, licensed under CC BY 3.0. https://creativecommons.org/licenses/by/3.0, via Wikimedia Commons

Image of Geoffrey Howe on p.90 and 91: Universitätsarchiv St.Gallen, licensed under CC-BY-SA 4.0. https://creativecommons.org/licenses/by-sa/4.0, via Wikimedia Commons

Image of Iain Duncan Smith on p.91: Chris McAndrew, licensed under CC BY 3.0. https://creativecommons.org/licenses/by/3.0, via Wikimedia Commons

Image of David Davis on p.91: Chris McAndrew, licensed under CC BY 3.0. https://creativecommons.org/licenses/by/3.0, via Wikimedia Commons

Image of Jo Johnson on p.91: Roger Harris, licensed under CC BY 3.0. https://creativecommons.org/licenses/by/3.0, via Wikimedia Commons

Image of Robert Jenrick on p.91: Chris McAndrew, CC BY 3.0. https://creativecommons.org/licenses/by/3.0, via Wikimedia Commons

Image of Penny Mordaunt on p.91: licensed under the Open Government Licence v3.0. https://www.nationalarchives.gov.uk/doc/open-government-licence/version/3/

Image of Claire Short on p.92: 5th EITI Global Conference, The EITI, 2011. https://www.flickr.com/photos/24432475@N03/5494065443. Licensed under CC BY-SA 2.0. https://creativecommons.org/licenses/by-sa/2.0/

Image of Edwina Currie on p.92: NHS Confederation, licensed under CC BY 2.0. https://creativecommons.org/licenses/by/2.0, via Wikimedia Commons

Image of Louise Haigh on p.93: Laurie Noble, licensed under CC BY 3.0. https://creativecommons.org/licenses/by/3.0, via Wikimedia Commons

Image of Chris Grayling in p.93: Chris McAndrew, licensed under CC BY 3.0. https://creativecommons.org/licenses/by/3.0, via Wikimedia Commons

Image of Priti Patel on p.93: Richard Townshend, licensed under CC BY 3.0. https://creativecommons.org/licenses/by/3.0, via Wikimedia Commons

Image of Nicola Sturgeon on p.98: Scottish Government, licensed under CC BY 2.0. https://creativecommons.org/licenses/by/2.0, via Wikimedia Commons

Image of Gina Miller on p.99: Keith Edkins, licensed under CC BY-SA 4.0. https://creativecommons.org/licenses/by-sa/4.0, via Wikimedia Commons

Image of press pack outside UK Supreme Court on p.101: Steve Nimmons, licensed under CC BY 2.0. https://creativecommons.org/licenses/by/2.0, via Wikimedia Commons

Image of UK Supreme Court on p.102: Rwendland, licensed under CC BY-SA 3.0. https://creativecommons.org/licenses/by-sa/3.0 , via Wikimedia Commons

Population data on p.103: © European Central Bank, Frankfurt am Main, Germany. https://www.ecb.europa.eu/ecb-and-you/explainers/tell-me-more/html/maastricht_treaty.en.html

EU member GDP figures on p.104: © European Union, 2022. https://www.europarl.europa.eu/RegData/etudes/BRIE/2022/730320/EPRS_BRI(2022)730320_EN.pdf#:~:text=The%20most%20recent%20estimations%20conclude%20that%20this%20has,of%20the%20analysis%20and%20on%20the%20model%20used

EU member employment figures on p.104: © European Union, 2017. https://www.europarl.europa.eu/RegData/etudes/BRIE/2017/611009/EPRS_BRI%282017%29611009_EN.pdf

Image on p.104: CJCE-ECT - Grand courtoom by Cédric Puisney, licensed under CC BY 2.0. https://creativecommons.org/licenses/by/2.0 , via Wikimedia Commons

GDP figures on p.105: World Economics and Information Sciences Limited.

Referendum data on p.105: United Nations, Department of Economic and Social Affairs, Population Division (2015). World Population Prospects: The 2015 Revision, Volume I: Comprehensive Tables (ST/ESA/SER.A/379).

Image on p.109: Respublika Narodnaya, licensed under CC BY-SA 4.0. https://creativecommons.org/licenses/by-sa/4.0, via Wikimedia Commons

Image on p.115 of Aldo Leopold: 1944, University of Wisconsin Libraries, licensed under CC BY 4.0. https://creativecommons.org/licenses/by/4.0/

Photo of Murray Bookchin on p.115: Janet Biehl, licensed under CC BY-SA 4.0. https://creativecommons.org/licenses/by-sa/4.0, via Wikimedia Commons

Photo of Carolyn Merchant on p.115: Sprockethead1, licensed under CC BY-SA 4.0. https://creativecommons.org/licenses/by-sa/4.0, via Wikimedia Commons

Photo of Jonathon Porritt on p.115: Tonylemesmerd at English Wikipedia, licensed under CC BY-SA 3.0. http://creativecommons.org/licenses/by-sa/3.0/, via Wikimedia Commons

Acknowledgements

Image of Kate Millett on p.123: Linda Wolf, licensed under CC BY-SA 3.0. https://creativecommons.org/licenses/by-sa/3.0, via Wikimedia Commons
Image of bell hooks on p.123: Alex Lozupone (Tduk), licensed under CC BY-SA 4.0. https://creativecommons.org/licenses/by-sa/4.0, via Wikimedia Commons
Photo of Charles Taylor on p.130: Léa-Kim Châteauneuf, licensed under CC BY-SA 4.0. https://creativecommons.org/licenses/by-sa/4.0, via Wikimedia Commons
Photo of Bhiku Parekh on p.130: Roger Harris, licensed under CC BY 3.0. https://creativecommons.org/licenses/by/3.0, via Wikimedia Commons
Photo of Marcus Garvey on p.137 and 138: A&E Television Networks, licensed under CC BY-SA 4.0 https://creativecommons.org/licenses/by-sa/4.0 , via Wikimedia Commons
Number of mass shootings from 2020-2023 on p.160: © Gun Violence Archive, 2025. https://www.gunviolencearchive.org/
Funds raised in Georgia senate race 2022 on p.167: FEC. https://www.fec.gov/data/elections/senate/GA/2022/#individual-contributions
Number of centrists across House & Senate in 2022 compared to 1972 on p.168: 'The polarization in today's Congress has roots that go back decades'. Pew Research Center, Washington, D.C. (March 10, 2022) https://www.pewresearch.org/short-reads/2022/03/10/the-polarization-in-todays-congress-has-roots-that-go-back-decades/
Information about how often senators voted with their party on pages 168 and 175: Roll call, 2022. https://rollcall.com/2022/03/01/party-unity-vote-studies-underscore-polarized-state-of-the-union/
Susan Collins earmark data on p.170: Citizens Against Government Waste, 2024. https://www.cagw.org/sites/default/files/pdf/CAGW_PigBook_2024.pdf
Chuck Schumer earmark data on p.170: The Hill, 2024. https://thehill.com/homenews/senate/597625-lawmakers-feast-on-pork-in-omnibus/
Percentage of time house committees spent overseeing executive branch on p.171: Brookings Institute, 2022. https://www.brookings.edu/articles/house-oversight-of-the-executive-branch-what-did-the-116th-and-117th-congresses-spend-their-time-on/
Total allocated to labour, health and education on p.171: House Appropriations Committee, 2024. https://appropriations.house.gov/news/press-releases/committee-approves-fy25-labor-health-and-human-services-education-and-related
Data on competitive congressional districts on p.174: Brennan Center for Justice, 2022. https://www.brennancenter.org/our-work/analysis-opinion/gerrymandering-competitive-districts-near-extinction
Congress demographic data on p.175: 'The changing face of Congress in 8 charts'. Pew Research Center, Washington, D.C. (February 7, 2023). https://www.pewresearch.org/short-reads/2023/02/07/the-changing-face-of-congress/3
Congressional polarization data on p.175: 'The polarization in today's Congress has roots that go back decades'. Pew Research Center, Washington, D.C. (March 10, 2022) https://www.pewresearch.org/short-reads/2022/03/10/the-polarization-in-todays-congress-has-roots-that-go-back-decades/
Details of Joe Biden's approval rating July 24 on p.186: Gallup. https://news.gallup.com/interactives/507569/presidential-job-approval-center.aspx
Details of George Bush's approval ratings on p.188: Gallup. https://news.gallup.com/poll/116500/presidential-approval-ratings-george-bush.aspx
Number of cases brought to and heard by the Supreme Court on p.192: © Georgetown Law Library.
Supreme Court nomination data on p.198: 'Up until the postwar era, U.S. Supreme Court confirmations usually were routine business'. Pew Research Center, Washington, D.C. (February 7, 2022) https://www.pewresearch.org/short-reads/2022/02/07/up-until-the-postwar-era-u-s-supreme-court-confirmations-usually-were-routine-business/.
Data on Supreme Court Cases decided on ideological lines on p.198: Politico, 2024. https://www.politico.com/news/magazine/2024/06/02/supreme-court-justice-math-00152188
Gun related deaths data on p.199: Center for Disease Control and Prevention, National Center for Health Statistics. National Vital Statistics System, Mortality Statistics on CDC WONDER. Data are from the Multiple Cause of Death Files, as compiled from data provided by the 57 vital statistics jurisdictions through the Vital Statistics Cooperative Program. Accessed at All Deaths of U.S. Residents with the Underlying Cause due to Firearm Injury, By Year. https://wonder.cdc.gov/controller/saved/D157/D418F753 on December 23, 2024.
Image of Pete Buttigieg on p.205: Gage Skidmore, licensed under CC BY-SA 2.0. https://creativecommons.org/licenses/by-sa/2.0 via Wikimedia Commons.
Campaign spending during 2020 elections on p.207: FEC. https://www.fec.gov/data/spending-bythenumbers/?election_year=2020
Campaign event data on p.208: Benjamin Oestericher, FairVote.org, 2020 and Deb Otis, FairVote.org, 2024
Spending of super PACs in 2020 on p.210: FEC. https://www.fec.gov/data/browse-data/?tab=committees
Details of Barack Obama's donors giving $100 or less on p.211: Politico, 2008. https://www.politico.com/story/2008/05/obamas-army-of-small-donors-010223
Presidential approval ratings data on p.211: The American Presidency Project, https://www.presidency.ucsb.edu/statistics/data/donald-j-trump-public-approval, https://www.presidency.ucsb.edu/statistics/data/george-bush-public-approval
Trump COVID 19 poll data on p.212: BBC News, 2020. https://www.bbc.co.uk/news/election-us-2020-53657174
Iraq war poll data on p.212: 'A Look Back at How Fear and False Beliefs Bolstered U.S. Public Support for War in Iraq'. (14 March 2023) Pew Research Center. https://www.pewresearch.org/politics/2023/03/14/a-look-back-at-how-fear-and-false-beliefs-bolstered-u-s-public-support-for-war-in-iraq/
UK 2024 general election campaign donation data on p.213: The Electoral Reform Society, https://www.electoral-reform.org.uk/how-big-donors-fund-our-political-parties/
Georgia senate race spending data on p.213: FEC. https://www.fec.gov/data/elections/senate/GA/2020/
Image of women's march on p.216: Jason Wu, licensed under CC BY 3.0. https://creativecommons.org/licenses/by/3.0, via Wikimedia Commons
Number of gun-related deaths in the US in 2023 on p.217: Association of Health Care Journalists, 2024. https://healthjournalism.org/blog/2024/02/nearly-43000-people-died-from-gun-violence-in-2023-how-to-tell-the-story/
Details of Lord Bamford donations to Conservative party on p.218: https://www.leasinglife.com/news/jcb-links-to-secret-club-of-tory-donors/?cf-view
Details of Greenpeace manifesto ranking on p.218: Greenpeace, 2024. https://www.greenpeace.org.uk/news/manifesto-rankings/
Scottish lobbyist data on p.219: Contains information licensed under the Scottish Parliament Copyright Licence.
Bipartisan Infrastructure Law information on p.220: Licensed under CC BY 3.0 US. https://creativecommons.org/licenses/by/3.0/us/
2024 Black voter demographic data on p.221: NBC News, 2024. https://www.nbcnews.com/politics/2024-elections/exit-polls
Demographic percentage of votes for Biden in 2020 on p.221: 'Behind Biden's 2020 Victory', June 30 2021, Pew Research Center. https://www.pewresearch.org/politics/2021/06/30/behind-bidens-2020-victory/
Demographic percentage of votes for Democrats in 2022 on p.221: 'Voting patterns in the 2022 elections', 12 July, 2023, Pew Research Center. https://www.pewresearch.org/politics/2023/07/12/voting-patterns-in-the-2022-elections/
Demographic percentage of votes for Trump in 2024 on p.222: NBC News, 2024. https://www.nbcnews.com/politics/2024-elections/exit-polls
Japan and South Korea population and ethnicity data on p.228: CIA.gov
Tunisia population data on p.228: UNdata. https://data.un.org/en/iso/tn.html
Image of Boris Johnson on p.232: Simon Dawson / No 10 Downing Street, licensed under CC BY 2.0. https://creativecommons.org/licenses/by/2.0/deed.en
Image of American restaurants in China on p.232: Chintunglee, licensed under CC BY-SA 4.0. https://creativecommons.org/licenses/by-sa/4.0 , via Wikimedia Commons
Image of Ajay Banga on p.235: kmu.gov.ua, licensed under CC BY 4.0. https://creativecommons.org/licenses/by/4.0/
Image of Greta Thunberg on p.236: European Parliament from EU, licensed under CC BY 2.0. https://creativecommons.org/licenses/by/2.0 , via Wikimedia Commons
Number of cases presided over by the ICJ on p.239: International Court of Justice, 2017-2025. https://www.icj-cij.org/cases
Data on extreme poverty levels and people's access to clean drinking water on p.241: MDG Monitor, 2017. https://www.mdgmonitor.org/millennium-development-goals/
Child mortality data on p.242: Our World in Data, licensed under CC BY 4.0. https://creativecommons.org/licenses/by/4.0/
Hottest 12-month period on record on p.243: Climate Copernicus, 2024. https://climate.copernicus.eu/may-2024-marks-12-months-record-breaking-global-temperatures
Defence spending of Luxembourg on p.245: NATO Defence expenditures of NATO Countries (2014-2023) https://www.nato.int/cps/en/natohq/news_216897.htm
Defence spending of Poland on p.245: SIPRI Fact Sheet: Trends in World Military Expenditure, 2023 by Nan Tian, Diego Lopes Da Silva, Xiao Liang and Lorenzo Scarazzato. Used with permission.
World Bank giving $12bn to 78 countries on p.247: World Bank, 2020. https://www.worldbank.org/en/news/press-release/2020/10/13/world-bank-approves-12-billion-for-covid-19-vaccines
IMF loans of $140 billion in 2022 on p.249: Financial Times, 2024. https://www.ft.com/content/eddedee3-669d-42cc-9597-33609a8bff99
EU subsidies data on p.251: OECD. "Agricultural Policies in OECD Countries: Monitoring and Evaluation 2003". https://cepr.net/publications/the-300-billion-question-how-much-do-high-income-countries-subsidize-agriculture/
Value of G20 stimulus package for Credit Crunch on p.253: Brookings Institute, 2009. https://www.brookings.edu/articles/understanding-the-g-20-economic-stimulus-plans/
Image on p.253 of Rishi Sunak and Emmanuel Macron: Licensed under CC BY 2.0. https://creativecommons.org/licenses/by/2.0, via Wikimedia Commons
Criteria for extreme poverty on p.255: World Bank, 2022. https://www.worldbank.org/en/news/factsheet/2022/05/02/fact-sheet-an-adjustment-to-global-poverty-lines
Image of Muammar al-Gaddafi on p.264: U.S. Navy photo by Mass Communication Specialist 2nd Class Jesse B. Awalt, Public Domain.
Data for graph of difference in annual temperatures 1900-2016 on p.266: NASA's Goddard Institute for Space Studies (GISS). © NASA/GISS.
CO2 concentration data on p.266: Climate Copernicus, 2023. https://climate.copernicus.eu/esotc/2023/greenhouse-gas-concentrations
USA being responsible for 36% of CO2 emissions p.268: U.S. Energy Information Administration, 2021. https://www.eia.gov/todayinenergy/detail.php?id=48856
Per capita emissions data on p.271: Our World in Data: Per Capita Consumption-based CO2 emissions, 2021 (Global Carbon Budget (2023); Population based on various sources (2023). https://ourworldindata.org/grapher/consumption-co2-per-capita#:~:text=Per%20capita%20emissions%20represent%20the,total%20emissions%20divided%20by%20population
Carbon emissions data on p.271: Global Carbon Project, 2024. Licensed under CC BY 4.0. https://creativecommons.org/licenses/by/4.0/.
India extreme poverty data on p.271: Business Standard, 2024. https://www.business-standard.com/economy/news/129-million-indians-live-in-extreme-poverty-in-2024-says-world-bank-124101501137_1.html
China, India, USA & Indonesia being four leading economies on p.275: PwC, 2017. https://www.pwc.com/gx/en/research-insights/economy/the-world-in-2050.html#:~:text=As%20a%20result%2C%20six%20of,fall%20below%2010%25%20by%202050
EU land mass on p.275: Eurostat, 2021. https://ec.europa.eu/eurostat/statistics-explained/index.php?title=Land_cover_statistics
EU population data on p.275: © Statistisches Bundesamt (Destatis), 2025. https://www.destatis.de/Europa/EN/Topic/Key-indicators/Population.html
US, Russia, India and China nuclear warhead data on p.276: Bulletin of the Atomic Scientists, 2024. https://thebulletin.org/premium/2024-05/united-states-nuclear-weapons-2024/ Russian nuclear weapons, 2024 - Bulletin of the Atomic Scientists. https://thebulletin.org/premium/2024-01/chinese-nuclear-weapons-2024/#:~:text=The%20modernization%20of%20China's%20nuclear,to%20arm%20future%20delivery%20systems.
Aircraft carrier data on p.276: SIPRI 'Aircraft Carrier Fleet Strength by Country (2024)'.
Population data on p.276: UN World Population Prospects 2024.
Active armed forces data on p.276: Statista, 2024. https://www.statista.com/statistics/264443/the-worlds-largest-armies-based-on-active-force-level/#:~:text=As%20of%20January%202024%2C%20China,the%20top%20five%20largest%20armies.
Military spending data on p.276: Global Firepower, 2025. https://www.globalfirepower.com/defense-spending-budget.php
Military base data on p.276: Al Jazeera, 2021. https://www.aljazeera.com/news/2021/9/10/infographic-us-military-presence-around-the-world-interactive
GDP export data on p.279: World Bank national accounts data, and OECD National Accounts data files. Licensed under CC BY 4.0. https://creativecommons.org/licenses/by/4.0/
Percentage of global output in 1913 and 1800 on p.279: Estevadeordal, A., Frantz, B., & Taylor, A. M. (2003). The Rise and Fall of World Trade, 1870-1939. The Quarterly Journal of Economics, 118(2), 359–407. http://www.jstor.org/stable/25053910
NAFTA data on p.285: US Chamber of Commerce, 2017. https://www.uschamber.com/assets/archived/images/the_facts_on_nafta_-_2017.pdf
World trade data on p.291: Eurostat, 2023. Licensed under CC BY 4.0. https://creativecommons.org/licenses/by/4.0/
Amount of aid EU provides on p.292: Press and information team of the Delegation to the UN in Geneva, 2023. https://www.eeas.europa.eu/delegations/un-geneva/humanitarian-aid-eu-increases-funding-%E2%82%AC17-billion-2023_en?s=62
John Rawls extract on p.317: John Rawls, "Justice as Fairness", in The Philosophical Review vol. 67, no. 2, pp. 164-194. Copyright 1958, Cornell University Press. All rights reserved. Republished by permission of the copyright holder, and the Publisher. www.dukeupress.edu.

Index

A
additional member system 25, 27, 31
affirmative action 128
African Union 286
alternative vote 25
altruism 108
amendments to US Constitution 147, 157, 159, 160
amicus curae brief 215, 216
anarchism 108-114
   anarcho-capitalism 113
   anarcho-communism 110-112
   anarcho-syndicalism 110-112
   collectivist 110-112
   egoism 113
   individualist 113
androcentric culture 125
anthropocentrism 116
Arab League 285
ASEAN 286
asymmetrical bicameralism 60, 161, 178
atomism 47

B
Bakunin, Mikhail 108, 110-112
battleground states 206, 208
Berlin, Isaiah 130, 132
Biden, Joe 186, 189
billiard ball model 259
bills 76, 169
biocentric equality 117
Blair, Tony 85, 89
Blue Dog Democrats 220
Bookchin, Murray 115, 119, 120
bourgeoisie 55
Brexit 33, 64, 105, 107
Brexit Party 16-18
Brown, Gordon 36, 84, 89, 95
Buddhist economics 117
Bull, Hedley 296
Burke, Edmund 44, 45
Bush, George W. 186, 188

C
cabinet government (theory of) 88
Callaghan, James 85
Cameron, David 84, 86
campaign finance 210, 211, 213
Carson, Rachel 115, 117, 118
Casey, Louise 131, 135
caucuses
   elections 205
   in government 175, 220-222, 226
chartists 6
chauvinism 137
climate change 266-268, 270-272
   UN conferences 268
Clinton, Bill 188
closed primaries 205
cobweb mode 259
codification 69
collective ministerial responsibility 91-93
collectivisation 111
Common Agricultural Policy (CAP) 251
complex interdependence 235
concurrent powers 167
confidence and supply deal 16
conservatism 19, 44-48
   New Right 47
   One Nation 19, 46
   traditional 45
Conservative Party 15, 16, 19, 22, 36, 37
Constitutional Reform Act (2005) 63, 97, 100
co-operative movements 57
Corbyn, Jeremy 20, 36
Crosland, Anthony 54, 57
cultural globalisation 232
cultural theory 145

D
dark money 210
Davey, Ed 36
de Beauvoir, Simone 123, 126
delegates 205
Democratic Party 220, 221
Democratic Unionist Party (DUP) 16, 21, 28
devolution 61, 62, 64-68
dialectical materialism 55
direct action 110, 216, 218
Disraeli, Benjamin 44, 46
domestic analogy 294

E
earmarking (bills) 168
ecocentrism 116
ecologism 115-122
   deep green ecology 117, 118
   eco-anarchism 119-121
   eco-feminism 119, 120
   eco-socialism 119, 120
   shallow green ecology 121
   social ecology 119, 120
Economic and Monetary Union 289, 290
economic globalisation 231
electioneering 216, 218
election performance
   of UK party leaders 23, 24, 36-43
   of US presidential candidates 211, 212
electoral college 206, 208, 209
empiricism 45
Engels, Friedrich 54-56
enumerated powers 181
environment 236, 266, 282, 293
   protest and campaign groups 272
environmental communalism 119
ethnonationalism 130, 134

European Convention on Human Rights 89, 260
European Court of Human Rights 260
European Economic Community 287, 288
European Union 103-105, 287-292
   as a global power 291, 292
   institutions 289, 290
   treaties 288
exclusive powers 167
executive agreement 181
executive departments 180
executive dominance 75
executive order 181

F
face-to-face assembly democracy 120
Farage, Nigel 36, 39, 41
feminism 123-129
   difference feminism 123
   equality feminism 123
   liberal feminism 125
   post-modern feminism 128
   radical feminism 127
   socialist feminism 126, 127
fiduciary power of government 50
filibuster 154, 168, 169
first-past-the-post 23, 25-27, 30, 31
Fixed-Term Parliaments Act (2011) 64
Ford, Gerald 186
Freedom Caucus 221
Friedan, Betty 49, 52

G
Garvey, Marcus 137, 138, 143
Giddens, Anthony 54, 56
globalisation 231-236
   liberal perspective 234, 294-297
   realist perspective 234, 294-297
   scepticism 234
   types of 231, 232
Goldman, Emma 108, 110-112
governing competency 38
green capitalism 116, 121
Green Party 21
Green, T. H. 51
group differentiated rights 132

H
Hard Left 20
Hardin, Garrett 270
hereditary peers 72
Hobbes, Thomas 44, 45
Hobhouse, L. T. 51
holism 116
hooks, bell 123, 128
House of Commons 70, 71, 74, 96
   legislative function 76, 77
   oversight 78-80
   representation 81, 82

House of Lords 63, 70-74, 96
   legislative function 76, 77
   oversight 80
   representation 81, 82
House of Representatives 166-168, 176
   legislative function 169, 170
   oversight 171-173
   political parties 175, 176
   representation 174, 175
humanitarian intervention 263, 264
human rights 235, 260-265, 282, 293
Human Rights Act (1998) 13, 62, 65, 98, 106
human sociability 111
Huntington, Samuel 131, 135
hyperglobalisers 234

I
implied powers 181
individual ministerial responsibility 91-93
informal powers 181
insurrection 113
integration 131
interest groups in the US 215-217
intergovernmental institutions 289, 290
Intergovernmental Panel on Climate Change (IPCC) 267
International Court of Justice (ICJ) 260
International Criminal Court (ICC) 262
international law 260-263
internationalism 138
intersectionality 123

J
Johnson, Boris 19, 80, 84, 86, 88, 90, 91, 93
judicial independence and neutrality 97, 101
judicial review power 98

K
Keynesian economics 52
Kropotkin, Peter 108, 110-112
Kymlicka, Will 130, 132

L
Labour Party 15, 20, 22, 36
laissez-faire government 47
leadership debates 42
League of Nations 237
Leopold, Aldo 115, 117
Liberal Democrats 16, 21, 22, 36
liberalism 49-53
   classical 50, 53
   in global politics 294-297
   modern 52, 53
libertarian municipalism 120
libertarianism 47

Index

life peers 72
Locke, John 49, 50
Lords Spiritual 72
Luxemburg, Rosa 54, 56

M

Macmillan, Harold 44, 46
Main Street Caucus 221
marginal seat 26
Marx, Karl 54-56
Maurras, Charles 137, 138, 141, 142
May, Theresa 86
Mazzini, Guiseppe 137-140
mechanistic theory 50, 116
Merchant, Carolyn 115, 119, 120
meritocracy 52
militarism 142
Mill, John Stuart 49, 50
Millennium Development Goals 241, 269
Millett, Kate 123, 127
mixed economy 46
mixed electoral systems 25
Modood, Tariq 130, 133
Montreal Protocol 266
motion of no confidence 79
multi-party system 15
multiculturalism 130-136
   cosmopolitan 134
   criticisms of 135
   liberal 132
   pluralist 133, 134
mutual aid 112
mutualism 108, 110-112, 114

N

Næss, Arne 269
NAFTA 285
national nominating conventions 206
nationalism 137-144
   conservative 141, 142
   exclusive 138
   expansionist 141,142
   inclusive 138
   liberal 139, 140
   post-colonial 143
   progressive 138
   regressive 138
negative liberty 51
neo-conservatism 19, 44, 47, 48
neo-liberalism 19, 44, 47, 48, 295
New Democrat Coalition 220
New Labour 20, 58
Nixon, Richard 187
noblesse oblige 45
non-state actors 231, 258, 272
Nozick, Robert 44, 47

O

Oakeshott, Michael 44, 45
Obama, Barack 187, 188
open primaries 205

P

Parekh, Bhikhu 130, 133
Parliament Act (1949) 76
parliamentary defeats (of governments) 84
parliamentary sovereignty 102, 106, 107
paternalism 44
Perkins Gilman, Charlotte 123, 125
Phillips, Trevor 131, 135
Plaid Cymru 21
political action committees 210
political globalisation 231
political representation 82
Porritt, Jonathon 115, 121
positive discrimination 125
positive liberty 51
post-materialism 116
power to persuade 181
pragmatism 44
prerogative powers 61, 84
presidential government (theory of) 88
presidential pardon 181
presidential reprieve 181
primaries 205
Prime Minister's Questions 78
private sphere 124
Progressive Caucus 220
proletariat 55, 56
Proudhon, Pierre-Joseph 108, 110-112
public sphere 124

Q

qualified majority voting 288
quasi-federalism 162

R

Rand, Ayn 44, 47
rational theory 145
rationalism 45
Rawls, John 49, 52
Reagan, Ronald 186
realism in global politics 294-297
recall elections 214
recess appointments 183, 184
referendums 5
   alternative vote 30
   and the media 41, 42
Reform UK 16, 36
regional bodies 285-288
regional party list 25, 27
regionalism (types of) 283
representative democracy 81, 82, 174-176
Republican Party 221, 222
Republican Study Committee 221
republicanism 140
Responsibility to Protect 264
Rocker, Rudolf 108, 110, 112
Rousseau, Jean-Jacques 137-140
Rowbotham, Sheila 123, 126, 127

S

Schumacher, E. F. 115, 117, 118
Scottish independence 21, 66
Scottish National Party (SNP) 16, 21, 22, 32
Scruton, Roger 44, 47
segregation 131
select committees 79
self-actualisation 49
Senate Majority Leader 166
single interest groups 215
single transferable vote 25, 28, 31
Sinn Féin 21, 22, 28
Smith, Adam 51, 254
Social Darwinism 51
social justice 49
social media
   influence on elections 41, 42
   influence on politics 43
socialism 54-59
   revolutionary 55, 56
   social democracy 57
   the Third Way 58
society of states 296
Soft Left 20
solidarity 112
sovereign equality 228
sovereignty 229, 230
Spencer, Herbert 51
Starmer, Keir 20, 39, 84
Stirner, Max 109, 113
structural realism 295
structural theory 145
suffrage 6
Sunak, Rishi 19, 37, 84, 87, 90
super political action committees 210
supplementary vote 25, 29, 31
supranational institutions 289, 290
surgeries 81
Sustainable Development Goals 269
swing justice 193, 198
swing states 208
Swinson, Jo 36
symmetrical bicameralism 167

T

Taylor, Charles 130, 133
Thatcher, Margaret 84, 85, 90
Thatcherite 19
tragedy of the commons 270
transformationalists 234
transnational corporations 258, 272
Treaty of Westphalia 229, 230
Trump, Donald 187, 189
Truss, Liz 19, 86, 247
two-party system 15, 16, 26

U

UK Cabinet 83, 88-90
UK elections 25-29
   campaigns 36
UK executive branch 70, 76, 77
   relationship with Parliament 96
   relationship with the judiciary 100
   relationship with the PM 83, 84
UK judicary 100-102
   relationship with Parliament 102
   relationship with the executive 100
UK Parliament 70
   relationship with the executive 96
   relationship with the judiciary 102
UK prime minister 83-95
   case studies 85-87
   power 94, 95
   relationship with the executive 83, 84
UK Supreme Court rulings 98, 99
UN Special Tribunals 261
Universal Declaration of Human Rights 261
universalism 133
US Cabinet 180
US Congress 166-176
   legislative function 169, 170
   oversight 171-173
   representation 174, 175
US elections 205-212, 220-222
US executive branch 179, 180
US political parties 175, 176, 220-222
US presidents 179-182, 186-189
   and Congress 183, 184
   and the Supreme Court 185
   election performance 211, 212
   evaluating presidencies 188, 189
   powers 181, 182, 186, 187
US Senate 166-168, 176
   legislative function 169, 170
   oversight 171-173
   political parties 175, 176
   representation 174, 175
US Supreme Court rulings 194, 195
USMCA 285

V

value pluralism 132
von Herder, Johan Gottfried 137, 138, 141, 142
voting demographics 34, 35

W

Waldron, Jeremy 130, 134
Webb, Beatrice 54, 57
Wollstonecraft, Mary 49, 50
world government 230